DSM-IV-TR™
in Action
Second Edition

SOPHIA F. DZIEGIELEWSKI

WILEY

John Wiley & Sons, Inc.

This book is printed on acid-free paper. ∞

Copyright © 2010 by John Wiley & Sons, Inc. All rights reserved.

Published by John Wiley & Sons, Inc., Hoboken, New Jersey.
Published simultaneously in Canada.

No part of this publication may be reproduced, stored in a retrieval system, or transmitted in any form or by any means, electronic, mechanical, photocopying, recording, scanning, or otherwise, except as permitted under Section 107 or 108 of the 1976 United States Copyright Act, without either the prior written permission of the Publisher, or authorization through payment of the appropriate per-copy fee to the Copyright Clearance Center, Inc., 222 Rosewood Drive, Danvers, MA 01923, (978) 750-8400, fax (978) 646-8600, or on the web at www.copyright.com. Requests to the Publisher for permission should be addressed to the Permissions Department, John Wiley & Sons, Inc., 111 River Street, Hoboken, NJ 07030, (201) 748-6011, fax (201) 748-6008.

Limit of Liability/Disclaimer of Warranty: While the publisher and author have used their best efforts in preparing this book, they make no representations or warranties with respect to the accuracy or completeness of the contents of this book and specifically disclaim any implied warranties of merchantability or fitness for a particular purpose. No warranty may be created or extended by sales representatives or written sales materials. The advice and strategies contained herein may not be suitable for your situation. You should consult with a professional where appropriate. Neither the publisher nor author shall be liable for any loss of profit or any other commercial damages, including but not limited to special, incidental, consequential, or other damages.

This publication is designed to provide accurate and authoritative information in regard to the subject matter covered. It is sold with the understanding that the publisher is not engaged in rendering professional services. If legal, accounting, medical, psychological or any other expert assistance is required, the services of a competent professional person should be sought.

Designations used by companies to distinguish their products are often claimed as trademarks. In all instances where John Wiley & Sons, Inc. is aware of a claim, the product names appear in initial capital or all capital letters. Readers, however, should contact the appropriate companies for more complete information regarding trademarks and registration.

For general information on our other products and services please contact our Customer Care Department within the U.S. at (800) 762-2974, outside the United States at (317) 572-3993 or fax (317) 572-4002.

Wiley also publishes its books in a variety of electronic formats. Some content that appears in print may not be available in electronic books. For more information about Wiley products, visit our website at www.wiley.com.

Library of Congress Cataloging-in-Publication Data:

Dziegielewski, Sophia F.
  DSM-IV-TR™ in action / Sophia F. Dziegielewski. – 2nd ed.
     p. ; cm.
  Includes bibliographical references and index.
  ISBN 978-0-470-55171-4 (pbk. : alk. paper); 978-0-470-64313-6 (ebk); 978-0-470-64314-3 (ebk);
978-0-470-64315-0 (ebk)
  1. Mental illness–Classification. 2. Mental illness–Diagnosis. I. Title.
     [DNLM: 1. Diagnostic and statistical manual of mental disorders. 4th ed., text revision. 2. Mental Disorders–
diagnosis. 3. Mental Disorders–classification. 4. Patient Care Planning. WM 141 D999d 2010]
  RC455.2.C4D95 2010
  616.89001'2–dc22
                                                                                              2010005950

Printed in the United States of America

10 9 8 7 6 5 4 3 2 1

A Tribute to Dr. Cheryl Green

I have come to believe that intelligence consists of the knowledge that one acquires over a lifetime. Wisdom, however, is far greater. Wisdom requires having intelligence but realizing it means nothing if it is not shared. In wisdom, there is a natural sense of giving where there is no fear of loss. It means realizing that the knowledge is measured purely by what we can teach and share with others.

For Dr. Cheryl Green, her intelligence made her a social work scholar. It was her wisdom, however, that touched my soul and made her one of my colleagues and dearest friends. Her sense of humor and ''Cherylisms'' made the time fly by. Cheryl passed on before the formulation of this second edition. Through her teaching and writing, the hearts of so many social workers like me will never be the same. Although not a day goes by that I do not miss my dearest friend, I remain comforted by the time we shared together.

Contents

SECTION I

Utilizing the *DSM-IV-TR*: Assessment, Planning, and Practice Strategy

Section II

Applications: Selected *DSM-IV-TR* Disorders

Preface

The pages that follow will introduce the reader to the diagnostic assessment, with its obvious strengths as well as its limitations. Although the concept of the diagnosis and assessment is rich in tradition, the connection between diagnostic procedures and behavioral-based outcomes requires practice strategy that is richly embedded in recognizing the importance of connecting the problems and concerns of the person as related to his or her environment. It is paramount to continually assess and reassess how to best address context changes related to emotional, physical, and situational factors regarding client well-being.

This book stresses a multidisciplinary or interdisciplinary focus that invites all medically and nonmedically trained professionals, social workers, and other mental health practitioners alike to join in a team-based approach. By working together, teams best serve the client's needs by providing a comprehensive diagnostic assessment that ensures quality care.

This book utilizes the diagnostic nomenclature outlined in the latest version of the *Diagnostic Manual of Mental Disorders* (*DSM*), sometimes referred to as a "bible" of mental health. To provide competent services, mental health counselors need to understand this information and how to incorporate it in order to provide competent, efficient, and effective practice strategy. To assist in this process, this book

outlines the basic diagnostic information related to the *DSM-IV-TR*.

This second edition serves as a handbook, creating an environment that extends beyond just learning the criteria for placing a diagnosis and includes the application phase. Intervention strategy and the creation of treatment plans include suggestions for the best therapeutic services available. As concerns continue to increase related to misdiagnosis, overdiagnosis, or labeling clients—all practices that can have severe repercussions personally, medically, socially, and occupationally—the need for informed ethical practice has never been more important. Mental health practitioners believe strongly in allowing ethical principles, environmental factors, and a respect for cultural diversity to guide all practice decisions. From this perspective, the diagnostic assessment described in this book embodies concepts such as individual dignity, worth, respect, and nonjudgmental attitudes. For social workers and other mental health counselors (often referred to as practitioners), recognition of these values provides the cornerstone from which all treatment planning and intervention stems. Many times these concepts remain subjective and require professional acknowledgment, interpretation, and application extending beyond the formal diagnostic criteria requiring interpretation and application strategies that lead to efficient and effective practice strategy.

OVERVIEW

To start this endeavor, Section I of the book includes four chapters that introduce the reader to the major diagnostic assessment schemes utilized in the profession and through this diagnostic lens outlines both support and resistance issues. In these introductory chapters, the basics of diagnosis and assessment are exemplified in relation to how these terms are applied in current health and mental health practice. Starting the learning process begins with an understanding of how terms such as diagnosis and assessment are combined in relation to current health and mental health practice. A historical perspective provides the history of the *DSM*, comparing the similarities and differences from the previous editions and the rationale for the latest version, the *DSM-IV-TR*. Further, this second edition speculates beyond the *DSM-IV-TR* and summarizes the current expectations and controversies surrounding the *DSM-5* and what the future may hold. Taken into account is the importance of including supporting information such as use of the defense mechanisms and how culture can influence behavior as noted in the cultural-bound syndromes. Ending the first section is an overview of how the "In Action" connection is made, linking the diagnostic impression to treatment planning and practice strategy. Case examples show the application of the theoretical concepts and demonstrate how these principles link to practice strategy.

Section II has been updated to provide comprehensive diagnostic information for each selected category of disorder identifying the most commonly seen psychiatric mental health conditions. Each chapter contains Quick References designed to highlight the most important diagnostic criteria in a clear and concise manner. The case examples show how the criteria can manifest. For each category of disorders outlined in the application chapters, at least one disorder

highlights the "In Action" focus of the book. The case example provides a comprehensive diagnostic assessment and treatment plan that reflects the related practice strategy.

Additional Treatment Plans were one of the most popular features of the first edition of the book, and they have been expanded. These treatment plans relative to the case examples are included in each chapter. In addition, the Appendix section covers selected disorders not addressed in the individual chapters, and also added are selected Quick References that clearly outline the criteria. Each treatment plan explains the signs and symptoms that should be recorded in the record, what the short- and long-range goals for the client are, and what needs to be done by the client, the practitioner, and the family.

WHAT IS NEW IN THE SECOND EDITION

This second edition of the book, like the first edition, supports the practitioner with current application principles relating psychopathology to clinical mental health practice. Section II chapters have been updated and expanded to provide the latest evidence-based treatment planning and practice strategy. Specific changes are discussed next.

- Chapter 4 includes numerous updates to the documentation and the practice strategies utilized, including information on computer-generated notes and assessing suicide potential with the latest expectations for ensuring a safety plan for the client and others.
- Chapter 5 focuses on the disruptive behavior disorders rather than conduct disorder alone. It has been expanded to include those disorders that are

considered the most difficult to treat: attention-deficit hyperactivity disorder, oppositional defiant disorder, and conduct disorder.

- Chapter 6 has been expanded to include descriptions of selected eating disorders in children: the conditions of pica and rumination disorder.
- Chapter 7 now covers all substance-related disorders, not just alcohol. The theories and etiology of the disorders and treatment strategy are discussed, with new and updated case examples. The chapter also includes information related to motivational enhancement therapies, integrated motivational enhancement therapy, motivational enhancement catalyst, and integrated approaches.
- Chapter 8 now includes descriptions of delusional disorder, schizoaffective disorder, shared psychotic disorder, psychotic disorder due to a general medical disorder, and substance-induced psychotic disorders not otherwise classified in addition to its original coverage of schizophrenia. A new section relates to schizophrenia in children and adolescents.
- In Chapter 9, selected mood disorder information was added related specifically to the unipolar and bipoloar disorders and the problems that can occur with self-reporting of symptoms.
- Chapter 10 has been expanded beyond its original coverage of obsessive-compulsive disorder to include panic disorder, phobia: specific and social, acute stress disorder, generalized anxiety disorder, anxiety disorder due to a general medical condition, substance-induced anxiety disorder, and anxiety disorder not otherwise specified.

- Chapter 11 is a new chapter on delirium, dementia, and amnestic and other cognitive disorders. This chapter introduces the reader to the disorders that fall in this category, such as major types of delirium and dementia. Numerous treatments are discussed, including psychosocial interventions, cognitive-behavioral therapy, reality orientation therapy, behavior therapy, bereavement therapy, and family therapy.
- Chapter 12 is a new chapter that outlines selected sexual disorders, an often overlooked area in treatment. This chapter includes an overview of each of the most common sexual dysfunctions, including the sexual dysfunctions as well as the orgasmic and sexual arousal and desire disorders. A completed diagnostic assessment and a case example are included.
- Chapter 13 is updated to include all three clusters related to the personality disorders. Each disorder is presented with the criteria first followed by a case example.
- The appendix contains additional treatment plans with the criteria provided for disorders not covered in the application chapters, such as the somatoform and factitious disorders and the sleep disorders.

UNIQUENESS OF BOOK

What remains unique about this book is that it challenges the practitioner to synthesize information into a complete diagnostic assessment that includes practice strategy. Each chapter, along with the Quick References, is designed to give health and mental health practitioners a sense of hands-on learning and participation. This book is not meant to include all aspects of a mental disorder and its subsequent treatment.

Rather, it provides a framework for approaching the disorder, with suggestions for the treatment that will follow.

Therefore, this book provides a reader-friendly comprehensive reference to the most commonly diagnosed mental disorders as well as specific applications designed to show how to apply the diagnostic framework toward current practice strategy. Each disorder was carefully selected based on what is most often seen in the field and taught in the graduate-level classroom. In addition, based on the prevalence of these diagnoses, the ones covered in this book are often included on social work and other mental health–related licensing exams.

On a personal note, I believe creating a reader-friendly, practice-based handbook of this nature is never easy—nor should it be. Creating the best diagnostic assessment takes a lot of hard work, and all practice wisdom must be grounded in evidence-based practice. Therefore, the actual drafting of chapters of this second edition from the first proposal to the end product covered a span of well over 2 years with numerous rewrites and edits. This book represents over 25 years of my professional practice and teaching experience. In addition, I have worked with all the contributing authors of the application chapters, all are fellow practitioners in the area, and together we have spent countless hours deciding on how best to transcribe practice experience into the written word. All the contributors of this text are passionate about our profession and agree that much needs to be learned from the clients served.

Case examples are used throughout this book to help the reader see the interface between what is written in the text and how it applies to practice. Many of the struggles that other professionals have noted are highlighted, and the case examples present information in a practical and informative way that is sensitive to the client's best interests while taking into account the reality of the practice environment. Thus, the contributors invite the reader to begin this adventure in learning and to realize that diagnostic assessment needs to be more than "the Blind Man and the Elephant."

There will always be a subjective nature to diagnosis and assessment, just as there is a subjective nature to individuals and the best-employed intervention strategy. This second edition, like the first edition, is intended to take the practitioner beyond the diagnostic assessment and ignite a creative fire for practice strategy and implementation, similar to what it has done for all of us. Welcome, and with each client served, I hope you never forget the importance of the three Rs: Recognition, Respect, and Responsibility.

Acknowledgments

I am very grateful for all the help I have received from the coauthors on the applications chapters included in this text. The sharing of firsthand experiences by such experienced practitioners has been invaluable. I would also like to thank the 17,000 social workers and counselors I have trained for professional practice in supervision and for taking licensing exams. Their wonderful feedback in terms of what they are seeing in the field and the problems they have encountered has helped me to become a stronger teacher and practitioner. For this input, I will always be thankful and intend to continue to give back to help others along their professional journey. As mental health practitioners, regardless of discipline, we have a clear path set before us. Not only must we deal with the challenges of this changing environment, but we bear the burden of exploring and subsequently influencing how these changes will affect our professional practice and the clients we serve.

I would like to thank my clients for teaching me the importance of going beyond what is expected and recognizing the uniqueness of each individual who I have had the privilege of serving. Seeing firsthand the stigma and subsequent danger of placing a label on a client has left me sensitive to ensuring the diagnostic assessment is not done haphazardly and always takes into account the person-in-situation or person-in-environment perspective. This means that each encounter must first recognize the uniqueness of the individual and show respect for the client and his or her situation. The practitioner must take responsibility for providing the most comprehensive diagnostic assessment and subsequent treatment available.

Furthermore, the final product is only as good as those who work diligently behind the scenes on the editing and production of this book. First, I would like to thank Barbara Maisevich, MSW, for her second set of eyes and technical support in completing this manuscript. I would also like to thank Kate Lindsay and especially Rachel Livsey, senior editor of Social Work and Counseling, at John Wiley & Sons, Inc. Rachel's openness to new ideas, high energy level, drive, ambition, and perseverance make her a wise teacher, mentor, colleague, and now my friend.

Last, I want to thank my family members, friends, and colleagues who understood and supported me when I said I could not participate because I had to work on this book. I am a firm believer that the more we share with others, the greater the gifts we receive in return. Therefore, it comes as no surprise that I am blessed with knowing and working with so many caring and supportive family members, friends, and colleagues. With that level of encouragement and support, all things really are possible.

Quick Reference List

UTILIZING THE
DSM-IV-TR
Assessment, Planning, and
Practice Strategy

Getting Started

INTRODUCTION

This chapter introduces the concepts and current application principles relating psychopathology to clinical mental health practice. This application is supported through the use and explication of diagnosis-assessment skills found in today's behavioral-based biopsychosocial field of practice. The major diagnostic assessment schemes utilized in the profession, along with support and resistance issues, are introduced. Diagnosis and assessment are applied to current mental health practice. A historical perspective is explored, and the type of diagnostic assessment most utilized today is outlined. Practice strategy is highlighted, and considerations for future exploration and refinement are noted.

BEGINNING THE PROCESS

The concept of formulating and completing a diagnostic assessment is embedded in the history and practice of the clinical mental health counseling strategy. Sadler (2002) defined the traditional purpose of the psychiatric diagnosis as providing efficient and effective communication among professionals; facilitating empirical research in psychopathology; and, assisting in the formulation of the appropriate treatment strategy for the client to be served. The importance of the diagnostic assessment is supported by estimates related to the prevalence of mental

disorders in our population and the effects it can have on human function and productivity. It is estimated that each year, one-quarter of Americans are noted as suffering from a clinical mental disorder. When looking specifically at this group, nearly half of these are diagnosed with two or more disorders (Kessler, Chiu, Demler, & Walters, 2005). Although on the surface these numbers may seem alarming, some researchers question whether these incidences of mental disorders are simply a product of our times and related primarily to the taxonomy used to define a mental disorder (Ahn & Kim, 2008). In practice, this rich tradition related to making the diagnostic impression has been clearly emphasized by compelling demands to address practice reimbursement (Braun & Cox, 2005; Davis & Meier, 2001; Kielbasa, Pomerantz, Krohn, & Sullivan, 2004; Sadler, 2002). For example, whether a client has health insurance can be a factor as to whether he or she gets a mental health diagnosis and the supporting treatment received (Pomerantz & Segrist, 2006).

To facilitate making the diagnostic impression, numerous types of diagnosis and assessment measurements are currently available—many of which are structured into unique categories and classification schemes. All mental health professionals need to be familiar with the texts often referred to by those in the field as the "bibles" of mental health treatment. These resources, representing the most prominent methods of diagnosis and assessment, are the ones that are most commonly used and accepted in the area of health service delivery. Although it is beyond our scope to describe the details and applications of all of these different tools and the criteria for each of the mental disorders described within, familiarity with those most commonly utilized is essential. Furthermore, this book takes the practicing professional beyond assessment by presenting the most current methods used to support the diagnostic assessment and introducing interventions based on current practice wisdom, focusing on the latest evidence-based interventions utilized in the field.

MAKING THE DIAGNOSTIC ASSESSMENT: TOOLS THAT FACILITATE THE ASSESSMENT PROCESS

Few professionals would debate that the most commonly used and accepted sources of diagnostic criteria are the *Diagnostic and Statistical Manual of Mental Disorders, Fourth Edition, Text Revision (DSM-IV-TR)* and the *International Classification of Diseases, Tenth Edition (ICD-10)*. Across the continents, especially in the United States, these books are considered reflective of the official nomenclature designed to better understand mental health phenomena and are used in most health-related facilities. The *DSM-IV-TR* (2000) is the most current version of the *Diagnostic and Statistical Manual* of the American Psychiatric Association (APA), and revision (*DSM-5*) to this edition is expected to be completed in 2013.

Today, the *DSM* is similar to the *ICD* in terms of diagnostic codes and the billing categories; however, this was not always the case. In the late 1980s, it was not unusual to hear complaints from other clinicians related to having to use the *ICD* for clarity in billing while referring to the

DSM for clarity of the diagnostic criteria. Psychiatrists, psychologists, social workers, and mental health technicians often complained about the lack of clarity and uniformity of criteria in both of these texts. Therefore, it comes as no surprise that later versions of these texts responded to the professional dissatisfaction over the disparity between the two texts as well as the clarity of the diagnostic criteria. To facilitate practice utility, these books now clearly relate to each other using almost identical criteria and descriptive classification systems that cross all theoretical orientations.

Historically, while most clinicians are knowledgeable about both books, the *DSM* is often the focus and has gained the greatest popularity in the United States making it the resource tool most often used by psychiatrists, psychologists, psychiatric nurses, social workers, and other mental health professionals.

ROLE OF SOCIAL WORKERS AND OTHER MENTAL HEALTH PROFESSIONALS

The publisher of the *DSM* is the American Psychiatric Association, a professional organization in the field of psychiatry. Nevertheless, the majority of copies bought and used are by individuals who are not psychiatrists. Early in the introductory pages of the book, the authors remind the reader that the book is designed to be utilized by professionals in all areas of mental health, including psychiatrists, physicians, psychiatric nurses, psychologists, social workers, and other mental health professionals (APA, 2000). Since there is a need for a system that accurately identifies and classifies biopsychosocial symptoms and for using this classification scheme as a basis for assessing mental health problems, it is no surprise that this book continues to gain popularity.

Of the documented 595,000 social workers in the United States, over 246,000 of them work in the area of mental health, substance abuse, medical social work, and public health, where many are directly involved in the diagnostic process (Bureau of Labor Statistics-Occupational Handbook, 2008–2009). When compared to psychiatrists, psychologists, and psychiatric nurses, social workers are the largest group of mental health providers having a significant effect on diagnostic impressions related to the current and continued mental health of all clients served.

Mental health practitioners, such as social workers, are active in clinical assessment and intervention planning. A past survey reported that for clinical social workers working in the area of mental health, the *DSM* was the publication used most often (Kutchins & Kirk, 1988). Furthermore, since all states in the United States and the District of Columbia require some form of licensing, certification, or registration to engage in professional practice as a social worker (Bureau of Labor Statistics-Occupational Handbook, 2008–2009), a thorough knowledge of the *DSM* is considered essential for competent clinical practice.

Because all professionals working in the area of mental health need to be capable of service reimbursement and to be proficient in diagnostic assessment and treatment planning, it is not surprising that the majority of mental health professionals support the use of this manual (Corey, 2001a; Dziegielewski, Johnson, & Webb, 2002). Nevertheless, historically some professionals, such as Carlton (1989), a social worker, questioned this choice. Carlton believed that all health and mental health intervention needed to go beyond the traditional bounds of simply diagnosing a client's mental health condition. From this perspective, social, situational, and environmental factors were considered key ingredients for addressing client problems. To remain consistent with the "person-in-situation" stance, utilizing the *DSM* as the path of least resistance might lead to a largely successful fight—yet would it win the war? Carlton, along with other professionals of his time, feared that the battle was being fought on the wrong battlefield and advocated for a more comprehensive system of reimbursement that took into account environmental aspects. Questions raised include: How is the *DSM* used? Is it actually used to direct clinical interventions when engaging in clinical practice? Or is the focus and use of the manual primarily limited to ensuring third-party reimbursements, qualifying for agency service, or to avoid placing a diagnostic label? Psychiatrists and psychologists also question how the *DSM* serves clients in terms of clinical utility (First & Westen, 2007; Hoffer, 2008). Concerns evolved that clients were not always given diagnoses based on diagnostic criteria and the diagnostic labels assigned were connected to unrelated factors, such as individual clinical judgment or simply to secure reimbursement. These concerns related directly to professional misconduct and caused ethical and legal dilemmas that affected billable and nonbillable conditions caused intended and unintended consequences for clients. To complicate the situation further, to provide the most relevant and affordable services many health care insurers require a diagnostic code. This can be problematic, from a social work perspective, when the assistance needed to improve mental health functioning may rest primarily in providing family support or working to increase support systems within the environment. The *DSM* is primarily descriptive with little if any attempt to look at underlying causes (R. S. Sommers-Flanagan & J. Sommers-Flanagan, 2007).

Therefore, some mental health professionals are pressured to pick the most severe diagnosis so their clients could qualify for agency services or insurance reimbursement. This is further complicated by just the opposite trend, which is where the mental health professional assigns the least severe diagnosis to avoid stigmatizing and labeling (Feisthamel & Schwartz, 2009; Kutchins & Kirk, 1986). According to Braun and Cox (2005), these violations include serious ethical violations, such as asking a client to collude with the assigning of mental disorders diagnosis for services. A client agreeing to this type of practice may be completely unaware of the long-term consequences this misdiagnosis can have regarding present, continued, and future employment as well as health, mental health, life, and automobile insurance service or premiums.

Regardless of the reasoning or intent, erroneous diagnoses can harm the clients we serve as well as the professionals who serve them (Feisthamel & Schwartz, 2009). How can professionals within the profession be trusted, if this type of behavior is engaged? It is easy to see how such practices can raise issues related to the ethical and the legal aspects that come with intentional misdiagnosing. These practices violate various aspects of the principles of the mental health profession.

Although use of the *DSM* is clearly evident in mental health practice, some professionals continue to question whether it is being utilized properly. For some, such as social workers, the controversy over using this system for diagnostic assessments remains. Regardless of the controversy in mental health practice and application, the continued and increased popularity of the *DSM* makes it the most frequently used publication in the field of mental health. One consistent theme in using this manual upon which most professionals agree is no single diagnostic system is completely acceptable by all. Some skepticism and questioning of the appropriateness of the use of the *DSM* is useful. This along with recognizing and questioning the changes and the updates needed makes the *DSM* a vibrant

and emerging document reflective of the times. One point most professionals can agree on is that an accurate, well-defined, and relevant diagnostic label needs to reach beyond ensuring service reimbursement. Knowledge of how to properly use the manual is needed. In addition, to discourage abuse, there must also be knowledge, concern, and continued professional debate about the appropriateness and the utility of certain diagnostic categories

DEVELOPMENT OF THE *DSM* CLASSIFICATION SYSTEM: HISTORY AND RESERVATIONS

The *DSM* was originally published in 1952, with the most recent version, the *DSM-IV-TR*, published in 2000. The publications of the *DSM* correspond to the publications of the *ICD* with the next version of the *DSM* scheduled for 2013, anticipated to follow the publication of the *ICD-11* by the World Health Organization.

DSM-I *and* DSM-II

The *ICD* is credited as the first official international classification system for mental disorders with its first edition published in 1948. The APA published the first edition of the *DSM* in 1952. This edition was an attempt to blend the psychological with the biological and provide the practitioner with a unified approach known as the psychobiological point of view. This first version of the *DSM* had outlined 60 mental disorders (APA, 1952). With the popularity of this first edition, the second edition of the book was published in 1968. Unlike its predecessor, the *DSM-II* did not reflect a particular point of view; it attempted to frame the diagnostic categories in a more scientific way. Both *DSM-I* and *DSM-II*, however, were criticized by many for being unscientific and for increasing the potential for negative labeling for the clients being served (Eysenck, Wakefield, & Friedman, 1983). The mind-set at the time centered on understanding the mental health of individuals based on clinical interpretation and judgment. From this perspective, symbolic and professional meaningful interpretations of symptoms were highlighted. This perspective relied heavily on clinical interpretation while taking into account the client's personal history, total personality, and life experiences (Mayes & Horwitz, 2005). With their focus on the etiological causations for identified mental disorders, these earliest editions were often criticized for the variance in the clinical and diagnostic interpretation within the categories. The fear of individual interpretation leading to a biased psychiatric label that could potentially harm clients made many professionals cautious. The situation was further complicated by the different mental health professionals who were using this book as a diagnostic tool. Originally designed by psychiatrists, for psychiatrists, the other related disciplines in mental health soon also began using the book to assist in the diagnostic process. These other disciplines, as well as some psychiatrists, warned of the dangers of using guides such as the *DSM*, arguing that the differences inherent in the basic philosophy of mental health practitioners could lead to interpretation problems. For example, Carlton (1984) and Dziegielewski (2004) felt that social workers, one of the major providers of mental health services, differed in purpose and philosophical orientation from psychiatrists. Since psychiatry is a medical specialty, the focus of its work would be pathology-based linking with the traditional medical model, a perspective very different from social work, a field whose strengths-based perspective historically has focused on how to help clients manage their lives effectively under conditions of physical or mental illness and disability. (See Quick Reference 1.1 below for a brief history on the *DSM*.)

QUICK REFERENCE 1.1

BRIEF HISTORY OF THE *DSM*

- *DSM-I* was first published by the American Psychiatric Association (APA) in 1952 and reflected a psychobiological point of view.

- *DSM-II* (1968) did not reflect a particular point of view. Many professionals criticized both *DSM-I* and *DSM-II* for being unscientific and for encouraging negative labeling.

- *DSM-III* (1980) claimed to be unbiased and more scientific. Many of the earlier problems still persisted, but they were overshadowed by an increasing demand for *DSM-III* diagnoses required for clients to qualify for reimbursement from private insurance companies or from governmental programs.

- *DSM-III-R* (1987) utilized data from field trials that the developers claimed validated the system on scientific grounds. Nevertheless, serious questions were raised about its diagnostic reliability, possible misuse, potential for misdiagnosis, and ethical use.

- *DSM-IV* (1994) sought to dispel earlier criticisms of the *DSM*. It included additional cultural information, diagnostic tests, and lab findings and was based on 500 clinical field trials.

- *DSM-IV-TR* (2000) does not change the diagnostic codes or criteria from the *DSM-IV*; however, it supplements the current categories with additional information based on research studies and field trials completed in each area.

DSM-III *and* DSM-III-R

According to Carlton (1984):

> Any diagnostic scheme must be relevant to the practice of the professionals who develop and use it. That is, the diagnosis must direct practitioners' interventions. If it does not do so, the diagnosis is irrelevant. *DSM-III*, despite the contributions of one of its editors, who is a social worker, remains essentially a psychiatric manual. How then can it direct social work interventions? (p. 85)

These professional disagreements in professional orientation continued with further divisions developing between psychiatrists and psychoanalysts on how to best categorize the symptoms of a mental disorder while taking into account the professional's theoretical orientations. Some professionals, particularly psychiatrists, argued that there was insufficient evidence that major mental disorders were caused by primarily psychological forces; other psychiatrists, especially those skilled in psychotherapy, and other mental health professionals refused to exclude experience and other etiological concepts rooted in psychoanalytic theory (Mayes & Horwitz, 2005).

Other professionals argued that the criteria for normalcy and pathology were biased and that sex-role stereotypes were embedded in the classification and categories of the mental disorders. These authors believed that women were being victimized by the alleged masculine bias of the system (Boggs, Morey, Skodol, Shea, et al., 2005; Braun & Cox, 2005; Kaplan, 1983a, 1983b; Kass, Spitzer, & Williams, 1983; Williams & Spitzer, 1983). The biggest argument in this area came from the contention that research conducted on the *DSM-III* (1980) was less biased and more scientific.

To address these growing concerns, the *DSM-III* (APA, 1980) was noted as being highly innovative. In this edition, a multiaxial system of diagnosis was introduced; specific and explicit criteria sets were included for almost all of the diagnoses; and a substantially expanded text discussion was included to assist with formalizing the diagnostic impression (Spitzer, Williams, & Skodol, 1980). It was in this edition that a clear emphasis was made on the importance of using criteria sets based in observational and empirically based research, disregarding underlying psychic mechanisms and causes (Helzer, Kraemer, Krueger, et al., 2008). This edition was considered an improvement over the earlier versions; however, even this shift from a psychodynamic perspective to the medical model failed to differentiate between classification of healthy and sick individuals (Mayes & Horwitz, 2005). Therefore, many professionals believed that the earlier problems persisted and that observation data and precise definitions were not really possible, as these criteria generally were not grounded in evidence-based practice principles. However, these concerns about application were overshadowed by an increasing demand for use of the *DSM-III* for clients to qualify for participation and reimbursement from insurance companies, governmental programs, and treatment requirements for managed care delivery systems and pharmaceutical companies.

The APA was challenged to address this issue by an immediate call for independent researchers to critically evaluate the diagnostic categories and test their reliability. The developers initiated a call of their own, seeking research that would support a new and improved revision of this edition of the manual called the *DSM-III-R* (APA, 1987). Some professionals, who had originally challenged the foundations of this edition, felt that this immediate designation for a revised manual circumvented attempts for independent research by aborting the process and making the proposed revision attempt obsolete. Therefore, all the complaints about the lack of reliability concerning the *DSM-III* became moot because all attention shifted to the revision.

The resulting revision, the *DSM-III-R* (1987) did not end the controversy. This edition did, however, start the emphasis on reporting the results of field trials sponsored by the National Institute of Mental Health (NIMH). According to Mayes and Horwitz (2005), these field trials included information from over 12,000 patients and over 500 psychiatrists from across the country. These researchers were familiar with the *DSM-II* and had actually participated in its preliminary drafts. Pleased to see the focus on research-based criteria, critics were still concerned that those who did the criteria verification were the same individuals who supported the narrowly defined set of criteria originally identified as the disorder symptoms (Mayes & Horwitz, 2005). Others felt strongly this was a positive step toward using field trials and evidence-based research, which would allow for a better statistical assessment of incidence and prevalence rates of mental disorders in the general population (Kraemer, Shrout, & Rubio-Stipec, 2007).

Despite these criticisms, *DSM-III* started the trend that was followed in later versions. It outlined a common language for all mental health providers to use and to define mental disorders for professionals using the book as well as for the systems in which it was to be utilized in the delivery of mental health services for all parties (Mayes & Horwitz, 2005).

The data gathered from these field trials helped to validate the system on scientific grounds while also raising serious questions about its diagnostic reliability, clinical misuse, potential for misdiagnosis, and ethics of its use (Dumont, 1987; Kutchins & Kirk, 1986; Mayes & Horwitz, 2005). Researchers, such as Kutchins and Kirk (1993), also noted that the new edition (*DSM-III-R*) preserved the same structure and all of the

innovations of the *DSM-III* yet there were many changes in specific diagnoses, resulting in over 100 categories altered, dropped, or added. The complaint noted that no one would ever know whether the changes improved or detracted from diagnostic reliability when comparing the new manual with the old. Attempts to follow up on the original complaints and concerns about the actual testing of overall reliability of the *DSM-III* were not addressed even after it was published. Specifically, Kutchins and Kirk (1997) continued to question whether these new revised versions still created an environment where diagnosis might be unnecessary or overapplied. Some researchers believe that these complaints may have evolved from a misunderstanding or misapplication of the statistical component of the *DSM* and how it related to the clinical decision making that was to result (Kraemer, Shrout, & Rubio-Stipec, 2007).

DSM-IV

Less than 1 year after the publication of the *DSM-III-R*, the APA initiated the next revision. *DSM-IV* was originally scheduled for publication in 1990, and the expectation was that it would carry a strong emphasis on the changes that occurred grounded by empirical evidence. In addition to the *DSM-IV* itself, a four-volume *DSM-IV* Sourcebook provided a comprehensive reference work that supported the research and clinical decisions made by the work groups and the task force responsible for updating the *DSM*. This publication included the results of over 150 literature reviews as well as reports outlining the data analysis and reanalysis and reports from the field trials. The four volumes of the sourcebook was the culmination of final decisions made by the task and work groups, presenting the rationale in an executive summary (APA, 1995). Because of this emphasis on evidence-based diagnostic categories and the resulting criteria, publication of *DSM-IV* was delayed until May 1994. The time period waiting its publication (1990–1994) caused some professionals to question whether this publication delay would detract attention and efforts toward substantiating earlier versions of the manual. It was felt that more was needed than simply waiting for this newer version of the *DSM*, and this lack of attention could have the same disruptive impact in regard to the manual's overall reliability (Zimmerman, 1988). Most professionals agreed that the *DSM-IV* (1994) did indeed place greater emphasis on empirical evidence as a basis to amend diagnostic rules. The short time period between *DSM-III* and *DSM-III-R* and the subsequent revisions, the paucity of relevant studies, as well as the lack of a coherent plan to involve statistical consultation in the process limited the feasibility and impact of statistical input (Kraemer, Shrout, & Rubio-Stipec, 2007, p. 259). The *DSM-IV* was hailed for its great improvements, but whether the research-based changes were really enough to address the shortfalls identified was questioned.

DSM-IV-TR: *Why Another Text Revision*

The latest revision of the *DSM* (the *Diagnostic and Statistical Manual of Mental Disorders, Fourth Edition*, text revision), upon which this text is based, was published in 2000. Although Chapter 2 discusses the application of this version of the text in greater detail, a brief summary of the changes related to the *DSM-IV-TR* is provided here. This newest version, with over 400 mental diagnoses, has come a long way from the original volume (*DSM-I*) with its 60. To prepare for the *DSM-IV-TR*, in 1997, the work and assignments for the new task groups for the text revision were assigned. Since the *DSM* has historically been used as an educational tool, it was felt that recent research might be overlooked if a revision was not published prior to *DSM-5* (originally expected in 2005), with the new delayed date

of 2013. Surprisingly, even though there has been much new research and information, the *DSM-IV* was still considered to be relatively up to date. (See Quick Reference 1.2, Reasons for Change in *DSM-IV-TR* and Quick Reference 1.3, Intent of the *DSM-IV-TR*.)

There were five reasons for this latest version of the *DSM-IV-TR*.

1. The authors corrected factual errors that cropped up in the *DSM-IV*. For example, under Pervasive Developmental Disorder Not Otherwise Specified, an error was corrected that had allowed the diagnosis to be given in cases in which there was a pervasive impairment in only one developmental area rather than multiple related areas (APA, 2000). Other areas in which factual inconsistencies were corrected included Personality Change due to a General Medical Condition and Bipolar Disorders with Melancholic Features. Comorbidity information related to a disorder was also an important addition in the *DSM-IV-TR*.

2. The authors updated the information in the *DSM-IV* with the latest supporting documentation. Better examples of the different types of behavior were added under Autistic Disorder. Similar data were added to many of the diagnostic categories to assist practitioners in forming a more accurate diagnostic impression.

3. At the time the *DSM-IV* was published in 1994, some of the field trials and literature reviews were still under way. The *DSM-IV-TR* includes the latest research results and integrates how this information relates to the clinical diagnostic category. The majority of the categories and information from the *DSM-IV* remained up to date without modification.

> ## QUICK REFERENCE 1.2
>
> ### REASONS FOR CHANGE IN *DSM-IV-TR*
>
> 1. Corrected factual errors.
> 2. Allowed the work study groups to review each diagnostic category to ensure that information was timely and updated.
> 3. Incorporated new information from literature reviews and research studies.
> 4. Enhanced the educational value of the book.
> 5. Incorporated the updated coding changes from *ICD-10-DCR*.

4. Since the *DSM* is often used in educational settings to teach professionals about diagnostic categories, more information was added to support this use.
5. Not all the *ICD* codes were available until 1996. Thus, those who bought early copies of the *DSM-IV* did not receive the complete *ICD* coding. Later printings included the *ICD* update. It is easy to check whether the *ICD* codes are included in the *DSM-IV*: Simply look at the front cover. If the coding update is included, the cover should have a round orange stamp stating "Updated with *ICD-10-DCR* Codes." The *DSM-IV-TR* incorporates the *ICD-10-DCR* codes into the text.

In summary, in formulating the text revisions, none of the categories, diagnostic codes, or criteria from the *DSM-IV* was changed. More supplemental information is now provided for many of the current categories. In addition, more information is provided on many of the field trials introduced in the *DSM-IV* but not yet completed by the original 1995 publication date. Publishing of the *DSM-IV-TR* allowed for the inclusion of updated research findings. Furthermore, special attention was paid to updating the sections in terms of diagnostic findings, cultural information, and other information to clarify the diagnostic categories (APA, 2000). Yet with all these changes, Muller (2008) still feels strongly that special caution is needed; regardless of the pronounced efforts to make the *DSM* more research based, it is still possible to take the reports of patients with abnormal thoughts, feelings, and behaviors and stretch them to fit the symptoms related to one or more checklists.

DSM-5: *What Does the Future Hold?*

Originally, the American Psychiatric Association developed the *DSM* for statistical, epidemiological,

> ## QUICK REFERENCE 1.3
>
> ### INTENT OF THE *DSM-IV-TR*
>
> According to the American Psychiatric Association, the intent of the latest revision is:
>
> - To review information and ensure that information is up to date, including the latest research and supporting information available.
> - To make educational improvements which enhance the value of the *DSM* as a teaching tool, and make sure the new *ICD-9-CM* codes were included in the text (as many of these codes did not become available until 1996—the year after publication of the *DSM-IV*).

and reporting purposes; the *ICD* was developed to reflect clinical approaches to diagnosis and training (Sorensen, Mors, & Thomsen, 2005). Today, with the revisions to the *DSM* that have been made over the years, the *DSM-IV-TR* is designed to be compatible with (but not identical to) the issues presented in the International Classification of Diseases (*ICD-10-DCR*). Significant differences in systems continue to remain, including differential diagnostic criteria in research and clinical practice, and how this affects problems in knowledge, reporting, and subsequent generalizability of findings to the general population (Sorensen, Mors, & Thomsen, 2005). These can be seen in studies documenting the impact of differing categorical criteria, with under- and overdiagnosing of mental disorders, as well as its impact on policy formulations of mental health treatment and services. Particularly in the classification of mental disorders in children, differences are noted between the *ICD-10-DCR* and the *DSM-IV-TR* criteria, whereby prevalence rates in diagnosis of Major Depressive Disorder (MDD), Attention Deficit Hyperactive Disorder (ADHD), and Oppositional Defiant Disorder (ODD) were higher when utilizing the moderate to severe specifiers when utilizing criteria in the *DSM-IV-TR* as opposed to the *ICD-10-DCR* (Sorensen, Mors, & Thomsen, 2005).

Some have grown increasingly frustrated with the delay in publication of the *DSM-5*, which is expected to address some of these shortcomings. On February 10, 2010, the American Psychiatric Association released the proposed draft criteria for the fifth edition. With an expected publication date of 2013, the gap between the *DSM-IV-TR* and the *DSM-5* will be over 13 years. Although already a decade worth of progress has occurred, the changes expected in the *DSM-5*, to date, still remain a work in progress. The APA states that major changes and clarifications are expected over the

next few years till its publication. These proposed revisions within the *DSM-5* are supported by a task force made up of over 160 world renowned clinicians and researchers constituting selected members of 13 work groups. These work groups will continue to review the research literature, consult with a number of experts, and for the first time also seek public comment. Changes expected for the *DSM-5* viewed on the web site for the manual (www.DSM5.org) welcomed public comment and review.

As these changes evolve, the number of diagnoses introduced will be monitored carefully, as it is never easy to replace or disregard a diagnosis, once it is introduced (Hoffer, 2008). Part of the reason for this reluctance to let go of what might not seem relevant is based in conflict of interest priorities in those who influence its content directly supporting what is stated in the *DSM-IV*. Cosgrove, Krinsky, Vijayaraqhavan, and Schneider (2006) reported that when they looked at studies conducted in support of the *DSM-IV* research-based changes, 170 panel members (56%) of the sample had direct financial associations with the big pharmaceutical companies; and all members on the mood disorder and the schizophrenia work groups had such ties.

Additionally, similar to previous versions of the *DSM*, the debates continue to rage. This revision's most active debate surrounds the categorical approach versus the dimensional (Helzer et al., 2008). It appears that the dimensional approach allows for greater flexibility and recognizes that mental disorders cannot be easily described by a single diagnostic category (Helzer et al., 2008). Mellsop, Menkes, and El-Badri (2007) believe that the diagnostic process should be broadened to include the treatment-relevant dimensions of observed motor, cognitive, and emotional functioning. From this perspective, individualized treatment will match symptoms, focusing on symptom suppression while enhancing global functioning (Mezzich, 2005).

Dimensional assessments also appear to permit the clinician to assess the severity of the symptoms in a particular client while "cross-cutting" or taking into account symptoms relative to a number of different diagnoses that can influence current presentation and behavior.

In summary, the generalities of what is to come are well debated but the exact changes are not clear or predictable. In terms of the future diagnostic changes expected, possible modifications will be discussed in the relative chapters. Changes in the area of the learning disorders, terminology (e.g., mental retardation will most likely be changed to intellectual disability) and the substance abuse and dependence categories remain hotly debated. Hoffer (2008) is hopeful, however, that with all the expected changes, certain additional medical and diagnostic tests will be included to support identified diagnoses. Sadler, Fulford, and Phil (2004) conclude that any changes need to include the perspective of patients and their families and that such an inclusion is supported in both sound policy and public requests. Shannon and Heckman (2007) warn that it still is important not to be too quick to "pathologize" behaviors and label them. In the midst of this discussion related to the needed changes, it is probably best to just accept that mental disorders are highly complicated concepts that need to be determined (Zachar & Kendler, 2007). With this recognition, it becomes possible to accept that some aspects of this mental disorder taxonomy will need to be determined (as opposed to discovered) with practical goals and concerns at the forefront of the diagnostic assessment (Ahn & Kim, 2008).

DIAGNOSTIC LABELS

Regardless of the controversy surrounding the use of the earlier, current, or future versions of the *DSM* as a diagnostic assessment tool, such

tools continue to be used. One of the biggest concerns remains: Categorizing an individual with a mental health diagnosis can result in a psychiatric label that is difficult to remove. Many clinicians believe that they must always consider the implications of making the diagnosis. When used properly, the identification of disorders and the acquisition and reimbursement of delivered services results. Consequences that are not intended can lead to social stigma and the loss of other opportunities (Moses, 2009). There is no question that labeling an individual with a mental health diagnosis can also result in the personal and public stigma (Hinshaw & Stier, 2008). In fact, some mental health professionals feel so strongly about labeling clients that they continue to resist the use of this assessment scheme in their practices. For example (as is discussed later in this text), if a child is given the diagnosis of conduct disorder in youth, many professionals believe that this condition will continue into adulthood, resulting in the classification of a lifelong mental health condition known as antisocial personality disorder. What complicates this diagnosing pattern further is that clients who receive such a diagnosis may start acting that way, creating a negative feedback loop that leads the individual to act in accordance with the condition given (Tsou, 2007). Such a label, whether accurately or inaccurately placed, can be very damaging to the client because of the negative connotations that characterize it and also because of what then becomes expected of the client for him- or herself and others. The negative connotations that sometimes accompany the diagnostic label of conduct disorder (i.e., generally nonresponsive to intervention, lack of moral standards, and lack of guilt) may result in conduct-disordered behaviors when these may not have been present to begin with (i.e., severe aggression toward people or animals). These types of behaviors are unacceptable by all societal standards yet if legitimized as part of a diagnosis, the effect can be twofold: If in conduct disorder it is expected that the client has no control over the behaviors exhibited, these overt actions may be viewed as acceptable or unchangeable in him/her. When unacceptable behaviors are considered an inevitable part of the diagnosis there may be less hope for the capacity of growth and change in the individual. Also, if the condition is not present but the individual was incorrectly classified with the diagnosis of conduct disorder, the client may begin to develop behaviors viewed as unacceptable and unchangeable, thus acting in accordance with the diagnosis. Regardless, these behaviors are accepted or tolerated because they are related to a mental disorder. (See Quick Reference 1.4 for a list of some Positive Aspects (pros) and Negative Aspects (cons) of the *DSM-IV-TR*.)

In addition, one common misconception about the *DSM* diagnostic scheme is that "the classification of mental disorders classifies people, when actually what are being classified are the disorders that people have" (APA, 2000, p. xxxi). Professionals must be sensitive to the labels placed and utilized when referring to people who suffer from a mental health disorder. For example, never refer to an individual as "a schizophrenic" but rather as "an individual with schizophrenia" or "an individual who suffers from schizophrenia." Consideration should always be used to ensure that terms are not used incorrectly and that individuals who suffer from a mental disorder are not referred to or treated in a careless or derogatory manner. It is important to guard against this type of labeling and to remind others to do so as well.

When mental health assessment schemes are utilized, a diagnostic label is placed on the client. In the ideal situation, labels would not exist; nor would treatment for certain mental health conditions be more likely than others to be reimbursed. Often in health and mental health practice, much of the assessment and diagnosis process is completed based on service reimbursement needs. Many health care professionals feel the pressure and focus on more reimbursable diagnostic categories, although there can be serious consequences for these pressures. For mental health practitioners, careful evaluation of what is actually happening with the client is essential. The diagnostic assessment starts with providing an accurate diagnosis (despite reimbursements as a criterion and incentive to diagnose). In this process, care is taken to prepare the client being served for the stigma that can occur with trying to overcome a diagnostic label with negative connotations or a label for which reimbursement is typically not allowed.

QUICK REFERENCE 1.4

DSM-IV-TR: Positive Aspects (PRO) and Negative Aspects (CON)

PRO: Leads to uniform and improved diagnosis.

CON: Leads to diagnostic labels.

PRO: Improves informed professional communication through uniformity.

CON: Provides limited information on the relationship between environmental considerations and aspects of the mental health condition.

PRO: Provides the basis for a comprehensive educational tool.

CON: Does not describe intervention strategy.

ANOTHER MENTAL HEALTH ASSESSMENT MEASURE

Social workers believe strongly in design, and base all practice strategy on the recognition of the person in the environment or person in the situation (Colby & Dziegielewski, 2010). From this perspective, the individual is believed to be part of the social environment, and his or her actions cannot be separated from this system. The individual is influenced by environmental factors in a reciprocal manner.

Impetus toward the development of this perspective may be partially related to dissatisfaction with the reliance on psychiatric-based typologies, which failed to account for environmental influences. The categorical approaches within the *DSM* did not appear to give such influences proper attention. Since these existing categories did not involve psychosocial situations or units larger than the individual within a system, problems were not viewed from an environmental context, thereby increasing the probability of such problems being classified as a mental illness (Braun & Cox, 2005; Carlton, 1984). In such a system, mental health practitioners could diagnose an individual with a mental health condition due to some general medical or symptom-based concern but were given no leeway to address a mental health condition based on life events and/or situational factors.

What transpired with the dynamic changes starting with the *DSM-III* encouraged social workers and other mental health professionals to provide aggregate parts to a diagnostic classification system. This focus on the individual tended to minimize the psychological and social causation, focusing more strongly on the reductive and biological causations of the disorders (hence its specific focus on symptom-based typologies) (Brendel, 2001). Clear demarcation of symptom-based criteria for diagnosing and

classification encouraged by insurance companies became an efficient and cost-effective measure for the treatment of mental disorders. Since insurance companies required a medical diagnosis before service reimbursement, social workers, psychologists, and other mental health professionals waged a long and difficult fight to use *DSM* independently for third-party payment purposes and their distinct services.

Developed through an award given to the California Chapter of the National Association of Social Workers (NASW) from the NASW Program Advancement Fund (Whiting, 1996), a new system was designed to focus on psychosocial aspects, situations, and units larger than the individual. It was called the Person-in-Environment Classification System, or PIE (Karls & Wandrei, 1996a, 1996b). It is built around two major premises: recognition of social considerations and the person-in-environment stance—the cornerstone on which all social work practice rests. Knowledge of the PIE is relevant for all mental health social workers regardless of educational level because of its emphasis on situational factors (Karls & O'Keefe, 2008, 2009).

The PIE system calls first for a social work assessment that is translated into a description of coding of the client's problems in social functioning. Social functioning is the client's ability to accomplish the activities necessary for daily living (e.g., obtaining food, shelter, and transportation) and fulfill major social roles as required by the client's subculture or community (Karls & Wandrei, 1996a, p. vi)

Originally designed to support the use of the *DSM-IV* rather than to substitute for it, the PIE's purpose was to evaluate the social environment and to influence the revisions of the *DSM*. Essentially, the PIE provided social workers and social work educators with a tool that allowed for environmental factors to be considered of primary importance. The PIE, an environmentally sensitive tool, supplemented the descriptive system of the *DSM* which related the mental illness to the human condition, utilizing a holistic, ecological, and pluralistic approach rather than just the diagnosis-focused (medical) foundational basis of the *DSM* (Satterly, 2007).

Social workers proposed an ecosystems perspective which incorporated the assumption that clinical practice needs to include the individual within his/her social environment and that his or her actions cannot be separated from his/her support system. Therefore, the PIE adopted features of the *DSM* multiaxis system in its assessment typology and had a notable influence on *DSM* revisions, particularly in the area of recognizing environmental problems. One concrete example of the PIE's influence on the *DSM-IV* is the change of Axis IV of the diagnostic system to reflect "psychosocial and environmental problems" where the problem is clearly listed; whereas in the past the *DSM-III-R* Axis IV merely listed the "severity of psychosocial stressors" and simply ranked the problem on a scale.

The PIE was formulated in response to the need to identify client problems in a way that health professionals could easily understand (Karls & Wandrei, 1996a, 1996b). As a form of classification system for adults, the PIE provides:

- A common language with which social workers in all settings can describe their clients' problems in social functioning.
- A common capsule description of social phenomena that can facilitate treatment or ameliorate problems presented by clients.
- A basis for gathering data to be used to measure the need for services and to design human service programs to evaluate effectiveness.
- A mechanism for clearer communication among social work practitioners and between practitioners, administrators, and researchers.

- A basis for clarifying the domain of social work in human service fields (Karls & Wandrei, 1996a).

In professional practice, tools such as the PIE can facilitate the identification and assessment of clients from a person-in-environment perspective that is easy for social workers to accept as comprehensive. When compared to the *DSM-IV* and the *DSM-IV-TR*, the PIE allows and provides mental health professionals with a classification system that enables them to codify the numerous environmental factors considered when looking at an individual's situation. Classification systems like the PIE offer mental health professionals a way first to recognize and later to systematically address social factors in the context of the client's environment. The PIE can help professionals to obtain a clearer sense of the relationship the problem has to the environment in a friendly and adaptable way.

PROFESSIONAL TRAINING IN THE PROFESSIONAL COUNSELING FIELDS

This book is written as a guide for several different disciplines of health and mental health professionals. Similar to the *DSM*, this book is designed to support usage in medicine and psychiatry, psychology, social work, nursing, and counseling. This type of integration, with so many diverse yet similar fields, is no easy task since different professions follow different practice models and methods. Yet regardless of which discipline a professional is trained in, there is often great overlap of therapeutic knowledge and skill. In the next chapter, special attention is given to how to apply the multiaxial diagnostic framework.

If professional practitioners are going to continue to utilize diagnostic assessment systems in the future, there are major implications for professional training and education. MacCluskie and Ingersoll (2001) are quick to remind us that, if professionals of different disciplines are going to use the *DSM*, training and adequate preparation in its use in classroom instruction and as part of a practicum or internship is required. This requires adoption of a more homogeneous approach to education and application among all helping disciplines. Other professionals, such as Horn (2008), remind us that all current interpretations must remain flexible and that, as we finalize the needed changes for the new version, *DSM-5*, we must remain vigilant of the ethical concerns that can result from misuse of this important diagnostic tool.

In today's practice environment, few would argue that the interdisciplinary approach of professionals working together to help the client is here to stay. To provide this homogeneity from a practice perspective, there is one goal that almost all professional helpers share: To "help clients manage their problems in living more effectively and develop unused or underused opportunities more fully" (Egan, 1998, p. 7). Now, to extend unification while ensuring competent, ethical and homogeneous practice, these helping disciplines will also need to unite in terms of professional education, mission, and goals. The first principle for the unification of professional education across disciplines is that (regardless of whether it is for social work, psychology, or other fields of professional counseling) training programs need to be more uniform and specific about what professional training entails and the effect it has on those who participate. When training can be defined in a reasonably specific manner and measured empirically, these professions will better assess its effects on client behavior. With the contemporary emphasis of professional accountability, the effort to predict and document specific outcomes of professional training is timely as well as warranted. The data also suggest that

one way in which professional training can be further enhanced is through differential selection of specified treatment methods. Training in these different treatment methods will allow for different causative variables (i.e., feelings and actions) to be identified in the course of assessing the client's behavior. Some researchers believe that sticking primarily to traditional methods, which still comprise a great part of professional training that emphasizes dispositional diagnoses (i.e., the direct relationship of the diagnosis and how it will relate to discharge), may result in diminishing accuracy of behavior assessment (Case & Lingerfelt, 1974; Dziegielewski, 2004).

Educators can improve the accuracy of client behavioral evaluations through the introduction of specific training in behavioral assessment. This may be the primary reason that in health care, the behaviorally based biopsychosocial approach has gained popularity. Clinical assessment, particularly when it emphasizes client behaviors, is a skill that can easily be taught, transmitted, and measured. Therefore, professional training that includes behavioral observation on how to construct observable and reliable categories of behavior and various systems of observation is recommended.

SUMMARY

As emphasized in this chapter, the *International Classification of Diseases, Tenth Edition (ICD-10)* and the *International Classification of Diseases, Ninth Edition, Clinical Modification (ICD-9-CM)* along with the *Diagnostic and Statistical Manual of Mental Disorders, Fourth Edition, Text Revision (DSM-IV-TR)*, reflect the official nomenclature used in mental health and other health-related facilities in the United States. Diagnostic assessment systems such as the *DSM*, the *ICD*, and the PIE are examples of three descriptive (categorical) classification schemes that cross all theoretical orientations.

The concept of understanding mental disorders, their taxonomical categorization, the formulating and completing of a diagnosis, assessment, or the diagnostic assessment and their definitions and meanings is embedded in the history of the *DSM*. The exact definition of what constitutes "diagnosis" and what constitutes "assessment" remains blurred and overlapping, with the words used interchangeably yet remaining distinct and interrelated (Dziegielewski, 1996, 1997a). For all professional practitioners, compelling demands and pressures related to practice reimbursement clearly emphasize the need for coordination in providing mental health care and subsequent intervention. Despite the differences currently existing among the disciplines, the degree to which a professional has power in the therapeutic marketplace rests on the degree to which a profession is licensed to apply the criteria used in the *DSM* diagnosis (MacCluskie & Ingersoll, 2001).

Because of the increasing demands related to evidence-based practice to achieve outcomes to assess quality, the effectiveness of service delivery, and the collection of data, numerous diagnosis and assessment measurements are currently available. Many are structured in unique categories and classification schemes. Whether this categorical approach used in the *DSM* is replaced by a dimensional one in the *DSM-5* still remains to be seen (Heizer et al., 2008). Utilizing the current system, this text demonstrates the application of these classification schemes and describes how assessment, treatment planning, and intervention become intertwined (Dziegielewski, 2008). Since assessment and treatment are based primarily on the practitioner's clinical judgment and interpretation, a thorough grounding in these classification systems will help him or her to make relevant, useful, and ethically sound evaluations of clients.

It is essential for the practitioner to be familiar with some of the major formal methods of diagnosis and assessment, especially the ones most commonly used and accepted in the area of mental health service delivery (Davis & Meier, 2001). The changes made over time and efforts toward the betterment within the criteria outlined in the *DSM* have served to move it toward becoming the best diagnostic tool possible. All mental health practitioners, regardless of discipline, can benefit by utilizing this information to systematically interpret and assist clients to understand what the results of the diagnostic assessment mean and how best to select empirically sound and ethically wise modes of practice intervention.

No matter whether we call what professional practitioners do assessment, diagnosis, or a combination of these resulting in the diagnostic assessment, the function remains a critical part of the helping process. Diagnosis and assessment constitute the critical first step that is essential to formulating the plan for intervention (Dziegielewski, Johnson, & Webb, 2002; Dziegielewski & Leon, 2001b). It is the plan for intervention that sets the entire tone for and circumstances of the professional helping process. As Dziegielewski (2004) has stated, based on the general context of reimbursement or fee for service, is it wise for all professionals to continue to struggle to differentiate diagnosis and assessment? Unfortunately, with the shift in mental health care to market-based services, practice and methods have evolved to reflect specialization, integration, and cost-effectiveness as part in parcel to service delivery. The question that now arises concerns who is eligible to make a diagnosis or an assessment. Professionals are lobbying and professional licensures reflect this transition, and can help to provide public accountability.

Today, the role of the professional practitioner is twofold: (1) Ensure that quality service is provided to the client, and (2) provide the client access and opportunity to see that his or her health and mental health needs are addressed. Neither of these tasks is easy or popular. Amid this turbulence, the role and necessity of the services that the professional practitioner provides in the area of assessment and intervention remain clear. All helping professionals must know and utilize the tools of diagnostic assessment and demonstrate competence in properly completing diagnostic assessment—the first step in the treatment hierarchy. To achieve this, it is crucial that health and mental health professionals have comprehensive training in this area to meet current requirements and service needs in an environment filled with limitations and shortages. The question remains: How can we best help the clients we serve?

QUESTIONS FOR —— FURTHER THOUGHT ——

1. Is there a difference between the terms diagnosis and assessment? How would you define the diagnostic assessment, and what client-relevant factors are the most important to identify?

2. Are these terms treated differently and assumed to have different meanings if the practitioner is in a particular health or mental health setting?

3. What do you believe is the most helpful aspect of using manuals such as the *DSM-IV-TR* in the diagnostic process?

4. What do you feel are the least helpful aspects of using manuals such as the *DSM-IV-TR* in professional practice?

5. Do you believe that use of the *DSM* as a diagnostic/assessment tool will facilitate your practice experience? Why or why not?

6. Taking into account the discussion related to the potential changes for the *DSM-5*, what do you see as the most critical changes that will best facilitate completion of the diagnostic assessment?

2 Basics and Application

The concept of formulating and completing a diagnostic assessment is richly embedded in the history of mental health practice (Ahn & Kim, 2008; Dziegielewski, 2010). The desire to master this process has been emphasized by compelling demands to address and meet required practice reimbursement (Dziegielewski, 2010). Therefore, all mental health practitioners need to become familiar with the major formal methods of diagnostic assessment, especially the ones used and accepted in the area of health and mental health service delivery. This chapter outlines the issues that contribute to the hesitancy and reluctance to differentiate between what constitutes a mental disorder and how the terms diagnosis and assessment relate. If these two terms are seen using a false dichotomy, obvious difficulty can result in practice focus and strategy. The purpose of this chapter is to explore the relationship between diagnosis and assessment and to introduce a more comprehensive term, the diagnostic assessment. The diagnostic assessment describes a combination approach that utilizes the meaning inherent in each term.

Once the terms are clearly defined, the information gathered during the diagnostic assessment becomes central for identifying and classifying mental health disorders as well as reporting this information systematically to insurance companies for reimbursement. In completing the diagnostic assessment, factors such as race, ethnicity, culture, and gender can affect the diagnostic impression derived. Recognition of this supporting information is essential to ensure a comprehensive diagnostic assessment vital for quality care. The information gathered through a comprehensive diagnostic assessment can also be utilized to understand the client and in turn better help the client understand him- or herself. Once completed, the diagnostic assessment becomes the foundation for identifying problem behaviors that will be utilized in establishing treatment plan considerations as well as the best course of intervention for a particular client. Since most fields of practice utilize the *DSM* as the basis of the formal diagnostic assessment system, this text focuses on this classification scheme.

UTILIZING THE *DSM-IV-TR* IN THE PRACTICE SETTING

In the United States, most health and mental health practitioners use the *DSM* to classify mental health problems. However, as described in Chapter 1, the *DSM*, which was originally designed for statistical and assessment purposes, does not suggest treatment approaches. This makes the *DSM* essential as a starting point for determining the nature of a client's problem as well as providing supportive information on prevalence rates within the larger population used to inform policy decisions. Thus, the book is valuable for both clinicians and researchers. For researchers, the interest lies in understanding the etiology and pathophysiology of the disorders;

for clinicians, the focus remains on the immediate and pragmatic, such as identifying clinically significant symptoms that affect human behavior and functioning (Nunes & Rounsaville, 2006). The *DSM* does, however, fall short on treatment strategy and options. Therefore, other supportive books are required to address this important aspect necessary for comprehensive, efficient, and effective care.

Therefore, in addition to the information provided in the *DSM-IV-TR*, practitioners need to be familiar with the latest and most effective forms of intervention based on relevant diagnostic criteria. Although the *ICD-10* and the *ICD-9-CM* are often used interchangeably, the *ICD-10* is most commonly referenced in the United States because of its direct relevance to clinical management. The *DSM-IV-TR*'s specific diagnostic coding system is most similar to the categories utilized in the *ICD-10-DCR*. In fact, the *ICD* clinical modification was developed to facilitate its use in practice and made it more relevant for practice in the United States. Many other countries, however, use the *ICD-10*, and it is a good idea for mental health practitioners to be familiar with both editions.

Professional Use: Who Can Use the DSM-IV-TR?

The *DSM-IV-TR* states clearly that it was designed to be used in a wide variety of settings, including inpatient and outpatient settings as well as consultation and liaison work. Furthermore, the *DSM-IV-TR* was designed for use by professionals, not as a self-help book for the lay public. The *DSM* is very complex and could overwhelm a client unfamiliar with the technical jargon. Therefore, use by the lay public is discouraged. The role of the professional is to interpret the diagnostic criteria, inform the client, and work with the client on what the best course of action would be.

The professional practitioners who use the *DSM-IV-TR* include psychiatrists and other physicians, psychologists, social workers, occupational and rehabilitation therapists, and other health and mental health professionals. Although these professionals can all have very different training and expertise, they still are expected to use this categorical approach by applying clinical skill and judgment to achieve similar determinations. These professionals need to be trained in how to use this categorical approach as well as being aware of the potential for misuse that exists before putting it into practice. Special care and consideration should always be given to protect the rights of clients while helping to identify issues needing to be addressed to ensure that client benefit and progress are obtained.

WORKING AS PART OF A TEAM: MULTIDISCIPLINARY AND INTERDISCIPLINARY TEAMS

Serving as part of a team, social workers and other mental health professionals have a unique role in the assessment and diagnostic process. Most professionals agree that a comprehensive diagnostic assessment starts with taking into account the complexity of the human condition and situational factors that affect behavioral health (Pearson, 2008). As part of either a multidisciplinary or interdisciplinary team, the mental health professional brings a wealth of information regarding the client's environment and family considerations essential to practice strategy.

To understand the term multidisciplinary, it can best be explained by dividing it into its two roots, multi and discipline. Multi means "many" or "multiple." Discipline means "the field of study a professional engages in." When combined, professionals from many or multiple disciplines work together to address a common problem. In health care settings, the use of multidisciplinary teams were part of a cost-effective practice response to the shifts from institutional care to community and home care through the delivery of specialized services (Rosen & Callaly, 2005). This type of team collaboration may also assist in improving patient care outcomes (Burns & Lloyd, 2004). The multidisciplinary team is often recognized as a preferred form of service delivery, especially when working in complex health and mental health service delivery systems (Orovwuje, 2008). Multidisciplinary teams are composed of health and social welfare professionals from various disciplines. These professionals include psychiatrists, physicians, nurses, social workers, physical therapists, occupational therapists, and so on.

When serving on a multidisciplinary team, each of the members has a distinct professional role, working independently, engaging in referrals to other professionals in inter-/intra-agencies, in a loose yet semistructured manner. Each professional generally works independently, sometimes in isolation, to solve the problems and related needs of the individual. At the same time, the professionals share what is learned about the client to improve treatment progress and overall team concerns. A key feature of multidisciplinary teams is a network-style group interaction of the participants of the team (Rosen & Callaly, 2005) in which the boundaries within professional disciplines are maintained, with each providing a perspective of the client's problem to address key features in the delivery of care. Patient care planning is brought together to provide a comprehensive method of service delivery for the client. In multidisciplinary teamwork, "a team manages its resources collectively according to client needs or along professional discipline boundaries" (Whyte & Brooker, 2001, p. 27). Communication and goals are consistent across disciplines, with each contributing to the overall welfare of the client.

In the current system of mental health care, which stresses evidence-based practices and outcomes to measure quality, multidisciplinary approaches are limited in meeting the current standards of care secondary to their structural makeup and style of approach to service delivery. Measurement is difficult to achieve when the interpretation of the stated goals and how to best achieve them differs among the different professionals. These professionals are all committed to working together to help the client, but in this type of teamwork there may still be different approaches and expectations for what is considered quality care and how to best achieve it. And while communication is evident, cohesion in multidisciplinary teams is not always feasible in services delivery, when normal differences occur in worldviews, professional identities, salaries, status and attitudes, and educational backgrounds emerge (Carpenter, Schneider, Brandon, & Wooff, 2003; Lankshear, 2003). The multidisciplinary team is still often used to provide services from a team perspective in mental health care, yet the focus toward a more collaborative and integrative approach, known as the interdisciplinary team approach, is gaining in popularity (Dziegielewski, 2004; Molodynski & Burns, 2008; Rosen & Callaly, 2005).

Similar to the multidisciplinary team, the interdisciplinary team consists of a variety of health care professionals. An interdisciplinary approach takes on a much more holistic approach to health care practice. "An interdisciplinary team in a modern mental health service brings specialist assessments and individualized care together in an integrated manner and is the underlying mechanism for case allocation, clinical decision-making, teaching, training and supervision and the application of the necessary skills mix for the best outcomes for service users" (Rosen & Callaly, 2005, p. 235). Interdisciplinary professionals work together throughout the process of service provision.

Generally, a plan of action is developed by the entire team. This type of teamwork involves a collaborative coordination of care, team-related activities, such as treatment planning, and shared leadership and power (Zeiss & Gallagher-Thompson, 2003).

In service provision, the skills and techniques that each professional provides often overlap. Interdependence is stressed throughout the referral, assessment, treatment, and planning process rather than through networking. This is different than the multidisciplinary team, where assessments and evaluations are often completed in isolation and later shared with the team. Boundaries in the formation of interdisciplinary teams are often blurred between members involved. In the interdisciplinary team process, each professional team member is encouraged to contribute, design, and implement the group goals for the health care service to be provided (Dziegielewski, 2004; Mezzich & Salloum, 2007).

Within the interdisciplinary team, each member may also supervise each other's work—a key difference from multidisciplinary teams, in which each member is measured and supervised independent of each discipline and agency (Rosen & Callaly, 2005). Interdisciplinary teams can facilitate the provision of quality care by gathering participatory information related to the analysis of the client's problem. A variety of multidisciplinary skills are available that work in a mutual and reciprocal educational fashion and produce viable and demonstrable results. This allows for implementation and problem-solving capabilities that encourage collaboration among providers to decrease and avoid isolation and generate new ideas.

Regardless of the type of team utilized, multidisciplinary or interdisciplinary, mental health professionals should always take the perspective that emphasizes client skill building and strength enhancement. If client needs are addressed from this perspective, each team member will be well equipped to contribute accordingly to the diagnostic assessment, supporting the development of the treatment plan, which will guide and determine future service delivery (Slomski, 2000). Providing attention to the dynamics of the team collaboration as well as the contributions each team member makes can only lead to enhanced service delivery for all served (Packard, Jones, & Nahrstedt, 2006).

DIAGNOSIS AND ASSESSMENT: IS THERE A DIFFERENCE?

Identifying a Mental Disorder

Diagnostic assessment starts with first defining what constitutes a mental disorder. The terms consistent with problematic behaviors within a mental disorder include distress and disability leading to a harmful dysfunction, abnormality, or aberration (Cooper, 2004; Kraemer, Shrout, & Rubic-Stipec, 2007). From a biological perspective, a mental disorder is generally defined as a biological or evolutionary disadvantage to an organism that interferes or reduces the quality of the life span or fitness (Lilienfeld & Landfield, 2008). Few would argue that utilizing a clear definition can help to guide decisions that determine the boundary between normality and pathology (American Psychiatric Association [APA], 2000). Yet clearly defining the criteria for a mental disorder is no simple task. Similar to the problems that occur when clearly trying to identify a medical disorder, the actual criteria can be subject to individual interpretation on the part of the client as well as the provider. For the client, self-reporting of symptoms can be confused by what the client thinks he or she is experiencing and what is actually happening. From the perspective of the practitioner, using a categorical approach to defining symptoms indicative of a mental disorder can also differ. Experienced practitioners can have very different interpretations on how symptoms are identified and what they believe meets the criteria for the diagnosis (Rashidian, Eccles, & Russell, 2008).

When starting with the definition of what constitutes a mental disorder, it is important to note the distinction between disorder and disease (Kraemer, Shrout, & Rubio-Stipec, 2007). Making this distinction plays a fundamental part in determining whether a disease or a disorder is present in the individual. According to Cooper (2004), making a distinction between these two terms is not easy because related disciplines continue to challenge what constitutes a mental disorder. Furthermore, there is disagreement about how using the taxonomy of categorizations within the *DSM* influences the subsequent diagnostic process. As early as the *DSM-II*, a condition was considered a disorder when the condition influenced role formulation and application of the diagnostic impression. Factors identified focused on distress or disability. Then starting with the publication of the *DSM-III*, the term disorder started to be used interchangeably with the term disease. Regardless, of the term used, disease or disorder, it relates directly to harmful dysfunctional behavior from an evolutionary psychology perspective (Cooper, 2004). To simplify the definition most often used today, it appears that disease indicates a known pathological process; a disorder may comprise two or more separate diseases but generally there is a known pathological process that is either known or unknown.

For medical professionals, especially those working in primary care, the difficulty in identifying what constitutes a mental disorder rests within the diagnostic impression and the variability that exists among professionals when identifying characteristics, traits, and behaviors relative to the disorder (Mitchell, Vaze, & Rao, 2009). Since identification and recognition rates can vary, the actual presence of a mental disorder can be difficult to ascertain, leading to incidents where professionals either overreport or underreport these symptoms. In addition, the flexibility within formulating the diagnostic impression leads to the question of what exactly is the diagnostic impression. And is the formulation of the evaluation completed by the mental health professional more accurately termed diagnosis or assessment?

In mental health practice, when looking specifically at terms like disease and disorder, confusion results when the two terms are not considered distinct. In such cases, the concepts inherent in each tend to blur and overlap in terms of application. This is complicated further by the multiplicity of meanings applied to the terms used to describe each aspect of what a client is experiencing and whether it is related to a disease or a disorder. The lack of clarity of definitions can result in applied social, personal, and professional interpretations in health and mental health practice that are varied and nonuniform. Similar to problems with defining disease and disorder, the debate on what to call the outlining of a client's mental health problems, such as diagnosis or assessment, continues to be examined. In today's practice environment, it is not uncommon to use these words interchangeably (Dziegielewski, 2004; Dziegielewski & Holliman, 2001).

A concrete definition for all these terms and for their relationship to each other facilitates the diagnostic process. Practitioners must be careful not to be too quick in categorizing an individual's problems; this may result in diagnostic bias and an inaccurate diagnostic label. The symptoms with which an individual may present for treatment may differ based on numerous variables, including psychological, social, cultural, and environmental circumstances.

Diagnosis and the Diagnostic Process It is easy to see how the actual definition, criteria, and subsequent tasks of assessment and diagnosis are viewed as similar and overlapping, thereby creating a shared definition. In most cases, if viewed separately, the assessment has been considered to come before the diagnosis and is the building block on which the diagnosis is established (Rankin, 1996). Regardless of whether health or mental health practitioners truly subscribe to or support the distinction between the terms assessment and diagnosis, awareness of the difficulty in trying to separate these two terms and announce their uniqueness continues. One commonly accepted diagnosis in the field of social work is in the *Social Work Dictionary* by Barker (2003):

Diagnosis: "The process of identifying a problem (social and mental, as well as medical) and its underlying causes and formulating a solution. In early social work delineation, it is one of the three processes, along with social study and treatment. Currently, many social workers prefer to call this process assessment because of the medical connotations that often accompany the term diagnosis. Other social workers think of diagnosis as the process of seeking underlying causes and assessment as having more to do with the analysis of relevant information." (Barker, 2003, p. 118)

The most widely accepted definition of diagnosis, however, rests within the medical model, because it is based on the representation of a presenting medical concern. Corey (2001b) states that the purpose of diagnosis in counseling and psychotherapy is to "identify the disruptions in a client's presenting behavior and lifestyle" (p. 52). Bridging the gap between viewing diagnoses in isolation, Perlman (1957) warned social workers not to perceive that determining and formulating a diagnosis "would magically yield a cure to a reluctance to come to any conclusion beyond an impression . . . grasping at ready-made labels" (p. 165). Perlman defined diagnosis as the identification of both process and product. According to

Perlman, the diagnostic process was defined as "examining the parts of a problem for the import of their particular nature and organization, for the interrelationship among them, for the relationships between them and the means to their solution" (p. 164).

In mental health assessment, historically the emphasis is placed on measuring the diagnostic product. Falk (1981, as cited in Carlton, 1984) suggested 14 areas to be addressed in providing diagnostic impressions: life stage, health condition, family and other memberships, racial and ethnic memberships, social class, occupation, financial situation, entitlements, transportation, housing, mental functioning, cognition (personal), cognition (capability), and psychosocial elements. Utilizing a biopsychosocial perspective, the areas are further broken down into three primary categories: biomedical, psychological, and social factors. Since all mental health professionals are responsible for assisting with the provision of concrete services, recognition of these factors is often considered part of the practitioner's role in assessment with the addition of a fourth area that addresses the functional/situational factors affecting the diagnostic process.

Historically, it has always been essential that the activity of diagnosis be related to the client's needs. A diagnosis is established to better understand and prepare to address the probable symptoms relative to the mental disorder. Factors resulting from the diagnostic procedure are shared with the client and assist in goals related to self-help or continued skill building. From a medical perspective, the diagnostic process is used to examine symptoms and the situation and provide the basis to initiate the helping process. The formal diagnostic process will yield and contribute to formal diagnostic and functional assessment based on the information learned. The diagnostic information gathered facilitates the establishment of the intervention plan.

Carlton (1984) further exemplified the issue of process in the diagnostic procedure:

> To be effective and responsive, any clinical social work diagnosis must be a diagnosis "for now"—a tentative diagnosis. It is the basis of joint problem solving work for the clinician and client. To serve this purpose, the diagnosis must be shared with the client(s) and, as their work gets under way and proceeds through the various time phases of clinical social work process, the diagnosis must change as the configuration of the elements of the problem change. Thus clinical social work diagnosis is evolutionary in character and responsive to the changing nature of the condition or problem in which it relates. (p. 77)

In addressing the diagnostic process, clear results that lead to a *diagnostic product* must be obtained. The diagnostic product is the obtained information gained through the diagnostic assessment. This includes drawing logically derived inferences and conclusions based on scientific principles from the information obtained. Corey (2001b) suggested that certain questions be asked:

- What is happening in the client's life now?
- What does the client want from therapy?
- What is the client learning from therapy?
- To what degree is the client applying what is learned?

Corey (2001b) believed that questions such as these allow for assessment and diagnosis to be joined in a tentative hypothesis and that these educated hunches can be formed and shared with the client throughout the treatment process. To establish a firm foundation for the diagnostic process, the professional therapist must be skilled in obtaining and interpreting the information acquired identifying the client's concerns while being able to rule out differential diagnoses (Owen, 2008). Carlton (1984) stressed the importance of recognizing three factors: biomedical, psychological, and social. He felt that it was essential for professionals to understand the biopsychosocial approach to health care practice and obtain balance between these factors. This balance does not have to be equal, and the area of emphasis can change. It is always the situation experienced by the client that places the most importance on what is the first area addressed.

For example, a client diagnosed with HIV can have many concerns that will need prioritization. First, practitioners must clarify what is related solely to the medical aspects of the condition and what is related to the mental health aspects. The information related to the biomedical area will stress the need to get the client information and implications of the positive findings of the medical test used. Medical tests will determine the t-cell count (a type of body protection factor) obtained and will establish a baseline for current and future levels of self-protection from the illness and opportunistic infectious diseases and treatment. Once the biomedical condition is clarified, emphasis will shift to education, providing information on the effects of the disease, what the illness means, and what to expect if the illness progresses. It is here that treatment adherence strategy becomes essential to making sure that clients get and continue to utilize the services they need. Adherence issues such as disease management, provider-client relationships, and other individual factors become essential to treatment success (Gilbert, Abel, Stewart, & Zilberman, 2007).

As the total needs of the client are taken into consideration, the diagnostic focus will shift to address the social aspects related to the client's condition. Components of transmission will be addressed, including sexual contacts and practices, and addressing these with the partners who are or have been sexually active with the client. Doing this will require educating the client on disclosure of the illness and the effects it presents to him or her and to all parties involved. The focus is how to explain to loved ones what has happened and address what this illness means for present and future social relationships. This focus involves a complex process of inter- and intrapersonal and emotional issues with the client that will occur in response to the illness and that must be resolved. Regardless of what area is emphasized and with what intensity, understanding and integration of the biopsychosocial approach is considered essential in the diagnostic assessment.

Overall, the mental health professions have embraced the necessity for diagnosis in practice—although this need is often recognized with caution. While accepting the requirement for completion of a diagnosis, much discontent and dissatisfaction among professionals continues to exist. Some mental health professionals fear that when the diagnosis is referred to in the most traditional sense, reflective of the medical or "illness" perspective, it will be inconsistent with professional values and ethics. For these professionals, an illness-focused perspective detracts from an individual's capacity for initiative based on self-will or rational choice. Today, however, this view is changing. Many mental health professionals, struggling for practice survival in a competitive, cost-driven health care system, disagree. They feel that practice reality requires that a traditional method of diagnosis be completed in order to receive reimbursement. It is this capacity for reimbursement that influences and determines who will be offered the opportunity to provide service (Steps Taken to Watchdog Managed Care, 1997).

When documenting treatment for reimbursement, however, it is probably better to use the term *assessment* or *diagnostic assessment* in place of *diagnosis* (Dziegielewski & Leon, 2001a). A reason is that *assessment* is often not directly related to the medical model, whereas the term *diagnosis* often is (Barker, 2003). Usually assessments are related to mental models, based on clinical expertise and training designed to recognize the patient's holistic situation and taking into account individual strengths and family support (Siebert, 2006).

Assessment   Most mental health practitioners are active in obtaining and completing assessment within the general context of diagnostic considerations (Corey, 2001a, 2001b). According to Barker (2003), *assessment* involves "determining the nature, cause, progression, and prognosis of a problem and the personalities and situations involved" as well as understanding and making changes to minimize or resolve it (p. 30). Assessment requires thinking and formulating from the facts within a client's situation to reach tentative hypotheses and a logical conclusion (Owen, 2008; Sheafor, C. R. Horejsi, & G. A. Horejsi, 1997). Therefore, assessment is an essential ingredient to the therapeutic process and is the hallmark of all mental health professional activity. An assessment is a collaborative process as it becomes part of the integrated interactions among client, therapist, multidisciplinary and interdisciplinary teams, and support systems (Corey, 2001a, 2001b). It controls and directs all aspects of practice, including the nature, direction, and scope; however, the assessment and diagnosis cannot be separated and must be continually updated as part of the intervention process (Corey, 2001b).

For professional practitioners who often fill many different roles as part of the interdisciplinary team, the process of assessment must reflect diversity and flexibility. Environmental pressures and changes in client problem situations require the examination and reexamination of the client's situation for accuracy. If the process of assessment is rushed, superficial factors may be highlighted while significant ones are deemphasized or overlooked. Professionals bear administrative and economic pressures to make recommendations for consumer protection while balancing fiscal and reimbursement concerns. Consumer protection is paramount and should never take second place to cutting costs—health care quality should always be preserved.

The problem of differentiating between diagnosis and assessment is not unique to any one of the counseling disciplines. Since none of the helping professions developed in isolation, the individual assessment process has been influenced by many disciplines, including medicine, psychiatry, nursing, psychology, and social work, as well as other counseling professionals. Historically, assessment has been referred to as *diagnosis* or the *psychosocial diagnosis* (Rauch, 1993). While further similarities seem to exist, professional helpers should not accept the terms as interchangeable. Diagnosis focuses on symptoms and assigns categories that best fit the symptoms the client is experiencing. Assessment, however, is broader and focuses on the functional ability of person-in-situation or person-in-environment stance to achieve activities of daily living.

This blurring of terminology is becoming customary that even the *DSM-IV* (1994) and *DSM-IV-TR* (2000) use both words. At times, it appears that these words are interchangeable throughout the books when used to describe the diagnostic impression. It appears that terminology as well as the resulting helping activities and subsequent practice strategies have been forced to adapt to the dominant culture (Dziegielewski, 2004) and the models for service delivery, which guide their structure and implementation. Since these expectations deal with the pressures of reimbursement for service, they influence and guide practice intervention and strategy. Pressure within the environment

supports the expectation to reduce services to clients, treat only those who are covered by insurance or can pay privately, and/or terminate clients because the services are too costly (Ethics Meet Managed Care, 1997). Therefore, the role of assessment and diagnosis, regardless of what we call it, is a critical one because it can determine what, when, and how services will be provided.

A COMBINATION APPROACH: THE DIAGNOSTIC ASSESSMENT

When looking specifically at the features inherent in a diagnostic assessment, the same features in technique remain and actually overlap. The distinction, which is present, is that the term *diagnosis* is utilized to describe a presenting condition while an *assessment* is utilized to acquire information to describe and/or verify the presence of a condition. Furthermore, *assessment* can be used more broadly to include taking into account a larger context at each step of the process, including understanding a client's personality, problems, strengths, and related information about relevant social and interpersonal considerations that influence his or her mental health (Jordan & Franklin, 2003). Therefore, these terms are often used interchangeably, but the primary difference lies in the fact that the focus of the assessment is applied. Therefore, in this text, the term *diagnostic assessment* is used simply as a combination of both terms.

In diagnostic assessments, the foundation and goals for therapy are established and confirmatory and discomfirmatory strategies are utilized to elicit information to confirm diagnosis and/or test the viability of an alternative diagnosis (Owen, 2008). Much of the client-provider interaction engages in asking questions, establishing mutual goals for therapy and alliance, and acquiring information to formulate a diagnostic impression. In addition to the diagnostic criteria, the diagnostic assessment goes further by also seeking information on a wide variety of personal and environmental factors contributing to the mental health disorder that can supplement the understanding of the treatment context within the individual's relational systems.

Dziegielewski (2004) outlined five factors that guide the initiation of accurate diagnostic assessment that will ultimately relate to the implementation of practice strategy. When working with individuals and preparing to complete the diagnostic assessment, professional practitioners should:

1. Examine carefully how much information the client is willing to share and the accuracy of that information. The information the client is willing to share and the accuracy of what is shared is essential to ensure the depth and application of what is presented as well as the subsequent motivation and behavioral changes that will be needed in the intervention process. Gathering information from the *DSM* and evaluating whether it matches what the client is reporting requires an awareness of this phenomena as it relates to how the symptoms are reported. Focusing on information that is readily available and forming quick impression and conclusions can lead to incomplete or inaccurate information (Owen, 2008). Special attention needs to be given not only to what the client is saying but also the context in which this information is revealed. What is going on in the client's life at this time? What are the systemic factors that could be influencing certain behaviors? What will revealing the information mean to family and friends, or how will it affect the client's support system? Gathering this information is important especially since a client may fear that stating accurate information could have negative consequences. For example, clients may withhold information if they feel revealing it may have legal ramifications (imprisonment), social consequences (rejection from family or friends), or medical implications (rehospitalization).

2. Gather as accurate a definition of the problem as possible. It will not only guide the diagnostic assessment, it will also guide the approach or method of intervention that will be used. Furthermore, the temptation should always be resisted to let the diagnostic impression or intervention approach guide the problem rather than allowing the problem to guide the approach (Sheafor et al., 1997). This is critical since so much of the problem identification process in assessment is an intellectual activity. The professional practitioner should never lose sight of the ultimate purpose of the assessment process, which is to complete an assessment that will help to establish a concrete service plan to address the client's needs.

3. Be aware of how their beliefs can influence or affect the interpretation of the problem or both. An individual's worldview or paradigm shapes the way the events that surround the situation are viewed. Most professionals agree that what an individual believes creates the foundation for who he or she is and influences how he or she learns. In ethical and moral professional practice, it is essential that these individual influences do not directly affect the assessment process. Therefore, the practitioner's values, beliefs, and practices influencing treatment outcomes need to be clearly identified at

the onset of treatment. Professional practitioners need to ask themselves: "What is my immediate reaction to the client and the problem expressed?" Clients have a right to make their own decisions, and the helping professional must do everything possible to ensure this right and not allow personal opinion to impair the completion of a proper assessment. Since counseling professionals often serve as part of an interdisciplinary team, the beliefs and values of the members of the team must also be considered. Awareness of value conflicts that might arise among team members is critical. This awareness allows practitioners to prepare for how personal feelings and resultant opinions might inhibit them from accurately perceiving and assessing the situation. As part of a team, each member holds the additional responsibility of helping others on the team be as objective as possible in the assessment process. Values and beliefs can be influential in identifying factors within individual decision-making strategies; they remain an important factor to consider and identify in the assessment process (D. W. Sue & D. Sue, 2008).

4. Address openly issues surrounding culture and race in the assessment phase to ensure that the most open and receptive environment is created. Simply stated, the professional practitioner needs to be aware of his or her own cultural limitations, open to cultural differences, and recognize the integrity and uniqueness of the client while utilizing the client's own learning style, including his or her own resources and supports (Dziegielewski, 1996, 1997a; D. W. Sue & D. Sue, 2008). Ethnic identity and cultural mores can influence behaviors and should never be overlooked or ignored.

For example, when utilizing the *DSM-IV*, cultural factors are stressed prior to establishing a diagnosis. The *DSM-IV-TR* emphasizes that delusions and hallucinations may be difficult to separate from the general beliefs or practices that are related to a client's specific cultural custom or lifestyle. For this reason, the *DSM-IV-TR* includes an appendix that describes and defines culture-bound syndromes affecting the diagnosis and assessment process (APA, 1995, 2000).

5. The assessment process must focus on client strengths and highlight the client's own resources for addressing problems that affect his or her activities of daily living and for providing continued support (Lum & Lu, 2003). Identifying strengths and resources and linking them to problem behaviors with individual, family, and social functioning may not be as easy as it sounds. There is a tendency to focus on the individual's negatives rather than praising the positives, which is further complicated by time-limited intervention settings where mental health professionals must quickly identify individual and collectively based strengths (Dziegielewski, 2008). The importance of accurately identifying client strengths and support networks in the diagnostic assessment is critical, as these will be incorporated into the suggested intervention plan providing a means for continued growth and wellness lasting beyond the formal treatment period.

In the diagnostic assessment, several aspects must always be considered:

1. Determine the existence of a disorder, disease, or illness supported by somatic, behavioral, or concrete features.

2. Ascertain the cause or etiology of the disorder, illness, or disease based on

features existing in the client that are severe enough to influence occupational and social functioning.

3. Base any diagnostic impression on a systematic scientific examination of the client's reported symptoms always taking into account the client's situation (Kraemer, Shrout, & Rubio-Stipec, 2007).

COMPLETING THE DIAGNOSTIC ASSESSMENT PROCESS

It is assumed here that the diagnostic assessment begins with the first client-practitioner interaction. The information gathered provides the data-based observations and reporting to be used to determine the requirements and direction of the helping process as well as the data collection. It is expected that the professional will gather information about the current situation, a history of past issues, and anticipate service expectations for the future. This diagnostic assessment should be multidimensional and include creative interpretation and provide the groundwork for the possible strategy for service delivery. Information gathered will follow a behavioral biopsychosocial approach to practice (Pearson, 2008).

Starting the Process: Gathering Information Related to the Biomedical, Psychological, and Situational Factors

In this type of assessment, the biomedical factors highlighted relate to the general physical health

or medical condition of the client. (See Quick Reference 2.1 for an explanation of biomedical factors in assessment.) Information should be considered from both the practitioner's perspective and the client's perception. All information gathered needs to show the relationship between the biological or medical factors as well as the functioning level to complete certain behaviors maximizing independence. Concrete tasks identify the focus of increased future change efforts.

The second area considered is psychological factors. Psychological functioning is noted, and cognitive health functioning is recorded along with its effects related to occupational and social functioning. Specific information related to lethality for a client that may be at risk for suicide or harming others must be gathered and processed. If these behaviors exist, immediate action will be needed. (See Quick Reference 2.2 for specifics on psychological factors in assessment.)

Last, behavioral-based biopsychosocial approaches to assessment emphasize identifying social and environmental factors. Most professionals would agree that environmental considerations are very important in measuring and assessing all other aspects of a client's needs. Identifying family, social supports, and cultural expectations are all important in helping the client ascertain the best course of action (Colby & Dziegielewski, 2010). (See Quick Reference 2.3 for how to assess for social and environmental considerations.) Assessing the situation is especially important when working with certain cultures. For example, Alegria et al. (2007) warn that living

QUICK REFERENCE 2.1
BIOMEDICAL FACTORS IN ASSESSMENT

General medical	The physical disability or illness the client reports and what specific ways it affects the client's social and occupational functioning and activities of daily living.
Perceived overall health status	Encourage the client to assess his or her own health status and what he or she is able to do to facilitate the change effort.

QUICK REFERENCE 2.2

PSYCHOLOGICAL FACTORS IN ASSESSMENT

Mental functioning	Describe the client's mental functioning. Complete a mental status assessment. Learn and utilize the multiaxis assessment system.
Cognitive functioning	Does the client have the ability to think and reason what is happening to him or her? Is the client able to participate and make decisions in regard to his or her own best interest?
Assessment of lethality	Would the client hurt him- or herself or anyone else because of the perception of the problem he or she is experiencing?

---

in what the client perceives as an unsafe area can clearly influence the behaviors the client exhibits.

Generally, the client is the primary source of data. Be sure to take the time to assess the accuracy of the information and determine whether the client may either willingly or inadvertently withhold or exaggerate the information presented. Assessment information is usually collected through verbal and written reports. Verbal reports may be gathered from the client, significant others, family, friends, or other helping professionals. Critical information can also be derived from written reports, such as medical documents, previous clinical assessments, lab tests, and other clinical and diagnostic methods. Furthermore, information about the client can be derived through direct observation of verbal or physical behaviors or interaction patterns between other interdisciplinary team members, family, significant others, or friends. When seeking evidence-based practice, recognizing directly what a client is doing can be a critical factor in the diagnostic assessment process. Viewing and recording these patterns of communication can be extremely helpful in later establishing and developing strengths and resources as well as utilizing and linking problem behaviors to concrete indicators reflecting a client's performance. Remember that in addition to verbal reports, written reports reflective of practice effectiveness often are expected. Background sheets, psychological tests, or tests to measure health status or level of daily function may be utilized to establish more concrete measurement of client problem behaviors.

Although the client is the first and primary source of data, the current emphasis on evidence-

---

QUICK REFERENCE 2.3

SOCIAL AND ENVIRONMENTAL FACTORS IN ASSESSMENT

Social/societal help seeking	Is the client open to outside help? What support system or helping networks are available to the client from those outside the immediate family or the community?
Occupational participation	How does a client's illness or disability impair or prohibit functioning in the work environment? Is the client in a supportive work environment?
Social support	Does the client have support from neighbors, friends, or community organizations (i.e., church membership, membership in professional clubs)?
Family support	What support or help is expected from relatives of the client?
Ethnic or religious affiliation	If the client is a member of a certain cultural or religious group, will this affiliation affect medical intervention and compliance issues?

based practice strategy necessitates gathering information from other sources. Taking a team approach involves sharing the responsibility for talking with the family, significant others, and other health providers to estimate planning support and assistance. From this perspective, task effectiveness is measured in how the team is successful in achieving its outcomes (Whyte & Brooker, 2001). As part of a team, it is important to gather information from other secondary sources, such as the client's medical record. To facilitate assessment, the nonmedically trained practitioner must work with those who are medically trained to make sure he or she understands the client's medical situation (Dziegielewski, 2006). Knowledge of certain medical conditions and when to refer to other health professionals for continued care is an essential part of the assessment process.

Considerations for Completing the Diagnostic Assessment

In completing a multidimensional diagnostic assessment, there are four primary steps for consideration (see Quick Reference 2.4 for important considerations in completing the assessment):

1. **The problem must be recognized as interfering with daily functioning.** Here the practitioner must be active in uncovering problems affecting daily living and engaging the client in self-help or skill building, changing behaviors, or both. It is important for the client to acknowledge that the problem exists. Once this is done, the definition of the problem will become clear, allowing for exploration (Hepworth, Rooney, & Larsen, 2002).

2. **The problem must be clearly identified.** The problem of concern is what the client sees as important; he or she is the one who is expected to create the behavior change. It is common to receive referrals from other health care professionals, and special attention should always be given to referrals that clearly recommend a course of treatment or intervention. This type of focused referral may limit the scope and intervention possibilities available. Often such focused referrals that limit intervention scope can provide the basis for reimbursement as well. Although referral information and suggestion should always be considered in your

---

QUICK REFERENCE 2.4

IMPORTANT CONSIDERATIONS FOR COMPLETING THE NEW DIAGNOSTIC ASSESSMENT

1. The problem must be recognized and linked to interferences with daily functioning.
2. Special consideration must be given to the environmental context in which the behaviors are occurring.
3. Cultural considerations for both the client and the practitioner should be addressed and when possible discussed openly. Once problem behaviors are noted, criterion for the diagnostic impression is important only as it leads to assisting with identifying the needs of the client for a problem-solving strategy.
4. A complete diagnostic assessment involves more than the diagnostic impression; it involves utilizing the information gathered to best help the client and, thereby, guide, enhance, and, in many cases, determine the course of treatment.

discussion with the client in identifying the problem, in terms of assessment and the resulting plan, the client's best interest is paramount, and he or she should participate to identify the end result.

3. **The problem strategy must be developed.** Here the professional practitioner must clearly focus on the goals and objectives to be followed in the intervention process. In the initial planning stage, identification of mutually agreed on, measurable goals and objective and concrete indicators of met goals and objectives will assist both the client and the practitioner to ensure practical, useful, and productive changes have been made.

4. **Once the problem strategy and plan are clearly identified, a diagnostic assessment plan must be implemented.** According to Sheafor, C. R. Horejsi, and G. A. Horejsi (1997), the plan of action is the "bridge between the assessment and the intervention" (p. 135). The outcome of the diagnostic assessment process is the completion of a plan that will guide, enhance, and determine the course of treatment to be implemented (Dziegielewski, 2010; Siebert, 2006). With the complexity of human beings and the problems they encounter, a properly prepared multidimensional diagnostic assessment is the essential first step for ensuring quality service delivery.

In summary, none of these classification systems suggests treatment approaches; all only provide diagnostic and assessment classifications. The intervention plan is derived from the assessment and depends on the practitioner's interpretation. Regardless of what type of diagnostic assessment tool is utilized, all practitioners need to be able to: (a) choose, gather, and report this information systematically; (b) be aware and assist other multidisciplinary or interdisciplinary team members in the diagnostic process; (c) interpret and assist the client to understand what the results of the diagnostic assessment mean; and (d) assist the client to choose evidence-based and ethically wise modes of practice intervention.

DSM-IV-TR ALONE IS NOT ENOUGH

For a diagnostic assessment to be completed, the actual information presented in each one of the criteria sets must be utilized. When the work groups of the *DSM-IV* and *DSM-IV-TR* were created, specific emphasis was given to ensure that the professionals engaging in this process had the latest in terms of information based on research and evidence-based practice. This allowed for work teams to complete: (a) comprehensive and systemic reviews of the published literature; (b) reanalysis of the already collected data sets; and (c) extensive issue-focused field trials (APA, 2000, p. xxvi). Projective testing alone was insufficient as supporting evidence for placement in a diagnostic category. In forensic settings and regardless of the supporting criteria, a diagnostic label cannot be utilized as a legal definition of a mental disorder or mental disability. Nor can a diagnosis of a mental disorder alone be used to determine competence, criminal responsibility, or disability. Information needs to describe a person's behavioral problems and other functional impairments.

DSM-IV-TR Is Based in Research and Evidence-Based Practice

As explained in Chapter 1, one of the major weaknesses in earlier editions of the *DSM* is that they generally focused on descriptive rather than etiological factors. It is important to note, however, that in the *DSM-IV*, this shortfall was addressed and was further modified in the

---

QUICK REFERENCE 2.5

BASIS FOR CHANGES IN THE *DSM-IV-TR*

The *DSM-IV-TR* changes are based on:

- Literature reviews
- Data analysis and reanalysis
- Field trials

DSM-IV-TR. The latest version of the *DSM* is now based on (a) literature reviews, (b) data analysis and reanalysis, and, (c) field trials (see Quick Reference 2.5).

In the *DSM-IV* and the *DSM-IV-TR* literature reviews were conducted to elicit clinical utility, reliability (i.e., did the same criteria continue to present from case to case), descriptive validity (did it actually describe what it was meant to describe), and psychometric performance criteria (were common characteristics of performance on psychometric tests listed in the criterion). Furthermore, a number of validating variables were identified and studied. This research, including systematic and computerized reviews, ensured that evidence-based information was utilized to support the suggestions made by the individual work groups.

A second area of research support included data analysis and reanalysis. Information from this source was particularly important when evidence was lacking to support work group recommendations. In addition to the original field trials in the *DSM-IV*, over 40 data sets were reexamined. The data reanalysis compared the impact of the probable changes suggested.

Finally, 12 field trials were also completed, each with 5 to 10 different sites and over 1,000 participants (APA, 2000). The field trials combined the knowledge gained from clinical practice with evidence-based procedures and research. Thus, the two most recent editions of the *DSM*, unlike their predecessors, have made efforts to incorporate the best mix of practice wisdom and research for determining the criteria and characteristics of categories presented.

Meaning of Clinically Significant

The practitioner needs to be well versed in the use of the *DSM* and situational factors that need to be part of the diagnostic assessment process. Knowing how to address these factors in clinical practice is critical. Knowledge of the potential damage that can occur from placing a diagnostic label inappropriately is essential. The term *clinically significant* indicates that a practitioner has clearly linked the symptoms present in the mental disorder with how these stop or impair a client's current level of functioning. An individual who exhibits the symptoms matching the criterion of a mental disorder yet his or her individual, social, or occupational functioning is not impaired should not be given a diagnosis. A diagnosis should be given only when the symptoms are severe enough to interfere with or disturb functioning. This makes the incorporation of environmental circumstances essential to support or negate the use of a diagnostic category. Next we introduce important sections and diagnostic features associated with the *DSM-IV-TR*. Remember, however, that regardless of the diagnostic symptoms a client is experiencing and whether these symptoms are related to factors such as culture, age, and gender, if the behavior is not considered clinically significant, no diagnosis should be given.

IMPORTANT SECTIONS IN THE *DSM-IV-TR*

For each disorder in the *DSM-IV-TR*, the authors describe the primary characteristics of the disorder and provide additional available diagnostic information. When additional information is available, the diagnostic criteria are divided under separate headings, such as "Diagnostic Features" and "Associated Features and Disorders." "Diagnostic Features" consists of examples of the disorder and the tests available to determine etiology (APA, 2000). When separate from the "Diagnostic Features," the "Associated Features and Disorders" is generally subdivided into three sections including descriptive features, laboratory findings, and information associated with features related to the physical examination or general medical conditions. For example, under the disorder vascular dementia (a type of dementia generally related to stroke), the diagnostic criteria are outlined. Under the "Associated Features," the text further highlights medical tests to confirm the presence of the disorder (e.g., computerized tomography of the head). Based on the information available, the "Diagnostic Features" section may be either combined or separate from the section on "Associated Features and Disorders."

"Associated Features" and lab findings presented in the text include three types of information.

1. The descriptive features of the mental disorder are presented as well as predisposing factors and complications.
2. Associated laboratory findings are listed (divided into three types of laboratory findings: diagnostic, abnormal to this group, and associated).
3. The physical exam and general medical conditions accompanying the condition are noted. The section on associated lab findings is further broken down into three areas: diagnostic (tests available to determine etiology); confirmatory of the diagnosis (tests supporting the diagnosis but not providing etiological basis); and complication(s) of the disorder (conditions often found in conjunction to or as a result of it, e.g., electrolyte imbalance and anorexia).

In the diagnostic assessment, the practitioner should be alert to these factors and how they affect the diagnostic criteria being exhibited (see Quick Reference 2.6).

QUICK REFERENCE 2.6

ASSOCIATED FEATURES AND DISORDERS

- **Associated descriptive features and mental disorders:** This category includes features associated with the disorder but not critical to making the diagnosis.
- **Associated laboratory findings:** This section provides information on three different types of laboratory findings. First, when diagnostic tests are presented in a section, they explain the cause of the etiology of the disorder. Second, the diagnostic tests presented may not clearly be related to the disorder but seem to appear in other groups of individuals that suffer from this disorder. Last, each section can present the laboratory findings that are associated with complications resulting directly from the disorder. These tests are presented as they help the practitioner make a more comprehensive diagnostic determination. But in all three areas, these findings are not required for a diagnosis to occur. For the most part, most of the tests in this category are associated with the diagnosis but do not necessarily reveal the cause of etiology (e.g., computerized tomography [CT] scans to assist in classification of types of dementia).
- **Associated physical exam findings and general medical conditions:** These findings are related to the disorder and have significance in treatment.

CULTURE, AGE, AND GENDER-RELATED INFORMATION

Culture has been defined as the "sum total of life patterns passed from generation to generation within a group of people and includes institutions, language, religious ideals, artistic expressions, and patterns of thinking, social and interpersonal relationships. Aspects of culture are often related to people's ethnic, racial and spiritual heritage" (Kirst-Ashman, 2008, p. 36). Many individuals get confused regarding the differences among culture, ethnicity, race, and the development of an ethnic identity.

Ethnicity generally refers to one's roots, ancestry, and heritage. *Culture* generally relates to values, understandings, behaviors, and practices (Ton & Lim, 2006). To provide a comprehensive diagnostic assessment, all social workers need to take into account clients' personal beliefs about the etiology and prognosis of their symptoms (Chang-Muy & Congress, 2009).

Race is defined as a "consciousness of status and identity based on ancestry and color," and ethnicity is all of that (e.g., religion, customs, geography, and historical events) minus color (Lee & Bean, 2004). Racial identity is not static and can be fluid depending on specific contexts. These certainly are influenced by location of residence, developmental stage, context of being asked, and the perceived benefit or loss in regard to this (Mays et al., 2003).

The development of *ethnic identity* stems from the continuum of acceptance of a person's ethnicity. *Ethnic identity* is generally defined as a common thread of heritage, customs, and values unique to a group of people (Casas, 1984; Queralt, 1996; Worden, 1999). These commonalities define and bond members producing an ethnic backdrop to everyday life. Ethnicity can influence thinking and feeling and pattern behaviors in both obvious and subtle ways (Canino & Alegria, 2008).

Many individuals either embrace or reject their ethnicity, relating it to personal and ascribed identity or a particular reference group, which dictates the primary support group to which they turn for clarity of decisions (Helms, 1990). No two people seem to experience their culture in the same way. And as race and ethnicity are more fluid than otherwise posited, *situational ethnicity* addresses changing of race or ethnic identity within specific contexts (Mays et al., 2003). This means that counselors must be careful not to approach the client with any preconceived bias or textbook definitions of exactly what to expect (Swartz-Kulstad & Martin, 1999).

The classifications of race and ethnicity change dramatically with the new fluctuations of immigration occurring in the United States as well as the frequency of intermarriages. A new cultural paradigm related to a blended society and multiracial considerations seems to be emerging. Every culture has processes, healers, medications, and prescribed medical practices that enter into the shared view of what constitutes daily living. These shared lifestyle patterns are reflected in daily behaviors. Patterns of response can easily be misinterpreted for something they are not (i.e., reflective of pathology).

Taking into account the possibility of this multifaceted presentation, practitioners continue to encounter a wide range of ethnic minority clients who present varied mental health problems and concerns. Although in this volume the author cannot do justice to the unique characteristics, issues, and challenges that each of these groups present, it is important to ensure that practitioners are aware of the major considerations related to mental health practice with these populations. This section of the chapter will sensitize the reader to some of these considerations and how they can affect the course of mental health treatment.

Addressing Cultural Aspects in the DSM-IV-TR

In the *DSM-IV-TR*, each diagnostic category seeks to be sensitive to issues related to culture, age, and gender and the effects these variables can have on the symptoms with which a client presents. This is particularly important in terms of cultural diversity. Possessing knowledge of and being sensitive to cultural aspects that can contribute to a client's overall diagnostic picture is critical in completing an accurate diagnostic assessment. (See Quick Reference 2.7 on how to identify cultural aspects below.) Each diagnostic category briefly addresses cultural variables. For additional information, clinicians are referred to an outline for cultural formulation and culture-bound syndromes found in Appendix I of the *DSM-IV-TR*.

Being culturally sensitive in completing the diagnostic assessment must clearly outline the client's culture-based behaviors that correspond to diagnostic criteria for a mental disorder. This will allow the practitioner to rule out disorders for which the client might otherwise qualify. This becomes more and more difficult as cultural practices and mores of different races and ethnic groups overlap.

The practitioner needs to work with the client to help him or her examine issues related to *personal identity*, where the individual sees him- or herself in a certain way(s), and *ascribed identity*, where the individual indicates how the society values or perceives behaviors and actions. In the current society, ethnic identity is not easily identified, and the degree to which it can influence life factors and behavior changes can remain elusive. Disparities related to poverty, lack of access, and lack of health care insurance can leave individuals without competent health care (Sutton, 2000), and a culturally sensitive approach can help reduce this.

Remember that both the client and the practitioner are products of the society in which they live. Societal influences, therefore, can directly affect individual cultural mores and beliefs predominant in the environmental system. Culture and its mechanisms of integration influence not only a client's behaviors but also the practitioner's. Most of the beliefs and values that helping professionals hold closely resembles those beliefs and values espoused by the greater

QUICK REFERENCE 2.7

IDENTIFYING CULTURAL ASPECTS

Practitioners Need to Help the Client:

- Identify and discuss the impact of current life circumstances that can affect daily functioning.
- Self-report race and ethnicity, respecting the self-identification of multiracial individuals, in a manner consistent with how the client thinks of him- or herself (Mays et al., 2003).
- Identify and acknowledge any psychological problems stemming from adaptation to a new environment.
- Identify and explore the degree to which the client has positive and supportive peer relationships contributing to or reducing feelings of isolation and facilitating transition.
- Identify social variables for which race or ethnicity serve as a proxy (e.g., social status, neighborhood context, perceived discrimination, social cohesion, social capital, social support, types of occupation, employment, emotional well-being, and perceived life opportunities) (Mays et al., 2003).
- Identify willingness to explore new coping skills that will help negotiate his or her environment.

society. Based on this assumption, practitioners from other ethnic groups, as well as those with heritage in a similar cultural group, may look at the client's behaviors through a culturally limited lens. Doing this may prevent the professional from gaining a clear picture of the importance of helping the client to differentiate that which is cultural and that which is a disorder. Professional helpers must be aware of a tendency to assess the client based on the professional's own values, beliefs, societal biases, and stereotypes (Dupper, 1992; Mays et al., 2003). If practitioners do not take care to avoid this bias, the lack of awareness of client ethnicity and culture may lead to distorted perceptions, misdiagnosing, and labeling of these clients and their family dynamics (Canino & Algeria, 2008; D. W. Sue & D. Sue, 2008).

The key to completing the best diagnostic assessment rests with addressing how to work best with the client in his or her cultural context (Congress, 2008). Some considerations for completing the diagnostic assessment and integrating helping activities with clients from different cultural backgrounds include: (a) becoming familiar with the client's cultural values and points of reference; (b) being aware of and sensitive to the traditional role of the client when in the client's environment; (c) identifying areas of conflict that can result from changes in environmental considerations; and (d) gaining familiarity with how the client is encouraged to express feelings of grief, stress, or unhappiness. To accomplish this, the mental health practitioner must first recognize aspects of the client's culture and incorporate this meaning into the diagnostic assessment and any change efforts to follow.

Countertransference problems may present challenges for both the client and the practitioner, especially when the practitioner is not familiar with the norms and mores of the client's culture. The best-meaning practitioner may assess and treat the client using his or her own cultural lens. It is also important to avoid *countertransference* related to overidentification with the client's culture and values, which may cause the practitioner to lose objectivity and not encourage the client to examine and make changes to improve psychological well-being. It is important not to accept a dysfunctional pattern as a cultural one; with this acceptance, the practitioner may not help to identify alternative coping strategies. This concept will be discussed further in the next section; however, the danger rests in the potential violation of the client's right to self-determination (Hepworth, Rooney, Rooney, Gottfried, & Larsen, 2010). Completing an ethnic-sensitive diagnostic assessment requires that the practitioner very clearly assess the client, his or her family, the role of culture and environment, and how each affects the client's behaviors and responses.

In terms of training professionals, in a study of 500 professional counselors, the majority perceived themselves to be culturally competent yet reported their multicultural training to be less than adequate (Holcomb-McCoy & Myers, 1999). In a similar study with social workers, Kaplan and Dziegielewski (1999) examined attitudes of MSW students that directly addressed issues of spirituality and religion and the degree to which these attitudes were incorporated into social work practice. Most graduate students reported valuing the role of spirituality and religion in their personal and professional lives. These social workers, like the professional counselors, reported a lack of adequate graduate education training and preparation to deal with issues such as culture supported by identification with spiritual or religious ties. These studies help to point out the importance of cultural sensitivity and training. Regardless of the helping discipline, cultural competence training focusing on cultural awareness and the various ways professionals can respond, as well as taking into account their preconceived

---

QUICK REFERENCE 2.8

CREATING CULTURAL COMPETENCE IN PRACTITIONERS

- Value diversity in all individuals and the strengths that can be found in differences.
- Seek out experiences and training that will facilitate the understanding of the needs of diverse populations.
- Conduct a cultural self-assessment, identifying one's own values, beliefs, and views.
- Be sure to include aspects of cultural identity, as self-reported and self-identified by the client, and the influences it can or does not have on the diagnostic assessment.
- Become aware of the limits of what one has competence and expertise in. If the problem behavior(s) the client is experiencing is beyond the understanding of the practitioner, it is up to the practitioner to seek ethnic group consultation or to make referrals to the more appropriate services or helping professionals.

---

notions, can lead to improvement in the diagnostic process and the subsequent psychiatric treatment (Qureshi, Collazos, Ramos, & Casas, 2008).

If mental health practitioners are truly committed to enhancing the lives of people—as individuals, groups, families, and communities—they must also be committed to enabling clients to maximize their capabilities as full and effective participants in society. If there is a spiritual aspect of human life, and it is interrelated with other aspects of life, practitioners need to be trained to take this into account in order to help clients reach their goals and potential. Although many practitioners may accurately assess relevant cultural, religious, or spiritual issues, they may not understand the relevance of a client's spiritual beliefs, values, and perceptions. What a client believes can influence the way he or she responds, and these behaviors may be inseparable from the environmental system. Without specific education, professional training, and preparation in this area, mental health practitioners are just as ill equipped to practice as they are to deal with policy issues or other types of psychological problems. Each professional must have both training education to assist the client in all areas taking into account a cultural perspective. Mental health practitioners need to be aware of their own strengths and limitations while remaining active in seeking education to prepare themselves to deal effectively with cultural, spiritual, and/or religious issues in the lives of the clients they serve. (See Quick Reference 2.8 creating cultural competence in practitioners.)

CULTURE-BOUND SYNDROMES

It is important for clinicians to be aware that viewing a client through a narrow cultural lens can lead to misinterpreting a client's cultural traditions and problem-solving processes as abnormal or dysfunctional. When examining the revisions and changes in the *DSM-III-R* (1987), *DSM-IV* (1994), and *DSM-IV-TR* (2000), experts clearly acknowledged that powerful cultural influences can and often do negate a mental health diagnosis. Taking a client's overall cultural influences into account does not equate directly to a culture–bound syndrome.

The term *culture-bound syndrome* denotes recurrent, locality-specific patterns of behavior that can result in troubling experience(s) potentially linked to a particular *DSM-IV* diagnostic category (APA, 2000). Culture-bound syndromes are examples of extreme forms of cultural expression that may be seen as dysfunctional in mainstream society. Yet when these forms of cultural expression are compared among various cultures, culture-bound syndromes share more similarities and commonalities than differences in physiological manifestations. This finding suggests that syndromes such as ataque de nervios, kyol goeu, ghost sickness, falling out, brain fag, hwa-byung, shenjing shuairou, shenkui, and shin byung may represent the same syndrome rather than different categorizations for each (Hsia & Barlow, 2001). Regardless of the exact definitions, however, if clinicians are not sensitive to these culture-bound syndromes and their limitations, they may inaccurately assess such symptoms as a *DSM-IV-TR* diagnostic category.

In culture-bound syndromes, cultural beliefs and mores influence the symptoms, course, and social response to the behaviors. Each family system seeks to maintain a homeostatic balance that is functional and adaptive for that system. The practitioner, therefore, must guard against impulses to reorganize a client's family system based on his or her expectations or standards set by the larger society.

Being aware of cultural differences and acceptance of diversity are essential in establishing a culturally sensitive practice (Congress, 2008; Sue & Sue, 2008). This awareness can prevent an inappropriate diagnostic label being given to a client. In addition, it may help to increase understanding of cultural expectations by examining culturally related behaviors and breaking them down into subgroupings since differences among groups that appear similar may also exist (Alegria, Shrout, Woo et al., 2007). Appendix I of the *DSM-IV-TR* lists some of the best-studied culture-bound syndromes and idioms of distress that may be encountered in clinical practice in North America. It includes relevant *DSM-IV-TR* categories and suggests that they should be considered in a diagnostic formulation. The quick references provided here give only some of the possible types of culture-bound syndromes identified. (See Quick Reference 2.9 for a list of selected Culture-Bound Syndromes.)

In summary, a comprehensive diagnostic assessment needs to take into account the cultural identity of the client being served. This is

---

QUICK REFERENCE 2.9

SELECTED CULTURE-BOUND SYNDROMES

Generally Related to American Indians

Ghost sickness: A preoccupation with death and the deceased (sometimes associated with witchcraft) frequently observed among members of many American Indian tribes. Various symptoms can be attributed to ghost sickness, including bad dreams, weakness, feelings of danger, loss of appetite, fainting, dizziness, fear, anxiety, hallucinations, loss of consciousness, confusion, feelings of futility, and a sense of suffocation.

Generally Related to Asians and Southeast Asians

Kyol goeu: Often found in refugees from the Khmer Rouge, symptoms are similar to panic attacks and anxiety disorders (Hsia & Barlow, 2001).

Generally Related to Regions of West Africa and Haiti

Boufee delirant: This French term (West Africa and Haiti) refers to a sudden outburst of agitated and aggressive behavior, marked confusion, and psychomotor excitement. Visual and auditory

(continued)

QUICK REFERENCE 2.9 (*Continued*)

hallucinations or paranoid ideation may sometimes accompany it. These episodes may resemble an episode of brief psychotic disorder.

Brain fag: A term initially used in West Africa to refer to a condition experienced by high school and university students in response to the challenges of schooling. Symptoms include difficulties in concentrating, remembering, and thinking. Students often state that their brains are "fatigued." Additional somatic symptoms are usually centered on the head and neck and include pain, pressure or tightness, blurring of vision, heat, or burning. "Brain tiredness" or fatigue from "too much thinking" is an idiom of distress in many cultures, and resulting syndromes can resemble certain anxiety, depressive, and somatoform disorders.

Generally Related to Hispanic Individuals

Ataque de nervios: An idiom of distress principally reported among Latinos from the Caribbean but recognized among many Latin American and Latin Mediterranean groups. Commonly reported symptoms include uncontrollable shouting, attacks of crying, trembling, heat in the chest rising into the head, and verbal or physical aggression. Dissociative experiences, seizure like or fainting episodes, and suicidal gestures are prominent in some attacks but absent in others. A general feature of an ataque de nervios is a sense of being out of control. Ataques de nervios frequently occur as a direct result of a stressful event relating to the family (e.g., news of the death of a close relative, a separation or divorce from a spouse, conflicts with a spouse or children, or witnessing an accident involving a family member). People may experience amnesia during the ataque de nervios but return rapidly to their usual level of functioning. Although descriptions of some ataques de nervios most closely fit with the *DSM-IV* description of panic attacks, the association of most ataques with a precipitating event and the frequent absence of the hallmark symptoms of acute fear or apprehension distinguish them from panic disorder. Ataques span the range from normal expressions of distress not associated with having a mental disorder to symptom presentations associated with the diagnoses of anxiety, mood, dissociative, or somatoform disorders.

Locura: A term used by Latinos in the United States and Latin America to refer to a severe form of chronic psychosis. The condition is attributed to an inherited vulnerability, to the effect of multiple life difficulties, or to a combination of both factors. Symptoms exhibited by persons with locura include incoherence, agitation, auditory and visual hallucinations, an inability to follow rules of social interaction, unpredictability, and possible violence.

Nervios: A common idiom of distress among Latinos in the United States and Latin America. A number of other ethnic groups have related, though often somewhat distinctive, ideas of "nerves" (such as "nevra" among Greeks in North America). The term *nervios* refers both to a general state of vulnerability to stressful life experiences and to a syndrome brought on by difficult life circumstances. It includes a wide range of symptoms of emotional distress, somatic disturbance, and inability to function. Common symptoms include headaches and "brain aches," irritability, stomach disturbances, sleep difficulties, nervousness, easy tearfulness, inability to concentrate, trembling, tingling sensations, and *mareos* (dizziness with occasional vertigolike exacerbations). Nervios tends to be an ongoing problem, although variable in the degree of disability manifested. Nervios is a broad syndrome that spans the range from cases free of a mental disorder to presentations resembling adjustment, anxiety, depressive, dissociative, somatoform, or psychotic disorders. Differential diagnosis will depend on the constellation of symptoms experienced, the kind of social events that are associated with the onset and progression of nervios, and the level of disability experienced.

Source: Selected definitions reprinted with permission from the *Diagnostic and Statistical Manual of Mental Disorders, Fourth Edition, Text Revision.* Copyright 2000 by the American Psychiatric Association.

particularly important for immigrants and ethnic minorities who exhibit communication problems in terms of foreign language acquisition, understanding, content, and stress due to the loss of social networks in new settings (Breslau et al., 2007; Leon & Dziegielewski, 1999). Also, adjusting to a new culture can cause acculturation adjustment problems serious enough to end in attempts of suicide (Leach, 2006).

The practitioner must also be sensitive to the predominant idioms of distress through which problematic behaviors are identified or communicated in what is called culture-bound syndromes, especially when clients report problems with nerves, being possessed by spirits, multiple somatic complaints, and a sense of inexplicable misfortune. The meaning that these symptoms have to the client, in relation to norms of his or her cultural reference group, need to be explored.

When addressing culture-bound syndromes, the practitioner should exercise care to interpret the symptoms displayed being careful not to use a bias cultural perspective that rests on stereotypes and pathologies rather than responding in a way that is responsive to the actual situational factor. For example, in ataque de nervios, found among people of Latin American, Central American, and Caribbean descent, what appears to be an extreme response that appears excessive to the situation of distress may occur. This extreme response can include dissociative symptoms, suicidal gestures, seizures, or fainting spells related to a distressing event such as interpersonal conflict or the death of a loved one (Keough, Timpano, & Schmidt, 2009). To take into account the cultural context of the client's response, the practitioner should examine: How is this extreme response influenced by the client's cultural surroundings and ethnic identity and how do these factors lead to the exhibited response of grief and loss? What makes this response a different cultural representation and/or syndrome? How does it differ from pathology? When examining these factors, connecting how these factors can be related to psychosocial and environmental stressors and the client's level of individual, social, or occupational functioning is important. Note differences in culture and social status between the client and the practitioner and problems these differences may cause in the diagnostic assessment. The diagnostic assessment should always conclude with an overall cultural assessment, acknowledging how these factors directly or indirectly influence behavior, and further comprehensive diagnosis and care.

DIAGNOSTIC ASSESSMENT FACTORS RELATED TO AGE

Regardless of their cultural or racial background, individuals both young and old use their cultural experiences to interpret their immediate surroundings, the interaction of others, and the interpersonal patterns of society (Bruner, 1991; Salesby, 1994). Culture and family are the first two powerful influences that determine how all individuals understand, internalize, and act on what is expected of them by their family, community, and the larger society (D. W. Sue & D. Sue, 2008). Discriminatory experiences may provide additional information and feelings to decipher and understand in individuals who are considered minorities. During times of emotional or psychological turmoil, human nature is such that all individuals, regardless of age, will strive for meaning in their lives using their "cultural lens": their values, beliefs, and experiences. In both the elderly and children in therapeutic situations, the practitioner must first accept that these individuals present a rich and complex picture, which requires examination of the biological, psychological, and social factors within a historical and cultural framework. During the diagnostic assessment, it is important to ensure that a lack of historical and cultural sensitivity by helping professionals does not hinder the good intentions of the intervention or the research process.

Recognizing age and culture in the diagnostic assessment are similar: Both areas need to be assessed and treated effectively and rapidly. Awareness of personal stereotypes to age and aging and discriminatory practices can affect the welfare and progress of the individual for whom assessment or treatment is provided (Dupper, 1992; Gaw, 1993; D. W. Sue & D. Sue, 2008; Willie, Kramer, & Brown, 1973).

Diagnostic Assessment With Children

Recognizing, understanding, and appreciating the effects that geographic and regional differences can have on children helps to develop age-sensitive practices and provides effective services. When assessing children, the family's place of origin should not be minimized. Family values may reflect differences in urban versus rural expectations and traditions. Congress (1997) recommends that practitioners identify appropriate tools to conduct culturally sensitive assessments. Children's actions are guided by the values and norms established within the family system. For example, if a child's family of origin is not supportive of mental health treatment and holds negative beliefs surrounding professional assistance, a child may not independently ask for help. If a parent does not support the provider's assessment or treatment for the child, gaining family support may be more complicated than simply having an uninvolved parent (Boyd-Franklin, 1989). It is possible to obtain a more accurate assessment in the parent's own home and/or through collaboration with other significant people in the community (e.g., clergy) who are part of the family's extended helping network and are trusted by the family (Congress, 1997; Harrison, Thyer, & Wodarski, 1996). See Quick Reference 2.10 diagnostic assessment with children below.

QUICK REFERENCE 2.10

DIAGNOSTIC ASSESSMENT WITH CHILDREN

- Carefully assess changes in self-esteem or confidence levels.
- Assess dysfunctional behavioral patterns, taking into account family system and other support system influences (including peer pressure).
- Be aware that the child is not solely responsible for many of the difficulties he or she encounters.
- Understand the role that cultural differences and expectations can play in each family system.

Diagnostic Assessment With Older Adults

Growing old often is viewed negatively in our society as well as by many health and mental health care professionals. Victimized by societal attitudes that devalue old age, many individuals (young and old) will do almost anything to avoid or deny old age. Such prejudices are the result of both rational and irrational fears. Rational fears about declining health and loss of income, loved ones, and social status can be exaggerated by negative stereotypes, as are irrational fears such as changes in physical appearance, loss of mobility, loss of masculinity or femininity, and perceived mental incompetence. Older adults continue to be oppressed by myths and misinformation and real obstacles imposed by various biological, psychological, social, and economic factors.

Practitioners need to examine their own attitudes toward aging. They need to recognize older adults as valuable resources in our society and provide services and advocacy assisting them in maximizing their degree of life satisfaction and well-being. Many older adults fear loss of activity and may deny the actual occurrence of such loss. Older adults may suffer from chronic conditions where probability of improvement is unlikely. They may also suffer from continuous life stresses, such as widowhood, social and occupational losses, and progressive and declining physical health problems. Lack of access and transportation create barriers for older adults with psychiatric problems who attend community mental health centers for checkups and medication.

Knowledge of the problems that elderly individuals face is critical. Loss of sexuality due to aging prevents many older men and women from engaging in sexual intercourse (Kelly & Rice, 1986). Perceptions and attitudes of ascribed asexuality in older adults ignore the sexual needs of elderly persons by family, friends,

peers, caregivers, and society in general (Hodson & Skeen, 1994). A patronizing attitude in relation to perceptions about elderly individuals increases the tendency to deny terminal problems rather than help them develop ways to cope. A diagnostic assessment should take into account the individual's health conditions and environmental factors among other aspects of their lives.

Assessing lethality with a suicidal older client is essential. Older adults may not openly discuss feelings of hopelessness and helplessness, and these must be screened. If suicidal ideation, thoughts of suicide, and a concrete plan are expressed (the way to carry out the suicidal act), steps to ensure hospitalization must be taken immediately, as for any client at serious risk for suicide. Many older adults may not be forthcoming with situational criteria and the practitioner may remain uncertain of the seriousness of the client's thoughts with regard to his or her actions. Regardless of whether the client's behavior is action focused or not, some type of immediate protective measure needs to be employed. This topic will be discussed in detail in the chapters on intervention strategy. (See Quick Reference 2.11 for a list of life circumstances that can complicate the diagnostic assessment with older adults.)

DIAGNOSTIC ASSESSMENT FACTORS RELATED TO GENDER

Most professionals would agree that girls and boys are often subjected to early differential treatment and identification. Parents and the larger societal network deal differently with girls and boys, and children often are expected to model themselves according to accepted gender lines. Most of the inquiry made into gender has focused on the importance of outlining the "actual" differences between male

---

QUICK REFERENCE 2.11

DIAGNOSTIC ASSESSMENT WITH OLDER ADULTS

Identify life circumstances that can complicate the diagnostic assessment process.

- **Retirement issues:** Identify problems with work role transition and retirement status.
- **Chronic conditions:** Identify chronic medical conditions that an individual may suffer from and how these conditions can affect his or her level of daily functioning.
- **Physical health conditions:** Identify physical health conditions, especially vision and hearing problems that can complicate or magnify current problems.
- **Mental health complaints:** Identify mental health problems, looking for signs such as feelings of sadness, loneliness, guilt, boredom, marked decrease or increase in appetite, change in sleep behavior, and a sense of worthlessness. Be aware that many times signs of depression in elderly persons can be situational (e.g., the etiology of the depression is related to life circumstances), and screen for problems related to tragic life experiences, including the loss of loved ones, job, status, independence, and other personal disappointments. Screen for confusion that may be a sign of dementia.
- **Medication use and misuse:** Identify the use and misuse of prescription medication because commonly prescribed medications can present such side effects as irritability, sexual dysfunction, memory lapses, a general feeling of tiredness, or a combination of these.
- **Sexual problems:** Be open to the identification of sexual problems.
- **Suicide:** Identify the probability of accumulated life losses and be cognizant of a client's abilities and/or problems in coping with grief.

---

and female characteristics and whether there are true physical, cognitive, and personality differences among the sexes. From a medical-biological perspective, most professionals would say that such differences do exist. Although the physical differences (e.g., physical structure and anatomy) between males and females are obvious, other differences are not. In medication use, when controlling for most factors (e.g., size, dose), therapeutic response to certain drugs can differ between males and females (*Physicians Desk Reference*, 2009). Furthermore, when viewing gender divergence from a social-psychological perspective, "broader social issues relating to sex and gender stereotyping can lead to unfair practices of sexism" (Dziegielewski, Resnick, & Krause, 1995, p. 169).

During the completion of the diagnostic assessment, it is difficult to avoid gender bias because of sex role representations. Even though "gender-neutral" influences may be

considered products of the society at large, individuals continue to have definite ideas about sex role deviance. It is critical to acknowledge the influences that gender may have on the diagnostic assessment process. Practitioners must be careful to rule out bias, such as viewing the male as the "doer" who is always rational, logical, and in control and the female as the "nurturer" who is often emotional, illogical, and dependent.

A gender-sensitive diagnostic assessment includes behaviors as naturally occurring phenomena. From a feminist perspective, gender and power relations are paramount to effective assessment and intervention. To summarize the feminist theory in our society, four elements are generally considered:

1. Gender inequality is highlighted and women are oppressed by a patriarchal society.

QUICK REFERENCE 2.12

GENDER AND THE DIAGNOSTIC ASSESSMENT I

Practitioners Need to:

- Identify the individual's perception of gender and how this belief affects values, beliefs, and behaviors.
- Identify an individual's traditional roots and acknowledge how that can influence the way issues are addressed and discussed.
- Identify adaptive and maladaptive behaviors.
- Identify the environmental or interpersonal circumstances supporting the behavior.
- Help the individual to acknowledge family or societal perceptions of his or her behavior, and how it may detract or contribute to current problem behaviors.

2. The individual experiences of men and women are considered the cornerstone of all social science understanding.
3. The primary emphasis is to improve the conditions women experience.
4. Feminism acknowledges that gender bias exists and that, as products of the society, practitioners cannot be objective observers (Concian, 1991).

Feminist contributions have been a major force in rethinking gender and power relations embedded in traditional methods of assessment and intervention and for developing new areas of inquiry and practice (Burck & Speed, 1995; Gilbert, 1991; Jones, 1995; Lott, 1991).

To be gender sensitive in the diagnostic assessment process, the practitioner must first identify power differentials contributing to the source of the problem area. According to feminist theory and thought, power differentials create and/or are the source of distress that the person experiences within the system. These may be found in relationships, roles, the cultural hegemony, and what is generally referred to as discourses. The primary focus is placed on power differentials and how these influence the individual as a source of distress and disorder. The practitioner would encourage the client to address how these power differentials affect and play a role in relation to

self and others. The practitioner is responsible for interpreting and finding meaning in what is said and must listen and respond by helping the client to problem-solve what is determined to be the "real" situation.

When practitioners complete the diagnostic assessment, they must consider gender as a basic building block, along with such concepts as generation (age) and ethnic and cultural implications. Operating with this foundation or mind-set, practitioners can assess the behavior patterns that are reinforced in this contingency pattern. (See Quick References 2.12 and 2.13, Gender and the Diagnostic Assessment I and II.)

In the diagnostic assessment process, the practitioner is responsible for interpreting and finding meaning in what the client says, and this interpretation is not based solely on what the client has stated. The practitioner must listen and respond by helping the client to problem-solve what is determined to be the "real" situation. Developing rapport during the diagnostic assessment is critical because it makes clients feel more comfortable and gives them permission to state how they feel and how those feelings are affecting behaviors (Friedman, 1997).

Although differences between men and women do exist, many differences can be traced to situations in which men and women find themselves; in these situations, even if they behave

---

QUICK REFERENCE 2.13

GENDER AND THE DIAGNOSTIC ASSESSMENT II

Practitioners Need to

- Realize that individuals are products of their family and societal context.
- Make a conscious attempt to recognize his or her own "behavior paradigms" and the sexual stereotypes that either consciously or unconsciously exist.
- Strive to be as objective and tolerant as possible regarding the uniqueness of clients and their rights, acknowledging that the behavioral paradigm of the practitioner is not necessarily the correct or ideal one.
- Be aware of how gender (the practitioner's or the client's) can affect the diagnostic assessment process and the information shared.
- Be aware of the personalities of those in the family and their effect, significant or otherwise, on the client, and how these personalities can influence views, actions, and performance of his or her activities of daily living.

---

identically, they are perceived and judged by different standards (Aronson, 2008). The practitioner is also a product of the social environment and influenced by the culture natural to him or her. It is important not to impose double standards of interpretation or, worse yet, interpretation without realizing the influence of gender at all. The inclusion of gender is imperative within the mind-set incorporated in diagnostic assessment.

SUBTYPES AND COURSE SPECIFIERS

In using the *DSM-IV-TR*, the use of subtypes and course specifiers is encouraged. A subtype helps clarify a diagnosis where the criteria are mutually exclusive and jointly exhaustive (APA, 2000). In schizophrenia, for example, the *DSM-IV* (1994) clearly establishes five identified subtypes (e.g., paranoid type, disorganized type, catatonic type, undifferentiated type, and residual type). The subtypes are defined by the prominent symptomology at the time of evaluation. (See Chapter 9 for further analysis and application.)

This example represents one of the major changes between the *DSM-IV* and the *DSM-IV-TR*. Based on the latest research, the subtypes of schizophrenia appear to be limited in terms of

stability and prognostic value. These subtypes are being evaluated and may be condensed in the *DSM-V* to more accurately reflect the research field trial results.

The second grouping for diagnostic categories is the course specifier. Contrary to the diagnostic subtype, the course specifier is not considered mutually exclusive and exhaustive. It is provided to show how criteria are similar and can be grouped. These homogenous (or similar) subgroupings can highlight certain shared features. For example, in the condition of major depressive disorder, the specifier "with melancholic features" can be added. Additional specifiers that may be listed after the diagnosis include mild, moderate, and severe, in partial remission, in full remission, and prior history. Since these specifiers help to clarify, specify, and note recurrence of a diagnostic mental disorder, the qualifiers of mild, moderate, and severe should be used only when the full criteria for the diagnosis is met. (See Quick Reference 2.14 for Severity and Course Specifiers.)

When it is considered important to the diagnostic assessment, the practitioner can note the recurrence of a mental disorder. If an individual has suffered from major depressive disorder in the past and met all the criteria at that time, yet currently shows signs of the disorder but not

---

QUICK REFERENCE 2.14

SEVERITY AND COURSE SPECIFIERS

Practitioners use qualifiers to clarify or specify a diagnosis, noting the recurrence and prior history of diagnoses:

- Is the condition mild, moderate, or severe?
- Is the condition in remission (i.e., partial or full remission)?
- Is there a prior history of the condition, and can this prior history have an effect on current level of functioning?

---

satisfy all related criteria for it, using the qualifier "recurrent" is considered appropriate; in this case, the diagnosis would be noted as major depressive disorder, *recurrent*. The term recurrent is particularly useful in assisting the practitioner when the criteria for a past disorder are not currently met, yet it appears supported by the practitioner's clinical judgment that the criteria will shortly be met, matching what has occurred before.

When applying any of the additional qualifiers or specifiers, the practitioner needs to make sure the application is related to the current level of problem behavior and must clearly document the frequency, intensity, and duration of why the specifier was noted. As will be discussed in more detail in Chapter 3, diagnostic codes, usually 3 to 5 digits, are often utilized to report statistical information and to facilitate retrieval of information. The fourth and fifth digits of the code can be assigned to the subtype. (See Quick Reference 2.15 for an example of diagnostic codes.)

Many of the subtypes and specifiers listed in the *DSM* are not listed in the *ICD-10-DRC* system; there are no corresponding codes for these subtypes and specifiers. When the practitioner wants to specify a client problem by utilizing the subtype or specifier, he or she should simply write it out (e.g., in the condition of obsessive compulsive disorder, include a 3-digit code, the subtype referred to as "with poor insight").

USE OF THE PRINCIPAL AND PROVISIONAL DIAGNOSIS

The reason an individual is seen by a mental health professional or admitted to an inpatient facility is often referred to as the *principal diagnosis*. Many times when a client is interviewed and the initial diagnostic assessment is completed, a principal diagnosis cannot be determined. In these cases, a provisional diagnosis can be assigned. A *provisional diagnosis* (often referred to in the field as the best-educated clinical guess) is based on clinical judgment and reflects a strong suspicion that an individual suffers from a type of disorder that, for some reason or another, the actual criteria are either not met or the

---

QUICK REFERENCE 2.15

EXAMPLE OF DIAGNOSTIC CODES

3-digit coding:	317 = Mild mental retardation (the diagnosis).
5-digit coding:	294.10 = Dementia of the Alzheimer's type (the diagnosis) without behavioral disturbance (the specifier).

QUICK REFERENCE 2.16

PRINCIPAL AND PROVISIONAL DIAGNOSIS

The practitioner can use either of these terms when the listed conditions are met:

Principal diagnosis: Symptoms related to the condition are the primary reason for the diagnostic assessment and the request for treatment/intervention.

Provisional diagnosis: Diagnosis is determined on the criteria used to verify the duration of the illness or when there is not enough information to substantiate a principal diagnosis.

---

practitioner does not have it available to make a more informed diagnostic assessment. In practice, a provisional diagnosis can be particularly helpful when information from family or the support system is not available to confirm the diagnosis. There are some disorders for which specific periods must be met to assign a diagnosis. In schizophrenia, regardless of the subtype, the criteria state that the duration of the illness must be approximately six months or more. With the first episode or the onset of the disorder, all criteria may be met except this one. Therefore, the provisional diagnosis allows the practitioner to use the term *schizophreniform disorder*, which also meets the same criteria as schizophrenia but has a lesser time frame (e.g., less than six months and remission does not occur). The most important thing for the practitioner to remember, however, is that a provisional diagnosis is *temporary*. This means that once a provisional diagnosis is given, every attempt must be made to monitor its course. When the needed information is gathered or the suggested time frame has been met, the provisional diagnosis should be changed to the primary diagnosis most relevant to current problem behaviors and future treatment. (See Quick Reference 2.16 for an overview of principal and provisional diagnosis.)

Several other diagnostic categories can also be used when diagnostic uncertainty as to an exact condition is noted. There are times when

there may not be a specific diagnosis relevant to a client's behaviors or actions, or the information gathered is so inadequate that the diagnostic criteria cannot be applied. At these times, simply coding "no diagnosis" or "diagnosis deferred" would be sufficient.

USE OF *NOT OTHERWISE SPECIFIED*

Since it is sometimes impossible for the practitioner completing the diagnostic assessment to categorize all the symptoms that a client is experiencing into one diagnostic category, the term *not otherwise specified* (NOS) was introduced. There are at least four situations in which a client with a disorder may be given this diagnosis. This option is provided at least once for every diagnostic category listed in the *DSM-IV-TR*. Even though the criteria for when to use it is outlined, they remain so subjective that clinical judgment is often the key factor to consider when making the determination for use.

The four situations that qualify for use of the NOS category include:

1. Client meets the general guidelines for a disorder yet not all of the criteria are met or the ones present are not considered clinically significant.
2. Significant behaviors are noted affecting social and occupational functioning but

---

are not considered part of the usual presentation for a disorder.

3. Uncertainty about etiology or the cause of the disorder exists. This is especially important when it is suspected that the disorder may be related to a general medical condition.
4. Insufficient information exists to fully support assigning behaviors to a particular mental disorder in the category, but the general criteria for the category of disorders are evident. For example, it is clear that an individual suffers from a type of bipolar disorder, but the specific criteria for a particular type cannot be clearly identified.

There are many reasons why the practitioner may have inaccurate information, including insufficient time to gather assessment information, individual client being unable to report symptoms accurately, and/or no family or support system available to help complete or verify accuracy and comprehensive information needed for the assessment.

Although using the NOS category is encouraged in the *DSM-IV-TR* when these considerations are met, a caution from an experienced practice reality must be noted. In billing and reimbursement practices, the NOS category is often very carefully scrutinized. Managed care companies and service providers are well aware of the criteria that do not have to be present for a diagnosis to be utilized for reimbursement. This means that medical reviewers will be looking closely to see that the client who is given an NOS category clearly needs to be given that diagnosis after a certain time frame, regardless of current criteria present and duration of symptoms. They will want to determine what circumstances make this diagnostic category more appropriate than the others in the same classification. Practice reality dictates the use of this diagnostic category cautiously. Practitioners must clearly link the choice of the NOS category to one of the four accepted reasons. (See Quick Reference 2.17 for a list of the accepted reasons for the use of the Not Otherwise Specified category [NOS].) See Quick Reference 2.18 for a full listing of the Appendices as listed in the *DSM-IV-TR*.

QUICK REFERENCE 2.18

DSM-IV AND *DSM-IV-TR* APPENDICES

A. Decision Trees for Differential Diagnosis: Utilizes decision trees to help the practitioner facilitate differential diagnosis.

B. Criteria Sets and Axes Provided for Further Study: Discusses several disorders that are being considered for possible inclusion as well as alternative dimensional criteria that can be used to support the diagnostic assessment process.

C. Glossary of Technical Terms: Particularly helpful in defining certain terms that are listed under the various disorders.

D. Highlights of Changes in *DSM-IV* Text Revision: Highlights the additions, modifications, and changes that were made within the latest revision of the *DSM*.

E. Alphabetical Listing of *DSM-IV-TR* Diagnoses and Codes: Lists both the *DSM-IV-TR* codes and the matching codes in the *ICD-10-DRC*.

F. Numerical Listing of *DSM-IV-TR* Diagnoses and Codes: The same as Appendix E, except that the codes are listed numerically rather than alphabetically. In billing, this appendix can be very helpful, especially when all a provider may be given is the diagnostic numerical code. Most practitioners do not memorize all the code numbers, although they may be very familiar with the diagnostic category once they see the name. This appendix allows the practitioner to look up the code directly and see what diagnostic category is associated with it.

G. *ICD-9-CM* Codes for Selected General Medical Conditions and Medication Induced Disorders: Lists the general medical conditions and matches these conditions with the *ICD-10-DRC* codes. This section also allows for coding concerning certain medications (prescribed at therapeutic doses) that can cause substance-induced disorders. The effects of these medications are coded (E-codes) as optional and when used would be listed on Axis I.

H. *DSM-IV* Classification with *ICD-10* Codes: Since much of the world is still using the *ICD-10-DRC* clinical codes, it is expected that soon they will be replaced with the *ICD-11-CM* that is due in 2010. Until that time, the *ICD-10* codes are listed in this appendix for clinical convenience.

I. Outline for Cultural Formulation and Glossary of Culture-Bound Syndromes: Divided into two parts, this outline facilitates cultural assessment and an actual glossary of culture-bound syndromes. The culture-bound syndromes often present similar to a mental disorder but, as discussed earlier in this chapter, are related directly to an individual's cultural beliefs.

J. *DSM-IV* Contributors: Lists the names of those who contributed to the formulation and development of the *DSM-IV* published in 1994.

K. *DSM-IV-TR* Advisers: Lists the names of those who contributed to the formulation and development of the *DSM-IV-TR* published in 2000.

Source: Reprinted with permission from the *Diagnostic and Statistical Manual of Mental Disorders, Fourth Edition, Text Revision.* Copyright 2000 by the American Psychiatric Association.

SUMMARY

This chapter gives the mental health practitioner the background information needed to complete the most accurate diagnostic assessment possible using the *DSM-IV-TR*. An accurate diagnostic assessment is the critical first step to identifying behaviors that disturb individual, occupational, and social functioning and formulating the plan for intervention. Thus, it is the diagnostic assessment that sets the tone for therapy. To compete in today's current mental health care service environment, the role of the practitioner is twofold: (1) ensure that quality service is provided to the client, and (2) ensure the client's access and opportunity to see that his or her health needs are addressed. Neither of these tasks is easy or popular in today's environment. The push for mental health practice to be conducted with limited resources and services and the resultant competition to be the provider have changed and stressed the role of the mental health service practitioner. Amid this turbulence, the role and necessity of the diagnostic assessment remains clear. Chapter 3 discusses in detail the application of the multiaxis diagnostic system in terms of documentation and the development of treatment plans that can assist and guide with the intervention process.

QUESTIONS FOR FURTHER THOUGHT

1. Is it important for mental health practitioners to be aware of the *DSM* and the *ICD*, and if so, why?
2. What is the difference among diagnosis, assessment, and diagnostic assessment?
3. Why is it critical to realize and incorporate the mind-body connection when completing the diagnostic assessment?
4. What is a culture-bound syndrome? Give an example of how this concept could be applied to the diagnostic assessment.
5. When is it best to use a principal diagnosis?
6. When is it best to use a Not Otherwise Specified diagnostic category?
7. Why was the *DSM-IV-TR* published? What are the substantial changes between the *DSM-IV* and the *DSM-IV-TR*? What are some of the expected changes related to *DSM-5*?

3 | Documentation and the Multiaxial Diagnostic Assessment

The purpose of this chapter is to use the multiaxial diagnostic assessment within the parameters of current mental health practice. Professional record keeping by all mental health practitioners in the twenty-first century is characterized by time-limited services, managed care requirements, quality assurance, and improvement procedures (Dziegielewski, 2008; Dziegielewski & Powers, 2000; Frager, 2000; Rudolph, 2000; Shlonsky, 2009). When diagnostic systems such as the multiaxial approach presented in the *DSM-IV-TR* are used, practitioner training in how to best utilize this system is mandatory. Skill in professional documentation in this area becomes essential for social workers, psychologists, mental health therapists, professional counselors, and other helping professionals. Training in this area constitutes a functional building block for effective, efficient, and cost-controlled service provision as well as representing the legal, ethical, and fiscal concerns inherent in all service provision (Braun & Cox, 2005; Dziegielewski, 2010; Sheafor et al., 1997).

In addition to presenting information on how to best utilize the multiaxial system, this chapter outlines the changes among *DSM-III-R* (1987), *DSM-IV* (1994), and *DSM-IV-TR* (2000) and awareness of these changes can influence proper use of this multiaxial diagnostic assessment. Each axis is presented with the changes between the earlier and later versions of the *DSM* described. The application of this information is highlighted, allowing practitioners to clearly identify and apply each step of the diagnostic system.

INTRODUCTION TO THE MULTIAXIAL ASSESSMENT SYSTEM

The information presented in this chapter is not meant to be inclusive of all the possibilities available for use of the *DSM-IV-TR* assessment system. It is, however, designed to give professional practitioners a practical introduction to facilitate and identify this multiaxial diagnostic system in the practice setting. Proper use of the *DSM-IV-TR* requires diagnostic classification on a multiaxial system that involves five separate axes. This chapter describes each axis and compares and contrasts what is required today within the assessment process to past requirements. (See Quick Reference 3.1 which lists the five axes and what is to be included.)

When and How to Use the Multiaxial System: Using All Five Axes

The *DSM-IV-TR* is a multiaxial assessment system that identifies five separate axes. In many practice settings in the 1980s and 1990s, the first three axes were considered sufficient to constitute the formal diagnostic process. The practitioner

---

QUICK REFERENCE 3.1

DSM-IV-TR: MULTIAXIAL ASSESSMENT

Axis I:	Clinical disorders, pervasive developmental disorders, learning, motor skills, and communication disorders.
	Other conditions that may be the focus of clinical attention.
Axis II:	Personality disorders. Mental retardation.
Axis III:	General medical conditions.
Axis IV:	Psychosocial and environmental problems.
Axis V:	Global assessment of functioning (GAF).

---

would complete a diagnostic impression of the client that involved Axis I, II, and III, leaving the use of Axis IV and V as optional. With the later additions of the *DSM* (*DSM-III* and *DSM-III-R)*, it was recommended that all five axes be addressed as part of the diagnostic assessment. In current practice, when utilizing the multiaxial system, the first three axes alone are no longer considered acceptable as a practice standard. With the advent of the *DSM-IV* in 1994 and in the *DSM-IV-TR* in 2000, working with the multiaxial framework requires addressing all five axes. Today, in most professional practice settings, a comprehensive diagnostic assessment should include all five areas, especially Axis IV and V because it relates directly to the derived practice plans.

When Is It Not Appropriate to Use the Multiaxial System?

There are times when using the multiaxial diagnostic assessment does not seem appropriate. For some practitioners, especially those who work with special groups (e.g., troubled youth) or in specialized settings (e.g., assisted residential care with elderly persons), the formal diagnostic assessment with diagnostic-related treatment plans may not be required. The use of the multiaxial diagnostic system may seem unnecessary. For example, practitioners in some counseling agencies may focus their efforts directly on problem solving, which entails helping individuals gain the resources needed to improve functioning. In this type of

setting or for this purpose, the complete multiaxis diagnostic system may not be appropriate, and a less formal system may be more advantageous.

Alternatives to the Multiaxial Assessment System

In situations where groups, settings, or agency function does not require it, the formal use of the multiaxial assessment system may not be needed. There may be interest in documenting some of the conditions or issues relative to the diagnostic assessment that prohibit improved problem-solving strategy. For example, if a client suffers from depression and this mental health condition is severe enough to impair occupational or social functioning, he or she may not be able to actively engage in problem solving. In such cases, a modified form of the multiaxial assessment system can be helpful. In these types of situations the practitioner is urged to consider the use of the *nonformal multiaxial assessment system.* (See Quick Reference 3.2 for how to document the assessment when utilizing the nonformal multiaxial assessment system.) This nonformal system can be beneficial when the multiaxial format is not outlined but specific categories are used to identify or classify the problems which the client experiences. To illustrate, the *other conditions that may be the focus of clinical* attention generally coded on Axis I may be of assistance. This category of mental health

---

QUICK REFERENCE 3.2

HELPFUL HINT: NONFORMAL MULTIAXIAL ASSESSMENT

When a practitioner does not use the formal multiaxial assessment system, this strategy for documentation is suggested:

- List the diagnostic category(s) that apply to the client being served.
- List the principal diagnosis or reason for visit first.
- List the mental disorders that interfere with functioning first and then list general medical condition(s) that are complicating or are directly/indirectly related to the mental health condition.

---

conditions is not considered representative of a major clinical syndrome, although the symptoms that the client is experiencing may be severe enough initially to make the professional consider assigning a diagnosis. For example, an elderly client's reaction to the death of a loved one may be significant enough to meet the criteria for bereavement (coded as V62.82), which is appropriate when the focus of clinical attention is related directly to the loss of a loved one (American Psychiatric Association [APA], 2000). As people age, they are more likely to experience repeated losses of partners, family, and friends. Repeated losses and the constant adjustment process can easily lead to feelings of sadness, disturbed sleep, and loss of appetite that resemble depression. Although the individual will eventually learn to cope with these changes and losses, the responses that occur in the adjustment process vary considerably. The non-formal multiaxial system can help the client and significant others (i.e., family and friends within his or her support system), as well as other professional and nonprofessional helpers, understand the client's behaviors. Using this diagnostic category can also help to avoid the client being given a label that might not be appropriate, such as major depressive disorder or an adjustment disorder, which are Axis I clinical syndromes.

It may also be helpful when working in settings where the full multiaxial diagnosis is not needed to use a categorical approach to describe other mental disorders, such as alcohol abuse or major depressive disorder, or to list a general medical condition troubling the individual. In these cases, the practitioner is urged simply to list the conditions that apply. The two guidelines to follow when using a nonformal assessment system are:

1. When there is more than one mental health condition, list the principal diagnosis or reason for visit first.
2. List the mental disorders or other conditions that interfere with functioning first and then list the general medical condition(s) that in the formal multiaxial system would be placed on Axis III.

Coding Within the Multiaxial Assessment System

All mental health practitioners must be familiar with the numeric coding utilized in the *DSM-IV-TR*. This coding provides quick and consistent recording leading to service recognition and reimbursement. Coding can also assist with describing the injury or illness a client suffers from. It also can be helpful in gathering prevalence and research information and can assist other health care professionals in providing continuity of care (Rudman, 2000). When a mental health practitioner completes or assists in completing a claim form, the proper diagnostic and procedural claim codes must be utilized. To facilitate this process, the creators of the *DSM-IV-TR* (APA, 2000) and the *ICD-9-CM* (World Health Organization with updates in coding provided by the American Medical Association, 2000) have collaborated to establish similar codes for each diagnostic system. When a mental health practitioner uses the *DSM-IV-TR* codes for reimbursement, he or she is in effect also using the *ICD-9-CM* codes.

There are two primary types of coding: diagnostic (what a client suffers from) and procedural (what will be done to treat it). The *DSM-IV-TR* and the *ICD-9-CM* are most concerned with the diagnostic codes. *Current procedural terminology* (CPT) codes are related to the services that mental health practitioners often use for assessing clients. Although closely linked to the *ICD-9-CM* codes, these codes correspond to procedures rather than to diagnostic categories.

CPT codes are divided into four procedural categories: (1) evaluation and management services, (2) surgical care, (3) diagnostic services, and (4) therapeutic services (Rudman, 2000). For example, when billing for Medicare reimbursement, the CPT codes are primarily responsible for documenting practice strategy.

CPT codes and the *ICD-9-CM* codes are updated regularly; therefore, keeping abreast of the latest procedural codes is a good idea (see Quick Reference 3.3). The CPT coding manual dated 1998 or later has the most comprehensive codes on the psychiatric disorders (APA Online, 2001a, http://www.apapracticecentral .org/reimbursement/billing/dsmiv-to-icd9cm-codes-chart.pdf). The *DSM-IV-TR* also has been updated with the latest diagnostic codes. Updated CPT codes assist with procedural recording in the inpatient and outpatient setting, denoting the setting where the service is provided (APA Online, 2001b). One myth in the practice setting is that, since the CPT codes represent procedure, the use of certain CPT codes can restrict reimbursement (see Quick Reference 3.3). Although there is some truth to this statement, it is not the code itself that restricts reimbursement—it is the reimbursement provider. Therefore, each insurance company or service reimbursement system will determine what service is covered and what is not. This makes it critical for the mental health practitioner who practices or facilitates billing to be aware not only of what the major service reimbursement systems utilized will cover but also which providers are authorized to dispense these services.

QUICK REFERENCE 3.3

HELPFUL HINTS: DIAGNOSTIC CODING

To purchase an updated *CPT* or *ICD-9-CM* manual, call the American Medical Association at (800) 621-8335.

E-mail address for APA, which may be helpful in obtaining coding changes:

www.apa.org/practice/cpt.html

and

www.apa.org/practice/pointer1295.html

Updated 2009 American Psychological Association

Copies can also be obtained through the Government Relations Office at: (202) 336-5889.

AXIS I AND AXIS II: MULTIAXIAL ASSESSMENT SYSTEM

In the *DSM-IV-TR*, all clinical disorders are coded on Axis I (e.g., mood disorders, schizo–phrenia, dementia, anxiety disorders, substance disorders, disruptive behavior disorders).

As can be seen from Quick Reference 3.4, of disorders on Axis I, there are a multitude of

conditions that if deemed appropriate can be placed there. Some of the disorders that in previous versions of the *DSM* were on Axis II, are now placed on Axis I. (See Quick Reference 3.5, for a summary of the changes between Axis I and II.) Examples of some of the most recent changes that were moved from Axis II to Axis I include the pervasive mental disorders and learning, motor skill disorders. In

---

QUICK REFERENCE 3.4

AXIS I: CLINICAL DISORDERS WITH MAJOR SUBSECTION HEADINGS

Disorders Usually First Diagnosed in Infancy, Childhood, and Adolescence

Learning disorders

Communication disorders

Feeding and eating disorders of infancy or early childhood

Motor skills disorders

Tic disorders

Pervasive developmental disorders

Elimination disorders

Attention-deficit and disruptive behavior disorders

Other disorders of infancy, childhood, and adolescence (separation anxiety disorder, selective mutism, reactive attachment disorder of infancy and early childhood, stereotypic movement disorder, disorder of infancy, childhood, and adolesence NOS)

Delirium, Dementia, and Amnestic and Other Cognitive Disorders

Delirium

Dementia

Amnestic disorders

Other cognitive disorders (NOS coded 294.9)

Mental Disorders Due to a General Medical Condition Not Elsewhere Classified

Catatonic disorder due to a general medical condition

Personality change due to a general medical condition

Mental disorder NOS

Substance-Related Disorders

Alcohol-related disorders

Amphetamine-related (or amphetamine-like) disorders

Caffeine-related disorders

Cannabis-related disorders

Cocaine-related disorders

Hallucinogen-related disorders

Inhalant-related disorders

Nicotine-related disorders

Opioid-related disorders

Phencyclidine-related (or phencyclidine-like) disorders

Sedative-, hypnotic-, or anxiolytic-related disorders

Polysubstance-related disorders

Other (or unknown) substance-related disorders

Schizophrenia and the Other Psychotic Disorders

Schizophrenia

Schizophreniform disorder

Schizoaffective disorder

Delusional disorder

Brief psychotic disorder

Shared psychotic disorder

Psychotic disorder due to . . . (indicate a general medical condition)

Psychotic disorder NOS

Mood Disorders

Depressive disorders

Bipolar disorders

Anxiety Disorders

Panic disorder with or without agoraphobia

Specific phobia

Social phobia

Obsessive-compulsive disorder

Posttraumatic stress disorder

(continued)

QUICK REFERENCE 3.4 (*Continued*)

Acute stress disorder

Generalized anxiety disorder

Anxiety disorder due to . . . general medical condition

Anxiety disorder NOS

Somatoform Disorders

Factitious Disorders

Dissociative Disorders

Sexual and Gender Identity Disorders

Sexual dysfunctions

Sexual desire disorders

Sexual arousal disorders

Orgasmic disorders

Sexual pain disorders

Sexual dysfunction due to a general medical condition

Paraphilias

Gender identity disorders

Eating Disorders

Anorexia nervosa

Bulimia nervosa

Eating disorder NOS

Sleep Disorders

Primary sleep disorders

Sleep disorders related to another mental disorder

Other sleep disorders

Impulse Control Disorders Not Otherwise Classified

Adjustment Disorders

Source: Information modified from the *Diagnostic and Statistical Manual of Mental Disorders, Fourth Edition, Text Revision.* Copyright 2000 by the American Psychiatric Association.

QUICK REFERENCE 3.5

Axis I and Axis II: Comparison of *DSM-II-R* and *DSM-IV-TR*

DSM-III-R Clinical Syndromes and V Codes.
Changed to:
DSM-IV Clinical disorders. Other disorders that may be focus of clinical treatment.
Axis II: Comparison of *DSM-III-R* AND *DSM-IV-TR*
DSM-III-R Developmental disorders and personality disorders.
Changed to:
DSM-IV Personality disorders and mental retardation.
Borderline intellectual functioning.*

---

* It remains unclear whether this category should be included on Axis II. In the *DSM-IV-TR* (p. 29), it is not listed, but the descriptive text (pp. 25, 740) states that it is to be listed on Axis II. Until this is clarified by the American Psychiatric Association, place this diagnosis based on practitioner judgment on either Axis I or Axis II.

---

addition, all other codes that are not attributed to a mental disorder but are the focus of intervention known as *Other conditions that may be a focus of clinical attention* are also coded on Axis I. Axis II is used to code personality disorders and mental retardation. It is important to remember that many changes occurred in the *DSM-IV* and this change was maintained in the *DSM-IV-TR* in terms of where diagnoses are coded. Therefore, the practitioner familiar with the coding scheme used in the *DSM-III-R* needs to look carefully as many diagnoses have been moved. If the experienced practitioner is not aware of this change, diagnoses may be inadvertently coded in the wrong place. The coding of several disorders has changed significantly with the new editions to the *DSM-IV* and *DSM-IV-TR*. For example, the classification of developmental disorders in the *DSM-III-R* included mental retardation, pervasive developmental disorders (e.g., autistic disorder), and the specific developmental disorders (aka academic skill disorders), all listed on Axis II (APA, 1987). This coding changed when the pervasive developmental disorders, learning disorders, motor skills disorders and communication disorders were moved from Axis II to Axis I in *DSM-IV*. Although there are no diagnostic

or multiaxial changes between the *DSM-IV* and *DSM-IV-TR*, it is a good idea to update professional knowledge and expertise in this area regularly as these coding systems can and do change.

For practitioners who are just learning to use the *DSM-IV-TR*, it may seem daunting to try to establish where to place a diagnostic condition. One simple way to do this is to first remember that all diagnostic mental health conditions and disorders, regardless of type, will be categorized on either Axis I or Axis II. Also, if the professional cannot remember all of the Axis I disorders, it may be easier simply remember what is to be placed on Axis II (personality disorders and mental retardation). All other mental health conditions should be placed on Axis I. (See Quick Reference 3.6, Helpful Hints for Coding on Axis I and Axis II.)

Practitioners who use this helpful hint find that remembering where to place the diagnostic category of mental retardation (with the subtypes mild, moderate, severe, or profound) is easy. Many professionals, however, get confused when it comes to what constitutes a personality disorder. Today it may seem simple, yet some practitioners may remember a time when the hint just provided was not applicable. For

---

QUICK REFERENCE 3.6

HELPFUL HINTS: CODING ON AXIS I AND AXIS II

When a professional is learning to use the *DSM-IV-TR* and is not sure where a diagnosis is to be placed and whether it should be placed on Axis I or Axis II, remember these simple rules.

- All diagnostic mental health disorders must be placed on either Axis I or Axis II.
- If the practitioner can remember what goes on Axis II (mental retardation and the personality disorders), everything else will go on Axis I.
- All disorders listed in *DSM-IV-TR* that end in the words *personality disorder* should be coded on Axis II.

---

example, the disorder currently known as dissociative identity disorder (where an individual has more than one distinct personality) was called multiple personality disorder in *DSM-III-R*. Even though the diagnosis ended in the words *personality disorder*, it was not classified as a personality disorder. It always has been and remains a clinical disorder to be coded on Axis I. To avoid confusion, the name of the disorder was changed in the *DSM-IV*. Now all mental disorders listed in the *DSM-IV-TR* that end in the words *personality disorder* represent personality disorders and need to be coded on Axis II. For example, if an individual suffers from obsessive compulsive disorder, what axis would it be coded on? If an individual suffers from obsessive compulsive personality disorder, what axis would it be coded on? The answer to the first question is Axis I, and the answer to the second is Axis II.

Are the Mental Health Diagnoses on Axis I More Severe Than Those Placed on Axis II?

There is a myth that coded Axis I diagnoses are the most serious mental disorders. This is not true. The multiaxial system is not based on severity of the illness; it is merely a classification system. Therefore, an Axis I diagnosis is not necessarily more serious than an Axis II diagnosis. This point is well supported when the two

categories of mental health conditions listed on Axis I are examined. For example, Axis I lists the clinical disorders and the other conditions that may be the focus of clinical attention. Both categories have many similar presenting symptoms, and these conditions can cause problems that are significant enough to affect individual, occupational, and social functioning. Other conditions that may be the focus of clinical attention, however, are not considered mental disorders. Although a mental disorder (e.g., major depressive disorder) may coexist with one of these conditions, if the condition identified as the focus of clinical attention (e.g., bereavement), and it is also the reason for the visit or treatment, it should not be confused with a mental disorder. Although many of the symptoms of mental disorder such as major depressive disorder may exist, since it is not related directly to the mental disorder but rather the death of the loved, the designation of bereavement is accurate and should be placed on Axis I. As explained earlier in this chapter, if we look at individuals who suffer from bereavement (formerly known as uncomplicated bereavement), although initial symptoms mimic depression, the symptoms will diminish as adjustment to the death of the loved one progresses. Another example of this category and how it can be utilized is in malingering (coded as V65.2). Although a client may present with multiple severe individual, occupational, and social problems, if the client meets the criteria for the condition of malingering, careful evaluation and documentation are required. Since malingering is not a mental disorder and it involves "the intentional production of false or grossly exaggerated physical or psychological symptoms, motivated by external incentives such as avoiding" (APA, 2000, p. 739), the practitioner must be sure to document clearly the external incentives. (See Quick Reference 3.7 for selected other conditions that may be a focus of clinical attention.)

To apply this further, imagine that a client wants to qualify for disability so he or she can receive a disability check. The client feigns or grossly exaggerates what he or she is feeling. In actuality, this client would not qualify as having a mental disorder related to the reason for visit, and his or her behaviors would be viewed as primarily manipulative in nature. In all fairness, and in support of the need for a thorough and comprehensive diagnostic assessment, this category should not be used haphazardly. The practitioner needs to be sure that the criteria to justify the diagnostic category are met. Often to support this effort, as will be discussed later in this chapter, supporting information gained through psychometric testing, such as rapid and self-administered assessment instruments, needs to be considered.

QUICK REFERENCE 3.7

AXIS I: OTHER CONDITIONS THAT MAY BE A FOCUS OF CLINICAL ATTENTION

Medication-Induced Movement Disorders

Neuroleptic-induced parkinsonism	Coded 332.1
Neuroleptic malignant syndrome	Coded 333.92
Neuroleptic-induced acute dystonia	Coded 333.7
Neuroleptic-induced acute akathisia	Coded 333.99
Neuroleptic-induced tardive dyskinesia	Coded 333.82
Medication-induced postural tremor	Coded 333.1
Medication-induced movement disorder NOS	Coded 333.90

Other Medication-Induced Disorders

Adverse effects of medication NOS	Coded 995.2

Relational Problems

Relational problems related to a mental disorder or general medical condition	Coded V61.9
Parent-child relational problem	Coded V61.20
Partner relational problem	Coded V61.10
Sibling relational problem	Coded V61.8
Relational problem NOS	Coded V62.81

Problems Related to Abuse or Neglect

Physical abuse of a child	Coded V61.21

(continued)

QUICK REFERENCE 3.7 *(Continued)*	
Sexual abuse of a child	Coded V61.21
Neglect of a child	Coded V61.21
Physical abuse of an adult	
Sexual abuse of an adult	
Additional Conditions That May Be a Focus of Clinical Attention	
Noncompliance with treatment	Coded V15.81
Malingering	Coded V65.2
Adult antisocial behavior	Coded V71.01
Child or adolescent antisocial behavior	Coded V71.02
Borderline intellectual functioning*	Coded V62.89
Age-related cognitive decline	Coded 780.9
Bereavement	Coded V62.82
Academic problem	Coded V62.3
Occupational problem	Coded V62.2
Identity problem	Coded 313.82
Religious and spiritual problem	Coded V62.89
Acculturation problem	Coded V62.4
Phase of life problem	Coded V62.89

*Can also be listed on Axis II.

Source: Listing of topics reprinted with permission from the *Diagnostic and Statistical Manual of Mental Disorders, Fourth Edition, Text Revision.* Copyright 2000 by the American Psychiatric Association.

Documentation of Information on Axis I

When documenting conditions on Axis I, the reason for the visit, generally referred to as the principal diagnosis, is listed first. When this is not the case and the principal diagnosis needs to be coded on Axis II, it would simply be listed there. One of the questions that professionals ask is: Why do most of the principal diagnoses almost always occur on Axis I rather than Axis II? The answer to this is not difficult, but it requires knowledge of both practice application (what diagnoses are placed on a particular axis) and some of the circumstances that surround why diagnoses are coded there.

In practice, most clients usually present with a principal diagnosis relative to Axis I. In adults, one of the major reasons for this prevalence is that many of the diagnoses coded on Axis II (i.e., the personality disorders) generally start in childhood or adolescence and persist in a stable form into adulthood with nonexistence or limited periods of remission. This would make it more unlikely, although not impossible, for an adult to come in for intervention with a presenting condition needing to be coded on Axis II. Furthermore, if an adult suffers from mental retardation (coded on Axis II), this is considered a lifelong condition that, although possible, usually would not in itself constitute the presenting problem. If the individual develops a condition resembling mental retardation in adulthood, it would not be diagnosed as mental retardation but as a specific type of dementia. (Both of these conditions are discussed in further detail in subsequent chapters.) In this case, once again an Axis I diagnosis would most likely result.

One example of an exception to this assumption is when an adult is given a principal diagnosis on Axis II, such as borderline personality disorder. Individuals diagnosed with this condition often have a pattern of "instability of interpersonal relationships, self-image, and affects and marked impulsivity" that might result in "frantic efforts to avoid abandonment [that] may include impulsive actions such as self-mutilating or suicidal behaviors" (APA, 2000, p. 706). Therefore, in this case, although the presenting diagnosis would be placed on Axis II because of self-harming behaviors, such as self-mutilating or suicidal threats or actions, the client likely would warrant admission for inpatient observation. This would make the Axis II diagnosis of a personality disorder the actual reason

for admission. When the principal diagnosis is listed on Axis II, it is always good practice to place the words *principal diagnosis* in parentheses after it. (See Quick Reference 3.8 for further clarification.)

In children, the same prevalence holds, and the presenting diagnosis is also more likely to be placed on Axis I. The reasons for this remain very similar to those just stated for adults. There is one additional reason, however, that is particularly important to remember when working with children. Since the personality disorders are generally considered to be representative of lifelong patterns of behavior, children often are too young to meet the foundational criteria for assignment of personality disorders.

Regardless of whether the practitioner is working with adults or children, acceptable proficient documentation of the provisional diagnosis requires that, if more than one diagnosis is noted (on either axis), the principal diagnosis should always be listed first. (See Quick Reference 3.8 on the principal diagnosis.)

As demonstrated in Quick Reference 3.9, whether a diagnosis is noted on Axis I or not, some type of coding will always need to be placed there. Therefore, the Axis I diagnosis

---

QUICK REFERENCE 3.8

EXAMPLE I: DOCUMENTATION OF PRINCIPAL DIAGNOSIS

When major depressive disorder is the principal diagnosis and there are two Axes I diagnoses, the reason for visit or principal diagnosis is listed first.

Axis I:	Major depressive disorder 296.xx
	Alcohol dependence 303.90

When the reason for visit or principal diagnosis is an Axis II diagnosis, be sure to identify it as the reason for the initial visit.

Axis I	V71.09 No diagnosis
Axis II:	Borderline personality disorder 301.83 (Principal Diagnosis)

QUICK REFERENCE 3.9

CODING ON AXIS I

Practitioners Need to Be Aware That:

- Some type of coding is always expected on Axis I.
- No diagnosis on Axis I is coded: V71.09.
- Lack of, or inaccurate information for, an Axis I diagnosis is to be coded: 799.9 (Diagnosis or condition deferred on Axis I).

---

should never be left blank. If there is no Axis I diagnosis, the practitioner should code No diagnosis on Axis I (V71.09). If the practitioner is uncertain of what diagnosis to place because of insufficient information (as explained in Chapter 2) he or she should code Diagnosis or condition deferred on Axis I (coded 799.9).

In completing the diagnostic assessment when working with Axis I conditions, three situations need to be examined.

1. The practitioner should note the major psychiatric symptoms a client is displaying. In the *DSM-IV-TR*, each diagnostic category has specific criteria associated with it.
2. These presenting symptoms should be clearly noted and documented concerning frequency, intensity, and duration.
   a. When looking at issues of frequency, it is critical to document how often the problem behaviors are happening (i.e., the rate of occurrence) during a specific time period. Are the behaviors happening, for example, once a week, or once a day? How does the frequency of occurrence of these problem behaviors directly affect individual, occupational, or social functioning? Many of the diagnostic categories say that the behaviors must occur once or more; others say they must be

frequent occurrences. To be safe, always document the frequency of the behavior and relate it directly to level of functioning.
   b. Intensity is another critical aspect needing to be clearly identified when assessing diagnostic criteria. To address intensity, the practitioner must gather information about the magnitude of the strength, power, or force with which a problem behavior is occurring and relate this directly to the way it affects daily functioning.
   c. For duration, the practitioner should document the time between the onset and stopping of the behavior (Ciminero, Calhoun, & Adams, 1986). Specifically, addressing duration requires that the period of time that something lasts or exists be measured. This period is very important in terms of identifying the criteria for a disorder because often specific time frames must be met (e.g., for schizophrenia the symptoms must last approximately 6 months; if less than 6 months, the diagnosis of schizophreniform is utilized).

Suggested measures, and standardized tools to assist the mental health practitioner in measuring incidence and problem behaviors (in terms of frequency, intensity, and duration) are presented in Chapter 4 as well as in each subsequent

---

QUICK REFERENCE 3.10

QUESTIONS TO GUIDE THE PROCESS

- What are the major psychiatric symptoms a client is displaying?
- What are the frequency, intensity, and duration of the symptoms or problem behavior?
- Have environmental factors, such as cultural and social factors, been considered as a possible explanation?

---

chapter as relevant along with the other rapid assessment instruments.

3. When substantiating the categorization of diagnostic criteria supportive of the Axis I diagnosis, environmental, cultural, and social factors must always be assessed. As discussed in Chapter 2, it can be difficult to separate behaviors that are culturally based from those that are not. It is critical to not diagnose Axis I disorder(s) when an individual's behaviors are related to a culture-bound syndrome. In the diagnostic assessment process, if the practitioner believes the behavior is "culture" related, no clinical syndrome or formal diagnosis constituting a mental disorder based on those symptoms alone is given. Practitioners should code an individual's behaviors that they consider to be culturally re-

lated under the category of other conditions that may be a focus of clinical attention as an Acculturation problem (coded V62.4). The individual should not be diagnosed with a mental disorder. Even though this condition is not considered a mental disorder, it would still be coded on Axis I. (See Quick Reference 3.10 for questions to guide the assessment process.)

Documentation of Information on Axis II

Axis II is used for reporting mental retardation and the personality disorders. Mental retardation is listed in terms of four degrees of severity (e.g., mild, moderate, severe, and profound with an additional classification when it is believed that mental retardation is present but the degree of severity cannot be assessed). (See Quick Reference 3.11 for the types of mental retardation and the codes used for documentation.)

QUICK REFERENCE 3.11

AXIS II: TYPES OF MENTAL RETARDATION

Mild mental retardation (IQ level 50–55 to approximately 70)	Coded 317
Moderate retardation (IQ 35–40 to 50–55)	Coded 318.0
Severe retardation (IQ level 20–25 to 35–40)	Coded 318.1
Profound mental retardation (IQ level below 20 or 25)	Coded 318.2
Mental retardation, severity unspecified	Coded 319
Borderline intellectual functioning (IQ level 71–84)	Coded 62.89

QUICK REFERENCE 3.12

Axis II: Types of Personality Disorders

Cluster A: Characteristics of Odd and Eccentric Behaviors

Paranoid personality disorder	301.0
Schizoid personality disorder	301.20
Schizotypal personality	301.22

Cluster B: Characteristic of Dramatic, Emotional, and Erratic Behaviors

Antisocial personality disorder	301.7
Borderline personality disorder	301.83
Histrionic personality disorder	301.50
Narcissistic personality disorder	301.81

Cluster C: Characteristic of Anxious and Fearful Behaviors

Avoidant personality disorder	301.82
Dependent personality disorder	301.6
Obsessive-compulsive personality disorder	301.4
Personality disorder NOS	301.9

Source: Listing of topics reprinted with permission from the *Diagnostic and Statistical Manual of Mental Disorders, Fourth Edition, Text Revision.* Copyright 2000 by the American Psychiatric Association.

Previously in the *DSM-III-R*, it was clearly documented that an additional condition called borderline intellectual functioning (coded V62.89) could also be coded on Axis II. Borderline intellectual functioning is one of the additional conditions that may be a focus of clinical attention. The main criterion for this category is the results of a standardized intelligence test. In borderline intellectual functioning, the Intelligence Quotient (IQ) range is between 71 and 84. This is the category of IQ scores directly above mild retardation and directly below what would be considered to fall within the normal intelligence range (85–115). Originally this diagnosis was placed on Axis II because it was similar to the other disorders in that the personality traits present are believed to be enduring

and pervasive. In *DSM-IV* and *DSM-IV-TR* (pp. 26, 27, and 29), it is no longer listed as a condition to be listed on Axis II. However, descriptive text within the *DSM-IV-TR* (APA, 2000) in the classification system (p. 25), and in the description of the disorder (p. 740) states that it is to be coded on Axis II. Most practitioners choose to place it on Axis II, but until the text is clarified clearly, coding on either Axis I or Axis II would suffice.

The second groups of disorders listed on Axis II are the personality disorders. (See Quick Reference 3.12 for a list of the disorders.) As mentioned earlier in this chapter, if a disorder is designated as a personality disorder in the *DSM-IV* and the *DSM-IV-TR*, the diagnosis will end in the two words *personality disorder*. In

QUICK REFERENCE 3.13

AXIS II: QUESTIONS ABOUT MENTAL RETARDATION

In completing the diagnostic assessment for mental retardation, these considerations should be taken into account:

- Is there a lifelong pattern of behavior with an onset of the condition prior to age 18?
- Is there significantly subaverage intelligence (IQ of 70 or below)?
- Is the subaverage intelligence concurrent with problems in adaptive functioning?
- What are the frequency, intensity, and duration of the presenting behaviors?

the *DSM-IV-TR*, although personality disorders continue to be grouped in clusters, the manual urges practitioners to be cautious using the cluster system. Although the cluster system may be helpful in terms of general categorizing of symptoms, in research and in educational settings, these groupings have not been proven to accurately measure what is expected (APA, 2000). In the *DSM-IV* and the *DSM-IV-TR*, there are now 11 different conditions related to personality. This is one fewer than was reported in the *DSM-III-R* (APA, 1987). The personality disorder known as passive aggressive personality disorder was removed from *DSM-IV* and *DSM-IV-TR* diagnostic categories and placed in the section with the criteria sets and axes provided for further study.

When working with the conditions to be listed on Axis II, the level of impairment and the onset and duration of the symptoms are important criteria that need to be evaluated. The practitioner should note the major psychiatric symptoms the client is displaying and whether these symptoms first started in childhood and continued into adulthood. (Dziegielewski, 2010). The greatest predictor related to conditions on Axis II is whether there is a lifelong pattern of behavior or whether the onset of the condition occurred before the ages of 18 to 21. This lifelong pattern, or an onset prior to age 18, is true for most individuals who suffer from mental retardation, and ages 18 to 21 better fit

those individuals who suffer from the personality disorders. In mental retardation, the practitioner should immediately look for significantly subaverage intelligence (IQ of 70 or below) with an age of onset younger than age 18. Also, it is critical to link the subaverage intelligence to concurrent problems in adaptive individual and social functioning. (See Quick Reference 3.13 for considerations to take into account when completing the diagnostic assessment for mental retardation.)

With personality disorders, individuals will often present with long-standing or enduring patterns of behavior and inner experiences that deviate markedly from expectations within the individual's cultural context. These behaviors remain pervasive and inflexible and cause the individual distress or impairment (APA, 2000, p. 685) Again, as with all diagnoses, the symptoms presented must be related directly to either adaptive or functional impairment. (See Quick Reference 3.14 for considerations to take into account when completing the diagnostic assessment for personality disorders.)

Similar to Axis I, all presenting symptoms for Axis II conditions should be clearly noted and documented regarding frequency, intensity, and duration of the problem behavior. Be sure to note the rate of occurrence of the problem behavior (frequency), the magnitude of the strength,

---

QUICK REFERENCE 3.14

AXIS II: QUESTIONS ABOUT PERSONALITY DISORDERS

In completing the diagnostic assessment for personality disorders, these considerations should be taken into account:

- Is there a pattern of behavior that develops in either adolescence or early adulthood?
- Is there an enduring pattern(s) of inner experience and behavior that deviates markedly from expectations of the individual's culture?
- Are the symptoms and behaviors pervasive and inflexible?
- How do these symptoms or behaviors relate to occupational and social functioning?
- What are the frequency, intensity, and duration of the presenting behaviors?

---

power, or force (intensity) with which a problem behavior is occurring, and the period of time the behavior exists (duration). When the symptoms exist but neither create marked distresses nor disturb or impair functioning, application of any diagnostic category is inappropriate. Similar to Axis I, Axis II needs to have a plan for addressing the disorders coded.

AXIS II: APPLICATION OF THE DEFENSE MECHANISMS

Defense mechanisms are a type of mental process or coping style that results in automatic psychological responses exhibited as a means of protecting the individual against anxiety. These coping styles and patterns of behavior help to safeguard the individual by keeping perceived internal and/or external stresses away from his or her awareness (APA, 2000; Barker, 2003). Since it is believed that many individuals either consciously or unconsciously develop defense mechanisms that can influence the diagnostic condition and impede progress, these psychological occurrences, when noted in a client, should be listed on Axis II. When defense mechanisms are present, it is very important for the practitioner to be aware and recognize how they may influence treatment because often the individual who is experiencing them is unaware of how these processes can affect his or her behavior. (See Quick Reference 3.15 for tips regarding coding on Axis II.) Defense mechanisms can influence an individual's reaction to emotional conflicts as well as responses toward

---

QUICK REFERENCE 3.15

CODING ON AXIS II

Practitioners need to be aware that:

- Similar to Axis I, some type of coding is always expected on Axis II.
- No diagnosis is to be coded: V71.09 Diagnosis on Axis II.
- Lack of, or inaccurate, information is to be coded: 799.9 Diagnosis or condition deferred on Axis II.
- Defense mechanisms can be coded on Axis II.

QUICK REFERENCE 3.16

EXAMPLE: RECORDING OF DEFENSE MECHANISMS

Axis	Coding	Description
Axis I:	V71.09	No diagnosis
Axis II:	301.83	Borderline personality disorder
Splitting (current defense mechanism)		
Axis III:	881.02	Lacerations of wrist
Axis IV:		Loss of employment
Axis V:		GAF = 45 (current)

---

internal and external stressors found in daily living. Therefore, identification and subsequent documentation of the defense mechanism(s) can facilitate the most accurate diagnostic assessment. When present, these mechanisms should be documented regardless of the fact that this type of coding holds no value in the billing process and is not considered a mandatory part of the multiaxial system.

The Defensive Functioning Scale, located in the appendix section of the *DSM-IV-TR*, can prove to be very helpful as a reference for practitioners. The scale identifies the defense mechanisms that an individual might develop as well as establishing the degree to which the defense mechanism or coping style may protect against anxiety or stress. Interpretation of defense mechanisms tends to be very subjective, and the definitions and subsequent application of these concepts can differ based on the source of the professional reference. Therefore, when using the defense mechanisms, it is important to identify coping styles and behaviors that can affect mental health–related behaviors utilizing similar definitions. Since most professionals in mental health use the *DSM* in practice, it makes sense to use the definitions of the terms described in the *DSM-IV-TR* to represent the coding placed within the multiaxis system. When noted, documentation of the occurrence of defense mechanisms in clients is usually listed

in order of prevalence and severity and placed on Axis II. Generally the defense mechanisms are listed beginning with those defenses or coping styles that are predominant and most representative of the client's current level of functioning. (See Quick Reference 3.16 for an example of recording defense mechanisms.)

To use the defense mechanisms, the Defensive Functioning Scale divides these coping styles into related groups referred to as *defense levels*. At the first defense level, the defensive mechanisms are related to *high adaptive functioning*. In this level of functioning, an individual is aware of what he or she is experiencing and uses it to promote a healthier sense of well-being. (See Quick Reference 3.17 for samples and definitions of the defense mechanisms occurring at this level.) For example, a common defense mechanism is known as *suppression*. According to the *DSM-IV-TR*, *suppression* is defined as "the individual deals with emotional conflict or internal or external stressors by intentionally avoiding thinking about disturbing problems, wishes, feelings, or experiences" (APA, 2000, p. 813). In this case, an individual may refuse to think about something that is painful and thereby refuse to discuss it. This can complicate the history taking of the diagnostic assessment, directly influencing the accuracy and relevance of what the client states as the presenting problem. This type of defense mechanism is considered higher level in

---

QUICK REFERENCE 3.17

Individual Defense Mechanisms: High Adaptive Level

High adaptive level: This level [category] of defensive functioning results in optimal adaptation in the handling of stressors. These defenses usually maximize gratification and allow the conscious awareness of feelings, ideas, and their consequences. They also promote an optimum balance among conflicting motives.

Selected definitions and examples of common defense mechanisms at this level include:

Affiliation: The individual deals with emotional conflict or internal or external stressors by turning to others for help or support. This involves sharing problems with others but does not imply trying to make someone else responsible for them.

Altruism: The individual deals with emotional conflict or internal or external stressors by dedication to meeting the needs of others. Unlike the self-sacrifice sometimes characteristic of reaction formation, the individual receives gratification either vicariously or from the response of others.

Anticipation: The individual deals with emotional conflict or internal or external stressors by experiencing emotional reactions in advance of, or anticipating consequences of, possible future events and considering realistic, alternative responses or solutions.

Humor: The individual deals with emotional conflict or external stressors by emphasizing the amusing or ironic aspects of the conflict or stressor.

Self-assertion: The individual deals with emotional conflict or stressors by expressing his or her feelings and thoughts directly in a way that is not coercive or manipulative.

Self-observation: The individual deals with emotional conflict or stressors by reflecting on his or her own thoughts, feelings, motivation, and behavior and responding appropriately.

Sublimation: The individual deals with emotional conflict or internal or external stressors by channeling potentially maladaptive feelings or impulses into socially acceptable behavior (e.g., contact sports to channel angry impulses).

Suppression: The individual deals with emotional conflict or internal or external stressors by intentionally avoiding thinking about disturbing problems, wishes, feelings, or experiences.

Source: Reprinted with permission from the *Diagnostic and Statistical Manual of Mental Disorders, Fourth Edition, Text Revision.* Copyright 2000 by the American Psychiatric Association.

---

terms of adaptive functioning, since the client is cognizant of the suppression. It can be helpful for professionals to help clients to address this coping style in subsequent treatment planning and intervention strategy. Other defense mechanisms that are considered to be of the highest adaptive level are *affiliation, altruism, anticipation, humor, self-assertion, self-observation,* and *sublimation.*

The second level of defense is referred to as *mental inhibitions (compromise formation).* When a client utilizes coping behaviors at this level, he or she is attempting to keep potentially threatening ideas, feelings, memories, wishes, or fears out of awareness (APA, 2001). For example, *repression* is a defense mechanism where "the individual deals with emotional conflict or internal or external stressors by expelling disturbing wishes, thoughts,

QUICK REFERENCE 3.18

INDIVIDUAL DEFENSE MECHANISMS: MENTAL INHIBITIONS LEVEL

Mental inhibitions (compromise formation) level: Defensive functioning at this level keeps potentially threatening ideas, feelings, memories, wishes, or fears out of awareness.

Selected definitions and examples of common defense mechanisms at this level include:

Displacement: The individual deals with emotional conflict or internal or external stressors by transferring a feeling about, or a response to, one object onto another (usually less threatening) substitute object.

Dissociation: The individual deals with emotional conflict or internal or external stressors with a breakdown in the usually integrated functions of consciousness, memory, perception of self or the environment, or sensory/motor behavior.

Intellectualization: The individual deals with emotional conflict or internal or external stressors by the excessive use of abstract thinking or the making of generalizations to control or minimize disturbing feelings.

Isolation of affect: The individual deals with emotional conflict or internal or external stressors by the separation of ideas from the feelings originally associated with them. The individual loses touch with the feelings associated with a given idea (e.g., a traumatic event) while remaining aware of the cognitive elements of it (e.g., descriptive details).

Reaction formation: The individual deals with emotional conflict or internal or external stressors by substituting behavior, thoughts, or feelings that are diametrically opposed to his or her own unacceptable thoughts or feelings (this usually occurs in conjunction with their repression).

Repression: The individual deals with emotional conflict or internal or external stressors by expelling disturbing wishes, thoughts, or experiences from conscious awareness. The feeling component may remain conscious, detached from its associated ideas.

Undoing: The individual deals with emotional conflict or internal or external stressors by words or behavior designed to negate or to make amends symbolically for unacceptable thoughts, feelings, or actions.

Source: Reprinted with permission from the *Diagnostic and Statistical Manual of Mental Disorders, Fourth Edition, Text Revision.* Copyright 2000 by the American Psychiatric Association.

or experiences from conscious awareness . . . [and] the feeling content may remain detached from its associated ideas" (APA, 2000, p. 813). When an individual practices these coping styles at this level, he or she may not be aware of what is happening (unconscious), although the feelings may come out in other ways. For example, in repression, a client may report that he loves and wants to protect his parents but is actually very angry and wants to punish them. He may report

that he is very close and wants to protect his family yet he continually practices behaviors that put his parents at risk. Other examples of defense mechanisms in this area include *displacement, dissociation, intellectualization, isolation of affect, reaction formation,* and *undoing.* (See Quick Reference 3.18 for this level of functioning and definitions.)

The third level of defense mechanisms identified in the *DSM-IV-TR* is the minor-image-

---

QUICK REFERENCE 3.19

INDIVIDUAL DEFENSE MECHANISMS: MINOR IMAGE DISTORTING-LEVEL

Minor image-distorting level: This level is characterized by distortions in the image of the self, body, or others that may be employed to regulate self-esteem.

Selected definitions and examples of common defense mechanisms at this level include:

Devaluation: The individual deals with emotional conflict or internal or external stressors by attributing exaggerated negative qualities to self or others.

Idealization: The individual deals with emotional conflict or internal or external stressors by attributing exaggerated positive qualities to others.

Omnipotence: The individual deals with emotional conflict or internal or external stressors by feeling or acting as if he or she possesses special powers or abilities and is superior to others.

Source: Reprinted with permission from the *Diagnostic and Statistical Manual of Mental Disorders, Fourth Edition, Text Revision.* Copyright 2000 by the American Psychiatric Association.

---

distorting level. (See Quick Reference 3.19 for examples of level at of functioning.) Clients who utilize coping styles and behaviors representative of this level of functioning exhibit behaviors that are characterized by distortions in self-image or self-esteem as well as distortions related to the way they perceive their body. For example, the defense mechanism *idealization* is defined as when an "individual deals with emotional conflict or internal or external stressors by attributing exaggerated positive qualities to others" (APA, 200, p. 812). In this case, when completing the diagnostic assessment, it may be difficult to assess the family and social influences that might affect a client's behavior because he or she cannot avoid or simply cannot accept the general perceptions of reality as shared by others.

When working with children, for example, idealization may be related to seeing a parent as a role model. The parent may be abusive, but because the child idealizes or sees the abusive actions as part of the expression of love and concern by the parent, the abuse is considered acceptable and tolerable. Because the parent is a role model, the behaviors exhibited by the abusive parent become viewed as acceptable expressions of love. The child may begin to see him- or herself as bad or undeserving of other types of love (e.g., the child may say to himself, "My father beats me, I respect him, so it must be done through love"). Another example that takes into account the distortions in body image that may occur when idealization is used is the condition of *anorexia*. Anorexia is an eating disorder in which a client idealizes the body image of being extremely thin and is willing to starve to achieve this perceived ideal body frame. Other examples of coping styles reflective of these types of behaviors are *devaluation, idealization,* and *omnipotence.*

At the fourth level, the individual develops defense mechanisms referred to as experiencing *disavowal,* characterized by "keeping unpleasant or unacceptable stressors, impulses, ideas, affects, or responsibility out of awareness with or without a misattribution of these to external causes" (APA, 2000, p. 809) (see Quick Reference 3.20). For example, in denial, the individual cannot or will not face emotional conflict or turmoil related to

---

QUICK REFERENCE 3.20

INDIVIDUAL DEFENSE MECHANISMS: DISAVOWAL LEVEL

Disavowal level: This level is characterized by keeping unpleasant or unacceptable stressors, impulses, ideas, affects, or responsibility out of awareness with or without a misattribution of these to external causes.

Selected definitions and examples of common defense mechanisms at this level include:

Denial: The individual deals with emotional conflict or internal or external stressors by refusing to acknowledge some painful aspect of external reality or subjective experience that would be apparent to others. The term *psychotic denial* is used when there is gross impairment in reality testing.

Projection: The individual deals with emotional conflict or internal or external stressors by falsely attributing to another his or her own unacceptable feelings, impulses, or thoughts.

Rationalization: The individual deals with emotional conflict or internal or external stressors by concealing the true motivations for his or her own thoughts, actions, or feelings through the elaboration of reassuring or self-serving but incorrect explanations.

Source: Reprinted with permission from the *Diagnostic and Statistical Manual of Mental Disorders, Fourth Edition, Text Revision.* Copyright 2000 by the American Psychiatric Association.

---

internal or external stressors and, based on this inability, refuses to acknowledge aspects or the entire situation or event because it is too painful. Generally, this lack of acknowledgment of the problem or situation is obvious and disconcerting to others in the client's environment. At times, when the defense mechanisms in this area are extreme, psychotic denial may result. When this happens, there is clearly gross impairment when discussing the problem or situation with the client in terms of reality testing. It is very important to note psychotic denial when completing the diagnostic assessment because the information received may be inaccurate where the client cannot or will not acknowledge it.

Recognition of these types of defense mechanisms clearly highlights the need for including environmental information from other sources, such as family and other individuals in the support system, to assess the reliability and validity of the information the client is sharing. Identifying these factors could also be especially helpful to other professionals working with the client in terms of treatment planning and strategy. For example, if a client is in denial and the practitioner does not gather additional information to supplement what is said, important factors that could guide the treatment process could be overlooked. Other examples of coping styles and strategies at this level include *projection* and *rationalization.*

The fifth defense level is referred to as *major image-distorting.* When experiencing defense mechanisms at this level, the client grossly distorts and misattributes actions or behaviors of the self or others. Examples are autistic fantasy, projective identification, and *splitting.* For example, when working with certain personality disorders (e.g., borderline personality disorder, which will be defined later in this text), the defense mechanism known as splitting may occur. When utilizing this coping style, the individual deals with emotional conflict or internal or external stressors by compartmentalizing opposite affect states and failing

---

QUICK REFERENCE 3.21

INDIVIDUAL DEFENSE MECHANISMS: MAJOR IMAGE-DISTORTING LEVEL

Major image-distorting level: This level is characterized by gross distortion or misattribution of the image of self or others.

Selected definitions and examples of common defense mechanisms at this level include:

Autistic fantasy: The individual deals with emotional conflict or internal or external stressors by excessive daydreaming as a substitute for human relationships, more effective action, or problem solving.

Projective identification: As in projection, the individual deals with emotional conflict or internal or external stressors by falsely attributing to another his or her own unacceptable feelings, impulses, or thoughts. Unlike simple projection, the individual does not fully disavow what is projected. Instead, the individual remains aware of his or her own affects or impulses but misattributes them as justifiable reactions to the other person. Not infrequently, the individual induces the very feelings in others that were first mistakenly believed to be there, making it difficult to clarify who did what to whom first.

Splitting: The individual deals with emotional conflict or internal or external stressors by compartmentalizing opposite affect states and failing to integrate the positive and negative qualities of the self or others into cohesive images. Because ambivalent affects cannot be experienced simultaneously, more balanced views and expectations of self or others are excluded from emotional awareness. Self and object images tend to alternate between polar opposites: exclusively loving, powerful, worthy, nurturing, and kind—or exclusively bad, hateful, angry, destructive, rejecting, or worthless.

Source: Reprinted with permission from the *Diagnostic and Statistical Manual of Mental Disorders, Fourth Edition, Text Revision.* Copyright 2000 by the American Psychiatric Association.

---

to integrate the positive and negative qualities of the self or others into cohesive images (APA, 2000). In this practice, ambivalent feelings result, and the client may focus on the extremes, avoiding more balanced views and expectations from self and others. This may lead the client to exhibit extreme behaviors such as being overly loving at times and at other times being extremely hateful and rejecting of others. Other defense mechanisms at the major image-distorting level include autistic fantasy and projective identification. (See Quick Reference 3.21 for definitions of the major image-distorting defense mechanisms.)

The sixth level is referred to as the *action level.* At this level, the client learns to deal with anxiety and internal and external stressors by withdrawing and running away or leaving the situation.

Acting out is a defense mechanism that can occur in clients who cannot accept or deal with certain emotions. For example, an adolescent may have contradictory feelings about his or her parents and, related to this internal or external struggle, may continually run away from home.

It is important to note, however, that the defense mechanism acting out cannot be summarized simply by identifying problematic behaviors. These problematic behaviors must be related directly to contradictory emotions and conflicts. Other defense mechanisms that fall at the action level are *apathetic withdrawal, help-rejecting complaining*, and *passive aggression* (see Quick Reference 3.22).

The last level of defensive functioning identified is referred to as *defensive dysregulation.* At

---

QUICK REFERENCE 3.22

INDIVIDUAL DEFENSE MECHANISMS: ACTION LEVEL

Action level: This level is characterized by defensive functioning that deals with internal or external stressors by action or withdrawal.

Selected definitions and examples of common defense mechanisms at this level include:

Acting out: The individual deals with emotional conflict or internal or external stressors by actions rather than reflections or feelings. This definition is broader than the original concept of the acting out of transference feelings or wishes during psychotherapy and is intended to include behavior arising both within and outside the transference relationship. Defensive acting out is not synonymous with "bad behavior" because it requires evidence that the behavior is related to emotional conflicts.

Help-rejecting complaining: The individual deals with emotional conflict or internal or external stressors by complaining or making repetitious requests for help that disguise covert feelings of hostility or reproach toward others, which are then expressed by rejecting the suggestions, advice, or help that others offer. The complaints or requests may involve physical or psychological symptoms or life problems.

Passive aggression: The individual deals with emotional conflict or internal or external stressors by indirectly and unassertively expressing aggression toward others. A facade of overt compliance masks covert resistance, resentment, or hostility. Passive aggression often occurs in response to demands for independent action or performance or the lack of gratification of dependent wishes but may be adaptive for individuals in subordinate positions who have no other way to express assertiveness more overtly.

Source: Reprinted with permission from the *Diagnostic and Statistical Manual of Mental Disorders, Fourth Edition, Text Revision.* Copyright 2000 by the American Psychiatric Association.

---

this level, coping styles break down in terms of the client's reaction to stressors. This breakdown is severe enough to distort perceptions of reality and cause the individual to lose objective reality. The individual denies what is happening around him or her and refuses to acknowledge the existence of certain factors related to emotional stressors or events in his or her internal or external reality. Examples of this level of defense mechanisms include *delusional projection*, where the individual holds on to beliefs even when evidence to the contrary is strong; *psychotic denial,* where there is a complete split from reality-based interpretation of activities and events; and *psychotic distortion*, where the individual cannot see things as others see them and misinterprets much

of what is happening to him– or herself. When a client is experiencing defense mechanisms at this level, information from outside sources (family, friends, social supports) is essential, as the history and interpretation are very likely to be confused.

AXIS III: THE MULTIAXIAL ASSESSMENT SYSTEM

Axis III lists the physical (medical) conditions that may be relevant to the condition being addressed. These medical or physical conditions are referred to as *general medical conditions* in the *DSM-IV* and the *DSM-IV-TR.* Previously, Axis III referred to these conditions as *physical disorders*

QUICK REFERENCE 3.23

AXIS III: COMPARISON OF *DSM-III-R* AND *DSM-IV* AND *DSM-IV-TR*

DSM-III-R	Physical Disorders and Related Conditions
Changed to:	
DSM-IV/DSM-IV-TR	General Medical Conditions

---

and related conditions. (See Quick Reference 3.23 for an outline of the changes.)

Since the term *mental disorder* means a condition that is not due to a medical condition, it is important for all practitioners to have some knowledge of the medical conditions listed in Axis III. Furthermore, the practitioner needs to be acquainted with the relationship that these conditions can have to a mental disorder. Pollak, Levy, and Breitholz (1999) were quick to warn that in the diagnostic assessment, alterations in behavior and mood that mimic a mental disorder may be directly related to a medical illness. This is particularly important to distinguish as many times clients suffering from a mental disorder may be confused about the symptoms they feel and may not report them clearly. Since most mental health practitioners do not have extensive training in medical disorders and what to expect when one occurs, the misdiagnosis of a medical disorder as a mental health disorder can be a fairly common occurrence. Clients at the greatest risk for misdiagnosis in this area include women who are pregnant or after pregnancy (e.g., prenatal, perinatal, or neonatal); indigent individuals because of limited resources and access to continued health care; individuals who engage in high-risk behaviors; individuals with a medical illness who exhibit symptoms that might be confused for mental illness; and individuals with chronic conditions, such as

those who suffer from major mental disorders and elderly clients (Hartmann, 1995; Pollak, Levy, & Breitholtz, 1999). For example, clients who have been diagnosed with mental disorders such as schizophrenia or bipolar disorder may be unable to perceive, misperceive, or simply ignore warning signs of a medical problem (Dziegielewski, 2010). Many of the chronic conditions that older adults exhibit may be deemphasized or ignored as a normal part of aging or chronic disease progression.

For all clients, misdiagnosis or absence of the proper diagnosis can have devastating effects. When a client is acting extremely agitated and uncooperative, the practitioner should assess to see if this type of behavior is characteristic of any other time in the client's life. If it is not, it is possible the behaviors could be related to an unknown trauma such as a closed head injury. Nonrecognition of the medical aspects of a mental disorder could also result in severe legal, ethical, and malpractice considerations. It is essential for nonmedically trained mental health practitioners to have some background in the medical conditions, particularly the influence these conditions have on mental health symptoms.

To guide the diagnostic assessment and screening inquiries that help to identify the relationship between medical factors and mental health–related behaviors, Pollak et al. (1999) suggests three guidelines:

QUICK REFERENCE 3.24

HELPFUL HINTS: CLINICAL PRESENTATIONS SUGGESTIVE OF A MENTAL DISORDER

- Previous psychosocial difficulties not related to a medical or neurodevelopmental disorder.
- Chronic unrelated complaints that cannot be linked to a satisfactory medical explanation.
- A history of object relations problems, such as help-rejecting behavior, co-dependency, and other interrelationship problems.
- A puzzling lack of concern on the part of the client as to the behaviors he or she is engaging in and a lack of concern with a tendency to minimize or deny the circumstances.
- Evidence of secondary gain where the client is reinforced by such behaviors by significant others, family, or members of the support system.
- A history of substance abuse problems (alcohol or medication abuse).
- A family history of similar symptoms and/or mental disorders.
- Cognitive or physical complaints that are more severe than what would be expected for someone in a similar situation.

---

1. The practitioner should look for risk factors and whether the client falls into a high-risk group as identified earlier.
2. The practitioner should consider whether the presentation is suspicious or inconsistent and therefore suggestive of a neurodevelopmental or medical condition.
3. After gathering initial screening information, the practitioner should decide whether further testing is warranted to address the physical or medical basis of the symptoms a client is experiencing. In this case, a physical exam should always be considered.

Once the practitioner makes a referral, a signed release from the client will be needed for the physician to share this information with the mental health practitioner. It is also recommended that the practitioner use client information from previous history and physical exams, medical history summaries, radiological reports, and lab findings. The most valuable advice for the practitioner is to first establish when the client last had a physical exam. When this information cannot be verified and the practitioner is not sure whether the condition is medically based, referral for a physical exam should be made. Although the mental health practitioner can assist in helping to identify and document medical conditions, remember that the original diagnosis of any such medical condition always rests with the physician (see Quick Reference 3.24 for helpful hints on identifying a mental disorder and its relationship to a physical disorder).

Pollak et al. (1999) suggest several factors to help a practitioner separate mental health clinical presentations that may have a medical contribution. Nine points should always be considered in completing the diagnostic assessment:

1. Give special attention to clients who present with the first episode of a major disorder. In these clients, particularly when symptoms are severe (e.g., psychotic, catatonic, and nonresponsive), close monitoring of the original presentation, when compared with previous behavior, is essential.
2. Note if the client's symptoms are acute (just started or relative to a certain situation) or abrupt with rapid changes

in mood or behavior. Examples of symptoms that would fall in this area include both cognitive and behavioral symptoms such as marked apathy, decreased drive and initiative, paranoia, labile mood or mood swings, and poorly controlled impulses.

3. Pay particular attention when the initial onset of a disorder or serious symptoms occur after the age of 40. Although this is not an iron-clad rule, most mental disorders become evident before the age of 40; thus onset of symptoms after 40 should be carefully examined to rule out social, situational stressors, cultural implications, and medical causes.

4. Note symptoms of a mental disorder that occur immediately preceding, during, or after the onset of a major medical illness. It is very possible the symptoms may be related to the progression of the medical condition. There is also the possibility that symptoms could be medication or substance related (Dziegielewski, 2010). Polypharmacy can be a real problem for many individuals who are unaware of the dangers of mixing certain medications and substances that they do not consider medications (i.e., herbal preparations) (Dziegielewski, 2001).

5. When gathering information for the diagnostic assessment, note whether there is an immediate psychosocial stressor or life circumstance that may contribute to the symptoms the client is experiencing. This is especially relevant when the stressors present are so minimal that a clear connection between the stressor and the reaction cannot be made. One very good general rule is to remember that anytime a client presents with extreme symptomology of any kind, with no previous history of such behaviors, attention and monitoring for medical causes is essential.

6. Pay particular attention in the screening process when a client suffers from a variety of different types of hallucinations. Basically, a hallucination is the misperception of a stimulus. In psychotic conditions, *auditory hallucinations* are most common. When a client presents with multiple types of hallucinations—such as visual (seeing things that are not there); tactile, which pertain to the sense of touch (e.g., bugs crawling on them); gustatory (pertaining to the sense of taste); or olfactory (relative to the sense of smell)—this is generally too extreme to be purely a mental health condition. Be sure a medically trained practitioner is aware of these symptoms and how it can relate to the mental health diagnosis.

7. Note any simple repetitive and purposeless movements of speech (e.g., stuttering or indistinct or unintelligible speech), the face (e.g., motor tightness or tremors), and hands and extremities (e.g., tremor, shaking, and unsteady gait). Also note any experiential phenomena such as derealization, depersonalization, and unexplained gastric or medical complaints and symptoms, such as new onset of headache accompanied by physical signs such as nausea and vomiting.

8. Note signs of cortical brain dysfunction, such as aphasia (language disturbance), apraxia (movement disturbance), agnosia (failure to recognize familiar objects despite intact sensory functioning), and visuo-constructional deficits (problems drawing or reproducing objects and patterns).

9. Note any signs associated with organ failure, such as jaundice related to

hepatic disease or dyspnea (difficulty breathing) associated with cardiac or pulmonary disease. For example, if a client is not getting proper oxygen, he or she may present as very confused and disoriented; when oxygen is regulated, the signs and symptoms begin to decrease and quickly subside.

Although mental health practitioners are not expected to be experts in diagnosing medical disorders, being aware of the medical complications that influence mental health presentations is necessary to facilitate the most accurate and complete diagnostic assessment possible.

Coding Medical Conditions on Axis III: Making the Mind-Body Connection

In using the *DSM-IV-TR*, several issues need to be explored. Perhaps most important is the need to remember the importance of *linking the mind and the body*. Individuals are complex beings. When a categorical approach to identifying and classifying disorders is utilized, the temptation is great to apply concrete and discrete criteria that do not include the full range of an individual's existence or situation.

Making the connection between mind and body and studying the resulting relationship is crucial to a comprehensive diagnostic assessment. Suffering from a medical disorder can clearly affect individual functioning and vice versa. The medical disorder and its subsequent symptoms as reported by the client can easily become confused. Simply having a medical disorder can affect the mental disorder, which in turn can influence the course of many diseases leading to short-term or long-term disability. In addition, mental health conditions can influence other medical conditions, such as cardiovascular disease, diabetes, HIV/AIDS, tuberculosis and malaria. According to Prince et al. (2007),

mental health conditions and the behaviors that are characteristic can also influence reproductive and sexual health with the development of conditions such as dysmenorrheal (disturbed menstrual cycles) and dyspareunia (genital pain during intercourse and other sexual activities).

In professional practice, it is easy to see how the line between what constitutes good *physical health* and what constitutes good *mental health* might be blurred (Dziegielewski, 2005). Just as it is impossible to separate the mind from the body, the concept of wholeness must also be considered. Current understanding demonstrates that achieving healthy outcomes requires positive and healthy mental health and vice versa. Integrating these medical components into the diagnostic assessment can increase the application of this connection. For example, a client may have all the symptoms of depression, but if he or she was also recently diagnosed with cancer, a mental health diagnosis of this nature could clearly be premature if not simply inaccurate. Just as a diagnosis alone is never enough, each practitioner must also assess a situation completely, taking into account system variables that include a person's physical health.

All relevant medical conditions should be listed on Axis III. These general medical conditions should be listed when (a) the mental disorder appears to have a physiological relationship or bearing on the mental health condition coded on Axis I and/or Axis II, and (b) when the medical condition actually causes or facilitates and is part of the reason for the development and continuation of the mental health condition. One sure way to establish this relationship is that when the general medical condition is resolved, the mental health condition is resolved as well. Although conclusive, it does not always happen so easily, or the damage from the general medical condition may not be curable. Regardless, it is important to document all related medical conditions when forming a diagnosis.

QUICK REFERENCE 3.25

Axis III: General Medical Conditions

Diagnostic categories include:

Diseases of the nervous system

Diseases of the circulatory system

Diseases of the respiratory system

Neoplasms

Endocrine diseases

Nutritional diseases

Metabolic diseases

Diseases of the digestive system

Genitourinary system diseases

Hematological diseases

Diseases of the eye

Diseases of the ear, nose, and throat

Musculoskeletal system and connective tissue diseases

Diseases of the skin

Congenital malformations, deformations, and chromosomal abnormalities

Diseases of pregnancy, childbirth, and the puerperium

Infectious diseases

Overdose

Additional codes for the medication-induced disorders

Source: Listing of topics reprinted with permission from the *Diagnostic and Statistical Manual of Mental Disorders, Fourth Edition, Text Revision,* Copyright 2000 by the American Psychiatric Association.

For example, if an individual suffers from dementia of the Alzheimer's type, which is coded on Axis I, then it is expected that one cause of the dementia (i.e., Alzheimer's disease) would be coded on Axis III. Similarly, when a mental disorder due to a general medical condition is coded on Axis I, the medical diagnosis that caused it should be reported on both Axis I and Axis III. (See Quick Reference 3.25 for the categories of general medical conditions listed on Axis III.) Appendix G (p. 867) of the *DSM-IV-TR* includes the complete list of general medical conditions that use the *ICD-9-CM* codes and are featured in the *DSM-IV-TR*. Some of the conditions listed in this appendix are further defined in the Glossary of this book.

QUICK REFERENCE 3.26

AXIS III: ASSESSMENT QUESTIONS

- Has the client had a recent physical exam? If not, suggest that one be ordered.
- Does the client have a summary of a recent history and physical exam that could be reviewed?
- Are there any laboratory findings or tests or any diagnostic reports that can assist in establishing a relationship between the mental and physiological consequences that result?

When making an Axis III diagnosis, mental health practitioners may find it helpful to receive support from an interdisciplinary or multidisciplinary team that includes a medical professional (Dziegielewski, 2006). Individuals who have training in the medical aspects of disease and illness can be valuable resources in understanding this mind-body connection. (See Quick Reference 3.26 for questions to help with an Axis III diagnosis and see Case Example 3.1.)

Before an Axis III diagnosis is recorded, there should always be some hard evidence to support its inclusion. The practitioner should query whether a recent history and physical has been conducted and, when one is available, review the written summary, which can be helpful in identifying medical conditions that may be related to the symptoms and behaviors a client is exhibiting. As stated earlier, if a physical exam has not been conducted prior to the assessment, it is always a good idea to either refer the client for a physical or suggest that the client see a physician for a routine examination. A review of the medical information available, such as lab reports and other findings, as well as consulting with a medical professional may also be helpful in identifying disorders that could complicate or prevent the client from achieving improved mental health. When utilizing this axis, mental health practitioners should be prepared to inquire into the signs and symptoms of these conditions and to assist in understanding the relationship of this medical condition to the diagnostic assessment and planning processes that evolve.

Special Considerations for Axis III

When completing the diagnostic assessment, there are two areas that are coded on Axis III which are often overlooked and neglected. Their importance is critical to a well-rounded comprehensive diagnostic assessment. The first falls under diseases of the eye and has to do with *visual loss* (coded 369.9) or *cataracts* (coded 366.9). Visual loss is related to a decrease in vision (sight) yet the apparent loss or visual acuity or visual field is not related directly to substantiating physical signs. This problem may be best addressed with client reassurance (WebMD, 2008). Cataracts relate to the loss of transparency in the lens of the eye. Both of these conditions result in vision impairment. Keep in mind that decreased or impaired vision may lead individuals to interpret daily events incorrectly. For example, have you ever sat near a window only to look up and be startled by your reflection? For a moment, you are shocked and frightened that someone is watching you. As you look closer, however, you realize that it is only your reflection. Now imagine that you are vision impaired and cannot see well. Or imagine that you are not wearing your glasses because you cannot remember where you put them. Or that you have developed a cataract that has grown so large your vision is obstructed, and what you can see is clouded or shadowed in appearance. Is it possible that no matter how hard you try, you are still unable to tell that reflection in the window is really you? Since you are unable to distinguish the shape in

---

QUICK REFERENCE 3.27

AXIS III: ASSESSING HEARING AND VISION PROBLEMS

In the diagnostic assessment process for hearing and vision, practitioners need to ask the client:

- Do you have any problems with your hearing or vision?
- How would you rate your current hearing and your vision?
- Can you give examples of specific problems you are having?
- When did you have your last vision or hearing checkup?

---

the window as your own, imagine how frightened you might become as you now convince yourself that a stranger is watching your every move? Would you not be suspicious of why you were being watched, and what this person or people might be after? Now imagine how someone who is vision impaired might feel if he or she is troubled by symptoms that cannot be easily explained. The frustration with the present situation can lead to symptoms being misperceived or misinterpreted. For mental health practitioners, the most salient issue to identify once the vision difficulty is recognized or corrected is whether the problem resolves itself. As part of the diagnostic assessment, special attention should always be given to screening for vision problems that may cause distress to the client in terms of individual and social functioning.

The second medical area that is often overlooked in the diagnostic assessment is related to hearing loss (Coded 389.9). A client with hearing impairment or hearing loss will experience a reduction in the ability to perceive sound that can range from slight impairment to complete deafness (WebMD, 2008). Many times a client who is having hearing difficulty may not want to admit it. Many individuals may rely on hearing enhancement devices such as hearing aids, which amplify sound more effectively into the ear. Such hearing aids may not be able to differentiate among selected pieces of information as well as the human ear. Furthermore, as a normal part of aging, high-frequency hearing loss can occur. Most noises in a person's environment, such as background noise, are low frequency. Therefore, an individual with high-frequency loss may not be able to tune out background noise, such as television sets or side conversations. He or she may get very angry over distractions that other people who do not have a similar hearing loss do not perceive. (See Quick Reference 3.27 to help with assessing for hearing and vision problems.)

CASE EXAMPLE 3.1- IMPORTANCE OF ASSESSING FOR MEDICAL FACTORS

In the multiaxial assessment, the importance of examining complicating or interacting medical conditions cannot be underestimated. Consider this example. Late one night a client who was extremely unkempt, delusional, and paranoid was brought to the emergency room. He reported bizarre delusions: Demons had invaded his teeth and were trying to capture his mind. The client had a past history of schizophrenia, paranoid type. This time, however, the delusions he was reporting were very extreme when compared with previous presentations. He was so convinced that demons were inside his teeth that he had started to tear at his gums with his fingers in an attempt to get at the demons inside. In his state of poor hygiene and malnourishment, it is not hard to see how he had managed to remove most of his teeth from his mouth, ripping them out with his fingers. Immediately on admission, a physical exam was ordered along with an X-ray of his teeth to see the extent of the damage he had created by ripping the teeth from his mouth. The X-ray revealed that the client had an extensive sinus infection. The X-ray report made it obvious how much pain was being caused by the untreated infection. The pressure the sinus discharge was placing on the roots of his teeth were causing him extensive pain and heightening the paranoid delusion of demons occupying his teeth. Once the sinus infection was treated, the severity of the paranoid delusions subsided.

As can be seen in this example, it is critical that medical issues, especially when clients present with extreme signs and symptoms, be clearly assessed and documented as part of the comprehensive diagnostic assessment process.

During the diagnostic assessment process, the practitioner should ask very specific questions about hearing and vision problems, as these medical problems can be misinterpreted as signs of a mental health problem.

AXIS IV: THE MULTIAXIAL ASSESSMENT SYSTEM

Axis IV is designed to address the severities of the psychosocial stressor(s) clients have experienced over the past year. Axis IV is particularly relevant when one considers the relationship between stresses in the environment and how these stresses can directly or indirectly influence mental health problems and symptoms. The use of this axis was strongly encouraged in *DSM-III* and later in *DSM-III-R*. In the *DSM-III*, the rating system was categorical (i.e., stressors were either listed as mild, moderate, severe, or catastrophic). This later changed to a numerical scale in *DSM-III-R*, in which the rating scale asked the practitioner to rate client problems on a scale from 1 (low) to 6 (high). In addition, a list of examples to help determine the proper number was given. A "0" was given if the information was unknown or repetitive. Generally, both the stressor and the severity were listed on this axis. In the formulation of *DSM-IV*, however, it was decided that a numeric scale allowed for too much ambiguousness in terms of coding and the rating scale was discontinued. In both the *DSM-IV* and the *DSM-IV-TR*, a list of stressors as factors contributing to life stress is included, and Axis IV was renamed *Psychosocial and Environmental Problems*. In addition, the stressors can be further clarified by listing the specific problem that results. It is important to discern how long the stressor(s) has been prevalent. An acute stressor has a better prognosis for recovery. For further clarification of the differences in Axis IV between *DSM-III-R* and *DSM-IV/DSM-IV-TR*, refer to Quick Reference 3.28.

QUICK REFERENCE 3.28
AXIS IV: CHANGES BETWEEN *DSM-III-R* AND *DSM-IV/DSM-IV-TR*

DSM-III-R	Severity of psychosocial stressors. (Scale rating I = low to 6 = high)
Changed to:	
	(continued)

QUICK REFERENCE 3.28 *(Continued)*	
DSM-IV-TR	Psychosocial and environmental problems.
Problems with primary support	
Problems related to social environment	
Educational problems	
Occupational problems	
Using problems	
Economic problems	
Problems with access to health care services	
Problems related to interaction with the legal system	
Other psychosocial problems	

AXIS V: THE MULTIAXIAL ASSESSMENT SYSTEM

Axis V is used to rate the client's psychosocial and occupational functioning for the past year. To complete this task, a scale known as the *Generalized Assessment of Functioning* (GAF) is used. Over the years, this measurement scale has gained in importance because it can be used to support measurement. Therefore, an increasing number of professionals are turning to the *DSM-IV-TR* and the GAF rating scores independent of the multiaxial diagnostic system as an aid for measuring and documenting client behaviors. Use of the GAF supports the current movement to enhance the diagnostic assessment by responding to the pressure to incorporate additional forms of measurement as part of the treatment plan (Dziegielewski, 2010). The pressure to achieve evidence-based practice has led to the incorporation of factors related to the individual, family, and social rankings to be included. These factors are now included in a reporting scale that provides a practitioner-driven measure capable of monitoring a client's functioning that can clearly be supported through direct client observation and recording.

Although the GAF was first described in the *DSM-III-R,* the range and the scaling descriptions were different. In the *DSM-III-R,* the scale ranged from 1 to 90 with the lowest scores representing poor functioning. The descriptions for each scale range were very limited. In *DSM-IV* and *DSM-IV-TR,* the scale of the GAF has been extended to 100 points; lower numbers continue to indicate lower functioning (e.g., 1 = minimal functioning, 100 = highest level of functioning). In addition, several other major changes have been made between the *DSM-IV* and the *DSM-IV-TR.* The modifications include: (1) changes related to the instructions for completing the scale; (2) minor changes and clarification in how to record the scores on the scale (i.e., past, current, at discharge); and (3) the addition of a function component reflective of the score range to the description section of the text.

When utilizing the GAF, the scale allows for assigning a number that represents a client's behaviors. The scale is designed to enable the practitioner to differentially rank identified behaviors from 1 to 100, with higher ratings indicating higher overall functioning and coping levels. By rating the highest level of functioning a client has attained over the past year and then comparing it to his or her current level of functioning, helpful comparisons can be made. For example, although the current level of functioning at time of assessment is expected, the practitioner can also gather information from the past year, upon admission or start of treatment (current level of functioning), and at discharge or termination. In this method, ratings of a client's functioning are assigned at the outset of therapy and again upon termination. It is particularly important to note, however, that in the *DSM-IV*, all assessments of functioning, current and past, were generally made recording the client's highest level of functioning observed. This differs from what is stated in the *DSM-IV-TR*, which encourages practitioners to note not only current level of functioning

but also the lowest level of functioning assessed during the weekly period prior to hospitalization or initiation of service. When other functioning times are assessed (over the past year, or on termination), the highest level of functioning is assessed.

The *DSM-IV-TR* also gives more detailed instructions on how to apply the GAF. According to the APA (2000), there are three steps to applying the GAF.

1. Always start at the top of the scale, and look at the numbers that denote the highest level of functioning possible. Now compare the behaviors that the client is exhibiting to the sample behaviors that appear in that category. (See Quick Reference 3.29 to become familiar with the categories of the GAF.)

2. Measure the individual's current level of functioning or severity of the behaviors. (When looking specifically at the behav-

---

QUICK REFERENCE 3.29

GLOBAL ASSESSMENT OF FUNCTIONING (GAF) SCALE

Consider psychological, social, and occupational functioning on a hypothetical continuum of mental health illness. Do not include impairment in functioning due to physical (or environmental) limitations.

Code   ***Note: Use intermediate codes when appropriate, e.g., 45, 68, 72***

Code	
100–91	Superior functioning in a wide range of activities, life's problems never seem to get out of hand, is sought out by others because of his or her many positive qualities. No symptoms.
90–81	Absent or minimal symptoms (e.g., mild anxiety before an exam).
80–71	If symptoms are present, they are transient and expectable reactions to psychosocial stressors (e.g., difficulty concentrating after family argument); no more than slight impairment in social, occupational, or school functioning (e.g., temporarily falling behind in schoolwork).
70–61	Some mild symptoms (e.g., depressed mood and mild insomnia) or some difficulty in social, occupational, or school functioning.
60–51	Moderate symptoms (e.g., flat affect and circumstantial speech, occasional panic attacks) or moderate difficulty in social, occupational, or school functioning (e.g., few friends, conflicts with peers or co-workers).

(continued)

QUICK REFERENCE 3.29 (*Continued*)

50–41	Serious symptoms (e.g., suicidal ideation, severe obsessional rituals, frequent shoplifting) or any serious impairment in social, occupational, or school functioning (e.g., no friends, unable to keep a job).
40–31	Some impairment in reality testing or communication (e.g., speech is at times illogical, obscure, or irrelevant) or major impairment in several areas, such as work or school, family relations, judgment, thinking, or mood (e.g., depressed man avoids friends, neglects family, and is unable to work; child frequently beats up younger children, is defiant at home, and is failing at school).
30–21	Behavior is considerably influenced by delusions or hallucinations or serious impairment in communication or judgment (e.g., stays in bed all day; no job, home, or friends).
20–11	Some danger of hurting self or others (e.g., suicide attempts without clear expectation of death, frequently violent, manic excitement) or occasionally fails to maintain minimal personal hygiene (e.g., smears feces) or gross impairment in communication (e.g., largely incoherent or mute).
10–1	Persistent danger of severely hurting self or others (e.g., recurrent violence) or persistent inability to maintain minimal personal hygiene or serious suicidal act with clear expectation of death.
0	Inadequate information.

Source: Reprinted with permission from the *Diagnostic and Statistical Manual of Mental Disorders, Fourth Edition, Text Revision.* Copyright 2000 by the American Psychiatric Association.

---

iors, if it appears more severe than outlined in that category, select a number from the next lower category.) Continue down the scale's score groupings until reaching the range that is most reflective of the client's behavior. If the severity of the symptoms and the level of functioning differ, the more dysfunctional aspect should be utilized to represent the number assigned.

3. To determine the appropriate number from the range, consider whether the individual's symptoms and level of functioning are at the higher or lower level of the range, and use that information in the selection of the number. For example, some professionals consider that a GAF score within the ranges of 30 to 40 or 41 to 50 is indicative of inpatient admission. According to the given criteria for these ranges, individuals with these scores are experiencing serious symptoms that disturb functioning. When a client has behaviors that fall into these ranges, the behaviors need to be clearly identified. Once this is accomplished, identify the exact number [e.g., GAF = 45 (current)] after assessing the symptoms and level of functioning. Next use this information to determine whether the client falls at the top, middle, or bottom of the range, and assign the number.

Utilization of the GAF can help practitioners both to quantify client problems and to document observable changes that may be attributable to the intervention efforts. Scales such as this allow practitioners to track performance variations across behaviors relative to client functioning.

QUICK REFERENCE 3.30

PRACTICE EXERCISE UTILIZING THE GAF, THE GLOBAL ASSESSMENT OF RELATIONAL FUNCTIONING (GARF), AND SOCIAL AND OCCUPATIONAL FUNCTIONING ASSESSMENT SCALE (SOFAS)

One of the hardest problems practitioners confront when utilizing therapist-driven scales, such as the GAF, GARF, and SOFAS, is ensuring that the documented behaviors are relevant to the clients who are being served. To facilitate documentation of client behaviors, try this exercise.

1. Ask to host an in-service training or to provide a segment of continuing education for your agency, inviting members of the interdisciplinary team. If you do not use a team approach, ask other colleagues and practitioners who work with the same population group as you. If you are working alone, try the same exercise by yourself.
2. Make a copy of the GAF, GARF, and SOFAS for each person who will be attending.
3. Lead the discussion and start with the GAF. For your population group, what behaviors do the majority of the clients served exhibit that represent the category discussed? What are the problem-solving skills an individual would have, what type of organizational skills would the individual have, and what type of emotional climate would be expected at that level?
   For example, take the GAF:
   > 100–91: Superior functioning in a wide range of activities, life's problems never seem to get out of hand, is sought out by others because of his or her many positive qualities. No symptoms.
   >
   > Review the criteria for this ranging, and write down the behaviors and indicators that would be typical of the client group being served that the individual might engage in. Starting at the top of the scale provides the perfect opportunity for participants to focus on strengths of the client and what they mean in terms of future progress and success.
4. Once done, write down the behaviors and skills that are agreed on for the group, and go to the next area. Once the GAF is done, do the same for the GARF and the SOFAS. Since coding on the GAF is considered mandatory, however, it is best to complete the GAF before trying the same activity for the other measures.

Professionals are not expected to memorize the GAF. The scale is clearly listed in the *DSM-IV-TR* and in this text as well. Practitioners may want to keep a copy of the GAF available so that it can be referred to as needed. Also, it is suggested strongly that when working as part of an interdisciplinary or a multidisciplinary team, all members sit down with a copy of the GAF and outline what behaviors, based on the specific population being served, would fall in the score range. All professionals would be looking at the same types of behaviors and could be aware of the relationship between the behavior and level of functioning specified for the particular population being served. Since the GAF

score may be used to justify the need for additional testing or assessment, careful documentation on this axis is critical to quality client care (Pollak et al., 1999). See Quick Reference 3.30 for an exercise that utilizes the GAF in the practice setting.

Supplements to AXIS V: GARF and SOFAS

In the *DSM-IV* "Criteria Sets and Axes Provided for Further Study," there are two scales that are not required for diagnosis yet can provide a format for ranking function that might be helpful to mental health professionals. The first of these optional scales is the relational functioning scale: Global

QUICK REFERENCE 3.31

GLOBAL ASSESSMENT OF RELATIONAL FUNCTIONING (GARF) SCALE

Instructions: The GARF Scale can be used to indicate an overall judgment of the functioning of a family or other ongoing relationship on a hypothetical continuum ranging from competent, optimal relational functioning to a disrupted, dysfunctional relationship. It is analogous to Axis V (Global Assessment of Functioning Scale) provided for individuals in *DSM-IV-TR* (p. 814). The GARF Scale permits the clinician to rate the degree to which a family or other ongoing relational unit meets the affective or instrumental needs of its members in these areas:

A.   Problem solving—skills in negotiating goals, rules, and routines; adaptability to stress; communication skills; ability to resolve conflict.
B.   Organization—maintenance of interpersonal roles and subsystem boundaries; hierarchical functioning; coalitions and distribution of power, control, and responsibility.
C.   Emotional climate—tone and range of feelings; quality of caring, empathy, involvement, and attachment/commitment; sharing of values; mutual affective responsiveness, respect, and regard; quality of sexual functioning.

In most instances, the GARF Scale should be used to rate functioning during the current period (i.e., the level of relational functioning at the time of the evaluation). In some settings, the GARF Scale may also be used to rate functioning for other time periods (i.e., the highest level of relational functioning for at least a few months during the past year).

Note: Use specific, intermediate codes when possible: for example, 45, 68, and 72. If detailed information is not adequate to make specific ratings, use midpoints of the five ranges, that is, 90, 70, 50, 30, or 10.

81–100 Overall: Relational unit is functioning satisfactorily from self-report of participants and from perspectives of observers.

Agreed-on patterns or routines exist that help meet the usual needs of each family/couple member; there is flexibility for change in response to unusual demands or events; and occasional conflicts and stressful transitions are resolved through problem-solving communication and negotiation.

There is a shared understanding and agreement about roles and appropriate tasks, decision making is established for each functional area, and there is recognition of the unique characteristics and merit of each subsystem (e.g., parents/spouses, siblings, and individuals).

There is a situational appropriate, optimistic atmosphere in the family; a wide range of feelings is freely expressed and managed within the family; and there is a general atmosphere of warmth, caring, and sharing of values among all family members. Sexual relations of adult members are satisfactory.

61–80 Overall: Functioning of relational unit is somewhat unsatisfactory. Over a period of time, many but not all difficulties are resolved without complaints.

Daily routines are present but there is some pain and difficulty in responding to the unusual. Some conflicts remain unresolved, but do not disrupt family functioning.

Decision making is unusually competent, but efforts at control of one another quite often are greater than necessary or are ineffective. Individuals and relationships are clearly demarcated but sometimes a specific subsystem is depreciated or scapegoated.

A range of feeling is expressed, but instances of emotional blocking or tension are evident. Warmth and caring are present but are marred by a family member's irritability and frustrations. Sexual activity of adult members may be reduced or problematic.

41–60 Overall: Relational unit has occasional times of satisfying and competent functioning together, but clearly dysfunctional, unsatisfying relationships tend to predominate.

Communication is frequently inhibited by unresolved conflicts that often interfere with daily routines; there is significant difficulty in adapting to family stress and transitional change.

Decision making is only intermittently competent and effective; either excessive rigidity or significant lack of structure is evident at these times. A partner or coalition quite often submerges individual needs.

Pain or ineffective anger or emotional deadness interferes with family enjoyment. Although there is some warmth and support for members, it is usually unequally distributed. Troublesome sexual difficulties between adults are often present.

21–40 Overall: Relational unit is obviously and seriously dysfunctional; forms and time periods of satisfactory relating are rare.

Family/couple routines do not meet the needs of members; they are grimly adhered to or blithely ignored. Life cycle changes, such as departures or entries into the relational unit, generate painful conflict and obviously frustrating failures of problem solving,

Decision making is tyrannical or quite ineffective. The unique characteristics of individuals are unappreciated or ignored by either rigid or confusingly fluid coalitions.

There are infrequent periods of enjoyment of life together; frequent distancing or open hostility reflects significant conflicts that remain unresolved and quite painful. Sexual dysfunction among adult members is commonplace.

1–20 Overall: Relational unit has become too dysfunctional to retain continuity of contact and attachment.

Family/couple routines are negligible (e.g., no mealtime, sleeping, or waking schedule); family members often do not know where others are or when they will be in or out; there is little effective communication among family members.

Family/couple members are not organized in such a way that personal or generational responsibilities are recognized. Boundaries of relational unit as a whole and subsystems cannot be identified or agreed on. Family members are physically endangered or injured or sexually attacked.

Despair and cynicism are pervasive; there is little attention to the emotional needs of others; there is almost no sense of attachment, commitment, or concern about one another's welfare.

0: Inadequate information.

Source: Reprinted with permission from the *Diagnostic and Statistical Manual of Mental Disorders, Fourth Edition, Text Revision.* Copyright 2000 by the American Psychiatric Association.

Assessment of Relational Functioning (GARF) (see Quick Reference 3.31). This index is used to address the status of family or other ongoing relationships on a hypothetical continuum from *competent* to *dysfunctional* (APA, 1994). The second index is the Social and Occupational Functioning Assessment Scale (SOFAS) (see Quick Reference 3.32). With this scale, an "individual's level of social and occupational functioning that is not directly influenced by overall severity of the individual's psychological symptoms" can be addressed (APA, 1994, p. 760). The complementary nature of these scales in identifying and assessing client

QUICK REFERENCE 3.32

SOCIAL AND OCCUPATIONAL FUNCTIONING ASSESSMENT SCALE (SOFAS)

Consider social and occupational functioning on a continuum from excellent functioning to grossly impaired functioning. Include impairments in functioning due to physical limitations, as well as those due to mental impairments. To be counted, impairment must be a direct consequence of mental and physical health problems; the effects of lack of opportunity and other environmental limitations are not to be considered.

Code   **Note: Use intermediate codes when appropriate, e.g., 45, 68, 72.**

Code	
100–91	Superior functioning in a wide range of activities.
90–81	Good functioning in all areas, occupationally and socially effective.
80–71	No more than a slight impairment in social, occupational, or school functioning (e.g., infrequent interpersonal conflict, temporarily falling behind in schoolwork).
70–61	Some difficulty in social, occupational, or school functioning, but generally functioning well, has some meaningful interpersonal relationships.
60–51	Moderate difficulty in social, occupational, or school functioning (e.g., few friends, conflicts with peers or coworkers).
50–41	Serious impairment in social, occupational, or school functioning (e.g., no friends, unable to keep a job).
40–31	Major impairment in several areas, such as work or school, family relations (e.g., depressed man avoids friends, neglects family, and is unable to work; child frequently beats up younger children, is defiant at home, and is failing at school).
30–21	Inability to function in almost all areas (e.g., stays in bed all day; no job, home, or friends).
20–11	Occasionally fails to maintain minimal personal hygiene; unable to function independently.
10–1	Persistent inability to maintain minimal personal hygiene. Unable to function without harming self or others or without considerable external supports (e.g., nursing care and supervision).
0	Inadequate information.

Source: Reprinted with permission from the *Diagnostic and Statistical Manual of Mental Disorders, Fourth Edition,* Text Revision. Copyright 2000 by the American Psychiatric Association.

problems is evident in the fact that all three scales—the GARF, GAF, and SOFAS—use the same rating system. The rankings for each scale range from 0 to 100, with lower numbers representing more severe problems. Collectively, these tools provide a viable framework within which mental health practitioners can apply concrete measures to a wide variety of practice situations. They also provide a multidimensional perspective that permits workers to document variations in levels of functioning across system sizes, including the individual (GAF), family (GARF), and social (SOFAS) perspectives. The same method of scoring as described for the GAF should be used with the GARF and SOFAS.

Standardized Measurements to Supplement the GAF, GARF, and SOFAS Since the GAF, GARF, and SOFAS are considered to be *therapist driven*, meaning that the practitioner uses clinical judgment to set the number and interpret all clinical information about symptom severity and level of functioning, it makes good practice sense to also consider the utilization of other standardized assessments to supplement the diagnostic assessment. Standardized measures can help to provide evidence for the development of operationally based terms. During the diagnostic assessment, symptom behaviors based on nebulous constructs such as stress, anxiety, and depression can be identified with subjective connotations. This semantic elusiveness when defining the symptom makes it very difficult to establish when change for the better has occurred. Success of the diagnostic assessment guiding intervention strategy relative to client progress can be determined only when problem behaviors are clearly and operationally defined. Standardized instruments can assist in this process when utilized as repeated measures to gather consistent data from baseline through termination and follow-up. Therefore, it is the responsibility of the practitioner to select, implement, and evaluate the appropriateness of the measurement instruments. Most professionals agree that standardized scales (i.e., those that have been assessed for reliability and validity) are generally preferred.

In recent years, mental health practitioners have begun to rely more heavily on standardized instruments in an effort to achieve greater accuracy and objectivity in their attempts to measure some of the more commonly encountered clinical problems. The most notable development in this regard has been the emergence of numerous brief pencil-and-paper assessment devices known as *rapid assessment instruments* (RAIs). As standardized measures, RAIs share a number of characteristics in common. They are brief; relatively easy to administer, score, and interpret; and they require very

little knowledge of testing procedures on the part of the clinician. For the most part, they are self-report measures that can be completed by the client, usually within 15 minutes. They are independent of any particular theoretical orientation and as such can be used with a variety of intervention methods. Since they provide a systematic overview of the client's problem, they often tend to stimulate discussion related to the information elicited by the instrument itself. The score that is generated provides an operational index of the frequency, duration, and intensity of the problem. Most RAIs can be used as repeated measures and thus are adaptable to the methodological requirements of both research design and goal assessment purposes. In addition to providing a standardized means by which change can be monitored over time with a single client, RAIs can also be used to make equivalent comparisons across clients experiencing a common problem (e.g., depression and marital conflict).

One of the major advantages of standardized RAIs is the availability of information concerning reliability and validity. *Reliability* refers to the stability of a measure. In other words, do the questions that comprise the instrument mean the same thing to the individual answering them at different times, and would different individuals interpret those same questions in a similar manner? Unless an instrument yields consistent data, it is impossible for it to be valid. But even highly reliable instruments are of little value unless their validity can also be demonstrated. *Validity* speaks to the general question of whether an instrument measures what it purports to measure.

There are several different approaches to establishing validity (Chen, 1997; Cone, 1998; Powers, Meenaghan, & Toomey, 1985; Schutte & Malouff, 1995), each of which is designed to provide information regarding how much confidence we can have in the instrument as an accurate indicator of the problem under consideration. While levels of reliability and validity vary greatly among available instruments, it is very helpful to know in advance the extent to which these issues have been addressed. Information concerning reliability and validity as well as other factors related to the standardization process (e.g., the procedures for administering, scoring, and interpreting the instrument) can help professionals make informed judgments concerning the appropriateness of any given instrument.

The key to selecting the best instrument to facilitate the diagnostic assessment is knowing where and how to access the relevant information concerning potentially useful measures. Fortunately, there are a number of excellent sources available to the clinician to help facilitate this process. One such compilation of standardized measures is *Measures for Clinical Practice* by Fischer and Corcoran (2007a, 2007b). These reference texts can serve as valuable resources for identifying useful rapid assessment instruments suited for the kinds of problems most commonly encountered in mental health practice.

Fischer and Corcoran have done an excellent job not only in identifying and evaluating a viable cross section of useful clinically grounded instruments but also in discussing a number of issues critical to their use. In addition, Schutte and Malouff (1995) provide a list of mental health–related measures for adults and guidelines for their use, with different types of practice-related problems. In addition to an introduction to the basic principles of measurement, these books discuss various types of measurement tools, including the advantages and disadvantages of RAIs. Fischer and Corcoran (2007a, 2007b) also provide some useful guidelines for locating, selecting, evaluating, and administering prospective measures. Furthermore, they divide the instruments into two volumes in relation to their appropriateness for use with certain target populations: couples, families, and children (Volume 1), and adults only (Volume 2). They are also

cross-indexed by problem area, which makes the selection process very easy.

To assist with identification of Axis III (general medical conditions) and Axis IV (psychosocial stressors) diagnoses, completing a neuropsychiatric history by utilizing screening instruments can be useful. These types of instruments can assist with family and health history as well as act as a checklist of neuropsychiatric complaints and symptoms. For example, health status instruments such as the short form SF-36 (Ware & Sherbourne, 1992) can be utilized to identify physical functioning and difficulties as well as psychiatric problems and social adaptation difficulties. The availability of these and numerous other references related to special interest areas greatly enhances the mental health professional's options with respect to monitoring and evaluation practice. Overall, the RAIs can serve as valuable adjuncts for evaluation efforts.

The helping relationship is a complex one that cannot be measured completely through the information gathered in the diagnostic assessment. This information is meant to serve as the basis for the development of intervention strategy. Gathering information through a diagnostic assessment needs to be intervention friendly, thereby outlining and providing the ingredients for the treatment planning and strategy to follow. The practitioner should always consider incorporating a number of evidence-based tools, such as direct behavioral observation techniques, self-anchored rating scales, client logs, projective tests, Q-sort techniques, unobtrusive measures, and personality tests as well as a variety of information that can be derived from mechanical devices for monitoring physiological functioning. Together these methods can provide a range of qualitative and quantitative measures for improving the overall diagnostic assessment process. Several are especially well suited for the assessment of practices based on the more phenomenological and existentially grounded theories. Space limitations do not permit a discussion of all of these methods in this chapter; however, a number of excellent sources discuss in detail the kinds of information needed in order to make informed decisions regarding selection and application (Bloom, Fischer, & Orme, 2009).

ETHICAL AND LEGAL CONSIDERATIONS

Professional efforts require that all activities performed and the judgments that are made be done within an ethical and legal framework. Practitioners must avoid any hint of malpractice. *Malpractice* is negligence in the exercise of one's profession. It is beyond the scope of this book to outline all the legal requirements and the problems that can occur. However, professionals should: (a) be aware of the rules and requirements that govern professional practice activity in their state, and (b) be well versed with the profession's code of ethics that represents the moral consensus of the profession (Reamer, 2001, 2009). It is not enough for helping professionals to assume that their ethical practice will be apparent on the basis of their adherence to their professional Code of Ethics.

> **Always Remember:** The client information you gather and document lives on and on and on.

Client information that is accurate and carefully documented and reflects the nature of the ethical client services provided can be the best way for mental health practitioners to protect against malpractice. Practitioner documents must ensure that client confidentiality and privacy are protected (Dziegielewski,

2004). One helpful rule is to remember that at any time, all records may be subpoenaed in a court of law where private client information may be divulged. Regardless of the employment setting, all helping professionals should consider maintaining personal malpractice insurance in addition to what may be provided through agency auspices. Even with the best of intentions, mental health practitioners may find themselves in legal proceedings defending the content of notes, subjective assessments, or terminology used in the diagnostic assessment. It is always best to record objective data and refrain from using terminology that may be subjective in nature (i.e., what you think is happening). When documenting, always use direct client statements; do not document hearsay or make interpretations based on subjective data (Dziegielewski, 2008). Practitioners need to be familiar with specific state statutes that do not allow professionals to elicit or document specific client information. For example, AIDS patients are protected by the prohibition against mental health professionals documenting their medical condition without client consent. In record keeping, the ultimate legal and ethical responsibility of all written diagnostic and assessment-based notes will always start and stop with the mental health practitioner.

PULLING IT ALL TOGETHER: USE OF THE MULTIAXIAL SYSTEM

To initiate utilization of the multiaxial system, it is assumed that the screening begins with the first client-mental health practitioner interaction. The information gathered by the mental health practitioner is assembled into a database that facilitates the diagnostic assessment and determines the requirements and direction of future treatment planning and intervention efforts. The diagnostic assessment assists in ordering information on the client's present situation and history in regard to how past behaviors can relate to present concerns. This assessment is multidimensional and includes creative clinically based judgments and interpretation of perspectives and alternatives for service delivery.

Generally, the client is the primary source of data, using either a verbal or written report. This information can be supplemented through direct observation of verbal or physical behaviors and through interaction patterns between other interdisciplinary team members, family, significant others, or friends. Viewing and recording these patterns of communication can be extremely helpful in later establishing and developing strength and resource considerations. In addition to verbal reports, written reports can also be utilized, such as background sheets, psychological tests, and tests to measure health status or level of daily functioning. Although the client is perceived as the first and primary source of data, the need to include information from other areas cannot be underestimated. This means talking with the family and significant others to estimate planning support and assistance. It is also important to gather information from other secondary sources, such as the client's medical record and other health care providers. To facilitate the diagnostic assessment, the practitioner must be able to understand the client's medical situation and the relationship that medical symptoms can have with mental health symptoms. Knowledge of what certain medical conditions are and when to refer to other health professionals for continued care is an essential part of the diagnostic assessment process.

In completing a multidimensional assessment, three primary steps can be adapted in the mental health setting:

1. Problem or behavior recognition. Here the practitioner must explore and be active in uncovering problems that affect daily living and will later be beneficial in engaging the client in self-help or skill-changing behaviors. It is important for the client to acknowledge that the problem exists. Once the problem is acknowledged, the boundaries related to the problem become clear (Hepworth, R. H. Rooney, G. Rooney, Gottfried, & Larsen, 2010).

2. Problem or behavior identification. In the diagnostic assessment, problems that affect daily functioning need to be identified. In addition, it is important to note what the client sees as the problem of concern, since this will assist later in helping the client to develop change behavior. In the mental health field, it is common to receive referrals that often provide the basis for reimbursement. Many times the referral source establishes how the problem is viewed and what should constitute the basis of intervention. Sound, efficient, cost-effective clinical practice needs to take referral information into account and can lead to better problem identification.

3. Treatment plan. Once the diagnostic assessment is complete, how will the information be related to the intervention plan and strategy to follow? According to Sheafor and coworkers (1997), the plan of action is the "bridge between the assessment and the intervention" (p. 135). Here the practitioner can help to clearly focus on the goals and objectives that will be followed in the intervention process. In the initial planning stage, emphasis on the outcome that is to be accomplished is essential.

The outcome of the diagnostic assessment process is the completion of a plan that will guide, enhance, and in many cases determine the course of intervention to be implemented. With the complexity of human beings and the problems that they encounter, a properly prepared multidimensional assessment is the essential first step for ensuring quality service delivery. Also, the diagnostic assessment should never be considered a static entity, or else it may become too narrow in focus, thereby decreasing its utility, relevance, and salience. Therefore, the process of diagnostic assessment must continually be examined and reexamined to ensure the quality of the practice provided. This process should not be rushed because when it is, superficial factors may be highlighted and significant ones deemphasized or overlooked. Mental health practitioners owe it to their clients to ensure that diagnostic efforts and the helping strategy that develops are quality driven, no matter what the administrative and economic pressures may be. To further support this, many mental health practitioners were active in supporting the creation of a commission to review changes in health care and make recommendations for consumer protection and health care quality (Steps Taken to Watchdog Managed Care, 1997). This support is just one of the ways practitioners are working not only to assist in developing a comprehensive strategy to help clients but also to ensure that quality service is made available and obtained.

SUMMARY

Mental health practitioners must be aware of how best to proceed with the diagnostic assessment that rests within the multiaxial assessment system. In mental health, all practitioners are expected to help their clients and other professionals in the area of diagnostic assessment and evaluation. For many professionals, the role of assessment leading to diagnosis in mental health counseling can be a complicated one; it can be particularly problematic for practitioners in solo practice who do not have either multidisciplinary or interdisciplinary team support to perform triage services or act as service brokers (Libassi & Parish, 1990). Regardless of the practice setting, all mental health practitioners are being called on to be more knowledgeable and interactive and to utilize evidence-based diagnostic tests to support practice strategy (Frances, Pincus, Davis, et al., 1991; Frances, Pincus, Widiger, et al., 1990; Siegelman, 1990). The role of the practitioner in linking the client to environmental considerations is an essential one. As well, all mental health practitioners need to be keenly aware and alert to updates in diagnostic criteria and act as advocates for the client throughout the diagnostic assessment and intervention process.

Equipped with a basic knowledge of the use and misuse of the *DSM-IV* as a tool in the creation of a diagnostic impression, the mental health practitioner can more constructively participate in the consultation process. Knowledge of diagnostic impressions and criteria can assist the practitioner in influencing and enhancing the client's overall functioning level. Since mental health practitioners often have regular and subsequent contacts with their clients, they can be essential in helping the interdisciplinary team to reexamine or reformulate previous diagnostic impressions and the relationship these original impressions can have on the client's future treatment potential. As a team member, the mental health practitioner is keenly aware of the environment and the importance of building and maintaining therapeutic rapport with the client. This makes the practitioner's input in understanding the mental disorder an essential contribution to intervention effectiveness. The mental health practitioner remains in a key position to allay the client's and his or her family's fears as well as elicit their help and support (Dziegielewski, 2004).

Moreover, with the increased emphasis on managed care and limiting time frames for treatment (Anderson, Berlant, Mauch, & Maloney, 1997; Dziegielewski, 2008), it is further postulated that increased emphasis on the conditions not attributable to a mental disorder, coded on Axis I, will also gain increased acceptance.

These are mental health conditions that are not attributable to a mental disorder yet remain the focus of clinical treatment. These mental health conditions are often referred to by clinicians in the field as the "V" codes and are coded on Axis I. Since these conditions historically have not been considered reimbursable, some practitioners have avoided their use. Nevertheless, the current practice emphasis based on brief time-limited treatment (Dziegielewski, 2008) makes awareness of these conditions essential.

Information gathered must always extend beyond the client. In doing so, special consideration should be given to the needs of family, significant others, and the client's identified support system. It is not uncommon for family members to have limited information in the area of mental health diagnosis and treatment. Family members may feel uncomfortable admitting to health care professionals that they believe another mode of treatment might be better (Wynne, 1987). The well-informed practitioner can correct distortions and foster cooperation in the treatment plan and among treatment team professionals (Dziegielewski, 2004). When practitioners are knowledgeable about the different mental health conditions, they can better serve their clients and make the most appropriate treatment decisions and system linkages. With an updated knowledge of mental health diagnosis and subsequent intervention, mental health practitioners can help prepare, as well as educate, clients and family members about the responsible use and expectations for psychiatric care. Professional schools that train mental health practitioners need to strongly encourage course work on use of the multiaxial assessment system. Since practitioners are held accountable for their own practice actions, they must strive to achieve the highest standards of their profession (Reamer, 2009).

QUESTIONS FOR FURTHER THOUGHT

1. Use of the nonformal multiaxial format can be helpful when identifying and addressing the mental health needs of a client. Give several examples of when, why, and where this nonformal system should be considered.

2. On Axis II, the defense mechanisms can be listed. When and why would it be advantageous to list these factors as part of the diagnostic assessment?

3. As a practitioner, what direct relationship exists between the diagnostic codes and the procedural codes? Apply a case example that highlights this relationship.

4. When utilizing the multiaxial system in the diagnostic assessment, all five axes are utilized. Why is it important to note Axis III, which involves the general medical conditions? Why are Axes IV and V important? What client information could be added to the documentation that supports the information provided on these axes?

CHAPTER

4 Applications: Beyond the Diagnostic Assessment

SOPHIA F. DZIEGIELEWSKI AND RUTHANNE VAN LOON

When utilizing the *DSM-IV-TR* in the diagnostic assessment, emphasis is placed on starting the diagnostic process by completing the initial assessment. Therefore, completing the initial diagnostic assessment is paramount, as it provides the foundation for the treatment planning and practice strategy that will follow. Accurate and successful documentation is critical to show what progress is being made in therapy and also to provide the groundwork for establishing efficiency and effectiveness of treatment. Many professionals falsely assume that the *DSM-IV-TR* suggests treatment strategy. This is not a correct assumption. Neither the *DSM-IV-TR* nor any of the previous versions of the *DSM* suggests treatment strategy or courses of action that can further highlight the intervention or treatment phases of the helping process. Since the mental health practitioner will be expected to assist in treatment planning as well as in the selection of the intervention and practice strategy, some background knowledge in this area is essential.

This chapter provides an overview of the importance of efficient and effective documentation in terms of treatment planning and practice strategy. In Section II of the volume, direct application is made to many of the specific diagnostic conditions that integrate many of the principles and practice techniques described in this chapter. Once the mental health practitioner has completed the diagnostic assessment,

this information must be recorded and applied accordingly.

DOCUMENTATION, TREATMENT PLANNING, AND PRACTICE STRATEGY

Throughout the history of mental health practice, practitioners have relied on some form of record keeping to clearly document information on client situations and problems (Dziegielewski, 2008). Although the formats used by professionals have changed, the value of documentation in maintaining case continuity has remained a professional priority (Dziegielewski, 2010). In its most basic form, case recording provides the helping professional with a map that indicates where the client and practitioner have traveled in their treatment journey (Dziegielewski & Leon, 2001b). Because experience is dynamic and words are static, the intervention process goes beyond what written words can describe (Lauver & Harvey, 1997). Understanding and recording the client's problems, the counseling interventions used, and the client's progress enables the practitioner to assess the interventions and to make necessary changes in counseling strategies. It is also crucial in terms of client safety. This is especially important when clients are depressed and might attempt to hurt themselves or someone else. As part of the assessment process, a culture of safety needs to be created (Yeager, Roberts, & Saveanu, 2009), taking into account the acute needs of the client being served (R. S. Sommers-Flanagan & J. Sommers-Flanagan, 2009).

In addition, especially when used in the courts, the medical record may be central to portraying and defending what was done or not done with a client in the treatment setting. The old saying "If you did not document it, it did not happen" remains an important reminder of the power of the written word. Therefore, the exact words used must be chosen carefully, making the primary goal of case documentation an evolving process. Reamer (2005) suggested thinking about the various audiences for the case record and then striking a balance between too little information, which might compromise the work of a team member or other professional who reviews the record, and too much information, which might prove detrimental to a client if the record is used for other purposes, such as a custody hearing.

Wiger (2005) outlined four functions of case documentation: (1) to monitor treatment, (2) to assist in determining treatment outcomes, (3) to aid in communicating with other professionals, and (4) to help with regulatory compliance. Additionally, case records serve as the basis for determining eligibility for services by managed care companies and provide evidence of the practitioner's accountability (Dziegielewski, 2008). Sheafor and Horejsi (2008) stated that good record keeping must provide an accurate and standardized account of the information gathered and support this information with introspective and retrospective data collection.

In the diagnostic assessment as well as throughout the intervention, practitioners must be aware that without accurate case documentation, most third-party payers will not reimburse for the start or continuation of services. Therefore, it is critical that all documentation within the diagnostic assessment and subsequent practice strategy clearly identify specific information related to problem severity that will lead and guide continued intervention efforts. This emphasis on accountability and reimbursement is mandated by managed care organizations and other external reviewing bodies that monitor client services (Dziegielewski & Holliman, 2001; J. Sommers-Flanagan & R. Sommers-Flanagan, 2009). All mental health practitioners are expected to justify and document client eligibility for service including diagnosis, symptoms, and functional impairment; appropriateness for specific services and their continuation based on client progress; the intensity of services including length of treatment and level of care; interventions provided; and the use of specific, objective, behavioral outcome criteria that serve as goals for discharge (Wiger, 2005).

Increasingly, managed care organizations expect mental health providers to justify treatment decisions in terms of medical or therapeutic necessity, which means that services are needed because of the severity of impairment or dysfunction rather than simply the diagnosis (Chambliss, 2000; Wiger, 2005). The case record is critical in demonstrating therapeutic necessity. Records that specifically document impairment and symptoms, and their persistence over time, can demonstrate the need for continuation of services. If a record lacks this level of specificity, a reviewer may conclude that the impairment no longer exists, and payment for services may be denied or discontinued (Wiger, 2005).

Utilizing a holistic framework that stresses the client's behavioral and biopsychosocial factors allows mental health practitioners to play an important role in the efficient delivery of interdisciplinary psychological and social services. Mental health practitioners can also assist other team members to document effectively while collaborating with them on client progress and problems (Dziegielewski, 2004). The importance of providing accurate, up-to-date, and informative records is vital to the coordinated planning efforts of the entire team. Comprehensive care that incorporates measurement instruments and other types of outcome verification has transformed mental health care and the services provided (Davidson, Tondora, Lawless, O'Connell, & Rowe, 2009).

With the advent of behavior-based systems of managed care, however, high caseloads and shorter lengths of stay have caused mental health practitioners to adopt a style of documentation that is brief yet informative (Dziegielewski, 2004; Dziegielewski & Holliman, 2001). The challenge is to summarize important client information in meaningful yet concise notes and treatment plans. Given the litigious nature of our society, informative records that demonstrate treatment interventions and reflect legal and ethical values and concerns become important documents in legal proceedings that can be recalled long after the therapeutic intervention has ended (Bernstein & Hartsell, 2004). The pressure for accurate documentation rests in the growing emphasis and pressure to utilize evidence-based professional practice and justification for the course of intervention that will follow. When utilizing evidence-based practice, clear documentation as reflected in the case record can be used for numerous purposes. Regardless of the helping discipline or practice setting, five generic rules for efficient and effective documentation must always be employed (Dziegielewski, 2008).

1. Clear and concise record keeping is essential to clearly document problem behaviors and coping styles.
2. The behavioral symptoms and impairments in functioning identified within

the diagnostic assessment will set the tone and provide concrete justification for the goals and objectives that will be highlighted within the treatment plan. Recording supporting information in the case file is essential for supplementation of the treatment plan. The relationship between case notes and the treatment plan is critical to the justification for service delivery.

3. The treatment plan will clearly reflect progress indicators and time frames, which once again must be supported in the written case record. In this section, the review of current goals and objectives as well as whether the therapeutic tasks assigned can be completed is discussed.
4. The case notes and the treatment plan must clearly document and show response to interventions and whether changes are needed to continue to help the client to progress.
5. Case notes are used to assess goal accomplishment and to evaluate the efficiency, treatment, and cost effectiveness of the service delivered (Chambliss, 2000).

See Quick Reference 4.1 for an overview of guiding principles for efficient documentation.

Problem-Oriented Recording

Among the various types of record-keeping formats, many mental health facilities commonly use problem-oriented recording (POR) (Dziegielewski, 2004, 2008, 2010). Developed first in health care or medical settings, this type of recording was used to encourage multidisciplinary and interdisciplinary collaboration and to train medical professionals. As members of either multidisciplinary or interdisciplinary teams, helping professionals find that problem-oriented case documentation enables them to maintain

---

QUICK REFERENCE 4.1

Overview of Guiding Principles for Efficient Documentation

- Use the information gathered in the diagnostic assessment as the foundation for treatment planning and practice strategy. Be sure to use concrete behaviors and impact on functioning as indicators of client progress when designing treatment or intervention plans.
- Complete periodic updates, and report and change those interventions and treatment strategies that do not appear to be working for the client.
- Be sure that the goals the client is to accomplish are stated in concrete, measurable terms and that the client can complete the therapeutic tasks assigned.
- Monitor problem behaviors and behavior changes to continually review and update the intervention process.
- Be sure to always assess goal accomplishment and evaluate the efficiency, treatment, and cost effectiveness of the service delivered.

---

documentation uniformity while remaining active within a team approach to care. Problem-oriented documentation also satisfies managed care organizations' demands for accountability (Kane, Houston-Vega, & Nuehring, 2002).

POR emphasizes practitioner accountability through brief and concise documentation of client problems, services, or interventions as well as client responses. Although there are numerous formats for POR, always keep comments brief, concrete, measurable, and concise. Many professionals feel strongly that POR is compatible with the increase in client caseloads, rapid assessments, and time-limited treatment. By maintaining brief but informative notes, practitioners are able to provide significant summaries of intervention progress. The mental health practitioner does not select the type of POR that will be utilized. The choice of a specific problem-oriented format for case recording is based on agency, clinic, or practice's function, need, and accountability. In today's practice environment, clear and concise documentation reflects the pressure indicative of evidence-based practice. This makes it critical that mental health practitioners be familiar with the basic types of POR and how to utilize this format within the case record.

One thing that all POR formats share in common is that they all start with a problem list that is clearly linked to the behavioral-based biopsychosocial intervention (Chambliss, 2000; Frager, 2000). This problem-oriented documentation helps the practitioner to focus directly on the presenting problems and coping styles that the client is exhibiting, thereby helping to limit abstractions and vague clinical judgments. (See Quick Reference 4.2 for information to be included in the POR.) This type of documentation should include an inventory reflective of current active problems that are periodically updated. While many client problems overlap and are interrelated, listing each problem separately allows for more focused treatment planning and intervention (Sheafor & Horejsi, 2008). When a problem is resolved, it is crossed off the list with the date of resolution clearly designated. Noting the active problems a client is experiencing and maintaining self-contained files are considered the basic building blocks for case recording within the problem-oriented record.

Although numerous formats for the actual progress note documentation can be selected, the subjective, objective assessment plan (SOAP) is the most commonly used. (See Quick

---

QUICK REFERENCE 4.2

INFORMATION TO BE INCLUDED IN THE POR

In a complete problem-oriented medical record, regardless of the recording format used, the following should always be included:

- Client identifying information.
- A complete behavioral-based biopsychosocial diagnostic assessment.
- A psychosocial history recording important past and present information.
- A list of client problems with suggestions for problem resolution.
- Progress notes that encapsulate intervention strategy and progress.
- A termination summary.
- Copies of supporting data and information (e.g., consent forms, releases, summaries of recent medical or physical exams, and laboratory results).
- Supervision and consultation reports (if applicable).

Reference 4.3 for a sample listing of the most common problem-oriented formats used today.)

The SOAP first became popular in the 1970s. In this format, the practitioner utilizes the S (subjective) to record the data relevant to the client's request for service and the things the client says and feels about the problem. The mental health professional can use his or her clinical judgment in terms of what appears to be happening with the client. Some professionals prefer to document this information in terms of major themes or general topics addressed rather than making specific statements about what they think is happening. Generally, intimate personal content or details of fantasies and process interactions should not be included here. When charting in this section of the SOAP, mental health practitioners should always ask

---

QUICK REFERENCE 4.3

SOAP, SOAPIE, AND SOAPIER RECORDING FORMATS

Subjective, Objective, Assessment, Plan (SOAP) or Subjective, Objective, Assessment, Plan, Implementation, Evaluation (SOAPIE) or Subjective, Objective, Assessment, Plan, Implementation, Evaluation, Review (SOAPIER)

S = Subjective data relevant to the client's request for service; client and practitioner impressions of the problem.

O = Objective data such as observable and measurable criteria related to the problem. If client statements are used, put the statement in quotes.

A = Assessment information of the underlying problems; diagnostic impression.

P = Plan outlines current intervention strategy and specific referrals for other needed services.

I = Implementation considerations of the service to be provided.

E = Evaluation of service provision.

R = Client's response to the diagnostic process, treatment planning, and intervention efforts.

themselves, "Could this statement that I record be open to misinterpretation?" If it is vulnerable to misinterpretation or it resembles a personal rather than professional reaction to what is said, it should not be included.

The O (objective) includes observable and measurable criteria related to the problem. These are symptoms, behaviors, and client-focused problems observed directly by the practitioner during the assessment and intervention process. In addition, some agencies, clinics, and practices have started to include client statements in this section as well. If a client statement is to be utilized as objective data, however, exact quotes must be used. For example, if in the session the client states that he will not harm himself, the practitioner must document exactly what the client has said. What is said must be placed within quotation marks. Under the objective section of the summary note, it is also possible to include the results from standardized assessment instruments designed to measure psychological or social functioning. These instruments can be helpful in supporting the process of gathering objective data.

The A (assessment) includes the therapist's assessment of the underlying problems, which often involves the development of a *DSM-IV-TR* diagnostic impression. As described in Chapter 3, when utilizing the multiaxial system, all five axes are utilized.

In P (plan), the practitioner records how treatment objectives will be carried out, areas for future interventions, and specific referrals to other services needed by the client. Time frames or deadlines for interventions are often included (Shaefor & Horejsi, 2006).

With today's increased emphasis on time-limited intervention efforts and accountability, two new areas have been added to the original SOAP format (Dziegielewski, 2004; Dziegielewski & Leon, 2001b). This extension, referred to as SOAPIE, identifies the first additional term

as I (implementation considerations of the service to be provided). Here the mental health practitioner explains exactly how, when, and who will implement the service. In the last section, an E is designated to represent service provision evaluation (Dziegielewski, 1998). It is here that all health care professionals are expected to identify specific actions related to direct evaluation of progress achieved after any interventions are provided. When treatment is considered successful, specific outcomes-based objectives established early in the treatment process are documented as progressing or checked off as attained. In some agencies, a modified version of the SOAPIE has been introduced and referred to as SOAPIER. In this version, the R outlines the client's response to the intervention provided.

A second popular problem-oriented recording format used in some health care facilities today is the data, assessment, and plan (DAP) format. The DAP encourages the mental health practitioner to identify only the most salient elements of a practitioner's client contact. Using the D (data), the practitioner is expected to record objective client data and statements related to the presenting problem and the focus of the therapeutic contact. The A (assessment) is used to record the diagnostic assessment intervention from the multiaxial format, the client's reactions to the service and intervention, and the practitioner's assessment of the client's overall progress toward the treatment goals and objectives. Specific information on all tasks, actions, or plans related to the presenting problem and to be carried out by either the client or the helping professional is recorded under P (plan). Also recorded under P is information on future issues related to the presenting problem to be explored at the next session and the specific date and time of the next appointment (Dziegielewski, 1998). Similar to the SOAP, the DAP format has undergone some changes. For example, some

---

QUICK REFERENCE 4.4

DAPE RECORDING FORMAT

Data, Assessment, and Plan (DAP) or Data, Assessment, Plan, and Education (DAPE)

D = Data that are gathered to provide information about the identified problem.

A = Assessment of the client in regard to his or her current problem or situation.

P = Plan for intervention and what will be completed to assist the client to achieve increased health status or functioning.

E = Professional education that is provided by the mental health practitioner to ensure that problem mediation has taken place or evaluation information to ensure practice accountability.

---

counseling professionals who generally apply the DAP are now being asked to add an additional section. This changes the DAP into the DAPE, where E reflects what type of educational and evaluative services have been conducted. (See Quick Reference 4.4 for this format.)

Two other forms of problem-based case recording formats are the problem, intervention, response, and plan (PIRP) and the assessed information, problems addressed, interventions provided, and evaluation (APIE). Both of these formats (see Quick Reference 4.5) can also be utilized for standardizing case notes. A structure similar to the SOAP and the DAP is employed. All four of these popular formats of problem-oriented case recording support increased problem identification, standardizing what and how client behaviors and coping styles are reported. Thus they provide a greater understanding of mental health problems and the various methods of managing them. This type of problem-oriented record brings the focus of clinical

---

QUICK REFERENCE 4.5

PIRP AND APIE RECORDING FORMAT

Problem, Intervention, Response, and Plan (PIRP)

P = Presenting problem(s) or the problem(s) to be addressed.

I = Intervention to be conducted by the mental health practitioner.

R = Response to the intervention by the client.

P = Plan to address the problems experienced by the client.

Assessed Information, Problems Addressed, Interventions Provided, and Evaluation (APIE)

A = Documentation of assessed information in regard to the client problem.

P = Explanation of the problem that is being addressed.

I = Intervention description and plan.

E = Evaluation of the problem once the intervention is completed.

attention to an often-neglected aspect of recording, which allows all helping professionals to familiarize themselves with a client's situation quickly (Dziegielewski, 2008).

For mental health practitioners, utilizing a problem-focused perspective must go beyond merely recording information that is limited to the client's problems. When the focus is limited to gathering only this information, important strengths and resources that clients bring to the therapeutic interview may not be validated (Dziegielewski, 1998). Furthermore, looking at a situation and not taking into account the situation that surrounds the problem, sometimes referred to as partialization of the problem, presents the potential risk that other significant aspects of a client's functioning will be overlooked in treatment planning and subsequent practice strategy. In an effort to understand the entire client situation and presenting problem, as mentioned in Chapter 3, all practitioners need to take into account a client's personal beliefs about the etiology and prognosis of symptoms (Chang-Muy & Congress, 2009). Therefore, problem-oriented forms of case recording need to extend beyond the immediate problem regardless of whether agencies require it (Dziegielewski, 2008; Rudolph, 2000).

In recent years, a number of sourcebooks for documentation of mental health services have been published (see, e.g., Jongsma, Peterson, & Bruce, 2006; Wiger, 2005). These sourcebooks provide templates for treatment plans and progress notes and can assist in meeting the requirements of third-party payers and regulatory agencies (Berghuis & Jongsma, 2008a, 2008b). In general, the templates provided fit within a problem-oriented recording framework.

Maintaining Clinical Records

Since records can be maintained in more than one medium, such as written case files, audio-

or videotaped material, and computer-generated notes, special attention needs to be given to ensuring confidentiality and the maintaining of ethical release of client information. Probably the greatest protection a mental health practitioner has in terms of risk management for all types of records is maintaining accurate, clear, and concise clinical records. This means that an unbroken chain of custody between the practitioner and the file must always be maintained. Since the mental health practitioner will ultimately be held responsible for producing a clinical record in case of litigation, this policy cannot be overemphasized.

Furthermore, documentation in the record should always be clearly sequenced and easy to follow. If a mistake occurs, never change a case note or treatment plan without acknowledging it. When changes need to be made to the diagnostic assessment, the treatment plan, or any other types of written case recording, clearly indicate that a change is being made by drawing a thin line through the mistake and dating and initialing it. When correcting computer-generated records, do not delete the mistake; instead, insert the correct information and include the date and your initials in parentheses (Bernstein & Hartsell, 2004). Records that are legible and cogent limit open interpretation of the services provided. (See Quick Reference 4.6 for some helpful hints on documentation.) In addition, the mental health practitioner is always required to keep clinical case records (including written records and computerized backup files) safeguarded in locked and fireproof cabinets. It can also benefit the mental health practitioner to consider using archiving types of storage systems, such as microfiche or microfilm, to preserve records and maximize space. States have varying legal requirements regarding the length of time records must be maintained. Many authorities, however, suggest that records be maintained indefinitely

---

QUICK REFERENCE 4.6

HELPFUL HINTS: DOCUMENTATION

Since accurate and ethical documentation ensures continuity of care and ethical and legal aspects of practice, and provides direction for the focus of intervention, some pointers on how to best write the information to be recorded in the client's file include:

- Date and time of entry.
- Interview notes that clearly describe the client's problems.
- A complete diagnostic assessment that is evidence based.
- A treatment plan with clearly established overall goals, objectives, and intervention tasks.
- Print and sign your name, title, and credentials with each entry that is made.
- Document all information in the case record as if you might someday have to defend it in a court of law.

Making Changes or Corrections in a Record:

- Always use ink that does not run (ballpoint pens are best).
- Never erase or use white-out to cover up mistakes.
- Draw a line through an error, mark it "error," and initial.

---

as a protection in the event of a lawsuit (Bernstein & Hartsell, 2004).

Computer-Generated Notes   As the use of computer-generated notes becomes more common, varying forms of problem-oriented case recording will be linked directly into computerized databases (Gingerich, 2002). In terms of convenience, this can mean easy and immediate access to the client's medical/treatment record as well as fiscal and billing information. When working with computerized records, Hartsell and Berstein (2008) suggest six pointers:

1. When recording client information on a hard drive or disk, be sure to store it in a safe and secure place.
2. Be sure to secure any passwords from detection.
3. If you are treating a celebrity or a famous individual, use a fictitious name and be sure to keep the "key" to the actual name in a protected place.
4. Always maintain a backup system and keep it secure.

5. Be sure that everyone who will have access to the client's case file reads and signs an established protocol concerning sanctity, privacy, and confidentiality of the records.
6. Take the potential of computer theft or crash seriously, and establish a policy that will safeguard the information being stored and what will need to happen if a breach of confidentiality should occur.

The convenience of electronic records produces another major concern. Since clinical case records are so easy to access and are portable, unauthorized access to recorded information presents a genuine problem. Every precaution should be taken to safeguard any information that is shared and stored electronically. In terms of convenience, this can mean immediate access to fiscal and billing information as well as client intervention strategy, documentation, and treatment planning. Caution, however, should always be used and although there is such easy access, one simple rule should always be applied: Never access anything unless there is a clearly identified clinical need to know that is related directly to patient care.

Protected Health Information

This easy accessibility, however, has fueled concerns about confidentiality and privacy. To address these concerns, Congress enacted the Health Insurance Portability and Accountability Act (HIPAA) in 1996, which established new rules for the privacy and security of electronic medical records. Under HIPPA, the Privacy Rule requires mental health practitioners to develop procedures for controlling the disclosure and use of client information, while the Security Rule requires the implementation of administrative, technical, and physical safeguards to protect client information (Bernstein & Hartsell, 2004). The term *protected health information* (PHI) is related to how private individual health information is recorded and processed.

The Privacy Rule requires practitioners and agencies to provide clients with a written notice of the providers' privacy policy about the disclosure of private health information. In general, providers can disclose this information without obtaining a specific consent for the purposes of treatment, payment, and health care operations, such as quality review. However, psychotherapy notes require a specific written authorization for disclosure or use (Bernstein & Hartsell, 2004; Yang & Kombarakaran, 2006). As medical records are kept for the benefit of the client, access to the record by the client is generally allowed without consent under HIPAA (Wiger, 2005). Some authorities, however, suggest that obtaining written consent from clients before allowing access to their records is always the best prudent policy. Practitioners should be familiar with HIPAA and state regulations that allow for withholding of information to clients when deemed harmful (Bernstein & Hartsell, 2004).

TREATMENT AND INTERVENTION PLANNING

Once the diagnostic assessment information has been gathered, this information will be utilized to start a treatment or intervention plan. When working with the client, it is important that each treatment plan be individualized. The plan also must reflect the general as well as the unique symptoms and needs the client is experiencing. The importance of a formal treatment plan cannot be overestimated as it will help to determine the structure and provide focus for any type of mental health intervention. Furthermore, a clearly established treatment plan can deter any litigation by either the client or a concerned family member (Bernstein & Hartsell, 2004; Reamer, 2005). When the treatment plan clearly delineates the intervention plan, family and friends of the client may feel more at ease and may agree to participate and assist in any behavioral interventions that will be applied.

Experts urge practitioners to adopt a risk-management approach to documentation (Reamer, 2005). Of particular importance is developing skills to assess and document threats of suicide or homicide. Any statements indicating a client's threat of violence to self or others should be documented in the case record without delay and preferably in the client's own words. Additionally, the record should reflect the practitioner's inquiry into the statement, such as asking the client about specific plans to act on the threat (Moline, Williams, & Austin, 1998). The practitioner's plan of action should also be documented. This may include consultation with supervisors or others, compliance with agency protocols for these situations, referrals for further evaluation, and compliance with state statutes regarding duty to warn potential victims and to notify police or other authorities (Bernstein & Hartsell, 2004). The client's reaction to these interventions should also be noted (Moline et al., 1998). Despite a practitioner's best efforts, a client may act violently. Documentation that reflects compliance with current standards of care and legal obligations can minimize the practitioner's risk.

Assessing for Suicide and Creating a Safety Plan

Regardless of the reason why the diagnostic assessment is being completed, the importance of assessing for the possibility of danger to self or others is essential. When danger to self is suspected, the first step is to screen for suicidal thoughts or plans. If the individual makes reference to suicide, appears seriously depressed, reports starting to feel better after experiencing a more pronounced depression with a return of energy, or has a history of suicide attempts, the practitioner needs to be sure to assess for the possibility of danger to self or others. For the most part, regardless of whether it is a child, adolescent, or adult, assessment for suicidal thoughts requires asking direct questions.

When asking direct questions, what is most important to clients in this situation is not just that they are listened to but that they are heard (Papadatou, 2009). Speaking clearly, slowly, and paraphrasing what is said in response will help the client to connect with the practitioner (Dziegielewski, 2010).

Critical questions to ask are:

- Have you considered harming yourself or someone else?
- If so, what would you do?
- How would you do it?
- Have you ever tried to do this before? What did you do that time?
- What would stop you from harming yourself?
- Have you ever considered harming anyone else? If so, what would you do, and why? (It is important to determine if clients have access to the means for action or self-harm and whether a concrete plan exists.)

If the potential for suicide is suspected, regardless of whether the client has a formal plan, a no-harm, no-risk agreement is recommended, whether in the form of a separate agreement or used as part of the record, all documentation needs to involve the development and implementation of acknowledgement of the symptoms and a clear safety plan. (See Quick Reference 4.7 for a sample of a No-Harm No-Risk agreement.)

QUICK REFERENCE 4.7

NO-HARM, NO-RISK AGREEMENT: SAMPLE SCRIPT

At present, I do not feel as though I could harm myself or someone else. As part of a safety plan, I have discussed with my counselor what to do if this changes. If I feel that I could be a danger to myself or someone else, I am aware of what the signs and symptoms are that could trigger a dangerous reaction in me and I agree to follow this safety plan. I [client's name] will not harm myself or someone else.

If I feel as though I could harm myself or someone else, I have been advised and I agree to call the police immediately and seek immediate mental health treatment from [list name, phone number and address for 24-hour facility that handles indigent clients if needed].

Client signature or documented agreement.
Family Member Acknowledgment*

---

*With client permission, family member to sign acknowledging awareness of the safety plan.

The effectiveness of a no-harm, no-risk agreement is only as strong as the safety plan that is attached (Dziegielewski, 2010). If this type of formalized agreement helps to clearly outline the safety plan, then use it. Be sure, however, that you also use referrals as needed and seek inpatient treatment when there is a clear plan. In order to have a comprehensive safety plan be sure that all questions related to safety have been asked, the responses addressed, and all information obtained is documented.

Always make sure family and others in the support system are aware of the safety concerns and the efforts in place to address them. Generally, the practitioner will need to get client permission to notify the family, but this is an important step to ensure that the support system is available to the client. On the surface the client may not show visible depressive symptoms; this may give family members a false sense of security that the family member is okay and any difficulties can be addressed. When family and other members of the support system are not aware of the difficulties the client is having, they may expect him or her to resume normal family and occupational activities, resulting in emotional overload for the client. Many times clients do not respond as actively to these expectations as they did in the past, which may result in frustration for the client and other members of the environmental support system (Dziegielewski, 2010).

Furthermore, there are inherent risks that once symptoms of depression lift, clients may want to discontinue their medication. While all clients have the right to self-determination in medication and other aspects of their treatment, practitioners can help to educate them about the triggers and risk of relapse (Dziegielewski, 2010). Grief and the interpretation of life circumstances can change across the life span. For more in-depth reading in this area, see the work of Walter and McCoyd (2009).

Honoring Self-Determination and Confidentiality: Danger to Self and Others

Many social workers struggle with what can be revealed and what should not be revealed when working with a suicidal client. Whether to involve family members and other members of the client's support system is always a difficult call to make, especially when the client does not want them notified. Questions in regard to what to reveal and what not to reveal can be difficult to determine. In terms of confidentiality, although statutory laws can differ across the states, Gamino and Ritter (2009) describe eight exceptions that allow the release of confidential information. They are:

1. Client authorized release of information
2. Danger to self
3. Danger to others
4. Neglect or abuse of children and vulnerable adults
5. Complaints or litigation against the counselor
6. Litigation concerning emotional pain and suffering
7. Court-ordered or statutory requirements to disclose
8. Requirements of third-party payers

For a complete discussion of these instances, the reader is referred to the work of these authors.

When releasing confidential information, always try to get a client-authorized release of information. For any safety plan, it is important to get client permission to contact the family and make sure they are aware of the situation, any intervention efforts, and the safety plan itself. In addition, when establishing a safety plan assessing for danger to self or others, it is crucial to make sure that not only does the assessment involve information about what a client might do to him- or herself but also whether others are at risk.

Many times social workers struggle with vague threats and whether the person would actually act on what he or she says would happen. Gamino and Ritter (2009) identify several factors that are particularly relevant to the seriousness of the threat. A combination of factors may complicate or worsen the potential for problems. For example, is the client male, recently divorced or separated, single, or widowed, over the age of 60, and lacking social support (especially no young children in the home)? Does the individual or other family members have a history of attempted suicide, unemployment, and financial difficulties? Is there a history of depression, a recent admission and discharge from a hospital, and/or alcohol use and abuse? Are firearms present?

When dealing with danger to self and others, issues surrounding the *Tarasoff v. the Regents of the University of California* (1976) is often stated. In this landmark case, an individual and the family were not warned by a therapist of a potential threat that was made by a client against another individual that resulted in death. To avoid the potential for harm, gathering a comprehensive summary of the situation while getting up-to-date information is essential. Since protecting clients and duty to warn expectations can differ among the states, researching this topic and relating this information directly back to professional conduct is paramount. Also, on legal issues always consult with an attorney. On professional or ethical issues consult with a colleague or supervisor before you act in good faith to protect another from harm. Based on the practitioner's field, addressing his or her professional code of ethics is mandatory. As a general rule when debating whether to take action on duty to warn and when ethics are involved, before taking a specific action, always ask this question:

- If I was held to a jury of my peers, would they do the same thing I am doing?

If so, be sure to outline the rationale for your decision.

Once professional ethical and legal implications have been addressed, when danger to self or others is suspected and ascertained, it is expected that the individual(s) at risk, the police, and those involved may need to be notified.

Gamino and Ritter (2009) remind the counselor to ask two critical questions before taking any action to protect others: (1) Is there a previous history of violent behavior toward people or animals? (2) Does the individual have possession of a firearm?

Last, if a client threatens to harm a vulnerable population, such as children, an elderly individual, or a mentally impaired adult, mandatory reporting requires that this be immediately addressed and the local protective agency be called.

DEVELOPING THE TREATMENT PLAN

In developing the treatment plan for clients who suffer from mental health problems, several critical steps need to be identified (Jongsma, Peterson, & Bruce, 2006).

1. Problem behaviors that are interfering with functioning must be identified. The ones that should receive the most attention are those that impair independent living skills or cause difficulties in completing tasks of daily living.
2. Once problem behaviors are identified, these behaviors need to be linked to the intervention process.
3. Involving the family and support system in treatment plan formulation and application can be especially helpful

First, problem behaviors that are interfering with functioning must be identified. In practice, it is essential that the client and his or her family participate and assist process as much as possible in identifying the issues, problem behaviors, and coping styles that are either causing or contributing to the client's discomfort. Of all of the problem behaviors a client may be experiencing, the ones that should receive the most attention are those that impair independent living skills or cause difficulties in completing tasks of daily living. Once identified, these behaviors need to be linked to the intervention process. The identification of specific problem behaviors or coping styles can provide an opportunity to facilitate educational and communicative interventions that can further enhance communication between the client and family members. Involving the family and support system in treatment plan formulation and application can be especially helpful and productive since at times individuals experiencing mental confusion and distortions of reality may exhibit bizarre and unpredictable symptoms. If support systems are not included in the intervention planning process, and the client's symptoms worsen, increased tension, frustration, fear, blame, and helplessness may develop in the connections between the client and the family-system. To avoid the client withdrawing from his or her support systems, all components of the family-system of support need to be made aware of the treatment plan goals and objectives that will be utilized with the client. Also, the client must agree to share this information with the family-system thereby gaining the client's consent allowing for current and continued involvement in each step of the intervention plan.

Second, not only do family and friends need to be aware of the treatment plan initiatives, they also need to be encouraged to share valuable input and support to ensure intervention progress and success. Family education and supportive interventions for family and significant others can be listed as part of the treatment plan for an individual client. It is beyond the scope of this chapter to discuss the multiple interventions available to the family members of the individual with mental illness; however, interested readers are encouraged to refer to Dziegielewski (2010), which provides an excellent strategy for working with individuals and families with a relative suffering from mental illness that is also under medication management.

Next, to assist in treatment plan development, it is critical to state the identified problem behaviors in terms of behavioral-based outcomes (Dziegielewski, 2008). In completing this process, the assessment data that led to the diagnostic impression as well as the specific problems often experienced by the client need to be outlined. Once identified, the client's problems are then prioritized so that goals, objectives, and action tasks may be developed. Fourth, the goals of intervention, which constitute the basis for the plan of intervention, must be clearly outlined and applied. These goals must be broken down into specific objective statements that reflect target behaviors to be changed and ways to measure the client's progress on each objective. As subcomponents to the objectives, action tasks must be included that clearly delineate the steps to be taken by the client and the helping professional to ensure successful completion of each objective.

Once the problem behaviors have been identified, the mental health practitioner must identify the goals and the behavioral-based objectives that can be used to measure whether the identified problems have been addressed and resolved (see Quick Reference 4.8, for assistance with recognizing identified problem behaviors). If the problem behavior is ambivalent feelings that impair general task completion, for example, the main goal may be to help the client decrease feelings of ambivalence. It is important to document a behavioral objective that clearly articulates a behavioral definition of ambivalence, ways

QUICK REFERENCE 4.8

SAMPLE OF IDENTIFIED PROBLEM BEHAVIORS

Identified problem behaviors often include:

- Ambivalent feelings that impair general task completion related to independent living skills.
- Affect disturbances, such as feelings of depression or a difficulty in controlling anger.
- Problems with coping related to poor concentration and limited insight. Associative disturbances, particularly in terms of inability to respond to being touched or approached by others.

that the ambivalence will be decreased, and the mechanisms used to determine if the behavior has been changed. The therapeutic intervention involves assisting the client to develop specific and concrete tasks that are geared toward decreasing this behavior and consequently meeting the objective. The outcome measure simply becomes establishing whether the task was completed. Each of the chapters in the applications section of this text and Appendix B include hints on creating sample intervention plans for dealing with clients who suffer from different types of mental disorders. The treatment plan is not designed to be all-inclusive; rather it is designed to provide the guidelines for effective documentation of the assessment and intervention process. Furthermore, treatment plans are to be viewed as starting points. Each diagnostic assessment and the treatment plan that results must be individualized for the client, outlining the specific problem behaviors and how each of these behaviors can be addressed.

In summary, the key to documenting the diagnostic assessment, treatment plan, and practice strategy is to maintain brevity while providing informative data. Documentation should record only the most salient issues relevant to client care and progress. Information should focus directly on content covered in the therapeutic sessions as well as the interplay of the client's progress with the counseling interventions. It is equally important for the practitioner to include the intervention strategies in the

primary treatment plan. Always link the therapeutic interventions to the original problems, goals, and objectives identified. Since today approval of services is often related directly to documented treatment progress, goals, and objectives, the need for clear documentation of these steps cannot be overemphasized (Russell-Chapin & Ivey, 2004).

Brief, accurate, and informative documentation that includes the diagnostic assessment, the treatment plan, and the practice strategy requires skill and training. Mental health practitioners must learn to document important information that will assist other professionals and oversight processes in providing the most effective interventions for clients. Doing this requires that vital client information gathered during the diagnostic assessment and intervention recommendations be combined in documentation that clearly identifies the client's problems, signs and symptoms, and past and current mental health history. While the specific type of documentation format used by mental health practitioners often is determined by the practice setting, practitioners should closely examine the format of choice and learn to integrate biopsychosocial and spiritual information that will be helpful in understanding the client and assist in formulating an effective intervention strategy.

Outcome Measures

With the emphasis on treatment efficacy and accountability in today's practice environment, it is essential that mental health practitioners learn to include objective measures that help to evaluate the effects of counseling therapies on the client's functioning. Included in these measures are standardized scales, surveys, and rapid assessment instruments (RAIs). These tools provide evidence-based data that identify the changes occurring over the course of the intervention. It is extremely important that mental health practitioners become familiar with and integrate measurement instruments in their practice and in their documentation to determine if treatment interventions have impacted baseline behaviors and problems (Dziegielewski, 2008). Furthermore, when working with specific populations, such as children, all measurement instruments are not created equal. Therefore, it is vital to make sure that the measurement tool selected is appropriate for the population being examined as well as the problem being elucidated. For more information on this topic, LeCroy and Okamoto (2009) outline specific considerations and measurement tools that are most sensitive to children.

Gathering pre- and postdata on a client's course of treatment enables both the practitioner and the client to examine whether progress has occurred and provides regulatory agencies with tangible objective evidence of client progress or decompensation. This single-system methodology, or the intensive or practice-oriented design, is used to help draw conclusions about effectiveness of individual cases over a period of time (Fischer, 2009). Utilization of designs such as this along with standardized instruments helps satisfy the requirements of managed care organizations (Kane, Houston-Vega, & Nuehring, 2002). When using a holistic framework that stresses the client's biopsychosocial factors, mental health practitioners play an important role in the efficient delivery of interdisciplinary health and mental health services.

Accurate record keeping increases effective communication and collaboration with other interdisciplinary health care team members on client progress and problems. The importance of providing accurate, up-to-date, informative records is vital to the coordinated health care planning efforts of the entire team and most important to the client's health. (Sample Treatment Plan 4.1 provides an example of how to define the condition and break down problem behaviors into goals, objectives, and interventions for the client.)

SAMPLE TREATMENT PLAN 4.1

BEREAVEMENT

Definition: Clinical attention focusing on an individual's reaction, emotionally, behaviorally, and cognitively, to the death of a loved one.

Signs and Symptoms to Note in the Record:

- Characteristics of a major depressive episode, including problems sleeping and eating, weight gain or loss.
- Guilt surrounding the death of the loved one.
- Conversational superficiality with respect to the loved one's death.
- Excessive emoting when the loved one's death is discussed.
- Feelings of worthlessness.
- Difficulty concentrating due to domination of thoughts surrounding loved one's death.
- Possible psychomotor retardation.
- Functional impairment(s).

Goals:

- Client will acknowledge and accept the death of loved one.
- Client will begin the grieving process.
- Client will resolve feelings over the death of loved one.
- Client will reconnect with old relationships and activities.

Objectives:

- Client will identify and state steps in the grieving process.
- Client will explore and express emotions and feelings associated with this loss.
- Client will resolve feelings of anger and guilt associated with loss of loved one.
- Client will interact with and discuss the death of loved one with others.

Interventions:

- Client will work with the therapist on gaining increased knowledge on the grieving process, specifically the stages of grief and how it relates to the client's thoughts and behaviors.
- Client will seek out others who have experienced the loss of a loved one to evaluate coping mechanisms used in dealing with this loss, and evaluate the use of these in individual therapy.
- Client will create a journal of emotions related to this loss to be discussed in individual therapy.
- Client will participate in "empty chair" exercise where he or she verbally expresses feelings not verbalized to the deceased loved one in life.
- Client will write a letter to the lost loved one expressing feelings and emotions, memories and regrets associated with loss to be discussed in individual therapy.
- Client will attend a bereavement support group.
- Client will interact with one mutual friend of the client and the deceased and share feelings about this loss, discussing the impact it has had on the living.

SELECTING AN INTERVENTION FRAMEWORK

Most counseling professionals, regardless of discipline, agree that all practitioners should be familiar with multiple practice modalities and frameworks for utilization in therapy. J. Sommers-Flanagan and R. Sommers-Flanagan (2009) state that a broad range of training experience in a variety of settings allows for the utilization of multiple methods. The mission of all helping professionals is to engage in activity that enhances opportunities for all people in an increasingly complex environment. Since mental health practitioners can work with a variety of human systems, including individuals, families, groups, organizations, and communities, some type of orientation that guides practice structure is needed. Fischer (2009) suggests that a framework needs to be utilized that can compare and analyze theories to determine which ones can best serve client need. Regardless of which overarching framework is eventually used, it needs to be consistent with the professional values and ethics of the practitioner's discipline and respect the cultural differences of all involved. Defined simply, a *theoretical practice framework* is the structured ideas or beliefs that provide the foundation for the helping activity that is to be preformed. Clients need assistance in functional recovery. Regardless of the method used, the emphasis on self-motivation and empowerment, especially for those that suffer from a mental disorder, should be at the heart of the strategy employed (Kern, Glynn, Horan, & Marder, 2009).

In mental health practice, many people use the words *theory* and *practice methods* or *strategy* interchangeably. Since they coexist (and in practice one without the other cannot exist for long), this linking is understandable. It is important to note, however, that theory and methods of practice strategy are not the same thing. A theoretical foundation provides the practitioner with the basics or the concepts of what can be done and why it is essential. The method or practice strategy, however, is the "doing" part of the helping relationship. It involves the outline or the plan for the helping activity that is generally guided by theoretical principles and concepts.

In mental health practice, attention needs to be given to selecting the best treatment approaches that form the basis for practice (Mandell & Schram, 2006). The diversity and uniqueness of each helping relationship requires that the practitioner be well versed in theory and practice and resilient in his or her ability to adapt this foundation to the needs of the client and the situation. For mental health practitioners, a delicate balancing act exists between blending theoretical concepts and frameworks that direct practice strategy. Doing this requires practitioners to be flexible in their approach as they deal with a multitude of different clients and different problems (Sommers-Flanagan & Sommers-Flanagan, 2009). To design and initiate professional practice strategy, practitioners must often go beyond the traditional bounds of their practice wisdom.

Utilizing the DSM-IV-TR and Selecting a Practice Framework

Although *DSM-IV-TR* is only a diagnostic tool, it can help practitioners develop an appropriate intervention plan for individual clients. Developing an intervention plan and selecting appropriate practice strategies is beyond the scope of

this book; however, helping professionals can use the information gathered from the diagnostic assessment to decide how to formulate the intervention plan and identify the best ways to engage the client. To begin this process, helping professionals must first be aware of the theoretical principles that underlie certain types of helping activity. Practitioners need to be prepared to pick and choose which theoretical concepts and practice strategies will offer the greatest assistance in formulating the helping process. Thus, practitioners should review the theoretical principles in terms of their application to the problem behaviors noted.

First and foremost, any helping strategy employed must be firmly based within the reality of the client's environment. At times, however, making this link may seem difficult or time consuming. Regardless, considering the impact of the client's environment on the practice method selected remains essential. For example, if a client is diagnosed with substance abuse and after receiving treatment is discharged back into an environment that is conducive to her once again beginning to abuse a substance, much of the influence of the intervention would be negated. In one case, a client diagnosed with substance dependence was admitted repeatedly to alcohol rehabilitation and treatment centers. The client always responded well to treatment while in the program but upon discharge quickly relapsed. After numerous intervention failures with this client, the mental health practitioner thoroughly assessed his situation and home environment. The practitioner quickly learned that the client was unable to maintain a bank account as a result of his instability and troubles with alcohol. So when it came time for him to cash his Social Security check, he used the local bar as his home address. When his check arrived each month, there was only one place to cash it: the local bar. To complicate matters further, the bar had a policy that it would cash checks only if a purchase was made, which led to the client's relapse. Being aware of the client's environment was a critical component in applying an appropriate helping strategy. Thus, anticipating the relationship that a client's environment can have on intervention outcome is essential (Colby & Dziegielewski, 2010; Dziegielewski, 2004).

In selecting a framework for the practice strategy, a second ingredient that is essential for formulating constructive helping activity is that all efforts be guided by theoretical concepts that are consistent with the needs and desires of the individual, group, family, or community being served (see Quick Reference 4.9). Furthermore, the theoretical framework must be consistent and reflective of the values and ethics of the practitioner's profession. It is important to recognize that selection of a theoretical framework to guide the interaction may not be as simple as knowing what models and methods are available and selecting one. When choosing a method of practice, it is not uncommon to

feel influenced and subsequently trapped within a system that is driven by social, political, cultural, and economic factors. With the numerous demands that are encountered in today's practice environment, it is difficult not to be influenced by these factors, and often they can dictate the practice basis that is employed. Mental health providers are often presented with problems as diverse as the individuals being treated. Once identified, these problems must be addressed within the framework of a client's unique circumstances (e.g., indigent or disadvantaged clients or clients who are culturally different from the majority culture in terms of ethnicity, race, or sexual orientation). How might all or any of these factors affect the helping relationship and practice strategy? How do mental health practitioners maintain the dignity and worth of each client served and balance their own feelings and possible prejudices so that those feelings and prejudices do not compromise the helping relationship? To address each of these questions thoroughly would fill several books. In short, each situation

---

QUICK REFERENCE 4.9

DEFINITIONS OF THEORETICAL CONCEPTS

Cognitive-behavioral therapy: A method of practice that uses the combination of selected techniques incorporating the theories of behaviorism, social learning theory, and cognition theories to understand and address a client's behavior.

Crisis intervention: A practice strategy used to help clients in crisis regain a sense of healthy equilibrium.

Educative counseling: A loosely defined approach to practice that focuses on helping the client to become an "educated consumer" and through this information is better able to address his or her own needs.

Interpersonal therapy: A form of time-limited treatment often used in the medical setting. Generally, this method involves an assessment that includes a diagnostic evaluation and psychiatric history. In this type of therapy the focus of treatment is directed toward interpersonal problem areas, such as grief, role disputes, role transitions, or deficits.

Psychotherapy: A form of therapy that involves understanding the individual in regard to his or her personal situation.

must be dealt with individually, and mental health practitioners should take care to identify potential problems and seek supervisory help when needed.

PRACTICE STRATEGY AND APPLICATION

Selecting the most appropriate practice method requires that helping professionals consider a multitude of factors relative to the individual and his or her family and support system. In addition to recognition of the support system, the importance of the helping activity and the importance of counseling that maximizes overall client well-being needs to be addressed. Clients or their families may be resistant to counseling and remain unconvinced that this type of intervention is necessary. In addition, other helping professionals may also not recognize the importance of mental health professionals in improving clients' functioning (Lambert, Bergin, & Garfield, 2004). As mental health services are demystified and affirmed by the media, public policy makers, and the general public, access to these types of services will continue to improve. Most clients and their families as well as other helping professionals now recognize the importance of counseling (Dziegielewski, 1997a; Gross, Rabinowitz, Feldman, & Boerma, 1996; Lambert, Bergin, & Garfield, 2004).

A basic assessment, intervention plan, and referral process initiated by the mental health professional can help clients promote and protect their physical as well as mental health. No matter how seasoned a practitioner may become, determining how to best handle a client's situation in the helping relationship will never be an easy task. It requires a constant process of assessing, reassessing, and collaborating with other professionals. Furthermore, when working as part of a professional team, professional opinions on how

to interpret, best select, and apply these strategies for helping will vary. Working together as a team and incorporating the helping ideas and strategies of each of the members will clearly improve the care available to vulnerable populations (Malone, Marriott, Newton-Howes, Simmonds, & Tyrer, 2009).

Although it is beyond the scope of this chapter to explain how to select from among the many theoretical and practice frameworks available to mental health practitioners, a brief presentation of several of the most common methods of practice, and how they can be related to client intervention, follows. Practice principles are presented to stress the importance of inclusion when selecting a practice method prior to embarking on the direct application of process to outcome.

Mixing Art and Science: Utilizing an Empowering Approach

In most schools that train mental health practitioners, students have traditionally been taught that the practice application can be defined in phases (even when they are not clearly established) with each application having a beginning, middle, and end. This is the format that is often presented in many time-limited practice models. One of the greatest lessons that professionals learn is that many times when applying the *science* of practice (i.e., identifying clear goals, objectives, and indicators for practice strategy), the intervention process will have a predictable beginning, middle, and end. At the same time, however, the *art* of practice acknowledges that at times nothing is predictable and even the best-made intervention plans will need constant modification and renegotiating. Balancing these two factors requires understanding that addressing and subsequently assisting to solve the problems of clients served will never be as easy as it might seem to the untrained observer.

In mental health practice today, *client empowerment* is very important. The uniqueness of the individual must always be accentuated and highlighted in each step of the helping process, regardless of the method of practice that is selected. Almost all clients respond favorably when they are acknowledged for their strengths and challenged to maximize their own potential.

Utilizing Time-Limited Practice and Managed Behavioral Care

Mental health practitioners must recognize that current practice will be brief and all intervention strategy must be linked to behavior-based outcomes (Dziegielewski, 2008). There are many reasons for this trend. For example, to receive reimbursement, practitioners must follow the expectations and subsequent limitations to service imposed by insurance reimbursement patterns (J. Sommers-Flanagan & R. Sommers-Flanagan, 2009). Insurance companies usually will not pay for long-term treatment. To ensure that practitioners will be reimbursed for their services, very specific time-limited approaches are essential. Following this trend, behavioral contracts have gained in popularity, as these clearly allow for outlining of costs for all, including the insurance provider, the program, and the client (Houmanfar, Maglieri, Roman, & Ward, 2008). In defense of this trend, many clients (especially the poor) simply do not have the time, desire, or money for long-term treatment. Many times individuals are not willing to commit the extra time or energy needed to go beyond addressing what is causing the problem. For many mental health practitioners who believe in long-term and comprehensive types of clinical helping relationships, this trend is very frustrating. Today, little emphasis exists in terms of amorphous clinical judgments and vague attempts at making clients "feel better," as these efforts will no longer be supported. In most areas of mental health practice, the days of insurance-covered long-term therapy encounters have ended.

For all professionals, starting the helping activity can be complicated by the fact that in today's turbulent and changing practice environment, selecting a practice framework remains dependent on more than just what is best for the client. With the advent of health care from a "managed care" perspective and restrictive cost-based service provision (J. Sommers-Flanagan & R. Sommers-Flanagan, 2009), this practice strategy must always be guided by balancing quality and effectiveness of the care provided with the cost effectiveness of the service being delivered. Since it is hard at times to quantify the helping benefits that clients receive, many professionals believe that when there is a battle between quality and cost effectiveness, generally the latter wins. Therefore, even the most seasoned practitioners are being forced to battle the expectation of providing what they believe is the most beneficial and ethical practice possible while being pressured to complete it as quickly and efficiently as reasonable.

A further complication when selecting a method of practice in mental health is that defending a type of treatment that is viewed as being in the best interest of the client may not truly reflect the client's wishes. The promise of lower premiums and less health care expenditures (Burner, Waldo, & McKusick, 1992) has changed clients' perspectives and expectations for treatment. This pressure makes it crucial for practitioners to work quickly in setting up and outlining a course of treatment (J. Sommers-Flanagan & R. Sommers-Flanagan, 2009). Clients now may request a specific type of intervention or therapy that addresses only certain problems because they are concerned about whether the service is covered by their insurance plan. It is not uncommon for many clients to be more interested in receiving a service that is time limited or reimbursable, regardless of the expected benefit that may be gained from an alternate, possibly longer-term, intervention strategy.

Practice reality dictates that the duration of most practice sessions, regardless of the methodology used or the orientation of the mental health practitioner, remain relatively brief. Research on treatment duration and effectiveness suggests that 13 to 18 sessions are needed for client change to occur, but in a large multisite study, the average number of sessions clients attended was less than 5 and a third attended only 1 (Hansen, Lambert, & Forman, 2002). For many practitioners, only seeing a client once is becoming commonplace. Furthermore, in health and mental health settings, so much of what practitioners do can no longer fall under the heading of brief therapy because much of intervention no longer has clear beginnings and endings. This has led the formal types of brief therapy to be replaced by intermittent types of therapy where intervention is provided when a client comes in and each session is considered to stand alone. Regardless of exactly what type of theoretical framework is to be utilized, a realization that most practice encounters are going to be brief and self-contained is essential (J. Sommers-Flanagan & R. Sommers-Flanagan, 2009). Planning for this short time or the single-session duration in implementing the helping strategy is critical (Dziegielewski, 2004). Without it, a lack of planning can result in numerous unexpected and unplanned endings for the client (Wells, 1994). It can also contribute to feelings of failure and decreased job satisfaction for the mental health and health care professionals (Resnick & Dziegielewski, 1996).

Time-Limited Brief Therapies

Many mental health practitioners who practice traditional forms of psychotherapy, particularly those who support psychoanalytic therapy, believe that managed care policies and subsequent counseling practice remain biased against them. For many practitioners trained in the more traditional forms of therapy and counseling, it is a common belief that making changes in a person takes time and that rushing into changes could lead to complications in a client's future health and wellness. Advocates for long-term approaches urge practitioners to realize this danger and advocate strongly for its continuance before it becomes an extinct mode of practice delivery in today's "big business" practice environment (Alperin, 1994).

For many practitioners, conducting traditional forms of psychotherapy remains problematic. Long-term therapy presents a particular problem for poor and disadvantaged clients. These individuals generally do not have the time or finances to afford long-term therapy, which has been referred to in some circles as a long-term luxury. Today, the majority of those in practice have for years shunned the more traditional approaches for a preferred emphasis on the applicability and effectiveness of time-limited methods of practice (Bloom, 1992; Dziegielewski, 1997, 1998; Epstein, 1994; Mancoske, Standifer, & Cauley, 1994; Wells, 1994). Studies suggest that practitioners who are successful in the managed care environment use problem-solving, short-term treatment models (Chambliss, 2000).

Based on the turbulence in our current practice environment, it is easy to see how time-limited therapies have gained in popularity, with their overall objective of bringing about positive changes in a client's current lifestyle with as little face-to-face contact as possible (Fanger, 1994). This emphasis on effectiveness and evidence-based treatments with applicability leading to increased positive change has helped to make briefer treatments popular (J. Sommers-Flanagan & R. Sommers-Flanagan, 2009). In general, time-limited approaches are the most often requested forms of practice in use today.

The foundation for traditional psychotherapy and time-limited or intermittent approaches is quite different. This difference requires practitioners to reexamine some basic premises in regard to long-term therapeutic models utilized in a more traditional format. According to Dziegielewski (1997b), seven factors can be identified that highlight the difference between these two methods.

1. **There is a primary difference in the way the client is viewed.** Traditional psychotherapeutic approaches often linked individual problems to personal pathology. This is not the case from a time-limited perspective, where the client is seen as a basically healthy individual with an interest in increasing personal or social changes or both (Budman & Gurman, 1988; Roberts & Dziegielewski, 1995). In current mental health practice, the focus on empowerment extends the belief that clients are not only capable of change, but they can be aware and active participants in this process. Traditional psychoanalytic approaches emphasize that the client is often unaware and unable to access this information because it lies beneath the surface of the client's awareness at a preconscious or unconscious level of awareness. These approaches make empowerment difficult to foster and do not highlight the strengths of the client in becoming an active participant in the practice strategy employed.

2. **Time-limited approaches are most helpful when administered during critical periods in a person's life** (Roberts & Dziegielewski, 1995). Utilizing a time-limited framework provides a basic difference from the use of traditional psychotherapies, which

are seen as necessary and continuing over a much longer period of time.

3. **In time-limited brief treatment, the goals and objectives of therapy are always mutually defined by both the client and the therapist** (Wells, 1994). In traditional psychotherapeutic approaches, goals are often first recognized and defined by the therapist and later shared with the client (Budman & Gurman, 1988).

4. **In time-limited therapy, goals are concretely defined and are often addressed outside the actual therapy session in the form of homework or other activities** (Epstein, 1994; Jacobs, 2008; Tompkins, 2004). One example of this is bibliotherapy (the use of outside reading materials as an adjunct to office sessions). In traditional psychotherapeutic approaches, issues are generally addressed during the sessions only, not outside of them (Budman & Gurman, 1988). This is because the presence of the therapist is seen as the catalyst for change. When bibliotherapy is used as part of the treatment, particularly in cognitive-behavioral approaches (CBT), treatment manuals that outline what is to be done are often used (Papworth, 2006).

5. **In time-limited intervention, regardless of the model, little emphasis is placed on insight.** This difference between brief approaches and traditional psychotherapy is one of the hardest to accept for mental health practitioners who were educated with a traditional psychotherapeutic methodology. In traditional psychotherapy, development of problem-oriented insight is considered necessary before any type of meaningful change can take place.

6. **Time-limited approaches to practice are seen as active and directive.** Here the mental health practitioner often goes beyond just active listening and assumes a consultative role with the client (Wells, 1994). This results in the development of concrete goals and problem-solving techniques and is very different from traditional psychotherapeutic approaches that emphasize a more nebulous inner representation of satisfaction.

7. **In brief time-limited settings, termination is discussed early in the therapeutic process** (Wells, 1994). Often the practitioner begins to plan for termination in the first session, and termination issues are discussed continually throughout the intervention process. By contrast, traditional psychotherapy may never address termination issues in advance. Preparation for termination is not typically considered an essential part of the therapy process.

TYPES OF TIME-LIMITED THERAPY IN MENTAL HEALTH PRACTICE

This section reviews several models usually linked to the provision of time-limited counseling services. However, these models do not represent all of the major models of practice for mental health counseling. This review briefly describes the types of models and methods available as well as the tradition from which they were developed. Regardless of the method used, one thing all practice approaches share is the desire for change that will reduce pain or suffering for the client (Herbert, Forman, & England, 2008). In Section II of this text, each of the mental health disorders and conditions presented describes a currently accepted treatment or

intervention strategy for the mental health condition or disorder presented. To assist and provide an overview of several current therapeutic approaches, these models for practice will be briefly summarized: interpersonal psychotherapeutic or psychodynamic approaches; strategic or solution-oriented therapies; cognitive-behavioral approaches; crisis intervention; and health, education, and wellness counseling. Cases are used to highlight each of these approaches. In the psychodynamic aspects of therapeutic practice, emphasis is placed on understanding the internal workings of the individual. In the solution-focused therapies, the solution (or course of action) is identified, and specific attempts are made to attain it. In the cognitive-behavioral approaches, the focus is on understanding the complex relationship between socialization and reinforcement as it affects thoughts and behaviors in the current environment. The final application is a form of time-limited therapy in which practitioners focus on providing health counseling and education based on the principle of creating and maintaining wellness.

Before discussing these methods, it is important to note that there is no method of practice that can alone call itself a "clean" mental health practice theory. In mental health practice, there has been a blending of ideas and theoretical concepts that are mixed and altered to best serve the client. For example, Brandell (2004) warns that even when looking directly at psychodynamic approaches, they too are compilations of multiple theories, models, and schemata. Thus, there is substantial overlap in the information that is presented for each approach. Although the practitioner may first start using one mode of practice, pieces of the other methods of intervention may also be incorporated to assist the client in the most efficient and effective way possible. Very often the mental health practitioner will be expected to mix and match practice strategies, using what works to help the client. Pieces or techniques alone, however, are not considered enough. There also needs to be some theoretical understanding of why certain techniques are being used and how selecting these methods must be consistent with the practitioner's professional ethics and standards. Also, when a type of therapy is used, the basic premises of the method should be reflective not only of the title but of what is actually being done (Simon, 2010).

Psychodynamic Approaches

Psychodynamic approaches allow for past experiences to be blended with present ones (Brandell, 2004). These approaches are often credited with being the foundation of mental health casework, and their premise is that focusing on history and past issues can lend credence to current problem-solving efforts. Furthermore, when utilizing a "biopsychosocial" perspective, this form of psychodynamic intervention has gained credibility and recognition among many health care professionals as an interdisciplinary approach. For example, historically this type of approach to practice was used in medical settings where interdisciplinary teams assisted clients in addressing their needs. In this practice framework, helping professionals are seen as active, supportive, and a contributing factor in therapeutic gain. In general, these models are often used to directly address symptom removal and prevention of relapse and to help clients having difficulty relating to significant others, careers, social roles, and/or life transitions (Goldstein & Noonan, 2001).

Psychodynamic approaches focus clinical attention on the conscious (individual awareness) and the unconscious (beyond individual awareness). Next, these factors are identified, outlined, reviewed, and addressed as part of the practice strategy. For the most part, as evidenced by Case Example 4.1, most of the psychodynamic approaches used in practice today portray the unconscious as immediately accessible and changeable (Goldstein & Noonan, 2001).

As in the case of John (see Case Example 4.1), the intervention addressed the client's present situation and focused on the "here and now"

CASE EXAMPLE 4.1 - CASE OF JOHN

Mr. Jones brought his 12-year-old son, John, in for assessment after he discovered that his son had been making obscene phone calls. John had never been in trouble before, and after being charged legally and sent to court, a judge decided that John could benefit from a mental health assessment rather than proceeding with further legal action. It was obvious during the interview that the father was extremely frustrated with the situation and could not understand why John had been engaging in this type of behavior. During his interview, John became very nervous. He seemed embarrassed to talk about what he had done and kept his head down, looking directly at the floor, as he spoke.

The mental health practitioner asked John what had happened. John described exactly what he had done, the phone calls he had made, and the obscene comments he had made to the women who answered the phone. John seemed embarrassed by his behavior but appeared honest in telling what he had done. When asked how he had gotten caught making the calls, John calmly stated that when asked, he gave his name. The practitioner was surprised by this and tried to clarify what he said. Again John stated that when the recipient of the obscene phone call asked who was calling, John told her his name. After hearing John tell of what he had done and how he had gotten caught, John's father voiced his frustration, anger, and shock with his son's

(continued)

CASE EXAMPLE 4.1 - CASE OF JOHN (*CONTINUED*)

behavior. He openly stated that he was alarmed by the behavior and could not understand it. The fact that John was leaving his name when asked caused the practitioner to feel that there was more here than simply "acting out," as the father had stated.

In gathering information for the diagnostic assessment, the practitioner asked if John had ever been in trouble before. John and his father agreed that he had not. Since this appeared inconsistent with his behavior, the practitioner asked if anything out of the ordinary had happened to upset John or disturb him. John stated he was not aware of anything. When asked specifically if there had been any changes in the past few months, John's father responded. According to the father, John's mother had died approximately 6 weeks before. Once the practitioner began to explore the death of the mother and the feelings of the child, it became clear that John was indeed having difficulty adjusting to his mother's death. It appeared as if John was making the phone calls and leaving his name as an attempt at crying out for attention or help. After beginning to discuss the death of his mother with the practitioner, John was also able to voice his fear that his father might die as well and leave him alone. The practitioner concluded that John did not suffer from a mental disorder at all but rather was suffering from bereavement (related to the death of his mother), and his reaction was an adolescent antisocial act (making the obscene phone calls).

The role of the mental health practitioner is to gather a comprehensive assessment exploring why things are happening as they are. In this case, many issues surrounding the death of the mother remained unresolved. Furthermore, it also appeared as if the child might in his own way be crying out for help and attention from the father. The approach the practitioner took was to explore the relationship between John and his father as well as to look at how their past relationship could balance and strengthen the present one. This approach utilized the concepts relevant in ego psychology, a form of psychodynamic therapy. In this approach, the practitioner helped to address the situation, plant a seed as to what was happening, create a release of tension and energy for John and his father, and later help them to reintegrate, address, and discontinue the problematic behaviors that had resulted.

It is important to note that although trained professionals do engage in these types of psychodynamic approaches, graduate-level training and expertise is usually required. Helping professionals without graduate training should refer clients to a qualified practitioner if they believe this type of approach would best serve the client. Overall, however, as can be seen in this case, the more a mental health practitioner knows in terms of practice strategy and frameworks, the more he or she can pick and choose the best helping approach. For John, exploring the reasons for his making the phone calls and the relationship between the problem behavior and the death of his mother was a crucial link. In making this connection, John was helped to address his feelings and he was able to stop making the phone calls as a means of getting attention.

(Weissman, Markowitz, & Klerman, 2007). Similar to what was done in this case, the focus of the intervention is on recent interpersonal events (the death of John's mother) with a clear effort to link the stressful event to John's current mood and actions (crying out for attention by making obscene phone calls).

Information is gathered in the diagnostic assessment along with a psychiatric history. When completing the diagnostic assessment,

the mental health practitioner is expected to pay particular attention to the client's family and support system interactions, including changes in relationships proximal to the onset of symptoms. In general, the focus of treatment is directed toward interpersonal problem areas such as grief, role disputes, role transitions, or deficits (Weissman et al., 2007). Focusing on one of these interpersonal areas will allow the practitioner to identify problems in the interpersonal and social context that need to be addressed (Weissman et al., 2007).

Utilizing a psychodynamic approach, the mental health practitioner and the client work together to identify issues for the treatment plan and establish the goals and objectives that will later be addressed in the practice strategy. Practice strategy must be directly related to the identified interpersonal problem. For example, if a role conflict exists between a client and his or her family member in regard to substance use and abuse, practice strategy would begin by clarifying the nature of the dispute. Discussion of the problem would result in an explanation of usual limitations that often are beyond the client's control. Limitations that are causing the greatest disagreements are identified and options to resolve the disputes are considered. If resolution does not appear possible, strategies or alternatives to replace the problematic behaviors are contemplated. In some cases, application manuals can be acquired and followed that give specific practice steps for approaching certain interpersonal problem areas (Weissman et al., 2007).

When applying the psychodynamic method of practice, mental health practitioners are expected to help clients identify issues of concern and provide the groundwork for how they can be addressed. Many times this includes helping the client to learn how to recognize the need for continued help and assistance through counseling, especially when problems seem greater than what the client is capable of handling at the time (Dziegielewski & Leon, 2010). Regardless of who is actually assisting the client, the role of the practitioner in this form of practice is an important one. Most important, the practitioner must always remain influential in helping the client feel comfortable about seeking additional help when needed. This help-seeking behavior is an important step in establishing and maintaining a basis for continued health and wellness.

Solution-Focused Approaches

Solution-focused brief therapy (SFBT) is a short-term treatment intervention that focuses on creating solutions to one's problems (de Shazer, 1988). From this perspective, solution building rather than problem solving is the focus (Iveson, 2002; Simon, 2010). In practice, solution-focused models are different in focus from the more traditional problem-solving methods because they do not spend much time on problem identification as the key ingredient to the practice encounter. The focus is on client's strengths and using these strengths to build solutions to current problems (Greenberg, Ganshorn & Danilkewich, 2001). Smock et al. (2008), similar to Metcalf (1998), believe SFBT is particularly helpful for individuals struggling with out-of-control behaviors such as substance abuse. This model is also used in settings such as schools where short-term types of interventions are the expectation (Brasher, 2009). Solution-focused models assume that clients are basically healthy individuals who possess the skills they need to address their problems and remain capable of change. Thus, this method focuses on identifying solutions to resolving the client's stated concern. This popular treatment strategy does not require there to be a causal link between the antecedent (what comes before the problem behavior) and the actual problem. Since this causal connection is not made, a direct link need not be established between the problem and the solution (de Shazer & Dolan, 2007). (See Case Example 4.2, the Case of Jim.)

Cognitive-Behavioral Approaches to Mental Health Practice

Cognitive-behavioral therapy often involves concrete and focused strategies to help clients change irrational thoughts or behaviors that can complicate the helping process. This type of

--------------- **CASE EXAMPLE 4.2 - CASE OF JIM** ---------------

Jim was referred for a mental health assessment requesting help because he was having difficulty interacting with his child. His wife constantly complained that he did not show enough attention and concern for their disabled child. Jim stated he loved his son very much but was not particularly comfortable showing it. He did not like the way his son, who was moderately mentally retarded, always demanded to be hugged after completing tasks. When asked whether he believed that it was important to show affection, Jim agreed but stated that he just was not sure how to go about it. Furthermore, he felt that his son was expecting too much love and attention and should be able to function without always requiring that it be given.

When Jim sought intervention assistance, he made it very clear that his insurance company would allow only three sessions and that was what he was going to stick with. After completing a diagnostic assessment, the mental health practitioner felt that a solution-focused approach to intervention would be best for Jim. Although his symptoms were problematic, they did not seem severe enough to affect Jim's overall functioning. In helping Jim to develop a change strategy, the practitioner (a) focused on what Jim saw as the problem, (b) let Jim establish what he perceived as the desired outcome, (c) helped Jim to begin to analyze and develop solutions focusing on his own individual strengths, (d) helped Jim to develop and implement a plan of action, and (e) assisted with termination and follow-up issues if needed (Dziegielewski, 1997b). In summary, in this case, the mental health practitioner was active in helping the client to find and identify strengths in his current functional patterns of behavior. A dialogue of "change talk" was created rather than "problem talk" (Walter & Peller, 1992). In change talk, the problem is viewed positively with patterns of change highlighted that appear successful for the client. Positive aspects and exceptions to the problem are explored, allowing for alternate views of the problem to develop. Once the small changes have been highlighted, the client becomes empowered to elicit larger ones (de Shazer & Dolan, 2007). Jim looked at what he was doing and the practitioner helped him to establish alternative ways of acting and behaving when his son approached him. They also developed ways for him to discuss with his wife his feelings and his strategy for building independence in his son.

---

practice approach gained popularity in the early 1970s when the focus was originally on the applied behavior and the power of reinforcement on the influence of human behavior (Skinner, 1953). However, many theorists believed that behavior alone was not enough and that human beings acted or reacted based on an analysis of the situation and the thought patterns that motivated them. Here the thought process, and how cognitive processes and structures influence individual emotions, was highlighted (Roberts & Dziegielewski, 1995; MacLaren & Freeman, 2007). Over the last decade a significant movement has emerged that focuses not only on changing cognitions but at times simply accepting them (Herbert, Forman & England, 2008). To understand the problem thoughts and

related behaviors, a schema is developed. The schema is generally referred to as the cognitive structure that organizes experience and behavior (Beck, Freeman, & Associates, 1990). When utilizing this perspective, the practitioner must be skilled and practice multiple approaches covering standard behavioral, cognitive, acceptance, and mindfulness strategies (O'Donohue & Fisher, 2008).

Overall, cognitive-behavioral approaches to practice focus on the present and seek to replace distorted thoughts and/or unwanted behaviors with clearly established goals (Fanger, 1994). In the cognitive-behavioral approach, the setting of goals and objectives is crucial for measuring the effectiveness of treatment provided (Brower & Nurius, 1993). These goals should always be stated positively and realistically so that motivation for completion will be increased. Also, to facilitate the measurement of effectiveness of what is being done, objectives must be stated in concrete and functional terms. In setting appropriate objectives, the focus is not necessarily on process but rather on the outcome that is desired (Roberts & Dziegielewski, 1995). Oftentimes a behavioral contract, either oral or written, is developed to clearly outline the expectations, plans, and/or contingencies for the behaviors. These contracts help to ensure that goals are agreed on; can assist to monitor progress; outline responsibilities such as time, effort, and money; and ensure all involved are committed to the plan that is to be completed (Houmanfar, Maglieri, Roman & Ward, 2008). Adapting cognitive and behavioral principles in the time-limited framework creates a viable climate for change (MacLaren & Freeman, 2007). (See Case Example 4.3, the Case of Jill.)

In working with client problems such as those experienced by Jill, a cognitive-behavioral approach can be very helpful. This is especially true for professionals who must deal with clients who are suffering from a variety of personal and situational problems. Thoughts can be difficult to control, and often clients may become extremely frustrated with their inability to control their own actions and behaviors and perform in areas in which they previously were proficient. When faced with a medical situation, they may develop negative schemata or ways of dealing with the situation that can clearly cause conflicts in their physical, interpersonal, and social relationships. Specific techniques such as identifying irrational beliefs, utilizing cognitive restructuring, behavioral role rehearsal, skill training, activity scheduling, self-reinforcement, and

---

CASE EXAMPLE 4.3 - CASE OF JILL

Jill sought the assistance of a mental health professional after becoming extremely frustrated with her ability to take tests in college. She often became so anxious that she could not focus or concentrate, thereby rendering her unable to put on paper what she really did know in her head. After interviewing Jill, the practitioner decided it would probably be best to use a type of cognitive-behavioral therapy to address her test anxiety.

As the first step in this helping process, the practitioner asked Jill to keep a diary. In the diary she was asked to record the specific thoughts, feelings, and emotions that she experienced when she was put in stressful situations—particularly testing situations. Jill kept the diary for 7 days and brought it to her next session. At that session, the practitioner reviewed the comments Jill had written and realized much of what was noted was self-defeating phrases and thoughts. For example, Jill often reported feeling stupid and useless. She also stated that she could remember her older brothers telling her how stupid she was.

Jill's schema revolved around her feelings of inadequacy and her belief that she was not smart enough to succeed in college. Once this was triggered by the stress of a test, she could no longer function. It was her interpretation of these events that influenced her reaction, resulting in cognitive distortion when interpreting a current situation or event. Therefore, the role of the mental health practitioner in this framework was to help Jill identify her negative and self-defeating thoughts and to replace them with more productive and fruitful ones.

The mental health practitioner helped Jill to look at each of the statements in her diary and analyze them. Many times they practiced rewriting the statements or inserting more positive self-statements. Basically, the practitioner helped Jill to rethink the comments she was saying to herself and replace them with more positive and productive statements.

systematic desensitization can assist clients to adjust and accommodate to the new life status that will result (MacLaren & Freeman, 2007). Cognitive and behavioral techniques can help clients to recognize these needs for change as well as assist with a plan to provide the behavior change needed for continued health and functioning.

Crisis Intervention Approaches to Mental Health Practice

A *crisis* is defined as a period psychological disequilibrium that results from a hazardous event or situation (Yeager, Roberts, & Grainger, 2008). Oftentimes the person in crisis becomes frustrated as his or her usual ways of coping simply do not seem to work. The practitioner assists clients in crisis by focusing on the immediate or acute problem situations. From this perspective, clients are helped to discover an adaptive means of coping with a particular life stage, tragic occurrence, or problem that generates a crisis situation. Crisis intervention techniques are employed in many settings: social and relief agencies, the military, private practice, shelters, hospitals (especially hospital emergency rooms), public health agencies, hospice services, home health care agencies, and almost all other agencies and services that utilize mental health professionals. Professionals have used crisis intervention techniques with migrant workers; rape survivors; domestic violence victims; death and dying; mental illness; event trauma, such as plane crashes, floods, and tornadoes; and in numerous other ways when immediate help and assistance is needed (Roberts, 2005).

By its very nature, crisis intervention is time limited. All efforts are directed at solving immediate problems, emotional conflicts, and distress (Green & Roberts, 2008). Therefore, the first criterion in this method of service

delivery is the realization that all practice approaches are often going to be intense over a time-limited duration (Roberts & Dziegielewski, 1995). In crisis intervention practice, strategy needs to accomplish a set of therapeutic objectives within a limited time frame while maintaining effectiveness in crisis management that appears to be indistinguishable from that of long-term treatment (Bloom, 1992). According to H. J. Parad and L. G. Parad (1990), utilizing minimum therapeutic practice strategy during the brief crisis period can often produce the maximum therapeutic effect. When a client is suffering from a crisis, an emphasis on utilizing supportive social resources and focused intervention techniques to facilitate practice effectiveness is highlighted (Green & Roberts, 2008). (See Case Example 4.4, the Case of Juan.)

For many clients, the psychological suffering that they experience following a traumatic event can be understood as an "affliction of the powerless" (Herman, 1992, p. 33). These are basically healthy people who are so disturbed by the event that functioning is impaired. If they are afraid of something, the threat to life and bodily integrity overwhelms normal adaptive capabilities, producing extensive symptomatology. For the mental health practitioner, an active problem-addressing and supportive role is essential. The practitioner helps the client to become empowered, recognizing that the symptoms that are being experienced can be viewed as signs of strength and the symptoms a client is experiencing are better related to understanding coping techniques developed by the survivor to adapt to a toxic environment (Roberts & Dziegielewski, 1995).

Educative Counseling

Through the document *Healthy People 2000* (Thomas, 2000), health promotion has been

---

CASE EXAMPLE 4.4 - CASE OF JUAN

Juan was referred for a mental health assessment after a devastating tornado. After the tornado, Juan was found wandering the neighborhood in a state of shock. For weeks he would return and wander through the rubble of what was once his home looking for belongings (now treasures) of a previous time. Although it had been a month since the event, Juan reported that he could not put it behind him and move forward. Juan sought intervention because his wife was very concerned about his behavior. He often woke up in the middle of the night in a cold sweat and could not go back to sleep. Juan reported that since his home was destroyed by the tornado, he often felt like he was in a daze. He reported having recurrent flashback episodes day and night in which he would relive the night the tornado destroyed his home. He reported that he now avoided driving to the construction site where his home was being rebuilt. Whenever he tried to go there, he would feel overwhelmed with anxious feelings and have to stop his car.

After completing a diagnostic assessment, the mental health practitioner felt that Juan was experiencing a stress reaction such as acute stress disorder (308.3). Although Juan was able to go to work, it was apparent that his reaction was severe enough to impair his overall functioning.

As part of the helping strategy, crisis intervention requires a dynamic form of practice that focuses on a wide range of phenomenon affecting individual, group, or family equilibrium. For Juan, the crisis was defined as a temporary state of upset and disequilibrium characterized chiefly by his inability to cope with a particular situation. During this crisis period, Juan's usual methods of coping and problem solving simply did not work. His perception was that the tornado was so devastating and intolerable that he could not cope with it. Juan viewed the tornado as a hazardous threatening event that left him vulnerable. He stated that no matter how hard he tried, he could not seem to control his fears.

To help Juan, crisis intervention techniques were applied to help him reformulate the crisis situation within the context of growth. Ultimately, the mental health practitioner needed to help Juan reach a healthy resolution where he could emerge with greater strength, self-trust, and a greater sense of freedom than before the crisis event (Gilliland & James, 1997).

When applied with clients such as Juan, crisis intervention techniques are centered on the assumption that acute crisis events can be concretely identified, controlled, and lessened. Successful resolution is therefore achieved when the practitioner helps the client to successfully reach a more healthy resolution of the problem.

For Juan, learning to deal with the physical devastation that resulted from the recent tornado was an area that needed to be addressed. A crisis such as this one was so unexpected that many families like Juan's lost their homes and their personal possessions. In some cases lives were lost. Juan worried repeatedly what he could have done differently and why this had to happen to him. With such an unanticipated catastrophe, Juan was concerned with understanding why this happened or how he could prevent it in the future. In situations such as these, the role of the helping professional is clear: to help the client once again return to that previous level of coping and adjustment.

---

incorporated into the nation's health delivery agenda. However, despite the growth and emphasis placed in this area, health promotion remains fragmented. Often its implementation is characterized by "poor communication between the many disciplines contributing to this area and little interaction between the research and the practitioner communities" (O'Donnell, 1994, p. ix).

Many times mental health professionals are called on to participate in a type of counseling that is not considered traditional. This type of

CASE EXAMPLE 4.5 - CASE OF BILL

Mental health practitioners can assist in providing education to clients in many different areas. Consider the case of Bill, who would not follow his diabetic diet. The medical condition resulting from his noncompliance was so severe that he was hospitalized repeatedly. During each hospitalization, he met with a dietitian and was given a copy of his diet before discharge, but was later readmitted for noncompliance. Upon referral to the mental health practitioner, a family assessment was completed. The practitioner discovered that the client's wife was responsible for preparing the family's meals. His wife had been handed the diet but was not really sure of the relevance of strict adherence to Bill's continued health. After meeting with the family and helping to educate his wife about the need for assisting, Bill's diet compliance increased dramatically.

counseling can include many different techniques. However, at a minimum, it must be time limited, goal directed, and objective focused and assist clients to address present and future health and wellness issues. More and more mental health practitioners are being called on to provide "educative counseling," and only recently has it been openly discussed and accepted as a method of providing practice (Cowles, 2003). Nor is its importance generally stressed or addressed in formal education through the curriculum in most schools. (See Case Example 4.5, the Case of Bill.)

Bill's case is just one example of how practitioners can assist clients by educating not only them and their families but also other members of a delivery team. Including a family member has been shown to increase patient adherence to treatment plans (Desmond & Copeland, 2000). It is also important for practitioners to be willing to educate clients in areas such as child abuse, domestic violence, and incest dynamics. Practitioners need to go beyond the traditional bounds of counseling and assist in educating clients to be better prepared for maintaining safety, security, and preparing for health and wellness for not only themselves but for their entire family system.

Openly acknowledging the importance of client education can assist practitioners in identifying the need for this commonly provided service. Mental health practitioners are in a unique position to participate in education, particularly in the areas of prevention and continued health and wellness. The overall practice of education in mental health is safety- and health-oriented, both conceptually and philosophically. This makes the mental health practitioner the link between the person and a system of support that maintains health (Skidmore, Thackeray, & Farley, 1997).

SUMMARY

Case documentation and using the information gathered to provide the basis for intervention planning and the practice strategy to follow is never simple. Numerous cases and individual situations arise that professionals are not sure how to handle. It is never easy to decide where to begin, what to write and what not to write in the case record, and what goals and objectives to process and apply to practice strategy. The science of intervention is important in starting the process, but it is the art that will carry it to a successful end. A delicate balancing act is required between the needs of the client, the demands of the environment, and the skills and helping knowledge available to the mental health practitioner.

Furthermore, the art and science within practice strategy is more involved than being familiar with the practice frameworks and simply choosing what works. It takes knowing the client and the strategies and methods available as well as how and when to best apply the theoretical foundations that underlie the practice techniques selected. In today's environment, many complicated problems need to be addressed and there is a real urgency to address them as quickly and effectively as possible. All mental health professionals, regardless of their discipline, need to be trained in these methods of helping. This training cannot be viewed as static. All professional helpers must continue learning and growing in order to anticipate the needs of our clients.

Dziegielewski (1998) identified five factors that must guide the initiation of the diagnostic assessment, treatment planning, and the practice strategy:

1. **Clients need to be active and motivated in the diagnostic assessment, treatment plan formulation, and intervention strategy.** Support and participation by the client will increase the likelihood of encouragement and completion of change efforts. Generally, the issues and behavioral problems a client is exhibiting may require him or her to exert serious energy in attempting to make behavioral change. This means that clients must not only agree to participate in the assessment process but be willing to embark on the intervention plan that will result in behavioral change.

2. **The information gathered in the diagnostic assessment will be used to guide the approach or method of intervention used.** Once symptoms are identified, different methods and approaches for clinical intervention can be selected. However, the approach should never guide the intervention chosen. Sheafor and Horejsi (2008) warn against practitioners becoming

over involved and wasting valuable clinical time by trying to match a particular problem to a particular theoretical approach, especially since so much of the problem-identification process in assessment is an intellectual activity. The practitioner should never lose sight of the ultimate purpose of the assessment process. Simply stated, the purpose is to complete an assessment that will help to establish a concrete service plan to address a client's needs.

3. **The influence and effects of values and beliefs should be made apparent in the process.** Each individual, professional or not, is influenced by his or her own values and beliefs (Colby & Dziegielewski, 2010). It is these beliefs that create the foundation for who we are and what we believe. In mental health practice, however, it is essential that these individual influences do not directly affect the assessment process. Therefore, the individual values, beliefs, and practices that can influence intervention outcomes must be clearly identified from the onset of treatment. For example, consider an unmarried client at a public health clinic who finds out she is pregnant. The practitioner assigned to her case personally believes that abortion is "murder" and cannot in good conscience recommend it as an option to the client. The client, however, is unsure of what to do and wants to explore every possible alternative. The plan that evolves must be based on the client's needs and desires, not the mental health practitioner's. Therefore, the practitioner ethically should advise the client of her prejudice and refer her to someone who can be more objective in exploring abortion as a possible course of action. Clients have a

right to make their own decisions, and mental health professionals must do everything possible to ensure this right and not allow personal opinion to impair the completion of a proper assessment.

In addition to the beliefs held by the practitioner and the client, the beliefs and values of the members of the inter-disciplinary team must also be considered. It is not uncommon for helping professionals to have value conflicts. These team members need to be aware of how their personal feelings and resultant opinions might inhibit them from addressing all of the possible options to a client. For example, in the case of the unmarried pregnant woman, a physician, nurse, or any other member of the health care delivery team who does not believe in abortion would also be obligated to refer the client. This is not to assume that mental health practitioners are more qualified to address this issue or that they always have an answer. The point is that mental health practitioners should always be available to assist other helping professionals and advocate for how to best serve the needs of the client. Values and beliefs can be influential in identification of factors within individual decision-making strategy and remain important factors to consider and identify in the assessment process.

4. **Issues surrounding culture and race should be addressed openly in the assessment phase.** The mental health practitioner needs to be aware of his or her own cultural heritages as well as the client's to ensure the most open and receptive environment is created. Dziegielewski (2004) suggested these considerations be established on the part of the health and mental health professionals:

a. Be aware of one's own cultural limitations.
b. Be open to cultural differences.
c. Recognize the integrity and the uniqueness of the client.
d. Utilize the client's learning style, including his or her own resources and supports.
e. Implement the behaviorally based biopsychosocial approach to practice from an integrated and as non-judgmental a format as possible.

For example, when utilizing the *DSM-IV-TR*, cultural factors should be stressed prior to establishing a formal diagnostic condition. As stated earlier in this book, delusions and hallucinations may be difficult to separate from general beliefs or practices related to a client's specific cultural custom or lifestyle. For this reason, the mental health practitioner should not forget that an appendix is included in the *DSM-IV-TR* that describes and defines culturally bound syndromes that might affect the diagnosis and assessment process and subsequent intervention strategy (American Psychiatric Association, 2000).

5. **The assessment must focus on client strengths and highlight the client's own resources for providing continued support.** One of the most difficult things for most individuals to do is to find, identify, and plan to use their own strengths. People, in general, have a tendency to focus on the negatives and rarely praise themselves for the good they do. With the advent of behavioral managed care, health and mental health care workers must quickly identify the individual and collectively based strengths of clients. Once this has been achieved, these strengths should

be highlighted and incorporated into the suggested treatment plan. The information gathered is utilized in the assessment and stressed in regard to the importance of individual support networks for the client. In this time-limited intervention environment, individual resources are essential for continued growth and maintenance of wellness after the formal intervention period has ended. In such settings, practitioners need to stay vigilant that quality of care is not compromised (J. Sommers-Flanagan & R. Sommers-Flanagan, 2009).

One such example in need of support and attention from practitioners is that of individuals suffering from AIDS. According to the Joint United Nations Programme on HIV/AIDS (UNAIDS, 2008) an estimated 30 to 36 million people around the globe are infected with HIV, the virus that causes AIDS, and more than 25 million have already died from the virus that rendered their immune systems defenseless. Many individuals are forced either to confront this generally terminal illness in themselves or see it progress in a loved one. Misconceptions and fear based on lack of education often stop family and friends from being supportive to individuals when they most need care and support. Practitioners must actively work to help these individuals and encourage support for them in their time of need. In this situation, practitioners need to be educated not only to varied theoretical approaches but be able to select which one to use and when. Psychodynamic approaches can be used to help clients to feel better about themselves and to help address previous relationship experiences that are affecting the development of new or current ones. Solution-focused methods can help individuals develop new ways of changing behavior, focusing positive

energy and attention on how to make things better. Cognitive-behavioral approaches can help individuals and family members to look at dysfunctional thought patterns and how they complicate current interactions. The crisis intervention approach can assist the client and his or her family to return to a previous or healthier level of coping. Education can provide client empowerment while enhancing independence and control. To become better equipped in the helping activity, practitioners must be aware of the multiple frameworks and practice methods available.

QUESTIONS FOR FURTHER THOUGHT

1. In this chapter, supporting information beyond that related directly to the diagnostic assessment is essential. List the types of supporting information that are most helpful for inclusion and explain why.

2. Apply the basics of the POR to a client you have seen or are seeing. Break down the factors in the case into either the SOAP or SOAPIE format.

3. When working with a client and gathering information, what is PHI, and how should it be handled?

4. Take a problem that a client could face and describe how you would approach it utilizing:
   Solution-focused therapy
   Cognitive-behavioral therapy
   Crisis intervention
   Educative counseling
   Interpersonal therapy

5. Compare and contrast the different types of therapy in handling clients.

6. Describe strategies you should use to protect client records and minimize your risk of legal action.

APPLICATIONS
Selected
DSM-IV-TR
Disorders

5 Overview of Selected Childhood Disorders: The Disruptive Behavior Disorders

SOPHIA F. DZIEGIELEWSKI AND SHIRLEYANN AMOS

Over the last few years there has been increased interest in causes, correlates, and factors related to child and adolescent mental health. This increased attention comes as no surprise as mental health can affect every area of an individual's functioning as well as that of the family. Disruptions in personal and peer-related activities can become commonplace, and disruptions to the family system and school functions can create situations that require immediate attention (Hinshaw, 2008). Disruptive behaviors in general can lead to "serious impairments in such crucial life domains as academic achievement, interpersonal competencies, and independent living skills" (p. 4).

When working with children and adolescents who suffer from mental illness, completing a proper diagnostic assessment must include many factors. Since children and adolescents are deemed vulnerable populations, special attention to protect them in the diagnostic assessment and clinical practice is warranted (Spetie & Arnold, 2007). Most mental health professionals acknowledge a need for increased research into the mental health needs of children and adolescents as well as increased access to mental health services. Researchers and clinicians who work with children and adolescents continue to strive to provide more inclusive information on effective mental health strategies (Beauchaine & Hinshaw, 2008).

It is beyond the purpose of this chapter to explore all of the diagnoses commonly applied to children. Rather, the purpose of this chapter is to introduce the reader to the primary disruptive behavior disorders: attention-deficit hyperactivity disorder (ADHD), oppositional defiant disorder (ODD), and conduct disorder (CD). These disorders remain some of the most common mental health disorders diagnosed in children. Discussion focuses on possible intervention and treatment planning that can best benefit the child as well as his or her family. The application section of this chapter focuses on what is considered the most severe of the disruptive behavior disorders, conduct disorder. The extent, importance, and the early predictors of problem behaviors and symptoms are explored. The various aspects of the disorder are presented with a case application that highlights the multiaxial diagnostic assessment, treatment planning, and evidence-based treatment strategy.

CHILDREN ARE NOT LITTLE ADULTS

When it comes to working with children and adolescents who may have a mental disorder, it is critical to emphasize that children should not be assessed as if they are simply small adults. Applying adult-based assessment strategy and theories directly to children or adolescents presents a challenge for many mental health practitioners (Prout, 2007). Developmental, social, and behavioral responses, peer influences, and influences of the family system make children and adolescents different from adults. This difference requires a comprehensive and creative approach to completing the diagnostic assessment and subsequent therapy. Consequently, each revision of the *DSM* has put forth more diagnostic criteria that take into account the developmental issues related to children and adolescents (Grills-Taquechel & Ollendick, 2008).

When looking specifically at individual behavior, developmentally the debate continues about the role of "nature" and "nurture" and how this affects child and adolescent behavior (Beauchaine, Hinshaw & Gatzke-Kopp, 2008). Given the mutual interdependence of these two factors and how genetic influences relate to environmental, to assess one without the other falls short of what is needed to complete a comprehensive diagnostic assessment. The childhood disorders outlined in this chapter are based on social and behavioral responses. These disruptive behavior disorders typically consist of diagnoses that contain distinguishing characteristics such as inattention, impulsivity, oppositional defiance, and aggressive behaviors. These difficult-to-control behaviors make these disruptive behaviors the most frequent reason children and adolescents are referred for services (Woo & Keatinge, 2008). Therefore, CD, ODD, and ADHD are disorders that are typically found in adolescents with social maladaptive behaviors.

Kearney, Cook, Wechsler, Haight, and Stowman (2008) believe that a behavioral assessment is the most important aspect of evaluation. The behavioral assessment starts with identifying the types of behavior that can be clearly defined and monitored over time. Characteristically, the behaviors exhibited within these diagnoses may at times coexist with overlapping features. This fact further complicates the behavioral assessment and the ability to make a clear diagnostic

impression. Furthermore, factors that complicate child development are ongoing, such as experiencing trauma as in childhood maltreatment (Wekerle, MacMillan, Leung, & Jamieson, 2008). Maltreatment in childhood increases the risk for the development of almost every disorder listed in the *DSM*, especially those related to mood, attention, and stress (Perry, 2008). Completing a behavioral assessment is further complicated by the subjective interpretation of the child's behaviors and how the behaviors exhibited are interpreted or possibly misinterpreted by the practitioner. Furthermore, could the age of the child complicate the way behaviors are interpreted? For example, what can be said about the level of understanding and comprehension of a 4-year-old (Lemke, 2006)?

Social factors that can influence a child or adolescent's behavior include peer relations, and how the perceptions of others within their peer-group can sway the child's perception of self and subsequent behavior in response to such influences. Other environmental aspects, such as unintentional injury, can affect the child's perception of self or social functioning (Faust & Stewart, 2008; Schwebel & Gaines, 2007; Zielinski & Bradshaw, 2006). Aggression, shyness, and a combination of low self-esteem and poor concentration are just some frequently seen behaviors. Children should have opportunities to develop the coping skills required for adjustment and adaptation to the world around them. Many normal behaviors that reflect conflict, lack of control, and opposition patterns may be mistaken for psychopathology by parents, school systems, and mental health professionals (Maxmen, Ward, & Kilgus, 2009).

Medication Use: When Should It Be a Critical Component of Treatment?

Over the years, concerns related to child and adolescent mental health treatment focusing on medication as a central component have intensified (Cooper et al., 2006; Noggle & Dean, 2009; Thomas, Conrad, Casler, & Goodman, 2006). It has become increasingly important for all helping professionals who work with children to become aware of the behavioral, cognitive, and physiological effects medications can have on children. It is not uncommon, especially when working in a school setting, to be expected to assist children who are taking medications. When medications are involved, the expectation is for the mental health professional to consult with other professionals and help make decisions about the use of medications or the modification of current medication-based treatment schemes (Dziegielewski, 2010).

Roemmelt (1998) and Woolston (1999) warned that addressing mental health conditions in children and adolescents by depending primarily on medications can disguise what the child is really experiencing and give parents and professionals a false sense of control that limits normal childhood development. Also, there is little information related to the subjective experience of these children and adolescents and whether they understand their illness or what the medications are designed to do (Floersch et al., 2009). Therefore, it is imperative, especially when medications are used as part of the treatment regime, to tread cautiously when assessing and treating the problems and disorders presented by children and adolescents and to utilize a team approach involving all the systems a child/adolescent is exposed to, including school, family system, and other providers.

Taking the Family System Into Account

It is the child's parents or guardians who generally determine such treatment issues as the duration of treatment and medication intervention. They are also the ones who select, arrange, and pay for the child's treatment experience (Bromfield, 2007). Therefore, parents or primary caretakers strongly influence the mental health process. This influence begins during the assessment phase and continues through the termination phase. Parents who do not fully understand or accept the value of counseling can change or terminate services for the child. For this reason, it is essential for practitioners to include parents or caregivers in the diagnostic assessment to ensure that they understand what is being completed and the results that are obtained. For example, if a child's family is not supportive of mental health treatment, the child learns not to ask for help (Dziegielewski, Leon, & Green, 1998). Oftentimes compliance issues emerge in relation to the parents' own perceptions of the diagnostic label and fears related to having this type of stigma placed on their child. Furthermore, parents' perceptions of the illness can affect how they support the child. When looking specifically at medication as part of the treatment, Gau et al. (2006) reported that tense parent-child interactions that are not properly addressed can result in poor compliance with physician-ordered medication use.

Utilizing a Cultural Lens

Since culture is the lens through which we view children and adolescents, "it provides the framework used to label, categorize and make sense of childhood development and behaviors" (Johnson & Tucker, 2008, p. 789). Therefore, the lack of culturally competent services can complicate treatment for those who seek mental health support within the context of their family, cultural beliefs, and community (Pumariega, Rogers, & Rothe, 2005). Johnson (1998) identified various steps that facilitate use of the *DSM-IV-TR* more effectively with minority children. He believed that cultural and ethnic factors can influence the manifestation of symptoms in children similar to the way they affect adults. This makes identification central to understanding how the child has acculturated to his or her environment and to mainstream society. Assessing acculturation and racial issues, and how they relate to symptom formation, can be better explained by taking into account information related directly to the appendix of culture-bound syndromes provided by the *DSM-IV-TR*.

Culture-bound syndromes identify any recurrent, aberrant behavior that is locality specific and not included in Western diagnostic nosology (Smith & Hughes, 1993). Utilizing the culture-bound syndromes to help explain behavior can help the practitioner understand and anticipate what might otherwise be seen as extreme forms of cultural expression. Using this classification scheme can help the practitioner to avoid incorrectly labeling behaviors as pathological or dysfunctional (Dziegielewski, 2010). Two examples of culture-bound syndromes identified in children are brain fag (American Psychiatric Association [APA], 2000, p. 900) and mal de ojo, or evil eye (APA, p. 901). According to the *DSM-IV-TR*, brain fag is a syndrome found among West African adolescents who react to school pressures. The symptoms are primarily somatic in nature and include blurred vision, neck and head pain, difficulty concentrating, and an overall sense of "brain tiredness." With increased pressure placed on children in the United States on test performance, this phenomenon warrants further attention. A careful evaluation to the actual cause of the depression or anxiety a child experiences should always be performed. When the pressure is great, and it becomes part of a child's ethnic identity, performing well becomes an expectation that some children may find hard to meet.

A second culture-bound syndrome for consideration is mal de ojo (the evil eye). This is a syndrome affecting many children in Caribbean and Mediterranean cultures. The belief is that, due to their physical and psychological vulnerabilities, children and infants are at high risk or serve as receptacles for evil thoughts or wishes intended for adult members of the family. Symptoms in this syndrome include disruptive sleep, crying without cause, vomiting, diarrhea, or fevers.

These are only two of the identified syndromes. What is most important to remember is that children are always part of a family system and do not operate in a vacuum. Recognizing cultural influences and belief systems is central to culturally sound practice (Canino & Spurlock, 1994; Thorens, Gex-Fabry, Zullino, & Eytan, 2008).

In summary, parental perceptions and contributions to care, as well as cultural factors that influence treatment, can be magnified when combined with other family issues and general life stressors. Divorce and family adjustments can clearly interfere with any treatment strategy as well as the short- and long-term development of the child (Johnston, Roseby, & Kuehnle, 2009). Family changes and stressors add to what children and adolescents—already presenting with a rich, complex, and evolving biopsychosocial picture—experience. This makes it essential for all professionals to recognize that these clients are an ongoing "work-in-progress" (McAdoo, 1997). Children are continuously developing and learning to understand their minds, bodies, emotions, and social patterns. Often children and adolescents feel they have little control over their lives. Just offering small choices can help the mental health practitioner to connect with the child and start the therapeutic process (Shapiro, Friedberg, & Bardenstein, 2006). When starting the diagnostic interview, for example, simply asking children where they want to sit, followed by whether they understand the purpose of the visit, can help them to feel a part of the process.

CHILDHOOD AND ADOLESCENT DISORDERS: ASSESSING MENTAL HEALTH FACTORS

The *Diagnostic and Statistical Manual for Mental Disorders (DSM-IV-TR)* is an important assessment tool used by social work practitioners. It includes certain diagnostic categories applicable to children and others that should be used with caution. There are some developmental differences that prevent the use of certain diagnostic codes with children (APA, 2000). Goldman (1998) proposes a quick and practical schema that allows the practitioner to apply *DSM-IV-TR* diagnoses to children. He proposes that the clinician first confirm the full criteria in the *DSM-IV-TR* and then consider these questions:

- **Where does the problem originate?** Distinguish between problems generated within the child, such as a mental health condition like ADHD, and problems that originate within the child's environment. Environmental concerns can include relationship problems with parents, siblings, peers, or adults in authority; problems related to abuse or neglect; or other conditions, such as antisocial behavior, academic problems, identity problems, acculturation problems, phase-of-life problems, or school-related difficulties.

- **Is the child's problem a reaction to a specific and identifiable stressor?** Once environmental problems are identified, special attention is given to determine what the stressor is that influences problem occurrence. If the stressor is clear, the social worker can use this information to rule out or defer specific mental health disorders such as adjustment disorders and posttraumatic stress disorders.

- **What are the basic areas affected and impaired by the problem?** How does this affect the child's school, home, or social play functioning? Goldman (1998) suggests the practitioner should distinguish among behavioral, mood, and dissociative disorders when answering this question.

- **Do the symptoms interfere with functioning, and are they reflective of long-standing difficulties?** Although many times it is too early to determine if a problematic behavior has the potential to be considered life-long, the practitioner still needs to be aware when observing behavioral characteristics identifying the behaviors that have the potential to continue into adulthood. If these behaviors continue to exist from childhood and beyond the teen years, they may be reflective of *DSM-IV-TR* Axis II and the personality disorders, which are usually diagnosed in young adults (approximately 21 years or older). These personality disorders often originate in childhood or adolescence and, when officially diagnosed in young adulthood, can continue to interfere with a person's social and occupational functioning (APA, 2000).

Maximizing Measurement

Today, health and mental health funding often focuses on discovering effective evidence-based practices. The MacArthur Foundation's Child System and Treatment Enhancement Projects (Child STEPs) have funded studies that identify "leverage points for, and barriers to, the adoption and implementation of evidence-based practices" in children's mental health services (Schoenwald, Kelleher, & Weisz, 2008, p. 66). Despite this increased attention, there is still much to be learned about mental health problems, effective counseling strategies, and patterns of medication use of children and adolescents (Dziegielewski, 2010). For example, children may not exhibit signs of depression in the same way as adults. Adults who are depressed might present as tearful and sad whereas adolescents often appear irritable, angry, and aggressive (Noggle & Dean, 2009). When symptoms are difficult to recognize and treat, practitioners can become frustrated, which may push them toward recommending medications to assist with these angry outbursts. During the last decade, this emphasis on both understanding the childhood psychiatric disorders and developing the evidence-based pharmacological and psychosocial treatments has been at an all-time high (Walkup et al., 2009).

LeCroy and Okamoto (2009) believe the most critical aspect for completing any child assessment is getting direct information from the child as well as seeking information from other sources in the child's environment. Practitioners can record and interpret the symptoms presented by children and can take note of environmental circumstances and how they influence the treatment process. To identify high-risk patterns, it is best to investigate functioning through examination of multiple domains utilizing multiple levels of analysis (Cicchetti, 2008). To facilitate a comprehensive assessment, practitioners must be aware of the various types of instruments that can assist with interpretation throughout the helping process.

The increase of time pressures—and the emphasis on rapid assessment and treatment—has forced mental health practitioners to shorten the length of biopsychosocial assessments to include only salient information on the child's past and current mental health functioning. This makes the assessment critical and forces practitioners to identify the significant aspects of the child's presenting problems and

the specific behaviors and circumstances of his or her impaired functioning. To facilitate the diagnostic assessment process, various self-report or rapid assessment instruments (RAIs) and other diagnostic tools are often used. The number of child-focused assessment and diagnostic instruments continues to grow and contribute to better evidence-based approaches. Shapiro, Friedberg, and Bardenstein (2006, pp. 245–246) compare these techniques to a "palette of colors that clinicians select, combine, and blend to paint their pictures of therapy with individual clients." These REIs can assist in all types of therapeutic settings especially when used in conjunction with the play therapy experience designed to decrease problematic behaviors (Baggerly, 2009). It is beyond the scope of this chapter to present criteria for using specific measurement instruments with children, but several texts are available that provide more information in this area. See Grigorenko (2009) for multicultural psychoeducational assessment strategy and Shapiro et al. (2006) for general mental health assessment with children and adolescents.

To facilitate an accurate and complete assessment of the child's behaviors, specific and behavior-focused information must be recorded. This information is needed for a complete assessment:

1. The problem presented by the child.
2. Behaviors that demonstrate the problem.
3. The intensity, frequency, duration, and specific environmental circumstances accompanying the problem.
4. Areas affected by the problem.
5. Previous coping skills and problem-solving methods used.
6. Any previous and current medication and counseling interventions prescribed.
7. Cultural factors affecting treatment compliance (Dziegielewski, 2010).

Gender Considerations

Gardner, Pajer, Kelleher, Scholle, and Wasserman (2002) reported that gender can also influence assessment and treatment. These researchers reported substantial gender differences in the way primary care professionals diagnose and treat mental disorders in children and adolescents. For example, girls with ADHD are more likely to present the inattentive symptoms of the disorder, while boys more often display overt learning and behavioral impairments that cause them to engage in disruptive classroom behavior. Since boys have more obvious symptoms, they are more readily diagnosed with CD and ODD. Therefore, girls may experience gender-based referral biases based on their lack of overt functional impairment even though both genders require the same type of treatment. This lack of recognition could adversely affect girls who suffer from ADHD (Biederman et al., 2002).

In assessing children, careful attention should be paid not to make general assumptions based on adult guidelines. Gender should always be taken into account in terms of how a child or adolescent presents in the clinical setting. Multiple factors can contribute to differences in symptoms and presenting problems among children, adolescents, and adults in the manifestation of psychological and emotional difficulties. A comprehensive assessment needs to include significant information on the specific behavioral, emotional, and psychological problems presented by children. The accuracy of this information will help the health care team, including the physician prescriber, to determine the nature of the child's mental disorder and whether medication therapy is indeed warranted.

Inclusion of Collateral Contacts

Another significant factor in the assessment and treatment of children and adolescents is the importance of information from collateral contacts, who include parents, the school system, the community, and other informants who can provide vital information pertaining to the child's difficulties and impact the treatment process (Dziegielewski, 2010). This process necessitates eliciting and incorporating feedback from these individuals in order to complete a comprehensive assessment of the child in his or her current environment (LeCroy & Okamoto, 2009). Last, to provide a comprehensive assessment, it is important to assess parents' knowledge and expectations of what constitutes "normal" behavior for a child of their child's age. Some parents may not understand what is considered normal development or behavior for a specific age, which may complicate their own expectations and any reported treatment gains (Wodarski & Dziegielewski, 2002).

ATTENTION-DEFICIT HYPERACTIVITY DISORDER

Attention-deficit hyperactivity disorder is one of the most common psychiatric diagnoses in childhood (Baldwin et al., 2004; Vaughan, Roberts, & Needelman, 2009). Estimates of prevalence range from 3% to 7% of school-age children (APA, 2000), to as high as 7% to 12% (Woodruff, et al., 2004). Many children are referred to health and mental health facilities for ADHD-like symptoms. Biederman (2003) estimates the incidence of ADHD in children to be slightly higher (4% to 12% of school-age children) when compared to 2% to 4% of adults. Froehlich and colleagues (2007) reported that poor children are more likely than wealthy children to meet the criteria for ADHD yet are less likely to receive expected medication treatment. They also reported that girls are less likely than boys to be diagnosed with ADHD even though they meet the *DSM-IV-TR* criteria. ADHD also seems to run in families. When one or more family members suffer from it, the incidence for occurrence in an individual is also higher. It is believed that ADHD starts in childhood and continues on into adulthood. If an individual is diagnosed in adulthood, it is expected that the symptoms originated in childhood but carried on into adulthood (WebMD, 2009a).

When present, ADHD can constitute a chronic neurobiological condition characterized by developmentally inappropriate attention skills, impulsivity, and/or hyperactivity (APA, 2000). This is a change from *DSM-III* (1980), where the disorder was termed attention deficit disorder (ADD) with two subtypes, with and without hyperactivity. Therefore, it is no surprise that some professionals and the lay public still use the term ADD to describe this condition. In *DSM-III-R* (1987), this term was eliminated and renamed ADHD. In *DSM-IV* (1994), the term ADHD was maintained but the subtypes were reintroduced in a modified form.

In current practice, ADHD is defined in the *DSM-IV-TR* (p. 85) as "a persistent pattern of inattention and/or hyperactivity-impulsivity that is more frequently displayed and more severe than is typically observed in individuals at a comparable level of development (Criterion A)". The *DSM-IV* and the *DSM-IV-TR* divides ADHD into three subtypes: (1) Attention-Deficit/Hyperactivity Disorder, Predominantly Inattentive (314.00); (2) Attention-Deficit/Hyperactivity Disorder, Predominantly Hyperactive-Impulsive Type (314.01); and (3) Attention-Deficit/Hyperactivity Disorder, Predominately Combined Type (314.01). Criterion B involves the age of onset for the diagnosis, where the child will generally have symptoms severe enough to cause impairment before the age of 7. In other cases, especially inattentive type, if the symptoms persist for a number of years, ADHD can still be diagnosed at a later age.

Criterion C states that some impairment must be present in at least two settings. Generally these settings include home and at school, or other places the child attends daily. The disorder must also manifest with clear evidence of how the functioning level is impaired thereby preventing developmentally appropriate, social, or occupational functioning. In selecting the proper and most relevant diagnosis for a client, other similar diagnoses need to be considered and appropriately ruled out. Similar to other diagnoses, the symptoms indicative of ADHD should not occur exclusively during the course of another disorder. Conditions that may present similarly at first but should not be the cause of the ADHD are symptoms related to a pervasive developmental disorder, schizophrenia, and other psychotic disorders. Also, the symptoms being exhibited should not be accounted for by another mental disorder, such as the mood disorders, the anxiety disorders, dissociative disorder, or a personality disorder (APA, 2000). Furthermore, children with ADHD often can have other comorbid diagnoses, such as the learning disorders, ODD, as well as symptoms related to anxiety and depression (Vaughan, Roberts, & Needelman, 2009).

When looking specifically at the predominantly inattentive type, this category is most like the older classification of ADD without hyperactivity. The child with the inattentive type often has trouble concentrating. This may manifest in difficulty maintaining attention in academic or social settings. It is not uncommon for the child with attention difficulties to perform poorly in school, although often teachers say that they are not sure why the child is having trouble as the child appears academically capable. If the child's attention is captured, he or she may get an A grade; if not, a dramatic shift to the F grade may result if the teacher cannot capture the child's attention. When the attention of the child is distracted he or she may be unable to complete the expected activities. In the hyperactive-impulsive type, the child suffers from problems with inattention but it is often the signs of hyperactivity and impulsivity that seem to cause the most problems for the child.

Although the causes of ADHD are still under investigation, there is widespread agreement that the validity of the disorder is clearly linked to how well the characteristics of the disorder are identified and how the impairment noted is related to familial patterns and influences (Faraone et al., 2005). Both theory and research have focused on neurochemical, anatomical, and genetic factors (Riccio, Hynd, Cohen, & Gonzalez, 1993). Some researchers (Lerner, Lowenthal, & Lerner, 1995) have suggested that ADHD may be caused by a chemical imbalance or deficiency in the area of the brain that is responsible for attention and response-related activity. Regardless of the exact cause, Nigg and Nikolas (2008) believe that major changes are needed in this category and adapting a dimensional approach in the *DSM-5* may help to address this current shortfall.

Since ADHD can originate in childhood and continue into adulthood, pharmacological treatments for both children and adults are often considered the treatment of choice (Adler et al., 2009). It is believed that stimulant medication is the most effective treatment for ADHD as it reduces the primary symptoms, such as hyperactivity, impulsivity, and inattention (Vaughan et al., 2009). Clinical management of medication treatment, however, is complicated. Some primary complications include patient and parent acceptance, individual variations in responses, and balancing stimulant efficacy with adverse effects (Olfson, Marcus, & Wan, 2009). The two types of medications most commonly used to treat ADHD include stimulants and antidepressants, which address the neurochemical imbalances thought to precipitate the symptoms (Anastopoulos, 1999; Greydanus, Nazeer, & Patel, 2009). Stimulants, which include Ritalin (methylphenidate) and

Dexedrine (d-amphetamine), are the most commonly used and have the best evidence-based support for the management of ADHD (Greydanus, Nazeer, & Patel, 2009). Antidepressants are generally considered second-line treatments.

Stimulants help children pay attention, stay calm, and follow instructions. For simplicity, it is easiest to classify stimulant medications into three areas: traditional short- and intermediate-acting stimulants, long-acting stimulants, and nonstimulants. The short- and intermediate-acting stimulants, such as Ritalin, are administered two to three times a day (Biederman, 2003). The effects of Ritalin generally last from 3 to 7 hours (Anastopoulos, 1999). This medication is available in tablet and capsule form and can be purchased in doses of 5, 10, or 15 mg. When used to treat ADHD, Ritalin and other stimulants need to be taken on a regular basis, and the prescriber should be contacted before the medication is adjusted (Kent, Blader, Koplewicz, Abikoff, & Foley, 1995).

The problem with clearly diagnosing ADHD is that it appears to be more than just one condition with several phenotypes, and it cannot be addressed in isolation (Nigg & Nikolas, 2008). Multiple factors shape the identification of the disorder. Consistent with this view, research supports the implications that family environment and parental style can be a key influence to the resulting behaviors of ADHD. Emphasis needs to be placed on distinguishing the partial independence of ADHD with other conditions, such as aggression and anxiety disorders. Comprehensive information is needed to make sure the possible subtypes are identified or else the practitioner may misattribute risk factors, underlying etiologic mechanisms, follow-up status, or treatment response patterns to ADHD, when these features more accurately pertain to other dimensions or disorders (Hinshaw, 1994; Nigg & Nikolas, 2008).

Children with ADHD present with many different types of symptoms, most of which are behavioral and cognitive in nature. According to Anastopoulos (1999), the clinical picture of ADHD is blurred by five factors: (1) the wide range of assessment instruments with varying levels of reliability and validity; (2) the fluctuation of ADHD symptoms dependent on specific situations; (3) the amount of structure provided in each situation; (4) the existence of comorbid conditions such as conduct disorders and learning disabilities; and (5) changes in living situations as well as parenting methods and styles.

In terms of counseling treatment, multiple forms are available. Most are offered on an individual basis to the child or adolescent suffering from ADHD. The intent is to improve problem solving and develop skills that will assist the child to concentrate on daily tasks, such as schoolwork or chores in the home (Jensen, 2004). Problem Solving Skills Training (PSST) is one of the cognitive-behavioral approaches that can teach children to define a problem, identify goals, generate and choose the best option, and discuss and determine the best outcomes (Seligman & Reichenberg, 2007). (Sample Treatment Plans 5.1 and 5.2 are designed to assist the practitioner to work with this type of disorder.)

SAMPLE TREATMENT PLAN 5.1

ATTENTION-DEFICIT HYPERACTIVITY DISORDER, PREDOMINANTLY HYPERACTIVE-IMPULSIVE TYPE

Definition: A disorder that becomes apparent in childhood, must be present before the age of 7, and is characterized by excessive motor activity as well as poor impulse control of emotional and physical behaviors.

Signs and Symptoms to Note in the Record:

- Inability to remain seated for an extended period of time.
- Excessive fidgeting.
- Excessive talking/noise.
- Blurting out of answers/inability to think before speaking/inability to raise hand and wait to be called on.
- Frequent interruption of conversations, activities, etc.
- Frequent accidents.

Goals:

- Client will take medication as prescribed by psychiatrist.
- Client will improve impulse control.
- Caretakers will set firm and consistent limits and reinforce positive behaviors of the child.
- Client will improve self-esteem.

Objectives:

- Parents will insure that medication is being taken in appropriate dosage and at specified times.
- Child will increase awareness of disruptive/impulsive behavior at home and in the classroom.
- Parents and teachers will establish and implement rules and limitations for child.
- Parents and teachers will decide on and implement consequences for inappropriate behaviors of the child.
- Parents and teachers will positively reinforce appropriate behaviors of the child.
- Child will improve self-confidence, self-regard, and self-worth.

Interventions:

- Client will adhere to a daily routine of taking prescribed medications as established by parents.
- Parents and teachers will develop a system responsible for immediately alerting the client to impulsive or off-task behaviors (i.e., attention training system) at home or in school.
- Assist parents and teachers in determining clear rules and boundaries for the client, and responsibilities of the client.
- Develop natural and meaningful consequences for noncompliance with rules.
- Utilize verbal praise to reward compliance with rules and appropriate behaviors.
- Increase the client's frequency of positive self-statements.
- Client will identify things that he or she does well.

SAMPLE TREATMENT PLAN 5.2

ATTENTION-DEFICIT HYPERACTIVITY DISORDER, PREDOMINANTLY INATTENTIVE TYPE

Definition: A disorder that becomes apparent in childhood, must be present before the age of 7, and is characterized by an inability to maintain focus/concentration, an inability to complete tasks, and poor organization skills.

Signs and Symptoms to Note in the Record:

- Inability to follow through on assignments/tasks from beginning to end.
- Inattention to detail/often makes careless mistakes.
- Loses interest in activities/frequent shifting of focus from one project to another without completion.
- Messy working space/area.
- Dislike of activities that require sustained attention.

Goals:

- Client will take medication as prescribed by psychiatrist.
- Client will increase attention/concentration span.
- Client will adhere to firm limits as established by parents and teachers.
- Client will increase self-esteem.

Objectives:

- Parents will insure that medication is being taken in appropriate dosage and at specified times.
- Client will maintain attention to activities for increasing intervals of time.
- Therapist will introduce and help the client utilize self-monitoring techniques to help client stay on task.
- Parents and teachers will establish and implement rules and consequences for the child.
- Parents and teachers will positively reinforce appropriate behaviors of the child.
- Client will improve self-confidence and self-worth.

Interventions:

- Child will adhere to a daily routine of taking medications as established by parents.
- Assist parents and child in developing a routine schedule of child's chores and assignments to be completed each day, and the time frame in which each is to be completed.

(continued)

SAMPLE TREATMENT PLAN 5.2 *(Continued)*

- Make recreational activities contingent on completion of daily assignment while systematically increasing the length of time required to complete such tasks.
- Introduce the client to a nondisruptive, self-repeating tape of tones that regularly reminds the client to ask him- or herself, "Am I working on my assigned task?"
- Assist the parents in determining clear rules for the child and developing a system of natural consequences for inappropriate behaviors.
- Utilize verbal praise to reward compliance with rules.
- Utilize a reward system to reinforce on-task behaviors and completion of tasks at home and in the classroom.
- Client will list, recognize, and focus on strengths, and utilize these in interpersonal relationships.

OPPOSITIONAL DEFIANT DISORDER AND CONDUCT DISORDER

Children and adolescents who persistently break important social roles put themselves at risk of incurring serious consequences, such as incarceration and violent death (Moffitt, Caspi, Rutter, & Silva, 2001). This type of antisocial behavior can also put others at risk from loss of property, violence, and in its most serious form, death by homicide (Loeber et al., 2005). In the *DSM-IV* and the *DSM-IV-TR*, two diagnoses are directly relevant to this type of problematic antisocial behavior in youths. In human growth and development, the early years can present a particularly sensitive time. In childhood, children must learn the importance of following the rules and the consequences for breaking them. Behavioral control and self-evaluative skills are central to learning how to comply and internalize these rules (Petitclerc, Boivin, Dionne, Zoccolillo, & Tremblay, 2009). It is believed that children with ODD and CD possess deficits in developing discrete skill sets that can lead to oppositional types of behavioral responses (Hamilton & Armando, 2008). Since resistance to these rules can be developmentally

appropriate and often occur in the preschool years, distinguishing between what is normal behaviors and what is beyond what can be expected can be a diagnostic challenge (Hamilton & Armando, 2008). When looking specifically at young children, it has been estimated that within samples of children ages 2 to 5 years, as many as 4% to 8% would meet the criteria for ODD and approximately 4% could meet the criteria for CD (Egger & Angold, 2006).

The first diagnosis in this area is usually considered the less severe, termed *ODD*. Oppositional defiant disorder is one of the most commonly diagnosed mental health conditions in childhood (Hamilton & Armando, 2008). Exhibited behaviors are considered developmentally inappropriate, and the recurrent nature of these negativistic behaviors can be particularly problematic for those individuals expected to teach and set appropriate limits with the child. In this disorder there is a clear pattern of negative, hostile, and defiant behavior with at least four or more symptoms (see Quick Reference 5.1). These behaviors have to be constant and beyond what would be expected of other youth at a similar developmental age.

QUICK REFERENCE 5.1

OPPOSITIONAL DEFIANT DISORDER

DEFINITION

A pattern of negativistic and hostile behavior, lasting at least 6 months, where four or more of the following are present:

1. Often loses temper.
2. Often argues with adults.
3. Often actively defies or refuses to comply with adult's requests or rules.
4. Often deliberately annoys people.
5. Often blames others for his or her mistakes or behaviors.
6. Is often touchy or easily annoyed by others.
7. Is often angry and resentful.
8. Is often spiteful and vindictive.

Similar to other diagnoses, the behavior needs to cause clinical significant impairment in social, academic, or occupational functioning.

The behaviors cannot occur at the same time as another mental disorder, such as a psychotic or a mood disorder

Criteria for CD are not met, and if older than age 20, criteria are not met for antisocial personality disorder.

Source: Summarized criteria from the *Diagnostic and Statistical Manual of Mental Disorders, Fourth Edition, Text Revision.* Copyright 2000 by the American Psychiatric Association.

The behaviors must be present for at least six months, and as with all diagnoses, it remains important to make sure that the resulting behaviors are not caused by another mental disorder, such as psychosis, a mood disorder, or other type of mental disorder. Also, all behaviors must be severe enough to influence social and academic functioning (APA, 2000).

Lahey (2008) warns that some researchers feel the criteria in the *DSM-IV-TR* are somewhat arbitrary and are concerned that it be made clear that youth do not suddenly shift from normality to abnormality when four of the needed criteria identified in Quick Reference 5.1 are met. Rather they believe that the emphasis should be placed on the more serious the behaviors exhibited by the child and when these behaviors result in serious consequences that can harm others.

CONDUCT DISORDER

The second disruptive behavior disorder in this area is termed conduct disorder. When compared to ODD, this diagnosis is considered more severe. Furthermore, the earlier the onset of ODD and the more severe the behaviors associated with it, the poorer the long-term prognosis. Most practitioners agree that previously diagnosed ODD that leads to CD has a poor prognosis and a complicated treatment strategy (Hamilton & Armando, 2008).

Conduct disorder is a diagnosis first made during childhood or adolescence and can result in barriers to individual and social functioning. Since first being introduced in the *DSM-III*, the diagnosis of CD continues to raise many questions for practitioners. Yet researchers continue to validate the application of *DSM-IV* and

DSM-IV-TR criteria. The greatest concern lies in the problems that can occur when trying to identify and define problematic behaviors and symptoms for children before and in preschool. In addition, continued concerns remain regarding the negative impact that placing this diagnosis can have on children. Placing a diagnosis of this type often results in a negative diagnostic label for the child, a label that may continue into adulthood. When the symptoms persist, the diagnosis would most likely be changed to antisocial personality disorder when the child reaches age 21. In a recent study, however, designed to examine when this diagnosis was given to children and adolescents involved with the legal system, no negative ramifications were found that negatively affected the judicial decisions made (Murrie, Boccaccini, McCoy, & Cornell, 2007).

Incidence and Prevalence of Conduct Disorder

What is the extent and importance of conduct problems or conduct disorders? More than 3 million children suffer from ADHD. An estimated 20% of children diagnosed with ADHD also have CD, and a significant number of children with ADHD also exhibit conduct problems and may later development CD. Conduct disorder can occur in preschoolers. When it does, it requires immediate and appropriate intervention to prevent educational and behavioral difficulties from escalating. Also, severe conduct problems or CD affects nearly 4% to 10% of children and adolescents.

Conduct disorder is one of the most frequently encountered diagnoses in mental health settings with one-third to one-half of children and adolescents suffering from mental health disorders presenting with these symptoms (Kazdin, 2002). They account for close to half of all referrals to mental health clinics. These children

have an increased risk for both juvenile delinquency and adult criminality. Children with severe conduct problems are likely to go on to have aggressive children, in this manner perpetuating these deviant patterns across generations. Therefore, CD in childhood, adolescence, and adults is a significant and costly problem to society since it can result in fighting, stealing, victimization, criminal behavior, unemployment, and substance use. Approximately 10% to 25% of those diagnosed develop substance-related problems (Barkley, 2006). The earlier the treatment and intervention, the better the chances are for the infant or child to understand and emulate acceptable behavior. There is already substantial evidence that the conduct symptoms of the *DSM-IV-TR* can be reliably applied and validly assessed in 2- to 5-year-old children (Keenan & Wakschlag, 2002, 2002; Kim-Cohen et al., 2005; Keenan et al., 2007).

Conduct disorder was first included in the *DSM-III* (APA, 1980). In *DSM-IV* and *DSM-IV-TR*, the age of onset of antisocial symptoms was added and is now used to subtype conduct disorder. Childhood-onset CD requires that at least one criterion characteristic (1 of 15 antisocial behaviors) is present before age 10 years; if the first antisocial behavior occurs at or after 10 years, the case is classified as adolescent onset (APA, 1994). The adoption of this subclassification in the *DSM-IV* was stimulated by reports of differences between early- and adolescent-onset cases, suggesting different causal pathways.

Children can start out with one disorder and advance to another such as CD especially when they already have ODD and ADHD or if they suffer from neuropsychological deficits, academic failures, poor school attendance, or family disadvantage. The *DSM-IV-TR* describes the difference between ODD and subsequent development of childhood-onset type of CD by explaining that those with CD have a persistent pattern of more serious forms of behavior, such as violating basic rights of others or age-appropriate societal norms or rules (Gelhorn et al., 2006). Childhood-onset and adolescent-onset subtypes have been enthusiastically embraced.

Gender can be a powerful predictor especially when found in the varying types of conduct problems. For example, when the disorder is considered childhood-onset, the cases identified are more likely to be males when compared to adolescent-onset cases. These males are also more aggressive and also more likely to have ADHD disorder. In addition, boys more commonly display confrontational aggression whereas girls tend to use more nonconfrontational behaviors. In boys, problematic behaviors such as frequently exhibiting fighting, stealing, vandalism, and school discipline problems are more common; whereas, girls are more likely to exhibit running away, substance use/abuse, truancy, lying, and prostitution (APA, 2000; Hartung & Widiger, 1998). Gender differences remain a crucial component for assessment in identifying CD behaviors (van Lier, van der Ende, Koot & Verhulst, 2007); and these conditions, especially in girls, can tend to be underdiagnosed because of the manifestation of aggression (Delligatti, Akin-Little, & Little, 2003).

Conduct Disorder: Factors Related to the Diagnostic Assessment

When looking specifically at diagnosing CD, most practitioners can agree that there is a "muddy" consensus as to what defines CD and how it will progress over time. Therefore, this remains a difficult diagnosis for researchers to study and confirm. To dispute the disagreements and support evidence-based conclusions, more research is needed that studies this disorder, and the children who suffer from it, over a continuous long-term period. Ongoing research of this type is vital to finding the actual etiology of this condition and to dispel concerns related to its ambiguous nature.

Practitioners completing the diagnostic assessment need to remain aware and understand the controversies surrounding placing such a diagnosis when utilizing the *DSM-IV* and *DSM-IV-TR* criteria. For example, clarity is needed in identifying and defining signs of aggression. Are the problematic behavioral acts reactive versus proactive, affective versus predatory, or hostile versus instrumental? Is the behavior the result of a direct action versus an indirect one? Is it done openly in an overt manner or secretively in a covert manner and hidden from others until randomly discovered by accident? Also, to avoid problems when identifying a client's aggressive and nonaggressive problematic behaviors, the practitioner should always try to determine the source and what is driving the aggression. Could there be an underlying cause for the problematic behavior? The identification and recognition of this cause may help to determine the best intervention to assist the client.

In addition to identifying the circumstances that surround acts of aggression, practitioners need to identify the risk as well as the protective factors that children with CD display. Identifying these risk factors sets the stage for determining who is most susceptible to developing CD. While developmentally expressing aggression may be a normal part of development, understanding what exceeds acceptable limits needs to be highlighted (Hamilton & Armando, 2008). Children, adolescents, and young adults with CD demonstrate behaviors that violate societal norms or the basic rights of others (Petitclerc et al., 2009). These negative behaviors can result from particular risk factors that have been noted to be precursors to CD. Numerous studies suggest children and youth exposed to a multitude of risk factors manifest symptoms that are the result of deficits in behavior and emotional functioning that were there already but not noticeable earlier (Keenan, et al., 2007). For example, witnessing family violence is such an important factor that in a study of children in foster care, 85% of school-age children in foster care or out-of home placement reported witnessing violence (Stein et al., 2001),

Keenan et al. (2007), summarizing other experts and researchers, report that taking into account the risk factors of development and environmental circumstances (i.e., the interactions of nature and nurture) can result in the following risk factors that lead to CD (see Quick Reference 5.2) A complete medical workup is always recommended, recognizing that neurochemical imbalances may result in cognitive delays or misperception of stimuli in the learning process.

QUICK REFERENCE 5.2

RISK FACTORS FOR CONDUCT DISORDER

- Biological factors such as genetics; abnormalities of prefrontal cortex; altered neurotransmitter function in the serotonergic, noradrenergic/dopaminergic systems; low cortisol; and elevated testosterone levels.
- Medical factors such as chronic illnesses, nutritional deficiencies, exposure to toxins, and cognitive delays.
- Individual psychological factors such as a lack of responsibility, problems processing information with underutilization of pertinent social clues, misattributing behaviors of others, generating few solutions to problems, and engaging in behaviors only if there is a reward expected.
- Behavioral functioning deficits include reading deficits, writing deficits, social problem-solving deficits, maladaptive peer relationships, temperament and control and moral reasoning problems, immaturity, excessive pleasure and sensation seeking behaviors, and association with a delinquent deviant peer group.
- Parental history—a history of mental health problems, substance abuse, maternal smoking during pregnancy, and if the child approaching puberty is depressed. Is there also a history of depression in the biological parents? Situational factors related to the parents include parental unemployment; high school drop-outs; marital discord; family history of criminal behavior and substance abuse; history of maltreatment (emotional neglect, sexual abuse, physical abuse, emotional abuse, physical neglect); witnessing violence; mother having children early (before completing high school); mother's or father's family of origin with coercive parenting behavior and family dysfunction.
- Family influences and concerns, such as familial factors that involve confrontational aggressive parent-child interactions, deficits in the caregiving environment, inconsistent and harsh discipline, young siblings in need of direction, family history of criminal behavior and substance abuse, victimization with physical/sexual/verbal abuse occurring in the home, ineffective communication, antisocial values, parents' failure to be involved in child's activities, not enough attention to prosocial behavior, and presence of firearms in the home, and family violence.
- Social and environmental factors such as poverty (e.g., children living under conditions of economic stress), lack of structure and high levels of stress, exposed to community violence, exposure to media violence, racial microaggression, and being a victim of physical/sexual/verbal abuse in the community.

Source: Information summarized from the work of Keenan et al. (2007) and others.

Negative interactions create pathways of behaviors exhibited in peer group, school, and other settings. Since one risk factor does not necessarily determine that a child or adolescent will have behavior problems, it is crucial for the practitioner to be aware that when the risk factors are combined, they magnify the potential for CD. This makes the development of protective factors, specifically personal characteristics that can help the child to avoid problematic behaviors essential. Once identified, these protective factors can interact with risk factors helping to improve outcomes for children and adolescents. Protective factors can also help to develop in the child increased levels of self-esteem and self-confidence. These children often have trouble controlling impulses and they need to develop mature characteristics, such as self-control. Once emotional control is enhanced, so is the ability to practice restraint. This helps children to develop greater ability for self-regulation and to address life issues with a deliberate, responsible intent engaging in behaviors reflective of accountability and responsibility.

There are multiple types of protective behaviors and one of the most important ones is making sure basic needs are met. This means that the family system is able to provide adequate food, shelter, clothing and medical care for the child. Other identified protective factors include developing resilience through peers who provide prosocial influences. Schools and other educational programs need to support the child and adolescent with services while providing advocacy, education, and skill building. The educational process needs to foster success, giving these children and adolescents the extra attention that may be needed to ensure that responsibility and self-discipline develop adequately.

Work with the family needs to involve helping to develop positive relationships within the family system (e.g., expressiveness and cohesion), where opportunities for personal growth are allowed to flourish. Children and adolescents need to develop a sense of independence while being allowed to question authority but not in a problematic, offensive, or defiant way. These children and adolescents, like all children, need the provision of structure. For those with CD, the focus on providing consistency and structure becomes essential. Developing a good relationship with an adult is central for role-modeling and future problem-solving abilities. Of course, no family system is ever ideal; however, these children and adolescents need positive relationships with primary caregivers, a stable family environment, consistent family discipline practices, and family characteristics that influence positive adaptation.

For many of these children and adolescents, living in a neighborhood where they feel as if they belong and where they feel safe and protected is central to treatment success. Being part of a positive community will help to enhance the knowledge of values, norms, morals, and beliefs, having community supports can help the child or adolescent to avoid quick and uncontrolled responses when confronted with negative messages that can lead to an unhealthy personal and group identity.

Once risk factors are coupled with protective factors, intervention support will consist of developmental education classes, medical services, social services, and support, and intervention programs can be used to improve the likelihood that a child diagnosed with ADHD will exhibit less disruptive behavior. Intervention may also help in decreasing the possibility of ODD behaviors becoming more severe and leading to a subsequent diagnosis of CD. Therefore, assessing risk and joining these problematic behaviors with protective factors that help to counteract the impulsiveness can assist with improvement of the disruptive behavior disorders and the symptoms relevant to it.

The next portion of this chapter discusses CD and the diagnostic assessment within the *DSM-IV* and *DSM-IV-TR* multiaxial system. This application section describes CD along with the associated conditions and problems. A case study is presented that outlines the decision process for the *DSM* diagnosis, treatment plan, and intervention components. The chapter concludes with a summary with future direction.

Conduct Disorder and Use of the DSM-IV-TR and the Multiaxial System

According to the *DSM-IV-TR* (APA, 2000), conduct disorder refers to a diverse cluster of problem behaviors involving persistent violations of the rights of others and of major social rules (Petitclerc et al., 2009). (See Quick Reference 5.3 for the criteria for diagnosing CD.)

Children and adolescents with this disorder often behave aggressively toward people and animals. For example, they may initiate frequent fights; bully, intimidate, or threaten others; or torture animals. In some cases, acts of aggression include rape, assault with a deadly weapon, or homicide. Children and adolescents with CD tend to engage in destructive behavior that results in loss or damage to other people's property. These children may vandalize public buildings, set fires, or break up furniture in the family home. They may also engage in deceitfulness as evidenced by chronic lying, breaking promises, or stealing. Finally, children with CD tend to violate important rules set by parents and school officials resulting in behaviors such as staying out late, running away overnight, or repeatedly failing to attend school. Overall, most children with CD tend to lack empathy for others and show poor frustration tolerance and high levels of irritability (APA, 2000).

QUICK REFERENCE 5.3

CONDUCT DISORDER

- Individuals who suffer from conduct disorder (CD) often exhibit a pattern of behavior that violates rights of others.
- Symptoms are grouped in four categories:
  1. Aggression to people and animals.
  2. Destruction of property.
  3. Deceitfulness or theft.
  4. Serious violations of rules.
- Two criteria were added to increase applicability to females: staying out at night and intimidating others.
- There are new subtypes based on age of onset: childhood and adolescent. (Onset prior to age 10 has a poor prognosis.)
- Historically, when a child turned the age of 18, the diagnosis was changed to antisocial personality disorder, but the criteria in the *DSM-IV* and *DSM-IV-TR* state that the diagnosis of CD can remain into the early 20s.
- Remember, not all CD will later develop antisocial personality disorder. CD is clearly more common in males.

Source: Summarized criteria from the *Diagnostic and Statistical Manual of Mental Disorders, Fourth Edition, Text Revision.* Copyright 2000 by the American Psychiatric Association.

Associated Conditions and Problems

Children and adolescents who suffer from CD often experience pervasive problems in social and academic functioning. Children with CD tend to show lower intelligence, achievement, and school adjustment than their peers who do not suffer from CD (APA, 2000). In addition, reading disabilities are especially prominent, and symptoms of emotional and behavioral maladjustment often lead to a high degree of overlap between CD and ADHD. Children with CD suffering from a dual diagnosis display more severe and persistent antisocial behaviors than those with a single diagnosis. Diagnosed children are also more likely than others to have fathers with severe antisocial psychopathology. A significant number of children with CD disorder qualify for a diagnosis of depressive disorder, particularly during adolescence. Finally, children approaching puberty who have relatives who also suffer from depression were significantly more likely to have higher rates of CD than children that did not have the same family prevalence (Wickramaratne, Greenwald, & Weissman, 2000).

Generally, cognitive and academic behavior problems begin early in life and remain chronic throughout the individual's school career. Children with CD show equally broad-ranging problems in their social adjustment. As previously described in this chapter, the risk factor in conduct problems tend to co-occur with a diverse range of overlapping familial and social-ecological stressors, including poor child management skills, parental psychopathology, marital distress and discord, poverty, and social isolation (Frances & Ross, 1996; Kim-Cohen et al., 2005; Thyer & Wodarski, 1998).

Moreover, children with CD experience high levels of peer rejection when they exhibit aggressive and annoying behaviors. Over time, peers begin to counterattack and provoke these children, thereby creating a negative spiral of aggression and rejection. In addition, children with CD often tend to have poor and nonsupportive relationships with their teachers and many significant individuals in their lives including parents, relatives or extended family, and school personnel. Not surprisingly, parents and school officials often clash over how to best address and deal with the child's behavior problems (First et al., 1995; Frances & Ross, 1996; Thyer & Wodarski, 1998). (See Case Example 5.1, Case of Charlie.)

CASE EXAMPLE 5.1 - CASE OF CHARLIE

An 11-year-old Caucasian boy named Charlie was always in trouble and had been brought to the attention of school authorities since age 7 for truancy, fights, and petty thefts. He is currently staying in a juvenile detention facility after hitting his older brother in the head with a can of soda while he was sleeping. Charlie is the youngest of three brothers and one sister. His mother and father stated that since Charlie attended first grade, they have received numerous calls and consultations for disruptive and aggressive behavior, school problems, and difficulties with peer relationships. They state that they are unable to control him. They report Charlie is a "fibber" and, when questioned about the truth of his statements, he becomes defiantly irate and walks away. In defiance of his parent's attempt to control his behaviors and actions, Charlie frequently stays out with friends without telling his parents where he is going or where he has been. His mother reported that he has run away twice from home after arguments with her and his dad. She also suspects that he often takes money from her purse or his father's wallet without permission.

Charlie was diagnosed with ADHD in the first grade because of home, school, and social disruptions. His behavior was reported to be inattentive, hyperactive, and impulsive and involved verbal and physical fights and

(continued)

CASE EXAMPLE 5.1
(*Continued*)

disruptions in classrooms, such as inattention, yelling, running, and jumping. He also stabbed another child in the hand with a pencil when he did not get his way. More recently, he was expelled from school when he and two friends were fighting in the school hallway and he and friends set fire to school property. He began stealing in the second grade. Related to both academic and social difficulties, he was held back 2 years in elementary school and now is failing in the fourth grade.

He refused to do homework when he was in school because he stated that schoolwork was boring and openly preferred to play video games that revolved around violence with "blood and guts." After school on several occasions, he chased classmates who had angered him. One child reported that he grabbed the sweatshirt string and deliberately pulled it tight across the child's neck when he grabbed him. Charlie reports that he often thinks about killing someone and when he does, he hopes the police will finally take him out of his house.

A series of thefts from neighborhood stores and classmates, fighting in the hallways at school, and the incident in which he and a companion set a fire at school resulted in pending criminal charges. The judge placed him in a juvenile detention facility and ordered that he have a mental health evaluation while there. In the juvenile detention facility, Charlie originally appeared to befriend other adolescents and several staff members; however, soon the staff reported that he was demanding, manipulative, and volatile. He frequently stormed out of supportive therapeutic groups and care plan meetings when decisions were made that did not go his way. He tried hard to ensure that all activities revolved around him and was enthusiastic about them at first. Later, however, he appeared angry and moped around when he was not permitted to monopolize the activity. Beneath his apparent bravado, however, the staff found him insecure and dependent.

Charlie slashed his wrist 2 months ago and ended up in the psychiatric ward of the hospital for an attempted suicide. He reported that he did not feel he could do anything right and being expelled from school put him over the edge. Environmental stresses increased 6 years ago, when Charlie's parents both had to take on extra work to adequately support the family. When Charlie was 5, his father had difficulty keeping employment because of his alcohol problem. It was not until Charlie was 8 that his father began treatment for alcoholism. Although Charlie wants to get along with his father, his father finds it difficult to cope with the boy's willfulness and anger. When verbal efforts at discipline fail, his father resorts to harsh corporal punishment, often with a switch. The family is plagued with financial hardships and moved six months ago for better-paying jobs and employment opportunities.

Charlie was court-ordered for an evaluation, assessment, and presentation of intervention options to this mental health agency. Once completed and an intervention plan has been established, the judge has agreed to court order Charlie to engage in and complete counseling and to remain in juvenile justice detention for the remainder of his probation period. Charlie's parents and his siblings are fearful of him and no longer trust the boy's unpredictable behavior. They want to discuss out-of-home placement options when he is ready for discharge.

Continuance of the Diagnostic Assessment

The diagnostic assessment began with the collection of biological and psychosocial information. Charlie is an 11-year-old boy with a history of ADHD that was present at age 5, with escalating disciplinary problems since age 7. He is the youngest of three brothers and one sister. There is a family history of antisocial disorder and alcoholism suggestive of a biological basis for ADHD that may place him and his other siblings at higher risk for developing CD. Charlie denies use of any illicit drugs or substances. He is currently in a juvenile detention facility after

---

QUICK REFERENCE 5.4

IDENTIFY PRIMARY AND PRESENTING PROBLEM

Primary problem:	Conduct disorder/childhood-onset type, severe.
Presenting problem:	Court-ordered mental health evaluation due to his involvement in thefts and fire setting.

---

expulsion from his home by both the judge and his parents as a result of him hitting an older brother over the head with a full can of soda while the brother was sleeping (see Quick Reference 5.4).

Once the primary and presenting problems have been identified, the first task of the mental health practitioner, especially with the child's history of violence toward self and others, is to complete a risk assessment. The practitioner needs to identify the risk of potential suicide, of violence to others, and whether there has been abuse of Charlie. These questions are asked in a straightforward and direct manner. Once identified, this information needs to be clearly recorded (see Quick Reference 5.5).

The second step for the mental health practitioner is to identify client strengths and behaviors that contribute to impairment in daily functioning. In addition, the clinician should observe the client's appearance, mood, attitude, affect, speech, motor activity, and orientation. Mental functioning should be assessed in terms of the client's ability to complete simple calculations, serial 7s, immediate memory, remote memory, general knowledge, proverb interpretation, and recognition of similarities and differences. In addition, questions

in regard to higher-order abilities and thought form and content need to be processed (see Quick Reference 5.6).

Application of the Multiaxial System

Charlie is given the Axis I diagnosis Conduct Disorder/childhood-onset type, severe (312.82). The placement of this diagnosis is supported by the fact that in the past 12 months, Charlie has exhibited more than three criteria of the disorder. During this time period, Charlie has practiced serious violations of rules by staying out at night; being truant from school; destroying siblings' and family belongings; being physically cruel to people; bullying, threatening, deceiving, and intimidating others; stealing from friends and family; and breaking into homes. Charlie also presented with more than one criterion present in the past 6 months reflective of aggression toward people. He states that he often gets what he wants through threats and intimidation of others, including starting verbal and physical fights. He has been caught destroying property, such as deliberately setting fire to school property. Other problematic behaviors include deceitfulness and theft by

---

QUICK REFERENCE 5.5

RISK ASSESSMENT

Document and assess suicide risk:	No evidence or none.
Document and assess violence risk:	Slight.
Document and assess child abuse risk:	Slight.

QUICK REFERENCE 5.6

MENTAL STATUS DESCRIPTION

Presentation	Mental Functioning	Higher-Order Abilities	Thought Form/Content
Appearance: Unkempt	Simple Calculations: Mostly accurate	Judgment: Impulsive	Thought Process: Logical and organized
Mood: Anxious	Serial 7s: Accurate	Insight: Intact	Delusions: None
Attitude: Guarded	Immediate Memory: Intact	Intelligence: Low	Hallucinations: None
Affect: Appropriate	Remote Memory: Intact		
Speech: Normal	General Knowledge: Mostly accurate		
Motor Activity: Restless	Proverb Interpretation: Mostly accurate		
Orientation: Fully oriented	Similarities/Differences: Mostly accurate		

---

breaking into homes and the school and stealing from parents. Charlie has a history of repetitive and persistent patterns of disturbed peer relationships, disobedience, and opposition to authority figures, lying, shoplifting, physical fighting, exhibition fighting, fire setting, stealing, vandalism, and school discipline problems since age 7. These conduct problems impair social and academic functioning, as evidenced by few friends, poor grades, school suspension, and being involved in numerous fights.

A second diagnosis to be included on Axis I is Adjustment Disorder, with depressed mood/acute (309.0). This second diagnosis is also placed on Axis I since Charlie demonstrates a typical pattern with depressive symptoms and suicidal ideation, and his behaviors rapidly escalate when he is frustrated or confronted by authorities after being caught in wrongdoing. This is supported by a suicide attempt he made two months ago by slashing his wrist. Self-esteem is low, despite the image of toughness presented to the public. Charlie's depression frequently manifests in his concurrent conduct and impulsivity problems. The co-occurring symptoms of conduct disorder and ADHD are indicators

of his depression. Other depressive symptoms appear related to the family's move, his disturbances in the home, and his statements that he is bored with school and schoolwork. The client's parents' report that Charlie isolated himself in his room for the past five months, has stopped being around friends, and has clinically significant impairment in social and academic functioning. Currently there are no severe symptoms to meet the criteria for a depressive disorder. For this reason, an additional diagnosis of adjustment disorder with depressed mood appears the most appropriate and provisional status to be considered.

On Axis II, No diagnosis (V71.09) will be recorded since there are no apparent personality disorders, borderline intellectual functioning, or mental retardation present. Defense mechanisms that can be coded on this axis include the following:

1. Dealing with emotional conflict and internal and external stressors indicates omnipotence by feeling or acting as if he possesses special powers and abilities and is superior to others.

2. His emotional conflict and internal and external stressors indicate devaluation by attributing exaggerated negative qualities to self and others.

3. His emotional conflict and internal and external stressors indicate idealization by attributing exaggerated positive qualities to gang leaders and troublemakers.

4. Addressing emotional conflict and internal and external stressors indicate projection identification as he falsely attributes his own unacceptable feelings, impulses, and thoughts to someone else.

5. He is frustrated by internal and external stressors and reacts by acting out with his actions rather than expressing his reflections or feelings.

6. His dealing with emotional conflict and internal and external stressors indicate denial by refusing to acknowledge some painful aspects of external and subjective experiences that would be apparent to others.

7. With difficulty adjusting to internal and external stressors he utilizes rationalization by concealing the true motivations for his own thoughts, actions, and feelings through elaboration of reassuring and self-serving but incorrect explanations.

On Axis III (F54), lacerations of the left wrist are noted from Charlie's attempted suicide 2 months ago.

On Axis IV, the clinician can note these issues: Charlie was recently arrested for setting a fire and fighting in school. The family moved 6 months ago. Charlie exhibits education deficits due to school change and nonattendance in class. His father admits using harsh discipline. Relationship conflicts due to aggressive and annoying behaviors and peer rejection exist along with expulsion from home by judge and parents for brutally hurting his brother. Charlie is experiencing social environmental pressures due to low income and a poor living environment. There is support group deficiency due to limited access to social welfare support and few family members or friends.

Current stress severity rating is moderate.

On Axis V, the global assessment of functioning (GAF), the current rating = 30. Family routines of mealtime and sleeping do not meet the needs of the children because rules are grimly adhered to or blithely ignored. Life cycle changes generate painful conflict, and there are obvious frustrating failures of problem solving. Parental decision making is tyrannical and ineffective. The unique characteristics of individuals are unappreciated or ignored, and there are confusing fluid coalitions among family members. Infrequent periods of enjoyment of family life together due to frequent distancing and hostility reflect significant conflicts that remain unresolved and quite painful.

Diagnostic Summary

The diagnosis for Charlie is CD, childhood-onset type, severe. Charlie has a seemingly charming personality but from an early age has been unable to follow home, school, or society's rules on a consistent basis. Incorrigibility, delinquency, and school problems such as truancy mark his childhood. Charlie's behavior problems affect every life area of functioning. Charlie remains aware of his own impulses but misattributes them as justifiable reactions to the other person. He induces the very feelings in others that were first mistakenly believed to be there, making it difficult to clarify who did what to whom first.

There are numerous complaints from parents and school that the boy fights, lies, steals, starts fires, cheats, and is abusive and destructive. Charlie glibly claims to have guilt feelings, but he does not appear to feel genuine remorse for his behavior. Charlie complains of multiple somatic problems and has made a suicide attempt. The manipulative nature of all his interactions with others makes it difficult to determine whether his complaints are genuine. Charlie has many conduct problems in excess of those required to make the diagnosis of CD, and the conduct problems have caused serious harm to his brother.

The additional diagnosis of *adjustment disorder with depressed mood/acute* appears appropriate. A mood disorder along with CD may often be overlooked. Usually there are so many pressing problems to sort out and so many different stressors that not until suicide is tried or talked about do many families, physicians, and other health professionals consider comorbid depression. Recent studies of teenagers who have committed suicide have found that these children were about three times more likely to have CD and 15 times more likely to abuse substances. Suicide is worth worrying about in chidlren diagnosed with CD and must be a part of treatment planning. In Charlie's case, he has attempted suicide, has low-self esteem, and is diagnosed with adjustment disorder with depressed mood. This is supported by symptoms of depressed mood, tearfulness, and current feelings of hopelessness (APA, 2000). (See Quick Reference 5.7 for the multiaxial diagnostic assessment of Charlie.)

QUICK REFERENCE 5.7

MULTIAXIAL DIAGNOSTIC ASSESSMENT (*DSM-IV-TR*)

Axis I: 312.82 Conduct disorder/childhood-onset type, severe.
            309.0   Adjustment disorder, with depressed mood.

Axis II: V71.09 No diagnosis.

            A. Current defenses or coping styles:
               1. Omnipotence.
               2. Devaluation.
               3. Idealization.
               4. Projection identification.
               5. Acting out.
               6. Denial.
               7. Rationalization.
            B. Predominant current defense level: Minor image-distorting level.

Axis III: Lacerations of left wrist.

Axis IV   Recent arrest for setting a fire and school fights.
            Family move 6 months ago.
            Educational deficits due to truancy and school change.
            Harsh discipline by father.
            Relationship conflicts with peers due to aggressive and annoying behaviors. Expulsion from home by parents and court.
            Social environment pressures of low income and poor environment.
            Support group deficient: Few family or friends and lack of access to social services.
            Stress severity rating: 3 (severe).

Axis V: GAF = 30 (current).
            GAF = 45 (past 6 months).
            GAF = 50 (past year).

Contributing Factors

The family history of antisocial disorder, physical abuse, and alcoholism suggests the possibility of a biological basis for ADHD and CD for the client. Also, the client has a history of ADHD that was present at age 5. Charlie's family and environmental surroundings are poor. Conflicting punitive measures and the lack of assistance from parents, teachers, and the legal system complicate the problems experienced by this client. Charlie has a poor frustration tolerance; irritability, temper outbursts, and reckless behaviors are common.

Further Information Needed

School and juvenile records will be requested to further validate the diagnosis and assist in treatment planning. Charlie's previous mental health records will be requested to see whether symptoms he had then could be those of depression when diagnosed with ADHD. Hospitalization records of the client's admittance to a mental health facility for suicide attempt will be requested. Educational testing and Intelligence tests will be requested to rule out pervasive problems in academic function. Referral for a medical exam and blood work will be requested of the parents.

Decision Process for **DSM** Diagnosis

In diagnostic formulation, five target symptoms require consideration:

1. Biopsychosocial stressors (especially sexual and physical abuse, separation, divorce, or death of key attachment figures).
2. Educational potential, disabilities, and achievement.
3. Peer, sibling, and family problems and strengths.
4. Environmental factors including disorganized home, lack of supervision, presence of child abuse or neglect, psychiatric illness (especially substance abuse) in parents, and environmental neurotoxins (e.g., lead intoxication).
5. Adolescent or child ego development, especially ability to form and maintain relationships.

A decision on the subtype of the disorder (childhood onset versus adolescent onset; overt versus covert versus authority; underrestrained versus overrestrained; socialized versus undersocialized; severity specifier of mild, moderate, or severe) is needed. Also, it is important to examine if there are any other possible alternate primary diagnoses with conduct symptoms complicating their presentation, especially in adolescents. To prevent a wrong diagnosis, it is essential to look carefully at syndromes that might be confused or concurrent with conduct disorder. These include:

1. Attention-deficit hyperactivity disorder.
2. Oppositional defiant disorder.
3. Intermittent explosive disorder.
4. Substance use disorders.
5. Mood disorders (bipolar and depressive).
6. Posttraumatic stress disorder and dissociative disorders.
7. Borderline personality disorder.
8. Adjustment disorder.
9. Dementia or delirium and seizure disorder.
10. Narcissistic personality disorder.
11. Specific developmental disorders (e.g., learning disabilities).
12. Mental retardation.
13. Schizophrenia (APA, 2000; First et al., 1995).

Treatment Plan and Intervention Components

In formulating the treatment plan, Charlie and his parents were interviewed together and separately to go over the history and check out all other possible contradictory information and comorbid conditions. School reports helped to verify truancy, behavior problems, and educational status. It is important for the practitioner to gather a comprehensive history that includes schoolwork, some parts of the physical exam, and both the child's and parents' perspectives. As noted earlier, lab tests and X-rays are needed to rule out neurological and/or biological components. In addition, the referral for a blood test will detect use or abuse of drugs or hormonal problems. Problem behaviors must be clearly identified, as these are the behaviors that will be reflected in terms of the intervention efforts. Practitioners should target the primary symptoms and behavior problems first. Using a multimodal intervention, they must target each domain assessed as dysfunctional.

Treatment time can vary among individuals with CD; however, it is rarely brief, since establishing new attitudes and behavior patterns take time. However, early intervention offers Charlie a better chance for considerable improvement and hope for a more successful future. Utilizing an eclectic approach might work best for Charlie, as this approach encourages practitioner responses that are based on differential assessments of the client's specific needs and problems (Fischer, 2009). Therefore, Charlie's treatment will combine medication, individual therapy, group therapy, behavioral therapy, social skills training, family support and family therapy, and, potentially, remedial education. While medication may be an important component of treating Charlie's behavior disorders, especially early on, it will work best as an adjunct to psychotherapy. Individual therapy can help Charlie gain greater self-control and insight into his social conduct and develop more thoughtful and efficient problem-solving strategies. (See Quick Reference 5.8 for a list of behavioral definitions.) Notably, this will give him the opportunity to understand and express his feelings with words instead of through behavior. Charlie's treatment will include behavior modification techniques, such as social skill training, through which he can learn to evaluate social situations and adjust his behavior accordingly. In addition, Charlie may need to have some kind of remedial education or special tutoring to compensate for any learning difficulties or to address any reading disorders, learning disabilities, or language delays that may be indicated following testing. It is important that the practitioner does not take on the attitude that some treatment is better than no treatment without evidence that the treatment is beneficial, effective, or that no harm or hindrances to the individual's progress will occur as a result. A client and parents deserve evidenced-based services, as do the public, as the other costs that CD has on society as a whole can be great.

Family therapy is an important component to treating CD. Family therapy and behavioral therapies, such as parent training programs, will address the family stress normally generated by living with a child or adolescent with CD. These treatment modalities will provide strategies for managing Charlie's behavior and may help the parents encourage appropriate behaviors in their other children and discipline them more effectively. By involving the entire family, this treatment will foster mutual support, positive reinforcement, direct communication, and more effective problem solving within the family (Braithwaite, Duff, & Westworth, 1999; Brunk, 1999).

Many target symptoms that may not have been apparent or acknowledged during the client interview may be discovered following interviews with parents, juvenile detention staff, and teachers. It is important to understand that caregivers, custodians, or even a parent may endorse symptoms that could be better conceptualized as normative manifestations of autonomy assertion and immature self-regulatory skills.

QUICK REFERENCE 5.8

BEHAVIORAL PROBLEM IDENTIFICATION

- Persistent failure to comply with rules or expectations in the home, school, and community.
- Excessive fighting, intimidation of others, cruelty and violence toward people, and deliberate fire setting with intention of causing damage and destruction of school property.
- History of breaking and entering and stealing from family, classmates, and neighbors.
- School adjustment characterized by repeated truancy, disrespectful attitude, and suspensions for misbehavior.
- Repeated conflict and confrontation with authority figures at home, school, and in the community.
- Failure to consider the consequences of actions, taking inappropriate risks, and engaging in thrill-seeking behaviors.
- Numerous attempts to deceive others through lying, conning, or manipulating.
- Consistent failure to accept responsibility for misbehavior accompanied by a pattern of blaming others.
- Little or no remorse for past misbehavior.
- Lack of sensitivity to the thoughts, feelings, and needs of other people.

It is necessary for the therapist to obtain additional information on the client and evaluate: (a) capacity for attachment, trust, and empathy; (b) tolerance for and discharge of impulses; (c) capacity for showing restraint, accepting responsibility for actions, experiencing guilt, using anger constructively, and acknowledging negative emotions; (d) cognitive functioning; (e) mood, affect, self-esteem, and suicide potential; (f) peer relationships (loner, popular, drug-, crime-, or gang-oriented friends); (g) disturbances of ideation (inappropriate reactions to environment, paranoia, dissociate episodes, and suggestibility); (h) history of early, persistent use of tobacco, alcohol, or other substances; and (i) psychometric self-report instruments.

In addition, Charlie's school records will provide a great deal of information, such as his academic functioning (IQ, achievement test data, academic performance, and behavior). Other data may be obtained in person, by phone, or through written reports from appropriate staff, such as school principal, psychologist, juvenile detention personnel, teachers, and school nurse. Any

standard parent and teacher rating scales of the patient's behavior would be useful. The practitioner should also make any referral for IQ, speech and language, and learning disability and neuropsychiatric testing if available test data are not sufficient. It may be necessary to look at physical evaluations, particularly any physical examination within the past 12 months (i.e., baseline pulse rate). A part of the treatment plan is to collaborate with the family doctor, pediatrician, or other health care providers. It is also important to conduct vision and hearing screenings. As records become available, it is necessary to evaluate medical and neurological conditions (e.g., head injury, seizure disorder, and chronic illnesses). The therapist will review any urine and blood drug screening, especially when clinical evidence suggests substance abuse that the client denies (Dziegielewski, 2005).

Treatment should be provided in a continuum of care that allows flexible application of modalities by a cohesive treatment plan. Selected outpatient treatment is planned for Charlie, including intervention in the family, school, and peer group. His predominance of externalizing symptoms in multiple domains of functioning requires the use of interpersonal psychoeducational modalities rather than an exclusive emphasis on intrapsychic treatment. This therapy needs to be provided in addition to psychopharmacological approaches. Because Charlie's CD is severe, it may require an extensive treatment and long-term follow-up. In preparing the treatment plan, the practitioner considered both treatment of comorbid disorders (e.g., ADHD, specific developmental disabilities, intermittent explosive disorder, affective or bipolar disorder, anxiety disorder, and substance use disorder) and possible family interventions, including parent guidance and family therapy to identify and work with parental strengths and parent training to help them establish consistent positive and negative consequences and well-defined expectations and rules. Addressing issues of noncompliance is central to treatment with Charlie and all children with this diagnosis. This is such an important area that these types of interventions can yield improvement in all areas of behavior (McMahon, Wells, & Kotler, 2006).

In this case, the practitioner decided to work to eliminate harsh, excessively permissive, and inconsistent behavior management practices. The clinician arranged for the father to receive individual substance abuse counseling and for Charlie to receive individual, peer support, and family group psychotherapy. Therapy focused on supportive, explorative, cognitive, and other behavioral techniques due to the client's age, processing style, and ability to engage in treatment. The combination of behavioral and explorative approaches is indicated because of internalizing and externalizing comorbidities (e.g., ADHD, specific developmental disabilities, intermittent explosive disorder, affective or bipolar disorder, anxiety disorder, and substance use disorder). Psychosocial skill-building training will be used to supplement therapy as well as

other psychosocial interventions. The use of a peer intervention was chosen to discourage deviant peer association and promote a socially appropriate peer network.

It also was important to establish and use a school intervention for appropriate placement, to promote an alliance between parents and school, and to promote prosocial peer group contact. Coordination and assistance in the juvenile justice system interventions may require the inclusion of court supervision and limit settings as well as other special programs when available. Social services referrals were needed to help the family to obtain benefits and service providers (e.g., case managers). As discharge nears there may be a need to consider other community resources, such as Big Brother and Big Sister programs and Friends Outside. There may come a time when it may be appropriate to use out-of-home placement (e.g., crisis shelters, group homes, or residential treatment).

As Charlie becomes older, he may require job and independent-living skills training. Psychopharmacology treatment generally starts with the minimum recommended starting daily dose for a child of the medication and at times medications such as Risperdal (risperidone) may be recommended for treatment of aggressive behaviors (Findling, 2000; Schur et al., 2003). Antidepressants that could be used for therapy include Eskalith (lithium carbonate), Tegretol (carbamazepine), and Inderal (propranolol). These medications are currently used clinically for the treatment of CD, but further rigorous scientific studies to demonstrate their efficacy still need to be performed. The risks of neuroleptics may outweigh their usefulness in the treatment of aggression in CD and require careful consideration before use.

Determining the best level of care and the criteria for hospitalization of this client can be complex, although the practitioner will choose the least restrictive level of intervention that fulfills both the short- and long-term needs of the client. When or if there is an imminent risk to self or others, such as suicidal, self-injurious, homicidal, or aggressive behavior, or imminent deterioration in the individual's medical status after completing juvenile detention, clear indications of the need for hospitalization exist. Inpatient, partial hospitalization, and residential treatment were considered: (a) therapeutic milieu, including community processes and structure (e.g., level system, behavior modification); and (b) significant family involvement tailored to the needs of the client (conjoint or without patient present), including parent training and family therapy. Because this is a young client, it is even more critical that the family be involved in the treatment process (Braithwaite et al., 1999; Brunk, 1999; First et al., 1995; Lewinsohn, 2000; Maxmen, Ward, & Kilgus, 2009). (See Sample Treatment Plan 5.3.)

In summary, there are a limited number of evidenced-based programs currently available for

the early predictors of early onset CD, but one deserves mentioning here. The Webster-Stratton Incredible Years Program: Parents, Teachers, and Children Training Series is an evidenced-based comprehensive prevention/intervention program to assist children ages 3 to 7 years. The program is designed to strengthen parent and teacher communication. Findings in four studies show that it effectively increases positive parenting practices and reduces antisocial behavior in children at risk for developing CD (August, Realmuto, Hektner, & Bloomquist, 2001; Barrera et al., 2002; Hutchings et al., 2007; Taylor, Schmidt, Pepler, & Hodgins, 1998). The New York University Child Study Center has developed and continues to study the efficacy of ParentCorps, a program that provides long-needed parent practices and child social competence for low-income families of preschool-age children. Evidence supports this as a promising outreach program for poor urban communities where children are at high risk of conduct problem behaviors and academic

SAMPLE TREATMENT PLAN 5.3
CHARLIE

Client Data:

Age: 11	Gender: Male
Race: Caucasian	Marital Status: Single
Admission Date: 8/7/2000	Discharge Date: 1/8/2001

Client Strengths: Intelligent, clear thinking, expressive/articulate, excellent manipulative abilities, excellent problem-solving abilities, motivated for change, physically healthy, supportive family, and varied interests.

Assessments Completed:
- Children's Depression Inventory (CDI): 32 depression and 10 positive.
- Neuropsychological questionnaire for children conducted by internal medicine physician: General health is good. Other testing pending.

Presenting Problems: Client reports that a judge has ordered him to get a mental health evaluation due to his involvement in thefts and fire setting.
Primary Problem: Conduct disorder/childhood-onset type, severe.

(continued)

SAMPLE TREATMENT PLAN 5.3 *(Continued)*

Mental Status Description

Presentation	Mental Functioning	Higher-Order Abilities	Thought Form/Content
Appearance: Unkempt	Simple Calculations: Mostly accurate	Judgment: Impulsive	Thought Process: Logical and Organized
Mood: Anxious	Serial Sevens: Accurate	Insight: Intact	Delusions: None
Attitude: Guarded	Immediate Memory: Intact	Intelligence: Low	Hallucinations: None
Affect: Appropriate	Remote Memory: Intact		
Speech: Normal	General Knowledge: Mostly Accurate		
Motor Activity: Restless	Proverb Interpretation: Mostly accurate		
Orientation: Fully oriented	Similarities/Differences: Mostly accurate		

Risk Assessment:

Suicide risk: None
Violence risk: Slight
Child abuse risk: Slight

Treatment Modalities and Approaches:

The following treatment approaches are being implemented:

- Individual: Cognitive restructuring and insight oriented.
- Group: Family, functional family, and peer group therapy.
- Behavioral: Token economy, behavioral techniques, relaxation training, and solution-oriented brief therapy.
- Social interventions: Supportive maintenance, Parent education, Social skills training, and Social skills building.
- Biological: Pharmacotherapy and medication management therapy.

Medication	Dosage	Frequency	Start Date	End Date
Risperidone	.25 mg/day	1 x in AM	7/5/2001	12/13/2001

MULTIAXIAL SYSTEM *(DSM-IV-TR)*

Axis I: 312.82 Conduct disorder/Childhood-onset type, severe.
           309.0   Adjustment disorder, with depressed mood.

Axis II: V71.09 No diagnosis.
           A. Current defenses of coping styles:
               1. Omnipotence.
               2. Devaluation.
               3. Idealization.
               4. Projection identification.
               5. Acting out.
               6. Denial.
               7. Rationalization.
           B. Predominant current defense level: Minor image-distorting level.

Axis III: Lacerations of left wrist.

Axis IV: Recent arrest for setting a fire and school fights.
Family move 6 months ago.
Educational deficits due to truancy and school change.
Harsh discipline by father.
Relationship conflicts with peers due to aggressive and annoying behaviors. Expulsion from home by parents and court.
Social environment pressures of low income and poor environment.
Support group deficient of few family or friends and lack of access to social services.
Stress Severity Rating: 3 (Severe).

Axis V: GAF = 30 (current).
GAF = 45 (past six months).
GAF = 50 (past year).

Treatment Plan:

Behavioral Definitions

- Persistent failure to comply with rules or expectations in the home, school, and community.
- Excessive fighting, intimidation of others, cruelty and violence toward people, and deliberate fire setting with intention of causing damage and destruction of school property.
- History of breaking and entering and stealing from family, classmates, and neighbors.
- School adjustment characterized by repeated truancy, disrespectful attitude, and suspensions for misbehavior.
- Repeated conflict and confrontations with authority figures at home, school, and in the community.
- Failure to consider the consequences of actions, taking inappropriate risks, and engaging in thrill-seeking behaviors.
- Numerous attempts to deceive others through lying, conning, or manipulating.
- Consistent failure to accept responsibility for misbehavior, accompanied by a pattern of blaming others.
- Little or no remorse for past misbehavior.
- Lack of sensitivity to the thoughts, feelings, and needs of other people.

Long-Term Goals (target dates must be given for each objective)

- The client will demonstrate increased honesty, compliance with rules, sensitivity to the feelings and rights of others; develop control over impulses and acceptance of responsibility for his behavior.
- The client will comply with rules and expectations in the home, school, and community on a consistent basis.
- The client will eliminate all illegal and antisocial behaviors.
- The client will terminate all acts of violence and cruelty toward people and the destruction of property.
- The client will express anger through appropriate verbalizations and healthy physical outlets on a consistent basis.
- The client will demonstrate marked improvement in impulse control.
- The client will resolve the core conflicts that contribute to the emergence of conduct problems.
- The parents will establish and maintain appropriate parent-child boundaries, setting firm consistent limits when the client acts out in an aggressive or rebellious manner.
- The client will demonstrate empathy, concern, and sensitivity for the thoughts, feelings, and needs of others on a regular basis.

(continued)

SAMPLE TREATMENT PLAN 5.3 (*Continued*)

Short-Term Objectives (target dates must be given for each objective)

- The client will complete psychological testing.
- The client will complete a psychoeducational evaluation.
- The client will complete a substance abuse evaluation and comply with the recommendations offered by the evaluation findings.
- The client will remain in the juvenile detention facility for the remainder of his probation term.
- The client will recognize and verbalize how feelings are connected to misbehavior.
- The client will increase the number of statements that reflect the acceptance of responsibility for misbehavior.
- The client will decrease the frequency of verbalizations that project the blame for the problems onto other people.
- The client will express anger through appropriate verbalization and healthy physical outlets.
- The client will reduce the frequency and severity of aggressive, destructive, and antisocial behaviors.
- The client will increase compliance with rules at home and at the alternative school.
- The client will increase the time spent with the parents in leisure and school activities.
- The client and his parents will cooperate with the recommendations or requirements mandated by the criminal justice system.
- The client and his parents agree to and follow through with the implementation of a reward system or contingency contract.
- The client will verbalize an understanding of how current acting-out and aggressive behaviors are associated with past neglect and harsh physical punishment.
- The client will identify and verbally express feelings associated with harsh physical abuse.
- The client will increase participation in extracurricular activities and positive peer group activities.
- The client will identify and verbalize how acting-out behaviors negatively affect others.
- The client will increase verbalizations of empathy and concern for other people.
- The parents will postpone recreational activity (e.g., playing basketball with friends) until after completing homework or chores when Charlie is at home.
- The parents will establish appropriate boundaries, develop clear rules, and follow through consistently with consequences for misbehavior when Charlie returns to home.
- The parents will increase the frequency of praise and positive reinforcement to the client.
- The parents will verbalize appropriate boundaries for discipline to prevent further occurrences of abuse and ensure the safety of the client and his siblings.
- The parents will watch the video Toughlove (1985) and share their understandings.
- The client will increase communication, intimacy, and consistency when addressing his or her parents.
- The client will take medication as prescribed by the physician.

Therapeutic Interventions (target dates must be given for each objective)

- The therapist will give a directive to parents to spend more time with the client in leisure, school, or other activities.
- The therapist will explore the client's family background for a history of physical, sexual, or substance abuse, which may contribute to his behavioral problems.
- The therapist will conduct a family therapy session in which the client's family members are given a task or problem to solve together (e.g., build a craft); will observe family interactions and process the experience with them afterward.

- The therapist will assist the client's parents to cease physically abusive or overly punitive methods of discipline.
- Charlie will remain in juvenile detention for the protection of siblings from further abuse until deemed unnecessary.
- The therapist will encourage and support the client in expressing feelings associated with neglect and harsh punishment.
- The therapist will utilize the family sculpting technique in which the client defines the roles and behaviors of each family member in a scene of his choosing to assess the family dynamics.
- The therapist will conduct family therapy sessions to explore the dynamics that contribute to the emergence of the client's behavioral problems.
- The therapist will assign the client's parents reading material and relevant books.
- The therapist will encourage the parents to provide frequent praise and positive reinforcement for the client's positive social behaviors and good impulse control.
- The therapist will design and implement a token economy to increase the client's positive social behaviors and deter impulsive, acting-out behaviors.
- The therapist will utilize the therapeutic game Talking, Feeling, Doing to increase the client's awareness of his thoughts and feelings.
- The therapist will arrange for the client to participate in group therapy to improve his social judgment and interpersonal skills.
- The therapist will assign the client the task of showing empathy, kindness, and sensitivity to the needs of others (e.g., read a bedtime story to a sibling, mow the lawn for the grandmother) after removal from juvenile detention.
- The therapist will encourage the client to participate in extracurricular or positive peer group activities to provide a healthy outlet for anger, improve social skills, and increase self-esteem.
- The therapist will provide the client with sex education and discuss the risks involved with sexually promiscuous behaviors.
- The therapist will explore the client's feelings, irrational beliefs, and unmet needs that contribute to the emergence of sexually promiscuous behaviors.
- The therapist will arrange for a medication evaluation of the client to improve his impulse control and stabilize moods.
- The therapist will arrange for a psychoeducational evaluation of the client to rule out the presence of a learning disability that may be contributing to the impulsivity and acting-out behaviors in the school setting.
- The therapist will firmly confront the client's antisocial behavior and attitude, pointing out consequences for him and others.
- The therapist will arrange for psychological testing of the client to assess whether emotional factors or attention-deficit/hyperactivity disorder is contributing to his impulsivity and acting-out behaviors.
- The therapist will provide feedback to the client, his parents, school officials, and criminal justice officials regarding psychological and/or psychoeducational testing.
- The therapist will arrange for substance abuse evaluation for the client.
- The therapist will consult with criminal justice officials about the appropriate consequences for the client's antisocial behaviors (e.g., pay restitution, community service, and probation).
- The therapist will encourage and challenge the parents not to protect the client from the legal consequences of his antisocial behaviors.
- The therapist will assist the client's parents in establishing clearly defined rules, boundaries, and consequences for misbehavior.

(*continued*)

SAMPLE TREATMENT PLAN 5.3 (*Continued*)

- The therapist will actively build the level of trust with the client in therapy sessions through consistent eye contact, active listening, unconditional positive regard, and warm acceptance to help increase his ability to identify and express feelings.
- The therapist will design a reward system and/or contingency contract for the client to reinforce identified positive behaviors and deter impulsive behaviors.
- The therapist will assist the client in making a connection between feelings and reactive behaviors.
- The therapist will confront statements in which the client blames others for his misbehavior and fails to accept responsibility for his actions.
- The therapist will explore and process the factors that contribute to the client's pattern of blaming others.
- The therapist will teach mediational and self-control strategies (e.g., relaxation, stop, look, listen, and think) to help the client express anger through appropriate verbalizations and healthy physical outlets.
- The therapist will encourage the client to use self-monitoring checklists at home and in the alternative school to develop more effective anger and impulse control.
- The therapist will teach the client effective communication and assertiveness skills to express feelings in a controlled fashion and meet his needs through more constructive actions.
- The therapist will assist the parents in increasing structure to help the client learn to delay gratification for longer-term goals (e.g., complete homework or chores before playing basketball).
- The therapist will establish clear rules for the client in home and school and ask him to repeat the rules to demonstrate an understanding of the expectations.

Prognosis:

The probability of successful achievement of treatment goals is fair. The rationale for this probability rating is due to a poor family economic situation and a limited means of family support. Increased use of parental support and assistance treatment that are at no cost to the family will be required and necessary. Substance abuse potential in the future is very high.

Discharge Criteria/Plan:

Aftercare plan: The client will continue attending peer support groups every two weeks and will continue with established extracurricular activities. The client will return to the clinic in six months for follow-up or when needed. He also states he will continue attending after-school programs so that he is not by himself.

Projected total number of sessions required for completion of treatment: Charlie will successfully achieve 100% of those short-term objectives that have been marked with a bullet before being considered for discharge from treatment.

Discharge Criteria:

- The client must attend school consistently without resistance.
- The client will comply with limits set by authority figures.
- The client will consistently abstain from mood-altering illicit drugs or alcohol.
- The client will demonstrate age-appropriate social skills.
- The client will demonstrate responsible, consistent medication-taking behavior.
- The client will engage in social interaction with appropriate eye contact and assertiveness.
- The client will have home visits completed without serious maladjustment.
- The client's mood, behavior, and thoughts will be stabilized sufficiently to independently carry out basic self-care.

- The client will have no exhibition of sexually inappropriate behavior.
- The client will have no expression of suicidal ideation.
- The client will have no expressions of a threat of physical aggression toward self or others.
- The client will have no violent outbursts of temper.
- The client will resolve conflicts peaceably and without aggression.
- The client will verbalize names of supportive resources that can be contacted if feeling suicidal.
- The client will verbalize plans for seeking continued emotional support after discharge.
- The client will verbalize positive plans for the future.

Client Response to Plan:

Patient response to treatment plan presentation: Client states that he wants to do whatever is needed to be a better child. He also understands that he needs to continue with extracurricular activities, support groups, and medication even after discharge from this facility.

Significant other response to treatment plan presentation: Mother and Father state that they are willing to try anything for their son's sake. Both parents report that they will be fully compliant with any and all requirements to get Charlie back into the family and home.

---

problems. A program that can address both of these aspects of the condition is desperately needed for economically disadvantaged children in every state throughout the United States.

Further research is needed to determine the long-term impact of the program on teaching practices, parenting practices, and parent-school involvement. Behavioral parent training is currently one of the most extensively well-validated interventions for children with aggressive and conduct problems. Inclusion of this type of supportive intervention may prevent the resulting behaviors from becoming severe enough to result in a dual diagnosis, such as ADHD and CD. Sadly, a majority of current intervention programs target school-age children, rather than reaching them at a much earlier age. Imagine what opportunities young children would have if their chances were improved by a parental program geared toward very early childhood for those who may be at risk of chronic disruptive behavior disorders. Early intervention can have more of an impact than interventions at age 5, 10, or in later years, when the behavior has become a way of life.

In the National Comorbidity Survey replication provided evidence that the prevalence and subtypes of CD for some age groups are well correlated within the *DSM-IV* (Nock, Kazdin, Hiripi, & Kessler, 2007). Despite those correlations, however, clinicians must be vigilant in the search for the newest findings in research, surveys, and evidence-based interventions and treatment (e.g., biological/psychological/social implications and medical studies). Because of the ever-changing advances being made to understand, treat, and prevent developmental disorders, more research is a necessary undertaking. Too, education should be a priority in maintaining evidence-based practices for the treatment and interventions that will improve services and identify mental health conditions such as CD.

SUMMARY AND FUTURE DIRECTIONS

CD is a complex problem with many forms. No one intervention can be used for every case, and evidence-based clinical diagnostics, treatment, intervention, and research is crucial. This chapter discussed selected disruptive behavior disorders in children with a focus on CD. What this chapter confirms is that disruptive behavior disorders start early in life. As such, early prevention and treatment is advantageous to the individual having any disruptive behavior disorder that prevents functioning because it increases the chances of overcoming dysfunctional behaviors. Controversies regarding the definition, etiology, and subtypes are continuously being researched and discussed; and conclusion does not appear to be in the near future.

Practitioners must look carefully at the risk factors and combine these with the protective factors that are evident in the child. Once combined into the diagnostic assessment, the identification of these factors remains a critical aspect of the therapeutic process. Instead of narrowing the assessment, it might be necessary to use computer technology to assist professionals in making more expedient and thorough assessments. As demonstrated through this case example, all aspects of the case could be shared with various professionals involved in the client's case, including practitioners, administrators, and researchers. A person-in-environment focus helps to attend to several interrelated dimensions of the client who suffers from CD, thereby focusing on the biological, intellectual, emotional, social, familial, spiritual, economic, communal, and so on, recognizing the client in relation to the immediate and distant environment.

The exact cause of the disruptive disorders is not known. It does appear, however, that there is a direct link to interactions of nature and nurture. Acknowledging these interactions can result in identifying biological, parental, psychological, behavioral, familial, and social environmental risk factors. These risk factors in turn result in a negative interaction that leads to behaviors that can follow the child into adulthood if left untreated. Correct identification of disruptive behaviors that lead to these disorders will benefit millions of children and

adolescents. More evidence-based programs that provide parent practices training and child social competence in low-income families of preschool-age children, as well as interventions, treatment, and prevention for this disorder are greatly needed.

The chapter discussed problem behaviors, symptoms, subtypes, associated conditions, and changes that have occurred in the *DSM* in diagnosing the disruptive behavior disorders. This was followed by a case study using the multiaxial system diagnosis guidelines with the condition of CD. The application of the multiaxial system, the diagnostic summary, examining contributing factors, and developing the treatment plan will aid in understanding the importance of following the guidelines provided by the *DSM*.

All mental health practitioners need to stay informed of the most up-to-date and evidence-based research on the interventions that can be used to treat clients who suffer from the disruptive behavior disorders. With the increase in managed behavioral care, it is imperative that mental health practitioners develop research that will clearly identify which treatment or combination of treatments is most cost effective to ensure that clients continue to receive coverage for the necessary treatments.

A number of things might happen in the future to improve our understanding of the etiology and nosology of disruptive behavior disorders, especially CD. A plethora of current research has demonstrated that mental health problems, disruptive behaviors, and CD can be identified and exhibit moderate stability as they emerge in children as young as 5 months old (Briggs-Gowan, Carter, Bosson-Heenan, Guyer, & Horwitz, 2006; Romano, Zoccolillo, & Paquette, 2006; Shaw, Gilliom, Ingoldsby, & Nagin, 2003; Skovgaard et al., 2007; Tremblay et al., 2004). Manifestations of early childhood behavior disorders and the future development of standardized methodology for clinically assessing preschool children would enhance not only research but the intervention and treatment efforts of clinicians.

Pottick, Kirk, Hsieh, and Tian (2007) found in a recent survey of 1,401 experienced psychologists, psychiatrists, and social workers that social workers were the least likely professionals to recognize a client suffering from mental illness. Survey results also indicated that psychologists were three times more likely and psychiatrists five times more likely to see mental illness than social workers. There can be a fine line between recognizing mental illness and overdiagnosing it. All mental health practitioners must strive for better education and training while reaching out to clients who want to overcome the persistent and severe symptoms that keep them from being functional and having the best life they can.

6

Selected Eating Disorders in Children and Adults

SOPHIA F. DZIEGIELEWSKI, JANICE L. RICKS, AND JANET D. MURRAY

Eating disorders are prevalent in today's society. For adults, the pressure to be thin can be so strong that many individuals, primarily women, do not eat enough, or practice fanatical eating or bingeing and purging in order to reach a state of thinness that for most is unachievable. From as early as the *DSM-I* (American Psychiatric Association [APA], 1952), problems with eating that resulted in disturbances of metabolism, growth, and nutrition were noted. Eating disorders can also occur in children, as outlined with the first inclusion of the eating disorders as a specific category in the *DSM-III*. The *DSM-III* acknowledged diagnoses such as anorexia nervosa and bulimia as well as childhood eating disorders such as pica (Woo & Keatinge, 2008).

Furthermore, the prevalence of eating disorders in adolescents who report physical neglect or sexual abuse points to the fact that environmental as well as social parental rearing practices also seem to be a factor (Johnson, Cohen, Kasen, & Brook, 2002). Research has shown that families can play an important role in the reduction of eating disorders. Developmental, social, and behavioral factors and influences of the family system make children and adolescents different from adults. This difference requires a comprehensive and creative approach to completing the diagnostic assessment and subsequent therapy. Consequently, each revision of the *DSM* has put forth more diagnostic criteria that take into account developmental issues related to the child (Grills-Taquechel & Ollendick, 2008). According to Loth, Neumark-Sztainer, and Croll (2009), research focused on the effects of family support show that the "parent child relationship can play a paramount role in the psychological and social well being of a child" (p. 150). It was also determined that eating disorders were more likely to develop when the individual was going through a challenging time. Other determining factors include "negative weight and body talk and teasing" (p. 150). When the practitioner addresses peer and societal pressures, parental intervention and family support become important factors, thereby reducing the likelihood of the child developing an eating disorder.

The focus of this chapter is to provide a brief overview of several of the most common eating disorders in children and adults. A more comprehensive application section related to the adult eating disorder anorexia nervosa is the focus of the application section of the chapter.

EATING DISORDERS IN CHILDREN: BRIEF OVERVIEW AND CRITERIA

In the past, children were not a primary focus when considering the severity of eating disorders. It has since become clear that this is not the case; eating disorders do not just affect adults but children as well. Although eating problems may be common in children, "Identification and diagnosis of eating disorders in children and adolescents are a major problem because . . . the DSM is not developmentally sensitive focusing on adults with long standing disorders" (Lock, 2009, p. 10). According to Lock, typically when diagnosed, children (approximately 60%) are given the diagnosis of Eating Disorder NOS because they do not meet the behavioral thresholds of a specific diagnosis. Two of the most common eating disorders in children include pica and rumination disorder.

In the *DSM-IV-TR* (APA, 2000), pica (307.52) is given the status of a distinct eating disorder, similar to rumination disorder of infancy and the adult-related eating disorders of anorexia nervosa and bulimia nervosa. Pica is the persistent eating of nonnutritive substances for a period of at least 1 month. Substances that are ingested vary with age. "Common forms of Pica includes geographia (ingestion of clay, sand or dirt), pagophagia (ice), trichophagy (hair) and amylophagia (laundry starch)" (Lemanek et al., 2002, p. 493). Prevalence estimates are that 25% to 50% of children under the age of 2 suffer from pica. It is also prevalent in children living in poverty and in African American children compared to Caucasian children (Lemanek et al., 2002). To date, the causes and risk factors of pica are not well established and no definitive answers have been provided for the behaviors associated with pica (Kislal et al., 2003). Pica is a serious disorder that can have deadly implications. According to Lemanek (2002), severe risks associated with pica include death due to intestinal obstruction and high blood levels of lead that may affect cognitive functioning.

Rumination disorder (307.53) is listed in the *DSM-IV-TR* as " . . . the repeated regurgitation and rechewing of food occurring after feeding that develops in an infant or child after a period of

normal functioning and lasts for at least 1 month" (APA, 2000, p. 105). The disorder may be seen in older individuals, particularly those with mental retardation. The act of rumination—the regurgitation and rechewing of digested food—appears to give pleasure. Infants suffering from this disorder often "display a characteristic position of straining and arching the back with the head back, making sucking movements with their tongues and give the impression of gaining satisfaction from the activity" (APA, 2000, p. 105). Infants or children suffering from a rumination disorder can present a particular challenge for the parent as they are often irritable and no matter how much they eat, hunger is always a problem. These children can suffer from malnutrition because they may eat but regurgitate it before proper nutrition can be obtained.

SELECTED CHILDHOOD EATING DISORDERS: ASSESSMENT AND DIAGNOSIS

Pica

The essential features of pica (307.52), as defined in the *DSM-IV-TR* (APA, 2000), include the persistent eating of nonnutritive substances for a period of at least 1 month. According to the *DSM-IV-TR*, young children and infants typically eat paint, plaster, string, hair, or cloth. Older children may eat animal droppings, sand, insects, leaves, or pebbles. Other nonnutritive substances that have been ingested include, but are not limited to, cigarette butts, chalk, and stick deodorant. (See Quick Reference 6.1 diagnostic criteria for pica.)

Associated features and disorders specified in the DSM-IV-TR (APA, 2000) state that pica is frequently associated with mental retardation. See Quick Reference 6.2 for criteria for mental retardation.

Although vitamin or mineral deficiencies have been reported in some instances, usually

QUICK REFERENCE 6.1

DIAGNOSTIC CRITERIA FOR PICA (307.52)

Criterion A Involves persistent eating of nonnutritive substances for a period of at least one month.

Criterion B When the eating of nonnutritive substances is inappropriate to the developmental level.

Criterion C When the eating behavior is not part of a culturally sanctioned practice.

Criterion D When the eating behavior occurs exclusively during the course of another mental disorder (e.g., Mental Retardation, Pervasive Developmental Disorder, and Schizophrenia), it is sufficiently severe to warrant independent clinical attention.

Source: Summarized criteria from the *Diagnostic and Statistical Manual of Mental Disorders, Fourth Edition, Text Revision.* Copyright 2000 by the American Psychiatric Association.

no specific biological abnormalities are found. Pica may come to clinical attention when an individual presents for other medical complications that are a result of them ingesting nonnutritional substances. Some medical conditions that may result from pica are lead poisoning caused by ingesting paint, mechanical bowel problems, intestinal obstruction resulting from hair-ball tumors, intestinal perforation, or infections such as toxoplasmosis and toxacariasis resulting from eating feces or dirt.

QUICK REFERENCE 6.2

DIAGNOSTIC CRITERIA FOR MENTAL RETARDATION

Abbreviated Guidelines:

- If this condition is present, after the intelligence levels have been confirmed, it should be diagnosed.
- Individuals must have significantly subaverage intelligence and deficits in adaptive functioning.
- Definition is compatible with AAMR definition except for subtyping.
- Onset prior to age 18; if later, the proper diagnosis is dementia.
- Must have IQ of 70 or below on an individual intelligence test (IQ).
- This disorder is slightly more common in males.

Borderline Intellectual Functioning

IQ 71–84, Can code on Axis II.

Mild

IQ approximately 50–55 to 70, considered educable, able to perform at sixth-grade level, can use minimal assistance, may need some supervision and guidance, can live in community or in supervised settings.

Moderate

IQ approximately 35–40 to 50–55, considered trainable, able to perform at second-grade level, with moderate supervision, can attend to their own personal care, can perform unskilled or semiskilled work, can live in the community.

(continued)

> ## QUICK REFERENCE 6.2 (*Continued*)
>
> ### Severe
>
> IQ approximately 20–25 to 35–40, generally institutionalized, have little or no communicative speech, possibly can live in a group home.
>
> ### Profound
>
> IQ below 20 or 25, generally total care required.
>
> ### Note
>
> All IQ score categories can have a margin of error equivalent to a 5-point overlap in the predicted IQ score, except for mild mental retardation, which starts at 70.
>
> ----
>
> *Source:* Summarized criteria from the *Diagnostic and Statistical Manual of Mental Disorders, Fourth Edition, Text Revision.* Copyright 2000 by the American Psychiatric Association.

The risk of developing pica is increased by poverty, neglect, lack of parental supervision, and developmental delay.

In terms of prevalence, according to the *DSM-IV-TR*, pica is more common in young children and occasionally is found in pregnant females. In some cultures, the eating of dirt or other nonnutritive substances is seen as valuable. According to Gavin (2007), while pica is most common in people with intellectual and developmental disabilities (IDD), it is believed that 25% to 30% of nondisabled children have pica. As reported in the *DSM-IV-TR*, the severity of the pica behavior increases with the severity of the retardation, with it being reported as high as 15% in adults with IDD. Pica usually begins in infancy and generally lasts for several months. It can continue into adolescence and with less frequency may continue into adulthood.

Rumination Disorder

The *DSM-IV-TR* describes disorders of feeding and eating that are generally diagnosed in infancy or early childhood. Rumination disorder (307.53) is included as Feeding and Eating Disorders of Infancy or Early Childhood. The essential features of rumination disorder as defined in the *DSM-IV-TR* (APA, 2000) include the repeated regurgitation and rechewing of food occurring after feeding that develops in an infant or child after a period of normal functioning and lasts for at least 1 month. Partially digested food is brought up into the mouth without apparent nausea, retching, disgust, or associated gastrointestinal disorder. The food is then either ejected from the mouth or, more frequently, chewed and reswallowed. The symptoms are not due to an associated gastrointestinal or other general medical condition (e.g., Sandifer's syndrome, esophageal reflux) and do not occur exclusively during the course of anorexia nervosa or bulimia nervosa. If the symptoms occur exclusively during the course of mental retardation or a pervasive developmental disorder, the disorder is most commonly observed in infants, but may be seen in older individuals, particularly those with mental retardation. In older children and adults, mental retardation is a predisposing factor. The act of rumination appears to be pleasurable in some instances: "infants display a characteristic position of straining and arching the back with the head back, making sucking movements with their tongues and give the impression of gaining satisfaction from the activity" (p. 105).

Infants with this disorder are generally irritable and hungry between episodes of regurgitation. Although they ingest large amounts of food, malnutrition may occur due to regurgitation immediately following the feedings. Weight loss, failure to make expected weight gains, and even death can result. Mortality rates as high as 25% have been reported. Malnutrition appears to be less likely in older children and adults in whom the disorder may be either continuous or episodic. Psychosocial problems, such as lack of stimulation, neglect, stressful life situations, and problems in the parent-child relationship, may be predisposing factors. Understimulation of the infant may result if the caregiver becomes discouraged and alienated because of the unsuccessful feeding experiences or the noxious odor of the regurgitated material. In some instances, feeding disorder of infancy or early childhood may also develop.

According to the *DSM-IV-TR*, rumination disorder appears to be uncommon. It may occur more often in males than in females. The onset may occur in the context of developmental delays. Onset is between ages 3 and 12 months, except in individuals with mental retardation, where the disorder may occur at a later developmental stage. In infants, the disorder frequently remits spontaneously. In some severe cases, the course is continuous.

EATING DISORDERS IN ADULTS

The exact definition of what constitutes thin can be elusive. This leaves food, weight, and body image an almost unavoidable preoccupation for many individuals. It is not unusual to use social comparisons to evaluate body image; women who compare their body shape and size to thinner women often develop a negative self-image (Bergstrom, Neighbors, & Malheim, 2009). According to Ivezaj et al. (2010), there is a strong relationship between binge eating and body image dissatisfaction. When individuals become dissatisfied with their weight and the way they look, this can result in the development of an eating disorder. In the last decades, the frequency of eating disorders has greatly increased, causing alarm among physicians (Daga, Boggio, Garzaro, & Pierò, 2004; Keski-Rahkonen et al., 2007; Klein & Walsh, 2003). Two common types of eating disorders are bulimia nervosa and anorexia nervosa.

Bulimia Nervosa

Bulimia nervosa (307.51) is a widespread eating disorder with symptom behaviors such as characteristic bouts of overeating and subsequent troublesome methods of controlling weight (i.e., self-induced vomiting, laxative abuse, and overexercise). According to Walsh (2008), individuals with bulimia nervosa appear to benefit from therapeutic interventions including antidepressant medications and cognitive-behavioral therapy. They continue to recover from their illness over time.

Eating disorders often occur in women, particularly Caucasian women, and it is this group that appears at the greatest risk for developing such disorders (Hoek, 2006; Wittchen & Jacobi, 2005). Although binge eating without purging is not uncommon among African American women, anorexia nervosa and purging behaviors are rare (Striegel-Moore et al., 2003, 2005). For African American women, multiple factors make up attractiveness. While body image is a component of attractiveness, it has been defined largely by Caucasian standards, overlooking African American women. For African American women, body image is defined by multiple factors, not just physical characteristics. These factors include how others react to them, comparisons of their bodies with those of others in their environment, and comparison to cultural ideals (Davis, Sbrocco, Odoms-Young, & Smith, 2010).

Prevalence and incidence is changing, and this is no longer a problem related solely to adult women. This trend can also be seen in girls as young as 6 and 7 who wish to be thinner than they are and acknowledge that they are dieting (Collins, 1991). Pollatos et al. (2008) found that "eating disorders are the most prevalent psychiatric disorder in females aged between 14 to 26" (p. 1). Girls, and increasingly boys, can become distressed over some aspect of their body that they believe is flawed, resulting in their feeling inadequate and unattractive (Hartley-Brewer, 2008). This increase in preoccupation with thinness and dieting in young girls and boys is an alarming trend. Current research indicates that body dissatisfaction and dieting are predictors of increased eating disorder symptoms among adolescent girls and boys (Field et al., 2002; Hartley-Brewer, 2008; Johnson & Wardle, 2005). It is estimated that among individuals who receive treatment for eating disorders, 40% to 50% of those treated for anorexia nervosa and 50% to 60% of those treated for bulimia nervosa will make a complete recovery (Loth et al., 2009).

The mass media and social norms dictate an unrealistic ideal of body shape and size that create impractical standards. According to Dittmar (2009), perfect body ideals are communicated to children early on—for example, through Barbie dolls. Girls as young as 5 to 7 years of age reported lower body esteem and a greater desire for a thinner body directly after exposure to such dolls. British researchers have found that girls between the ages of 14 and 17 experienced increased body consciousness when they idolized a celebrity. This can result in a negative body image on the part of the young woman if the celebrity is unrealistically thin. Ultimately the resulting body dissatisfaction can trigger an eating disorder (Vandereycken, 2006). Biological and genetic factors tell us that the current "thin is beautiful" ideals describe a body weight for most women that is unrealistically low and unhealthy

(Wilfley & Rodin, 1995). Women constantly confronted with the media's slender and beautiful ideals thus aspire to a standard that is impossible for most to achieve (Bergstrom et al., 2009; Pliner, Chaiken, & Flett, 1990). Mass media objectification of the female body contributes to teach girls and women that their value is based primarily on their looks (Moradi, Dirks, & Matteson, 2005).

Men are not immune to the pressures of culture and increased personal pressure to achieve unrealistic physical standards. In the past decades, males have also been targeted in the media, "which is a particularly potent and pervasive source of influence" (Dittmar, 2009, p. 2). Consequently, they have slowly begun to succumb to cultural pressures with many individuals becoming preoccupied with attractiveness (Dittmar, 2009; Pope, Phillips, & Olivardia, 2000). To ascribe to this expectation, they have increased their efforts to build muscle and stay lean (Leit, Pope, & Gray, 2001). Ochner, Gray, and Brickner (2009) report that men desire to gain more lean muscle and maintain a lean muscular build known as the "mesomorphic" body type. Taken to extremes, this can lead to depression and muscle dysmorphia in men. Men share body image concerns much as women do (Furnham, Badmin, & Sneade, 2002; Pope, Phillips, & Olivardia, 2000), and evidence suggests that men and women are growing increasingly dissatisfied with their bodies (Adams, Turner, & Bucks, 2005; Ochner et al., 2009).

According to Peplau, Frederick, Yee, Maisel, Lever, and Ghavami (2009), gay men are at greater risk for body dissatisfaction, which makes them more susceptible to developing eating disorders. One reason for this may be the value that is placed on attractiveness and good looks within the gay community. Boroughs and Thompson (2002) report that, especially in males, excessive exercise can be another important aspect of the gay community related to the preoccupation with body image and staying fit to remain attractive. In addition, Feldman and Meyer (2007) found sexual orientation to be a prominent risk factor.

Attention to the psychological and physiological development of eating disorders is critical because eating disorders are associated with serious and even fatal medical complications. Courtney, Gamboz, and Johnson (2008) found that the co-occurrence of eating disorders with other pathologies exists: Eating pathology is associated with depression, substance abuse, and anxiety disorder.

Anorexia Nervosa

In anorexia nervosa, the essential feature is refusal to maintain a minimum body weight. Lifetime prevalence rates of anorexia nervosa are 0.3% for men and 0.9% for women (Hoek, 2006; Wittchen & Jacobi, 2005). Death from starvation is a realistic concern for individuals who suffer from anorexia nervosa—mortality rates are the highest of any psychiatric disorder, ranging from 6% to 20% (Mitchell & Bulik, 2006; Pomeroy, 1996; Steinhausen, 2002).

Denial is a hallmark of anorexia nervosa, which leaves many individuals refusing to acknowledge or simply unaware that they have the disorder (Mitchell & Bulik, 2006). Treating anorexia can be problematic even with active client participation. Only one-half of the individuals who suffer from anorexia nervosa recover. Of those who do recover, up to 30% live with residual symptoms and as many as 20% experience severe disabilities from the chronic nature and severity of the disease (Pomeroy, 1996; Steinhausen, 2002). In addition, women with this disorder have a suicide risk that is 50 times higher than the general population (Keel et al., 2003).

According to Mitchell and Bulik (2006), low self-esteem and body image dissatisfaction have been consistent predictors of problem dieting and eating disorders. Katsounari (2009) states that self-esteem is central to how people see themselves as far as their capacity to do things

as well as the value they place on themselves. Self-esteem means respecting oneself. Often women receive mixed messages about what is desirable. "Women are convinced of the thinness ideal while living in a society of abundance and increasing obesity. The idealization of thinness has a strong appeal because it is associated with the idea of happiness and success" (Karpowicz, Skärsäter, & Nevonen, 2009, p. 319). Furthermore, Karpowicz et al. report that body image is a core aspect of mental and physical well-being and body dissatisfaction is linked to many physical and mental health problems including obesity, body dysmorphic disorder, depression, and low self-esteem.

Eating Disorders and Body Image

According to Dittmar (2009), although all individuals are exposed to mass media and cultural messages about physical appearance, some will actually develop eating disorders or could have serious body image problems, or both. Research has shown that the media's portrayal of body image and the comparison that is made to thin models as the ideal body shape contributes to body image disturbance (Bergstrom, 2009). Negative or traumatic experiences associated with appearance can be internalized triggering negative assumptions about an individual's own body shape. These assumptions influence self-esteem, personality, and behavior. Over time, an individual may rehearse negative and distorted self-statements about his or her appearance until they become unconsciously held beliefs. In both bulimia and anorexia, this sets up behavior patterns that maintain the preoccupation with appearance.

When an individual is diagnosed with an eating disorder, numerous things must be taken into account, and intervention options can vary. The application of this chapter discusses one of the most common forms of eating disorders, anorexia nervosa, and addresses related issues from a community and societal perspective. To reduce the magnitude of disturbances this disorder can have on the individual, the family, and society, it is critical that practitioners complete a thorough diagnostic assessment, treatment plan, and practice strategy that can efficiently embrace, identify, and effectively treat individuals who suffer from anorexia nervosa. Family-related factors, such as support and willingness for treatment assistance, are an important dynamic that should always be taken into account to facilitate treatment success (Kluck, 2008).

Anorexia and Use of the DSM-IV-TR Multiaxial System

The essential features of anorexia nervosa (307.1) as defined in the *DSM-IV-TR* (APA, 2000) include the individual's refusal to maintain a minimally normal body weight. (See Quick Reference 6.3 for the criterion needed to make the diagnosis.)

Individuals with this type of eating disorder look in the mirror and believe their reflection is too heavy for their body frame and height. They have a distorted body image—a significant disturbance in the perception of the shape or size of their body. This leads to adopting methods that contribute to severe weight reduction (see Criterion A). Weight loss is achieved by reduction in total food intake, although it could also occur through purging, such as self-induced vomiting or misuse of laxatives or diuretics, and excessive exercise. Minimal body weight is reached when the individual weighs 85% less than what is considered normal for age and weight based on published charts, such as the Metropolitan Life Insurance tables. In the diagnostic assessment, it is important that the individual's body build and weight history be considered when evaluating this criterion.

Individuals suffering from anorexia nervosa also have an intense fear of gaining weight (see Criterion B). This intense fear is not alleviated by weight loss but often increases as the individual's weight decreases, often leading to desperate measures to control weight. In addition, the self-esteem of anorexic individuals is critically tied to their body weight and size. These individuals perceive weight loss as an impressive achievement and a feat of great self-discipline and self-control. Some individuals may feel globally overweight while others recognize that they are thin but focus on certain body parts that they consider "too fat" (Criterion C). Techniques used by these individuals to monitor their weight and size include weighing themselves numerous times per day, obsessive measuring of body parts, and constant checking in the mirror for fat. In addition, they may participate in avoidance behaviors that help them maintain their drive to lose weight. For

---

QUICK REFERENCE 6.3

CRITERIA FOR ANOREXIA NERVOSA (307.1)

Criterion A	Maintaining a body weight that is below normal.
Criterion B	Intense fear of gaining weight.
Criterion C	Distortion of the significance of body weight and shape.
Criterion D	Amenorrhea.

Source: Summarized criteria from the *Diagnostic and Statistical Manual of Mental Disorders, Fourth Edition, Text Revision.* Copyright 2000 by the American Psychiatric Association.

example, they often avoid situations where they may be expected to eat or where others may view them eating, or they wear loose-fitting clothing to disguise their diminishing shape.

The strong denial component combined with the severe weight loss associated with anorexia nervosa often results in the cessation or disruption of menstrual cycles (amenorrhea) in postmenarcheal females (Criterion D). Abnormally low levels of estrogen secretion bring about amenorrhea, and the cessation of menstruation is a physical indication of significant physiological dysfunction. Many anorexic women judge success at losing and maintaining their desired weight only when their menstrual cycle stops.

When these women are of childbearing age, this disturbance in the menstrual cycle will also disturb attempts at pregnancy and affect childbearing.

Two primary subtypes of anorexia nervosa focus on the current or presenting symptoms or episode. (See Quick Reference 6.4 for a brief discussion of the various subtypes.) The first subtype is the restricting type. In this subtype, the individual does not regularly engage in binge eating or purging to maintain weight but rather focuses primary attention and efforts on restriction of food intake. In the second subtype, the binge eating/purging type, the individual regularly engages in binge eating or purging (or both). Generally, a binge is defined as eating in a discrete period of time (usually less than 2 hours) an amount of food that is definitely larger than most individuals would eat under similar circumstances. If the individual binges, she will also purge by self-induced vomiting or the misuse of laxatives, diuretics, or enemas. Many will purge without bingeing.

Anorexia Nervosa: Associated Conditions and Features

Associated conditions and features that are supplemental but not essential to making the diagnosis of anorexia nervosa include associated laboratory findings and general medical conditions that may present on a physical exam. For many individuals who suffer from this disorder, depressive features, such as depressed mood, social withdrawal, irritability, insomnia, and diminished interest in sex, may coexist. This is why in the diagnostic assessment it is important to assess symptoms of depression and whether the criteria for a comorbid diagnosis of major depressive disorder may be met.

In addition, the client may be so consumed with the thought of controlling food intake that obsessive-compulsive features may also exist. Furthermore, the need to control may be so strong that, at times, these behaviors may also be unrelated to food. Since clients are preoccupied with thoughts of food, it is not uncommon for some to collect or hoard food. Other features of the disorder include concerns about eating in public, feelings of ineffectiveness, a strong need to control one's environment, inflexible thinking, limited social spontaneity, and overly restrained initiative and emotional expression.

One important aspect of completing the diagnostic assessment is looking carefully at the general medical conditions coded on Axis III. Assessment and documentation on this axis are important because the semistarvation state can affect most major organs and produce a variety of serious medical disturbances. Induced vomiting and use of laxatives, diuretics, and enemas associated with anorexia nervosa can also cause a number of physical disturbances, including severe anemia and hepatic, thyroid, cardiovascular, dental, and hormone disturbances. Every possible attempt should be made to include information in the diagnostic assessment from associated laboratory and medical findings. Furthermore, a physical exam should always be the first referral if one has not already been completed.

QUICK REFERENCE 6.4

SUBTYPES FOR ANOREXIA

Restricting type: During the current episode, the individual has not regularly engaged in binge eating or purging, and weight loss is primarily accomplished through restriction of food intake.

Binge eating/purging type: During the current episode, the individual has regularly engaged in binge eating or purging (or both).

Source: Summarized criteria from the *Diagnostic and Statistical Manual of Mental Disorders, Fourth Edition, Text Revision*. Copyright 2000 by the American Psychiatric Association.

Anorexia Nervosa: Specific Culture, Age, and Gender Features

Prevalence studies show that 0.5% to 1.0% of the population meets the full criteria and many more are on the threshold for the disorder. Although often body image concerns may begin in late childhood or early adolescence, anorexia nervosa symptoms rarely begin before puberty. Although men also suffer from this disorder, more than 90% of the cases occur in females (APA, 2000). Generally, anorexia nervosa appears more frequently in industrialized societies where there is an abundance of food and where being considered attractive is linked to being extremely thin.

For most individuals who suffer from this disorder, the mean (average) age at onset is approximately 17 years, although some individuals start earlier. Peaks in the disorder occur at ages 14 and 18. According to Lewinsohn and Striegel-Moore (2000), middle to late adolescence is most likely the period of greatest vulnerability for the onset of eating disorders. The course and outcome of this disorder are variable; some individuals experience only one episode while others experience a chronically deteriorating course over many years. It is not uncommon for hospitalization to be required in order to maintain weight and restore body functioning. The long-term mortality rate is 10%, and death commonly results from starvation, suicide, or electrolyte imbalance. In terms of familial pattern, there is an increased risk of anorexia nervosa among the first-degree biological relatives of individuals with the disorder. According to Mitchell and Bulik (2006), family studies show that there is a greater lifetime prevalence of eating disorders among relatives of individuals with an eating disorder. Studies have shown that there is a strong genetic link between the children who have an eating disorder and the child's mother. Therefore, having a parent with an eating disorder may constitute an at-risk group, and children of mothers with eating disorders should be monitored closely.

Probably one of the biggest factors to consider when first meeting with a client who suffers from this disorder is that most times individuals do not generally seek treatment on their own. Instead, individuals with anorexia nervosa are often brought to treatment by a concerned family member or a friend. Individuals with anorexia will rarely seek help on their own because they fear that getting help will lead to weight gain. In addition, they frequently lack insight into their problem, and the overriding characteristic is denial. In completing the diagnostic assessment, accurate information regarding symptoms and duration should be collected from family members or other outside sources in addition to what is stated by the client.

Historical Aspects and Intervention with Anorexia Nervosa

Research shows that anorexia nervosa has an estimated prevalence rate of 0.5% to 1.0% (Herzog & Eddy, 2009). Considering the lethality of this disorder, these statistics are alarming. Low self-esteem has been identified as a primary factor in the development of eating disorders. From childhood, individuals have a tendency to evaluate their appearance in relation to ideal physical standards set by society. Self-worth is often based on how closely these standards are met. Socialization, particularly influences from parents, peers, and the media, contributes to the acquisition of values and attitudes about appearance. Messages that convey the importance of appearance contribute to ongoing social comparison and beliefs that looks and body shape and size symbolize a person's worth.

Normal developmental changes brought about by puberty often bring on an intense preoccupation with changes in the body and concern about how one will be perceived by others. According to Newman and Newman (2009), adolescent girls who are attempting to reduce negative feelings about themselves due to body dissatisfaction may begin restrictive diets, denying their bodies of the increased calorie intake that is needed during this time of rapid growth. Normal changes in the body, such as menstruation and increases in body fat in the breasts or hips as a girl matures, often precipitate persistent negative body image disturbances (Byely et al., 2000; Cash, 1996). Personality traits also provide a moderating influence on body image development. Individuals may define themselves in terms of their physical attributes, which contributes to a substantial negative impact on self-esteem and social confidence. These individuals have developed negative perceptions or schemata and are more vulnerable to societal "shoulds" that define their physical acceptability.

Cognitive-behavioral therapy formats are effective interventions for avoiding negative thinking patterns. Changes such as fewer cognitive body image errors, less frequent negative body image thoughts, and less preoccupation with weight are addressed. Cognitive-behavioral therapy appears to be effective in improving cognitive, evaluative, effective, perceptual, and self-reported behavioral aspects of body image. According to Schapman-Williams and Lock (2007), cognitive-behavioral therapy is superior to other treatments when working with eating disorders. To understand the development of this eating disorder, current research has examined the relationship of familial influences on the development of one's body image and dieting patterns. Allen, Byrne, Forbes, and Oddy (2009) found that there is a strong relationship between parental approval and eating behavior. When parents perceive a child as overweight, there is an increase in the risk of developing an eating disorder. Often a girl will believe that the only aspect of her life that she can control is her own weight. Thus, family involvement in treatment of the anorexic individual is often an essential component in recovery and prevention of relapse.

Regarding recovery:

[I]t appears that with an adolescent onset and a shorter duration of symptoms there are favorable prognostic signs among individuals with anorexia nervosa. However, once the symptoms of anorexia nervosa have persisted for some years, the illness seems to take on an impressive refractoriness. Seemingly appropriate therapeutic interventions such as antidepressant medications and cognitive behavioral therapy have, at most, modest impact among adults with anorexia nervosa. (Walsh, 2008, p. 95)

─────────── **CASE EXAMPLE 6.1 - CASE EXAMPLE OF M** ───────────

M is a 19-year-old Caucasian female college sophomore who came to the University Counseling Clinic at the urging of her friends. She was alert and oriented to person, place, time, and situation (oriented x4), and her speech was of normal rate and rhythm. Upon interview, M looked thin and pale, and when asked her weight she was reluctant to state what it was. When asked why she was so reluctant, she said it was because her family, especially her mother, was always asking, and this made her feel uncomfortable. According to the nurse's initial documentation she was 5 feet, 9 inches tall and weighed approximately 110 pounds. She stated her preferred weight was 100 pounds but the last time she got close to it her mother insisted that she would be hospitalized unless she started eating. To please her mother and get her to leave her alone, M said she ate rice and milk. This made her sick to her stomach as soon as her mother had left her apartment. When asked what had brought her to the clinic, at first M was resistant and stated that her only reason for coming in was to "talk to someone" to please her friends and family.

During the initial session, she also admitted feeling frustrated with herself and her physical appearance. She stated that she was experiencing problems with eating and had lost her appetite. She said she exercised daily and sometimes ran 2 to 5 miles twice a day if possible. She stated that she had given up meat and bread and now was having a hard time finding something that she could eat that would not upset her stomach. She said that her mother tried to get her to take vitamins, but they upset her stomach even more. Although she does not tell many people, she almost enjoys getting sick and throwing up her food because this way she knows that she is free to eat again later if she so chooses without having to worry about gaining weight. She reported that she did not see her current weight as a problem and wanted everyone to know that she did not plan to start eating anything that she did not like. She said she realized that she was having "some problems" with school but stated that she felt she could handle them, even though her family and friends were concerned. When discussing her weight she said, "They're just making a big deal out of this." When asked what her goal was for coming, she stated that she had an interest in wanting to learn how to "lose weight in a healthy way."

M also reported that at times she has "anger at food" and cannot stop thinking about eating. M reported that she lost 10 pounds in the last 2 weeks and, although she wishes to lose more weight, she realizes how concerned her family is that she has lost too much weight. She stated, "It is not easy for me to lose weight but if I stick to a strict routine I am sure it can be done."

Completion of the Diagnostic Assessment for M The first step in starting the diagnostic assessment is to identify the presenting problem (see Case Example 6.1, Case Example of M). To complete this information, the initial assessment includes factual information about the client and her behaviors. See Quick Reference 6.5, which outlines the presenting problems.

Once the primary and presenting problems have been identified, the first task of the mental health practitioner, especially in regard to the client's desire to stop eating and continue losing weight, is to complete a risk assessment. Key questions will identify if there is a potential for self-harm or suicide. These questions are always asked in a straightforward and direct manner. Once identified, this information should be clearly recorded in the client's file. In this case, while assessing lethality, M reported having thoughts of suicide while in high school. She stated that although she never attempted to harm herself, she has thought about it seriously since she was in high school. Upon interview, she denied any suicidal or homicidal thoughts and stated, "I have too much to live for and don't want to end my life." (See Quick

---

QUICK REFERENCE 6.5

IDENTIFY PRIMARY AND PRESENTING PROBLEMS

Primary problem: A sincere desire to lose weight and refusal to maintain a normal healthy weight.

Presenting problems: Preoccupation with eating and weight reduction, anger at food.

Low body weight with minimal weight loss causing considerable concern.

Lack of appetite and consumption of food, overexercises.

Strong denial of the presenting problem.

Reference 6.6 for an overview of the risk assessment.)

The mental status exam report described M as below normal weight for her height, well groomed, neatly and appropriately dressed. She was cooperative and spoke willingly and openly. Her thought processes and speech were logical and coherent, with occasional tangential drifts when giving details. Her mood fluctuated between moderate calmness, anxiety, and frustration as she described her concerns. Her affect fluctuated between appropriate and somewhat dramatic, particularly when speaking about her anger regarding food and eating. Motor movement was within expected limits, and there was no evidence of delusions or hallucinations; however, she exhibited pronounced preoccupation with food and the eating behaviors of herself and others. M appeared to be of above-average intelligence; however, her insight and judgment appeared somewhat limited, particularly concerning eating and weight.

In gathering history information, M stated that she grew up in a small town, with still-married parents and a brother 6 years younger. Her mother is a registered nurse and her father is an engineer. She voiced a strong sense of obligation to please her parents and stated that her biggest fear was disappointing them. M reported that she was not fat as a child but always felt that she was. Although she stated that she was not teased as a child and had many friends, she began to experience strong anger, resentment, hurt, and a sense of unfairness when she compared herself to her peers during her first years in high school. M reported that when she was a sophomore in high school, she hated herself and had thoughts of suicide. Nevertheless, she did not make an attempt, and then felt even more anger at herself that she could not follow through with it. She wrote of her anger at herself and her wish for death in journals and stated that after two years, she "let go" of the anger.

M reported that at that time, she also developed an aversion to using public bathrooms and reported that she was able to control her bowel habits, refraining from having a bowel movement for numerous days or possibly 2 weeks if

---

QUICK REFERENCE 6.6

RISK ASSESSMENT

Document and assess suicide risk: Previous history of ideation, no previous attempts, no current ideation, no evidence of current attempts.

Document and assess violence risk: None.

she wished. She admitted that she felt powerful controlling her body in this way and also in her ability to limit her food intake. By the end of her junior year in high school, her concerns about food led her to consult with a practitioner of alternative medicine, who helped her to learn about all the unhealthy additives and chemicals in foods. Using this information as rationale, she began eliminating more and more foods from her diet. When she did this, she began to lose weight. She stated that she set a goal of attaining a size 3, which she selected because "it represented the tall but petite size." Throughout her senior year in high school and by the end of her freshman year at college, she had started losing weight where others would notice. Some of her friends complimented her, and she said it felt good. She stated that she did this by limiting her intake of food, exercising every day, and occasionally purging by vomiting. She became a vegetarian 5 months ago, further restricting the foods she "allows" herself to eat. Fearing her parents' disapproval, when she occasionally goes to her hometown for a weekend, she stays with friends and often she does not let her parents know that she is in town.

Family history of psychopathology reveals that her mother has experienced depressive symptoms for more than 10 years; however, it is unknown if she was ever diagnosed with a mental health condition or has taken psychotropic medication. M stated that her father's psychiatric history is unremarkable.

Based on the chronic nature and negative effects that can result from limiting food intake, a complete medical and dental history was suggested. M denied any significant medical history. She reported a dislike of and distrust with traditional medicine and medical providers and preferred alternate methods, such as herbs, vitamins, and meditation. M reported that she had a strong aversion to menstruation. She stated that this aversion was so great in high school that she

would constantly clean herself, changing clothes and bathing frequently. She reported that in the past, she has had amenorrhea for a period of time (unknown duration) and currently has very irregular periods. She stated that she thinks she may be infertile because of this.

Although she denied having allergies, she voiced a strong aversion to preservatives, dyes, and other chemical additives to foods and is fearful of eating foods containing them. For example, she stated she could eat white rice that she has prepared, but worried that it contained additives if she purchased it from a restaurant and would not eat it. Although she denied purging behavior at this time, her front teeth appear uneven and have moderate calcification. M denied any psychiatric treatment in the past. She stated that she has not had a physical examination recently but would be willing to get one if it would help her family and friends feel better about her.

When assessing her daily functioning ability, the client stated she felt a great deal of anger and this anger is directed primarily at food. M reported feeling angry when watching others eat or when others watch her eat, and is also angry and resentful that others can eat "bad" things and not have a "problem" as she does. She reported feelings of guilt if she eats something "unhealthy" and maintains rigid rules for what she considers healthy or okay to eat. M reported that she refuses to eat food that she has not prepared herself or has not watched as others prepared it, voicing a fear that there may be "bad" things in the food. She identified these bad things as additives, chemicals, fat, or animal products. Currently, she stated that it is easier for her to fast than it is to eat and that she has difficulty keeping food down when she does try to eat. M reported feeling uncomfortably full and very guilty when she eats even small amounts (e.g., a cup of plain pasta or white rice). She stated that she consumes vitamins and herbs. She admitted that she stores food in her room but that she rarely eats it because she feels it is "old." M reported that she weighs herself three to five times a day and that she now wishes to attain a dress size of 1 within 2 months. M reported that she drinks large amount of liquids, primarily water, sugar-free caffeine drinks, and coffee, and does not smoke cigarettes. She reported having good grades in high school, taking many advanced placement classes, and currently has a 3.2 college grade point average.

She reported that, at this time, she feels happier with herself and her life and attributes this to her dedicated routines that led to her weight loss plan. Although she reported that she belongs to a sorority and has many caring friends, she also spoke of a sense of not belonging or fitting in. She reported dating occasionally but stated that she has never had a steady boyfriend or serious dating experience. At this time, M reported a general feeling of tiredness and concern that her grades are slipping. She admitted that she is extremely concerned about her appearance and will not go out of her room if her clothing, hair, and makeup are not exactly the way she wants. Although she attends classes most days, she stated that she skips class if she does not have enough time to dress and groom properly. Although she voiced an extreme concern for health, this does not generalize to concern about drinking caffeine. She reported that she has no difficulty falling asleep; however, feels that she is getting less sleep than she would like. M reported that she rarely gets to bed before 2 A.M. and admitted that much of her time is spent doing favors for her friends and listening to their problems and counseling them. She denies problems with dreams or nightmares.

Although she stated that she does not have an eating disorder, she mentioned that some of her behaviors are "similar to those of a person with an eating disorder," and she voiced concern that she

may be losing control of eating. When asked what would she like to achieve from mental health intervention, M stated that her goal is to "decrease her weight in a way that is healthy and to understand more about her anger at food."

Application of the Multiaxial Format with M
After compiling the information for the diagnostic assessment, it appears as if M disguises and justifies her extreme fear of weight gain and her extreme restriction of foods into more acceptable terms that she refers to as "maintaining health consciousness." She constantly attempts to rationalize systematically (uses the defense mechanism, rationalization) by limiting her range of allowable foods in the name of good health. She displays many of the classic symptomatic behaviors of anorexia nervosa, such as hoarding but not eating food; avoiding eating when others can observe her; feelings of power only when she controls her body; feelings of guilt about eating; feeling overfull after eating tiny amounts of food; as well as many monitoring, restricting, and purging behaviors. Although M is minimally below normal weight at this time, her eating-disordered behaviors appear to be escalating. Since M does not meet all the *DSM-IV-TR* criteria for anorexia nervosa at this time, this diagnosis will not be recorded on Axis I. However, since there is strong evidence of anorexia-like symptoms that should be monitored closely, the most appropriate Axis I diagnosis appears to be eating disorder not otherwise specified. The reason for this diagnosis opposed to anorexia nervosa is that all of the criteria for anorexia nervosa are met except that, despite significant weight loss, the individual's current weight is in the normal range. If her weight falls below 85% of normal weight, she would then fit the criteria for anorexia nervosa.

It is important to note, however, that in actual practice, the diagnosis of anorexia nervosa might be given regardless of whether the full criteria are met or not. Clinical practice justification for this may include: (a) the symptoms are progressing so rapidly that it is possible all criteria will be met shortly; and (b) insurance reimbursement or hospital admission may be complicated by an NOS diagnosis since the criteria are often screened very thoroughly because of the flexibility allowed in establishing the criteria. Regardless of billing or system concerns, however, good practice would lend itself to starting out with the NOS diagnosis and later when the criteria are met, changing to the subsequent diagnosis of anorexia nervosa.

Furthermore, M's recent decision to become a vegetarian also appears to be of concern because it contributes to the compilation of increasing evidence of an eating disorder. According to Trautmann, Rau, Wilson, and Walters (2008), several studies on the risk of disordered eating behaviors have found that vegetarianism may be a means to justify and mask disordered eating behaviors in a socially acceptable manner, without raising questions from peers or family. Special caution should be raised as individuals with anorexia nervosa may turn to vegetarianism as part of their symptomolgy. Yackobovitch-Gavan et al. (2009) conducted research to identify factors that influenced the course of anorexia nervosa over time and found that "vegetarianism can develop rapidly in clients with Anorexia Nervosa to become a rigid change-resistant behavior. As such, although geared toward anxiety reduction, it can likely lead to its perpetuation" (p. 315). Vegetarianism may provide anorexic individuals with more "valid" or more easily defended reasons to support a food-centered lifestyle, avoidance of social eating situations, and general dietary restraint. (See Quick Reference 6.7, Multiaxial Diagnosis for M.)

No diagnosis is listed on Axis II. Although the client has obsessive-compulsive personality traits, there is not enough to substantiate a diagnosis. Also, often these types of traits can accompany or result from the primary diagnosis. In addition, the client also appears to practice several defense mechanisms that can directly affect her daily level of functioning. The use of defense mechanisms represents mental processes or coping styles that result in automatic psychological responses that are exhibited as a means of protecting her against anxiety. Since the behaviors are automatic, she is having difficulty identifying when these defenses are being used and how to control them. It is believed that, in this case, identification of these defense mechanisms is essential because either consciously or unconsciously developed defense mechanisms can influence the diagnostic condition and impede intervention progress. Current defense mechanisms for this client include: displacement, intellectualization, idealization, rationalization, and denial. (See Quick Reference 6.8 for definitions and application of these defense mechanisms.)

On Axis III, a careful review of medical conditions is critical, given the seriousness of the physical complications that can occur from depriving the body of adequate nutrition. Assurance of a recent physical should be verified and if absent a referral should be made. For M, a diagnosis on Axis III to rule out dysmenorrhea (625.3) seems most appropriate. Medical attention is necessary as problems with menstruation can stem from multiple causes.

On Axis IV, the client's psychosocial and environmental problems and stressors are identified. For M, one of her primary stressors appears to be her own self-inflicted maintenance of high standards and her fear that she will disappoint those she loves if she does not maintain these unrealistic standards. M also seems to involve herself actively in the life problems of her friends and places a great deal of her energy toward solving the problems of others, thus avoiding addressing issues in her own life that

QUICK REFERENCE 6.7

MULTIAXIAL DIAGNOSIS FOR M

Axis I: Clinical Disorders

307. 50 Eating disorder not otherwise specified, with obsessive/compulsive features.

Diagnosis deferred/rule out 307.4 anorexia nervosa, restricting type.

Axis II: Personality Disorders - No Diagnosis

Current defense mechanisms:

Displacement.

Intellectualization.

Idealization.

Rationalization.

Denial.

Axis III: General Medical Conditions

Rule out 625.3 dysmenorrhea.

Axis IV: Psychosocial and Environmental Problems

Stressors: Self-inflicted maintenance of high standards; fear of disappointing parents; overinvolvement with problem solving for friends; living in sorority house with no food preparation site available to her; forced to eat in a communal setting.

Axis V: Global Assessment of Functioning

GAF on service admission = 61 (current).

are causing her distress. Another significant stressor for M is that she now lives in a communal setting where she does not have complete control over meal preparation. She reported she cannot control the way the food is prepared and uses this to rationalize her food intake avoidance behaviors.

Axis V describes the client's psychosocial and occupational functioning for the past year. In the diagnostic assessment, this requires that M's behaviors and coping styles be identified and compared to the severity of the behaviors that are rated on the Generalized Assessment of Functioning (GAF) scale. Assessment of Axis

V for M is particularly important because it will later be used to support concrete measurement of the increase or decline of problem behaviors. In *DSM-IV* and *DSM-IV-TR*, the GAF scale has a maximum of 100 points. The lower the number, the lower the level of functioning (1 = minimal functioning, 100 = highest level of functioning). Using the GAF scale, the number 61 is assigned to represent the current severity of M's behaviors. Although it is not clear, it appears that M has had a higher level of functioning in the past (possibly an 81), but it is difficult to tell as the historical information has been obtained only from the client, not from

QUICK REFERENCE 6.8

DEFENSE MECHANISMS EXHIBITED

Displacement: M often deals with emotional conflict or internal or external stressors by transferring a feeling about food or a response to food to her distaste for food or anger about food.

Intellectualization: M often deals with emotional conflict or internal or external stressors by the excessive use of abstract thinking or the making of generalizations to control or minimize disturbing feelings. She reports that so much of food is not healthy and she tries to make eating into a "science," ensuring her own protection from unhealthy things.

Idealization: Is a defense mechanism that is considered to be minor image distorting. M's behaviors are often characterized by distortions in self-image, in terms of self-worth and self-esteem as well as body image. She often tries to regulate her eating behaviors and relates eating patterns directly to her own self-esteem. She also deals with internal or external stressors by attributing exaggerated positive qualities to the ability to control her eating habits and other body functions and feelings that, by doing this, her problems will also resolve.

Rationalization: M deals with internal or external stressors by concealing the true motivations of her own actions or feelings through the elaboration of reassuring or self-serving but incorrect explanations about her eating behavior and her concern for good health.

Denial: M deals with emotional conflict or internal or external stressors by refusing to acknowledge that she may have a serious problem regarding her eating behaviors. Although it is apparent to friends and family that she has a problem, the client does not believe she "really" has one and is seeking treatment primarily to appease family and friends.

Source: The exact definition of the defense mechanisms were summarized from the *Diagnostic and Statistical Manual of Mental Disorders, Fourth Edition, Text Revision.* Copyright 2000, by the American Psychiatric Association.

family members or other collateral supports. (See Quick Reference 6.9, application of the GAF to the case of M.)

Standardized Assessments: Self-Report Measures
Utilizing standardized measurements can be helpful when working with people who suffer from eating disorders. A self-report measure that can be utilized is the Eating Disorder Inventory-2 (EDI-2), which is a widely used questionnaire for assessing psychological and behavioral features of eating disorders (Garner, 1991; Garner, Olmsted, & Polivy, 1983; Villa et al., 2009). This measure may be particularly relevant for differentiating severity as well as subtypes of the disorder.

Another relevant measure is the Mizes Anorectic Cognitions Scale, which measures cognitions associated with anorexia nervosa and bulimia nervosa.

The Self-Esteem Rating Scale (SERS) developed by Nugent and Thomas is a relevant scale to utilize. This 40-item scale was created to measure the construct of self-esteem (Nugent, 2004). It may be particularly helpful as a pretest and posttest measure for self-esteem. The SERS provides scores ranging from −120 to +120; the more positive the score, the more positive the self-esteem, and the more negative the score, the more negative the self-esteem. The SERS has an excellent reliability rating. Its internal

---

QUICK REFERENCE 6.9

CASE APPLICATION OF THE GAF

M's possible range for past behaviors. Score of 81.

80–71   If symptoms are present, they are transient and expectable reactions to psychosocial stressors (e.g., difficulty concentrating after family argument); no more than slight impairment in social, occupational, and school functioning (e.g., temporarily falling behind in schoolwork).

M's current range for current behaviors. Score of 61.

70–61   Some mild symptoms (e.g., depressed mood and mild insomnia) OR some difficulty in social, occupational, and school functioning.

---

consistency has an alpha of 0.97. The SERS correlates significantly with the Index of Self-Esteem and the Generalized Contentment Scale for good construct validity. This instrument is reported to be indicative of problems in self-esteem as well as positive or nonproblematic attitudes (Fischer & Corcoran, 2007b; Nugent, 2004).

According to Maïano et al. (2009), the most widely used instrument to measure the behavioral component of body image disturbances is the Body Image Avoidance Questionnaire (BIAQ). The BIAQ contains 19 items that deal with "avoidance of situations that provoke concern about physical appearance." Totaling the points on each of the six items scores the questionnaire. The possible range is 0 to 94. The higher the score, the more avoidance behaviors are used. The internal consistency for the BIAQ is excellent, with a Cronbach's alpha of 0.89. It has a stable 2-week, test-retest reliability coefficient of 0.87. Further, the BIAQ has fair to good concurrent validity, with a low but significant correlation of 0.22 with body size estimation and a correlation of 0.78. The scale also has good known group validity, significantly distinguishing between clinical (bulimia nervosa) and nonclinical populations, and has been shown to be sensitive to changes in clients with body image disturbance (Fischer & Corcoran, 2007b).

Daily Body Satisfaction Logs   To aid in data collection and self-monitoring of behaviors, a computer-supported data collection system known as the Self-Monitoring Analysis System (SMAS) (Schlundt, 1989) may be used. When a computerized system is not available, Dziegielewski and Wolfe (2000) suggest the creation of a Daily Body Satisfaction Log (see Figure 6.1). This log can be used to record baseline data regarding personal body satisfaction. Body satisfaction is rated on a scale of 1 to 10 (1 = "very satisfied with my body," 10 = "totally dissatisfied with my body"). Individuals are instructed to rate body satisfaction three times a day: after breakfast, lunch, and dinner. This log should be kept throughout the measurement process. Overall, concrete and standardized measures such as these can help support the diagnostic assessment, lead to more successful treatment planning and strategy, and provide measurement of progress during treatment.

Self-Monitoring of Food Intake Log   Because of the strong cognitive component in anorexia nervosa (intense and irrational fear of gaining weight, low self-esteem, distortion of body weight and shape), the identification of dysfunctional thoughts, schemas, and thinking patterns is of critical importance. Having the individual recognize the patterns of thoughts and feelings that accompany eating and

Figure 6.1   Daily Body Satisfaction Log

Instructions: Please circle a number from 1–10 that best represents how you feel about the appearance of your body after each mealtime. 1 = "very satisfied with my body" and 10 = "totally dissatisfied with my body." Use a separate log for each day.

DAY #

Breakfast

1 2 3 4 5 6 7 8 9 10

"*Very satisfied* with how my body looks"   "Totally *dissatisfied* with how my body looks"

Lunch

1 2 3 4 5 6 7 8 9 10

"*Very satisfied* with how my body looks"   "Totally *dissatisfied* with how my body looks"

Dinner

1 2 3 4 5 6 7 8 9 10

"*Very satisfied* with how my body looks"   "Totally *dissatisfied* with how my body looks"

compensatory behavior episodes will illuminate cognitive distortions (see Figure 6.2).

Treatment Plan and Intervention

A complete treatment plan with M's goals and objectives and practice strategy is included at the end of this section. Treatment should be provided in a continuum of care that allows flexible application of modalities by a cohesive treatment plan. In developing the treatment plan for M, it is important for the practitioner to gather a comprehensive history that includes information about medical conditions and, if possible, additional information from family and friends. On some occasions, lab tests and X-rays are needed to rule out biological complications that can occur from the nutritional deprivation that is a symptom of anorexia nervosa. Referral for a blood test should be considered to detect use or abuse of drugs or hormonal problems. In addition, a referral to a dentist should be made

to evaluate the possibility of dental damage due to purging techniques.

Problem behaviors must be clearly identified and related directly to the stated goals of the client as this relationship is critical to formulation of the intervention process.

When working with an individual suffering from anorexia nervosa, intervention time can vary. However, it is rarely brief, since breaking ritualistic patterns of behavior and establishing new attitudes and behavior patterns take time. Planned and early intervention, however, can offer the client a better chance for considerable improvement. Often intervention with individuals diagnosed with this mental disorder requires a comprehensive approach that combines individual therapy and family supports.

Body dissatisfaction is linked to a range of physical and mental health problems including disordered eating, obesity, body dimorphic disorder, depression, and low self-esteem. It has also been linked to "cosmetic surgery,

Figure 6.2   Self-Monitoring of Food Intake

For one week, record all of your food intake and associated thoughts and feelings as soon as possible after eating. In the first column, record the time of the eating episode. In the second column, record all foods and liquids consumed. Record where the eating took place, if the eating was part of a binge, and whether you engaged in vomiting/laxative/excessive exercise or any other compensatory behavior. Finally, record your thoughts and feelings before, during, and after the eating episode.

Name: _____ Day: _____ Date: _____

Time	Food and Liquid	Place	Binge?	Compensatory Behavior	Thoughts and Feelings

unbalanced diet regimes, and steroid abuse" (Dittmar, 2009, p. 1). Thus, accurate assessment of self-esteem, depression, and body image is an important ingredient for establishing the best intervention efforts possible (See Quick Reference 6.10). Body image, weight, and dieting habits can be examined by using a variety of self-report or standard measures. The treatment plan for M should include interventions to improve both self-esteem and body image. Also important is continued assessment for depression and the effects it could have on the intervention plan.

Another factor to be considered in treating individuals with eating disorders is whether the symptoms such as amenorrhea, exhibited in severe cases of anorexia nervosa, serve as a method of avoiding development as a sexually mature individual (Ghizzani & Montomoli, 2000). Since these women often feel they have little or no control over external events and their own lives, the resultant changes in sexual characteristics brought on by decreased body fat, and thus decreased estrogen, are often a desperate attempt to achieve bodily control. Psychosexual attitudes of women with anorexia nervosa endorse ambivalence toward menstruation, pregnancy, and seeking and maintaining mature sexual relationships. Since these women often consider their sexual experiences in a negative way or experience extreme guilt feelings, individual intervention strategy can be geared toward helping the client to identify and address these issues as well.

QUICK REFERENCE 6.10

M's IDENTIFIED GOALS

1. Diminish feelings of anger and guilt, particularly regarding food and eating.
2. Establish healthy eating patterns.
3. Change beliefs related to food and weight.
4. Establish a sense of self-worth that is not paired with weight and body image.

Last, to facilitate the initiation of treatment strategy, it must be determined whether the client will benefit most from either inpatient or outpatient treatment. Since anorexia nervosa and bulimia nervosa are complex and almost always chronic disorders, an assessment as to whether the physical problems that result from nutritional deprivation must be stabilized in the inpatient setting must be made. Furthermore, considering that death due to starvation can occur in 10% of cases, the decision for inpatient versus outpatient treatment remains a critical one. Although determining the best level of care and the criteria for hospitalization of a client can be complex, the practitioner should consider the least restrictive level of intervention that can fulfill both the short- and long-term needs of the client. When or if there is an imminent risk to the client, such as suicidal or self-injurious behavior, or extreme weight loss leading to possible starvation, the practitioner is justified in limiting intervention to the inpatient setting where the client can be monitored closely by a medical team.

Whether it is implemented in an inpatient or outpatient setting, the intervention strategy will follow a similar path. All efforts for intervention strategy should include: (a) education about the condition of anorexia nervosa; (b) individual therapy to address issues of self-esteem, body image, dysfunctional eating attitudes and patterns of behavior, and teaching healthy patterns for eating; and (c) significant family involvement tailored to the needs of the client (conjoint or without the client present), including education

on eating disorders, how to recognize signs and symptoms of increased severity, and supportive family therapy.

Sample Treatment Plan 6.1 is a sample of suggestions for inclusion in treatment. Note that specific dates to complete goals are required in an actual treatment plan. If it was an actual treatment plan, goals and dates for completion would have been indicated.

Psychopharmacology It is common for those who plan to implement psychosocial strategies when treating eating disorders to initially review the benefits of also starting a course of medication therapy. Unfortunately, however, psychopharmacological treatment of eating disorders has not met with widespread success (Kaye et al., 2001; Strober, Freeman, DeAntonio, Lampert, & Diamond, 1997; Walsh et al., 2006). Crow et al. (2009) report that, to date, pharmacotherapy research for anorexia nervosa has been extensive (at least in terms of variety of agents examined), yet effective agents have not been identified. They go on to say that "strategies to remedy this problem might include developing new treatment targets, new measurement strategies, and new mechanisms or networks for conducting trials" (p. 6). The medications that are often utilized are not designed specifically for treating eating disorders but rather for the symptoms that often accompany them. For example, antidepressants, such as specific serotonin reuptake inhibitors (SSRI) or tricyclics, designed to address the depressive symptoms that often are comorbid to eating disorders, are often

SAMPLE TREATMENT PLAN 6.1

Goals:

1. Diminish feelings of anger and guilt, particularly regarding food and eating.
2. Establish healthy eating patterns.
3. Change beliefs related to food and weight.
4. Establish a sense of self-worth that is not paired with weight and body image.

Objectives	Interventions
1. Support and increase motivation to change; heighten awareness of the disadvantages of eating disorders.	Share and discuss educational information regarding disadvantages of disordered eating (physical problems such as skin tone and color, hair loss, halitosis, low energy, lack of concentration, etc.).
2. Analyze the pros and cons of maintaining the disordered eating patterns—identifying functional higher-order goals of behavioral patterns and beliefs.	Develop a detailed list of the pros and cons of maintaining the disordered eating habits at this time—recognizing the adaptive nature of the symptoms.
3. Introduce a consideration of irrational beliefs.	Begin to introduce doubt about the practicality and utility of eating habits as a means of meeting goals—examining the evidence of the nonadaptive factors of the disorder. Provide list of cognitive distortions that may be related to M's beliefs about her body shape and eating.
4. Identify specific targets of anger—increase awareness of the antecedents to her feelings of anger. Pair anger and pleasure with noneating activities.	Keep lists of all the possible targets of anger (which foods, when, what other than food, how angry did you feel, how long did the anger last) throughout the day. Complete Self-Monitoring of Food Intake Log for 2 weeks.
5. Increase understanding of the development of her body image disturbance and eating disorder.	Write a developmental history of her body image—include physical appearance and important events that influenced her body image as she developed.
6. Change beliefs regarding body image perceptions.	Keep record of negative "body talk" and create a positive or neutral statement to counter each negative statement.

used. (See Quick Reference 6.11 for a list of SSRIs and tricyclics that can be used.)

In addition, a few successful cases have been reported using the antipsychotic medicine olanzapine (Zyprexa). For example, Ridley-Siegert (2000) discussed three cases of chronic anorexia nervosa that were successfully treated after 2 to 9 months of a trial with this medication. However, pharmacological treatments have been found to be ineffective for restoring weight in the underweight stage of anorexia nervosa (Attia, Haiman, Walsh, & Flater, 1998; Barbarich et al., 2004) and showed mixed effectiveness for preventing relapse in weight-restored individuals (Kaye et al., 2001; Strober et al., 1997; Walsh et al., 2006).

According to Mitchell and Bulik (2006), when treating bulimia nervosa, cognitive-behavioral therapy is the treatment of choice and fluoxetine (Prozac) is a medication approved by the Food and Drug Administration for its treatment. In summary, it appears that further research is needed before conclusions can be drawn regarding the possibility for successful pharmacological treatment with individuals who suffer from anorexia nervosa. Furthermore, once a medication is started, mental health practitioners still need to encourage clients to supplement this intervention with psychosocial strategies designed to address problem behaviors. Therefore, while medication may be an important

QUICK REFERENCE 6.11

SSRIs AND TRICYCLICS

Selective Serotonin Reuptake Inhibitors		Maximum Daily Dosage
Fluoxetine (Prozac)		80 mg
Paroxetine hydrochloride (Paxil)		50 mg
Sertraline (Zoloft)		200 mg
Fluvoxamine (Luvox)		200–300 mg
Citalopram (Celexa)		40 mg
Tricyclics	**Sedative Effect**	**Dosage Range**
Amitriptyline (Elavil)	Strong	150–300 mg a day
Imipramine (Tofranil)	Moderate	150–300 mg a day
Nortriptyline (Pamelor/Aventyl)	Mild	50–150 mg a day
Desipramine (Norpramine/Pertofrane)	Mild	100–300 mg a day

component of treating this eating disorder, medications generally are prescribed to address the behaviors that are manifested by the condition rather than the condition itself. Thus, medications are most effective when utilized as an adjunct to psychotherapy.

Strategies for Individual Therapy and Intervention Individual therapy may help client M gain greater insight into her dysfunctional behaviors and develop more thoughtful and efficient problem-solving strategies. But perhaps most important, it will give M the opportunity to better understand and express her feelings with words instead of avoidance behaviors, such as denying herself food. At this time, cognitive-behavioral approaches for providing individual therapy appear to have the best track record for control of the disorder, helping individuals with an eating disorder to return to normal weight and eating behaviors (Fairburn, Cooper, & Shafran, 2003; Garner & Garfinkel, 1997; Schapman-Williams & Lock, 2007). Emphasis is placed on enhancing motivation for change and engaging individuals as active

collaborators in their treatment (Vitousek, Watson, & Wilson, 1998). Therefore, to help M achieve success, a cognitive-behavioral approach such as that developed by Cash (1996) may be helpful to address low self-esteem, locus of control, shape and weight concerns, and fears.

To begin the cognitive-behavioral strategy, the client will be assisted to identify her cognitive distortions and negative self-thoughts, and apply behavioral change talk to social situations, allowing her to adjust her problem behaviors accordingly. (See Quick Reference 6.12 for list of some of the common cognitive distortions associated with eating disorders.) In addition, she will use self-monitoring, tracking techniques, and problem-solving skills to clearly identify triggers related to the occurrence of problematic behaviors. She will be assisted in learning alternate behaviors and identifying clearly and preparing for any negative or devastating consequences that can result if certain behaviors continue.

Strategies for Family Therapy and Intervention When addressing issues with M's family, special attention needs to be given to her

---

QUICK REFERENCE 6.12

BODY IMAGE COGNITIVE DISTORTIONS

All-or-nothing thinking: This can also be referred to as black-and-white thinking. Rigid rules are part of all-or-nothing thinking, and no allowance is made for a middle ground. Perfectionism is a prime example of this type of reasoning. Either one's body perfectly matches the ideal, or the individual feels like a failure.

Catastrophizing: This is related to magnification in the tendency to exaggerate the probability that something terrible will happen. This occurs when someone magnifies the importance of something and then predicts the worst—for example, if an individual decides not to go to the beach because he is afraid that he would look like a whale and everyone would notice (magnification) and that this would result in his being dumped by a new girlfriend.

Filtering: This involves paying attention only to certain information while ignoring contradictory information that would challenge existing beliefs. For example, this is illustrated by the belief that thinness is the sole parameter on which to base one's self-worth.

Superstitious thinking: Also called magical thinking. This occurs when individuals act as if there is a cause-and-effect relationship between two events or outcomes that really are not at all linked—for example, believing that eating a brownie will result in gaining 5 pounds.

---

relationship with her mother. M has reported that she often avoids visiting with her parents and that she is afraid of their reaction and refuses to share her current eating difficulties with them. Research conducted by Cunha, Relvas, and Soares (2009) regarding family functioning found that patients with anorexia nervosa perceived less emotional involvement among family members, and they seemed to distrust their mothers and peers. They also communicated less with their peers and showed more detachment to mothers, fathers, and peers. M's relationship with her parents may be a significant factor in her eating disorder. Working with the whole family (i.e., family therapy) is essential to facilitate a more positive prognosis, particularly when working with adolescents.

According to Lock (2009), the best treatment for adolescents with eating disorders is family therapy, which is intended to help parents learn how to manage their child's symptoms. One of the best-studied approaches to family

therapy is the Maudsley Model, which involves 10 to 20 conjoint (all family members present) family sessions spaced over 6 to 12 months and moves through three distinct phases (Dare & Eisler, 1997; Lock & Le Grange, 2005; Lock, Le Grange, Agras, & Dare, 2001). In phase 1, parents are directed and coached to take complete control over their eating-disordered child's eating and weight. Siblings are encouraged to participate and join in the creative solutions developed as a family. Phase 2 begins when the adolescent begins to accept parental authority and gradually regains control over her own eating. Throughout this process, blaming the parent is always avoided (Nichols & Schwartz, 2005).

The individual gains age-appropriate autonomy expressly linked to the resolution of her eating disorder in the final phase of the treatment. Although this treatment method has not proved to be beneficial for older individuals or those with a longer history of the illness, adolescents with short-duration symptoms have an expected rate of recovery that exceeds the aggregate 50% rate cited for all individuals with anorexia nervosa (Le Grange, Binford, & Loeb, 2005; Lock, Agras, Bryson, & Kramer, 2005; Nilsson & Hagglof, 2005; Steinhausen, 2002). In fact, the National Institute for Clinical Excellence (2004) recommends that in addition to individual therapy, family interventions that directly address the eating disorder should be offered to all adolescents suffering with anorexia nervosa. Interest in family therapy approaches, whether short- or long-term appears to be growing (Kraemer, 2005).

These treatment modalities will provide strategies for managing M's behavior and may help the parents identify and encourage appropriate behaviors for their daughter. By involving the entire family, this treatment will foster mutual support, positive reinforcement, direct communication, and more effective problem solving within the family (Braithwaite, Duff, & Westworth, 1999; Brunk, 1999).

Cognitive Restructuring and EMDR with Eating Disorders

Eye movement desensitization and reprocessing (EMDR) is an intervention tool that combines aspects of cognitive restructuring. Although eye movement, or other forms of dual stimulation, has garnered the most attention, the method actually consists of eight phases and numerous procedural elements that all contribute to its efficacy (Shapiro, 2001). EMDR is being widely used and tested as an effective brief therapy for clinically challenging issues, such as posttraumatic stress disorders, anxiety disorders, and phobias. In addition, Brown, McGoldrick, and Buchanan (1997) used EMDR with seven cases of body-dysmorphic disorder. These authors used between one and three EMDR sessions and reported improvements in six of the seven clients. Five of the seven clients reported complete resolution of symptoms. Although the symptoms of body-dysmorphic disorder should not be confused with a diagnosed eating disorder, its similarity of interest is in the "preoccupation with an imagined defect in appearance" (APA, 1994, p. 468).

In practice with individuals who suffer from an eating disorder, the relationship among body image, weight, and dieting is pronounced. However, most studies attempted measurement but not treatment or improvement of either body image or self-esteem, even though both factors are targeted in treatment plans and research related to eating disorder symptoms (McAllister & Caltabiano, 1994; McCaulay et al., 1988; Rosen, 1995).

According to Dziegielewski and Wolf (2000), however, the EMDR method of brief therapy can also be used with clients who suffer from problems related to distorted body image and low self-esteem. Remember, however, that special training is required to use EMDR to implement the step-by-step approach (Shapiro, 2001; Shapiro, Kaslow & Maxfield, 2007).

Their study emphasized a single subject design for improvement of both self-esteem and body image in a non-eating-disordered subject who reported eating disorder symptoms. EMDR with cognitive restructuring was introduced as the treatment intervention. Body image and self-esteem were pre- and posttested using standardized scales. Weight and dieting habits were not the focus of this study. The EMDR intervention consisted of an eight-phase treatment plan: (1) client history and treatment planning; (2) preparation for EMDR (includes explanation of the procedure, relaxation training); (3) assessment (identifying a target negative and positive cognition and establishing a baseline response on the Subjective Units of Disturbance and Validity of Cognition scales before processing); (4) desensitization (eye movements or other bilateral stimulation); (5) installation

---

QUICK REFERENCE 6.13

SUDS Scale Development

To develop a SUDS scale, the client is asked to focus directly on a recent event that is believed to be tantrum-like. For example, if the client identifies the statement "I hate the way my body looks now," this statement would be rated prior to processing on the SUD scale, with 0 = No disturbance, and 10 = Highest disturbance imaginable. Negative cognitions are identified and scaled throughout the intervention process.

(strengthening of identified positive cognition to replace negative cognition); (6) body scan (target residual tension in the form of body sensations); (7) closure; and (8) reevaluation (Shapiro, 2001).

In addition, Dziegielewski and Wolfe (2000) utilized the SUD (Subjective Units of Disturbance) and the VOC (Validity of Cognition) scales to rate emotional and cognitive functioning related to the treatment target. The subject selected an image or picture as the disturbing or target event and rated the level of disturbance on the 10-point SUDS scale (see Quick Reference 6.13). After identifying the negative statement, the client is asked to change it to a positive statement. This can be formed as an "I statement" and represents what the client would like to believe. All statements must be realistic and obtainable. In turn, positive cognitions can be rated on a 7-point VOC scale, which constitutes a baseline before processing begins (see Quick Reference 6.14).

For a sample EMDR Session Worksheet, which includes the VOC and SUD scales, see Sample Treatment Plan 6.2. A more thorough explanation of EMDR protocols and procedures can be found in Shapiro (2001) and Dziegielewski and Wolfe (2000).

The use of EMDR as a treatment intervention for eating disorder symptoms merits consideration for future practice intervention. According to Dziegielewski and Wolfe (2000), when using this method, the subject's increase in self-esteem and decrease in body-image avoidance behaviors indicated positive progress after only two scheduled sessions. The combination of cognitive restructuring and EMDR may be of particular importance to practitioners who are constantly challenged to do more, with less time, for less money and at the same time asked to provide concrete indications of their effectiveness (Dziegielewski, 2004). By using standardized scales along with clear treatment protocols, clinicians can document this effectiveness in a way that is acceptable to the managed care milieu. It is further recommended that only practitioners trained by the EMDR International Institute use the EMDR protocols in treatment or research.

QUICK REFERENCE 6.14

VOC Scale

To develop a VOC scale, the client is asked to take a negative cognition related to body image, such as "I'm ugly/I have no control," and turn it into a positive statement. The positive cognition now becomes "I have control over my feelings about how I look," and this statement is rated on the VOC scale. On the VOC scale, 1 = Completely false, and 7 = Completely true.

SAMPLE TREATMENT PLAN 6.2

SAMPLE EMDR SESSIONS WORKSHEET

EMDR Session #:
Client:
Name:
Date:

"What we will be doing often is a check on what you are experiencing. I need to know from you exactly what is going on with as clear feedback as possible. Sometimes things will change and sometimes they won't. Just give as accurate feedback as you can as to what is happening without judging whether it should be happening or not. Just let what ever happens happen." *Remember the STOP signal. Choose a metaphor. Remember a safe place.*

Presenting Issue or Memory

Picture

Emotions/Feelings: When you bring up that picture/incident and those words (previous negative comments), what emotion(s) do you feel now?"

SUD: "On a scale of 0 to 10, where 0 is no disturbance or neutral and 10 is the highest disturbance you can imagine, how disturbing does the incident feel to you now?"

0 1 2 3 4 5 6 7 8 9 10

No disturbance/neutral   highest disturbance

Negative Cognition: "What words go best with that picture incident that expresses your negative belief about yourself now?"

Location of Body Sensation: "Where do you feel the disturbance in your body?"

Positive Cognition: "When you bring up that picture/incident, what would you like to believe about yourself now?"

Desensitize: Check SUD—should be down to 0 or 1 before continuing with process to desensitize.

VOC: "When you think of that picture/incident, how true does that [repeat previous cognition] feel to you now on a scale of 1 to 7, where 1 feels completely false and 7 feels completely true?"

1   2   3   4   5   6   7
Completely false   Completely true

Body Scan: Access any material from original target—hold with positive cognition—if residual discomfort, reprocess until discomfort subsides.

Closure: Debrief. Explain there may be after-session processing; ask to keep a log. New material will be targets for future sessions.

Source: Sample form adapted from Dziegielewski and Wolfe (2000).

Environmental Considerations When working with an individual who suffers from an eating disorder, the factors in the environmental context that can influence intervention whether positive or negative must be identified. This can be accomplished by identifying the assets or strengths the client has in her support system and potential barriers that may exist (See Quick Reference 6.15).

In terms of assets or strengths, M has her parents as well as several friends who are concerned for her and have encouraged her to seek

---

QUICK REFERENCE 6.15

ENVIRONMENTAL CONSIDERATIONS

Client Strengths and Assets for Intervention Include:

- M has several friends who are concerned about her and who have encouraged her to seek help.
- M acknowledges their caring, values, and continued concern and support.
- M voices a desire to meet her weight goals in a healthy way.
- M recognizes that she is demonstrating behaviors that could ultimately be dangerous.

Barriers to Intervention Include:

- M believes with strong conviction that she can only have a sense of control when she controls her body.
- M pairs food restriction and food rituals with healthfulness.
- M uses food as a focus for her feelings of anger and frustration related to internal and external life stressors.
- M avoids trying to identify and focus her attention on other factors that may be contributing to her anger.

---

help. She has acknowledged that her parents and friends care for her and considers that the input of her parents and peers is a very important part of her life. This makes it essential to consider the impact of her peer social supports at school and the influence of her family as treatment progresses. Sociocultural factors contribute substantially to the development of body image disturbance and eating disorders. To facilitate a more global treatment of M, it would be valuable to have more information regarding her relationships with her family and peers.

Since peer support is also a critical factor, outreach programs to educate social groups such as sororities may help to alert women to the signs and symptoms of eating disorders. Education would heighten awareness and may contribute to identification of eating difficulties before they become disorders. Since M is a student, several university resources are recommended. Upon evaluation, M initially refused to use her own family physician for a medical consultation and physical exam, which is not uncommon with individuals who suffer from this type of eating disorder because there is

such strong denial that a problem exists. Keeping this in mind, special attention was given to finding an acceptable medical referral for M. After discussion of the options, she agreed to go to the student health services clinic for a checkup with a nurse practitioner. She also could benefit from a program that encourages healthy eating and weight reduction. An example of such a program for this client was available on campus. This particular program monitors weight and exercise, provides consultation with a dietitian, and encourages peer-to-peer "buddies" who are available to address a wide range of typical student problems or concerns. Programs like this can be invaluable to clients who are obsessed with food and are prone to unhealthy eating patterns.

SUMMARY AND FUTURE DIRECTIONS

Since the media and societal expectations continue to remain prominent in the promotion of "thin is beautiful, perfect, and desirable," mental health practitioners must be prepared to intervene in the predictable increase in chronic eating disorders. Doing this requires a thorough diagnostic assessment, documented clearly in the multiaxial system and supplemented with standardized assessment measures.

The *DSM-5* is scheduled to be published in 2013, 19 years after the *DSM-IV* criteria were distributed and 12 years after the text was revised into the *DSM-IV-TR* (Walsh, 2009). According to Attia and Roberto (2009), the removal of the amenorrhea criterion for anorexia nervosa is being considered for the fifth edition. Becker, Eddy, and Perloe (2009) state that the text addressing diagnostic features of anorexia and bulimia in the *DSM-5* should be augmented to provide guidelines for ascertainment of cognitive-based signs and symptoms in the absence of client endorsement of them. In addition, replacement of terms relating to the word refusal relevant to anorexia on Criterion A should be considered. Another concern raised by Becker, Eddy, and Perloe concerns cultural variation in the presentation of anorexia nervosa that have been reported with respect to the rationale for food refusal.

Intervention plans and strategy must incorporate evidence-based practice principles and techniques especially when working with self-esteem, body image disturbance, and other eating disorder symptoms. More research in this area is needed to anchor and support the treatment strategies that are being employed. Medications, although considered an essential intervention strategy with many mental disorders, clearly fall short in this area.

By using the ideas presented in this chapter and incorporating these suggestions with evidence-based efforts supported by client-reported gain, mental health practitioners can have an impact on the development and subsequent treatment of the mental health problems experienced by individuals who suffer from an eating disorder.

Substance-Related Disorders: Alcohol and Other Drugs

CARMEN P. CHANG-ARRATIA AND SOPHIA F. DZIEGIELEWSKI

As a public health concern, the misuse of alcohol and other drugs (AOD) poses a serious peril in the form of social, economic, and human welfare costs. Recognizing the impact and costs to the individual, relationships, community, and society make focusing on this area central for research, intervention, and prevention efforts. According to the World Health Organization (WHO) (2009c), it is estimated 76.3 million individuals worldwide suffer from an alcohol use disorder. In addition, 15.3 million have a reported drug use disorder of which 93 out of 136 countries report concurrent HIV infection secondary to injection drug usage. When addressing mortality rates in 2000, it was estimated that AOD account for 12.4% of all deaths worldwide; the percentage of total life lost is 8.9% (WHO, 2009d). This may be considered a conservative estimate since substance users typically use more than one substance. These numbers also may be underreported as they may not take into account excessive use of dependence-producing prescribed drugs.

Considering alcohol consumption alone, the effects it poses to individual health can include chronic and debilitating diseases, interpersonal violence, accidents, disability, and mortality. Harmful and hazardous drinking and

associated behaviors such as aggression and involvement with the criminal justice system also produce secondary consequences, such as violations of the law and subsequent injuries. "Injuries may be divided into two categories: Unintentional injuries, drowning, burns, poisoning and falls; and intentional injuries, which result from deliberate acts of violence against oneself or others" (WHO, 2007, p. 1). Approximately 1.8 million deaths are alcohol related. A third are included as unintentional injuries in the sum total of deaths worldwide; and 58.3 million account for disability (WHO, 2007, 2009a).

The disproportional distribution of alcohol consumption in developing countries and in countries where the pattern of alcohol use is hazardous, rather than a part of daily routine (e.g., alcohol use with mealtimes), are believed to contribute to associated consequences. When the patterns of total alcohol consumption are compared with per capita income distributions and how much people age 15 and above drink annually (per pure liter of alcohol), results vary. The poorest countries and emerging economies (e.g., Africa, South and Central America, Asia, and Pacific) as well as countries with higher incomes but low mortality (e.g., North America, Europe, Australasia, Eastern Europe, and Central Asia) tend to have the highest alcohol-associated patterns related to use and mortality (WHO, 2007, 2009d).

Special thanks to Julie Wenglinsky for her contributions to the earlier version of this chapter.

In the United States, approximately 8 million people meet the diagnostic criteria for alcohol dependence with approximately 700,000 in treatment at any given time (Evans, Levin, Brooks, & Garawi, 2007). Determinants of alcohol use, such as demographics and socioeconomic factors, policies, education, and living standards, can affect the frequency of alcohol consumption and influence the type of beverage consumed (Poznyak et al., 2005). These determinants often serve as targets for intervention and prevention efforts and as strategies to address, minimize, and ameliorate continued social problems and risk factors associated with alcohol consumption. Important intervention targets related to identification and modification of care need to take into account factors such as age, gender, and marital status to name a few. Once identified, these targets need to be related to policy initiatives, implementation of services, and access to care.

These same venues and factors are applicable to illicit and psychoactive substance use. In developed countries with high mortality rates, the rate of illicit and psychoactive drug use is high. Accounting for earlier loss of life, illicit drug use affects mortality rates before the age of 60. Again, this may be underestimated because it may not address other associated risk factors, such as disease, injuries, and violence (WHO, 2009d). There is limited information overall on the prevalence of illicit drug and alcohol use, but from 2006 to 2007 concurrent use was reported at 5.6%, which is equivalent to 7.1 million people between the ages of 12 to 25 respectively (Substance Abuse and Mental Health Services Administration [SAMHSA], 2009a). In 2000 as in 2008, attributable deaths due to psychoactive use remained high in males with 80% for illicit drug use to 90% for alcohol use worldwide and in women the numbers also remained significant with estimates ranging from 9.9 to 6.3% (SAMHSA, 2009a, 2009b; Schulte, Ramo, & Brown, 2009; WHO, 2009f). Furthermore, when looking specifically at psychotherapeutic drug use, similar rates of use are evident between the sexes (2.6% for females and 2.4% for males), which is causing significant alarm as it is indicative of the development of a new trend in disorders (SAMHSA, 2009c).

In the United States, findings from the 2008 National Survey of Drug Use and Health estimated that 20.1 million people age 12 and older were illicit drug users at the time of the survey. Of the substances recorded, marijuana use attained the highest prevalence (15.2 million users), followed by psychotherapeutic drugs (6.2 million), cocaine (1.9 million), and hallucinogens (1.1. million). Consumption trends in countries where excessive availability and inadequate regulation of drugs are present show patterns of increased drug abuse. Other substances of concern related to use and dependence include the benzodiazepines and other anxiolytics acquired through prescriptions, illegal street vendors, and the Internet. "In developed countries . . . the prevalence of anxiety and insomnia and the consumption of sedative hypnotics are growing, the elderly being the main group of consumers. The INCB [International Narcotics Control Board] notes with concern the frequent long-term use (beyond one year and sometimes indefinitely) of psychotropic substances for treating psychological reactions to social pressure without a diagnosis for a specific disorder" (WHO, 2010, p. 1). Legally approved and prescribed medications are being used for nonmedical recreational use. In full-time college students ages 18 to 23, Adderall, a prescribed medication for the treatment of attention deficit hyperactivity disorder and a stimulant, is a concern. The addictive nature of Adderall when combined with alcohol and other drugs can lead to adverse health and safety consequences (SAMHSA, 2009c).

This chapter describes the *DSM-IV-TR* diagnostic criteria for the taxonomical classification of Substance-Related Disorders. Included is the application of diagnostic criteria to the application of alcohol use disorders. A brief overview of the clinical presentations and treatments utilized to assist individuals suffering from alcohol abuse or dependence through various approaches is provided and discussed. Causes and risk factors associated with alcohol use are included, and factors in the diagnostic assessment and treatment strategy are presented, exploring the use of the biopsychosocial approach, brief interventions, motivational enhancement therapies, cognitive-behavioral therapy, systems, and the self-help approach. Case examples with applications to the multiaxial system, explanation of application to that system, and sample treatment plans are included. The chapter concludes with current approaches and practice implications.

INTRODUCTION TO DIAGNOSTIC CLASSIFICATION AND DEFINITIONS FOR SUBSTANCE-RELATED DISORDERS

Substance-related disorders is the taxonomical category for disorders that addresses substances (e.g., medications, drugs of abuse, or toxins) and the affects these substances can have on the system. In the *DSM-IV-TR* (American Psychiatric Association [APA] (2000) this category is applied with classifications related to 11 classes of substances that share similar features: alcohol, amphetamines, caffeine, hallucinogens, inhalants, nicotine, opioids, phencyclidine (PCP), sedatives, hypnotics, and anxiolytics (see Quick Reference 7.1).

The *DSM-IV-TR* provides examples of medications and selected other substances that can cause substance-related disorders. For example, medications such as anesthetics, muscle relaxants, over-the-counter medications, antidepressants, and corticosteroids can cause substance-related disorders. Other substances such as toxins, including lead, carbon monoxide, and nerve gases, can be directly related to accidental intoxication, and inhalants such as fuel and paint used intentionally for the purpose of becoming intoxicated can cause poisoning.

To help clarify the substance-related terminology further, differentiation between two subsets within the taxonomical category of substance-related disorders are included (i.e., substance-use disorders and substance-induced disorders). These two subsets set the diagnostic criteria for disorders that fall under the substance-use disorders (substance dependence and substance abuse) and substance-induced disorders (substance intoxication, substance withdrawal, substance-induced delirium, substance-induced persisting dementia, substance-induced persisting amnesic disorder, substance-induced psychotic disorder, substance-induced mood disorder, substance-induced anxiety disorder, substance-induced sexual dysfunction, and substance-induced sleep disorder) (APA, 2000).

These differentiations allow for the phenomenological analysis of co-occurrence and comorbidity. These differentials also help to determine between primary or independent considerations of substance-induced disorders and how it relates to other classifications of *DSM* disorders and syndromes, such as other mental disorders (APA, 2000; Nunes & Rounsaville, 2006). This is particularly helpful because it provides clinicians with a tool for making a distinction between whether a mental disorder or a substance-induced disorder precedes the diagnosis of the presenting condition, its subsequent prognosis, and the type of treatment needed.

The definition for substance use disorder applies to two qualifiers: dependence and abuse. When referring specifically to the features of dependence, the term is applied to a "cluster of cognitive, behavioral, and physiological symptoms indicating that the individual continues use

QUICK REFERENCE 7.1

SUBSTANCE-RELATED DISORDERS

Eleven classes of substances of use in the DSM-IV-TR:

Alcohol	Sedatives	Nicotine
Caffeine	Anxiolytics	Phencyclidine (PCP)
Inhalants	Amphetamines	Hypnotics
Opioids	Hallucinogens	

All substances are associated with:

Substance Use Disorders

Abuse: Harmful and hazardous interpersonal and social consequences due to use, not indicative of tolerance or withdrawal, and absent of dependence. (Not applicable to caffeine and nicotine.)

Dependence: Maladaptive cognitive and behavioral consecutive responses to use, indicative of tolerance and withdrawal with inability to cease or diminish use, impairing multiple domains of individual functioning, and marked by dependence, a demonstrative physiological response due to a lack of the presence of the substance.

Substance-Induced Disorders

Intoxication: Reversible maladaptive behavioral, psychological, and physical induced changes to recent exposure or ingestion of a substance (excluding caffeine and nicotine) resulting in increased risk factors and impairments in functioning, not attributed to a medical condition or mental disorder.

Withdrawal: Maladaptive psychological, physiological, and behavioral responses to reduction or lack of ingestion of a substance, without being attributed to a medical condition or mental disorder, and causing social and occupational impairments.

Source: Summarized criteria from the *Diagnostic and Statistical Manual of Mental* Disorders, *Fourth Edition, Text Revision.* Copyright 2000 by the American Psychiatric Association.

of the substance despite significant substance-related problems" (APA, 2000, pg. 192). Tolerance, withdrawal, and compulsive drug-taking behavior are three important criteria of six in the *DSM-IV-TR* for meeting the diagnosis for dependence, if these symptoms are present at any time during a 12-month period.

Tolerance is the continued use with an increased amount of consumption of the same substance to achieve prior desired effects. *Withdrawal* is the physiological, cognitive, and subsequent maladaptive behavioral responses to a decline in amount and consumption of the

substance of abuse. Stated simply, in withdrawal the concentration of the substance in the blood and tissue of an individual declines after prolonged heavy use of a substance, therefore it takes more of a substance to get the same response. Specifiers for the physiological response to withdrawal in the *DSM-IV-TR*, as applied to the criterion for tolerance, include *with physiological dependence* or *without physiological dependence* (if criteria for tolerance is not present) (APA, 2000). While tolerance and withdrawal may be present, these do not provide the basis for meeting the diagnosis of substance use dependence. To further specify the compulsive drug-taking behavior and the criterion for the diagnosis of dependence, there needs to be involvement of the substance with the desire to increase the amounts of the substance over longer periods of time, while also having concerns related to continued use. This concern about the desire for continued use must also invoke a persistent desire to decrease or cut down use.

In dependence, the individual should demonstrate evidence of repeated unsuccessful attempts to cut down or cease use. Preoccupation with obtaining the substance, using, and recovering from use of the substance further extends the criteria to meet dependence. For example, the individual plans and builds all social activities around the substance of use, which impairs other areas of the individual's social, occupational, and personal life.

In the current edition of the *DSM-IV-TR*, there is no qualifier in the nomenclature for addiction, only abuse and dependence. There has been some contention that replacing the terminology of dependence with addiction would shift the impact of disorder from chronic use and physical dependence to one of associated harmful effects and addictive processes. From this perspective, using the term *addiction* would help to limit the diagnostic confusion between the specifiers for physical dependence, the classification of dependence in relation to certain substances, and *DSM* criteria for diagnosis (Potenza, 2006). The addition of the terminology of addiction would also include nondrug behaviors/disorders (e.g., pathological gambling, obesity) within the category. Currently, these nondrug behaviors are addressed categorically or separately or are simply not addressed within the *DSM*. Proponents of the replacement of the terminology of addiction state that changes would follow shifts in the *DSM-III* to the present and reduce interventions deemed controversial (e.g., methadone

maintenance). Other authors believe that addressing this term may unintentionally increase rather than decrease the stigma often associated with the term *addiction* (Nunes & Rounsaville, 2006; Potenza, 2006). If the term *addiction* was added to the nomenclature in *DSM-5*, it would assist to address the core components indicative of a subset of other co-occurring disorders (e.g., impulse disorders) and those not defined (obesity).

Core components of the terminology used to define addiction include cravings prior to behavioral engagement, compulsive engagement, impaired control over behavioral engagement, and continued behaviors despite negative consequences (Potenza, 2006). If implemented in the *DSM-5*, application of the term *addiction* can assist in examining the relationship between the substance disorders and their primary or independent effect on the presenting problem. Consequently, if this shift was made in the *DSM-5*, it would require that the existing nomenclature undergo major revisions making a direct connection between addiction to the existing categories. If and when this term is included in *DSM-5*, providers will have to be trained on the ontology of new specifications and diagnosing, and new measurements will be needed. In practice today, however, while the term *addiction* is often used when addressing substance-related disorders, currently the term is not included in the *DSM-IV-TR*.

Unlike dependence, the features for abuse focus on the maladaptive behaviors and adverse and harmful consequences related to use. In abuse, however, not noted are the specifications for tolerance, withdrawal, or compulsive drug-taking behavior. Following a period of 12 months or persistence of the same factors, two defining criteria are specified for abuse: (1) a repeated failure to meet major role obligations, situations involving physical hazard, multiple legal problems, and social and interpersonal problems; and (2) the patterns of use did not meet the criteria for *dependence* (APA, 2000). The *DSM-IV-TR* excludes the application of the term *abuse* and in the diagnostic impression it cannot be applied to caffeine and nicotine, although nicotine can be applied to the dependence category only.

In the assessment and application of abuse, the individual who is experiencing substance abuse will find him- or herself intoxicated in situations where risky behaviors will occur. Occurrences of violence or assaults may result with legal ramifications resulting from the behaviors. In the workplace, there may be frequent absences. Social and relational problems can also result from being intoxicated, including marital difficulties, divorce, verbal and/or physical fights. The major constellation that will determine whether something is defined as abuse or dependence is when there is an absence of dependence to the substance as well as the pronounced desire for use of the substance and this desire overrides concerns with consequences to the individual and others.

The criteria and qualifiers for substance-induced disorders can overlap with the disorders found in the category of substance use disorders. This overlap focuses on reversible and presenting factors related to the reaction to the substance that can affect individual functioning and can have other social consequences. Included in the taxonomical category of substance-induced disorders are substance intoxication, substance withdrawal, and substance-induced mental disorders included elsewhere in the manual (e.g., substance-induced delirium, substance-induced mood disorder, substance-induced sexual dysfunction, etc.). While these overlap with substance use disorders, the phenomenological characteristics of each disorder presented in this section can also be attributable to other disorders within the *DSM-IV-TR*.

Substance intoxication is the reversible yet recent ingestion of a substance with cognitive and behavioral maladaptive responses directly attributed to the physiological effects to the central nervous system (APA, 2000). The substances not included in responses to intoxication are caffeine and nicotine. The *DSM-IV-TR* outlines three criteria for the classification of intoxication: (1) a recent exposure or ingestion to a substance; (2) maladaptive behavioral, physiological, and psychological responses to exposure or ingestion to the substance; and (3) the present symptoms are not accounted for by a medical condition or mental disorder.

The changes an individual experiences that produce *intoxication* must result in maladaptive responses or dysfunctions (harmful ones). These responses to substances do not necessarily qualify as resulting in maladaptation. Since substances are different and the effects they can have on the body differ, the variability among individuals resulting in common changes and disturbances during intoxication that result can also be varied. The resultant cognitive processes (e.g., impaired and disturbed executive functions) and physical and behavioral processes (e.g., psychomotor retardation) remain dependent on the variability among substances, amount of use, duration of use, situational and environmental context of use, and associated risk factors (e.g., legal problems, interpersonal conflicts, financial difficulties) (APA, 2000; Room, 2006). The brevity of the *intoxication* within this classification requires that after intake of the substance there be a recent substance reaction, which can be minor, acute, or chronic. *Intoxication* and the resultant behaviors often result in problematic repercussions of use. These symptoms can include maladaptive induced cognitive and behavioral changes that manifest subsequent risk factors which can affect the individual's interpersonal and social circumstances.

Slightly more severe and associated with substance dependence, secondary to heavy and prolonged substance use, *substance withdrawal* is the induced behavioral, psychological, and physical changes that do not cease after dosing stops. Whereas in intoxication, changes resulting from exposure or ingestion cease after the effect of the substance has worn off, in withdrawal, these changes persist, and remain indicative of the severity and duration of use. Three important criteria related to intoxication are necessary to warrant the diagnosis of withdrawal: (1) there must be a behavioral, psychological, and physiological change and response to a reduction in or cessation of substance use; (2) there needs to be significant impairment to other functional areas that are developed secondary to use; and (3) the symptoms exhibited should not be caused by a medical condition or a related mental disorder (APA, 2000). Furthermore, to accurately make the diagnostic impression the *DSM-IV-TR* specifies symptoms and ingestion and duration levels for withdrawal from certain groups of substances.

All the relevant criteria applicable to dependence, abuse, intoxication, and withdrawal are applied to the 11 substances specified in the *DSM-IV-TR*. The *DSM-IV-TR* recommends laboratory findings, urinalysis, and history to indicate the presence and use, severity, and tolerance of substance of use in the assessment. In relation to the specifications set in *DSM-IV-TR* for an accurate diagnosis and in this book, a thorough assessment will include background information of the client, demographics (context and situation, cultural variations toward substance consumptions, age, gender), route of administration of substance, substance of choice, onset and duration of use, associated and differential medical and/or mental health conditions, impairments to global functioning and health, family patterns of use, and exposure and utilization of medications and toxins.

If in the assessment the presence of *at least three* substances is found repeatedly within a 12-month period with no single substance predominating, the *DSM* specifies the application and diagnosis of a polysubstance-related disorder (i.e., *Polysubstance Dependence* [Code 304.80]) (APA, 2000). It is recommended that each individual substance be specified and listed in the assessment.

Some measurements that can be used to assist in the assessments include the Alcohol Use Disorders Identification Test (AUDIT); Drug Abuse Screening Test (DAST); Alcohol, Smoking, and Substance Involvement Screening Test (ASSIST); and Cut-Down, Annoyed, Guilt, Eye-Opener (CAGE) (with the inclusion of drugs [CAGE-AID]). These self-report measures, with the ASSIST as an interviewer-based measure, can be useful in research and practice to assist in acquiring information regarding the level of substance-related dependence or abuse. These instruments take anywhere from 15 to 20 minutes to an hour to administer. Currently the AUDIT and DAST are primarily utilized for assessment and physician billing for extended or brief interventions for substance abuse. Popularity for use has increased since the Wellstone-Domenici Mental Health and Addictions Equity Parity Act of 2008 and the introduction of corresponding new current procedural terminology (CPT) codes. The AUDIT's primary function is to assess problems that can occur from alcohol use; it can be used in conjunction with other measurements. AUDIT, which is available in all major languages, has information supporting its reliability and validity with various populations and cultural groups. It is used widely throughout the world in health screenings and primary brief intervention programs (Foxcroft, Kypri, & Simonite, 2009; Humeniuk et al., 2008; Parker, Marshall, & Ball, 2008). There are a total of 10 Likert-based questions, with a score range of 0 to 40 (two supplemental questions are included but these are not scored), and a threshold score of 8 or more demonstrating risk for alcohol problems. Each measurement's subscales measure alcohol-related consumption, dependence, and alcohol-related problems requiring further inquiry. The AUDIT is considered superior to other self-report measures such as the CAGE in detecting hazardous and harmful drinking (Parker et al., 2008).

Often used in conjunction with the AUDIT, the DAST measures illicit and psychoactive use particularly in the general assessment of medical, social, and behavioral events attributed to use (Newcomb, Humeniuk, & Ali, 2005). The DAST is a 28-item, "yes/no" nominal-base questionnaire, with a score range of 1 and 28, and a score of 6 or more indicative of a substance abuse or dependence problem. A shortened version of the DAST, the DAST-10, is also available for the assessment and measurement of abuse or dependence on illicit and psychoactive drugs.

Due to the success of the these measurements, particularly the AUDIT in health screening and brief intervention programs, the ASSIST has been developed to screen and identify people with moderate and severe substance abuse problems identifying behaviors related to risk and hazardous substance use. It has also been used to determine appropriate treatment levels secondary to risk (Humeniuk et al., 2008). The ASSIST is an interview-administered measurement comprised of eight Likert-based questions, score ranging from 0 to 40. The ASSIST covers 10 substance areas (tobacco, alcohol, cannabis, cocaine, amphetamine-type stimulants, inhalants, sedatives, hallucinogens, opioids, and other drugs) and assesses frequency of use and associated problems. Each substance is scored separately with a threshold score for alcohol at 11 to 26 for moderate risk and 4 to 26 for illicit and psychoactive substances. The ASSIST also includes questions related to injection drug use.

The CAGE has been used to briefly assess alcohol dependence concerns, with the introduction of the CAGE-AID to assess illicit and psychoactive drug use. The CAGE scale, however, does not focus on detecting risk or problematic drug use in nondependent people (Newcombe et al., 2005).

When these and other measurements are used in conjunction with the biopsychosocial assessment, they can provide a useful self-reported baseline analysis to address and supplement findings of dependence and abuse.

DSM-IV-TR: Definition of Alcohol-Related Disorders: Problematic Misuse

Dependence, abuse, intoxication, withdrawal, and a cumulative pattern of behaviors interfering with socialization, relationships, and work are key areas of concern when addressing alcohol-related disorders. Individuals with alcohol-related conditions and impairments can experience legal consequences resulting from driving while intoxicated and disorderly conduct. Physiological-related ailments in relation to severe and chronic debilitating conditions such as cardiac problems and cirrhosis of the liver are only two of the conditions associated with alcohol misuse. Tracking the true effects of alcohol misuse can be difficult because some individuals seek medical treatment for reasons unrelated to their abuse and dependence. They can also present with different explanations of the cause related to direct or indirect involvement with the criminal justice system. The consumption of alcohol exceeding the limits of accepted social and cultural norms that also impairs health and social relationships defines an alcohol use disorder. Alcohol use disorders include the classifications of alcohol abuse, alcohol dependence, and alcohol-induced disorders. The *DSM-IV-TR* describes two primary qualifiers for alcohol use disorders: alcohol abuse and

QUICK REFERENCE 7.2

CRITERIA FOR ALCOHOL USE DISORDERS

Alcohol Abuse

Role Impairment

Impaired and inability to fulfill major role obligations due to use (e.g., school, work, or home).

Legal Problems

Alcohol-related legal problems due to hazardous use.

Social Problems

Continued drinking despite recurrent social and/or interpersonal problems caused or exacerbated by alcohol use.

Hazardous Use

Recurrent use with physical risks (e.g., driving while intoxicated).

No diagnosis of dependence in the past 12 months.

Alcohol Dependence

Tolerance

Need to increase consumption by 50% or more to achieve the same desired effects.

Markedly reduced effects when drinking the same amount.

Withdrawal

Physiological indicators and responses due to lack of alcohol ingestion.

Drinking to avoid or relieve withdrawal.

Recurrent drinking of larger amounts or for a longer period of time than intended.

Desire to Quit

Unsuccessful attempts or a persistent desire to quit or cut down on drinking.

Reduced Activities and Social Problems

Time spent using, obtaining, or recovering from the effects of alcohol.

Important social or recreational activities given up or reduced in favor of alcohol use.

Psychological/Physical Problems

Continued drinking despite knowledge of a recurrent or persistent psychological or physical problem caused or exacerbated by alcohol use.

Source: Summarized criteria from the *Diagnostic and Statistical Manual of Mental Disorders, Fourth Edition, Text Revision.* Copyright 2000 by the American Psychiatric Association.

alcohol dependence. As specified in the criteria defined in the *DSM-IV-TR* for abuse, a diagnosis of alcohol abuse is given if the person experiences all of the maladaptive cognitive and behavioral components of abuse, including impairment in interpersonal and social relationships, inability to perform major obligations, engagement in physically hazardous and risky behaviors, and legal difficulties due to alcohol use. Despite the psychosocial problems resulting from abuse, alcohol abuse does not include the same compulsive drinking patterns or physiological components of tolerance and withdrawal seen in alcohol dependence (Schulte et al., 2009). As shown in Quick Reference 7.2, the primary disorders of abuse and dependence have their own differentiating criteria, symptomatology, and duration.

Alcohol dependence is defined as the constellation of maladaptive cognitive, behavioral, and physiological symptoms related to physical dependence as well as compulsive alcohol-seeking patterns of use. These result in the severe and persistent pattern of use that results in psychosocial and medical impairments (Schulte et al., 2009). To qualify for a *DSM-IV-TR* diagnosis of alcohol dependence, a person must exhibit at least three or more symptoms within a 12-month period: (1) physiological dependence (tolerance and withdrawal); (2) inability to control amount of use; (3) inability to cut down or fail to quit drinking when experiencing problems; (4) spending and using most of time drinking in larger quantities; and (5) giving up and/or building relationships and social events around alcohol use (APA, 2000; Schulte et al., 2009).

The practitioner must also identify the differences between two common disorders: intoxication and withdrawal. Intoxication is reversible and induced cognitive and behavioral changes occurring due to overingestion of the substance. This may be accompanied by a lower threshold for anger and violence but usually results in generalized disinhibition. Intoxication is related to harmful and hazardous use with complications related to social and occupational function. It does not have the severe and long-lasting symptoms of withdrawal.

Withdrawal is the biophysical reaction and syndrome related to the reduction of a chemical stimulus in the body. This reaction requires medical attention by an appropriate provider to rule out complications. A clinical feature and predictor of the presence of withdrawal is a high pulse rate indicating severity of withdrawal. Oftentimes this is followed by overactivity of the autonomous central nervous system and the physiological manifestation of alcohol withdrawal syndrome (or delirium tremens [DTs]). DTs are characterized by tremors, sweating, anxiety, nausea, vomiting, agitation, insomnia, seizure tachycardia, and respiratory failure.

There may also be a previous history of DTs (APA, 1994, 2000; Lee et al., 2005; Maxmen & Ward, 1995; Parker et al., 2008; Zuckerman, 1995). These symptoms overlap with other clinical presentations of severity and can result in serious and permanent complications.

Wernicke's encephalopathy is a complication of withdrawal due to chronic alcohol dependence, stemming from a thiamine deficiency that presents with a classic triad symptoms: confusion, ataxia, and opthalmophegia (Parker et al., 2008). Other symptoms of Wernicke's encephalopathy include DTs, hypothermia, hypotension, memory disturbance, coma, and unconsciousness. While reversible, if left untreated, Wernicke's encephalopathy results in permanent brain damage (Korsakoff's psychosis) resulting in severe short-term memory loss and functional impairment (Parker et al., 2008). It is not uncommon that the individual experiences a loss of pleasure and desire, almost equivalent to a melancholic depression or similar to the negative symptoms of schizophrenia.

Alcohol withdrawal can present with auditory and visual hallucinations, disorientation, confusion, anhedonia, clouding of consciousness, impaired attention, and autonomic hyperactivity in psychological alterations due to use (Lee et al., 2005; Pozzi et al., 2008). Care should be exercised that these symptoms are a response to the withdrawal rather than suspect immediately that these symptoms may be related to other mental health or medical conditions. (See Quick Reference 7.2 for a summary of the criteria for the alcohol use disorders.)

THEORIES AND ETIOLOGY OF ALCOHOL USE DISORDERS

Descriptions and definitions of alcoholism are varied and come from various sociological, physiological, and psychological theoretical perspectives.

People with alcohol problems are found in all social classes and cultures, from different demographical backgrounds (e.g., genders, ages, and religions or atheists), in various systems, such as individuals, couples, families, and groups, in a variety of settings. Earlier theories and theorists related alcohol use problems as having a direct relationship with morality, failed duty to self, a lack of personal self-control, and a lacking of will. Furthermore, it was postulated that an inability to attain role functioning due to alcohol use was not only a sign of a "sick person" but that the individual with an alcohol use problem accepted and benefited from the "sick person" role. As early as 1969, this perspective had changed, and theorists began to regard individuals suffering from alcohol-related disorders as medically ill rather than weak or immoral (Jones, 1969). From this newer perspective, alcohol use is a medical condition requiring physical treatment to gain respite. Other theories highlight the relationship between individuals and the environment, asserting that alcohol use is a learned response from watching and learning drinking behaviors and patterns (positive and negative ones) through individual expectancies, family systems, and socialization. These theoretical frameworks assert the relationship and consequences among alcohol use, the individual, and society.

The motivational aspects, personality and traits, and characteristics of individuals who suffer from an alcohol use disorder can share similarities especially regarding interpersonal factors related to use. Similarities include feelings of incompleteness, imperfection, and emptiness where the individual is desperate to find a sense of wholeness and completion. This sense of completion may rest in finding and holding on to an external source, such as a person or an object. Guilt and shame become prominent emotions. To cope, a variety of defense mechanisms are utilized that are indicative of the intrapsychic aspects of personality development and sustainment in continued alcohol use. From this perspective, defense mechanisms such as denial may be used to control anxiety. Other defense mechanisms that may be present in severe and chronic alcohol use are rationalization and intellectualization (Modesto-Lowe & Kranzler, 1999).

Studies examining personality and alcohol use demonstrate that certain traits are present in those with alcohol use and substance disorders. The Myers-Briggs Type Indicator (MBTI) personality test outlines personality traits found in the normal population. These include:

1. Extroversion—individuals who are sociable interactive, externally oriented, gregarious, and enjoying multiple relationships.
2. Introversion—individuals who are intense, internally oriented, enjoy limited number of relationships, and reflective.
3. Sensing—individuals who like to deal with the here and now, focusing on experience, are realistic, hardworking, and practical.
4. Intuition—individuals who are future oriented, trust their hunches and are inspirational, ingenious, imaginative, and active.
5. Thinking—individuals who use cognitive processes to engage in decision making
6. Feeling—individuals who are subjective, intimate, persuasive, personable, harmony oriented, and sympathetic.
7. Judging—individuals who are settled, decided, fixed, like to plan ahead, enjoy closure.
8. Perceiving—individuals who are open-minded, tentative, and like to keep their options open (Janowsky, Hong, Morter, & Howe, 1999).

In their study of 90 participants admitted to a psychiatric facility with alcohol-related disorders (e.g., abuse and dependence),

Janowsky et al. (1999) noted that individuals with alcohol-related substance abuse problems only exhibited a high degree of traits for sensing, feeling, perceiving, and extroversion, similar to traits found within the normal population; yet of those with substance abuse and mood disorders, traits higher in introversion, sensing, feeling, and perceiving were found. This research highlights a strong relationship between the domain of personality traits and multiple types of risk-taking behaviors and offers an explanation to the role of temperament and possible etiology of alcohol-related approaches to behaviors (Schulte et al., 2009). Furthermore, personality and how temperament relates to problem use may be clinically useful in determining the type of treatment modality (e.g., individual, group, or self-help) for those with alcohol problems. In treatment, however, it should always be recognized that personality characteristics often remain consistent but behavioral patterns can change and vary with time (Schulte et al., 2009).

Another delineation worth noting is between the Type I and Type II and Types A and B personalities and alcohol use. Type A personalities have later onsets of alcohol use and fewer disturbance of psychosocial functioning. Type B have an earlier onset (>25 years old) and increased psychosocial interference. According to Zuckerman (1995), the preferred mode of treatment is matched to the typology (p. 160). In the Type I as in Type A personalities, there is a later onset of drinking, a strong genetic effect, and a low probability of risk-taking behavior, such as fighting or arrest. Type II matches the Type B personalities in that there is an earlier onset of alcohol use and frequent risk-taking behaviors. Neither typology appears to be statistically linked to etiology of disorders and/or observed behavioral outcomes (Dawson, 2000; Kirst-Ashman, 2007; Pagan et al., 2006).

Substance Disorders: Etiology of the Problem

Many different factors contribute to etiological factors of alcoholism. The factors resulting in alcoholism remain individually unique; however, commonalties exist.

Genetics and the Environment
Alcohol dependence is influenced by genetics with heritability estimates ranging from 50% to 70%, genetic factors accounting for 40% to 56% of variance, and influences remaining fairly constant across adulthood (Pagan et al., 2006). Genetic expression is influenced by environmental agents, and environmental influences rather than just strictly genetic factors play a major role in the decision to initiate substance use. Environmental influences account for 55% to 80% of variance with the initiation of alcohol use, with genetic factors accounting for variance in frequency of use and transition from initiation and experimental alcohol use to regular and problematic use (Pagan et al., 2006). The manifestation and expression of genes in alcohol use increase the propensity and importance of drinking behavior once initiation has begun in response to the environmental stimuli.

In the longitudinal research analysis of twins, Pagan et al. (2006) concluded:

Shared environmental influences were less important for frequency of use, while the influence of additive genetic factors and unique environmental factors were more influential contributors to the frequency of alcohol use. Genetic factors important at initiation overlapped to a small degree with the genetic factors influencing the frequency of use, but we found no overlap of unique environmental factors across stages of use. Genetic factors play the largest role in problematic drinking at age 25 in both men and women, whereas common environmental influences were non-significant in both sexes. For both sexes genetic factors influencing alcohol problems overlapped substantially with those influencing frequency of use at age 25, and shared environmental influence on initiation overlapped moderately with the relatively small shared environmental influences on frequency of use at 25. (p. 496)

Studies addressing the impact of variants in genes associated with encoding alcohol-metabolizing enzymes (ADH1B, ADH1C, and ALDH2) help to explain variations of alcohol use disorders and risks among different individuals and certain groups (Schulte et al., 2009). The inability to break down alcohol in the body leads to rapid intoxication, which sustains the propensity for dependence.

Family Systems   Noting disturbed familial patterns is of particular importance, especially poor parental relations, poor parental supervision, harsh parental physical punishment, and parental conflict contributing to the individual coming from a broken home. In the alcohol use disorders, other factors include coming from a family with a large number of children, mothers of a young age, single-parent households, low socioeconomic status, and other associated alcohol use disorders increase within a conflicted family environment (Swendsen et al., 2009; WHO, 2006a). Modeling of parental alcohol use has a direct effect on children's alcohol use and misuse. There is a direct relationship between parental monitoring and alcohol use in children; if children are monitored, this protective factor can help to reduce and control hazardous and harmful drinking behavior patterns (Schulte et al., 2009). Furthermore, there

is also a connection between alcohol and substance-related use during pregnancy as it can be related to fetal alcohol spectrum disorders (FASD), learning disabilities, mental retardation and developmental disabilities (MR/DD). It can also increase the future risk that these individuals will develop an alcohol and substance-related disorder themselves (Campbell, Essex, & Held, 1994; Huggins, Grant, O'Malley, & Streissguth, 2008; Janikowski, Donnelly, & Lawrence, 2007; Robertson, Davis, Sneed, Koch, & Boston, 2009).

Social Stressors   Associations between community and societal factors have been found in alcohol use problems. Social stressors such as gangs, delinquent friends, availability of alcohol, and poor social integration can all be problematic (Swendsen et al., 2009; WHO, 2006b). In affiliations with deviant peer groups, harmful alcohol use increases by modeling alcohol drinking behaviors as a way to cope with stress, especially in individuals who lack or have limited self-regulation to cope with emotional effects (Schulte et al., 2009). This modeling effect has an impact on violence and the availability and consumption of alcohol. When under the influence a person may experience poor social integration due to the effects that alcohol use has on the processing of perceived emotional cues. For example, the processing of emotional facial cues following alcohol consumption may become impaired, causing the individual to misattribute facial cues and thereby increasing the likelihood of inappropriate behavioral responses, such as aggression (Craig, Attwood, Benton, Peton-Voak, & Munafo, 2009). Combining misattributed emotional states and harmful and hazardous drinking when individuals have limited self-regulation can be problematic. In addition, if violence and witnessing of violence is commonplace in a cultural context where these stressors are sanctioned, it will only add to subsequent alcohol use problems and increased risks of developing alcohol-related problems.

RISK FACTORS AND CHARACTERISTICS

Age Difference: Youth Versus Adults

Variations of drinking patterns emerge in the transition from adolescence to adulthood. Experimentation is a normal developmental pattern among adolescence but can lead to problem drinking into adulthood if onset of drinking begins at earlier ages. Early age of first use is a significant predictor of subsequent transitions from alcohol (or drug use) to dependence (Pagan et al., 2006; Swendsen et al., 2009). Divergence from experimentation to problem use may be attributed to developmental biological changes and environmental factors influencing use, including hormone fluctuations that impact alcohol sensitivities and neurocognitive development. Alcohol sensitivity increases with age, which accounts for the intense and quick sedation that occurs in adults rather than in adolescents and causes adults to stop drinking after shorter periods of time than in adolescents (Schulte et al., 2009). This may also explain the increased tolerance developed with earlier-age drinking leading to dependence into adulthood.

Gender: Males Versus Females

Prevalence rates for alcohol use disorders remain higher in males when compared to females. Attributable deaths due to alcohol use remain higher in males at 90% for alcohol use worldwide and respectively 9.9% to 6.3% in women (SAMHSA, 2009a, 2009b; Schulte et al., 2009; WHO, 2009d). Biological differences in gender allow for differences to alcohol reactivity and how these relate to problem drinking. Alcohol sensitivity in drinking affects women nonlinearly more in the realm of negative motor and cognitive deficits than men, with women suffering greater task completion impairment relative to men at similar levels of alcohol concentration (Schulte et al., 2009; Sohrabji, 2002). This may explain why men develop higher rates of alcohol use disorders than women. Generally, men consume more alcohol when compared to women to achieve the same effects that result in alcohol intoxication. These greater amounts of consumption increase their level of tolerance and consequently the development of dependence. Looking at volume of alcohol consumed and the effects of alcohol sensitivity to cognition in men and women, when 0.5 liter is consumed (3 drinks or less), cognitive abilities improved for both compared to those not drinking whereas drinking 1 liter (6 or more drinks) impaired cognitive ability in both sexes. When the volume of alcohol falls within the range of 0.5 to 1 liter, however, cognitive ability improves for men but not for women, resulting in susceptibility to alcohol-related cognitive dementia (Sohrabji, 2002). Physiological difference in gender in body mass ratio also may explain protective differences to the effects of alcohol. Greater body fat in women and hormonal changes reduce water levels in the body, increasing sensitivity to alcohol and thus increasing blood alcohol concentrations (BAC) compared to males with proportional body weight (Schulte et al., 2009). As this sensitivity is higher in women than men, it decreases women's propensity for dependence. This is attributed to differences in metabolic rates, where females have slower elimination rates of alcohol than males, due to enzymes and hormone fluctuations during reproductive cycles. Alcohol is metabolized earlier in men because the enzymes of dehydrogenase needed to break down acetaldehyde are higher in men than in women; alcohol metabolism is further affected in women by the presence of estrogen during the reproductive cycle—a hormone not present in males (Sohrabji,

2002). Due to the low elimination rates, secondary conditions related to alcohol-consumption in women can lead to breast cancer, loss of bone density (osteoporosis), and Alzheimer's disease. These differences should be taken into consideration when assessing for substance-related disorders and subsequent treatment. Yet despite these differences, disparities in treatment and access to care are more pronounced in gender. This situation can be attributed to the difference in rates of stigma between the sexes when addressing alcohol-related concerns.

Disabilities

Certain conditions that result in disability, such as learning disorders, sensory impairments (e.g., blindness and deafness), developmental disabilities, mental retardation, and postinjury disabilities (e.g., brain injury or spinal cord injury), increase the risk for substance-related disorders. Of these conditions, learning disabilities account for 40% to 60% prevalence rates of AOD, sensory impairments account for 35% to 50%, postinjury disabilities account for 25% to 75%, mental retardation accounts for approximately 10%, with an unidentified estimate of prevalence rates for individuals with other coexisting disabilities, such as borderline intellectual functioning and developmental disabilities (Janikowski et al., 2007; Robertson et al., 2009). Fifty percent of traumatic brain injury and spinal injuries are related to alcohol-related circumstances, and many of these individuals may return to alcohol use poststabilization. When abstinence is achieved, negative physical circumstances (e.g., seizures) may lead to the need for residential treatment care. Facilities to assist these individuals in recovery are limited, especially when there is a coexisting mental health condition and alcohol and other substance-related conditions (Huggins et al., 2008; Janikowski et al., 2007; Robertson et al., 2009).

Some of the disabilities individuals present with also have a history of alcohol- and substance-related concerns within the family system and this pattern of behavior can have a lifelong course; for example, prenatal substance abuse and FASD, learning disorders, MR/DD, neurodevelopmental deficits, limited and/or impairment in a triad of function impairment (e.g., executive functions, communication, and behaviors), and limited social interactions place a higher stress on emotion regulation already limited in those with these impairments. Paradoxically, these limitations require prescribed treatment and management for alcohol and substance-related abstinence, including finding alternatives to lifestyle (a limitation in the life domain and occupation), alternatives through problem solving (a cognitive deficit), and substituting peer using and places of use (and emotional difficulty for those with already limited social interactions) (Campbell et al., 1994; Janikowski et al., 2007). Taken advantage of and exploited due to their learning differential, functional limitations, and communication barriers, individuals with learning disabilities, MR/DD, and neurophysiological disabilities present with challenges in clinical presentation but require assessment and treatment due to the risk factors involved.

COMPLETION OF THE DIAGNOSTIC ASSESSMENT

A clear understanding of the diagnostic assessment leading to the treatment process is essential. Although treatment can be initiated at any stage, due to the severe medical complications resulting from this illness, the goal is to intervene in the early progression to prevent permanent brain damage or death (See Quick Reference 7.3).

In treatment, the first stage is completion of the diagnostic assessment. A complete

QUICK REFERENCE 7.3

EARLY RECOGNITION OF ALCOHOL-RELATED PROBLEMS

Early Indicators

- Heavy drinking (more than 6 drinks per day (i.e., greater than 60 grams per day of ethanol for men) and more than 4 drinks per day for women (i.e., greater than 40 grams of ethanol).
- Concern about drinking by self, family, or both.
- Intellectual impairment, especially in the abstracting, planning, organizing, and adaptive skills.
- Eating lightly or skipping meals.
- Drinking alcohol rapidly.
- Increased tolerance to alcohol.

Psychosocial Factors

- Accidents and injuries related to drinking.
- Absence from work related to drinking.
- Majority of friends and acquaintances are heavy drinkers; most leisure activities and sports center on drinking.
- Attempts to cut down on drinking have had limited success.
- Frequent use of alcohol to deal with stressful situations.
- Frequent drinking during the workday, especially at lunch break.
- Heavy smoking.

Investigation Factors

- Macrocytosis (MCV of red cells more than 100) in the absence of anemia.
- An elevated GGT (gamma-glut amyl transpeptidase).

- Elevated serum uric acid level.
- Elevated high density lipoprotein.
- Random blood alcohol level (BAC) greater than 0.05 g %.

Clinical Symptoms and Signs

- Trauma
- Scars unrelated to surgery
- Elevated pulse
- Hand tremor and sweating
- Psoriasis
- Alcohol smell on the breath during the day
- Dyspepsia
- Morning nausea and vomiting
- Recurring diarrhea

- Pancreatitis
- Hepatomegaly
- Impotence
- Palpitations
- Hypertension
- Insomnia
- Nightmares

understanding of the biological, psychological, and sociocultural perspectives is important in the assessment. The *DSM-IV-TR* provides an outline of important factors to consider as does this book. Identifying these factors and the use of a number of measurement tools can assist the mental health practitioner. As with any disorder, basic facts to obtain and consider about the individual include age, culture, gender, socioeconomic status, marital status, family history, developmental or childhood history, incidence of abuse or neglect (including domestic violence), and educational status. Level of motivation for starting treatment is an important factor to engage the client as it will set the stage for what is to come. Other factors to assess include: age of first use, attitude toward use, honesty about usage, social and occupational

---

QUICK REFERENCE 7.4

General Concerns

- Isolation from family and community.
- Life events revolving around drinking activities.
- Increased frequency of accidents and injuries.

- Acts of violence and crime.
- Financial problems
- Legal problems.

At Work

- Frequent absenteeism, especially Monday and Friday, and after payday.
- Frequent and varied medical reasons for absence from work.
- Promotion failure, impaired job performance.

- A history of gaps in work, frequent changes of employment, and the threat of job loss.
- Industrial accidents.
- Early retirement

---

functioning while using the substance, amount used, frequency of use, duration of use, changes in use over time, attitudes of family and others toward use, recreational activities, composition of social circle, availability of the substance, mental health disorders issues (e.g., depression, anxiety, disability), medical issues (e.g., withdrawal syndrome symptoms), issues of mental status, (e.g., orientation to person, place, and time), and drug of choice and/or secondary drugs. (See Quick References 7.4 and 7.5 for identification of general concerns, and see Case Example 7.1.)

QUICK REFERENCE 7.5

COMMON EFFECTS OF EXCESSIVE ALCOHOL CONSUMPTION WITHIN THE FAMILY

The alcohol-dependent person:

- Denies the alcohol problem, minimizes use, blames others, is forgetful, and employs defense mechanisms to protect the self (ego).
- Receives criticism from others and from the family.
- Spends money needed on alcohol rather than for necessities.
- Financially irresponsible, prioritizing use over bills.
- Is unpredictable and impulsive.
- Resorts to verbal and physical abuse in place of honest and open talk.
- Loses the trust of family, relatives, and friends.
- Experiences increased sexual arousal but reduced function.
- Has unpredictable mood swings—Jekyll-and-Hyde personality.
- Suffers from depression, guilt, shame.

The spouse or partner:

- Often hides and denies the problem of the partner.

- Takes on the other person's responsibilities, perpetuating the spouse/partner's dependence.
- Takes a job to get away from the problem and/or to maintain financial security.
- Has difficulty being open and honest because of resentment, anger, hurt, and shame.
- Avoids sexual contact, seeking separation or divorce.
- Engages in overprotection of the children, neglect, and/or uses them for emotional support.
- Shows gradual social withdrawal and isolation.
- May lose feelings of self-respect and self-worth.
- May use alcohol or prescription drugs to cope.
- May use alcohol to share a relationship with substance dependent spouse.
- May present to the doctor with anxiety, depression, psychosomatic symptoms, or evidence of domestic violence.

The children have an increased risk of developing alcohol dependency themselves. They may be:

- Victims of birth defects (from maternal alcohol use).
- Torn between parental conflicts.
- Deprived of emotional and physical support and nurture.
- Lacking trust in anyone.
- Avoidant of peer group activities, out of fear and shame.
- Destructive and negative dealing with problems and getting attention.
- Shortsighted in goals, losing sight of values and standards because of a lack of consistent parental monitoring or harsh discipline.
- Truant or fail in school.
- Indulge in petty crimes.
- Suffering from a diminishing sense of self-worth as a significant member of the family.
- Presenting with learning difficulties, enuresis, or sleep disorders.

CASE EXAMPLE 7.1 - CASE OF ROBERT

Robert is a 56-year-old Caucasian male, of average height and weight, appearing older than stated age. He is being admitted to the chemical dependency unit at a hospital on a voluntary basis reporting that he is not "handling things well." He reports that he is feeling suicidal and verbalizes plans of driving a truck into a tree or using a gun. He reports ongoing difficulties with alcohol and substance abuse for over 2 years. Robert was intoxicated at time of admission with a blood alcohol level of .436, five times the legal limit, and testing positive for cocaine and marijuana. Precipitating factors to the hospitalization included loss of residence, marital separation, financial stressors, and loss of employment. Within 48 hours prior to admission, Robert reports having moved out of his daughter's home and unsuccessfully attempting to move in with a friend. He reports feeling depressed, using cocaine to excess and marijuana, and experiencing insomnia. He reports having snorted cocaine earlier and drinking all day long from morning to evening, presenting inebriated at the time of interview at the chemical dependency unit.

Robert reports a long history of outpatient chemical dependency treatment, with multiple detoxification admissions. He reports multiple attempts at sobriety, with attendance to Alcoholics Anonymous (AA), but

(continued)

CASE EXAMPLE 7.1
(*CONTINUED*)

none was successful. Robert reports feeling depressed at the time of interview and admits to experiencing suicidal ideation. He denies any past history of suicide attempts. He has had thoughts of killing himself while driving. He denies having access to a weapon at the time of the interview. He denies any visual, auditory, tactile, olfactory, and/or gustatory hallucinations at the time of admission.

He reports a current history of alcohol and illicit drug use of cocaine and marijuana. He drinks on a daily basis, stating he drinks approximately a case of beer and at least a pint of vodka daily. He snorts cocaine almost daily, using with friends, and buying and spending weekly approximately $100 to $150. He smokes "a joint" with friends when available, sometimes 2 to 3 times per week. He reports he does not have a problem with marijuana and states that his cocaine use has increased in this past year. He is experiencing difficulties when not drinking or using, experiencing "shakes, sweats, and vomiting." He reports there is frequently blood when vomiting. He denies a seizure disorder but received medical treatment for seizures he suffered last year due to his use. He reports he was stabilized but refused treatment for his substance-related concerns at that time. He has difficulty with sleeping secondary to his use. He denies issues of gambling at the time of the interview.

In gathering history information, Robert states that his parents were divorced days after his birth. He has a positive family history for substance-related concerns. Robert's birth father is deceased due to liver complications from alcohol use. He had limited contact with his father, citing that his father was absent in his life. Roberts states his mother remarried to his stepfather and stayed married for 20 years, but they are now divorced. He has limited contact with them individually since his use worsened. Robert's stepfather was in the Navy, and the family traveled often. He states his childhood was unproblematic and denies any abuse issues. Robert states that he has two half brothers from his mother and stepfather's union and two half brothers from his birth father's second marriage. Robert denies contact with his biological father's sons. He has one deceased half brother, his youngest, who died of cancer. He states he had a close relationship with his younger brother and has been affected by this loss. His other half brother, George, is "not very social" and Robert has little contact with him. He does state that George has had problems with drugs, mostly marijuana, including legal problems. He is unable to provide information due to limited contact with his brother at the time of the interview. When asked about family history for substance abuse, he reports only his biological father had problems with alcohol and his brother, Greg, has problems related to marijuana use. He reports his stepfather was a "social" drinker as was his mother and denied substance abuse problems with them at the time of the interview. Robert denies substance abuse treatment for his family members but reports being unsure of treatment received by his brother Greg. When asked about a past family history for mental illness, Robert denies knowledge of mental illness and states that no one in his family has received treatment for mental illness at the time of the interview.

Robert reports medical concerns currently affecting him. He reports a diagnosis of liver cirrhosis and seizures. He states he has not been compliant with his medical treatment secondary to his alcohol and illicit drug use. According to the physical that was conducted and upon observation, he demonstrates jaundice and abdominal swelling at the time of this interview. Robert has experienced seizures secondary to his substance-related concerns and received medical treatment for these at that time. He has allergies to sulfa medications.

Robert is currently married but has been separated from his second wife for a year. He had one previous marriage that resulted in divorce. He has two adult daughters from his first marriage. He also reports a third adult daughter from a relationship with another woman, not his previous or current wife, whom he states was a result of "a minor indiscretion." Robert states that his current wife has three minor children from her previous marriage (two boys and a girl). No difficulties are noted with his relationship with his minor stepchildren at the time of this interview. Robert reports marital difficulties related to his substance-related use and subsequent problems he is experiencing. He has been separated from his current wife for approximately a year, with frequent fighting and arguing with his wife secondary to his drinking. He reports having "pushed" her on a "few occasions" and "I never slapped her" when having been drinking. He has sexual difficulties in the marriage secondary to his drinking, stating a loss of desire and performance concerns, which has further affected his marriage. When his financial problems worsened, his wife "kicked me out." He is vague regarding what precipitated him leaving, citing only that his wife was angry about financial matters. At the time of the interview, he denies substance-related concerns to be the issue for the present separation and his inability to return home.

Robert reports a lengthy history of vocational jobs after having completed military service in the Navy. During his time in military service he worked as an assembler, a seaman, and was last promoted to a higher-rank position in operations prior to leaving service. He denies any problems with substance abuse and having any social or occupational concerns during his time of enlistment. After his enlistment, he reports completing and acquiring a bachelor's degree and then pursuing a chiropractor degree, which he obtained in 1990. He has been successful in this occupation, including opening his own practice, until his problems with alcohol and other substances worsened. He denies being currently employed, citing having lost his practice and currently facing a malpractice suit. He reports sporadic income from working "odd jobs" for friends for cash. He denies actively seeking employment at the time of the interview.

Robert reports extensive legal problems secondary to his substance-related concerns. He is currently facing charges for reckless driving, reckless endangerment, and driving without a license for which he has a pending criminal case. He has legal problems related to multiple driving under the influence charges for which his license was revoked and reports criminal cases against him pending this and other charges, for which he may suffer incarceration. He also suffered a malpractice suit for which he may also lose his chiropractor's license. Secondary to his legal problems and loss of income, he filed for bankruptcy. He acknowledges that these legal difficulties are the result of his use. He states that he presently does not have a source of income. Robert states he was denied Social Security due to his multiple legal problems and current and past substance abuse concerns. Robert feels that the strain of these concerns has added enormous pressure on him, which he acknowledges has further increased his drinking and drug use.

Significant events include death of a brother with whom he had a close relationship, multiple pending legal problems with possible incarceration, loss of income, bankruptcy, and separation from current wife. He has housing concerns secondary to his marital problems, and that recently he moved into his daughter and son-in-law's home. Due to his drinking and drug use and their concerns for their infant son, his grandson, he was asked to leave. He recently talked to a friend who stated that he could stay with him, but upon arriving, the friend notified him that he could not stay. He worries about having a place to stay after he leaves the hospital and is currently homeless.

Robert has few social contacts but these are related to his alcohol and drug use. He has ceased contact with former friends but is vague regarding why. He reports residing with his friends when available, and with this last stay he reports having been asked to leave his daughter's house. He reports engaging in alcohol and cocaine use with this friend on the day of his admission to the chemical dependency unit. He engages in marijuana use with this friend. He denies buying drugs from his friends, saying they give these to him for "free." When asked if he acquires his illicit drugs from these friends, he reports he has "other friends" but does not provide any information regarding these. Robert identifies his spirituality or religious system as a "spiritualist." He feels that his beliefs do not cause any problems for him (see Table 7.1).

(continued)

CASE EXAMPLE 7.1
(CONTINUED)

Table 7.1.   Mental Status Description

Presentation	Mental Functioning	Higher-Order Abilities	Thought Form/Content
Appearance: Unkempt	Simple Calculations: Accurate but slowed	Similarities/Differences: Accurate	Judgment: Fair to poor
Mood: Anxious and depressed	Serial 7s: Limited		Insight: Limited
Attitude: Cooperative	Immediate Memory: Needed prompts to remain on task, some vagueness to detail		Intelligence: High
Affect: Congruent, sad, blunted			Thought Process: Logical but slowness noted
Speech: Slurred and slow	Remote Memory: Impairment noted		Difficulty with concentration noted.
Motor Activity: Retarded	General Knowledge: Accurate yet slow to respond		Delusions: None
Orientation: Oriented X 4	Proverb Interpretation: Accurate yet slow processing		Hallucinations: None
	Insight: Limited		
	Intelligence: High		
	Thought Process: Logical but slowness noted; difficulty with concentration noted		
	Delusions: None		
	Hallucinations: None		

Application of Multiaxial Assessment: Robert

Based on the accumulated data, laboratory findings, and completion of the AUDIT, the client is diagnosed on Axis I with alcohol dependence with physiologic dependence, cocaine dependence, and cannabis abuse. Justification for each listing follows. Alcohol dependence with physiologic dependence is diagnosed secondary to the presenting pathologic amount of alcohol consumed with a resultant blood alcohol level of .436, reported daily use of large quantities of alcohol with tolerance, and Robert's report of a past and current history of withdrawal symptoms and past medical hospitalization related to his withdrawal symptoms (e.g., elevated pulse, sweating, vomiting with blood, tremors, and seizures). He has a diagnosis of liver cirrhosis secondary to his alcohol use, substantiated by hematology and past medical records. He reports multiple failed attempts at sobriety with detoxification, counseling, and

AA. His employment, social, and intimate relationships have been impaired secondary to his inability to cease his alcohol use. He continues to engage in compulsive, alcohol-seeking behaviors despite acknowledging the physical, psychological, and social/occupational consequences his alcohol use continues to cause. Second to alcohol dependence is the issue of cocaine and cannabis use. Robert reported using cocaine daily for a 12-month period, has been unable to maintain work and relationships, and has demonstrated poor performance issues regarding professional functioning, decision making, and coping skills. His cocaine use continues despite lacking financial means, current legal issues, and problems he could incur from buying illicit drugs. He presented with a positive result for cocaine upon this admission. While it is difficult to show singularly if cocaine is affecting his withdrawal syndromes as required in the diagnostic criterion for physiologic signs (secondary to current and concurrent use of alcohol), because of his daily continued use for the past

12 months and multiple impairments to all areas of functioning, cocaine dependence is also added to the Axis I diagnostic criteria.

With respect to cannabis use, Robert reports smoking only with friends on a weekly basis at the time of the interview. While he is currently using three substances on a regular basis, the diagnosis of polysubstance dependence can be ruled out as he reports not utilizing cannabis daily and does not cite the psychological and/or physiological aspects of tolerance and withdrawal as he reports with alcohol and cocaine at the time of interview. He also denies compulsive seeking of cannabis, which would continue to further affect his social and occupational functioning as he presents with his use of alcohol and cocaine. Because he does engage in cannabis use, which is harmful use secondary to the risk behaviors he incurs socially and occupationally, he is given the diagnosis of cannabis abuse.

Axis II will reflect the V Code of 71.09 of no diagnosis as on this examination it cannot be determined that he has a personality disorder. At the time of admission, he demonstrates some avoidant and antisocial traits; however, these are in relation to his current substance dependence (e.g., legal difficulties, financial matters, relationship problems, and compulsive seeking of substance in response to his psychological and physical dependence to them). Prior to his substance use disorder, Robert denies any personal, legal, financial, and/or occupational concerns. While co-occurrence of personality and mood disorders are evident in the phenomenological analysis of substance use disorders, accuracy of personality disorders and traits are assessed when client is in full remission of dependence concerns. A scheduled psychological assessment should be arranged postdependence and medical stabilization to rule out disability factors such as developmental delays and learning disorders.

On Axis III, the diagnosis is liver cirrhosis, history of seizures, and allergy to sulfa drugs. It is important to note these medical conditions and concerns because when medications are prescribed for this client, the prescriber will need to take into account his compromised liver functioning and minimize prescription errors and medication side effects. Generally, to make sure attention is brought to the allergies in particular, important points are often capitalized in the medical record to alert the team to potential problems and concerns.

The diagnosis of alcohol liver disease, such as liver cirrhosis, requires that specific criteria are met: Heavy drinking for more than 5 years in the amount of over 40 grams/day in men (and over 20 g/day for women) of drinking over 80 grams/day for two weeks, jaundice, weight loss, elevated serum levels, and the exclusion of hepatotrophic virus infection and drug-induced and toxic liver injuries to explain for abnormal findings (Zeng et al., 2008). The presence of liver cirrhosis is an additionally conclusive sign that the patient has been accurately diagnosed with alcohol dependence. Monitoring for the potential of seizures by physicians, nurses, and social workers can further decrease medical errors due to prescriptions.

The recording of Axis IV demonstrates issues in almost all of the psychosocial domains. Based on the details of the assessment, the social stressors are listed according to level of severity of how these affect the client the most on Axis IV:

1. Multiple legal problems with possible incarceration.
2. Medical concerns, chronic and debilitating conditions.
3. Occupational difficulties with loss of career and current unemployment.
4. Inadequate support system, with substance-using peers.
5. Marital conflict with current separation of 1 year.
6. Social isolation.
7. Lack of housing.

QUICK REFERENCE 7.6

ROBERT'S MULTIAXIAL ASSESSMENT

Axis I   Alcohol dependence with physiological dependence 303.90.
              Cocaine dependence 304.20.
              Cannabis abuse 305.20.

Axis II: V71.09 No diagnosis.

Axis III: Liver cirrhosis.
              History of seizures.
              Allergy to sulfa drugs.

Axis IV: Multiple legal problems with possible incarceration.
              Medical concerns, chronic and debilitating conditions.
              Occupational difficulties with loss of career and current unemployment.
              Inadequate support system, with substance-using peers.
              Marital conflict with current separation of 1 year.
              Social isolation.
              Lack of housing.

Axis V: 45 (current).

Axis V looks at the client's global functioning, which in this case is impaired on the psychological and psychosocial functioning domains (although cognitive functioning remains fairly intact). Because of his suicidal ideation and his compulsive drug-seeking behaviors, he demonstrates serious psychological symptoms despite these being attributed to his presenting substance-related concerns. These are present in level of functioning. He has serious impairments to his social and occupational functioning secondary to his own behaviors and that of his peer-using friends, his loss of employment and career, and multiple legal difficulties relating to his use. He is given a current Generalized Assessment of Functioning (GAF) score of 45 due to the severity of his presenting symptoms and impaired social/occupational functioning, omission of hallucination and delusions with no impairment in reality testing, and with the presence of awareness of problem with resulting voluntary admission to treatment. (See Quick Reference 7.6 for Robert's multiaxial assessment.)

TREATMENT PLANNING, IMPLEMENTATION, AND EVALUATION

Effective treatment planning for clients such as Robert and others suffering from abuse and dependence must take into account environmental agents and all of the information discussed in the assessment when planning for the intervention. In formulating a treatment plan in this area, the plan of intervention—short-term sample treatment goals should reflect the client's immediate presenting problems. Longer-term functional goals need to directly address reducing alcohol consumption, obtaining and maintaining sobriety, resolving legal issues, improving social and coping skills, and acquiring employment. It is important to assure that the goals are realistic, match the assessment, and reflect the desires of the patient initially upon diagnostic assessment and throughout treatment. Additionally, factors such as strengths, support systems, dual diagnoses, and culture are taken into consideration when developing the treatment plan.

Objectives for the alcohol-related disorder should be clear and concise. These should take into consideration where the client is beginning treatment, immediate needs, and address the potential of relapse to support the client's desire of sobriety. This will help him to not be set up for failure. (See Sample Treatment Plan 7.1.) Ascertaining the client's attitude about treatment is essential in engaging the client, assessing level of motivation, and developing a successful plan. Upon the initial formulation of the treatment plan, the first stage of implementation is generally detoxification for alcohol dependence as for any substance-related dependence concern.

Detoxification and Withdrawal

Detoxification is the medically assisted process during which the client removes all substances and toxins from his or her system. Completion of this phase usually occurs in an inpatient hospital (Henderson, Landry, Phillips, & Shuman, 1994). The risk associated with detoxification of alcohol is the potential dangers of withdrawal syndromes and mortality, leaving the client in critical need of immediate medical attention (Fuller & Hiller-Sturmhofel, 1999; Wesson, 1995). These withdrawal syndromes are characterized by a continuum of signs and symptoms usually beginning 12 to 48 hours after cessation of intake. The mild withdrawal syndrome includes tremor, weakness, sweating, hyperreflexia, and gastrointestinal symptoms. Some patients have generalized tonic-clonic seizures (alcoholic epilepsy or rum fits), usually not more than two in short succession (APA, 1994, 2000; Mattoo et al., 2009; Wesson, 1995) (See Sample Treatment Plan 7.2 for dependence).

Medical evaluation is needed to detect coexisting illness mimicking the withdrawal

---

SAMPLE TREATMENT PLAN 7.1

GENERAL TREATMENT PLAN FOR ALCOHOL USE (ABUSE)

Definition: Harmful and hazardous interpersonal and social consequences due to use, not indicative of tolerance or withdrawal, and absent of dependence.

Signs and Symptoms:

- Risk behaviors due to drinking (e.g., binge drinking).
- Impairment in memory.
- Neglected responsibilities.
- Absences from school or work.
- Anxiety.
- Legal difficulties.
- Relationship problems, violence, verbal, and physical fights.
- Slurred speech.
- Financial difficulties.

Goals:

1. Abstinence from harmful and hazardous drinking.
2. Medical assessment.
3. Introduce new coping skills and/or build existing coping skills.

(continued)

SAMPLE TREATMENT PLAN 7.1 *(Continued)*

Objectives	Interventions
1. Evaluate amount and type of consumption of client's alcohol intake.	Encourage client to self-report drinking patterns (e.g., binge drinking).
	Encourage client to verbalize beliefs regarding drinking patterns.
	Provide education to client regarding drinking patterns, use, and consequences.
	Encourage to connect beliefs and consequences to increase awareness of use and patterns.
	Assist the client to problem-solve and develop strategies to reduce harmful use.
2. Client will reduce risk factors associated with problem use.	Encourage client to report behaviors due to use that risk client's well-being, interpersonal relationships, and occupational status.
	Encourage client to verbalize thoughts, feelings, and emotions in response to risk factors due to use.
	Provide education to client regarding drinking patterns, use, and consequences.
	Assist client in developing problem-solving strategies to reduce risk behaviors and ameliorate consequences.
3. Client will establish a support system to utilize and depend on during recovery.	Develop with the client a list of friends and family members who provide positive support.
	Contact friends/relatives and ask for input on client's substance use.
	Contact these people and attempt to meet or speak to them about the importance of recovery for client.
4. Client will have a physical examination completed by a physician.	Refer client to his primary physician for evaluation.

SAMPLE TREATMENT PLAN 7.2

GENERAL TREATMENT PLAN FOR ALCOHOL USE (DEPENDENCE)

Definition: Substance dependence on alcohol is indicated by the individual's maladaptive psychological and physical response, with continued compulsive seeking and use of the substance, despite significant substance-related problems. There is a pattern of repeated self-administration resulting in tolerance and withdrawal. Evidence of tolerance or symptoms of withdrawal indicate physiological dependence on alcohol. Alcohol-dependent individuals continue to use despite evidence of the adverse psychological or physical consequences (e.g., permanent brain damage, cancer, liver disease, depression, psychosis). Consumption of alcohol continues to avoid or relieve withdrawal symptoms. A minority of individuals with alcohol dependence never experience clinically relevant levels of alcohol withdrawal (withdrawal symptoms that develop 4 to 12 hours after the reduction of intake following prolonged, heavy, alcohol ingestion); only about 5% of individuals with alcohol dependence ever experience severe complications of withdrawal (i.e., delirium, grand mal seizures).

Signs and Symptoms to Note and Document in the Record:

- Withdrawal syndrome symptoms, such as delirium tremens, sleep problems, vomiting.
- Periods of time devoted to obtaining and consuming alcoholic beverages.

- School or job performance deterioration.
- Alcohol-related absences from school or occupation.
- Neglect of child care or household responsibilities.
- Legal difficulties arising from alcohol-related use.

Goals:

1. Assist client in abstaining from alcohol.
2. Reduce psychological and behavior mechanisms that increase hazardous drinking.
3. Increase client's problem-solving capabilities to implement supportive systems of action.
4. Increase family functioning and support.

Objectives	Interventions
1. Assist client with alcohol withdrawal syndrome symptoms.	Refer and/or schedule a medically assisted detoxification.
	Provide education to client regarding alcohol withdrawal syndrome to understand expected symptoms.
	Encourage client to verbalize and express emotions and concerns related to withdrawal.
	Encourage client to follow medical regimen for detoxification as prescribed.
2. Address maladaptive psychological responses to dependency.	Encourage client to verbalize beliefs about alcohol use.
	Encourage client to verbalize thoughts, feelings, and emotions regarding use.
	Encourage client to verbalize pros and cons to cessation of alcohol use.
	Provide education to client regarding dependence and long-term complications and consequences.
	Assist client to identify thoughts that decrease desire to engage in problem use.
	Assist client to develop alternate thoughts that increase self-regulation and self-efficacy to cease use.
3. Address compulsive seeking behaviors related to dependency.	Assist client to report awareness of how compulsive behaviors are related to use.
	Educate client regarding behaviors, dependency, and consequences to use.
	Assist client to connect behaviors and consequences to use.
	Assist client to develop problem-solving strategies to assist client in situations and contexts related to use.
	Assist client to develop alternate support system strategies (e.g., AA).
4. Address the needs of the alcohol-dependent client's family.	Arrange family sessions to address dependency and substance-related concerns and participation.
	Provide education to family members regarding dependency, substance-related concerns, and support.
	Encourage and provide feedback to family members at all stages of treatment.
	Assist family to develop and implement supportive mechanisms (e.g., Al-Anon).

syndrome and rule out other conditions, such as traumatic brain injury. Often these conditions coexist with alcohol and other substance-related concerns, serving as the primary cause for the initial disability and continuation of use. Yet it is important to note that when not due to substance-related factors, symptoms such as confusion, impaired memory, mood changes, alteration in speech, and gait difficulties are symptoms also evident in other medical conditions (e.g., brain injury, heart conditions).

INTERVENTION STRATEGIES: MODELS AND TREATMENT MODALITIES

Alcohol-related disorders and treatment planning methods are diverse and complex and often brief interventions are used. A brief summary of several popular approaches is provided.

Biopsychosocial Model

The biopsychosocial approach incorporates the physical with the psychosocial to understand the person as a whole. When looking specifically at alcohol abuse and dependence, it is essential to classify alcoholism as a medical condition related to biomedical factors beyond the control of the individual (Yalisove, 1998). This practice approach supports the importance of observing factors such as the deficiency in natural body chemicals, like serotonin. Wild and Cunningham (2001) investigated the determinants of perceived vulnerability and found a statistical link between a person's perception of potential harm and potential social implications for potential harm. "The biopsychosocial model for understanding and treatment of alcohol problems is a concept with much utility in primary care settings. This approach takes into account the interaction of physiological, behavioral,

social, and environmental factors in the etiology of disease. It is a concept with relevance to interventions as well, since behavioral and medical management techniques are closely interrelated" (Mendelson & Mello, 1992, p. 481).

Family System Approach

According to the family system perspective, successful treatment of alcoholism requires a multidimensional approach involving the abuser, his or her family, and the environment. The client suffering from alcohol abuse or dependence is viewed as a human system that requires more than one and often a combination of intervention approaches. The family is viewed as a set of interconnected individuals acting together to maintain a homeostatic balance. The basic premise of this model is to allow each member of the family to achieve a higher level of functioning and emotional security (Curtis, 1999; Van Wormer, 2008). The view of the family as a system is essential to accomplish the intended outcome. The substance user does not exist in a vacuum. Rather, the person and his or her addiction are living, breathing, interacting elements of the environment and the family's environment, and the exclusionary observation of the person without these factors is impossible in this model. From this perspective, the substance being abused is seen as a family disease. Significant others and any other persons close to the individual suffering from substance abuse also need to benefit from treatment. Milkman and Sederer (1990) discuss the possible need to restructure the family and need to adjust to the recovery of the family member. The support system is a vital and powerful aspect of the client's ability for recovery, and intervention strategies not including the client's family system offer poor prognosis for long-term recovery (Parker et al., 2008; Van Wormer, 2008). A further understanding of familial stages and elderly families or patients must be included in further interventions (Zimberg, 1996).

Studying a single variable in isolation cannot reveal the information needed about the system as a whole, because the nature of the relationships between components of a system is interactional (Kilpatrick & Holland, 1999). Duncan, Duncan, and Hops (1999) agreed with this belief and stated that a thorough analysis of the cognitive, social, and behavioral aspects of the abuser's drinking behavior has been shown through research to be essential before intervention can be undertaken. The observation of the system in the environment and the use of homeostasis in perpetuating addiction are of special consideration to the practitioner utilizing this approach.

Pharmacotherapy

Medications in the detoxification and ongoing treatment of substance disorders such as alcohol abuse and dependence have continued to emerge as a prominent treatment approach. While mental health practitioners cannot prescribe medications, it would be a noticeable deficit if they were uneducated in this approach (Dziegielewski, 2010). The brain consists of multiple neurotransmitter systems that modulate various bodily functions. These include opioids, glutamate, serotonin (5HT), and dopamine (Johnson & Ait-Daoud, 1999). Opioids are pain blockers with similar effects as morphine or heroin occurring naturally in the brain. In alcohol use, these pain blockers appear to increase the sense of rewarding effects when alcohol is consumed. GABA (gamma-amino butyric acid) inhibited responses are a key component in aversive pharmacological treatments. Growing evidence demonstrates that the modulation of glutamatergic neurotransmission receptor agonists with N-methyl-D-aspartate (NMDA) to inhibit GABA attenuate operant responding for alcohol and prevent alcohol dependence (Evans, Levin, Brooks, & Garawi, 2007). When combined to block GABA and decrease NMDA, these blockers provide a decreased response to cravings to alcohol. Glutamate is an excitatory transmitter that works with brain receptor sites increasing the effects of intoxication, cognitive impairment, and some symptoms of withdrawal in alcohol consumption. Serotonin affects bodily functioning in varied psychological and physiological ways, including cognition, mood sleep, and appetite. Dopamine is linked to higher brain functioning and organization of thought and perception (Johnson & Ait-Daud, 1999).

Three medications approved by the FDA to treat alcohol dependence are disulfiram (Antabuse), naltrexone (ReVia), and acamprosate (Campral) with the longest-standing medication used in treatment to prevent relapse from alcohol use being disulfiram. Disulfiram, often known in the lay community as Antabuse, is referred to as aversive because it produces unpleasant reactions to alcohol when consumed (Evans et al., 2007; Parker et al., 2008). This medication can result in negative physiological reactions including nausea, vomiting, and increased blood pressure and heart rate. Disturbances can also cause dissociation, cognitive disturbances, and memory impairments (Evans et al., 2007). However, problems with poor compliance decrease the medication's effectiveness. Safety concerns regarding contraindications in people with cardiovascular disease, a history of cardiovascular accident (CVA), hypertension, pregnancy, or psychosis have resulted in the reduced use of disulfiram (Evans et al., 2007; Parker et al., 2008). Naltrexone and acamprosate are considered safer than disulfiram and produce the same effects with minimal contraindications. Naltrexone, an opiate-blocking agent, and acamprosate modulates GABA/glutamate (Bonn, 1999; Petrakis & Krystal, 1997). Memantine (known as Namenda) is used in Europe to treat alcohol dependence, it was approved by the Food and

Drug Administration (FDA) in 2003 and also results in decreased craving. It is reported that with memantine, the aversive response is not as severe as the other pharmacological treatments yet comparison of the same positive response warrants further study (Evans et al., 2007).

Some pharmacological treatments used to treat alcohol withdrawal are central nervous system depressants, also known as psychotherapeutics (e.g., benzodiazepines). These reduce the signs and symptoms of withdrawal, with longer-acting benzodiazepines (e.g., chlordiazepoxide [Librium], diazepam [Valium] may assist with preventing seizures, and shorter-acting benzodiazepines (e.g., lorazepam [Ativan], oxazepam [Serax] may assist with preventing the significant liver disease (Parker et al., 2008). The main problems with benzodiazepines in alcohol use disorders and in other areas of substance-related concerns is intoxication, dependence, and withdrawal; hence, there is a secondary further addiction problem (Hood, O'Neil, & Hulse, 2009; Miller & Gold, 1998; Myrick & Anton, 1998; Wesson et al., 1995). Medication Assisted Therapy (MAT), which utilizes medications such as methadone and buprenorphine, are designed to assist with withdrawal and reduce the cravings related to substance dependence; however, this medication-focused treatment alone does not create a lifestyle supportive of recovery, and other supplemental approaches may be indicated (Rabinowitz, 2009).

Cognitive-Behavioral Therapy

Management of stress reactions, anxiety, tension, panic, worry, emotional pressure are important in this treatment. Considering the principle that a person's emotional and behavioral reactions are determined by the relationship between his or her cognitions and subsequent behaviors, the cognitive-behavioral approach to treatment continues to be utilized as the primary intervention

model. Cognitive-behavioral therapy (CBT) has been proven effective in numerous outcome research studies in problems such as anxiety disorders, sexual problems, psychosis, gerontology, depression, obesity, and substance-related disorders. Treatment rests with education, supportive therapy, and techniques that teach individuals the relationship among thoughts, emotions, and behaviors and how these are interconnected to factors related to problem areas. Individuals learn self-regulation, problem-solving strategies, and coping skills.

According to Turner (1996), cognitive therapy methods utilized by practitioners must relate to the client on the basis of behavior and stated thoughts, emotions, and goals, without postulating unconscious forces. The diagnosis is made based on the distortions or limitations in the client's thinking. This perspective looks at the client's strengths rather than pathology and puts those strengths to use. The clinician guides the client into trying selected experiences that may alter his or her inaccurate perceptions. Recognition is made that each client's behavior is shaped by personal goals rather than by universal biological drives. The focus is on helping clients to realize that to achieve changes, they need to expand this consciousness of self, others, and the world around them. Also, Turner (1996) states that it is important to get clients to take responsibility for their behavior, not allowing the past or the "unconscious" to excuse current conduct (p. 102).

The first step toward intervention is to help clients become aware of the beliefs that guide the substance-related condition. Once these beliefs are recognized, clients are assisted to recognize the circumstances related to use while being supported in problem-solving alternatives to these circumstances. Some clients will be successful at integrating lifestyle changes, and others will need more time to acquire awareness to integrate changes related to use. Behavior modification and changes in cognitive processes are effective in achieving these goals. These are really guided self-help steps, and clients must work actively to achieve them, with responsibility for commitment to the goals and taking charge of recovery from the substance-related disorder determining the degree of success.

Identifying negative self-statements, private thoughts, or negative self-talk that in some manner inhibit client performance and maintain use can be cognitively restructured into positive, constructive statements, and combined with a perceptual redefinition of clients' reality in the inhibiting situation. Learning to use the positive self-statements increases self-regulation and confidence in reinforcing new behaviors. These are important for clients to achieve self-control and manage the implementation of alternatives to use.

Expectancies play an important role in cognitive-behavioral therapy. The theory proposes that people act in accordance with expected outcomes, rationally selecting among a set of options that will gain the most and best results. Expectancies can be positive or negative and four types of expectancies exist. First, the stimuli associated with the effects of drinking may become cues for seeking out anticipated rewards from alcohol or for avoiding the negative consequences of drinking. Second, physiological withdrawal symptoms become cues for drinking to achieve temporary reduction of aversive physical symptoms. A third influence in outcome expectancies consists of social environmental factors. For instance, an individual may develop alcohol outcome expectations specific to peer affiliations in a particular context or situation. A fourth source of alcohol outcome expectancies consists of the beliefs an individual holds about the effects of alcohol and what he or she perceives as a benefit or cost from its use. Cognitive-behavior theory suggests that people are more likely to abuse alcohol if they lack self-efficacy to enable them to achieve the desired outcome.

Social skills training and development and redevelopment of problem-solving strategies are components of restructuring beliefs, attitudes, and actions that the individual will use to achieve the desired effects.

Motivational Enhancement Therapies

DiClemente, Bellino, and Neavins (1999) state that "motivation is an important step toward changing any action or behavior" (p. 86). "Motivation appears to be a critical dimension in influencing patients to seek, comply with, and complete treatment as well as to make successful long term changes in their drinking" (p. 87). Determining the level of motivation involves assessment of internal and external motivators. In the assessment as in practice, each stage of practice intervention allows for the provider to assess attitude and level of motivation that will lead to engagement and change. To facilitate the assessment process DiClemente et al., identify five stages that outline the decision-making process for the individual when contemplating any change. These five stages are: (1) precontemplation, (2) contemplation, (3) preparation, (4) action, and (5) maintenance.

According to McMaster (2004), the five stages of DiClemente and Prochaska's 1997 Stages of Change Model (known also as the Transtheoretical Model [TTM]) are as follows: In the precontemplation stage, the client has no intent to change, is usually pressured to attend treatment, and does not recognize the substance-related use as a problem. In the contemplation phase, the client has begun to become aware of the substance-related problem, still has no intent to change, but is weighing the pros and cons to change. The preparation stage signals the client's plans to change the substance-related problem in the near future with behavioral goals set but no action implemented. The action stage implements the client's plans to change, with behavioral goals in place, modifying lifestyle, experiences, and settings associated with substance-related use. In the maintenance phase, the client maintains lifestyle changes to prevent relapses or associated risks with substance-related use. These lifestyle changes are differentiated by the source of the desire to effect change from within the person or from external or environmental sources.

Once the baseline for level of motivation is established through assessment, intervention begins. There are several intervention approaches to utilize. Brief motivational intervention consists of educating patients about the negative effects of alcohol abuse to motivate them to stop or reduce drinking. This approach is indicated for the nondependent alcohol use disorders. The course is generally 1 to 4 sessions lasting 10 to 40 minutes each. The setting is generally substance abuse outpatient or primary care offices (DiClemente et al., 1999).

The second motivational intervention approach is motivational interviewing. The application involves educating clients on the stages of change and the experiencing feelings of denial and ambivalence are viewed as natural components of these stages. Clients are assisted to work through ambivalence toward sobriety. Taken from social psychology, motivation theory is based on the premise of: How can I get someone to do something actively on their own without constraints or duress? This is an important question to address because when the person becomes empowered the changes will be made for and by the client without or due to fear, coercion, or force.

Techniques used include four motivational interviewing principles: (1) encouraging clients to develop an awareness of the discrepancy between goals and behaviors that obstruct goals; (2) expressing empathy toward clients and their situation; (3) rolling with resistance instead of arguing or confronting clients; and (4) reflective

listening. In addition, the pros and cons of change are examined with support of clients' self-efficacy and ability to change and overcome difficulty. All behaviors are assessed (i.e., ABC) charting, behavioral counts), and counselors give feedback on problem behaviors. Last, counselors elicit self-motivational statements or affirmations from patient (Van Wormer, 2008). The length of treatment is undefined and can be as long as needed to effect change. Sessions last from 30 to 60 minutes and are generally once a week (DiClemente et al., 1999).

The third approach in motivational therapy is motivational enhancement therapy (MET). This method was developed as a treatment modality with subcomponents combining motivational interviewing with a less intensive setting. It has three types of modalities: brief intervention, integrated motivational enhancement therapy, and motivational enhancement catalyst (Walker et al., 2007). In MET, enhancing the therapeutic alliance stresses the avoidance of confrontational approaches when it might lead to a premature focus on the addictive behavior and labeling that force clients to accept labels such as addict or alcoholic. Often in sessions the counselor asks questions that can be answered with yes/no, and tries to avoid the "expert trap" where clients are put down rather than collaboratively exchange information (Van Wormer, 2008). Resistance is addressed in a similar manner to modalities such as Rational Emotive Behavior Therapy (REBT) and CBT, treating skepticism and rejection as normal components of self-determination. It is natural for clients to experience trust concerns regarding the treatment modality as it is as equally valid for clients to reject therapeutic services that do not meet their needs or concerns or that make them feel worse. Through this approach, a client who engages in change without coercion or through mandated means will have longer-lasting and more effective changes.

MET was found effective and provided treatment success to the extent that the client's social support network was supportive for sobriety. (Follow-up studies on subjects found that emotional partner support was a key factor in long-term recovery) (Van Wormer, 2008). Applying motivational interviewing techniques, MET is particularly useful with clients whose motivation to change is minimal or changeable (Parker et al., 2008; Walker, Roffman, Picciano, & Stephens, 2007).

INTEGRATED MOTIVATIONAL ENHANCEMENT THERAPY AND MOTIVATIONAL ENHANCEMENT CATALYST: BRIEF INTERVENTIONS

To assist clients with hazardous and harmful drinking in nondependence alcohol use disorders, brief interventions may prove helpful. These approaches are often used in primary care and accident and emergency settings by general practitioners and nurses, requiring minimal training and lasting anywhere from a few minutes to 20 to 30 minutes or for extended brief interventions lasting for four sessions or more (Parker et al., 2008; Walker et al., 2007). Parker et al. (2008) outline brief interventions consisting of educating clients about the negative effects of alcohol abuse and motivating them to reduce consumption of alcohol to sensible or less risky levels, providing the tools for change, and indicating underlying problems using a model of intervention termed *frames*. In the *frames* delivery of intervention: (1) *feedback* is respectfully given that outlines the concerns of the client that will provide structure and reduce harm; (2) emphasis is placed on the client's accepting *responsibility* for change; (3) clear *advice* is given to make a change in drinking; (4) discuss a *menu* of options for making change; (5) listen and express *empathy* and be nonjudgmental; and (6) reinforce the

patient's *self-efficacy*, stressing that positive change is possible and when made that it will be beneficial (p. 498).

Integrated Motivational Enhancement Therapy

Integrated motivational enhancement therapy (IMET) combines multiple clinical components for individuals with more severe dependency issues. Included in this therapy model is MET, cognitive-behavioral skills training, and case management for nine intervention sessions or more (Walker et al., 2007).

Motivational Enhancement Catalyst

The purpose of motivational enhancement catalyst (MEC) is to induce motivation for change for individuals not ready for treatment. To start this process individuals are screened and if found to have risk factors, free-standing invitations are given to those who are interested making them aware that services are available and how to contact programs for more information (Walker et al., 2007). Once requests for services are received these interventions can be delivered through computerized checkups where mini-assessments with feedback are given. This information can be used to help individuals determine or confirm whether they actually have a problem severe enough to require intervention. The personalized feedbacks, referred to as Personalized Feedback Reports (PFRs) includes normative data, graphics use to enhance self-appraisal, risk-related indices, and identification of the client's anticipated pro/con consequences from changing (Walker et al., 2007). According to Walker et al., there are five variants to this free-standing MEC approach:

1. *In-Person Driver's Checkup (DCU):* This approach is intended to reach problem

drinkers not interested in formal treatment but concerned about having a problem. Provides a voluntary assessment of how alcohol use is influencing areas of their lives. Includes structured interviews, neuropsychological assessment, feedback on client's alcohol consumption per week in comparison to the average drinker with peak blood alcohol concentrations per week, and risk of family problems and associated problems related to research norms and cut-points.

2. *Computer-Based Driver's Checkup (CDCU):* This approach is also intended to reach problem drinking via computer. The CDCU administers a computerized assessment and feedback session, consisting of a screening using the AUDIT; if the threshold score is higher than 8, modules continue to acquire peak blood alcohol concentrations given from demographic information provided. The participants engage in a decision-making module that gives a set of exercises regarding the positive and negative aspects of drinking, assessing clients' ambivalence with feedback then provided.

3. *In-Person Marijuana Checkup (MCU):* Similar to the DCU and intended to attract adult users of marijuana not seeking treatment or change but experience negative consequences from use, the assessment provides opportunity for reflection. Feedback is given based on scientific educational information about marijuana.

4. *In-School Teen Marijuana Checkup (TMCU):* Through waivers with parental permission, the TMCU is intended to reach adolescents in school settings, encouraging exploration of ambivalent attitudes and offering support and strategies for change through a computerized and self-administered assessment. Personalized feedback is given with a counselor and teen after computerized assessment is completed, who is then given educational information offering change strategies and tips.

5. *Telephone Delivered Sex Checkup (SCU):* Attempting to attract men seeking men (MSM) and reduce incidences of HIV due to high risk sexual behaviors, the assessment relies on a telephone intervention that provides the opportunity to talk about ambivalent feelings toward unsafe sexual practices. Participants can enroll anonymously by renting of a post office box (for which they are reimbursed). Educational materials are then delivered with possibilities for a follow-up interview.

These MET interventions reach various populations, with varying needs and through different methods. These applications are available to providers to address the needs of alcohol- and substance-related concerns at varying stages of change and need. Four sessions are offered over a 12-week period with initiation occurring after completion of an intensive assessment process. The use of standardized measures occurs at session 1, and clear, concise feedback about the patient's addiction behavior is relayed to the patient in each session. Session 2 is intended for the purpose of developing a change plan. Session 3 is used for reinforcement and enhancing commitment to motivation and change. Session 4 is termination (DiClemente et al., 1999). In assessing the model, research indicates that each individual intervention approach shows promise for a variety of clients suffering from alcohol abuse. In terms of future interventions, more information on the use of combination therapies, such as cognitive and motivation techniques is needed.

Traditional Self-Help Approach

One approach is most often considered as a primary intervention strategy for those suffering from alcohol abuse and dependence. This approach, referred to as the traditional approach or the disease model, is provided through Alcoholics Anonymous and is the major nonmedical support system for substance-related use concerns. Other systems offer emotional support and practical advice in similar circumstances, and many, but not all, alcoholics can be helped by the mutual/self-help fellowship of AA (J. Mendelson & Mello, 1992; Tonigan, Connors, & Miller, 1998). It is the most extensive model of mutual peer-to-peer self-help group worldwide (described as horizontal clinical relationship

services), with more than 100,000 groups, and involvement associated with long-term abstinence (Parker et al., 2008; Carroll, 2009).

The 12-Steps model (See Quick Reference 7.7) forbids promotion and anonymity is of paramount importance. "While some addicted individuals, for various reasons, will not accept or engage in self-help programs in a manner that produces a good experience, the great majority of addicted men and women will obtain support, encouragement, information, insight, guidance, friendship, genuine caring, and occasionally a much needed friendly kick in the ass from their self-help programs" (Carroll, 2009, p. 331). AA also differentiates religion from spirituality, and bases beliefs in a "higher power of one's own understanding." Alcoholics Anonymous also urges participation in Al-Anon for family members. Despite criticisms, there are many who feel strongly this model of intervention works.

QUICK REFERENCE 7.7

12 STEPS TO RECOVERY

1. We admitted we were powerless over alcohol—that our lives had become unmanageable.
2. Came to believe that a power greater than ourselves could restore us to sanity.
3. Made a decision to turn our will, and our lives, over to the care of God as we understood Him.
4. Made a searching and fearless moral inventory of ourselves.
5. Admitted to God, to ourselves, and to another human being the exact nature of our wrongs.
6. Were entirely ready to have God remove all these defects of character
7. Humbly asked Him to remove our shortcomings.
8. Made a list of all persons we had harmed, and became willing to make amends to them all.
9. Made direct amends to such people wherever possible, except when to do so would injure them or others.
10. Continued to take personal inventory and when we were wrong promptly admit it.
11. Sought through prayer and meditation to improve our conscious contact with God, as we understood Him, praying only for knowledge of His will for us and the power to carry that out.
12. Having had a spiritual awakening as the result of these steps, we tried to carry this message to alcoholics and to practice these principles in all our affairs.

Source: National Institute on Alcohol Abuse and Alcoholism, No. 30 PH 359, October 1995.

INTEGRATED APPROACH: IMPLICATIONS FOR PRACTICE

Substance use is a multifaceted problem that results from elements of conditioning and of social learning as well as from neurobiological processes, genetics, cognitive processes, and influences from family systems, society, and culture (Latorre, 2000; Wallace, 1989). Turner (1996) explains that for "too long we have labored under an impression that adherence to one approach to practice by definition excluded others; there was some component of disloyalty or some quality of Machiavellian manipulation to attempt to move from one approach to another depending on the situation" (p. 709). Therefore, when separating these perspectives for practice, each intervention strategy has its own strengths and limitations. For example, the best plan of cognitive-behavioral intervention can easily go astray if environmental agents and family supports are ignored. Incorporating the ideas from systems theory as part of the intervention process allows the mental health practitioner to acknowledge the importance of the situational context, taking into account the whole situation. Intervention needs to include more than just the individual and always involves the systems that will affect family behavior change strategy.

The most popular intervention strategy, with current emphasis on evidence-based practices, needs to include a harm reduction approach, which addresses substance-related concerns from a public health model of care. Harm reduction seeks to decrease harms incurred from use without denying services or care based on continued substance-related use. "It is more important to provide services that target the individual's stage of change and try to increase the client's motivation to make continued changes. Thus, harm reduction provides a framework for services [for] users at earlier stages" (McMaster, 2004, p. 357). Services

included in the harm reduction model include needle exchange programs for intravenous (IV) drug users, teaching IV drug injectors how to clean needles, methadone maintenance programs, providing condoms to sexually active clients, psychotropic medications for those with co-occurring disorders, and facilitating access and opportunity to treatment to anyone seeking it (Carroll, 2009).

Harm reduction rests on five assumptions, as described by McMaster (2004):

1. Focus on reducing drug-related harm rather than focus on drug use reduction.
2. Abstinence is effective at reducing substance-related harms, but there are other possible services and objectives to address that can reduce substance-related harm.
3. Substance abuse and dependence is harmful, but some of their more harmful consequences (e.g., HIV/AIDS, hepatitis) can be eliminated without having to achieve complete abstinence.
4. Services for substance-related problems need to be relevant to substance-related concerns and be user friendly to be most effectiveness at minimizing harm.
5. The focus of substance abuse and dependence should be understood from a broad perspective rather than focusing on the problem as an individual act, shifting substance-related solutions away from coercive practices and a criminal justice system.

The harm reduction framework and approach to treatment utilizes the stage-based model of treatment (e.g., motivational enhancement therapies), providing assessment of clients' motivational states and gearing interventions according to their level of motivation and readiness. From this perspective, individuals are supported during the decision-making process, receiving all substance-related services despite active use. This approach is central to integrated care and integrated team treatment and is used with concurrent integrated approaches to public health. Because of its emphasis on effective measures, quality of care, and cost-effective measures, harm reduction is favored by insurance companies and managed care organizations. Likewise, with the Wellstone-Domenici Mental Health and Addiction Equity Parity Act of 2008, in principle, the harm reduction model also integrates rather than differentiates medical from mental health and substance abuse services.

Use of harm reduction, however, is not without disagreement. Programs known as abstinence-based programs are at odds with the harm reduction model. Abstinence-based programs require that clients abstain from use, and if the client has been unable to achieve this, then it is thought best that the client "hit rock bottom" before he or she can fully begin to accept and recognize the need for change (Van Wormer, 2008). Others also contest this approach by citing that these programs do not discharge or "drop-out" nonabstinent clients. Rather, abstinence-based programs require that clients remain abstinent while in treatment; if they relapse while in treatment, they are transferred to other care options (Carroll, 2009).

In addressing harm reduction, the position of care is that demanding abstinence is an unrealistic position that fails to understand the severity and complications of what a substance-related disorder is while acknowledging the *DSM* definition. Addressing abstinence-based programs, the position of care is that substance use has become a problem, and according to the *DSM* definition of a substance use problem, abstinence is the means to achieve control because moderation cannot be achieved. Each approach is centered on the client's problem with

substance-related use. The abstinence-based approach implies that each failed opportunity is a learning experience, which should motivate the client more quickly to desire abstinence (often due to the consequences suffered with each learning experience). The abstinence-based approach focuses solely on individual acts and effects of use on the individual and immediate social relations but does not actively intervene in these acts. The harm reduction approach implies that motivation to change can be enacted at any point without having to fail to achieve the desired result; it supports clients who already suffer from the experience of abuse and dependence without applying further consequences. This focuses on individual acts and social relations and unrelated extended social relations affected by substance-related use. In harm reduction programs, needle exchanges are implemented as a preventive measure (e.g., decrease the incidence of HIV/AIDS, staph infections, and other communicable diseases to others within the population).

Last, with respect to integrated care and the integration of services, the changes to a market-based delivery of services has continued to shift health and allied professional services to specialized care (attributed to insurance and managed care billing and reimbursement requirements and restrictions). This places a greater demand on provider professional education and training requirements to provide outcome-based services in substance-related programs. The harm reduction-based programs emphasize these stipulations in their approaches and implementation of service provision. Providers from abstinence-based programs sometimes use peer-to-peer providers who provide counseling but do not have the educational requirements of a trained professional. This has caused providers of abstinence programs who formerly did not require educational training in order to provide substance-use related services to now require counselors to acquire specialized training and certifications (e.g., Credentialed Alcohol and Substance Abuse Counseling Programs [CASAC]) so the facility can seek reimbursement for the services provided.

The challenge for the mental health practitioner is to approach the client's entire system in unison with a multidimensional treatment strategy. Doing this involves more than just using the principles inherent in cognitive-behavioral therapy, where the role of the practitioner is primarily that of an educator who expects clients to set their own standards, monitor their own performance, and reward or reinforce themselves appropriately. In this respect, the counselor strives to help clients become their own therapist (Milkman & Sederer, 1990). According to Watson (1991), the preferable strategy is empowerment of people who feel spiritually and personally empty and giving this area ample attention. Latorre (2000) concurs with this approach: "We are dealing with a system, not just a collection of parts, a system that continually strives to balance itself using symptoms as a way to self heal" (p. 67). Furthermore, although easily forgotten, effective treatment must include the client's family. Westermeyer (1990) explains that as drug and alcohol addicts recover, there is a need for involvement of an individual's own social identity groups as well as the communities in which the individual lives and functions (Arredondo, 1998).

An integrated approach that involves family education and support combined with self-help groups is particularly important to patients in treatment. Alcoholism is a family disease. Significant others and any other persons close to the person with alcoholism typically also benefit from treatment. Milkman and Sederer (1990) relate the possible need to restructure the family to adjust to the recovery of the family member. The family and the client's support system is a vital and powerful aspect of his or her ability for recovery. If the intervention strategy does not include the client's family system, the prognosis

for long-term recovery from the illness is greatly decreased. Understanding of familial stages and elderly families or patients must also be included in further interventions (Zimberg, 1996). From the traditional perspective, AA urges participation in Al-Anon for family members. In addition to the need for counselors treating clients with alcoholism to include the family, the social worker who specializes in family therapy needs training in the awareness, and diagnosis, of addiction problems in families (Steinglass, 1976).

Mendelson and Mello (1992) believe that the diagnosis of the disease is complicated by the intense denial evidenced by the individual suffering from an alcohol problem, by his or her family, and by society. The use of a genogram is suggested when working with a troubled family. Although the family may deny the possibility of a chemical abuse problem, a genogram that reports chemical abuse in previous generations is at least an indicator of the strong possibility of prevalence of this condition in this family. Among the tasks of the worker are: (a) helping the client and the family accept that alcoholism is the primary problem, (b) recommending treatment options, and (c) instilling hope for recovery. Therapeutic alternatives are the use of Antabuse, individual therapy, family therapy, and AA. Relapses, when properly handled, can help the individual with substance abuse to accept his or her powerlessness over alcohol. Treatment manuals free to the public for working with specialized populations are listed next. All are available from the U.S. Department of Health and Human Services, Center for Substance Abuse, 1 Choke Cherry Road, Rockville, MD 20857 (www.samsha.gov).

- Detoxification and Substance Abuse Treatment: A Treatment Improvement Protocol (TIP). (2006). N. S. Miller and S. S. Kipnis.

- A Provider's Introduction to Substance Abuse Treatment for Lesbian, Gay, Bisexual and Transgender Individuals. (2009).
- Substance Abuse Treatment for Persons with HIV and AIDS: Treatment Improvement Protocol Series (37). (2008). S. L. Batki and P. A. Selwyn, Consensus Panel Co-Chairs.

MISUSE OF PRESCRIPTION MEDICATIONS AND PSYCHOTHERAPEUTIC DRUGS: AN EMERGING PROBLEM

Psychotherapeutic drug use has developed into a new trend of substance-related disorders, accounting for 6.2 million people in the United States in the age bracket of 12 and above with abuse and dependence problems (SAMHSA, 2009b; WHO, 2009b). It is the second-highest substance use problem after marijuana use. Excessive availability and inadequate regulation have increased the consumption of psychotherapeutic drugs through prescriptions, illegal street vendors, and the Internet. These modes of acquisition have led to an increased use of benzodiazepines and other anxiolytics. It is estimated that 15% to 44% of chronic benzodiazepine users become addicted and upon cessation experience severe withdrawal symptoms, including emergent anxiety and depressive symptoms (Hood et al., 2009).

The *DSM-IV-TR* identifies Sedatives-, Hypnotic-, and Anxiolytic-related disorders under the 11 classes of substances found in the classification for substance-related disorders (APA, 2000). Included in this category are medications such as the benzodiazepines (e.g., clonazepam [Klonopin], zolpidem [Ambien]), carbamates (e.g., glutethimide), barbiturates (e.g., secobarbital), and barbiturate-like hypnotics,

including all prescription sleeping medications (e.g., eszopiclone [Lunesta]) and almost all prescription anti-anxiety medications excluding non-benzodiazepine anti-anxiety agents (e.g, buspirone [Buspar], gepirone). When used properly, psychotherapeutic medications can alleviate suffering associated with symptoms of mental disorders and/or neurological disorders for those who truly suffer from them. Long-term use of these drugs prescribed for psychosocial stressors rather than for mental disorders has created problems, including dependence. Moreover, nonmedical use of psychotherapeutic drugs have also increased in use for recreational purposes in youths rather than for intended use (e.g., amphetamine and dextroamphetamine [Adderall] and methylphenidate [Ritalin]).

There are three reasons why this area has become so controversial.

1. The use and misuse of psychotherapeutic medications has caused major shifts in the structure and delivery of services for mental disorders. This has required a restructuring in the system of care that has resulted in a changing of the epistemological basis of the *DSM*. Subsequently, this change has resulted in modifications to the ontological understanding of mental disorders and classifications, as well as the treatments. To state that these drugs were instrumental in providing solutions to alter an entire structural system is an understatement. The increased availability and unmonitored consumption is an unintended and an unexpected consequence.

2. The social sanctioning of psychotherapeutic medications (unlike illicit drugs) leads the consumer to believe that these medications approved by trusted institutions (such as the FDA), which act on the behalf of consumers to

secure the public health and welfare, are safe. These medications are seen as cures rather than causes of a social ill. Yet because of the concerns and the large number of people who use psychotherapeutic drugs, their safety and efficacy has become the subject of great discussion. The FDA has authorized label revisions for antidepressants that list stimulant effects, as too many providers are unaware of some adverse and intoxicating effects of these medications (especially the newer psychotherapeutics) (Breggin, 2006).

3. Limited emphasis is placed on the addiction, dependence, and withdrawal that can result from the use of prescription medications. Oftentimes, intoxication and dependence are associated primarily with street drugs and alcohol, not with prescription medications. Public perceptions of prescriptions are associated with cures; illicit drugs and alcohol are not—despite the fact that their composition and effects are quite similar if not the same. The majority of people who take prescribed psychotherapeutic medications

have no prior experience with the intoxicating effects of these drugs; nor do their families and friends, but most can easily recognize the intoxicating effects of alcohol or other types of drug use (e.g., slurred speech, gait disturbance) (Breggin, 2006).

Criteria specific for diagnosing psychotherapeutic-related use is categorized under the sedative, hypnotic, or anxiolitic use disorders, following specification as stipulated in the nomenclature of substance-related disorders. As with all 11 substances in the *DSM-IV-TR*, sedative, hypnotic, or anxiolytic use disorders is a classification of disorders within the taxonomical representation of substance-related disorders. Use disorders are sedative, hypnotic, or anxiolytic dependence and sedative, hypnotic, or anxiolytic abuse; induced disorders are sedative, hypnotic, or anxiolytic intoxication; sedative, hypnotic, or anxiolytic withdrawal; and other sedative, hypnotic, or anxiolytic-induced disorders (APA, 2000). A case example (see Case Example 7.2) of psychotherapeutic drug use is presented in this section with application of the multiaxial system, a sample treatment plan, and an intervention strategy.

CASE EXAMPLE 7.2 - MRS. BROWN

Mrs. Brown is a 53-year-old African American female of short stature. She is overweight and appears her stated age. She presents to a community-based clinic secondary to a referral from her primary care physician for a mental health referral. Referral concerns expressed by her primary care physician involve Mrs. Brown's problems taking prescribed medication and her continued demands for prescription benzodiazepines to treat her anxiety concerns and her citing a lack of response to nonbenzodiazepine anti-anxiety agents. Mrs. Brown is asked to describe some of the current symptoms she is experiencing. She reports insomnia, restlessness, agitation, crying spells, low frustration tolerance, anger, agoraphobia, nervousness, headaches, frequent urination, and constipation. She reports these symptoms have been present for over a month since she last acquired her prescription for Xanax and says symptoms having increased in severity in the last 2 weeks. At the time of the interview, Mrs. Brown is restless and agitated and repeatedly asks when she will see a physician to acquire Xanax. She repeatedly states at time of interview that she has only been prescribed Xanax and that this is the only medication that works. She reports she is prescribed 10 mg Xanax.

Mrs. Brown has several medical problems for which she is receiving medical care. She has multiple sclerosis and demonstrates difficulty with mobility due to curvature of the spine. She has swelling in her left knee and employs an assistance device to aid her with moving. She is overweight and is a non-insulin-dependent Type II diabetic. She has her condition under medical control taking glucophage and monitoring her blood sugar. She suffers from hypertension, with a family history of high blood pressure. She denies taking nitrates at the time of this interview and states she has in the past for this concern. She denies taking pain medication and has her condition in control. She denies allergies to medications. She denies medical concerns, citing repeatedly that her main concern is her prescription for Xanax.

When addressing issues of mental health, Mrs. Brown denies mental health problems at the time of the interview. She reports feeling concerned about her son as he will soon be graduating high school, possibly moving out of the apartment to live with his girlfriend. She is concerned that her son is too young to engage in these commitments but supports him in these matters. She reports that she likes the girlfriend. Her son is her main companion as her husband is deceased. When asked if she has received inpatient treatment for any mental health concerns, she denies any mental health hospitalizations at the time of this interview. When asked if she has received mental health treatment for any concerns, she reports she has only received medical treatment to "take the edge off" and that for this concern she is prescribed "only Xanax." When asked if she has been prescribed medication for this concern by any provider other than her current physician, she reports visiting other clinics to acquire her prescription, citing that other providers have refused to prescribe her desired medication after a time. She states this is her first psychiatric referral to address medication management concerns related to this current prescription need.

Mrs. Brown reports a decrease in her social activities since her stated present concerns. She enjoys hobbies such as crocheting and playing bingo with her cousins. She enjoys spending time with her son. She reports she has been unable to engage in these activities since the worsening of her symptoms. She reports that her prescription allowed her to engage in these activities and cites the importance of seeing the physician to acquire this medication. She denies financial concerns, stating that she receives disability for her medical condition and a pension from her deceased husband.

Mrs. Brown reports she is currently experiencing symptoms of nervousness, "anxiety," crying spells, low frustration tolerance, anger, insomnia, restlessness, frequent urination, constipation, and headaches with duration of symptoms present for over 2 months and worsening in the last 2 weeks, per her verbalizations at the time of this interview. She denies auditory, visual, tactile, gustatory, and/or olfactory hallucinations at the time of this interview. She denies delusions at the time of this interview. Client is oriented x 4. Judgment and insight is limited. Psychomotor function is intact and within normal limits. She denies suicidal ideation, morbid, and/or homicidal ideation at the time of this interview.

Application of Multiaxial Assessment: Mrs. Brown

From the information provided by Mrs. Brown and the referral from her primary physician, Mrs. Brown's presenting problems and symptoms appear secondary to withdrawal from her prescription medication, Xanax. This is attributed to her verbalization that her symptoms began since her last acquisition of her prescription with subsequent worsening. She reports frequenting other clinics to acquire her medication and reports that other nonbenzodiazepine anti-anxiety agents cannot alleviate her symptoms. She reports she has been refused her prescription by physicians secondary to concerns related to her use. She is referred by her primary physician due to concern regarding her behaviors and response to her demand for prescription Xanax.

Mrs. Brown has not taken her prescribed high dose of Xanax for over a month, during which time her symptoms worsened. After she stopped taking the medication she has experienced insomnia, anxiety, agitation, and restlessness that has persisted since her last dosage. She reports that these symptoms have worsened in the past 2 months; she has experienced crying spells, agoraphobia, and impaired social functioning, being unable to attend her bingo functions with her cousins, to enjoy the company of her son, her crochet, and has difficulty leaving her apartment. Her medical conditions are stabilized and do not account for her presenting issues. She has no mental health concerns present except for the "anxiety" related to her use.

She has behaviors indicative of compulsive-seeking behaviors, demonstrative of withdrawal symptoms of dependence. Based on this strong desire to again start taking the medication, she has frequented various clinics to acquire this prescription. This behavior continues even when refused by other prescribers and she refuses to consider nonbenzodiazepine anti-anxiety agents to address her presenting symptoms. Under the criteria of substance-related disorders, withdrawal with psychological and physical symptoms is criteria for dependence for the 11 substances listed in the *DSM-IV-TR*. The criteria for sedative, hypnotic, or anxiolytic withdrawal are inclusive and overlap with criteria for withdrawal for substance-related disorders and as a qualifier for dependence. Mrs. Brown meets the criteria for withdrawal with physical symptoms, as she has also been experiencing frequent urination, headaches, and constipation related to her presenting concerns. She is cleared medically, despite her condition of hypertension without medication,

and her headaches are not attributed to her blood pressure.

She has been prescribed other nonbenzodiazepine anti-anxiety medications but reports these do not function or alleviate her symptoms, indicative of tolerance to stronger and faster-acting agents. She has reported "anxiety," nervousness, low frustration tolerance, and anger; according to the *DSM-IV-TR*, such symptoms may persist for months: "these lingering withdrawal symptoms (e.g., anxiety, moodiness, and trouble sleeping) can be mistaken for non–substance induced Anxiety or Depressive Disorder" (APA, 2000, p. 288). Mrs. Brown's symptoms are not indicative of these concerns although they share phenomenology; rather they are related to her present withdrawal from benzodiazepines.

Axis I: Due to these presenting concerns, Mrs. Brown can be diagnosed with sedative, hypnotic, or anxiolytic dependence (304.10), with physiological dependence.

Axis II: No Diagnosis code of V71.09 is given although when she reaches full remission of her presenting condition, any present personality issues or concerns can be reassessed.

Axis III: Documented medical conditions include multiple sclerosis with curvature of her spine and she reports non-insulin-dependent diabetic (Type II) and reports a history of hypertension.

Axis IV: Medical concerns and increased social isolation. Mrs. Brown reports that she used to have active involvement with her cousins playing bingo, enjoyed crocheting, and family relationships primarily with her son, but now this has decreased significantly secondary to her current symptoms.

Axis V: GAF 50 (current)

Rationale: She is given a score of 50 as she presents with serious symptoms: She is not suicidal but has compulsive-seeking behaviors of clinic frequenting to acquire her prescription medication. She also has serious impairment

---

QUICK REFERENCE 7.8

MRS. BROWN

Axis I: Sedative, hypnotic, or anxiolytic dependence, 304.10.

Axis II: V71.09 No diagnosis.

Axis III: 1. Multiple sclerosis, with curvature of spine.
             2. Swelling in left knee, with assistance for mobility.
             3. Non-insulin dependent diabetes mellitus (Type II).
             4. Hypertension.
             5. NO KNOWN ALLERGIES (NKA).

Axis IV: 1. Medical concerns.
             2. Increased social isolation.

Axis V: 50 current (Past 50).

---

to her social functioning (she does not have an occupation and does not attend school), as she has ceased her social activities and hobbies, which she enjoyed secondary to her current symptoms related to her withdrawal from Xanax (see Quick Reference 7.8).

Intervention strategies can be applied, as stated in this chapter, to provide psychosocial interventions. These include cognitive-behavioral, brief intervention, and motivational enhancement therapy. With psychotherapeutic-related use, intervention often involves tapering (titrating of the dosage) from higher to lower dosages until Mrs. Brown's system is clear of the substance. To help to decrease her symptoms, she might be prescribed a nonbenzodiazepine in conjunction with her Xanax, as this may assist to help with her anxiety but not cause the same dependence symptoms noted with the Xanax. Once complete, she can then have all substances removed that are not related to a true mental health concern (see Sample Treatment Plan 7.3).

SAMPLE TREATMENT PLAN 7.3

MRS. BROWN

Address Prescription Medication Dependence:

- Schedule appointment with psychiatrist to taper dosage of Xanax until substance is able to be removed.
- Monitor medication management and contraindications per psychiatrist recommendations.
- Encourage client to follow medical protocols as related to cessation of substance per physician.
- Coordinate physician and psychiatric services to assure compliance with reduction of prescription medication.
- Address physical symptoms related to psychotherapeutic medications.
- Provide information regarding physical symptoms of dependence of Xanax.

(continued)

SAMPLE TREATMENT PLAN 7.3 (*Continued*)

- Encourage client to verbalize physical symptoms she experiences when taking and not taking Xanax.
- Encourage client to verbalize beliefs she has about Xanax and her use of Xanax.
- Encourage client to weigh the pros and cons of utilizing Xanax.
- Assist client in developing alternatives to utilizing Xanax.
- Encourage client to see the connection of use to compulsive behaviors.
- Provide information regarding behaviors of dependence on substances, including psychotherapeutics such as Xanax.
- Encourage client to become aware of Xanax use and how it influences behaviors.
- Encourage client to identify beliefs she has regarding psychotherapeutic use, particularly her Xanax.
- Encourage client to become aware of behaviors related to dependence and how these are related to Xanax.
- Assist client in developing strategies to avoid redeveloping patterns of use related to Xanax dependence.
- Assist client in problem-solving alternatives to behaviors that perpetuate compulsiveness.

For the purposes of this case example, and in conjunction with the *DSM-IV-TR*, dependence to benzodiazepine was presented. In other clinical situations, use of the benzodiazepines may coexist with other psychotherapeutic drugs and when multiple substances are involved, more complex treatment might be required. This case example was included because psychotherapeutic-related disorders are rising in terms of incidence rates in the United States and developed nations, where greater availability and high consumption of these medications with little or no monitoring occur. In the suggested revisions for the *DSM-5* this diagnostic category may be modified to include elimination of the substance abuse and dependence categories, replacing it with a new category termed the "addiction and related disorders" (News Release, APA, 2010). The hope is that eliminating the category of dependence will allow for a more clear distinction between compulsive, drug-seeking behavior related to addiction (as in this case example) and the normal or expected responses to tolerance and withdrawal that can affect the central nervous system.

SUMMARY AND FUTURE DIRECTIONS

Substance use and dependence can create a social, psychological, and physical affliction that is difficult to define yet can have a profound impact on individuals, their families, and society. Individuals with alcohol problems (and other substance-related problems) who recover need involvement both with their own special social identity groups and with others broadly representative of the communities in which they live and function (Westermeyer, 1990). The substance-related disorders are a taxonomical classification of disorders assessed and diagnosed with criteria set in the *DSM-IV-TR*. The criteria specified are also applied for the classification of alcohol use disorders as given in the case example of Robert. The etiology of alcohol-related disorders is attributed to genetics and the environment, social stressors, family systems with associated risk factors of age, gender, and disability. Theories from sociology and psychology related to alcohol use guide models, practice, treatment interventions, and prevention efforts. Causes of alcoholism are as diverse as those afflicted.

If intervention is initiated early it can assist to minimize cognitive and biological deterioration especially with the substances that can lead to withdrawal.

Various treatment modalities can assist clients at various stages of the recovery process (e.g., medically assisted detoxification and pharmacology). These approaches can assist in teaching clients to change maladaptive and harmful and hazardous substance use patterns to adaptive alternatives. Models such as cognitive-behavioral therapy, motivational enhancement therapy, and self-help groups can assist. Current approaches utilizing harm reduction versus abstinence-based approaches are available to help the counselor determine which can be of the most service to a client. Regardless of the treatment approach selected, one aspect remains clear. It is imperative that all practitioners possess knowledge about substance-related disorders, processes, and the impacts substances can have on both the individual and his or her support system as this information is imperative for effective practice and service.

8

Schizophrenia and the Psychotic Disorders

SOPHIA F. DZIEGIELEWSKI, SHIRLEYANN AMOS, AND GEORGE JACINTO

INTRODUCTION

This chapter provides information on children, adolescents, and adults with schizophrenia as well as an overview of the other psychotic disorders. These devastating illnesses can have far-reaching effects that clearly go beyond the client. They can touch the very core of the individual, affecting the development of close relationships, developing talents, family relations, and economic independence. Further complicating schizophrenia is the fact that even with the best treatments known, repeated episodes of the illness will occur throughout a client's life (Menezes, Arenovich, & Zipursky, 2006).

Since the psychotic disorders involve some level of *psychosis* that results in distorted perceptions and affects the way an individual perceives reality (Walker, et al., 2008), when experiencing these incorrect impressions, individuals often cannot function as others do. They often become lost in a world where they cannot communicate their basic needs. These types of communications are so basic to daily functioning and survival that many family members are left to question how this could happen. This lack of understanding of the symptoms related to the disease and impaired communication further disturbs family relationships and thereby alienates support systems critical to enhanced functioning (Dziegielewski, 2007).

This chapter highlights the guidelines for using the *Diagnostic and Statistical Manual of Mental Disorders* (*DSM-IV-TR*; American Psychiatric

Association [APA], 2000) to better understand and assess these conditions. Of all the psychotic disorders, schizophrenia is the most common (Walker, Mittal, Tessner, & Trotman, 2008). Although this chapter presents a brief overview of all the psychotic disorders, the diagnosis and treatment of schizophrenia is the central focus. The latest practice methods and newest research and findings are highlighted to further the understanding of these often-devastating illnesses.

SCHIZOPHRENIA AND THE PSYCHOTIC DISORDERS

When reading the work of diverse ancient cultures (e.g., Egypt, India, Greece, and China), it becomes clear that strange and bizarre behavior often referred to as "madness" or "lunacy" has existed for thousands of years (Woo & Keatinge, 2008, p.470). The term demence precoce, or early dementia (dementia praecox), was the general term for what we today call schizophrenia. Within the psychotic disorders, the condition of schizophrenia historically has always been the most clearly defined. Several subtypes that can occur within schizophrenia were identified and described by Kraepelin in 1899. Emil Kraepelin (1809-1926), using the earlier work of Morel, developed a formal diagnostic category where he broke dementia praecox into different subtypes: disorganized type (previously known as hebephrenia), paranoid, and catatonic. This classification system lasted for many years. It was not until a new generation of researchers, who voiced concerns with the consistency and uniformity of these earlier classification schemes, developed the *DSM* definition most similar to what we utilize today (Walker, Mittal, Tessner & Trotman, 2008).

Today, many theories about the causes of these mental health conditions have evolved (Lehmann & Ban, 1997). Some of the more current theories of causation include: oxygen deficiency; biological causes related to the biological similarity of epilepsy and schizophrenia; and an imbalance with natural neurochemical balances within the brain, such as serotonin or dopamine disturbance or both (Hong, Lee, Sim, & Hwu, 1997; Lehmann & Ban, 1997). One reason it may be so difficult to define the disorder is that when most researchers think of the psychotic disorders, they immediately think of schizophrenia; and to complicate the matter further, many professionals agree that schizophrenia is an illness with a complex and heterogeneous nature (Glick, 2005; National Institute of Mental Health [NIMH], 2009d). Based on recent research, the conceptual definition of schizophrenia has broadened to include awareness that it is not one singular disease (Walker et al., 2008). Walker et al. acknowledge this research and agree that trying to make schizophrenia into one disorder might confuse and complicate the diagnostic assessment process. Rather, it might be easier to classify the disorder as a group or cluster of disorders that lack a single cause.

UNDERSTANDING INDIVIDUALS WHO SUFFER FROM THE PSYCHOTIC DISORDERS

Receiving a diagnosis of schizophrenia or one of the psychotic disorders can be one of the most devastating experiences for an individual and his or her family. Unfortunately, no known prevention or cure exists for these disorders (Woo & Keatinge, 2008). The behaviors and coping styles characteristic of psychotic disorders such as schizophrenia, which include symptoms such as hallucinations, delusions, and bizarre or inappropriate behavior, can be problematic. The word psychotic can easily be misinterpreted. In the psychotic disorders, individual criteria must be met, and the definition and meaning of what constitutes a psychotic symptom can change based on the diagnosis being considered. Further, the disorders in this category do not always stem from a common etiology. What diagnoses in this category clearly share are the problems that can occur with performing daily tasks, particularly those that involve interpersonal relationships. Symptoms related to the psychotic disorders often appear as a thought disorder, with poor reality testing, social isolation, poor self-image, problems in relating with family, and problems at work (Woo & Keatinge, 2008).

The individual who suffers from one of these disorders can experience states of terror that prevent daily interactions and create difficulty in distinguishing fantasy from reality. This resulting separation from reality makes the symptoms that an individual client suffers extend far beyond personal discomfort. The symptoms related to the individual's mental disorder also affect the support system and all of the people who come into contact with him or her. This disorder has far-reaching effects; not only does it disrupt the life of the individual, but it can tear apart support systems and alienate the client from daily contacts with family and friends. Not knowing the actual cause of psychotic disorders and misinterpreting the signs and symptoms may frustrate both family and friends. Therefore, it is not surprising that this category of mental disorders, especially schizophrenia, has been documented as a leading, worldwide public health problem.

The often-negative reaction by lay individuals, peer relations, family, and professionals toward individuals who suffer from schizophrenia and other psychotic disorders is extreme when compared to what might be experienced by individuals who suffer from depression. Once diagnosed, clients with these disorders often need extensive monitoring and support that most primary care physicians and other practitioners are not able to provide or interested in providing (Dziegielewski, 2008). Furthermore, although they might not openly admit it, few professionals actually seek out this type of client to work with, unless they are working in a mental health setting. Many professionals simply prefer not to work with clients suffering from a psychotic disorder because of the monitoring problems and the unpredictability of client responses, which makes it difficult to provide the support and supervision required in a nonspecialized treatment environment. On the more optimistic side, it appears that practitioner views toward this population are changing somewhat, although the process of professionals developing a greater interest in working with these clients will continue to be a slow one. Psychopharmacology is one area in which new medications have brought about relief for many clients who suffer from this chronic and debilitating condition (Dziegielewski, 2010).

In summary, since first being introduced in the earliest versions of the *DSM* (APA, 1952), the diagnostic category of the psychotic disorders, especially schizophrenia, continues to raise many questions for practitioners. Concerns center on its validity and application of criteria as well as the detrimental and negative impact that this diagnosis can have on the future life of the individual. In addition, many mental health practitioners remain leery of working with these individuals because of the unpredictability and uncertainty of their behavior. For many individuals who suffer from this disorder, complete or total remission is rare, and a chronic yet variable

course of the illness is to be expected. Furthermore, schizophrenia appears to be an equal opportunity illness that affects rich and poor alike. There are over 2.2 million individuals with schizophrenia in the United States, or 1.1% of the U.S. population 18 years of age or older (NIMH, 2008).

OVERVIEW OF SCHIZOPHRENIA AND THE PRIMARY PSYCHOTIC DISORDERS

According to the *DSM-IV-TR*, the primary psychotic disorders include brief psychotic disorder, schizophreniform disorder, delusional disorder, schizoaffective disorder, shared psychotic disorder, psychotic disorder due to a general medical condition, substance-induced psychotic disorder, psychotic disorder not otherwise specified (NOS), and the five subtypes of schizophrenia. The characteristic symptom of psychosis experienced by clients is being out of touch with reality, and this can be magnified by five subtypes of schizophrenia. These five subtypes include: paranoid type, disorganized type, catatonic type, undifferentiated, and residual type. Although it is beyond the scope of this chapter to define all psychotic disorders, a brief definition of criteria for each is included in Quick Reference 8.1.

Hallucinations are basically sensory experiences that happen without the support of the appropriate stimuli (Woo & Keatinge, 2008). The majority of hallucinations exhibited are usually auditory (70-90%), but can more rarely manifest as visual, olfactory (related to smell), gustatory (related to taste), or tactile (related to touch). Visual hallucinations may exist but are less common than auditory. When a client is experiencing visual hallucinations, an assessment to rule out potential organic brain damage is generally warranted. Less common forms of hallucinations

QUICK REFERENCE 8.1

TYPES OF PSYCHOTIC DISORDERS

Schizophrenia: In this mental health condition, individuals suffer from characteristic psychotic symptoms and a noted deterioration in adaptive functioning. The time frame consists of an active phase of the disorder that must last at least 1 month with a time frame of at least 6 months in duration. As identified in the *DSM-IV* and the *DSM-IV-TR* there are five subtypes:

1. **Disorganized type:** Characterized by a marked incoherence, lack of systematized delusions, and blunted, disturbed, or inappropriate affect.
2. **Catatonic type:** Characterized by negativism and psychomotor disturbances such as stupor, negativism, rigidity, and bizarre posturing.
3. **Paranoid type:** Individuals experience one or more systematized delusions or auditory hallucinations with a similar theme.
4. **Undifferentiated type:** Sometimes referred to as the "garbage can" as there is an overlapping of symptoms related to the other disorders in this category.
5. **Residual type:** Not currently displaying symptoms displayed in the past.

Brief psychotic disorder: A disorder in which a symptom generally lasts at least 1 day (24 hours) but no longer than 1 month. Sudden onset is generally linked to some type of psychosocial stressor.

Schizophreniform disorder: Diagnosis is usually considered provisional because it generally relates to the first episode of psychosis that has lasted at least 1 month, and there was an absence of the requirement that there be a decline in functioning. Reflective of the criteria for schizophrenia, when the active phase of the episode extends beyond 6 months, the diagnosis will be changed to schizophrenia.

Delusional disorder: A disorder in which an individual suffers from nonbizarre delusions that last approximately 1 month; however, many of the other active-phase symptoms of schizophrenia are not present.

Schizoaffective disorder: A disorder in which the individual suffers from the signs and symptoms prevalent in both the schizophrenic disorder and the mood disorder, with the schizophrenic symptoms being prevalent.

Shared psychotic disorder (induced psychotic disorder): In this condition, delusions are present in an individual who is clearly influenced by someone else who has a longer-standing delusional system.

Psychotic disorder due to a general medical condition: Disorder in which the psychotic symptoms an individual is experiencing are related directly to a medical condition.

Substance-induced psychotic disorder: In this condition, the psychotic symptoms an individual is experiencing are related directly to drug abuse, a medication, or toxin exposure.

Psychotic disorder not otherwise specified (NOS): In this condition, the psychotic symptoms and client's presentation of them do not meet all the criteria for any of the specific psychotic disorders, or information is either inadequate or contradictory to confirm a clear diagnosis.*

---

*What each of these disorders share is characterized by what is often referred to as positive and negative symptoms. Basically, a positive symptom involves the development of delusions (distortions of thought content), conceptual disorganization (grossly disorganized speech or grossly disorganized or catatonic behavior), hallucinatory behavior (distortions of perception), excitement, grandiosity, suspiciousness/persecution, and hostility.

(continued)

QUICK REFERENCE 8.1 *(Continued)*

Positive symptoms are further divided into two categories: the psychotic and the disorganized. The psychotic dimension relates directly to positive symptoms such as hallucinations and delusions. A basic definition of a delusion is simply a strong belief by an individual that will not wavier after being presented with evidence to the contrary. Delusions often contain ideas of reference, which have a theme or involve one certain idea. A variety of themes may occur such as religious, persecutory, or grandiose. There are two types of delusions: bizarre and non-bizarre. The ones that are termed as bizarre are the most pathological because they are not plausible on any level of understanding (Woo & Keatinge, 2008). Thought insertion or thought broadcasting are generally considered bizarre, whereas, the more believable ones such as the "police are after me" tend to be considered nonbizarre.

Source: Summarized criteria from the *Diagnostic and Statistical Manual of Mental Disorders, Fourth Edition, Text Revision.* Copyright 2000 by the American Psychiatric Association.

in schizophrenia include tactile (touch), taste, and smell (olfactory) sensations.

Experiencing tactile or olfactory hallucinations may also be indicative of an organic problem. In some cases, clients may report feeling tactile misperceptions, such as bugs crawling on them. In this case, a simple rule that may be helpful to remember is that clients' reporting of "bugs" on them may be related to substance use and abuse. Substance abuse can be a sincere problem in schizophrenia and when it is a co-occurrence with the disorder, negative consequences can result that influence all aspects of the treatment process (Green, 2007). In these cases, a client should immediately be referred for a drug screen, physical examination, or both to determine if the resulting psychosis is possibly related to the side effects of using prescription medications, drug abuse, or a related type of delirium.

The disorganized dimension of a client's behavior can be seen in his or her disordered patterns of speech. Disordered speech can be expressed in a variety of ways. For example, clients may make loose associations and jump from one topic to another, or their speech may be tangential or even incoherent. The disorganized dimension of a client's thought process relates to the primary symptoms most relevant to problematic behaviors that occur through speech and behavior. For the mental health practitioner, these symptoms are often very obvious and easy to detect in the diagnostic assessment process.

In contrast, the negative symptoms often seen in these disorders are often more common than the positive symptoms, although they remain harder to detect. This is because negative symptoms involve behaviors that should be present but are absent. For example, one symptom may be a flat or blunted affect, which involves restrictions in the range or intensity of facial expressions. Additional negative symptoms include avolition (lack of goal-directed behavior), emotional withdrawal, poor rapport, passivity, apathy, social withdrawal, difficulty in abstract thinking, lack of spontaneity, and stereotyped thinking patterns. In addition, the *DSM-IV-TR* included two new negative symptoms: alogia and avolition (APA, 2000). Alogia deals primarily with the fluency and productivity of speech, and avolition relates directly to goal-directed behavior and drive.

Since the negative symptoms commonly occur but are often more subtle than the positive symptoms, the inability to control these symptoms often prevents clients from leading fruitful and productive lives (Malhotra, Pinsky, & Breier, 1996). Often the negative symptoms overlap with symptoms that also occur in individuals who are depressed, such as reduced appetite, lack of energy, lack of pleasure, and inattention. Medications appear to be most helpful in controlling the positive symptoms but less effective in controlling the negative ones (Dziegielewski, 2010).

In summary, these disorders share the fact that they are generally characterized by symptoms such as delusions, hallucinations, and disorganized speech and behavior as well as numerous negative symptoms. (See Quick Reference 8.2 for a general listing of the positive and negative signs and symptoms often present in these disorders.)

Delusional Disorder

Delusional disorder is diagnosed when the client has none of the symptoms of schizophrenia other than delusional thinking. As the name indicates, delusional disorder is characterized by persistent delusions that may seem believable and not bizarre. In delusional disorder, the individual often suffers from nonbizarre delusions that last approximately 1 month, although many of the other active-phase symptoms of schizophrenia are not present. These individuals often perform well at work or in certain situations where the delusional beliefs can be controlled. However, when something happens to change this situation or disturb the individual's usual coping styles, problems with social or occupational functioning often result (Munro & Mok, 2006).

QUICK REFERENCE 8.2

PSYCHOTIC CHARACTERISTICS AND SYMPTOMS

Positive Symptoms

Delusions—strong beliefs held in spite of strong evidence to the contrary.

Hallucinations—misperceptions.

Disorganized speech.

Disorganized or catatonic behavior.

Negative Symptoms

Blunted affect.

Poor rapport.

Apathy.

Difficulty in abstract thinking.

Stereotyped thinking patterns.

Avolition—the lack of goal-directed behavior.

*Alogia—deals primarily with the fluency and productivity of speech.

*Volition—relates directly to goal-directed behavior and drive.

Emotional withdrawal. Passivity.

Social withdrawal.

Lack of spontaneity.

---

* These two negative symptoms have been included in the *DSM-IV-TR* (APA, 2000).

This disorder usually starts late in life. Although it does not generally cause problems with intellect or work-related deterioration, it does cause frequent domestic problems. Family members close to the client may constantly listen to the delusional train of thought and become frustrated because although it may sound believable to some, they know it is not true. Efforts to convince the client suffering from the disorder generally fall on deaf ears as the delusional thinking, although it is not bizarre, is a critical part of the client's belief system than cannot be shaken. Based on their strong beliefs, these clients are often involved in litigation within the legal system for what they believe are crimes committed against them. When the delusions are psychosomatic and they believe what has happened to them is medically related, they may have endless medical tests.

The chronic reduction of sensory input (e.g., blindness or deafness) may also contribute to misinterpretations and the eventual development of what seem to be hallucinations and delusions. In addition, further misinterpretations may occur in conjunction with the client's experiences, especially when there is social isolation as when an immigrant tries to adjust to a different culture. It is important to note that the client may not meet Criterion A for Schizophrenia. The clinician should always check for any general medical conditions and for substance abuse whether prescribed or illegal that may contribute to the symptoms that are presented by the individual (APA, 2000; Morrison, 1995).

Schizoaffective Disorder

The description of schizoaffective disorder clearly distinguishes it from the other psychotic disorders, and it is increasingly assigned to individuals in clinical settings. Schizoaffective disorder addresses individuals who have prominent features of both schizophrenia and major mood disorders. Prior to *DSM-III*, this diagnostic category was often used to classify anyone who had symptoms of mood-incongruent psychotic features together with signs of an affective disorder (Woo & Keatinge, 2008). Clients suffering from this disorder were considered to have a subtype of dementia praecox, yet they experienced good premorbid adjustment, rapid recovery, and subsequent achievement of good social and occupational function (APA, 2000). To clarify this disorder, the *DSM-III-R* identified this disorder in relation to the timing and duration of the mood episodes that accompany the psychotic symptoms (APA, 1987).

In *DSM-IV* and *DSM-IV-TR*, the individual must meet the criteria for the occurrence of both the psychotic and the affective symptoms. Symptomolgy for both disorders (schizophrenia and the mood disorder) must be clear, but schizophenia is always prominent, while at the same time it meets the criteria for a manic, mixed, or depressive episode (APA, 2000). It is important that the depressive episode meets the full criteria for the mood episode, as some of the negative symptoms are prominent in schizophrenia as well. This fact makes it difficult to tell if the depressive symptoms actually coexist as depression may be a co-occurring condition.

DSM-IV-TR does not specify the prevalence, although it does note that schizoaffective disorder is less common than schizophrenia (APA, 2000). One of the biggest concerns with this diagnosis is the overlap of symptoms and the confusion that can occur when putting these two major clinical syndromes into one (Woo & Keatinge, 2008). This leaves the practitioner to question whether the psychosis and affective components of these two conditions are really separate and how best to treat them to address all aspects of the condition and the symptoms being experienced. More research in this area is needed that clearly looks at the treatment options for this group and how best to take into account the positive symptoms characteristic of this disorder along with the affective component, which can clearly affect mood and presentation.

Shared Psychotic Disorder

In terms of prevalence, shared psychotic disorder, or folie à deux (French for "madness of two"), is presumed to be extremely rare. The disorder was once called induced psychotic disorder, double insanity, or folie à deux. Shared psychotic disorder is dramatic and inherently interesting because it usually involves two people sharing the same delusional system. It is possible, however, that it can involve as many as four people or an entire family, generally living in close proximity or the same household (Oshodi, Bangaru, & Benbow, 2005). Often this disorder develops within families, although whether there is a genetic connection is not clear.

Shared psychotic disorder appears to develop in clients with a history of social isolation. These individuals will slowly disconnect from family and friends and anyone who may threaten or challenge the nonbizarre delusions that are present and guide their daily routines. When looking at individuals who share this disorder, the delusional system of one individual influences the other party, such that the other person grows to share the primary individual's delusional beliefs. In these cases, one individual grows in prominence and power within the relationship and is said to be primary or the leader, and the other individual increasingly takes on a secondary role. The primary individual leads the secondary; often the secondary does not originally believe the delusional themes of the primary. Eventually, however, the secondary later compromises and accepts it to be an accurate perception. Often the secondary has some form of cognitive impairment or may simply become vulnerable to repeated, unchallenged, delusional themes that

later result in acceptance and compromise (Woo & Keatinge, 2008). If the secondary is removed from the situation, he or she may be able to remit the delusion thinking patterns and recover. The primary will have a much harder time in treatment as the convictions are so much more pronounced (Munro, 1999).

This nonbizarre delusional system serves to protect the individuals and keep them in isolation. An example of this might be two sisters living alone, one of whom believes that the neighbors and the landlord are sneaking into the house when they leave it and are touching and rearranging things. The primary continually tells the other sister (the secondary) that this is happening. At first the secondary disputes the claims, then later she slowly and progressively begins to accept them as real. Eventually, the sister in the secondary role compromises and accepts this is happening. To avoid it happening again, they must barricade their home to keep out all intruders who may sneak in during the night. To protect themselves, they isolate themselves inside the home.

This disorder appears to affect women more often than men. Aside from the delusions, the thoughts and behaviors of those with shared psychotic disorder are usually quite normal. This normalcy in some areas may confuse others regarding the seriousness of the situation. The cause of shared psychotic disorder has yet to be identified, but stress appears to play a key role. Being in and maintaining isolation can also contribute to the development of this disorder. People who have shared psychotic disorder simply grow to share the same delusional system. These delusions are not the result of any other mental health disorder, a medical condition, or drug taking (either prescribed or illegal) (Abramowitz, 2009).

Individuals who suffer from this type of disorder often live in isolated or rural settings where the belief system can remain undisturbed for long periods by outside influences. In these settings, outside influences are not present to question or directly challenge the delusional beliefs, thereby allowing these patterns of coping and behavior to grow and strengthen. These individuals rarely seek treatment as they do not see their behavior as problematic and may isolate from all that challenges the ingrained belief system.

Psychotic Disorder Due to a General Medical Disorder or Substance Induced

Descriptions of psychotic disorder due to a general medical condition can fill many pages. Currently one of the most common problems is HIV disease, which is associated with major mental health disorders, such as psychosis. Cancer may accompany psychotic illness, which can affect the treatment of mind, mood, body, and behavior. General Medical Condition has two subgroups: with hallucinations and with delusions. Examples of causes of psychoses that are secondary to a general medical condition include: trauma or structural changes of the brain, such as space-occupying lesions; biochemical changes; organ failure; infections; and nutritional deficiencies. Also, a number of medications (prescription and over the counter) that will sometimes induce a psychotic episode when taken alone, in excess, or in combination with other medications. Common psychiatric comorbidities associated with insomnia can include psychotic symptoms resulting in a psychotic disorder.

A wide variety of central nervous system diseases, from both external poisons and internal physiologic illness, can produce symptoms of psychosis. The numbers of medical conditions that can cause or induce a psychotic disorder are many. To be classified as a psychotic disorder due to a general medical condition, however, the psychotic symptoms an individual is experiencing must be related directly to a medical condition.

In substance-induced psychotic disorder, the psychotic symptoms an individual is experiencing are related directly to abuse of a drug, a medication, or toxin exposure. Primary features of a substance-induced psychotic disorder are prominent psychotic symptoms, such as hallucinations and/or delusions (depending on the substance). A substance-induced psychotic disorder is subtyped or categorized based on whether the prominent feature is delusions or hallucinations. As described, delusions are fixed, false beliefs whereas hallucinations involve seeing, hearing, feeling, tasting, or smelling things that are not there.

Psychotic Disorder Not Otherwise Classified

Psychotic disorder not otherwise specified (NOS) includes the psychotic symptoms of delusions, hallucinations, disorganized speech, or grossly disorganized or catatonic behavior when there is inadequate information to make a specific diagnosis. Generally, there may also be contradictory information, or disorders with psychotic symptoms that do not meet the criteria for any specific psychotic disorder. Professionals choose this category for symptoms or syndromes that do not meet the criteria for any of the disorders previously described for psychotic disorder. Charles Bonnet syndrome, postpartum psychosis, and auditory hallucinations are in this category. Psychotic disorder NOS is the category assigned to a client who is psychotic, but there is inadequate information to make a definitive diagnosis or there is conflicting information.

DIFFERENTIATING AMONG BRIEF PSYCHOTIC DISORDER, SCHIZOPHRENIFORM, AND SCHIZOPHRENIA

The key feature of brief psychotic disorder is that the disturbance is the result of a sudden onset of at least one of the positive psychotic symptoms:

delusions, hallucinations, markedly disorganized speech (e.g., frequent derailment or incoherence), or grossly disorganized or catatonic behavior (Criterion A). An episode of the disturbance lasts at least 1 day but less than 1 month, and the individual eventually has a full return to the premorbid level of functioning (Criterion B). The disturbance is not better accounted for by a mood disorder with psychotic features, by schizoaffective disorder, or by schizophrenia and is not due to the direct physiological effects of a substance (e.g., a hallucinogen) or a general medical condition (e.g., subdural hematoma) (Criterion C) (APA, 2000). Brief psychotic disorder may be more common among teenagers, young adults, and clients who have preexisting personality disorders (Morrison, 1995).

The condition of schizophreniform may at first be confused with the condition of schizophrenia because of the overlap of criteria, but there is a difference in duration. This diagnosis is important because it can prevent case closure and alerts all practitioners that an underlying cause of psychosis has not become clear. The diagnosis of schizophreniform is used to describe clients who recover completely within the 6-month period and have no residual effects. The criteria for schizophreniform disorder are the same as those of schizophrenia (Criterion A) except for two differences: the total duration of the illness (including prodromal, active, and residual phases) and impaired social or occupational functioning during some part of the illness is not required (although it may occur). The duration requirement for schizophreniform disorder is considered intermediate between that for brief psychotic disorder (less than 1 month) and schizophrenia (more than 6 months) (APA, 2000). Because of the brief period and the fact that it is not clear whether schizophrenia could resolve in a client, this diagnosis is often given first and characterizes the beginning phase of the disease.

Since so many mental health practitioners confuse brief psychotic disorder, schizophreniform disorder, and schizophrenia, these disorders are differentiated with a brief case example. The most important thing to remember when approaching a client who may suffer from one of these disorders is to look carefully at the time frame in which the client experienced the active problematic symptoms for each disorder:

- Brief psychotic disorder: less than 1 month.
- Schizophreniform disorder: less than 6 months.
- Schizophrenia: more than 6 months.

In brief psychotic disorder, the symptoms are often severe but generally are brief in nature, lasting at least 24 hours (1 day) but less than 1 month. When the symptoms subside, the client generally returns to the premorbid level of functioning. In addition to the time frame criteria, in brief psychotic disorder there may or may not be a stressor, although if there is a precipitating stressor, it should be clearly identified. Onset of brief psychotic disorder is sudden and accompanied by positive symptoms such as hallucinations, delusions, or disorganized speech. In schizophreniform disorder, the symptoms are very similar to schizophrenia; however, this provisional diagnosis is usually applied to the first psychotic break. In a diagnosis of schizophreniform disorder, the criterion of 1 month has been met but the 6-month period has not. In addition, there is no requirement in schizophreniform disorder, as in the criteria for schizophrenia, that there be a decline in either social or occupational functioning during some point in the illness. Schizophreniform disorder is considered primarily a provisional diagnosis because if the criteria and the time frame of 6 months are met, the diagnosis will be changed to schizophrenia.

To highlight the relationship of these three psychotic disorders, a brief clinical case example is provided of a military recruit. It is not uncommon for a recruit to experience his or her first psychotic breakdown during military basic training. In this 6-week, intensive training experience, new recruits are placed under considerable stress, and extreme pressure is applied to change their usual style of coping and patterns of behavior. Recruits are forced to abruptly learn and adopt an entirely new lifestyle. Emphasis on the individual is negated in an effort to have recruits form a group identity. This pressure to conform is so intense that it is not uncommon for some new recruits to experience what would appear to be a psychotic break. In this case, a female recruit became hysterical and actively delusional. When told that she would have to take a shower in a communal setting with other female recruits, she experienced auditory hallucinations that told her that others were plotting against her. She became so uncontrollable and volatile that after weeks of trying to calm her within the unit, she was referred for inpatient admission and evaluation. After completing the initial evaluation, it was clear that the client met the criteria for schizophrenia except that there was no documented history of this disorder. She had been experiencing the symptoms for almost 1 month; the 6-month period had not been met. Thus, the diagnosis of either schizophreniform or brief reactive psychosis seemed more appropriate.

In looking at the recruit's symptoms, there was clearly a severe stressor related to the incident; within several hours after she was placed in an inpatient setting and after problem-solving the situation, the positive symptoms resided. Within 1 week, all previous discomfort was resolved. This would make the diagnosis of schizophrenia or schizophreniform inappropriate because of the short time frame and the complete remission. The recruit's symptoms supported neither

diagnosis. In addition to duration of symptoms, cultural factors should always be taken into account when making a diagnosis (Woo & Keatinge, 2008). This particular client, during an interview, stated that she was always taught that the naked body was sacred and should be viewed only by her mate. The recruit believed that by taking a communal shower, she would be violating this sacred trust and tainting her physical body, which she was saving for marriage. When she was permitted to take showers alone, the symptoms disappeared. Nevertheless, one additional condition that may be the focus of clinical attention in this case is Acculturation Problem (coded V62.4). According to the *DSM-IV-TR* (APA, 2000), this category can be used when the focus of clinical attention is adjustment to a different culture. In the example, the recruit's difficulties occurred because of adjustment problems related to rapid integration into the military culture.

If the client had been diagnosed with schizophrenia (at that time it was military policy to do so), she would have immediately been processed for discharge. However, by carefully looking at her symptoms and taking into account environmental and cultural factors, it was determined that the diagnosis of schizophrenia was inappropriate. This is an excellent example of how the mental health practitioner's clinical judgment will always need to include a mixture of both art and science when completing an assessment.

FACTORS RELATED TO SCHIZOPHRENIA

To better understand the condition of schizophrenia, it is necessary to examine the risk factors and symptoms, the diagnostic criteria, the problems identifying the disorder, and the different interventions that have been used for treatment of persons with this disorder. This section discusses the condition of schizophrenia from a personal, community, and societal perspective. Based on this information, a treatment plan and practice strategy is developed that can efficiently embrace, identify, and effectively treat individuals who suffer from psychotic disorders such as schizophrenia.

It is common for a diagnosis of schizophrenia to be based on the presence of positive symptoms in juxtaposition with impaired social function and the absence of significant mood symptoms. The practitioner should always make sure that a physical exam has been conducted to rule out any recognizable neurological illness or substance use that can account for the psychotic symptoms. Generally, the first onset of the symptoms of this disorder usually occur during late adolescence or early adulthood. There may be an overlap with other disorders, and diagnosing schizophrenia in particular may be complicated because of the overlapping of symptoms mentioned earlier in this chapter. Recent research has begun to show connections between the etiology and the disease boundaries between schizophrenia and several other mental health disorders. For example, recent genetic research involving studies of the brain support similar causes among schizophrenia, autism spectrum disorders, and mental retardation (Guilmatre et al., 2009). Continuous research and development of a database to keep up with the various studies and findings holds much promise for the care of these clients.

Characteristically, schizophrenia is a disturbance in perception, thought, emotion, affect, and social relatedness. The *DSM-IV-TR* (2000) reports the median age of adult onset for the first episode of schizophrenia is the early to mid-20s for men and the middle to late 20s for women. Adult-onset schizophrenia is often accompanied by positive (hallucinations, delusions, racing thoughts) and negative (lack of emotion, poor social functioning, apathy, loss of motivation)

symptoms (*DSM-IV-TR*, 2000). Early-onset schizophrenia (EOS) is defined by the onset of the disorder occurring before age 18. Childhood-onset schizophrenia (COS) presents at age 12 or younger. COS is a severe form of a psychotic disorder that rarely occurs since symptoms and characteristics are difficult to pinpoint without extensive testing over a 6- to 12-month period. The first psychotic break often occurs in the early 20s; however, the severity of symptoms of the disease appear to stabilize to some extent after the age of 30.

The potential severity of schizophrenia and its associated problems make the information gathered in the diagnostic assessment and treatment plan crucial for an accurate diagnosis, especially as it relates to the identification of environmental factors that are important in the early assessment, prevention, and treatment of this disorder. Individuals who suffer from schizophrenia and members of their support systems can all benefit from educational interventions and other types of intervention programs. The majority of individuals experience some type of prodromal phase characterized by the slow and gradual development of several signs and symptoms. Most studies report that the course of schizophrenia may be inconsistent, with some experiencing exacerbation and remission of the disease and others remaining chronically ill (APA, 2000).

Biology and Etiology of Schizophrenia

Support for the belief that there is a biological component to schizophrenia increased substantially when psychotropic medication showed a decrease in symptoms related to the disorder (Dziegielewski, 2010; Lehmann & Ban, 1997). Subsequently, the medications that had an effect on these symptoms also opened the window for further understanding of the biological dynamics of schizophrenia (Lehmann & Ban, 1997). Researchers took great interest in the role that neurotransmitters such as serotonin and dopamine as well as noradrenaline, acetylcholine, and glutamate had related to establishing a biological basis for schizophrenia (Bishara & Taylor, 2009). For example, when the brains of individuals who suffered from schizophrenia were examined during autopsy, it was found that the D-4 (dopamine) receptors (members of the G-protein family that bind with antipsychotic medications) were 6 times denser than in the brains of nondisordered individuals (Hong et al., 1997). In turn, this discovery led to the biological or dopamine D-4 hypothesis of schizophrenia (Lehman & Ban, 1997). Regardless of the exact relationship, it is clear that there is a connection between schizophrenia and the neurochemical dopamine. This connection remains ambiguous because many of the medications taken to treat the disorder can also increase dopamine receptor density. What does remain clear, however, is that even never-medicated patients with schizophrenia still show elevations in the dopamine receptors (Walker et al., 2008).

Studies on the structure and function in the amygdala and anterior segment of the hippocampus, basal ganglia, and thalamus have noted differences in individuals with schizophrenia and their siblings versus the control group (Qiu et al., 2009). Qiu and colleagues concluded that there may be a schizophrenia-related endophenotype. Neuroendocrinology studies have offered another perspective on the etiology of schizophrenia. These studies focus on the relationship of the workings of the pituitary gland to the hypothalamus and the central nervous system (CNS). These studies have studied growth hormone (GH) and thyroid-releasing hormone (TRH), but results linked directly to a causal interpretation have been mixed (Keshavan et al., 1988; Lieberman et al., 1992).

Neuroimaging studies, first introduced in the 1970s, have also been helpful in identifying the possible causative factors related to

schizophrenia (S. Raz & N. Raz, 1990). These studies are helpful in exploring both the functional and the structural changes that can occur in the brains of individuals who suffer from schizophrenia. Through these studies (e.g., magnetic resonance imaging [MRI], or cerebral blood flow [CBF]), specific areas of the brain can be identified and studied (Gur & Pearlson, 1993; Keshavan et al., 1997). For example, MRIs used to look specifically at individuals who suffer from schizophrenia revealed decreased frontal, temporal, and whole-brain volume (Lawrie & Abukmeil, 1998). Also, the hippocampus has consistently been identified as one important place where distinctions can be made distinguishing people with schizophrenia from people without it (Schmajuk, 2001).

Some researchers believe that a genetic link contributes to the subsequent risk of developing schizophrenia (Brzustowicz, Hodgkinson, Chow, Honer, & Bassett, 2000; Kendler & Diehl, 1993; Nauert, 2007; Tsuang, 2004). Furthermore, researchers conducting studies in the United States, Germany, Greece, and Ireland affirm findings that schizophrenia strongly runs in families (Baron et al., 1985; Kendler et al., 1993; Kendler, Gruenberg, & Tsuang, 1985; Maier, Hallmayer, Minges, & Lichtermann, 1990; Tsuang, 2004).

In addition, twin studies also appear to support a link toward genetic transmission of schizophrenia; however, not all individuals who possess a genetic predisposition will experience symptoms of schizophrenia (Kendler & Diehl, 1993). Several accounts for this discrepancy have been posited, including the interplay of genetic and environmental considerations, where a biological child of an individual with schizophrenia has a similar risk for developing the disorder whether the child grows up in a home with that parent or not (Altschule et al., 1976; Gottesman, 1991). Brzustowicz et al. (2000) found that there is a susceptibility point on a particular gene for schizophrenia, which lends support to the theory that schizophrenia is related to genetic as well as environmental factors.

Furthermore, environmental issues are highlighted by family response to a person diagnosed with schizophrenia and how soon the person relapses following hospitalization. It appears that relapse occurs most quickly if there is a hostile family environment that is nonsupportive or over-controlling (Weisman, 1997). Recent research on the brain supports that neurodevelopmental damage during childhood is a possible antecedent to the diagnosis of schizophrenia in children, adolescents, and adults (Dutta et al., 2007; Hollis, 1995; Mental Health America, 2009; University of Virginia Health System, 2006). These environmental events associated with developmental delays or permanent neurological damage can increase the occurence of schizophrenia as well as the possibility of an individual being most susceptible to developing other mental illnesses.

Nonetheless, it is fairly well accepted that genetics may be a necessary, but not a sufficient, cause for schizophrenia (Kendler & Diehl, 1993). To acknowledge this link between the individual and the family, the term schizophrenia spectrum was added to the *DSM-IV-TR* (APA, 2000) under the familial pattern section. Schizophrenia spectrum represents the range of mental disorders that are more likely to occur in family members of individuals with schizophrenia, such as schizoaffective disorder and schizotypal personality disorder.

Concerns Regarding Misdiagnosis and Treatment

Over the years, misunderstandings surrounding schizophrenia have resulted in individuals being treated primarily by trial and error with a variety of supposed remedies to alter body states. Some examples include substances such as cocaine, castor oil, turpentine oil, sulfur oil, and barbiturates; the injection of animal blood; and carbon dioxide inhalation and various methods designed to induce convulsions (Lehmann & Ban, 1997).

Schizophrenia has a lifelong chronic prevalence with 20% to 30% showing continuing moderate-level symptoms for the rest of their lives (Walker et al., 2008). It is estimated that 50% of individuals with this diagnosis will suffer from relapse within the first year of their most recent episode, regardless of whether they are taking medication. In fact, relapse occurs so often that sufferers can expect to be in the hospital 15% to 20% of their lives. If a person with schizophrenia stops taking his or her medication, relapse tends to be longer, and most do not return to previous baseline functioning (Ayuso-Gutierrez & del Rio Vega, 1997). This finding is complicated further by what is often referred to as treatment-resistant schizophrenia. From 10% to 30% of patients prescribed antipsychotic medications have little if any response, and an additional 30% have only a partial response (APA, 2004). This makes using medication alone problematic and the use of supportive care essential. Many individuals with schizophrenia, especially those with treatment resistance, may have such poor responses to medications that they may be destined to suffer chronic yet variable courses of illness.

The chronic course of treatment and the high relapse rate make care for the individual who suffers from schizophrenia extremely costly within the health care system (Ayuso-Gutierrez & del Rio Vega, 1997). In the United States, it is estimated that mental health disorders are one of the most costly health care expenditures (Soni, 2009). According to the Medical Expenditure Panel Survey (MEPS), from 1996 to 2006, the expenses in this area went from $19.3 million to $36.2 million (Soni, 2009). Mental disorders have also been linked to the loss of $193 billion annually in terms of lost wages (Kessler et al., 2008).

In summary, clients who suffer from schizophrenia and other psychotic disorders are usually thought to be out of touch with reality and to have an impaired ability to evaluate the environment around them. Often these clients are not receptive to the intervention that the mental health practitioner may try to provide, even though they require help. Schizophrenia remains a very complex disease that can manifest itself in numerous ways. Overall, the general understanding of schizophrenia and the related psychotic disorders has improved; however, schizophrenia and the psychotic disorders still remain a significant challenge for those who try to provide therapeutic treatment. To achieve a current, ethical, and efficacious practice, mental health practitioners must have a general understanding of the condition of schizophrenia and the resulting behaviors in order to accurately complete or facilitate the diagnostic assessment.

Schizophrenia in Children and Adolescents

The prevalence of schizophrenia is rare prior to age 12; however, between ages 13 and 19, the diagnosis increases 50-fold for those who are older than 15 years of age (Clark, 2006). In adults, the prevalence of schizophrenia is reported to range from 0.5% to 1.5% of the population (*DSM-IV-TR*, 2000). Each of the age groups has different indicators associated with the onset of schizophrenia. The psychosis related to schizophrenia develops gradually in children, without the sudden psychotic break that may happen in adolescents and adults. The behavior of children with this illness may change over time and in fact often does.

Childhood-onset schizophrenia (COS) research has confirmed that those with early-onset schizophrenia will experience a more complicated clinically severe problem than those with the adult-onset disorder. COS continues into adulthood yet manifests with special developmental and social challenges (APA, 2000). For this reason, COS is often chronic, persistently debilitating, and overwhelming to support systems. It affects the client's continuous quality of life unless well followed by combined medical, physical, social, and environmental treatments. Glick (2005) presented an etiologic pathway of targeted features of schizophrenia that discusses intervention at every level. He asserts that there is a hopeful picture for the natural course of the disease and that it tends to stabilize with age.

While childhood schizophrenia is rarely diagnosed, there appear to be several antecedent neurodevelopmental issues related to the condition (Mental Health America, 2009; Weiner, 1987). These neurodevelopmental antecedents include developmental delays in speech and motor development, problems with behavior and social development, emotional problems, and reports of psychotic-like experiences, and encounters (Hollis, 1995; Laurens, Hodgins, & Maughan, et al., 2009; Weiner, 1987).

Adolescent onset of schizophrenia is treatable, and early intervention can prevent the damage associated with lack of treatment and recurrence of uncontrolled schizophrenic episodes (Keeping Kids Healthy, 2009). In adolescents, schizophrenia may develop over time or have a rapid onset (University of Virginia Health System, 2006). The assessment of the adolescent for a diagnosis of schizophrenia must include a discussion of the adolescent's history and current functioning, such as: disorganized thinking; poor interpersonal skills; inability to control ideas, behavior, and emotions; and impaired reality perception (Weiner, 1987). All adolescents have specific life circumstances and experiences that contribute to the symptoms they may experience in the development of schizophrenia.

DSM-IV-TR AND THE DEFINITION OF SCHIZOPHRENIA

Since schizophrenia was first introduced in the *DSM*, many changes have occurred in practice related to this disorder, requiring revisions in the *DSM*. The *DSM-IV* (APA, 1994) and the *DSM-IV-TR* (APA, 2000) combine three sections (e.g., schizophrenia, delusional disorder, and psychotic disorder not elsewhere classified) that were listed separately in the *DSM-III-R* (APA, 1987). In the *DSM-IV* and the *DSM-IV-TR*, the essential features of schizophrenia are a mixture of characteristic signs and symptoms (Criterion A). The magnitude of the symptoms must be significant enough to impair occupational and social functioning (Criterion B). Furthermore, the duration of the symptoms must be at least 6 months and include a period of 1 month with active-phase symptoms. This period can be less than 1 month if successfully treated with medication and may include periods of prodromal or residual symptoms (Criterion C). It is important to note that the 1-month criterion is different from older versions of the *DSM*, which listed it as 1 week. Other conditions such as schizoaffective and mood disorder must be ruled out (Criterion D), and what the client is experiencing cannot be related to a substance abuse problem or a general medical condition (Criterion E). Last, the relationship between the pervasive developmental disorder known as autism must be clearly identified, and in schizophrenia it must be determined that the client is experiencing hallucinations and delusions (Criterion F).

To diagnose the individual who suffers from schizophrenia, the characteristic signs and symptoms (Criterion A) must be identified. Since these signs and symptoms are often multifaceted, careful identification is required. In schizophrenia, as described earlier in this chapter, different positive and negative symptoms will always occur. In the *DSM-IV-TR*, there are five identified subtypes of schizophrenia. These include paranoid type (coded 295.30), disorganized type (coded 295.10), catatonic type (coded 295.20), undifferentiated type (coded 295.90), and residual type (coded 295.60). It is suspected, however, that in the modifications that will occur in the *DSM-5*, these subtypes will either be revised or discontinued. Current research used to support the diagnostic categories does not appear to find these subtypes stable, nor do they appear to have clear diagnostic value.

In the paranoid type, individuals have a preoccupation with one or more delusions or frequent auditory hallucinations; however, these individuals do not have prominent symptoms related to disorganized speech or behavior or flat or inappropriate affect. Many times clients of the paranoid type will present with numerous complaints about being watched, plotted against, or both. In the disorganized type, disorganized speech and behavior are apparent, as is flat or inappropriate affect. Catatonic behaviors, however, should not be present. The catatonic subtype presents with at least two of the following symptoms: extreme negativism or mutism; excessive, purposeless motor activity; peculiarities of involuntary movement; and catalepsy, stupor, or motoric immobility. The client can also present with echolalia (parrotlike representation of someone's speech) and/or echopraxia (parrotlike repetition of someone's speech and movements). In the undifferentiated type, delusions and hallucinations are present, but the criteria are not met for the other types. Finally, the residual type is diagnosed when the active-phase symptoms are not present, but there is continuing evidence of the disturbance.

DIFFERENTIAL DIAGNOSTIC CONSIDERATIONS

The diagnosis of schizophrenia is often complicated by the fact that symptoms remain susceptible to change during subsequent assessment. Depression and the symptoms relevant to it occur in 25% of the cases in which there is clear documentation of schizophrenia (Siris, 2000). To provide the best care, mental health practitioners need to realize that negative symptoms can overlap, and therefore can be easily confused with other mental health conditions, such as depression (Woo & Keatinge, 2008).

Generally, most individuals who suffer from schizophrenia experience a characteristic deterioration in adaptive functioning that accompanies the psychotic symptoms. The first psychosis, or "break with reality," usually occurs between ages 17 and 30 in men and 20 and 40 in women (Carpenter, Conley, & Buchanan, 1998). The course and variation of schizophrenia remain extremely variable. The first episode of this illness should always be assessed carefully because, after one episode, some individuals may not become psychotic again. The majority of individuals with schizophrenia improve after the first episode but continue to manifest symptoms and remain unpredictable with future occurrences.

Schizophrenia can have either a gradual and insidious onset or a rapid and sudden onset. As noted earlier, in order for a diagnosis of schizophrenia to be given, the active phase must last approximately 6 months and the person must present with psychotic symptoms for a significant portion of time during a 1-month period or less if the client responds to treatment. If the time period is less, the individual should be diagnosed with schizophreniform disorder or brief psychotic disorder.

Mood disorders, substance abuse, and medical conditions can imitate schizophrenia and must be ruled out. Individuals who suffer from schizophrenia can also abuse alcohol and other drugs. In addition, since substance abuse can reduce effectiveness of treatment, a clear and comprehensive assessment to rule out co-occurring conditions and complicating factors must be conducted (National Institute of Mental Health, 2009c).

SCHIZOPHRENIA AND FACTORS FOR CONSIDERATION IN THE DIAGNOSTIC ASSESSMENT

When starting the diagnostic assessment for this disorder, two factors must be clearly understood:

1. Identification of a Single Disorder: Schizophrenia is probably not a single disorder (Woo and Keatinge, 2008). In professional practice, mental health practitioners quickly realize that the client with a single problem does not exist, nor does the client who clearly and concisely fits perfectly into an identified diagnostic category. Clients often have multiple problems that require a multifaceted approach to intervention. The same can be said for clients with schizophrenia who have multiple mental health problems and difficulties (Dziegielewski, 2010). Some of these problems can easily overlap with other mental health conditions, such as the affective disorders (bipolar and depression) or the dementia- or delirium-based disorders. Since the etiology of schizophrenia is not yet fully understood, the use of medications to control the little we do understand is essential. As an understanding of the causes and origins of schizophrenia and the psychotic disorders increases, so will the ability of mental health professionals to better treat this illness.

2. Cultural Considerations: Since the diagnostic assessment will serve as the foundation for intervention with an

individual who has schizophrenia, it is imperative to consider the cultural background and experiences of the client and how the client's culture may influence or affect subsequent behavior (Brekke & Barrio, 1997; Dutta et al., 2007). Research suggests that there is a better prognosis for schizophrenia in developing societies than in societies that are more industrial (Cohen, Patel, Thara, & Gureje, 2008). Furthermore, some theorists have postulated that cultural factors can be directly involved with the expression of positive (Weisman, 1997) and negative symptoms (Dassori et al., 1998).

Ethnic group identity, religion, and spirituality can help to establish culturally sanctioned behaviors that appear to be different from behaviors demonstrated in the dominant culture. For the practitioner, "cultural context or knowledge of the cultural environment is a critical determinant of how one evolves as a cultural being" (Lum, 2003, p. 77). For example, for those who practice Catholicism in the Latino culture, mental health difficulties are often explained as "God's will" (Lefley & Pederson, 1986; Weisman, 1997). Typically, Latinos first confer with indigenous healers (curanderos or espiritistas) or Catholic leaders, or both, before discussing mental health symptoms with mental health practitioners (Weaver & Wodarski, 1996). For Mexican Americans who suffer from schizophrenia, there appears to be a greater manifestation of cognitive negative symptoms when compared to their Caucasian American counterparts (Dassori et al., 1998).

For African Americans, controversy continues about the relevance of culture as related to the diagnosis of schizophrenia.

It is believed that African Americans are more likely to be incorrectly diagnosed as suffering from schizophrenia than other minority groups (Weaver & Wodarski, 1996). Although the actual reason for this is not known, it may be influenced by misperceptions of African American clients as having limited abilities or being excessively suspicious and hostile (Wodarski & Megget, 1996). Samoan culture tends to view mental health disturbances as spiritual; Samoans thus often attribute symptoms to possession by spirits (Weisman, 1997). Vietnamese and Chinese cultures tend to view expressions of psychotic symptomology as uncontrollable, linking it to supernatural causes (Hong et al., 1997; Weisman, 1997).

It is important to note that a study by Brekke and Barrio (1997) did not find any racial differences among individuals who suffered from schizophrenia. Regardless of this study's conclusions, the authors found that cultural factors are important in both the diagnostic assessment and the intervention plan. Cultural factors always need to be identified and taken into account when working with individuals. The ways in which cultural factors can affect or contribute to problematic behavior should not be underestimated. Grigorenko (2009) provides an excellent edited resource for assisting practitioners to make culturally sensitive assessments.

APPLICATION OF THE MULTIAXIAL DIAGNOSTIC SYSTEM

Given the behaviors that Jacob has exhibited and his past history (Case Example 8.1), as well as the symptoms that he is now experiencing, Jacob's diagnosis, diagnosed according to the

CASE EXAMPLE 8.1 - CASE OF JACOB

Jacob is a 48-year-old divorced Caucasian man. He is of large build and tall, with brown hair and brown eyes. He is unshaven, with long greasy hair, and appears to care little about his personal hygiene, as evidenced by his dirty and disheveled appearance and layers of sloppy clothing. Jacob was recently released from jail after being arrested for vagrancy and resisting arrest. Currently Jacob states he was evicted from his apartment by his landlord several weeks ago and has been homeless and living on the streets.

Upon interviewing Jacob, he appeared guarded and suspicious of the police and his previous landlord. While in jail, Jacob had gotten into a fight with another inmate and suffered a black eye and two broken ribs. Officers in the jail referred him for an evaluation, as he appeared to have limited insight and judgment and also stated that the prisoner who beat him up was taking orders from the devil.

Upon arrival at the crisis stabilization unit, Jacob displayed suspiciousness and refused to answer any questions that could reveal any personal information about himself or his behaviors. He appeared agitated, showed bizarre posturing, and appeared unpredictable in terms of his reactions and movement. When left alone for a few moments, Jacob was observed talking to himself. When he was finally able to talk, Jacob told the practitioner that he played backup music for Dylan in the 1960s. Jacob stated that his being locked up in jail was a plot to keep him away from his real brother in music, Elvis, who really was not dead, as everyone thought.

After obtaining permission from Jacob to call his family, his father related that Jacob had a long history of mental illness since age 25 and had been previously diagnosed with schizophrenia, paranoid type, and it was chronic. Jacob had reportedly been in and out of the state mental hospital, the Veterans Administration hospital, his parents' house, and various assisted living facilities for the past 15 years. Recently, Jacob had been doing so much better that he was discharged from an assisted living facility and moved into his own apartment. According to his father, it was around this time that Jacob started hanging around with the wrong crowd, and on occasion he would drink wine and smoke marijuana. His new friends would help him cash his disability check; they would then buy wine and then drink the wine and smoke the cigarettes that he would buy. According to his father, Jacob constantly reported that he could not sleep, as he often had nightmares of bombs exploding. Jacob's father suspected that Jacob had stopped taking his antipsychotic medication shortly after he got into his apartment, but he could not be sure of exactly when. After Jacob failed to pay his rent, his landlord threw him out. This led to Jacob being on the street and his subsequent arrest for vagrancy. According to his father, Jacob had become quite paranoid and frightened in jail. Jacob had never had any legal problems prior to being arrested for vagrancy.

Jacob is a Vietnam veteran who did not have direct combat experience but spent a great deal of time on tactical training maneuvers. His father insists that Jacob was fine until he was discharged from the military at age 21. After leaving the military, Jacob had gradually increasing symptoms, particularly hearing voices. Jacob told family and friends that he was discharged from the military because he was caught trying to help the North Vietnamese people. After the military discharge, he began to stay in his room all of the time and his hygiene became very poor. Jacob began to express bizarre and paranoid thoughts. The family tried to ignore Jacob's behavior until one night, when he had a psychotic episode, Jacob threatened to stab his mother with a kitchen knife while alternating between cries for help and fiendish ranting. After this incident, Jacob was hospitalized numerous times with delusions and hallucinations.

Jacob was married for 6 months to another patient whom he met during one of his hospitalizations. Between his times in the hospital, Jacob has usually lived with his parents or alone. He has no children. Jacob's last hospitalization was 1 year ago. His father states that Jacob feels overwhelmed and does not know what to do. Jacob's father is elderly, legally blind, and feels that he cannot handle Jacob anymore. He asked if permanent placement in the state hospital could be an option for Jacob because, if it was, then he would know that Jacob was safe. After a 3-day course of antipsychotic medication, Jacob presents as more friendly and cooperative, although his affect is flat and he complains of being sleepy. Jacob says that he knows that he is a worry to his father but begs not to be put back in the state hospital. He asserts that he goes off his medication because it has such terrible side effects, and then he smokes and drinks in an attempt to self-medicate.

DSM-IV-TR, continues to be schizophrenia, paranoid type, and this is placed on Axis I of the multiaxial system. The diagnosis of post-traumatic stress disorder (PTSD) is given provisionally, as there is not enough information to determine whether some of his behaviors may be related to stressors that originally surfaced from his military experiences. In speaking with the client, Jacob said that he had never been diagnosed with or treated for PTSD. It is possible, however, that although Jacob presents with symptoms that seem indicative of schizophrenia, he could also being experiencing PTSD based on his military experiences. The medications for schizophrenia and PTSD differ, and if the client does also suffer from PTSD, he might benefit from an antianxiety medication along with his antipsychotics. There is also some concern noted that he is drinking wine with his friends, although he and his father both deny that alcohol or marijuana is a problem. Both say that when Jacob buys wine, his friends generally drink it, not him. Also, Jacob reports the wine could be poisoned; he generally will not eat or drink anything that his mother has not prepared. Therefore, a diagnosis of substance abuse for alcohol and/or marijuana is not warranted at this time.

On Axis II, no diagnosis (V71.09) is recorded since there are no apparent personality disorders, borderline intellectual functioning, or mental retardation present. On Axis III, there are no medical conditions noted, and Jacob has recently had a physical exam that did not reveal any significant results. On Axis IV, the psychosocial stressors include problems with primary support (strained family relations); problems related to the social environment (recent arrest for vagrancy, fighting, and resisting arrest); housing problems (recent eviction); and economic problems (inability to manage disability income). On Axis V, the Global Assessment of Functioning (GAF) rating for current = 35 is noted (See Quick Reference 8.3 for the multiaxial assessment of Jocab).

The assignment of the Axis I diagnosis (schizophrenia, paranoid, chronic) is supported by the long chronic history of positive and negative symptoms. These symptoms have clearly lasted for a period of at least 6 months and have continued for approximately 1 month

---

QUICK REFERENCE 8.3

MULTIAXIAL ASSESSMENT

Axis I:	295.30 Schizophrenia, Paranoid Type, Chronic.
	309.8l Posttraumatic Stress Disorder, Provisional.
Axis II:	No diagnosis.
Axis III:	No diagnosis.
Axis IV:	Problems with primary support.
	Strained family relations.
	Problems related to the social environment.
	Recent arrest for vagrancy, fighting, and resisting arrest.
	Housing problems.
	Recent eviction.
	Economic problems.
	Inability to manage disability income.
Axis V:	GAF = 35 (current).

unless Jacob was given antipsychotic medication (APA, 2000).

In terms of addressing Jacob's symptoms, his condition seemed consistent with four negative symptoms that are important for determining and influencing the intervention process (Woo & Keatinge, 2009). The first consideration is that Jacob appears to be suffering from associative disturbances. His associative disturbances were related directly to how he interacts within the environmental context. Very often he is unsure of the best way to relate to others, as evidenced by his behaviors with his new friends. To win their friendship, he would try either to "buy" their allegiance or withdraw from all social contact. He also would not allow his mother or father to touch or hug him and, according to them, would often think nothing of getting up in their faces when he wanted something. After talking with Jacob's family, it is understandable how disturbing these behaviors seem. See Quick Reference 8.4 for a list of the negative symptoms he was displaying. Jacob's behaviors have become so dysfunctional that they clearly disturb his social and occupational functioning and have resulted in his isolation from others within his environmental context.

The second associated feature relative to the assessment of Jacob is related to affective disturbances. Jacob often exhibits unpredictable moods and emotions, and at times he appears to have a splitting of affect. In this type of splitting, Jacob exhibits polarities in showing his emotions. Although his overall mood appears depressed, he can be angry one minute and laughing the next. The incongruence between the emotions

Jacob is exhibiting and the actual situation is very alarming to his family and friends. This unpredictability of actions led to Jacob's immediate hospitalization and his parents' reluctance to let him live with them at their home.

The third associated feature, in addition to associative and affective disturbances, is that Jacob also suffered from autistic-like symptoms, which involve a separation or lack of responsiveness to the reality surrounding him. This makes it difficult to communicate with him and to determine exactly how much he is actually able to comprehend. Jacob's father describes him as being in a world of his own; the father cannot communicate with Jacob or get him to respond appropriately to conversation or requests needed to facilitate his personal care.

Jacob also appeared extremely ambivalent, having a great deal of difficulty in making decisions or adhering to structure in terms of completing his own activities of daily living. He consistently expressed willingness to do something but moments later changed his mind and refused to go somewhere or participate in an activity. For Jacob, simple tasks, such as dressing himself or deciding whether to go outside or not, may be daunting activities. He also repeatedly changed his mind about taking his medicine, getting out of bed, or walking in the yard.

For Jacob, the secondary symptoms included delusions. Jacob had many beliefs that he felt were true despite evidence to the contrary. He was so convinced that "people" were out to get him that this belief clearly disturbed his daily functioning ability. Jacob believed that the

---

QUICK REFERENCE 8.4
GAF SCORE RANGE 40–35

40–35   Some impairment in reality testing or communication (e.g., speech is at times illogical, obscure, or irrelevant) or major impairment in several areas, such as work or school, family relations, judgment, thinking, or mood (e.g., depressed man avoids friends, neglects family, and is unable to work; child frequently beats up younger children, is defiant at home, and is failing at school).

Table 8.1.   Mental Status Description

Presentation	Mental Functioning	Higher-Order Abilities	Thought Form/Content
Appearance: Unkempt	Simple Calculations: Mostly accurate	Judgment: Impulsive	Thought Process: Disorganized and tangential
Mood: Anxious	Serial Sevens: Accurate	Insight: Poor	Delusions: Paranoid Hallucinations: Auditory
Attitude: Guarded	Immediate Memory: Intact	Intelligence: Low to average	
Affect: Blunted/flat Speech: Guarded	Remote Memory: Intact		
Motor Activity: Restless	General Knowledge: Mostly accurate		
Orientation: Fully oriented	Proverb Interpretation: Refused		
	Similarities/Differences: Refused		

police, his family, and his friends were against him and he could never trust any of them, often refusing their efforts to help him. Jacob also appeared to be having auditory hallucinations as evidenced by his talking to himself. He had suffered from what are often referred to as delusions of reference. In this type of paranoid delusional thinking, he was convinced that others were out to get him—even his mother, whom he believed tried to poison him. It is important to differentiate the delusions of reference, so common in schizophrenic conditions, from ideas of reference as experienced in some of the personality disorders. For example, in the schizotypal personality disorder, there is often social withdrawal from family and friends accompanied by ideas of reference.

An idea of reference is different from a delusion of reference in that the idea of reference is much more individualized. An idea of reference often refers to a specific, individual event or item that can be surrounded by magical thinking or involve a certain degree of exaggerated importance. An example of an idea of reference is the client who believes that because his father had a heart attack, he will also have one, regardless of his state of health. However, other areas of the client's life are not affected by such beliefs. This is very different from the more extensive

condition known as schizophrenia, where the client can exhibit delusions of reference. Jacob, in the case example, suffered from delusions of reference where police, family, and friends were all out to get him. Delusions of reference are much more pervasive and affect almost every part of the client's life. (See Table 8.1 for an example of a mental status description.)

Most often medications are used to help clients gain control of this aspect of the illness, and it is important to determine how long Jacob had not been taking his antipsychotic medications. In schizophrenia, it appears that auditory hallucinations (e.g., inaccurately hearing spoken speech or voices) are the most common types experienced by clients, making up almost 70% of all reported hallucinatory symptoms (Hoffman, 2000). This means that Jacob will often struggle with addressing these auditory hallucinations and how the voices relate to what he is experiencing. Jacob did not report being commanded by these voices to engage in certain behaviors, but this area needs further assessment.

When working with clients such as Jacob, it is important to realize that many can experience disturbances in motor behavior, such as bizarre posturing, catalepsy (a state of stupor), and waxy flexibility. For example, in waxy flexibility, a client may appear somewhat rigid and may seem to be stuck in certain positions or stay frozen in these positions for a long period of time. Waxy flexibility and catalepsy are both characterized by a state of continual and unusual muscle tension (Moore & Jefferson, 1997). If you view a client in this state, he or she appears to be stuck, soldered in place, and unable to move on his or her own. This type of behavior can be very frightening to inexperienced mental health practitioners, family, or friends. The bizarre nature of the behavior often results in the client posturing and being unable to respond. This can cause family members to withdraw support from the client. Therefore, if this does occur in a client being served, it is essential to educate the client, his or her family, and professionals about the condition of schizophrenia, the possible signs and symptoms, and the interventions that work best to address them.

For Jacob and so many other individuals who suffer from schizophrenia, the symptoms tend to be so arbitrary and susceptible to change that the course of the illness can remain unpredictable. The mental health practitioner must be aware of current and past symptoms and anticipate changes in symptoms that may develop during the intervention process as well as in the future course of the illness. This understanding of schizophrenia becomes particularly important when gaining an increased knowledge about the disease process and the mechanisms that lead to development of difficulties (Flaum, 1995).

TREATMENT PLANNING AND INTERVENTION STRATEGY

A complete treatment plan with Jacob's goals and objectives is addressed in Quick Reference 8.5. With the information gathered during the diagnostic assessment as the basis of treatment, the intervention plan allows for application. As part of the intervention process, problem behaviors must be clearly identified and related directly to the stated goals and objectives. Treatment should be provided in a continuum of care that allows flexible application of modalities based on a cohesive treatment plan. In developing the treatment plan for Jacob, it is important for the practitioner to gather a comprehensive history, which includes information about medical conditions. Since Jacob has difficulty recalling his treatment history, supplemental information is needed from family and others in his immediate support system. Information about whether Jacob has had a recent medical exam is important, especially since he does not appear motivated for self-care. It is not known whether he is eating and sleeping; Jacob's overall nutritional status is questionable. In addition, a referral for a blood test should be considered to detect use or abuse of drugs or hormonal problems.

In schizophrenia, planned and early intervention can offer the client a better chance for considerable improvement. Often intervention with individuals diagnosed with this mental

---

QUICK REFERENCE 8.5

Jacob's Identified Goals

To help John stabilize with a plan that allows him to return to the most appropriate and least restrictive environment possible.

Objectives:

- To help Jacob reduce his feelings of agitation and paranoia.
- To help Jacob get control of his behaviors and activities of daily living (ADL).
- To help Jacob find an appropriate place to live upon discharge.

disorder requires a comprehensive approach that will primarily combine individual therapy, case management, family supports, and medication management.

Acute Treatment Plan and Intervention

To best assist a client diagnosed with schizophrenia, two treatment plans are recommended. The first is an acute care plan, and the second is to assist with transitional or continued care needs of the client. In the acute care plan, the primary goal is stabilization. The initial acute care plan will serve as the transitional plan for the client when he or she is discharged. Some type of long-term supervised care or community case management to assist the client with necessary linkages for successful return to the community should follow this. At discharge, the decrease in or elimination of the client's agitation, paranoia, and incoherence needs to be documented. Also, as the client stabilizes (before discharge), the mental health practitioner will need to meet with the client to discuss his or her discharge plans and to plan the transition care part of the treatment plan (see Sample Treatment Plans 8.1 and 8.2).

SAMPLE TREATMENT PLAN 8.1

SAMPLE ACUTE CARE GOALS AND INTERVENTION PROVIDED

Goal:

To stabilize Jacob and discharge him to the least restrictive environment.

Objectives:

- To help Jacob reduce agitation and paranoia.
- To help Jacob get control of his behaviors and activities of daily living (ADL).
- To help Jacob find an appropriate place to live upon discharge.

Treatment Provided:

- Psychiatric evaluation and consultation.
- Prescribed medication and monitoring for mental status and side effects. Nursing assessment and ongoing nursing care.
- Contacts with clinician for counseling.
- Participation in therapeutic and psychoeducational group meetings as scheduled.
- Observation and, as needed, other care by the treatment team.

Sample Application of Acute Plan:

- Medication compliance.
  Objective: Monitor and evaluate medication effectiveness, side effects, and compliance and report observations to social worker once a month.
- Stabilization of schizophrenia.
  Objective: As client moves up the levels in the program, he will take progressively more responsibility for making sure that he takes his medication.
- Linkage with community resources.
  Objective: During the next month, the client will phone a self-help group for schizophrenics in the area and inquire about meetings. He will report back to the worker on this task when they meet.

(continued)

- Development of a support system.
  Objective: The client will phone and inquire about a day treatment program run by the facility, and decide if he wants to participate in the program (1-month time frame).
- Education about medications.
  Objective: The client will attend all psychoeducational group meetings at the facility and meet with his social worker once a month for counseling.
  Objective: The client will be prepared to discuss with the worker the above objectives and the progress he has made during the month.

SAMPLE TREATMENT PLAN 8.2

TREATMENT PLAN DEVELOPMENT TOPIC: SCHIZOPHRENIA

Definition: Two or more characteristic symptoms (delusions, hallucinations, disorganized speech, grossly disorganized or catatonic behavior, or negative symptoms) that persist for at least 6 months, 1 month of which must include the characteristic symptoms, and the person must experience a decline in two or more areas of functioning. Symptoms may not be associated with a general medical condition, schizoaffective, mood disorder, substance abuse, or withdrawal. If a pervasive developmental disorder exists, a diagnosis of schizophrenia can be made only if the symptoms are prominent and are present for at least 1 month (and last over 6 months).

Signs and Symptoms:

- Delusions.
- Hallucinations.
- Disorganized speech.
- Disorganized behavior.
- Catatonic behavior.
- Negative symptoms (flatted affect, alogia, avolition).
- One or more areas of functioning are disturbed (self-care activities, work, social, and academic).
- Persists continuously for 6 months (can shift between symptoms).
- At least 1 month of symptoms from Criterion A (delusions, hallucinations, etc.).
- Inappropriate affect.

Goals:

1. Client will not pose danger to self or others.
2. Client will independently perform self-care activities.
3. Client will maintain prescribed medication regimen after discharge.
4. Client will increase adaptive functioning.

Objectives	Interventions
1. Client will not exhibit symptoms of psychosis (hallucinations and delusions), as measured by observations of psychiatric staff and self-reports by client, during the course of treatment and after release.	Psychiatric staff to record behaviors associated with hallucinations or delusions in chart every day.

(continued)

SAMPLE TREATMENT PLAN 8.2 (*Continued*)

Objectives	Interventions
2. Client will increase cooperation (with taking prescribed medications) from zero compliance before hospitalization (self and family reported) to full cooperation (taking medications as prescribed), as reported by hospital staff in client's chart.	Client will take his medication as prescribed each day.
3. Client will increase his performance of self-care activities from 0 per day to 5 per day, as measured by staff behavior count, by the end of treatment.	Clinician to contract with client specific self-care behaviors to be learned and performed daily. Clinician to apply a cognitive-behavioral approach to teach/ train client to perform self-care activities (teeth-brushing, combing hair, bathing, dressing, etc.) Clinician will work with client and family of client to reinforce, maintain, and expand on self-care activities when released from the hospital.
4. Client will maintain taking prescribed meds after discharge, as evidenced by record of full compliance in case management record and family reports (indefinitely).	Case manager will monitor client's compliance with medication protocol through 2 times/week contact with client and family members.
5. Client to increase social functioning from a score of 15 at pretest to a score of 55 by the end of treatment on the Social Adjustment Scale for Self-Report (SAS-SR).	Client will receive positive reinforcement from family members and clinician for behaving in a socially positive way. Client will participate in at least 12 weeks of social skills classes.
6. Client's family members will increase in adaptive functioning, as measured by a score of 55 to a posttest score of 250 by the end of treatment on the Social Behavior and Adjustment Scale (SBAS).	Client's family will participate in a 6-week educational program about schizophrenia. Client's family will network with other families who share similar stressors.
7. Family of client will increase existing household income by $500/month through SS Disability to help care for client in the home, within 6 months.	Family of client will be assisted in filing for SS Disability for client's special needs.

Transition Care Treatment Planning and Strategy

With his permission, while Jacob was still hospitalized, the mental health practitioner began to make telephone calls to family members and various assisted living facilities. After an honest and comprehensive presentation of Jacob's case with the potential representative of the services, Jacob was accepted into a community-based program provided by the mental health center in his area. This program offered a stepwise approach designed to assist individuals with chronic mental health problems, allowing the client to return to the community. In this program, clients such as Jacob start out in a more restrictive atmosphere and go through stages of training that allow for less restrictive facilities until they end up in apartments, either alone or with a roommate, operated by the center. If Jacob fails to meet the goals for a particular level of care, he will remain at the highest level that he can achieve until he is ready to progress further. It is highly recommended that the client and his family make arrangements to visit the program. Jacob's father agreed to visit him and to lend support while Jacob is in the program.

Chronic Care Treatment Planning and Strategy

Treatment planning for people with schizophrenia will require a combination of medication, psychosocial intervention, and the development of adequate social support (Grohol, 2006). Bola (2006) suggests, however, that before immediately starting a course of medication therapy, especially in acute early-episode psychotic disorders such as schizophrenia, developing and implementing a psychosocial treatment might provide a safe alternative to medication intervention. When the disorder progresses and the client needs more supervised placement, other facilities that offer more supportive and intensive levels of care may need to be considered. When a client is placed in these more restrictive residential settings, it is expected that a case manager will monitor the client once a month. By the time that the client is on the last level, the case manager will be helping only with minimal problems, such as medication monitoring and facilitating community linkage. If Jacob's medication compliance was still a problem, an injectable medication with a longer-lasting effect would be suggested. In addition, medication monitoring would include suggesting adjustments or changes if the client was not receiving the desired effect. The client would be monitored for medication-related conditions, such as tardive dyskinesia, as well as side effects, such as dystonia and akathisia. If these conditions were present, newer antipsychotic medications would be considered and an evaluation for PTSD would be recommended. A referral to attend Alcoholic Anonymous (AA) or Narcotics Anonymous (NA) may also be considered if the drinking or substance use becomes increasing problematic. Continual assessment for suicidal thoughts and ideation will need to be conducted. Although this was not a direct consideration in this case, suicide is the leading cause of death in schizophrenia (Walker et al., 2008). The media provides a disservice when they present mentally-ill persons as dangerous individuals; in reality, people without such illnesses commit 95% of all homicides (Ferriman, 2000). Those with schizophrenia are more likely to harm themselves than someone else. Furthermore, it is possible that this tendency to harm themselves rests with the guilt many clients feel for the burdens they put on their family, as many clients blame themselves for their illness. The negative portrayal by the media has only recently started to change (Frese, Knight, & Saks, 2009).

Generally, the individual treatment provided for people who suffer from schizophrenia is supportive in nature. Other methods, however, are being tried and explored. For example, Lukoff (2007) advocates a spiritually focused recovery model. This empowers persons with schizophrenia to manage their own rehabilitation plan and attempts to achieve their treatment goals. Other programs have focused on intensive treatment milieus with minimal use of medications (Bola & Mosher, 2002; Calton & Spandler, 2009; Ciompi & Hoffman, 2004). The Soteria program sponsored two programs in the United States (Bola & Mosher, 2002) and one program in Switzerland (Ciompi & Hoffman, 2004) with significant results at the 2-year follow-up. Participants in the Soteria program demonstrated significant improvement in global psychopathology; combination outcomes including social functioning, employment, independent living; and fewer readmissions to inpatient settings when compared with the control group (Bola & Moser, 2003).

Other alternative therapies suggested to treat schizophrenia include acupuncture, magnetic field therapy, naturopathic medicine, sound therapy, and traditional Chinese medicine (Chopra, 1994). In addition to those of Lukoff (2007), other approaches to the treatment of schizophrenia incorporate spirituality and religion in treatment (Huguelet, Mohr, & Borras, 2009). An aspect of spirituality and religion includes the cultural lens through which clients understand illness or disease, and the way the client responds often follows this cultural expectation. None of the alternative therapy methods described should be attempted without the supervision and specification of a licensed health practitioner.

Family and Support Systems

Special attention and emphasis should always be given to building the client's family and community support systems. Schizophrenia is a disease that can cause its victims to feel lonely and isolated, and due to its unpredictable course, this chronic illness can manifest behaviors that alienate family and friends. It is important to ensure that the family does not burn out or withdraw support from the client. Support groups can help the family members to see that they are not alone and that others are also struggling. In addition, family members need to be educated that the condition of schizophrenia is real and that their loved one is not just making it up to gain attention. Learning to identify the unusual behaviors associated with this condition may help family members to better understand and accept their loved one's behaviors (NIMH, 2009d). In addition, myths about schizophrenia in which persons with this illness are portrayed as menacing figures also need to be addressed because these depictions are often violent and may lead to the belief that all individuals suffering from schizophrenia are violent (Long, 2000). One factor that is associated with violence among persons diagnosed with schizophrenia is substance abuse comorbidity; however, the risk factor for those with substance abuse comorbidity is similar to the substance-abusing population who are not diagnosed with psychosis (Fazel et al., 2009: Tracker, 2009).

Family members must also be encouraged to remain part of the support system, and strategies need to be used to keep the family involved (e.g., case management support, community residential placement). Most of the therapeutic interventions used with individuals suffering from schizophrenia are intended to be supportive in nature. For instance, in the case of Jacob, most of the practitioner's goals, for example, were directed toward helping him to develop and sustain his social support system. Supportive therapy may provide the client with friendship and encouragement; it may also give the client practical advice about how to access community resources, information on how to develop a more active social life, vocational counseling, suggestions for minimizing friction with family members, and, above all, hope that his or her life circumstance will improve (Long, 2000).

Medication as a Treatment Modality

Over the years, the treatment for the individual who has suffered from schizophrenia has involved primarily supportive therapy, family and community supports, and psychopharmacology. In schizophrenia, the mystery surrounding what the disease entails has led to its being treated by trial and error with a variety of supposed remedies that can assist to control behaviors and alter body states (Lehmann & Ban, 1997). For the most part, medications often used as the primary treatment modality for individuals that suffer from schizophrenia focus on controlling symptoms.

Older Typical Neuroleptic Medications

The primary medications used for this condition were first introduced in 1952, with one of the first documented cases being how the medication chlorpromazine (Thorazine) was used accidently as an antipsychotic (neuroleptic) medication (Bishara & Taylor, 2009). This medication is a combination of narcotic, sedative, and hypnotic drugs and was used with a client suffering from schizophrenia in Paris (Lehmann & Ban, 1997). Often referred to as the typical antipsychotic medications, this older group of drugs was labeled neuroleptics because of the side effects that affect the nervous system.

QUICK REFERENCE 8.6

OLDER OR TYPICAL ANTIPSYCHOTIC MEDICATIONS IN SCHIZOPHRENIA

MEDICATIONS USED WITH THE PSYCHOTIC DISORDERS

Antipsychotic Drugs (Neuroleptic Drugs):

Used to treat severe psychotic disorders (i.e., schizophrenia). Generally, symptoms include: hallucinations, delusions, psychotic behaviors, and a depressed flat affect. Peak concentrations occur between 2 and 4 hours. Generally, two antipsychotic medications are not prescribed at the same time. After discharge, wait aprroximately 3 to 6 months before considering changing the medication to ensure that the client has gotten the full affect.

Old or Typical Antipsychotic Medications:

Chlorpromazine/Thorazine

Thioridazine/Mellaril

Trifluoperazine/Stelazine

Phenazine/Prolixin

Haloperidol/Haldol

Loxapine/Loxitane

Thiothixene/Navane

Chlorpromazine (Thorazine) was followed by the development of other neuroleptics such as trifluoperazine (Stelazine), haloperidol (Haldol), fluphenazine (Prolixin), thiothixene (Navane), and thioridazine (Mellaril) (WebMD, 2009b). Being the first medications introduced in this area, these traditional or typical antipsychotics became the state of practice. These medications worked directly as dopamine inhibitors that block other neurotransmitters, including acetylcholine, histamine, and norepinephrine. After 30-plus years of use, this group of older neuroleptic drugs started to fall from favor and today is no longer considered the first line of treatment for schizophrenia and the psychotic disorders. The primary reason that these medications lost their favor within the medical community was because of complicated side effect profiles and the feelings of tiredness. These pervasive side effects often disturbed client performance, motivation or emotional responsiveness (WebMD, 2009b). (See Quick Reference 8.6 for a list of some of these older antipsychotic medications.)

Extrapyramidal symptoms (EPS), which affect the motor system, are a common side effect with these medications. *Dystonia,* characterized by sudden and painful muscle stiffness (National Alliance on Mental Illness [NAMI], 2003), may present as grimacing, difficulty with speech or swallowing, oculogyric crisis (upward rotation of the eyeballs), muscle spasms of the neck and throat, and extensor rigidity of the back muscles (Carpenter, Conley, & Buchanan, 1998). These reactions will often occur within the first few days of treatment. *Akathisia* is less obvious than dystonia, although it is the most common form of EPS. Akathisia is an extreme form of motor restlessness that may be mistaken for agitation (NAMI, 2003). The individual feels

QUICK REFERENCE 8.7

GENERAL SIDE EFFECTS, CONDITIONS, AND MEDICATIONS TO CONTROL THE SIDE EFFECTS WITH TYPICAL ANTIPSYCHOTIC MEDICATIONS

General Side Effects with Antipsychotic Medications:

Most common side effect is drowsiness or sleepiness.

General Conditions Related to Medication Use:

Parkinsonian or extrapyramidal (EPS) side effects include:

Dystonia—Acute contractions of the tongue (stiff or thick tongue).

Akathisia—Most common form of EPS (e.g., inner restlessness).

Tardive Dyskinesia:

A permanent neurological condition that can result from using the older antipsychotic medications and not taking anything to help control the EPS side effects.

Some Anti-Parkinsonian Medications Used to Decrease EPS Side Effects:

Benzotripine/Cogentin

Biperiden/Akineton

Trihexyphenidyl/Artane

Diphenhydramine/Benadryl

---

compelled to a constant state of movement, and many times clients will report an "inner restlessness" evidenced by a shaking leg or constant pacing. During assessment, these clients cannot sit still and often exhibit restless legs or uncontrollable foot tapping.

Another form of EPS, which results from long-term treatment with these older antipsychotic medications, is a condition called tardive dyskinesia (TD). This condition involves pronounced involuntary movements of any group of muscles, most commonly the mouth and tongue (NIMH, 2009f). This syndrome generally occurs with elderly individuals, especially women (NIMH, 2009d). TD is a negative consequence of taking long-term conventional antipsychotic medications, with intervention duration being

the primary developmental factor (Carpenter, Conley, & Buchanan, 1998). Awareness of the development of TD is particularly important because preventing it is far more desirable than treating it, as it can be nonreversible (NAMI, 2003). One way to address this issue is to prescribe the medication in lower doses, but for chronic schizophrenia, this may not be an option. (See Quick Reference 8.7 for a list of the general conditions and side effects related to the use of these older, typical antipsychotic medications.)

These typical, older antipsychotics tend to have a high potential for developing EPS side effects (Lambert, 1998). The medications often prescribed to decrease or control movement-related side effects are referred to as *anti-Parkinson medications*. When a client is receiving

QUICK REFERENCE 8.8

SELECTED ANTI-PARKINSON MEDICATIONS

Brand Name (Generic Name)

Cogentin (benztropine)

Akineton (biperiden)

Benadryl (diphenhydramine)

Artane (trihexyphenidyl)

Newer Atypical Neuroleptic Medications: The oldest medication in this category is known by the brand name Clozaril (clozapine). Relative to documented deaths being attributed to infections secondary to clozapine-induced agranulocytosis, this medication was at one time withdrawn from unrestricted use (Davis & Casper, 1977). This unfortunate side effect caused a severe reduction in the number of granulocytes, a type of white blood cell. Without these granulocytes, the body is unable to fight life-threatening infections. Today, when this medication is used, strict monitoring is required to be sure this condition does not develop. Therefore, this medication is primarily used for treatment-resistant schizophrenia and this strict monitoring of blood levels is required since the Food and Drug Administration (FDA) approved it for use in the United States in 1990 (NIMH, 2009). Other atypical antipsychotic medications that soon followed included Risperidone (Risperdal), Olanzapine (Zyprexa), Quetiapine (Seroquel), Ziprasidone (Geodon), Aripiprazole (Abilify) and Paliperidone (Invega).

a traditional or typical antipsychotic medicine, it is essential to determine if other medication has been prescribed to assist and counter the side effects that might result. (The medications often used to avoid these types of side effect profiles are listed in Quick Reference 8.8.) Special care should be noted as some of these consumers might consider selling these medications on the streets. This is particularly true for benztropine and trihexyphenidyl, which may have a high potential for abuse on the streets. When the potential for abuse is suspected, it is always best for the practitioner to share this information with the treatment team or with the prescriber and consider an over-the-counter medication, such as diphenhydramine, to help control the symptoms of EPS.

The 1990s saw the development of several new drugs to treat schizophrenia and other psychotic disorders. These are known as atypical or nontraditional antipsychotic medications (NIMH, 2009d). These medications have gained popularity because they appeared to have lower side effect profiles when compared to the traditional antipsychotic medications. Popularity increased rapidly as they clearly were able to help consumers feel less sleepy while assisting with thought clarity and interpreting emotion more accurately (Lambert, 1998). For these reasons, they are often used as the first line of treatment (See Quick Reference 8.9 for list of newer atypical medications.)

Risperidone (Risperdal) was introduced as one of the first official atypical antipsychotic medications in 1992 (Schulz, 2000). In studies, risperidone seemed more effective in reducing positive and negative symptoms than older, more traditional medications such as Haldol (Armenteros, 1997). Risperidone has been used with schizotypal personality disorder to decrease the

---

QUICK REFERENCE 8.9

Newer or Atypical Antipsychotic Medications

Clozapine/Clozaril*

Risperdone/Risperdal

Olanzapine/Zyprexa

Risperidone (Risperdal)

Olanzapine (Zyprexa)

Quetiapine (Seroquel)

Ziprasidone (Geodon)

Aripiprazole (Abilify)

Paliperidone (Invega)

---

* Side effect for Clozaril is agranulocytosis, which affects white blood cells and requires weekly monitoring.

---

psychotic-like, or positive, symptoms of the condition as well as negative symptoms, such as cognitive impairment (Saklad, 2000). Another atypical antipsychotic, olanzapine (Zyprexa), appears to be well tolerated and readily accepted by clients, especially because of its low incidence of EPS and its ability to address the negative symptoms of schizophrenia when given at higher doses. All practitioners should be aware, however, that olanzapine and any of the other newer atypicals may increase blood glucose levels in individuals with diabetes (Physicians Desk Reference, 2009). Quetiapine (Seroquel) is an atypical antipsychotic medication that was introduced in the United States in 1998. It has fewer side effects than some of the other antipsychotic medications but does cause considerable sedation in the early stages of treatment (Schulz, 2000). Newer atypicals include ziprasidone (Geodon), aripiprazole (Abilify), and paliperidone (Invega). Two additional medications in this area approved by the FDA in 2009 are iloperidone (Fanapt) and asenapine (Saphris)

(Drugs.com, 2009a). The side effects associated with iloperidone include dizziness, dry mouth, fatigue, nasal congestion, a sudden decrease in blood pressure (orthostatic hypotension), sleepiness, rapid heart rate (tachycardia), and weight increase. The side effects for asenapine include the inability to sit "motionless (akathisia), a decrease in oral sensitivity (oral hypoesthesia), and drowsiness (somnolence)" (Drugs.com, 2009a, 2009b).

When using these antipsychotic medications with elderly clients, it is important to note that the FDA has issued a public health advisory regarding an increased incidence of death with elderly individuals who suffer from dementia. Therefore, these medications are no longer prescribed for elderly individuals who have problematic behavioral symptoms and suffer from dementia (NIMH, 2009f).

It is beyond the scope of this chapter to discuss all the medications used to treat the psychotic disorders; for a more comprehensive review, see Dziegielewski (2006, 2010). For the most part, these medications enable people to stabilize symptoms and return to their homes, allowing them to live within their community of origin (WebMD, 2009b).

For mental health practitioners, it is critical to educate clients and their family members that taking these medicines will not result in a "quick fix." Depending on the specific medication, peak concentrations in the system can vary, resulting in varied time periods before therapeutic effects can be detected. Also, the relief gained based on the use of antipsychotic medications does not cure but only helps to control the symptoms. Further, although the side effect profiles associated with these medications show a lower incidence of EPS, there can be other disturbing side effects.

Medications play such an important role in management of psychosis that it is impossible to cover all the newer medications and side effect profiles. Therefore, it is recommended that the reader refer to Dziegielewski (2010), which presents psychopharmacological information to the nonmedically trained practitioner. In addition, companies such as Janssen Pharmaceutics have established programs, such as "Pathways to Change," to offer support and assistance to those diagnosed with psychosis, their families, caregivers, and mental health providers. In these programs, particular attention is given to medication compliance, relapse prevention, remaining in mental health treatment, and return to the community (Easing the Emotional Cost of Schizophrenia, 1997).

SUMMARY AND FUTURE DIRECTIONS

Although great strides are being made in the field of research in understanding the psychotic disorders, particularly schizophrenia, we are only at the forefront of what can be learned. Since 2.5

million Americans have schizophrenia, this mental disorder either directly or indirectly costs taxpayers $65 billion a year, or 2.5 percent of all U.S. health care costs (Walker, 2000). Schizcophrenia and the psychotic disorders present as chronic and disabling illnesses that can separate the individual from reality and treating the symptoms holds little promise for cure. Management of clients suffering from the psychotic disorders generally includes psychopharmacological as well as psychosocial approaches. In addition to these types of treatments, however, a broad array of services may be needed to address housing and social support needs. Furthermore, many clients suffering from psychotic symptoms may only get limited relief. When medication and counseling together are not enough, clients suffering from these disorders are often termed partial responders (Dziegielewski, 2010). Unfortunately, this leaves many individuals who are not helped substantially by the traditional courses of supportive therapy or medication intervention.

In mental health practice, the debate continues as to what constitutes relief or good outcomes for the client who suffers from a psychotic disorder. When treating any of the psychotic disorders, the ultimate goal of intervention is to help the client to be free from the usual debilitating problems that can accompany symptom occurrence. In addition, intervention is designed to help the client feel better and be more productive in dealing with his or her life expectations and tasks. The skills of the mental health practitioner need to be directed toward helping clients to gain some semblance of control over life events and tasks. Furthermore, in addition to improvements in medication use, recent developments in the treatment of psychotic symptoms has led to a sincere interest in using diagnostic information to assist both professionals and family members in understanding these often-devastating conditions. However, despite the advent of new medications and the greater understanding of how these disorders can affect the individual, there is still much to be learned. The role of the mental health practitioner is essential in ensuring that quality of life issues are considered; and their primary duties cannot be focused on how to measure and cut costs (Walker, 2000). In addition, when working with individuals who suffer from any of the psychotic disorders, especially schizophrenia, mental health practitioners are central to confronting the stigma often associated with this illness. Practitioners can help clients and their families avoid the negative stereotypes associated with these psychotic disorders and avoid blame-seeking behavior and misperceptions that the disorder could simply be avoided if there was motivation to change.

CHAPTER 9

Selected Mood Disorders

INTRODUCTION

Families and communities pay a heavy toll when a disorder involving an individual's mood is not recognized and treated. For so many individuals who suffer from these disorders, problems with family relations and support systems are common as well as the potential for suicide. In adults, adolescents, and children who suffer from a mood disorder, legal difficulties can develop along with employment and school difficulties that can have devastating affects on the client, his or her family, and the eventual involvement of the judicial system. Promptly recognizing a mood disorder in children, adolescents, and adults is imperative. Furthermore, no single medicine, treatment, or therapy holds the key to success, and all options should be used to assist this population.

This chapter presents a brief overview of the mood disorders listed in the *Diagnostic and Statistical Manual of Mental Disorders, Fourth Edition, Text Revision* (*DSM-IV-TR*; American Psychiatric Association [APA], 2000) with an overview of the selected unipolar or depressive disorders (major depressive disorder, dysthymic disorder, and depressive disorder not otherwise specified) and the bipolar disorders (bipolar I

disorder, bipolar II disorder, cyclothymic disorder, and bipolar disorder not otherwise specified). In terms of application, specific attention is made to the application of the bipolar disorders concerning adults. In addition, since the diagnosis of bipolar disorder is becoming increasingly more common with children and adolescents, a case example in this area has been included. Discussion of the bipolar disorders from a community and societal perspective identify how critical it is for mental health practitioners to complete a thorough diagnostic assessment, treatment plan, and practice strategy. It is important to identify and effectively treat the mood disorders in adults and children while attempting to reduce the magnitude of disturbances these disorders can have on the individual and his or her support system.

A number of treatment methods exist for mood disorders, and several are discussed throughout this chapter. The focus of this chapter rests on the fact that mood disturbances can be difficult to define and once clarified may still require professionals to realize that not only one method of treatment works for all clients and that it may take several different methods to assist clients with mood disturbances. Making an individualized treatment plan to work with clients is essential in successfully assisting them in improving their functioning in society and enjoying life.

With special thanks for the previous first edition version of this chapter to Shirleyann Amos, Jennifer Loflin, and Karen Simons.

OVERVIEW OF MOOD DISORDERS

According to the *DSM-IV-TR*, several disorders fall into this category. The most prominent characteristic that these entire disorders share in common is that there is a disturbance of mood (APA, 2000). The World Health Organization (WHO) (2009b) reports that today, approximately 121 million people worldwide are affected by depression, and the depressive disorders are the leading cause of disability, constituting 33% of those living with a disability. For the bipolar disorders, it is estimated that 10 million individuals in the United States alone are affected with this illness (Torpy, 2009). For the mental health practitioner, these clients may be seen as especially frustrating to deal with as these complaints (generally somatic in nature) usually result in negative medical work-ups. Addressing these multifaceted disorders gives way to fertile ground for misunderstandings and frustration on the part of both health care providers and the clients served (National Institute of Mental Health [NIMH], 2000). To further complicate this scenario, about 70% of the individuals who have suffered from a mood disorder related to depression once can expect a recurrence (Resnick & Carson, 1996).

In the diagnostic assessment of an individual who suffers from any type of mood disorder, depression is a primary symptom. When clients report the symptoms of depression, however, the lack of clarity and problems in semantics related to defining what the terms such as depression mean can be problematic. Feelings of depression can frequently be overstated or understated, influenced by the definition and normalcy standards set within an individual's unique social and environmental context. For many individuals, depression can mean feeling sad, blue, or down in the dumps; for others, it constitutes clearly established criteria that reflect consistent patterns, signs, and symptoms relative to a mood disorder. Furthermore, some form of depression

(also referred to as dysphoric mood) characteristic of the mood disorders is also present in almost all other mental health conditions, with the only possible exceptions being some forms of mania, schizophrenia, and dementia (Gitlin, 1996).

Therefore, in understanding mood disorders the first step involves becoming aware of the different mood episodes that can characterize these disorders. In the *DSM-IV* and the *DSM-IV-TR*, mood episodes are not considered diagnostic conditions. One simple way to think of these episodes is that they are the basic ingredients or the building blocks for the disorders that follow. (See Quick Reference 9.1 for a description of the mood episodes.) The types of mood episodes that make up the mood disorders are the manic, hypomanic, major depressive, or mixed episodes (APA, 2000).

In a manic episode, the client's mood is persistently elevated expansive, and irritable, but the predominant mood disturbance is irritability, especially when others do not fulfill the client's wishes or meet his or her expectations. Along with elevated mood, the client must also exhibit at least three of these symptoms: increased involvement in goal-related activities or psychomotor agitation, distractibility, pressure of speech, flight of ideas, decreased need for sleep, and inflated self-esteem or grandiosity. Clients in this phase often show little restraint and may exceed the limits on their credit cards, spending extravagantly. They may show little regard for the safety of others and drive recklessly. They may also act indiscriminately, engaging in sexually promiscuous behaviors that might lead to unsafe sexual practices. These expansive symptoms should last for at least one week; the criteria could be less than one week or any time frame when the symptoms are severe enough that there is a need for hospitalization.

In a hypomanic episode, the symptoms initially may appear similar to the manic episode as it involves persistently elevated, expansive, or

---

QUICK REFERENCE 9.1

TYPES OF MOOD EPISODES

Manic episode: Present mood is persistently elevated, irritable, and expansive with severe mood disturbance and that leads to impaired functioning. There must also be at least three of these symptoms: pressured speech, increased psychomotor agitation, flight of ideas, decreased need for sleep, increased involvement in goal-oriented activities, distractibility, inflated self-esteem or grandiosity, and so on. There is also excessive involvement in pleasurable activities, which have the potential for high risk and negative consequences. The time frame for the episode lasts at least 1 week. If hospitalization to control or address behaviors occurs, the 1-week time frame is not needed. Or if there are psychotic features that cause serious impairment.

Hypomanic episode: Similar to manic, but all features and symptoms are less severe although they still interfere with functioning. Criteria for hypomanic include a distinct period of persistently expansive, irritable, elevated mood that lasts at least 4 days but less than 1 week. There must be the presence of at least three symptoms (whereas four symptoms are required if there is [predominantly and irritable mood]). Symptoms include: pressured speech, increased involvement in goal-oriented activities, psychomotor agitation, distractibility, decreased need for sleep, inflated self-esteem or grandiosity. There is also excessive involvement in pleasurable activities, which have the potential for high risk and negative consequences.

Major depressive episode: Depressed mood for at least 2 weeks or a loss of interest or pleasure in nearly all activities and with the lack of pleasure or interest exists at least four additional symptoms experienced by the client almost daily for at least 2 consecutive weeks. Other associate features include: sleeping and appetite disturbances (very common symptoms); decreased energy or fatigue; changes in sleep; changes in psychomotor activity; reduced ability to think, concentrate, or make decisions; feelings of worthlessness or guilt; morbid ideation or suicidal ideation, plans, or attempts; irritable mood; and so on.

Mixed episode: Alternating moods of sadness, irritability, and euphoria that last at least one week and also meet criteria for both manic episode and depressive episode. General symptoms include agitation, appetite dysregulation, insomnia, psychotic features, and suicidal thinking.

Clinical note when depression occurs in children, it is almost always related to agitation and irritable mood rather than sad mood as often occurs in adults.

Source: Summarized criteria from the *Diagnostic and Statistical Manual of Mental Disorders, Fourth Edition, Text Revision.* Copyright 2000 by the American Psychiatric Association.

---

irritable mood. In addition, this period of abnormal mood is accompanied by a minimum of three additional symptoms from a selected list such as nondelusional grandiosity, inflated self-esteem, pressured speech, a flight of ideas, and increased involvement in goal-directed activities or psychomotor agitation (APA, 2000). There is often a decreased need for sleep, where the individual reports trouble either falling or staying asleep. These individuals may take on projects and tasks that keep them very busy, although they may become distracted and not finish the commitments originally made. Similar to the manic episode, during a hypomanic episode the individual also may engage in high-risk behaviors that he or she finds pleasurable while ignoring the potential harmful consequences that may result. Clients often report experiencing a euphoric mood. Although some interactions may involve sarcasm, overall the individuals may appear cheerful. Often while in the hypomanic episode, individuals report feeling self-confident and good.

The time period for this mood episode to last is approximately 4 days, and during this time it is clear that the individual is exhibiting signs that remain uncharacteristic of previous levels of functioning. Individuals experiencing a hypomanic mood episode rarely need to be hospitalized; although the symptoms may impair functioning, marked impairment is not noted. What differentiates the hypomanic episode from the manic episode is the absence of sophisticated and pronounced delusional thinking. Furthermore, individuals experiencing a hypomanic episode also do not show evidence of psychotic features, even though others interacting with them are aware that the behaviors they are exhibiting are uncharacteristic.

The third type of mood episode, the major depressive episode, generally involves five or more signs in addition to the first sign of depressed mood or loss of pleasure and interest which is always needed. The first criterion, considered mandatory for the episode to be assessed, involves a clear loss of interest or pleasure in nearly all activities. Similar to many other mental disorders, the diagnostic criteria of loss of interest must be significant enough to interfere with the client and his or her performing usual activities. In addition, four additional symptoms must be present. Two common symptoms that are generally part of the four required symptoms include appetite and sleep disturbances.

Often individuals suffering from the major depressive episode report having appetite disturbances that occur on almost a daily basis. At times these eating patterns involve consuming too much food, resulting in weight gain (5% of body weight in one month); if they involve eating too little, they may result in weight loss. The weight loss has to be significant, and a specific amount is outlined that is

reflective of this. To facilitate the assessment of this symptom, these questions are suggested: Has the client gained or lost weight recently (focusing on the last month)? If so, how much weight has been lost or gained? The answer to these questions will help the practitioner to determine if the client is suffering from anorexia (eating less) or hyperphagia (overeating [in lay terminology, gluttony]) to cope with the depressive feelings.

A second common symptom is sleep disturbance, either sleeping too much (hypersomnia), or experiencing an inability to sleep or disturbance in sleep patterns (insomnia). To facilitate the assessment of this symptom, these questions are suggested: Is the client sleeping at night? If so, for how long? How does the client feel when he or she wakes up? Does he or she report feeling refreshed? Disturbances in eating and sleeping common in this disorder are often assessed first. Symptoms such as eating and sleeping are considered basic for survival. Therefore, when referring specifically to insomnia and the loss of appetite, the term used to describe these symptoms are *vegetative*. When it involves oversleeping (hypersomnia) and overeating (hyperphagia), this is referred to as *reversed vegetative symptoms*.

Other signs and symptoms include: daily bouts of depressed mood; markedly diminished interest or pleasure in activities that usually are pleasurable (anhedonia); psychomotor agitation or changes in psychomotor activity; agitation or retardation nearly every day; fatigue or loss of energy; feelings of worthlessness or guilt; difficulty thinking, concentrating, or making decisions; and other related symptoms. Furthermore, it is not uncommon for individuals experiencing these symptoms to consider suicide and experience recurrent thoughts of death (morbid ideation) or suicidal ideation, plans, or attempts. In addition, as with all diagnoses, the symptoms experienced must be significant enough to impair occupational and social functioning and in this case last for a period of at least 2 weeks and involve the expectation of depressed mood or loss of interest or pleasure.

The last type of mood episode is referred to as the mixed episode that needs to occur nearly every day for at least a 1-week period. The mixed episode generally meets the criteria for the manic and the depressive episodes along with the individual experiencing rapidly alternating moods such as sadness, irritability, and euphoria (APA, 2000). Symptoms present include agitation, psychotic features, appetite disturbance, and insomnia. When suicidal thoughts and intent are present, these symptoms should always be assessed. In the mixed episode, as in the other episodes, the symptoms must be severe enough to cause impairments in social and occupational functioning or require hospitalization.

Although it is beyond the scope of this chapter to discuss all the signs and characteristic symptoms of all the mood disorders, the societal context and a brief overview of the most common ones are presented.

CLINICAL DEPRESSION AND THE UNIPOLAR DISORDERS

For many mental health practitioners, clients who report symptoms of depression are commonplace. When these feelings become pervasive and disturb almost every aspect of functioning, clinically depressed mood is noted. In this type of depressive symptomology, an individual's basic needs are affected, including disturbances in sleeping and eating, loss of interest or pleasure in previously satisfying situations and activities, feelings of guilt, low self-worth, and poor concentration and depressed mood. The term unipolar is used to identify the specific mental health conditions that are characterized by occurrences of depressed mood.

According to the World Health Organization (WHO, 2009b), 120 million people are suffering from unipolar depression. Nearly 30 million of the U.S. adult population are affected with major depression, with one-third of those classified as severely depressed (Nemeroff, 2007). Furthermore, it is estimated that approximately 16% of the population will suffer from depression at some point in their lives (Capriotti, 2006; Hansen, Gartlehner, Lohr, Gaynes, & Carey, 2005). When depression is linked to suicide, it becomes a tragic fatality that results in approximately 850,000 lives lost each year (WHO, 2009b).

In terms of prevalence, children are often affected; it is estimated that 2% to 6% of children and adolescents suffer from depression (Whittington et al., 2004). About 25% of people over the age of 65 with a chronic medical illness suffer from depressive symptoms and approximately 15% suffer from major depressive disorder (Sheikh et al., 2004). These symptoms are reported so frequently during routine medical visits and throughout the course of psychological treatment that they can seem like the common cold of mental health. Reports of depressive symptoms in older adults range from 10% to 25% in community and primary care settings to 50% in nursing homes and medical settings (Skultety & Zeiss, 2006). Treatment for unipolar illness is lacking. According to WHO (2009b), fewer than 25% of those suffering from severe depressive symptoms will have proper access to care. Of the clients who seek treatment to address their depression, it is further noted that 50% to 80% go unrecognized or misdiagnosed (Higgins, 1994). Unfortunately, about 70% of the individuals who have suffered from depression once can expect to suffer from it again (Resnick & Carson, 1996).

THE DEPRESSIVE DISORDERS AND THE DIAGNOSTIC ASSESSMENT

The clinical picture for depression can be somewhat complicated as at times some people report both manic and depressive symptoms. This subjectivity in reporting makes determining a clear, succinct diagnosis of unipolar disorder challenging. Further, in cases where symptoms seem to fluctuate between the highs and lows, mood bipolarity rather than a unipolar disorder should be considered. When the reported symptoms are clear and depressed mood is the only sign noted, the diagnosis of a unipolar disorder seems most appropriate.

Undetected depression in primary care settings ranges from approximately 30% to 70%; of those whose depression is detected, less than 50% receive adequate treatment (Liu et al., 2006). Yet depression is a common problem. Research has indicated the rate of depression to be 5% to 10% for patients with multiple health-care issues in primary care and 10% to 14% for patients under general hospital care (Timonen & Liukkonen, 2008). When looking specifically at race, it appears African Americans are one-third less likely to receive medication treatment for depression and anxiety than Caucasian Americans (Gonzalez et al., 2008). Furthermore, when working specifically with males, depressive symptoms can be masked in angry responses, and depression may be assessed as less severe although serious deficits in functioning may exist.

Problems With Self-Reporting of Symptoms

One reason this lack of proper assessment of symptoms is so problematic rests in the symptoms that clients self-report. Much of what we know about a client suffering from depression—or any mental health condition, for that matter—comes from self-report. How the client interprets and reports the symptoms being experienced can be misleading because feelings of depression often are overstated or understated. The client's subjective experience is being reported; this interpretation will need to be combined to reflect the definition and standards of normalcy within an individual's unique social and environmental context.

The symptom of *anhedonia,* which indicates a complete loss of pleasure in all activities, may be another factor that affects self-report. Anhedonia clearly affects how events and symptoms are perceived and expressed. Since often depressed individuals maintain some capacity of experiencing pleasure (Woo & Keatinge, 2008), the degree to which this impression affects self-report can be variable. Therefore, the reporting of symptoms can be confusing: Is the individual feeling pleasure from certain activities or not? Is he reporting what he is feeling now or what he remembers feeling in the past? Therefore, the first step toward effective treatment is identifying a clear, concise, psychosocial criteria-based diagnostic standard.

The influence of life factors on self-report cannot be overestimated. Reported symptoms are always influenced by many factors, including current or past relationship problems, irritability with the situation, and work-related conflicts. All diagnostic interpretations must be sensitive to the influence of cultural and stress-related environmental and social factors. Some ethnic minority groups are exposed to tremendous contextual stressors that figure prominently in depression, including poverty, poor and rundown neighborhoods, acculturation, and loss associated with "never going home again" (White, Roosa, Weaver, & Nair, 2009). Similarly, the social context needs to be assessed when working with immigrants, as their depressive symptoms may stem from a conflict of values from their country of origin and American customs and values, problems speaking the English language, parenting stress, and conflict between children's and parents' beliefs and customs.

Therefore, in assessing depression, it is important to consider not only what symptoms a client reports but also cultural influences and complexities relative to the client's cultural identity (McGoldrick, Giordano, & Garcia-Preto, 2005). McGoldrick and colleagues point out that ethnicity is not the only dimension of culture but that it is a necessary component in understanding an immigrant's adjustment to his or her new life and the losses experienced to get there. Social workers must also be willing to consider how gender, socioeconomic status, social class, geography, race, religion, and politics influence that adjustment; how important these factors are in accurately assessing depression; and how to best use a client-oriented support system as part of the treatment process.

Clients suffering from depression can also become frustrated with medial providers because the complaints reported are somatic in nature and no physical causes are revealed. In turn, providers can also be frustrated because, after completion of a medical examination, no physical causes for the problem are revealed. In research on the opinions of general practitioners, Krupinski and Tiller (2001) discovered that assessment was limited to a specific set of symptoms. These symptoms included sleep disturbances, insomnia, early wakening, loss of appetite, overeating, weight changes, depressed mood, hopelessness, and sad and gloomy feelings.

In addition to problems with the subjectivity of reporting by clients and negative medical findings is lack of clarity in identifying the condition of depression. For many individuals, depression can mean feeling sad, blue, or down in the dumps. From a professional perspective, however, there must be clearly established criteria that reflect consistent patterns, signs, and symptoms relative to the mood disorder. This is further complicated by the simple fact that some form of depression (also referred to as *dysphoric mood*) is present in virtually all mental health conditions with few exceptions (mania, hypomania, and certain forms of schizophrenia and dementia). For these reasons, it is recommended that enhancing self-report requires gathering clear, concise, psychosocial criteria-

based diagnostic standards as well as gathering collateral information and perceptions of significant others, family, coworkers, and friends (Woo & Keatinge, 2008).

ENDOGENOUS AND EXOGENOUS DEPRESSION: MAKING A DISTINCTION

To date, there are two types of serious depression that constitute a severe form of affective illness. The first is often referred to as *endogenous* or *melancholic depression* (Woo & Keatinge, 2008). In this type of major depression, symptoms of depressed mood are related directly to internal biologic factors, such as neurotransmitter dysfunction (Sadock & Sadock, 2008; Tierney, McPhee, & Papadakis, 1997). Individuals who experience this type of depression often report a loss of pleasure in almost all their usual activities and symptoms of severe anhedonia, hopelessness, and inappropriate guilt. Suicidal symptoms may become a concern (Woo & Keatinge, 2008). Electroconvulsive therapy (ECT), referred to historically as shock treatment, is often considered an endogenous treatment. This treatment strategy involves direct (biologic) stimulation of the neurotransmission process. Similar to ECT, antidepressant medications also are successful in lifting endogenous depression; however, they affect the neurochemical pathways chemically rather than electrically (Maxmen, Ward, & Kilgus, 2009).

In the second type of major depression, there is a primary relationship between personal character-related factors or neurotic responses and precipitating events. This form of *exogenous*, or environmental depression is referred to as *reactive depression*, and the signs and symptoms manifested relate directly to life stressors or other psychosocial factors (e.g., divorce, unemployment, or injury) (Tierney, McPhee, &

Papdakis, 1997). Bettmann (2006) conceptualized understanding utilizing attachment theory where, in response to stressors, clients respond by experiencing depression through isolating themselves from social contact. They feel unlovable and unworthy and show this insecurity by withdrawing. When a traumatic experience with loss or grief occurs, these individuals do not know how to reach out to others in their support system. For this reason, Tierney and colleagues (2006) cautioned mental health practitioners to differentiate between normal grief symptoms, which at first resemble major depression, and actual depression symptomatology. They believe grief and sadness are normal responses to loss, whereas severe depression is not. In depression, the survivor feels a marked sense of worthlessness and guilt, but with grief, individual self-esteem remains intact.

There are a variety of symptoms, including anxiety, chronic nervousness, insomnia, agitation, restlessness, and physical symptoms (Capriotti, 2006). This can lead to confusing the signs of depression with anxiety or bipolar disorder. When physical signs mask depression, assessing depressive factors beyond the anxiety and worry and beyond the headaches and the complaints of chronic pain, fatigue, and eating problems may be relevant to the emotions an individual is feeling inside.

Whether depression is *endogenous* (related to internal causes), *exogenous* (related to external or environmental causes), or a combination of both, the first clinical feature usually presented in major depression is *dysphoria* (a disturbance in mood) or *anhedonia* (a loss of pleasure or interest in normally enjoyable activities) (Maxmen, Ward, & Kilgus, 2009). Besides dysphoria or anhedonia, depressed individuals present with a wide range of complaints that include feelings of guilt, the inability to concentrate, feelings of worthlessness, somatic complaints, feelings of anxiety, chronic fatigue, and loss of sexual desire (Woo & Keatinge, 2008).

As with any mental health problem, an accurate diagnosis of major depressive disorder requires clear documentation of the client's cognitive, behavioral, and somatic complaints.

COMPLETING THE DIAGNOSTIC ASSESSMENT FOR THE UNIPOLAR MOOD DISORDERS

The mood episodes identified in the *DSM-IV-TR* that constitute the building blocks of the mood disorders are classified as major depressive, manic, hypoma or mixed, with each episode coinciding to its predominant features. In the depressive disorders, these individuals all experience some degree of depressive symptoms that are characteristic of the depressive episode. In each of the depressive disorders, some level of interpretation related to the criteria relevant to the depressive episode will be noted. (See Quick Reference 9.1, listed in previous section, for a brief description of the depressive episodes.)

Common unipolar or depressive disorders listed in the *DSM-IV-TR* include: major depressive disorder, dysthymic disorder, and depressive disorder not otherwise specified. What these disorders all share in common is depressed mood with subsequent changes in eating, sleeping, and energy levels; impairments in executive function and attention; and changes in self-awareness and perception (APA, 2000). When suffering from a depressed mood, clients often report feeling a loss of interest or pleasure in activities. Difficulty concentrating can lead to problems with performing activities of daily living (ADLs) and making decisions.

Careful attention should be given to assess properly any recurrent thoughts of death or suicide. One rule to remember is that an individual is most likely to harm him- or herself not while in the throws of a depressive episode but rather when the feelings of depression begin to lift. The return of energy gives the client the initiative to act on thoughts and feelings expressed. If there is suicidal ideation, it is critical to watch for the return of energy, as now the client may have the energy to act with intent.

Like almost all the other mental health diagnoses, these unipolar disorders cannot be attributed to a medical condition, substance use disorder, another mood disorder, another mental disorder, or bereavement. To support and substantiate diagnostic categories as described in the *DSM-IV-TR*, mood disorder field trials that investigated the reliability and validity of the diagnostic categories were implemented (Keller et al., 1995; Keller, Hanks, & Klein, 1996). This resulted in research support for the classification system of major depressive disorders.

Major Depressive Disorder

According to the *DSM-IV-TR*, an individual who suffers from major depressive disorder must have either a depressed mood or a loss of interest or pleasure in daily activities consistently for at least a 2-week period (APA, 2000). This must represent a change from the individual's normal mood. It must also affect social, occupational, educational, or other important functioning and the individual must report distress due to this change in mood. This disorder is characterized by depressed mood most of the day, nearly every day. Clients report these symptoms and often state that they are feeling sad, lost, and alone. Often they might appear sad and tearful upon discussion of the simple unassociated events or issues. These individuals report markedly diminished interest or pleasure in all, or almost all activities most of the day, nearly every day. Appetite and weight loss or gain may occur. Guilt and feelings of worthlessness or excessive or inappropriate guilt occur nearly every day with difficulty concentrating.

Similar to the other mental disorders, the depressed mood in this disorder cannot be caused by substances (such as drugs, alcohol, medications) and it cannot be caused by or part of a general medical condition. This diagnosis cannot be given if there is a history of manic, hypomanic, or mixed episodes. It cannot be affected by a bipolar disorder or any of the psychotic disorders. Furthermore, the symptoms cannot be accounted for by bereavement, which can mimic severe depression but is related directly to the death of a loved one.

Diagnosing major depressive disorder and the characteristics found in the major depressive episode involves identifying two or more major depressive episodes, without the presence or history of manic, mixed, or hypomanic episodes and unattributed to schizoaffective disorder or superimposed on schizophrenia, schizophreniform disorder, delusional disorder, or psychotic disorder not otherwise specified.

Several risk factors associated with major depressive disorder include:

- There is a higher risk of developing depression in families where a biological relative also has the disorder.
- Stress-related events can account for 50% of all depression in early life and increases the risk for the development in later life as well (MacPhee & Andrews, 2006).
- Traumatic events can include exposure to combat or terrorist attacks, rape, mugging, robberies and assault, natural disasters, and car accidents, plane crashes, and so on. Experiencing these events increase the risk of developing major depressive disorder as well as the related onset of posttraumatic stress disorder (PTSD) (APA, 2000).

When assessing for major depressive disorder, careful consideration is needed to differentiate the presence of these risk factors.

When documenting major depressive disorder, the *DSM-IV-TR* establishes diagnostic codes. In major depressive disorder (single episode or recurrent), this coding scheme is used:

1. For the diagnosis major depressive disorder, the first three digits are always 296.
   Major Depressive Disorder 296.xx
2. The fourth digit denotes whether it is a single (denoted with the number 2) or recurrent (denoted with a 3) major depressive episode.
   296.2x single/296.3x recurrent
3. The fifth digit indicates the severity.
   - 296.x1 mild severity
   - 296.x2 moderate severity
   - 296.x3 severe without psychotic features
   - 296.x4 severe with psychotic features
   - 296.x5 in partial remission
   - 296.x6 in full remission
   - 296.x0 if unspecified

The other specifiers for major depressive disorder (with melancholic features, with postpartum onset, etc.) cannot be coded within the numbering system. They are to be written out and listed after the official diagnosis. (See Quick Reference 9.2 for list of specifiers used in major depressive disorder.) Most professionals agree that normal life situations and developmental phases can create feelings of sadness or depressed moods in everyone. A depressed mood becomes pathological only when the magnitude or duration of the experience exceeds normal limits, taking into account the precipitating event.

QUICK REFERENCE 9.2

DEPRESSIVE DISORDERS AND SPECIFIERS

SPECIFIERS DESCRIBING MAJOR DEPRESSIVE DISORDER: RECURRENT

1. **Longitudinal:** These specifiers are used to describe remission patterns. The two types include "with full inter-episode recovery" (i.e., full remission was attained between the two most recent episodes) and "without full inter-episode recovery" (i.e., remission was not attained between the two most recent episodes).
2. **Seasonal pattern specifier:** These specifiers link a time of year or season directly to the depressive episode. The term *seasonal affective disorder* (SAD) is often used to describe this type of depression.
3. **With melancholic features:** Loss of pleasure in almost all activities and lack of reactivity to pleasurable stimuli can occur at any time throughout the depressive episodes. In addition, three or more of the following are present: distinct quality of depressed mood, early-morning worsening, marked psychomotor agitation or retardation, disturbance in appetite with weight gain or loss, and excessive and inappropriate guilt.
4. **With atypical features:** Within this specifier, there are incongruent findings to some of the established criteria (e.g., mood brightens when exposed to a pleasant event) or unusual features related to the condition (e.g., overeating, oversleeping, or patterns of hypersubjectivity to rejection).

Source: Summarized criteria from the *Diagnostic and Statistical Manual of Mental Disorders, Fourth Edition, Text Revision.* Copyright 2000 by the American Psychiatric Association.

Dysthymic Disorder

Dysthymic disorder is a depressive mood disorder characterized by a long and chronic course. To receive this disorder, the depressive symptoms must continue to interfere with functioning most of the day, on more days than not, for at least 2 years. According to the *DSM-IV-TR*, this diagnosis is not given if there are any other mood episodes present other than the features present in the depressive episode. If there are hypomanic, manic, or mixed episodes, this diagnosis should not be made. Also, this disorder's depressive symptoms cannot be due to a medical condition, medication, illegal drug, or psychotic disorder. Similar to the major depressive disorder found within the major depressive episode, accompany symptoms include: disturbances in appetite (lack of appetite or overeating) and sleep (insomnia or hypersomnia); low energy or fatigue; low self-esteem; poor concentration; difficulty making decisions; and feelings of hopelessness.

Although the symptoms of dysthymia have traditionally been considered less severe when compared to major depressive disorder, it can still have grave consequences, including severe functional impairment and increased morbidity from physical disease. The same concerns with major depressive disorder are also noted with dysthymic disorder in terms of an increased risk of suicide.

Dysthymia can also occur in children. The mood children display, however, usually differs from that of adults. In children suffering from dysthymic disorder, the mood is often irritable and may appear to be an angry depression. Children and adolescents usually exhibit the symptoms differently from the majority of adults with this disorder. This agitated or angry form of depression often seen in children and adolescents coincides with their own feeling of pessimism, low self-esteem, and poor social skills. When children are sad, agitated, or angry displays of behavior

in can be different from adults. When adults are sad they often appear with blunt or flat affect and may not display agitation. Also, the *DSM-IV-TR* applies different criteria for children with dysthymia where the depressive symptoms exhibited need to have a required minimum duration of only 1 year as opposed to 2 years in adults. In dysthymia this disorder is constant; during the 2-year period (1 year for children or adolescents), symptom-free periods cannot last longer than 2 months. In the adult, occupational and social functioning are impaired, but in the children and adolescents, the primary indicator will be impaired school performance and poor social interaction (APA, 2000).

It is possible that if, in the first 2 years of this disorder, the depressive symptoms intensify and meet the full criteria for the major depressive episode, the diagnosis would be changed to major depressive disorder. Unfortunately, this disorder has a chronic history and if it continues for 2 or more years and then later meets the criteria for a full major depressive episode, the term *double depression* may be applied. In this clinical situation, the diagnosis of both major depressive disorder and dysthymic disorder may be applied. Once the major depressive episode resides, however, and some of the depression-related criteria still remain, a return to the diagnosis of dysthymic disorder will need to be considered. Although it does not meet the criteria for a personality disorder, dysthymia has been referred to as the "mood disorder that can act like a personality disorder" because of its long chronic duration and symptom displays that interfere with functioning.

Depressive Disorder Not Otherwise Specified

Depressive disorder not otherwise specified (NOS) has clusters of symptoms that impair an individual's functioning; however, it does not officially meet the criteria for major depressive disorder, dysthymic disorder, adjustment disorder with depressed mood, or mixed anxiety and depressed mood (APA, 2000). This mental disorder is characteristic of an all-encompassing low mood where the individual also has low self-esteem and loss of interest or pleasure in normally enjoyable activities. According to the *DSM-IV-TR*, two other conditions that need to be considered for symptom exclusion are: brief depressive disorder (lasts only 2 days to 2 weeks) and premenstrual dysphoric disorder (a disorder that involves a depressed mood with anxiety and decreased interest in activities that occurs only during the menstrual cycle beginning in the luteal phase and resolving within a few days after the onset of menses). In addition, the symptoms a client is experiencing cannot be related to a medical condition or other mental disorders, as noted in the *DSM-IV-TR*.

TREATMENT FOR THE UNIPOLAR DISORDERS

Psychopharmacology

When depression is severe and exercise, sleep adjustments, and diet do not seem to be working, treatment guidelines suggest drug therapy is a possibility. Prior to resorting to medication, however, a complete assessment of factors related to levels of exercise, and considerations for achieving restful sleep and controlling diet are always suggested (Dziegielewski, 2010). Once the assessment is complete, medication management is one of the primary treatments for the depressive disorders and the person who responds best to utilizing medication for the treatment of depression is someone who suffers from more than just the blues. A prolonged depressed mood that does not respond to short-term psychotherapy or crisis intervention and that

interferes with a person's family life and mental, physical, job, and social functioning indicates the need for antidepressant medication (Shindul-Rothschild & Rothschild, 1998). Further, most medically trained professionals agree that practice guidelines indicate that when an individual fails to respond to two or more trials on an antidepressant using this as monotherapy (medications alone) or when clients fail to achieve full remission using medications alone, other types of treatment interventions are suggested (Valenstein et al., 2006).

When depression runs in families, particularly for those whose mothers were depressed, or when there is a first-generation family history of major depression, drug therapy is often recommended by the medical community (Goodman & Tully, 2006). Antidepressant medications have resulted in approximately $12 billion in annual sales in the United States (Schatzberg, Cole, & Debattista, 2007). The consensus is that depression has been underdiagnosed and inadequately treated in the United States; it is estimated that fewer than 10% of people suffering from major depression receive an appropriate therapeutic dose of medication (Capriotti, 2006). Before prescribing an antidepressant, the prescriber needs to take into account factors such as drug side effect profiles, the potential for toxicity or overdose, and other client characteristics, such as presentation of symptoms, other medical conditions, and general health and age (Schatzberg, Cole, & Debattista, 2007).

Schatzberg, Cole, and Debattista (2007) suggested that 50% to 65% of patients are expected to respond to any given trial of an antidepressant. However, not all clients will respond to medication. It is estimated that between 29% and 46% of people with major depression fail to respond to antidepressants and half of those who do not respond to the first antidepressant fail to respond to a second (Corya et al., 2006). Antidepressants work by attempting to normalize naturally occurring brain chemicals called neurotransmitters, specifically serotonin and norepinephrine, which are neurotransmitters involved in mental health. Other antidepressants work on the neurotransmitter dopamine (Cheung, Emslie, & Mayes, 2006).

Although classification systems can differ slightly, generally antidepressant drugs can be classified into three major groups: (1) tricyclic antidepressants; (2) monoamine oxidase inhibitors; and (3) newer antidepressants, which include serotonin-selective reuptake inhibitors (SSRIs) and other similar drugs (Brophy, 1991; Tierney, McPhee, & Papdakis, 1997; Woo & Keatinge, 2008). The popularity of these medications, especially the newer generation antidepressants, has risen dramatically, which can be seen in recent sales figures and profits noted by pharmaceutical companies (IMS, 2009).

A multitude of studies have examined the efficacy of antidepressants (Debonnel et al., 2006; Kennedy, Anderson, & Lam, 2005; Segal, Vincent, & Levitt, 2002) and the efficacy of medications on severely depressed individuals (Versiani, Moreno, Ramakers-van Moorsel, & Schutte, 2006). Some studies focus on different age groups, such as the use of antidepressants in elderly persons (Sheikh et al., 2004) and children and adolescents (Cheung, Emslie, & Mayes, 2006; Moreno, Arango, Parellada, Shaffer, & Bird, 2007). Serious concerns have been noted when using these medications (particularly the SSRIs) with children and adolescents. The concerns in this area were so severe that, in 2004, the Food and Drug Administration instructed manufacturers to include "black box warnings" about the risks of suicidal thoughts and behaviors on all antidepressants for children and adolescents and in 2006 extended this warning to include young adults (ages 18–24). For more information on this topic, see Dziegielewski (2010) or Jureidini (2009). Additional studies examined the use

of medications with depressive symptoms in PTSD (Smajkic et al., 2001) and suicidal patients (Simon & Savarino, 2007).

Utilizing psychopharmacological treatment for depression has three major purposes: (1) to treat an acute episode, (2) to prevent a relapse, and (3) to prevent future episodes (Gitlin, 1996). Depression is often marked by recurrence and chronicity (Hirschfeld et al., 1997). A general three-phase framework for understanding the treatment of depression contains these phases: acute, continuation, and maintenance (Hirschfeld et al., 2007). A single client could move through all three phases of treatment under the care of one clinician or three different therapists. In the acute phase, the primary goal is to stabilize symptoms, which could include suicidal ideation, inability to sleep, or other severe symptoms that impair daily functioning. As a rule for practice, when suicidal thoughts are present, a complete assessment and safety plan are always needed and considered the first priority (Seligman & Reichenberg, 2007). At this point, medications such as the SSRIs are used (NIMH, 2009e) (see Quick Reference 9.3).

Once stabilized, the goal in the continuation phase is to sustain the stabilization. At this point psychotherapy is often combined with pharmacological treatment, and cognitive-behavioral therapy is often the treatment of choice (Rude & Bates, 2005; Vidair & Gunlicks-Stoessel, 2009). The maintenance phase is focused on prevention. In maintenance, the goal is to prevent the client from experiencing another depressive episode (Hirschfeld et al., 1997). Therefore, maintenance treatment is synonymous with prevention.

When medication is used as a primary treatment modality in depression, social workers and other mental health practitioners often serve as part of an interdisciplinary team. Understanding the role of medications in treatment and what is realistic for clients to expect in benefit is

---

QUICK REFERENCE 9.3

SELECTIVE SEROTONIN REUPTAKE INHIBITORS

Drug

fluoxetine (Prozac)

paroxetine hydrochloride (Paxil)

sertraline (Zoloft)

fluvoxamine (Luvox)

citalopram (Celexa)

For current dosage information, please see the *Physicians' Desk Reference* (2009).

---

essential. The practitioner often spends the most quality time with clients, increasing the likelihood that he or she may be one of the first team members to become aware of regimen problems, possible side effects, or medication reactions (Dziegielewski, 2010). Simple education concerning realistic expectations about what the medications can do to assist with depressed mood is essential. In youth, for example, it is not uncommon for many to have the expectation that if they do not feel good something is wrong. This expectation allows them to avoid having to deal with uncomfortable feelings that may be a normal part of life experience (Jureidini, 2009). All nonmedically trained practitioners need to understand the antidepressant medications their clients are taking and assist with realistic impressions of what a medication can or should do as well as with compliance issues, pharmacy shopping, side effect profiles, and medication insurance coverage. In addition, they must provide education, information, and support (Dziegielewski, 2006, 2010).

Verbal Therapy Models: Cognitive-Behavioral Therapy

Individuals with depression have internal working models that include cognitive schemas about themselves and the world around them (McBride, Atkinson, Quilty, & Bagby, 2006). The theoretical rationale of using cognitive-behavioral therapy rests with how individuals cognitively structure their view of the world and how their unique patterns of thinking influence their affect and behavior (Hamamci, 2006). In comparing medication to cognitive-behavioral therapy, at 8 weeks patients taking medication had response rates of 50% compared to 43% of individuals who received cognitive-behavioral therapy alone (DeRubeis et al., 2005).

Antidepressant medications also can be used to treat related conditions, such as obsessive-compulsive disorder and symptoms of anxiety while blocking the symptoms of panic and assisting with medical complications, such as rapid heartbeat, terror, dizziness, chest pains, nausea, and breathing problems. What studies seem to support is that cognitive therapy with a highly trained therapist can be very effective over using just medications in moderately and mildly depressed individuals (Seligman & Reichenberg, 2007). Cognitive-behavioral therapy focuses on the interaction of the individual's thoughts, emotions, and behaviors (Rude & Bates, 2005). The primary principles of cognitive therapy are teaching clients how to identify their dysfunctional thoughts and beliefs and how they contribute to their depression (Vidair & Gunlicks-Stoessel, 2009).

Seligman and Reichenberg (2007) reported that individual psychotherapy alone is appropriate for mild to moderate uncomplicated forms of depression while the more severe forms do better utilizing a combination approach of both medication and psychotherapy. Some professionals fear, however, that use of these newer antidepressants will become too familiar and more change-related behaviors such as those related to exercise, sleep and diet will take second place.

Special Topics: Addressing Sexuality

Traditionally, mental health practitioners have used a biopsychosocial approach (Hepworth, Rooney, & Larsen, 2002) to understand the difficulties experienced by clients and to empower them to take charge of their lives and strive for new and improved levels of health and mental health satisfaction and functioning (Dziegielewski, 2004). When treating clients with depression, expanding the biopsychosocial model includes the assessment of sexuality and spirituality.

To assess the impact of depression on sexuality, careful accumulation of data that is likely to affect sexual response is needed. The multitude of factors include: age; marital status; religious beliefs; intimate relationships; socioeconomic status; education level of both partners; nature of the marital relationship; functional ability of the male partner; levels of anxiety; type of anorgasmia (primary versus secondary); and gynecological, physiological, and medical conditions (Dziegielewski, Jacinto, Dick, & Resnick-Cortes, 2007). In assessing depression and sexual functioning, the level of sexual performance prior to the current onset of depression is gathered to determine changes in arousal, desire, or performance. It is important to distinguish between loss of libido versus a sexual disorder. In males, a loss of libido may be attributed to a decrease in testosterone combined

with depression, anxiety, low self-esteem, work-related stress, and relationship problems (Dziegielewski, Turnage, Dick, & Resnick-Cortes, 2007). These combined factors may interact with one another in contributing to a sexual dysfunction; therefore, it is important to determine which came first.

DSM-IV-TR AND THE DEFINITION OF BIPOLAR DISORDERS

Bipolar disorder is a severe, recurrent psychiatric illness characterized by extreme fluctuations in mood with vacillating episodes of major depression and mania (Basco, Ladd, Myers, & Tyler, 2007). Bipolar disorder is often referred to as *manic depression* or *bipolar affective disorder,* and is the second grouping of diagnoses in the mood disorders in the *DSM-IV* and *DSM-IV-TR* (APA, 1994, 2000). According to Leahy (2007), bipolar disorder afflicts 3% to 5% of the U.S. population. What is particularly concerning to mental health professionals is that the rates for completed suicide for persons suffering from bipolar disorder are 60 times higher than in the general population, making bipolar disorder a chronic, devastating, and often underdiagnosed mental health disorder (Leahy, 2007).

When suffering from one of the bipolar disorders, clients can experience recurrent psychiatric episodes with high levels of hospitalization, long-term morbidity, comorbidity, and disability (Baldessarini, Perry, & Pike, 2007). Multitudes of symptoms can occur in quick succession (Farrelly, Dibben, & Hunt, 2006). Despite the availability of psychotropic medications and increased research supporting treatment efficacy, the majority of people with bipolar disorder are not able to maintain long-term remission (Vieta, Suppes, Eggens, et al., 2008). It is estimated that even with good medication maintenance, 75% of people with bipolar disorder relapse within 5 years (Williams et al., 2008). There is an increase in mortality rates and risky behaviors can result in accidents making individuals who suffer from bipolar disorder and the problems they experience a major concern for the health care system (Baldessarini et al., 2007). This is further complicated by the fact that controlling the symptoms can be difficult and those who suffer from the bipolar disorders are responsible for 5% to 15% of new and longer psychiatric hospitalizations (Miasso, Cassiani, & Pedrao, 2008).

In all of the bipolar disorders, individuals suffering from them have at least one or some degree of symptoms related to mania, in contrast to those who suffer from the depressive or unipolar disorders. The episodes, as stated earlier, are classified as depressive, manic, or mixed, coinciding with its predominant features. Even when a client initially presents with only manic symptoms, it is assumed that a bipolar disorder exists and that a depressive episode will eventually occur.

The symptoms of the depressive form of bipolar disorder are usually clinically indistinguishable from those exhibited in the major depressive disorders, although psychomotor retardation and hypersomnia may also occur in the depressed phase of bipolar disorder. The essential difference between the major depressive disorders and the bipolar disorders is that the depressive episodes only have a depressive component (thus the term unipolar) whereas the bipolar disorder has both phases (thus the term bipolar). Manic episodes either immediately precede or immediately follow a depressive episode. In some cases the manic and depressive episodes are separated by intervals of relatively normal functioning (APA, 2000). Harel and Levkovitz (2008) state that "although abnormal mood elevation is the cardinal diagnostic feature that distinguishes bipolar disorder from recurrent major depressive disorder, depression more than mania is the leading cause

of impairment and death among patients" suffering from a bipolar disorder (p. 121).

According to the *DSM-IV-TR*, there are four primary types of bipolar disorders: bipolar I, bipolar II, cyclothymia, and bipolar disorder NOS. (See Quick Reference 9.4 for brief descriptions of each.)

The *DSM-IV-TR* identifies six subgroups of bipolar I disorders. Each of these subgroups include criteria to determine if a client is experiencing a single manic episode and identifying the most recent episode. In addition, there are specifiers that mental health practitioners can use to describe the episode recurrence. Badger and Rand (1998) identify these specifiers as "rapid cycling, which indicates at least four episodes in a year; the presence or absence of inter-episode recovery; and the emergence of a seasonal pattern in the depressed episodes"(p. 83). (See Quick Reference 9.5 for subgroupings.) When working with the bipolar I disorders, it appears that either depressive episodes, manic episodes, or mixed episodes can be involved (Maxmen, Ward, & Kilgus, 2009).

Practitioners should keep in mind that clients with bipolar I disorders frequently report depressive episodes as well as symptoms such as agitation and hyperactivity that often are associated with it. In this condition, a full depressive episode is also reported. Between episodes, 20 to 30% of clients may continue to suffer from labile mood (mood lability or fluctuations) that is significant enough to disturb interpersonal or occupational relations. In some cases, the development of psychotic features may occur. When this happens, subsequent manic episodes are more likely to have psychotic features.

The manic episodes characteristic of bipolar I disorder tend to be extreme, and there is a significant impairment of occupational and social functioning. A person who experiences a manic episode has a marked elevated, euphoric, and expansive mood, frequently interrupted by

QUICK REFERENCE 9.4

DESCRIPTION OF BIPOLAR MOOD DISORDERS

In the bipolar mood disorders, at least one or more manic or hypomanic episodes with a history of depressive symptoms is present.

Bipolar Disorders: Mixed, manic, and depressed.

Bipolar I Disorder: This disorder is considered the most severe and is characterized by one or more manic episodes and also consists of a history of depressive episodes. Psychosis as evidenced by psychotic features may also be present in the manic stage.

Bipolar II Disorder: This disorder is characterized by one or more depressive episodes with at least one hypomanic episode.

Cyclothymic Disorder: This disorder is characterized by a persistent mood disturbance lasting at least 2 years, and the individual must not be without the symptoms for 2 months. This disorder, although considered more chronic because of the duration of the symptoms, is considered less severe because the symptoms are not nearly as intense as Bipolar I or Bipolar II.

Bipolar Disorder NOS: This disorder is similar to the other NOS categories as individuals in this area do not meet the full criteria for one of the other mood disorders listed.

———————

Source: Summarized criteria from the *Diagnostic and Statistical Manual of Mental Disorders, Fourth Edition, Text Revision.* Copyright 2000 by the American Psychiatric Association.

QUICK REFERENCE 9.5

SIX SUBGROUPS OF BIPOLAR I DISORDER

1. Bipolar I Disorder, Single Manic Episode 296.0x
   Presence of only one manic episode and no past major depressive episodes.
2. Bipolar I Disorder, Most Recent Episode Hypomanic 296.40
   Currently (or most recently) in a hypomanic episode.
   There has previously been at least one manic episode or mixed episode.
3. Bipolar I Disorder, Most Recent Episode Manic 296.4x
   Currently (or most recently) in a manic episode.
   There has previously been at least one major depressive episode.
4. Bipolar I Disorder, Most Recent Episode Mixed 296.6x
   Currently (or most recently) in a mixed episode.
   There has previously been at least one major depressive episode.
5. Bipolar I Disorder, Most Recent Episode Depressed 296.5x
   Currently (or most recently) in a major depressive episode.
   There has previously been at least one manic episode or mixed episode.
6. Bipolar I Disorder, Most Recent Episode Unspecified 296.7
   Criteria, except for duration, are currently (or most recently) met for a manic, a hypomanic, or a
       major depressive episode.
   There has previously been at least one manic episode or mixed episode.

———————

Source: Summarized criteria from the *Diagnostic and Statistical Manual of Mental Disorders, Fourth Edition, Text Revision.* Copyright 2000 by the American Psychiatric Association.

outbursts of irritability or even violence, particularly when others refuse to go along with the manic person's antics and schemes. For a manic episode to exist, the mood must persist for at least 1 week. In addition, three of these symptoms must also occur in the same time period.

1. There is a notable increase in goal-directed activity, which sometimes may appear to be a nonrelievable restlessness.
2. Thoughts and mental activity may appear to speed up, so that the individual appears to exhibit a "flight of ideas" or thoughts that "race" through the brain.
3. Distractibility, high levels of verbal output in speech or in writing, and a severely decreased need for sleep may also occur.
4. Inflated self-esteem is common and, when severe, becomes delusional, so that the person harbors feelings of enormous grandeur and power.
5. Personal and cultural inhibitions loosen, and the person may indulge in foolish ventures with a high potential for painful consequences, such as foolish business ventures, major spending sprees, and sexual indiscretions (APA, 2000).

In bipolar II, a clinical course is characterized by the occurrence of one or more major depressive episodes accompanied by at least one hypomanic episode. Furthermore, the presence of a manic or mixed episode precludes the diagnosis of bipolar II disorder. The presence of the hypomanic episode as opposed to the manic episode is a critical factor for differentiating between these two conditions. In bipolar II, the symptoms must cause clinically significant distress or impairment in social, educational, or occupational functioning, although in some cases the hypomanic episodes themselves do not cause the impairment. Often this impairment results from major depressive episodes or from a chronic pattern of unpredictable mood episodes that cause unreliable interpersonal or occupational functioning. Furthermore, according to the *DSM-IV-TR*, bipolar II disorder may be gender related. This disorder occurs more commonly in women than in men; and the *DSM-IV-TR* notes that women with the disorder may be at risk of developing subsequent episodes in the immediate postpartum period. (See Quick Reference 9.6 for diagnostic criteria for bipolar II disorder.)

In both bipolar I and bipolar II disorders, symptoms of persistent depressed mood, loss of interest in activities, poor concentration, feelings of hopelessness, and changes in eating and sleeping patterns characterize the depressive phase. In contrast, the hypomanic client usually exhibits increased levels of energy, irritability, decreased need for sleep, changes in eating patterns, increases in activities (including spending), and increases in pressured verbalization. Because of the increase in energy and activities, many individuals become quite creative during these spurts and later experience the depressive trend. Individuals with bipolar II disorder are at higher risk for suicide and usually have a strong family history of bipolar or depressive disorders (McElroy, Strakowski, West, & Keck, 1997).

Cyclothymic Disorder

According to the *DSM-IV* and the *DSM-IV-TR*, clients with a diagnosis of cyclothymic disorder have milder symptoms than those who suffer from the other types of bipolar disorders, although the symptoms are more consistent and last for approximately 2 years. In order to be diagnosed with cyclothymic disorder, the client's history must indicate that he or she has not been without hypomanic and depressive symptoms for a period of 2 months (APA, 1994, 2000); a person who experiences a clear

---

QUICK REFERENCE 9.6

DIAGNOSTIC CRITERIA FOR BIPOLAR II DISORDER

- Presence (or history) of one or more major depressive episodes.
- Presence (or history) of at least one hypomanic episode.
- There has never been a manic episode or a mixed episode.
- The mood symptoms in Criteria A and B are not better accounted for by schizoaffective disorder and are not superimposed on schizophrenia, schizophreniform disorder, delusional disorder, or psychotic disorder not otherwise specified.
- The symptoms cause clinically significant distress or impairment in social, occupational, or other important areas of functioning.

Source: Summarized criteria from the *Diagnostic and Statistical Manual of Mental Disorders, Fourth Edition, Text Revision.* Copyright 2000 by the American Psychiatric Association.

---

major depressive episode only should not be diagnosed as cyclothymia. Although it is a milder form of mood disorder, cyclothymia is considered chronic. Clients may experience less severe mood swings, but they are not free of symptoms for more than 2 months over a 2-year period (Austrian, 2005).

In order to be diagnosed with cyclothymia disorder, the client's history has to indicate that he or she has not been without hypomanic and depressive symptoms for a period of 2 months (APA, 2000); however, a client with only a major depressive episode should not be diagnosed with cyclothymia. Remember that although this is a milder form of mood disorder, individuals with this disorder are not free of symptoms for more than 2 months over a 2-year period. It is commonly referred to as a chronic disorder (Austrian, 2005).

Bipolar Disorder Not Otherwise Specified

Caution should always be exercised when diagnosing bipolar disorder not otherwise specified (NOS), because of the variety of symptoms that can be included. In clinical practice, this diagnosis is generally used with clients who do not meet all of the criteria described for the bipolar disorders yet still exhibit some of the basic symptoms evident in manic, major depressive, or mixed episodes (APA, 1994, 2000).

Summary of Bipolar Disorders

Adults with bipolar disorder seem in some ways to be more unfortunate than those who suffer from recurrent major depression because more than 90% of those who have one manic episode will go on to have further episodes (APA, 2000). Overall, the probabilities of "full recovery" for bipolar and unipolar disorder are equally discouraging; about 40% of individuals experience another manic episode within 1 to 2 years following hospitalization and lithium therapy (Harrow, Goldberg, Grossman, & Meltzer, 1990).

DIAGNOSTIC ASSESSMENT IN ADULTS WITH BIPOLAR DISORDER

Regardless of the type of bipolar disorder, it is important during assessment to remember that variability in the client's behavior and actions is expected and these changes in behavior and energy level can occur gradually or quite suddenly. One factor to consider during the assessment phase is whether the client is experiencing rapid cycling. This refers to four or more complete mood cycles within a year's time, within days, or in some cases within hours (Badger & Rand, 1998). Some clients with bipolar disorder may be in a mixed state, which indicates that their mood reflects concurrent depressive, manic, or hypomanic symptoms. For those individuals who experience a mixed state, rapid cycling affects approximately 33% of people with bipolar II. Rapid cycling is a risk factor for recurrence, suicidal behavior, comorbidity, poor outcome, decreased functioning, and resistance to lithium treatment (Hajeka et al., 2008).

When a diagnosis of bipolar disorder is confirmed using the *DSM-IV-TR* criteria (APA, 1994, 2000), attention focuses almost immediately on determining whether the client meets the criteria for depressive, manic, hypomanic, or mixed episodes. In addition, every mental health practitioner should also assess for critical symptoms that could be reflective of other mental health problems and how these exogenous factors can influence the resulting episode. The complex and multifaceted symptoms can be complicated with other psychiatric problems that also require attention and treatment. For example, priority is given to identifying substance-related disorders important during the assessment phase continuing on through the treatment phase. When there is a history of alcohol and drug use, special attention must be paid when prescribing medications for treatment of this disorder. Failure to obtain substance use information at the point of assessment can become harmful if the client uses medications while taking these substances.

Once the diagnosis has been confirmed, assessments include suicide potential, history and risk of violence, psychotic symptoms, risk-taking behaviors that can include sexual acting out, and assessing for substance and

alcohol abuse (Gitlin, 1996). Suicide assessment is critical as the risk for suicide is 37 times higher when the client is in the combined mixed state followed by the depressive state when compared to 18 times higher when clients are in the depressed state (Valtonen et al., 2008). For example, in their study of 176 individuals with bipolar disorders I and II, Valtonen et al., found that over an 18-month period, females were more than twice as likely to attempt suicide than males. In addition, those with bipolar disorder II were twice as likely to attempt suicide than those with bipolar I. Other risk factors related to increased suicide were anxiety disorders and comorbid personality disorders. Since research has demonstrated that depressive episodes usually follow manic phases (APA, 1994, 2000), watching for this trend can lessen the high risk of suicidal thoughts and attempts at suicide. Clients who already rely on alcohol and drugs have easy access to substances that can be used in a suicide attempt.

The immediate plan for the bipolar client who appears to be a danger to self or others should be to assess rapidly what appears to be occurring, to protect the client from harm, to begin a medication regimen, and to stabilize the dangerous symptoms. Hospitalization is usually recommended because it can ensure an environment where these objectives can be met and where the client can continue therapeutic work. Furthermore, allowing time to adjust medications in a supervised setting may help contribute to continued medication compliance and management upon discharge to a less restrictive environment. The period of hospitalization can also serve as a time when clients and family members become educated about the nature of the illness and the treatment alternatives. Having family understanding and support can help to facilitate discharge.

To facilitate and provide direct application of the diagnostic assessment with an adult, an in-depth biopsychosocial analysis of a case involving a male client with bipolar disorder is presented. (See Case Example 9.1, the Case of D.) Issues critical for the diagnostic assessment are outlined, including how to elicit important factors that affect treatment planning and intervention strategy.

Completion of the Diagnostic Assessment for D

Given the behaviors that D exhibited on intake at the crisis unit, hospitalization became necessary. For D, the diagnosis placed on Axis I diagnosis was Bipolar I Disorder, Most Recent

—————— CASE EXAMPLE 9.1 – CASE OF D ——————

D, a 50-year-old Caucasian male who owns his own landscaping business, was brought to a crisis assessment unit by the police because he was found naked in a neighbor's yard. When the police questioned him as to what he was doing, he told them "he was God and fertilizing the ground." Per the police report, it was documented that D was found planting a tree in his neighbor's yard, without permission, at midnight, under a spotlight in the nude. The neighbor's adult daughter also told police that she saw him from the window masturbating in the hole he had dug to plant the tree. When the police arrived on the scene, the neighbor told them that he did not want to press charges and that D was a nice guy most of the time. He and his family just wanted to see him get help. The police stated that D did not resist arrest, and his bizarre ramblings led them to believe he needed mental health treatment rather than being arrested and sent to jail.

Upon interview in the crisis unit, D reported that he felt great and his neighbor had contracted with him to plant some trees for him earlier in the week. His speech would start out coherent and then he would begin rambling. The content of his speech was pressured as he started to describe how he was "Johnny Appleseed" and then begin to talk about time factors and other hard-to-follow irrelevant information. At times he would make jokes, laugh at them, and be very surprised that the social worker doing the interview was not laughing, too. He became easily distracted by the slightest noise in the hallway, and these distractions disturbed his trend of thought. When the social worker completing the initial assessment tried to bring him back on task, he became irritated and asked bluntly "Do you have a brain?" He reported no suicidal ideation or intent, but his judgment and insight were impaired. When asked what he would do when he left the unit, he said he would plant more trees as he wanted to take care of the world and make it a better place. When asked about his previous behavior, he stated that he saw nothing wrong with spreading a little love seed with his love tool. He then asked the social worker if she wanted to see it. She said, "No, thank you" and told him that was unacceptable behavior. He replied with "Sorry, just trying to loosen you up a little as you are way too serious." When told that hospitalization was recommended and asked if he would sign himself in voluntarily, he agreed and said he would just have to bring his cheer to the inpatient unit. The social worker phoned the psychiatrist on call, and D was admitted to the unit with a plan to restabilize him again on lithium.

Several weeks later D was brought to the unit again but this time by his brother. His brother said that he was very concerned about D as he had refused to eat for the last 2 days and was not willing to get out of bed. He said his brother's employees from the nursery called and told him to check on D. The employees told him that just the week before, D had opened the nursery store and started giving away plants, telling customers their purchases were on the house. After giving away numerous expensive plants and refusing to take money when offered, his employees questioned his behavior. He threatened to fire them if they interfered. Also, later in the same day, he offered to give them early Christmas bonuses because business was improving so much. Further, after staying at work for a couple of hours that day, he told them all to take the day off and celebrate life. They had not seen him since, and that was a week ago. An employee who often ran the nursery went by to check on him and noticed his car was at his home but no one answered the door. He reported this to the brother and asked him to go check on D. When his brother went to the house and knocked on the door, no one answered. D lives alone but his brother had a key. When he opened the door and entered the house, D was sitting on the floor with his head in his hands. He was surrounded by boxes of seeds and other packages of items he must have purchased at the local store. His brother was frustrated as he described the situation to the intake social worker, stating that he has no idea how his brother is going to pay his credit card bills and commenting that he had unopened boxes for six (on-sale) brand-new electric can openers.

This time in the clinical interview, D presented a very different picture. His mood was clearly depressed, affect was flat, and he suffered from alogia (poverty of speech). He made no eye contact and refused to respond to questions by the social worker or his brother. He muttered very softly in a low, monotone voice "I wish I was dead . . . I wish I was dead." When asked if he would harm himself, he said yes, he would shoot himself if he had a gun. When asked if he had a gun at home he said no, but when his brother was asked outside the individual interview with D, his brother said that D had several guns. The social worker explained to the brother that she was going call the psychiatrist for an assessment and medication evaluation, get the on-staff nurse practitioner to provide a medical clearance, and seek inpatient admission for his brother. In addition, the social worker told the brother to make sure that the inpatient unit mental health practitioner was aware that his brother had guns at home so this could be addressed upon discharge. The social worker would be sure to also pass this information along in her report and ask that the client be placed on "suicide watch" and precautions be taken for his safety upon admission to the unit.

Episode Depressed. In making this diagnostic impression, it appeared that there was at least one manic episode documented 2 weeks earlier by the same social worker at the crisis unit. This previous episode also resulted in hospital admission. In gathering history from his brother, it does not appear that D has a history of schizophrenia or any other psychotic disorder. Per his brother, it is only during these episodes of bizarre behavior that he is most concerned. His brother states that for the most part, his brother is a solid businessman and his employees really like him. His brother says sometimes he can go a year or more and be normal, even when he knows his brother is functioning without his lithium, and then something will happen. He is not sure what triggers it; it could be a call from his ex-wife or visiting his adult son who is diagnosed with bipolar II disorder (See Quick Reference 9.7 for application of the multiaxial diagnosis of D.)

On Axis II, no diagnosis (V71.09) is recorded since there are no apparent personality disorders or mental retardation present. On Axis III, there are no medical conditions noted on this assessment or during his past psychiatric hospitalization. On Axis IV, the psychosocial stressors include problems with primary support (strained family and employee/work relations); problems related to the social environment (recent incidents with the police); and occupational problems as he is the boss with his employees. On Axis V, the Global Assessment of Functioning (GAF) rating for current = 30 is noted.

When D starts to feel better, a more extensive history can be gathered. At that time. D reports that for the past 10 years he has been admitted several times to the inpatient unit and stabilized upon discharge. He has a regular psychiatrist and reports taking lithium "only when he has to as it makes him too thirsty." He states that his moods can change and sometimes

QUICK REFERENCE 9.7

APPLICATION OF *DSM-IV-TR* MULTIAXIAL SYSTEM FOR D

Diagnostic Impressions

AXIS I: 296.6 Bipolar I disorder, most recent episode depressed.

AXIS II: None (V71.09 No diagnosis).

AXIS III: Deferred.

AXIS IV: Problems with primary support.
              Problems related to the social environment.
              Occupational problems: Discord as boss
              with employee problems.
              Economic Problems: Overspending and impulsive
              buying resulting in large debt.

AXIS V: GAF (current/highest in past year) = 30/70.

he feels as if he is going to fall off the edge of the earth and prefers his previous elevated mood to his more depressed ones. When asked about treatment and if he is taking medications to help with his reported feelings of highs and lows, he says that he has a medicine cabinet full of medications. He states that he prefers exercise to medications and therapy. D reports that he does not take his medications regularly due to various side effects and an inability to tolerate many of the medications prescribed. According to D, it appears that many of the antipsychotics and mood stabilizers sedate him and make him so depressed he has no energy. He keeps repeating how good he felt last week and really does not want to take anything to change that. He said one time when he was given a selective serotonin reuptake inhibitor by his general medicine physician, he became very excited. He is convinced he triggered his own manic episode.

When D feels extremely energetic, the mania has manifested itself with delusions, compulsions, argumentative behavior, paranoia, dissociation, anxiety, and obsessions. D reports that the first severe symptoms presented at around age 30; this

is confirmed in his documented medical history. Medications that have been prescribed but that have not stabilized him include lithium (which he still takes), valproic acid, (Depakote), amitriptyline (Elavil), queiapine (Seroquel), citalopram (Celexa), fluoxetine (Prozac), paroxetine hydrochloride (Paxil), sertaline (Zoloft), nefazodone hydrochloride (Serzone), mirtazapine (Remeron), bupropin hydrocholoride (Wellbutrin), gabapentin (Neurotin), alprazolam (Zanax), and zolpidem (Ambien) (for sleep).

Once the initial information about the client's symptoms has been obtained, it is important to guide the remainder of the interview to yield information that will facilitate the diagnostic assessment process. When completing an assessment with clients who suffer from a mood disorder, special attention needs to be given to identifying the mood episodes that are being exhibited. Once the mood episode is established, the criteria are later applied to the existence of a mood disorder. When determining whether the criteria for a mood episode are met, it is important to realize that the disturbance in mood must be severe enough to affect many areas of an individual's functioning. Current and past

Table 9.1. Substance Use/Abuse

Drug Substance	Age of First Use	Frequency	Usual Amount	Date of Last Use
Marijuana	13	occasionally	1 to 2 joints	2/2010
Alcohol	12	1 to 2 times per week	1 to 2 wine coolers/beer	1/27/2010
Hallucinogens	17			1993
Amphetamine	19			1985
Cocaine	Spring 1999			Summer 1999
Ecstasy	January 2005			2/2008
Nicotine	12	Weekly	Pack a week	Regular

behaviors must be considered when identifying a mood episode.

While the *DSM-IV-TR* provides technical definitions of what constitutes manic and hypomanic episodes, it is helpful for the practitioner to know the kinds of symptoms such clients regularly present. During the assessment process, to confirm the presence of a manic or hypomanic episode, the mental health practitioner should elicit information about changes in these areas: sleeping and eating habits/patterns, levels of energy and restlessness, increase in activities (especially in those that are considered risk taking or destructive), problems concentrating, and when the client becomes easily distracted. Mood changes include: instances of extreme feelings of happiness and laughing inappropriately (usually accompanied with agitation). The client may become very talkative, and speech takes on a pressured quality with racing thoughts where the client reports that he or she cannot keep up with the influx of ideas. Other factors include assessing for impaired judgment, grandiose thinking, inflated self-esteem, increased irritability and impatience with others, easy excitability, and indications of violent behavior. Disorientation, incoherent speech, and bizarre hallucinations are not uncommon, and often individuals will have impaired social relationships characterized by a lack of interest.

For clients with a poor history of treatment compliance, it is important early on to assess whether a substance abuse history may be complicating the diagnostic or intervention process. Always ask the client what substances are used and the date of first and most recent use. In this case, D denied any and all other substance use or experimentation besides experimentation with marijuana and weekly use of alcohol. A sample chart like this one may be of help to organize this information (see Table 9.1).

In the diagnostic assessment, it is critical to get a complete medical and medication history, asking the client questions about health conditions as well as using medical records and previous history and physicals to substantiate information received. When gathering the medical history, if clients are able to do so, ask if they have any specific allergies and write them down so you can alert the team.

In assessing his socialization and support system resources, D states he has very few friends and his employees do not associate with him outside of work. He reports numerous relationships with women, but these relationships never last as he believes they use him for his money. He reports that he has an undeserved reputation of being deceitful and misleading and as a result has difficulty keeping and maintaining relationships with others. D reports that he feels "dumped" by his last four relationships. He is unable to identify any social or recreational interests. When discussing sociable manners and involvement with others, it became clear that D frequently feels inferior when socializing with people except for his brother. It is further clear that D's inappropriate delusional behavior during the manic episodes and suicidal thoughts during the depressive ones create stressors in social situations. D appears very suspicious of different social circumstances and is unwilling to enter into situations where friendships can result. When asked about excessive spending, D agrees that he compulsively goes on shopping binges, which frequently prevent him from paying his bills. D's legal history involves being arrested once for writing a check with insufficient funds that was settled with the receiver and the bank without legal involvement, and no arrests thus far. Law enforcement, however, has been called numerous times to his home over the years due to reports of bizarre behavior. The police in his neighborhood all know him for his bizarre behavior, but he has never become violent to self or others.

Due to the instability of the client and his moods, a clear risk and suicide assessment is needed. On this last interview, when D started to feel better, he reported that he was not currently suicidal. On this admission, however, he was admitted voicing suicidal ideation and probable intent. As part of the discharge plan, the mental health practitioner will need to ensure that any weapons he may have at home are no longer available to D. As a result, D agrees to give the weapons to a trusted family member or friend prior to returning home. Since D has a very good relationship with his brother, permission from D will be obtained to invite his brother to participate in any available family-group support sessions.

Upon discharge, it is documented that his appetite has increased and he has gained several pounds while in the hospital. He states he has had problems with insomnia for years. The mental status exam revealed that D is aware of his name

(orientation to person); where he is (orientation to place: city, state, name of the facility); what day and time it is (orientation to time: time, day, day of week, month, year); and spatial or situational orientation (his current situation, serial sevens, spell WORLD backward, medications taken, age, year born, last meal, count backward from 10, three-object recall, etc.). He was thus oriented times four (oriented x4). His eye contact strayed often and was fair. On this third assessment prior to discharge, his motor activity was normal and he denied suicidal ideation and intent. Speech was still somewhat pressured but more goal directed. There was no abnormality of thought content, ideas of reference, or obsessions/compulsions. His concentration is adequate to the interview; in general, his insight still appears to be poor.

Treatment Planning and Intervention Strategy for D

A complete treatment plan with D with goals, objectives, and practice strategy is included in Sample Treatment Plan 9.1. With the information gathered during the diagnostic assessment as the basis of treatment, the intervention plan allows for application. As part of the intervention process, problem behaviors must be clearly identified and related directly to the stated goals and objectives. Treatment should be provided in a continuum of care that allows flexible application of modalities based on a cohesive treatment plan. In developing the treatment plan for D, it is important for the practitioner to gather a comprehensive history, which includes information about medical conditions (see Quick Reference 9.8). Once treatment planning is complete, options for counseling strategy are outlined in Quick Reference 9.9.

Since D has difficulty recalling his treatment history, supplemental information is needed from family and others in his immediate support system.

SAMPLE TREATMENT PLAN 9.1

Bipolar I Disorder, Most Recent Depressive Episode for D

Definition: Bipolar I Disorder, Most Recent Episode Depressed, characterized by the presence of a previous manic episode. There previously were several times where there has been a major depressive episode, manic episode, or mixed episode, but the client is presently in a depressed episode. A depressed episode consists of a depressed mood or loss of interest or pleasure in nearly all activities for at least 2 weeks and when at least four additional symptoms are experienced by the client almost daily for at least 2 consecutive weeks. Other associated features related to this client are: sleeping and appetite disturbances (very common symptoms); decreased energy or fatigue; reduced ability to think, concentrate, or make decisions; feelings of worthlessness or guilt, morbid ideation; suicidal ideation and possible intent with means available (guns in the home).

Signs and Symptoms to Note in the Record:

- Inflated self-esteem or grandiosity when in the manic episode.
- Decreased need for sleep when in the manic and the depressed episodes.
- Pressured speech in the manic episode, alogia in the depressed.
- Flight of ideas or racing thoughts in the manic episode.
- Distractibility in both the manic and the depressed episode.
- Psychomotor agitation in the manic episode retarded and delayed in the depressed.
- Excessive involvement in pleasurable activities that may have harmful consequences, such as sexual promiscuity or impulse buying in the manic episode, severe depressed response to this behavior when in the depressed phase.

Goals:

1. Help client to become aware of triggers for the manic episode, thereby allowing for a return to a normal activity level, and increase good judgment.
2. Reduce agitation, impulsive behaviors, and pressured speech and increase sensitivity to consequences of behaviors.
3. Cope with underlying feelings of low self-esteem and fears of rejection or abandonment.
4. Increase controlled behavior, achieve a more stable mood, and develop more deliberate speech and thought processes.

Objectives	Efforts and Interventions by Practitioner
1. Client will cooperate with a psychiatric evaluation and ongoing treatment and take medications as prescribed.	Arrange for a psychiatric evaluation for psychotropic medications and follow-up to monitor client's reaction to the medication.
2. Client will reduce impulsive behaviors and establish a clear safety plan to reduce the potential for harm to self or others.	Develop a clear no-harm, no-risk agreement and safety plan. This will involve the client as well as others in his support system with a focus on recognizing triggers that will require psychiatric support and follow-up as well as inpatient admission.
3. Client will decrease grandiosity and express self more realistically.	Confront the client's grandiosity through supportive counseling and reinforce more realistic self-statements.

(continued)

SAMPLE TREATMENT PLAN 9.1 (*Continued*)

Objectives	Efforts and Interventions by Practitioner
4. Client will be able to discuss behaviors and recognize triggers for the start of a mood episode.	Discuss with client triggers that lead to expansive behaviors and what to do when this occurs.
5. Client will speak more slowly and maintain focus on one subject at a time.	Provide structure for the client's thought processes and actions by directing the course of the conversation and developing plans for the client's behaviors. Plan will be simple and focus on identifying triggers and calling for help when triggers occur. In this case client will call brother first as agreed on by both client and brother.
6. Client will address feelings of low self-esteem and fear or rejection with an effort to expand his support system.	Psychotherapy to explore the psychosocial stressors that are precipitating the client's manic behaviors.

QUICK REFERENCE 9.8

CHARACTERIZATIONS, SYMPTOMS, AND BEHAVIORS FOR D

During periods of manic episodes, D has shown the following symptoms

- Inflated self-esteem and delusional behavior.
- Periods of decreased need for sleep, difficulty falling asleep, and other times has inexhaustible energy and goes without sleep for several days (evidenced by his delusional activity at night).
- Periods of being more talkative than usual with a need to keep talking. Inappropriate conversations with pressured speech and irrelevant joking.
- During communications with others there is flight of ideas and speech becomes disorganized and incoherent.
- Easily distracted and does not take into account rules and social expectations evidenced by his bizarre behaviors.
- Increase in bizarre goal-related activities at work and at home.
- Excessive involvement in pleasurable activities with high potential for painful consequences.
- Frequently does not accept responsibility for his behaviors nor sees a problem with exhibiting them, lack of insight.
- Sexual interest is excessive with poor impulse control resulting in public and private masturbation attempts.
- No medical conditions noted that influence behavior.

During depressive episodes, D has shown the following symptoms

- Depressed all day, nearly every day, as evidenced by reports of feelings of sadness and observed by others.
- Marked diminished interest or pleasure in all, or almost all, activities most of the day as evidenced by inability to answer his door or perform basic activities of daily living (ADLs).
- Insomnia or hypersomnia nearly every day.
- Experiences fatigue and loss of energy every day.
- Experiences feeling worthless with suicidal ideation on admission.
- Diminished ability to think or concentrate and is indecisive.
- Suicidal ideation with possible intent and guns at home. Denies danger to others.

QUICK REFERENCE 9.9

Counseling Strategies for Cognitive Therapy for D

- Identify with D the cognitive distortions that occur in the manic and depressive phases and are factors for his development and maintenance of mood disorders. Look at mania characteristics of self, especially those that trigger delusional thinking and inappropriate sexual acting out.
- Discuss negative distortions related to expectations of the environment, self, and future that contribute to depression.
- Examine D's perceptions of the environment and activities that are seen as unsatisfying or unrealistic. Review work- and social-related behaviors, identifying why they are problematic and developing a plan to address them.
- Identify dysfunctional patterns of thinking and behaving, and guide the client to evidence and logic that test the validity of the dysfunctional thinking.
- Assist D in understanding automatic thoughts that occur spontaneously and contribute to the distorted affect (e.g., personalizing, all or nothing, mind reading, discounting negatives), looking specifically at situations, thoughts, and consequences. If this technique is not helpful or does not work for D, help him to understand and explore other possibilities.
- Help D to use "I" statements in identifying feelings and reactions.

Peer Support Group Therapy

- Such therapy will help D to develop social relationships and provide a format for learning how to better communicate and increase social interaction.
- Also, this group will help D in discussing medication-related issues and serve as an avenue for promoting education related to the affective disorder and its treatment. D often stops taking his medications and does not like the side effects; discussion regarding the danger and the consequences of this behavior can be outlined.

Family Therapy for Depression and Mania

- Involve D's brother in treatment planning designed to formulate a therapeutic plan to resolve symptoms and restore or create adaptive family and work-related function.
- Build an alliance with the client and the family members. It is important to establish a positive working relationship between the client and his family.
- Combine psychotherapeutic and pharmacotherapeutic treatment education. This is especially important because of the variable and small therapeutic window of effectiveness with lithium use.
- Obtain the brother's view of the situation and specify problems, clarify each individual's needs and desires. Allow the family members to vent about the chronic burden they have experienced and problem-solve ways to address this.
- Decrease the use of coercion and blaming.
- Increase cooperative problem solving.
- Increase each member's ability to express feeling clearly and directly and to hear others accurately.

Information about whether D has had a recent medical exam is important, especially since upon this admission he does not appear motivated for self-care. It is not known whether he is eating and sleeping, and D's overall nutritional status is questionable. In addition, a referral for a blood test should be considered to detect use or abuse of drugs and monitor his lithium levels. Careful evaluation of the medications he is taking and has taken in the past needs to be ongoing.

BIPOLAR DISORDER IN CHILDHOOD AND ADOLESCENCE

Between 10 and 15% of adolescents with recurrent major depressive episodes may also later develop bipolar disorder. With the average age of 20 for the onset for bipolar disorder, a client can have a differential diagnosis of attention-deficit hyperactivity disorder (ADHD), conduct disorder, and schizophrenia. Also, bipolar symptoms may be easily misunderstood if there are no distinguishing symptoms of risk-taking behavior from the reckless nature of manic symptoms of the adolescent. If agitation is prominent in bipolar disorder, hypomanic symptoms may be misunderstood as reflecting an anxiety state (APA, 2000). When the diagnosis of bipolar disorder in children is presented, careful attention to other more common conditions, such as ADHD or conduct disorder, can present with similar symptoms (Carlson, 1998; Netherton, Holmes, & Walker, 1999; Weller, 1995). For additional information on existing co-conditions and complications, see Chapter 5.

The existence of the mania episode of bipolar in children and adolescents remains controversial. In the data that are available, bipolar disorder resembling the adult form of the illness is rare in prepubertal children, yet if an expanded phenotype is accepted, this disorder may be more common. Until these

questions are answered or resolved, identifying bipolar in children will remain controversial (Keltner & Folks, 2001). Recent research on bipolar disorders in children and adolescents appears to support an increased prevalence of this disorder. In several studies, it appears that most adults diagnosed with bipolar disorders in the United States experienced the onset of illness in their teen years or before. Bipolar disorder has frequently been misdiagnosed as ADHD or oppositional defiant disorder (ODD), conduct disorder (CD), or depression. Until recently, it was rare that a diagnosis of bipolar disorder was made in childhood, yet the best chance for children with emerging bipolar symptoms is early identification and intervention (National Institute of Mental Health [NIMH], 2000).

Although the *DSM-IV* and *DSM-IV-TR* (APA, 1994, 2000) does not indicate separate criteria for diagnosing bipolar disorder in children and adolescents, it considers developmental parameters when using the adult criteria of the disorder in children (Kronenberger & Meyer, 1996; Netherton, Holmes, & Walker, 1999). For example, Kronenberger and Meyer state that "mixed episodes occur when a child meets the criteria for a manic episode and a major depressive episode 'nearly every day' for 1 week or more, with marked impairment in functioning" (p. 156). When working with children and adolescents, Fountoulakis (2008) warns that a diagnosis is often difficult because the symptoms they experience can manifest periodically. When the symptoms of the disorder, however, constitute repeated occurrences and result in obvious decline, bipolarity should be suspected. Symptoms often exhibited in this population include: marked decline in school performance; restlessness; pulling or rubbing of hair, skin, and clothes; excessive complaining and shouting; crying; aggressive outbursts; and antisocial behaviors.

Adults and children may both present with grandiosity, but the way these symptoms present can differ. For example, adults often engage in behaviors like excessive spending, inflated self-esteem, and inappropriate attire. Children and adolescents who also are grandiose may exhibit these symptoms by being argumentative, bossy, and showing attitudes of superiority to other children and adults (Hamrin & Pachler, 2007). Furthermore, according to Fountoulakis (2008), these children may initially present as quite personable and well liked by friends despite the grandiose and overconfident behaviors.

Generally, it is more common for adolescents over the age of 13 to be diagnosed with bipolar disorders (Keller & Wunder, 1990; Kronenberger & Meyer, 1996). Axelson and colleagues (2006) found that in a study of 255 children and adolescents with bipolar disorder, the mean age of onset was 12.9 years. For adults, the median age of onset has been documented as approximately 18 years with a range from 18 to 22.7 years of age (C. K. Burke, J. D. Burke, Reiger, & Rae, 1990; Colom et al., 2005; Goldberg & Garno, 2009). Nevertheless, there has been a 40-fold increase in pediatric diagnosis of bipolar disorder (Baroni et al., 2009). Furthermore, consistent with a person-in-situation stance, social workers should ensure that a diagnosis is not reached too quickly or that it is based solely on behaviors exhibited in isolation or the behaviors are not more extreme variations of symptoms associated with ADHD, conduct disorder, anxiety, or aggression. Making an accurate diagnostic impression is important because if a child or adolescent is misdiagnosed with ADHD instead of bipolar disorder and a stimulant is given, the clinical picture might worsen considerably (Fountoulakis, 2008).

In this case example (see Case Example 9.2), J has engaged in hyperactive and distractible actions that lead to poor judgments on his part which resulted in probation from the Department of Juvenile Justice and his subsequent care at a mental health facility. These behaviors provide rationale and supportive information for the manic episode. A major depressive episode is supported as the client attempted to cut his wrist related to his not wanting to live. Other signs of his depressed mood include weight gain, marked appetite increase, excessive sleep, fatigue, difficulty concentrating, and low self-worth.

––––––––––––––– **CASE EXAMPLE 9.2 - CASE OF J** –––––––––––––––

J, a 12-year-old overweight boy, arrived at the clinic with his head down and a refusal to look up for the first 10 minutes of the session. Over the past 2 years, he explained, he was afraid that people were out to hurt or harm him and he did not like looking at people. After the mental health practitioner explained that looking at a person who was speaking was a way of showing courtesy and that the individual was listening, he eventually lifted his head and began to talk. J reported that people are watching him and talking about him out on the streets. He describes his mood as feeling sad and empty and that he felt angry inside at the whole world. In the past 2 years, he indicated that when he gets depressed, the feelings could last several weeks. Since his appetite has increased, he has gained weight, sleeps excessively, and because of fatigue wants to remain in bed the majority of the day. J reports that he has difficulty concentrating, is bored, and has a loss of interest in most of his usual activities. Although J does not admit directly to suicidal thoughts, he states openly he does not like himself or others and many times wishes he were dead. His mother and his sister confirm J's self-statements. Fifteen minutes into the session, the client excused himself for a drink of water and took a bathroom break for 10 minutes. His mother explained that in the past 2 years he has

(continued)

CASE EXAMPLE 9.2
(CONTINUED)

had bouts of unresponsiveness and that he appears to feel worse in the evening and better in the morning. She also explained that in the past year he has been cruel to animals and killed several cats and birds in the neighborhood in the past couple of years. Six months ago, he was hospitalized for attempted suicide; he slit his wrist with a kitchen knife. He was also hospitalized a year ago for a similar attempt. When asked why he did it, he states he just feels so angry inside he wanted it to stop. Shortly after J returned to the session, he left again for another drink of water and a walk down the hallway. His mother stated that during the past 2 years, J can be fine one month and totally depressed the next. Additionally, the mother says that he can also rapidly cycle through episodes of irritability, depression, disruptive behaviors, and temper tantrums.

J's mother states that his behavior scares her because he often engages in unexpected reckless behaviors. To support this statement, she describes several incidents. The first occurred when her son jumped on the back of her vehicle for a ride as she was pulling out of the driveway. Another occurred when he was caught walking on the ledge of a building two stories high. She explained that at times he seems very excited; however, irritability surfaces quickly when what he wants is refused, and he can become unpredictable with changing moods. Some days she says he can go on a few hours of sleep, and on other days he does not sleep at all. The family states that he will not stop talking; he will jump from one topic to another; and what he says can be unorganized and difficult to understand. At times during the past 2 years, he has been unable to complete something because he cannot concentrate or stay with it long enough; at other times he will not stop what he is doing until completion. At other times and for long periods, 3 or 4 months, he does not show any signs of this type of behavior at home or in school. This is what is so confusing to his mother because at times he seems fine. Yet other times he is uncontrollable. His mother reports that over the past year and a half, he has called total strangers, which has resulted in expensive telephone bills. In the past 2 years, he has had bouts where he is outrageously excitable, intrusive, and demanding. During this session, he stated that he was currently seeking a girlfriend with whom he could have a sexual relationship.

Six months ago, his behaviors resulted in arrest on simple assault for chasing his mother and sister around the house with a fork. His family members have lost patience with his habitual moaning and complaining as well as his angry outbursts related to events that other family members consider trivial matters. His sister and mother say he will argue, make verbal threats, and show rage for hours over simple things like not getting a glass of milk, a sandwich, or a television program when he wants it. Two weeks ago, he got on a city bus, put on headphones and listened to music at top volume, but when he was asked to turn his music down, he became irritable, nasty, and cruel to the passengers. This resulted in another arrest, and he was placed in an inpatient mental health facility for several days. The mother now involves the police in transporting her son to a hospital or residential treatment when there have been physical threats or he becomes irrational. The mother has petitioned the court for her son's admission to a psychiatric unit or into residential treatment for his protection and the protection of others. The family is very frustrated and no longer wants J in the home.

Completion of the Diagnostic Assessment for J

Since it is unusual for a child or adolescent to be given a diagnosis of bipolar disorder, and individual and collateral information (i.e., actual behavior in school setting) in this case is limited, it is critical that clear justification occurs for the use of this diagnostic category. Therefore, in completing the diagnostic assessment, the problematic behaviors the client is exhibiting need to be identified and clearly documented. J appears to meet the criteria for bipolar I disorder by exhibiting distinct behavioral periods of mood swings (at least six) from profound depression to extreme euphoria and irritability (mania, if not the less severe hypomania) with intervening periods of normalcy in the past 3 years. During these periods of mood disturbance, he has shown these symptoms:

- Inflated self-esteem as evidenced by his demanding others to do things for him and his inability to express or understand shame/guilt. At times he experiences euphoria and elation; however, irritability surfaces rapidly when his wishes and desires go unfulfilled, and he becomes very volatile as his mood fluctuates.
- Periods where he has a decreased need for sleep, difficulty falling asleep, and an inexhaustible energy as evidenced by his feeling rested after only 2 or 3 hours of sleep. He also has periods where he goes without sleep for several days. These periods appear cyclic in nature and not typical of his personality. Yet at times these bouts of energy change very quickly, alternating rapidly over days or even during one day.
- Periods of being more talkative than usual and with the need to keep talking.
- During communications with others, he demonstrates flight of ideas and his speech becomes disorganized and incoherent.
- Easily distracted and frequently leaves those who are around him to tend to unimportant or irrelevant external stimuli. Becomes paranoid and states that he hears voices. Goal-directed activities become difficult.

- Increase in goal-directed activities at home/school as evidenced by extensive computer use and playing video games.
- Excessive involvement in pleasurable activities that have a high potential for painful consequences evident by his unrestrained listening to music at extreme levels in public. He seldom accepts responsibility for his own behaviors and sexual interest is excessive. He also suffers from poor impulse control that results in his becoming socially uninhibited.

Overall, these problematic behaviors are severe enough to cause marked impairment in usual social activities and relationships at home and school. For example, J has been arrested for crimes such as assault and battery and disturbing the peace. He was hospitalized to prevent harm to others. In the past 3 years, he has made two suicide attempts; the most recent 6 months ago required hospitalization. He displays impaired social interaction related to narcissistic behavior evidenced by inability to develop satisfying relationships. He also displays impaired social interactions because he manipulates others to carry out his wishes. If things go wrong, he is skillful at projecting the responsibility for the failure onto them (APA, 2000). Since many of these symptoms overlap with conduct disorder and ADHD, careful attention to recording these symptoms is needed and additional information is required before a diagnosis of bipolar disorder is placed. (See Quick Reference 9.10 for a description of the multiaxial assessment for J.)

In addition, J meets the criteria for major depressive episodes; he exhibits many symptoms during depressive episodes that are present during 2- to 3-week periods and a change from previous function due to depressed mood. A detailed list of his symptoms follows:

QUICK REFERENCE 9.10

MULTIAXIAL ASSESSMENT FOR J

Axis I: 296.80 Bipolar disorder not otherwise specified (provisional).

            Diagnosis deferred: ADHD, hyperactive impulsive type and conduct/oppositional disorder.*

Axis II: None.

Axis III: None.

Axis IV: Psychosocial and environmental problems.

            A problem with primary support is evident by his not being able to get along with and making threats to his sibling and his mother.

            Problems related to the social environment as evidenced by being removed from a city bus and having no friends.

            Educational problems as evidenced by poor performance, being expelled from school, and inability to follow directions and rules.

            Problems related to interaction with the legal system as evidenced by recent arrest and a charge of simple assault, Department of Juvenile Justice resulting in probation, and his inability to comply with probationary stipulations.

            Mother is working toward expulsion from home.

Axis V: Global Assessment of Functioning Scale (GAF) = 30 (current).

---

*More information is needed to completely rule out ADHD and/or conduct/oppositional disorder.

1. Depressed all day, nearly every day, as evidenced by reports of feelings of sadness and observed by family members, schoolmates, and teachers.

2. Marked diminished interest or pleasure in all, or almost all, activities most of the day as witnessed by family members, schoolmates, and teachers.

3. He has had a significant weight gain with an increase in appetite daily.

4. Insomnia or hypersomnia nearly every day.

5. Psychomotor agitation exists, although he and his family report that he is restless and slow to accomplish assigned tasks.

6. During these periods he experiences fatigue and loss of energy every day.

7. He experiences feeling of worthlessness nearly every day with hypersensitivity to criticism.

8. Client and family members state that he has a diminished ability to think or concentrate and that he is indecisive.

9. Recurrent suicidal attempts and threats as evidenced by stabbing himself with a knife on several occasions, resulting in hospitalization. It is unclear, however, whether these are serious and controlled attempts to harm himself or whether these attempts might be better explained as inappropriate and dangerous attention-seeking behaviors. (See Quick Reference 9.11 for reported characteristic symptoms.)

QUICK REFERENCE 9.11

CHARACTERIZATIONS, SYMPTOMS, AND BEHAVIORS FOR J (CHILD)

During periods of manic-like episodes, J has shown these symptoms:

■ Inflated self-esteem and very volatile, and this mood fluctuates.

■ Periods of decreased need for sleep and difficulty falling asleep; other times has inexhaustible energy and goes without sleep for several days.

■ Periods of being more talkative than usual with a need to keep talking.

■ During communications with others, there is flight of ideas and speech becomes disorganized and incoherent.

■ Easily distracted and frequently leaves those who are around him to tend to unimportant or irrelevant external stimuli.

■ Increase in goal-directed activities at home/school as evidenced by extensive computer use and playing video games.

■ Excessive involvement in pleasurable activities with high potential for painful consequences.

■ Frequently does not accept responsibility for his behaviors.

■ Unusual or uncharacteristic symptoms include rapid alteration of symptoms in a 1-day period, going from very angry and irritable with lots of energy to becoming extremely depressed and going to bed.

During depressive episodes, J has shown these symptoms:

■ Depressed all day, nearly every day, as evidenced by reports of feelings of sadness and as observed by others.

■ Marked diminished interest or pleasure in all, or almost all, activities most of the day as evidenced by others.

■ Significant weight gain with an increase in appetite daily.

■ Insomnia or hypersomnia nearly every day.

■ Experiences fatigue and loss of energy every day.

■ Experiences feeling worthless nearly every day with hypersensitivity to criticism.

■ Diminished ability to think or concentrate and is indecisive.

■ Recurrent suicidal attempts and threats with more impulse control.

■ Angry and agitated symptoms during depressive phase similar to what is often seen in children and adolescents.

Treatment Planning and Documentation for J

A treatment plan with the client's goals and objectives needs to be formulated. With the information gathered during the diagnostic assessment as the basis for treatment, the intervention plan allows for application. In the diagnostic assessment, information given by the client is supplemented with other resources to confirm history and check out all other possible contradictory information and comorbid conditions. Client should undergo a complete physical examination, complete blood count and general chemistry screening, a thyroid function test, and if substance abuse is suspected a test of urine toxicology. In addition, the referral for a blood test should be considered to detect use or abuse of drugs or hormonal problems (APA, 2000). If the client is taking or will be taking medications, serum levels should be considered especially if the medications include valproic acid (Depakene), carbamazepine (Tegretol), or venlafaxine (Effexor). If the client is treatment resistant, medically trained practitioners can use the results from more standardized radiological tests, such as computed tomography or magnetic resonance imaging and electroencephalography, as second-line options in the evaluation (Griswold & Pessar, 2000).

Problem behaviors must be clearly identified in terms of the intervention efforts. While a clinical interview is often an adequate method to assess the treatment needs of a bipolar patient, rapid assessment instruments may assist the therapist in arriving at a more careful and comprehensive assessment and treatment plan. The Mood Disorder Questionnaire developed by Hirschfeld, Williams, Spitzer, Calabrese, et al. (2000) offers an overall assessment of the client's symptoms and functioning. Semantic Differential and Mood Scales (SDFMS)

developed by Lorr and Wunderlich (1998) permit a therapist to measure changes on various dimensions of symptoms relevant to depression and mania. The Mood Related Pleasant Events Schedule (MRPES) developed by MacPhillamy and Lewinsohn (1982) can be used to measure changes in the client's perception of life events and provide the clinician with quantifiable data in making modifications to treatment plans. The Family Sense of Coherence (FSOC) and Family Adaption Scales (FAS) used together and designed by Antonovsky and Sourani (1988) can be used to evaluate the family's sense of coherence and adaption helping the therapist to better understand family dynamics and functioning. (See Sample Treatment Plan 9.2 and Quick Reference 9.12 for treatment aspects for J.) (Quick Reference 9.12 highlights goals that can be addressed in counseling strategies for cognitive therapy. Other approaches include peer support group therapy, family therapy, and family support group therapy.)

SAMPLE TREATMENT PLAN 9.2

BIPOLAR DISORDER NOT OTHERWISE SPECIFIED FOR J

Definition: This disorder is characterized by symptoms that do not meet the criteria for all of the mood episodes for any of the bipolar disorders. The reason for this classification is that J presents with very rapid alteration of symptoms, sometimes within hours or days, yet all the other symptoms are met. There has previously been at least one major depressive episode, manic episode or mixed episode, but the client is presently in a manic episode and is very angry and agitated. It is difficult to get a full assessment or collateral information. The diagnosis of bipolar disorder NOS is not deferred at this time as almost all the other symptoms of bipolar disorder are met except for the alternating of mood and the preoccupation with severe and aggressive behaviors toward others.

Signs and Symptoms to Note in the Record:

- Inflated self-esteem or grandiosity.
- Decreased need for sleep.
- Pressured speech.
- Flight of ideas or racing thoughts.
- Distractibility.
- Psychomotor agitation.
- Excessive involvement in pleasurable activities that may have harmful consequences, such as sexual promiscuity or impulse buying.

Goals:

1. Reduce uncontrollable energy, return to a normal activity level, and increase good judgment.

2. Reduce agitation, impulsive behaviors, and pressured speech and increase sensitivity to consequences of behaviors.

3. Cope with underlying feelings of low self-esteem and fears of rejection or abandonment.

4. Increase controlled behavior, achieve a more stable mood, and develop more deliberate speech and thought processes.

Objectives	Interventions
1. Client will cooperate with a psychiatric evaluation and take medications as prescribed.	Arrange for a psychiatric evaluation for psychotropic medications and monitor patient's reaction to the medication. Request a no-harm, no-risk safety plan be put in place.
2. Client will reduce impulsive behaviors.	Psychotherapy to address consequences of behaviors.
3. Client will decrease grandiosity and express self more realistically.	Confront the client's grandiosity through psychotherapy and reinforce more realistic self-statements.
4. Client will be able to sit calmly for 30 minutes without agitation or distractibility.	Reinforce client's increased control over his energy, and help the client set attainable goals and limits on his agitation and distractibility.
5. Client will speak more slowly and maintain focus on one subject at a time.	Provide structure for the client's thought processes and actions by directing the course of the conversation and developing plans for the client's behaviors.
6. Client will acknowledge the low self-esteem and fear or rejection that underlies his grandiosity.	Psychotherapy to explore the psychosocial stressors that are precipitating the client's manic behaviors, such as rejection by peers or past traumas.

QUICK REFERENCE 9.12

COUNSELING STRATEGIES

Cognitive Therapy

- Help J identify cognitive distortions that support the development and maintenance of problematic thoughts and behaviors. Examine unrealistic cognitive distortions related to the mania.
- Discuss negative distortions related to expectations of the environment, self, and future that contribute to depression.
- Examine J's perceptions of the environment and activities that are seen as unsatisfying or unrealistic.
- Identify dysfunctional patterns of thinking and behaving, and guide the client to evidence and logic that test the validity of the dysfunctional thinking.
- Assist in understanding "automatic" thoughts that occur spontaneously and contribute to the distorted affect (e.g., personalizing, all or nothing, mind reading, discounting negatives) looking specifically at situations, thoughts, and consequences. If this technique is not helpful or does not work for J, help him to understand and explore other possibilities.
- Help J use "I" statements in identifying feelings and reactions.

QUICK REFERENCE 9.12 (*Continued*)

Peer Support Group Therapy

- Provides clients with a feeling of security when discussing troublesome or embarrassing issues. Also, this group will help J in discussing medication-related issues and serve as an avenue for promoting education related to the affective disorder and its treatment.
- This group will help J gain a sense of perspective on his condition and tangibly encourage him to link up with others who have common problems. A sense of hope is conveyed when an individual is able to see that he is not alone or unique in experiencing affective illness.

Family Therapy for Depression and Mania

- Work with families to formulate a therapeutic plan to resolve symptoms and restore or create adaptive family function.
- Build an alliance with the client and the family members establishing a positive working relationship between the client and his family.
- Combine psychotherapeutic and pharmocotherapeutic treatment education.
- Obtain each family member's view of the situation and specify problems seeking understanding and shared meaning of events among the members. Encourage a nonblaming and accepting therapeutic atmosphere for the client and the family. Assure the family members that they did not cause the condition. Allow family members to ventilate about the chronic burden they have experienced.
- Review ambient family stress. Examine any objective and subjective burdens the family is experiencing due to observable aspects of the illness and the need to provide caregiving. Look for criticism or emotional overinvolvement of family members in response to J's illness.
- Help to redefine the nature of the family's difficulties.
- Encourage recognition of each member's contribution to the discord.
- Recognize and modify communication patterns, rules, and interactional patterns.
- Increase reciprocity through mutual exchange of privileges.
- Decrease the use of coercion and blaming and increase cooperative problem solving.
- Increase each member's ability to express feelings clearly and directly and to hear others accurately.

Family Support Group Therapy

- Provide an atmosphere for growth and change and discuss importance of complying with the treatment strategy outlined.
- Provide family members with a feeling of security when discussing troublesome or embarrassing issues. Also, this group will help family members in discussing medication-related issues and serve as an avenue for promoting education related to the identified mood disorder and its treatment.
- This group will help family members gain a sense of perspective on J's condition and tangibly encourage the family members to link up with others who have common problems. A sense of hope is conveyed when family members are able to see that they are not alone or unique in experiencing affective illness.

Source: Griswold and Pessar (2000).

TREATMENT STRATEGY FOR THE BIPOLAR DISORDERS

Bipolar disorder generally worsens over time, and as a chronic illness, the severity and frequency of episodes can increase. Individuals with bipolar disorder potentially can lose 14 years of effective living and die 9 years early (Jones, Sellwood, & McGovern, 2005). The bipolar disorders present with a variety of symptoms that often cause major functioning problems across a vast array of psychosocial domains. This leads to frustration for the individual, the family, and other support systems (Jones, 2003). Clients with this disorder are often overwhelmed by the symptoms associated with their fluctuating moods, vacillating energy levels, and repeated disruptions when trying to complete the tasks of daily living. The client who suffers from bipolar disorder is faced with the challenge of understanding and tracking two separate sets of symptoms within one illness: those that arise during a manic state and those reflected in the depressive phase (Jones et al., 2005).

For many clients with bipolar disorders, the challenge is learning how to determine whether their cheery disposition or depressed states are within normal limits or indicative of a manic swing or a depressive downtrend. The client may not be able to depend on his or her own assessment to detect the changes in mood, but relatives and friends can be very helpful in identifying the mild mood fluctuations and changes that appear to represent an unusual state for the client. Although support systems can become taxed by these behaviors, collateral supporting reports are always helpful. It is common for these clients to become resistant to seeking and maintaining treatment, especially those who are in the manic or elevated high states of the illness. There is a high degree of comorbid disorders, such as personality disorder, generalized anxiety, panic disorder, and substance abuse (Leahy, 2007). In a study of 429 individuals with bipolar disorder, 32.9% reported having discontinued all medications for the disorder at some point in the past without informing the physician (Baldessarini, Perry, & Pike, 2007). Clients in the manic phase of the illness often avoid or refuse support during these periods. When social workers understand the differences that can occur in mood states and the specific criteria that characterize each of the bipolar disorders, they are in a better position to assist clients and their families in accepting, monitoring, and treating this form of mental illness. Understanding and managing this symptomlogy medically can be difficult for clients, their relatives, and other support systems.

A thorough assessment that leads to an accurate diagnosis is only the beginning phase of the intervention. It can be difficult to convince a client with a bipolar disorder that he or she is in fact experiencing serious changes in mood states and that help is necessary. Other reasons for treatment nonadherence include psychiatric and substance abuse use comorbidities and the client's attitudes toward the treatments and medications (Sajatovic, Valenstein, & Blow, et al., 2007). Miasso, Cassiani, and Pedrao (2008) report that nonadherence can be directly related to how clients perceive taking medication and the social stigma as well as the side effects of the medications that can affect their overall performance.

Psychopharmacological Treatments: Lithium

In both children and adults, the main goal of psychological and psychopharmacological treatment is to prevent relapse and improve psychosocial functioning. Medications are frequently utilized as either the sole treatment strategy or as a supplemental treatment strategy for the bipolar disorders in adults and adolescents and children. The same medications are often used for the disorder regardless of a client's age. Miklowitz (2008) warns, however, that "despite significant strides in pharmacological treatment of bipolar disorder, most bipolar patients cannot be maintained on drug treatments alone" (p. 1408).

Of the bipolar disorders, bipolar I is recognized as the easiest to treat with medications; the other types of the disorder present a much greater challenge for health care providers (Fountoulakis, 2008). Individuals with bipolar disorder experience significantly greater impairment from depressive episodes and take longer times to recover than from manic episodes. Due to the limited efficacy of pharmacotherapy, adjunctive psychosocial treatments are often utilized (Miklowitz et al., 2007).

Because bipolar disorders are recurring illnesses with remissions and relapses or recurrences of both depressive and manic or hypomanic episodes, clients often require an ongoing regimen of medication. Most people with bipolar disorder may have to take medications throughout their life. The goal of medication therapy is to (a) stabilize the depressive or manic symptoms, (b) prevent relapse of depressive or manic episodes, (c) reduce subthreshold symptoms, (d) decrease suicide risk, (e) reduce cycling frequency, and (f) improve overall functioning (Usery, Lobo, & Self, 2008). Various categories of psychotropic medications are used in the treatment of bipolar disorders, yet the majority of individuals with bipolar disorder need to be monitored carefully, as many are not able to maintain remission in the long term (Vieta et al., 2008).

The medications used to treat bipolar disorder fall into four groups: (1) mood stabilizers, (2) atypical antipsychotics, (3) anticonvulsants, and (4) antidepressants. Of these medications, the most common are mood stabilizers (Dulcan, 2006), yet their efficacy can be limited and they often produce side effects. The oldest of the mood stabilizers and still the most commonly

prescribed is lithium (Eskalith or Lithobid). It is beyond the capacity of this chapter to discuss all of these medications categories; for a more comprehensive review for the nonmedically trained, see Dziegielewski (2006, 2010). Furthermore, the antipsychotic medication risperidone (Risperdal) for the treatment of acute mania in children and adolescents with bipolar disorder appears to hold promise (Haas et al., 2009).

Lithium is used with all ages; however, caution is stressed when used with children and adolescents. Dulcan (2006) recommends a course of only up to 2 years. Over the last few years this medication has been used with children and adolescents to control behavioral outbursts or rage. When it is used for this purpose, the medication is generally prescribed only until more appropriate ways to control the child's anger (such as problem-solving and coping skills or another, safer medication) can be found (Dulcan, 2006).

Lithium can assist the client by providing symptomatic control of both the manic and depressive phases of bipolar disorder and in long-term prophylaxis against condition recurrence (Karper & Krystal, 1996). Lithium is less effective in treatment of acute depressive episodes compared to manic episodes (Keck, 2005). Despite the side effects, lithium remains among the most widely used medications along with antidepressants for depression. Lithium can reduce impulsivity and aggression, thus reducing suicidal behavior. It is established as having efficacy against recurrent manic or depressive episodes (Goldberg, 2007). Although lithium should diminish manic symptoms in 5 to 14 days, it may take months before the condition is fully controlled (Dulcan, 2006). Since lithium has a short half-life, it is rapidly excreted from the system. Caution should be used as the drug is highly toxic and must be monitored regularly by medically trained professionals. Furthermore, with its high toxicity and excretion rate, lithium can be particularly problematic in older people (PDR, 2009), who should take it only if they have normal sodium intake and normal heart and kidney function. Since the therapeutic range for lithium is limited, there is a fine line between the therapeutic dose and a toxic one (Usery et al., 2008). Maintaining a safe and therapeutic dose requires routine monitoring of lithium levels and at minimum an established baseline between other recommended tests (white blood cell, calcium, kidney function, thyroid function, etc.) (Dulcan, 2006). It is beyond the scope of this chapter to describe all the side effects of this medication; the National Institute of Mental Health (2009b) gives a very comprehensive and simple-to-understand summary.

With lithium as with any medication regime, a complete medical history needs to be taken to ensure other factors, such as potential thyroid or renal problems and possible pregnancy, have been assessed (NIMH, 2009b). Concerning women of childbearing years, Einarson (2009) believes many psychotropic drugs are generally safe; however, he states strongly that a woman with a serious psychiatric disorder should always be considered high risk, and both she and the fetus should be monitored carefully during and after pregnancy. In addition, there should be frequent monitoring of potential problems every 2 to 3 months while a client is taking lithium. Overdosing with lithium can be fatal (PDR, 2009), and the need to properly educate clients and family members to the dangers of using this medication cannot be overemphasized.

Counseling Strategy

Several different types of counseling are frequently considered when working with individuals who suffer from the mood disorders. A complete diagnostic assessment can help the mental health practitioner decide what problem behaviors are most prominent and how to address what is identified. Leahy (2007) recommended eight lessons essential for clinicians working with clients who suffer from bipolar disorder:

1. Learn to adequately diagnose hypomania and mania prior to the client taking medications.
2. Bipolar has a high genetic component, which helps to medicalize the problem, normalize the use of medication, and reduce moralization.
3. Realize that psychological therapy involves recognizing and treating the specific episode while working toward maintenance treatment goals over the long term.
4. Pharmacological treatment is important for bipolar disorder.
5. A psychoeducational component is necessary so the client understands the illness.
6. Mental health practitioners should work closely with the prescribing psychiatrist in addressing the specific problems of the current episode.
7. Despite the strong genetic component to bipolar disorder, life events, coping skills, and family environment may play a part in the expression of depressive and manic episodes.
8. Cognitive therapy can help clients understand aspects of both their depressive and manic episodes.

Electroconvulsive Therapy for Depression and Mania

Electroconvulsive therapy (ECT) is a form of treatment for depression and other mental illnesses that involves the introduction of a series of brain seizures in the patient (Pandya, Pozuelo, & Malone, 2007; West, Prado, & Krystal, 1999). The fact that ECT has such an undeservedly bad reputation can deter its use as an effective treatment for a number of mental health disorders (Pandya et al., 2007). To date there is no definitive explanation as to how or why ECT works. Yet there are numerous neurochemical, neuro-endocrine, and neurophysiologic hypotheses concerning this matter (Willoughby, Hradek, & Richards, 1997). What is known is that it is not the electrical shock that causes the therapeutic effect but rather the resulting seizure, which is a rapid firing of neurons in the brain (Fischer, 2000).

Unfortunately, no nationwide figures show the true frequency of ECT usage. Yet it is probable that ECT usage has increased during the past two decades due to its efficiency and resulting shorter hospital stay (Willoughby et al., 1997). A study by Reid, Keller, Leatherman, and Mason (1998) showed that between September 1993 and April 1995, more than 2,500 people received ECT in state psychiatric hospitals in Texas. With this information and other statistics, Fischer (2000) concluded that more than 100,000 patients receive ECT every year. Society's stigma against ECT has inhibited its use. Not only do many public and rural hospitals not offer it as a treatment, but many doctors are never taught how to perform the procedure. As a result, ECT is considered a treatment of last resort.

ECT is not without its risks and, similar to medications, side effects are possible. There are no absolute contraindications for using ECT; however, a complete medical workup is always indicated. "The cardiovascular, central nervous, and pulmonary systems carry the highest risk from general anesthesia and the induction of generalized seizure activity" (Pandya et al., 2007, p. 680). According to Willoughby and coworkers (1997), "Adverse effects of ECT

may include apprehension or fear, headache, muscle soreness, nausea, cardiovascular dysfunction, prolonged apnea, prolonged seizures, and emergent mania" (p. 11). The most troubling of these affects is cognitive dysfunction, which many times entails memory loss for a period of time before and after the procedure. This memory loss frequently lasts several weeks but can extend up to 6 months. In some cases, the memory loss persists longer. Research has shown that the cognitive dysfunction caused by ECT does not adversely affect functions not associated with memory, such as intelligence and judgment, in any lasting way. According to Johnstone (1999), approximately 80% of patients report some side effects; memory impairment is the most frequent with a range of responses including fear, humiliation, increased compliance, failure, worthlessness, betrayal, lack of confidence, and degradation as well as a sense of having been abused and assaulted.

According to Willoughby and coworkers (1997), despite all the controversy surrounding ECT, the APA has determined that ECT is an effective treatment option for people suffering from the mood disorders as well as several of the psychotic disorders. ECT can also be used with affective disorders and psychotic depression, which is seldom responsive to medications. In addition, ECT can lead to significant improvement of patients with severe affective disorders. Reid and coworkers (1998) found that 90% of all patients they reviewed who had undergone ECT had been diagnosed with a severe mood disorder and the remaining 10% had schizophrenia. With the research supporting the effectiveness of ECT with mood disorders, specifically bipolar disorder and depression, ECT can be viewed as an appropriate treatment option (Fischer, 2000).

ECT is effective with clients who are acutely suicidal and in the treatment of severe depression, particularly in those clients who are also experiencing psychotic symptoms and those with psychomotor retardation in sleep, appetite, and energy. It is often considered for treatment only after a trial of therapy with antidepressant medication has proved ineffective (Griswold & Pessar, 2000). Although ECT is still considered an effective treatment for the mood disorders, other neuromodulatory treatment techniques are being explored. Pandya and colleagues (2007) report that popularity of several other treatments used in this area is increasing, but these treatments are often not considered unless several unsuccessful trials with an antidepressant medication have been used. Promising treatments on the horizon include vagus nerve stimulation (an implanted pacemaker–like device that stimulates the vagus nerve), deep brain stimulation (electrodes implanted in precise areas of the brain), and repetitive transcranial magnetic stimulation (uses an induction coil delivered in brief daily sessions). For a brief description and further information regarding the future of these treatments, see Pandya et al. (2007).

SUMMARY AND FUTURE DIRECTIONS

Dealing with any form of mental illness is a major challenge for clients, mental health practitioners, and family members. Bipolar disorders, with their varying mood episodes, present a unique challenge because symptoms may not be addressed until clients reach acute episodes of mania. In addition, clients with this disorder often present with coexisting psychiatric disorders that require concurrent attention. The assessment process in diagnosing bipolar disorder is an essential component of treatment. Assessing the client for critical or harmful problems such as suicidal ideation during a depressive episode may require addressing these problems first as a way of securing the client's safety. Assessment also

includes the appropriate use of the criteria provided by the *DSM-IV* and *DSM-IV-TR* manuals and the inclusion of medication as the first priority in treatment strategy.

Regardless of the type of mood disorder a client is suffering from, during assessment, it is important to remember the variability that can result in the client's behaviors and actions that is indicative of the mental disorder. Mental health practitioners need to be well versed in the signs and symptoms identified in the *DSM-IV-TR* and be able to use this manual to facilitate the diagnostic assessment, treatment planning, and intervention that will follow. If a mental health practitioner suspects that any client, regardless of age, may suffer from bipolar disorder, it is critical to confirm this diagnosis using the *DSM-IV-TR* criteria (APA, 2000; Meeks, 1999). Doing this requires determining that the client meets the criteria for one of the mood states of bipolar disorder. In other words, does the client meet criteria for depressive, manic, hypomanic, or mixed episodes? In addition, every practitioner should also assess for critical symptoms reflective of other mental health problems that a client can exhibit (Cassano, Pini, Saettoni, & Dell'Osso, 1999). There are limitations because every individual is unique. Mood disorders, and the bipolar disorders in particular, can be complex, and more research is needed to establish the best evidence-based practices. In addition, more research is needed in the area of children and adolescents. Accurate measurements of problem behaviors and social problems provide fuel for the most comprehensive approaches to quality client care.

Mental health practitioners are in a unique position not only to provide services to those with bipolar disorders but to advocate for the needs of the client that are going unmet. Many families struggle with someone with bipolar disorder and need the support of the community, physicians, and mental health organizations.

Support groups for both client and family can provide low-cost assistance. In addition, the legal justice system and medical society red tape must be removed or simplified to expedite aid and assistance to clients with bipolar disorder and to their families. Finally, in the diagnostic assessment, mood variability makes it imperative to teach individuals in the client's support system to be aware of suicidal indications. Mental health practitioners spend a great deal of time with clients; it is criticals that they understand the intricate nature of mood disorders as they teach clients and their families about the disorder and help clients accept intervention efforts.

10

Anxiety Disorders

CARMEN P. CHANG-ARRATIA AND SOPHIA F. DZIEGIELEWSKI

INTRODUCTION

Stress is a subjective emotional state experienced by all that constitutes a normal part of everyday life. When stress and anxiety occur, an uncomfortable feeling often results that causes a response to the situation, event, or circumstance. When this response becomes excessive, however, it can become problematic affecting an individual's cognitive, behavioral, physiological, biological, and social responses. The *Diagnostic and Statistical Manual of Mental Disorders, Fourth Edition, Text Revision* (*DSM-IV-TR*; American Psychiatric Association [APA], 2000) has categorized these extreme responses as anxiety disorders. Included in these disorders are panic attack, panic disorder without agoraphobia, agoraphobia without history of panic disorder, phobia (specific or social), obsessive-compulsive disorder, post-traumatic stress disorder, acute stress disorder, generalized anxiety disorder, anxiety disorders due to a general medical condition, substance-induced anxiety disorder, and anxiety disorder not otherwise specified.

According to the National Institute of Mental Health (NIMH; 2008), anxiety disorders are estimated to affect over 50 million people over age 18 in the United States. Many have a median onset as early as 13 years of age (approximately 34 million people). As late as 2004, the indirect and direct economic costs associated with the treatment of anxiety disorders was $46.6 billion per year—a third of all mental health expenditures allotted for that year. When looking at individual factors, anxiety disorders can begin with an individual treatment cost of at least $350 and above per year (NIMH, 2008). For those affected and/or suffering from an anxiety disorder, the economic impact and social costs incurred are profound.

Expenditures aside, the unintended social impact of these disorders can prove even more hazardous. When an individual is socially and situationally bound by thoughts, impaired cognitive processes, and emotions that cause worry, fear, and distress, the ability to socialize and meet others is hindered. So is the ability to perform optimally in occupational and educational settings, and overall personal health is compromised. In terms of quality of life, these life circumstances result in the individual being unable to form and sustain relationships and can lead to subsequent withdrawal from family and friends. When the anxious feelings are great, the individual may become unable to seek, obtain, or sustain employment. When employed, the fear and anxiety can lead to withdrawal and absences from work. There may also be an avoidance of participation in scholastic pursuits, all of which can affect the individual's economic standing. Excessive stress and anxiety can also lead to immediate and prolonged health, mental health, and substance abuse concerns that could

Special thanks to Jennifer Loflin and Carol (Jan) Vaughn for the earlier version of this chapter.

result in physical deficiencies, other social problems, and possible death.

This chapter introduces the *DSM-IV-TR* taxonomical classification of the anxiety disorders, and provides a concise explanation of the disorders listed under this category. An extensive focus on obsessive-compulsive disorders (OCD) and posttraumatic stress disorder (PTSD) is included in this chapter. Theories and etiology related to the anxiety disorders as they guide and inform practice, treatment, interventions, and preventions are addressed. Case presentations are included that demonstrate the application of the multiaxial system and each example has corresponding sample treatment plans. Popular interventions for anxiety disorders are included, as is a discussion on an integrated approach to care, ending the chapter with current and future implications and directions.

DSM-IV-TR CLASSIFICATION AND DEFINITION FOR THE ANXIETY DISORDERS

Included in the *DSM-IV-TR* classification of anxiety disorders are several disorders that share featured characteristics and criteria that specify common metacognitions and physiological responses. Metacognitions involve the processing of emotional and situational states which provide the basis for an individual's trust and safety assessments. Inappropriate allocation of attentive processing and disordered information processing (e.g., breakdown in adaptive "signal" to "noise" discrimination), with inappropriate and exaggerated innocuous body sensations are central to understanding the clinical phenomenology of the anxiety disorders (Wise, McFarlane, Clark, & Battersby, 2009). Processing stressful events requires executive functions such as interpretation, attention and memory, and these functions are applied when threat and

danger assessments and responsive actions are formed (i.e., as in fight or flight). When excited, the individual then tries to regulate these emotions, invoking compensatory emotions such as fear, worry, distress, terror, or despair. What the individual attributes to the situation provides the basis for anxious responses. If any component of these processes is impaired, then judgment and decision making in these situations becomes inaccurate. When judgment and interpretation of a situation is impaired, the individual will actually believe, assess, and feel that their own perception is accurate. Responses to stress and anxiety, especially when severe, can include physiological reactions that stimulate the sympathetic and parasympathetic nervous system, resulting in increased heart rate, trembling, sweating, nausea, shortness of breath, dizziness, headaches, and diarrhea.

Anxiety is the sum total of all of these components; its symptomology is observed in its frequency and intensity, its excessiveness and unreasonableness, and its intrusiveness and inappropriateness to the domain of the individual's life. These shared components are found in the disorders listed in this taxonomical category: panic attack, agoraphobia, panic disorder without agoraphobia, agoraphobia without history of panic disorder, phobia (specific and social), obsessive-compulsive disorder (OCD), posttraumatic stress disorder (PTSD), generalized anxiety disorder (GAD), anxiety disorder due to a general medical condition, substance-induced anxiety disorder, and anxiety disorder not otherwise specified (see Quick Reference 10.1). Symptoms of all of these disorders include but are not limited to fear, worry, preoccupation, restlessness, irritability, anger, terror, distress, helplessness, horror, poor concentration, hypervigilance, motor restlessness, disturbed sleep, fatigue, shortness of breath, dizziness, palpitations, trembling, and muscle tension (APA, 2000).

Of the disorders presented in the *DSM-IV-TR*, the origin identified for the clinical presentation of anxiety disorders begins with the experience of panic and two clinical features: panic attacks and agoraphobia. This intense fear, panic, and apprehension results in the first feature of an anxiety disorder, known as the panic attack. Since it constitutes a clinical feature of all the anxiety disorders, the *DSM-IV-TR* does not code panic attacks. These attacks, however, can be unexpected, situational (cued), or predisposed situational (recurrent). The presence of these panic attacks and their clinical expression indicate the type of disorder and process of interaction affecting the individual. For example, processing the interaction can be unexpected (an internal process, such as in generalized anxiety disorder), cued (a predominately external process with an immediate reaction, such as in phobias and OCD), or predisposed situational (an episodic and specific reaction to internal and external interactions as those found in PTSD). Much like the appraisal that generates the presence of this acute response, a preventive measure accompanies these reactions leading to the further detriment of the individual's suffering. A discrete period of fear must exist where the individual must experience at least 4 of 13 somatic or cognitive symptoms. (See Quick Reference 10.1 for symptoms evident in the panic attack.)

The second feature related to the anxiety disorders is agoraphobia where there is a pronounced fear of being in places where escape may be difficult. Agoraphobia involves excessive anxiety that leads to an avoidance of persons or places where escape could be difficult or embarrassing (APA, 2000). The feelings of anxiety become so overwhelming the individual will avoid the situation for fear that if needed help might not be available, a panic attack might result. Similar to the anxiety disorder feature panic attack, the *DSM-IV-TR* also does not have a specific diagnostic code for agoraphobia. When experienced as a disorder, agoraphobia is expected to occur either with panic disorder (300.21) or without panic disorder (300.22). When an anxious reaction accentuates the interaction between situational and cognitive factors, the individual will try to avoid the feared situation. A friend or companion may assist or the individual may just try to endure the experience although great distress is noted. The individual worries about his or her responses to situations where strategy and problem solving is limited and will restrict potential interactions to avoid the occurrence or reoccurrence of processes and ensued responses. The *DSM-IV-TR* further specifies that the presence of the anxiety and avoidance cannot be accounted for by another specific anxiety disorder (e.g., phobia, obsessive-compulsive disorder, posttraumatic stress disorder, or separation anxiety disorder).

QUICK REFERENCE 10.1

COMMON SOMATIC OR COGNITIVE SYMPTOMS NOTED IN A PANIC ATTACK

Somatic symptoms: palpitations, sweating, trembling or shaking, sensations of shortness of breath, chest pain or discomfort, abdominal pain or distress, nausea, dizziness, lightheadedness, paresthesias, chills or hot flashes.

Cognitive symptoms: feelings of being smothered or choked, derealization, depersonalization, fear of losing control or going crazy, and the fear of dying.

Source: Summarized from the *Diagnostic and Statistical Manual of Mental Disorders, Fourth Edition, Text Revision,* Copyright 2000 by the American Psychiatric Association.

QUICK REFERENCE 10.2

PRESENTATION OF ANXIETY

- Clients who are anxious often seek the help of a primary care physician before seeing a mental health practitioner.
- Clients often initially attribute signs and symptoms experienced to medical factors rather than to nervous problems.
- Clients present with both physical and mental symptoms (e.g., tremors, dyspnea, dizziness, sweating, irritability, restlessness, hyperventilation, pain, heartburn).

Experiencing the symptoms related to the anxiety disorders along with the features of panic attacks and agoraphobia may seem overwhelming and confusing. Not sure what is causing the problem, many individuals may seek medical attention for answers. The individual as well as the practitioner may at first be confused as to whether the symptoms being experienced may be medically related (see Quick Reference 10.2). When a physical exam has been completed and no medical reason can be determined for the symptoms displayed, a referral to a mental health practitioner may be made.

Understanding the clinical features of panic and subsequent agoraphobia provides the basic information for understanding the anxiety disorders. A concise explanation of the anxiety disorders is presented in this section. Special consideration is given to OCD and PTSD in separate sections of this chapter. All of the disorders presented in this section cause clinically significant distress, interfere with normal daily functioning, and impair the ability to pursue necessary tasks. (See Quick Reference 10.3.)

Panic Disorder

The presence of worry of recurrent and unexpected (uncued) panic attacks—"out-of-the-blue" attacks not due to the direct physiological effects of substance abuse or a general medical condition—forms the basis and characteristic

hallmark of panic disorder (PD) (APA, 2000). PD has a prevalence rate of 6 million people in the United States ages 18 and above with a median onset in late adolescence and mid-30s (APA, 2000; NIMH, 2008). There is an abnormal speed of processing of information present in PD, and event-related processing is disturbed as well as autonomic maladaptive physiological responses (Wise et al., 2009). The attack is usually attributed to fears of an undiagnosed terminal medical condition. The individual often fears that this experience is a sign of losing one's mind, going crazy, or a signal of emotional weakness. This multitude of symptoms includes shortness of breath, heart palpitations, chest pain, choking, smothering sensations, paresthesias, fear of dying, and feelings of losing control (APA, 2000; Hurley, 2007). To be considered a significant finding, worry regarding the onset of the attack must be present for at least 1 month.

The *DSM-IV-TR* presents two conditions of panic disorder: panic disorder with agoraphobia and without agoraphobia. With agoraphobia, panic is exacerbated by fears involving situations where space and escape is confined and restricted. For example, the fear occurs when the individual is in a crowd; standing in a line; traveling in a bus, train, or automobile; being outside the home alone; or being on a bridge (APA, 2000). "Indirect evidence of the over-inclusion of certain types of environmental stimuli is the clinical observation that panic disordered individuals frequently experience heightened anxiety and panic in complex environments of particularly high sensory load: common agoraphobic and panic-triggering situations such as supermarkets, shopping malls, and crowds" (Wise et al., 2009, p. 35). With PD's comorbidity with other anxiety disorders and medical conditions, the *DSM-IV-TR* has no laboratory findings to support diagnostic identification of PD except for elevated blood pressure and transient tachycardia in medical examinations.

Phobia: Specific and Social

Two types of phobias are specified under this category: specific (also known as simple phobia) and social phobia. Within the United States alone, phobias account for a prevalence rate of 34.2 million people diagnosed at age 18 and above, with a median onset in early childhood and peaking in early adulthood (APA, 2000; NIMH, 2008). The *DSM-IV-TR* defines subtypes of specific phobias and includes animal type, natural environment type, blood-injection type, situation type, and other type. Phobias are defined by their intense anxiety response when in the presence of an anxiety-provoking stimuli (i.e., object, situation, or social circumstance). The defining feature of the phobias is that there is a persistent fear of the interaction with a clearly specified object, a situation, or a social performance situation (APA, 2000; Walsh, 2002). When exposed to anxiety-provoking stimuli, the individual suffering from a phobia will have an immediate anxiety response to avoid stimuli; if avoidance is unavoidable, it is endured with dread.

In social phobias, a specifier for generalized phobia to most related social situations is defined. In social phobias, the stark fear of being judged negatively by others, a belief that the person will act inappropriately, and feelings of inadequacy resulting in catastrophic social consequences cause distress, embarrassment, humiliation, and

depression (Spokas, Rodebaugh, & Heimberg, 2004; Walsh, 2002). According to Spokas et al., a bias in attention, interpretation, and memory results in the negative reinforcement of self-image, evaluations, poor performance, and avoidance. These authors contend that the cognitive process of phobias is the increased attention to negative information, selecting specific and selected aspects of information (situational or social) as negative, threatening, or dangerous. Trying to make sense of the environment, the person subsequently perceives social cues, interprets them based on recall of past events, and anticipates a reaction. The emotions occurring cause fear and avoidance of the situations, social circumstances, and/or objects. In both specific and social phobias, the fear is recognized as excessive and/or unreasonable. Comorbidity with other anxiety disorders, mood disorders, and substance use disorders is present. No laboratory tests exist to determine the presence of the phobias, except in medical examinations where elevated blood pressure and vasovagal fainting is present and occur in relation to the specific phobia of the blood injection injury type (APA, 2000).

Acute Stress Disorder

The onset of acute stress disorder (ASD) is characterized by exposure to an extreme traumatic stressor and the development of recurrent anxiety, dissociative, and other symptoms of which reminders of the stressor are avoided subsequent to the hyperarousal experienced (APA, 2000). Symptoms present in ASD—also found in PTSD, discussed later in this chapter—can include difficulty sleeping, irritability, poor concentration, hypervigilence, and motor restlessness. Included in the *DSM-IV-TR* criteria for ASD is the experiencing of a traumatic event with the individual reexperiencing a minimum of three dissociative symptoms lasting anywhere from 2 days to a maximum of 1 month after the event. For example, the individual may suffer from a subjective sense of numbing, detachment (emotional and physical), absence of emotional awareness of his or her surroundings, derealization, depersonalization, or dissociative amnesia. Comorbidity with other disorders is present as are medical conditions resulting from trauma (e.g., head injury) (APA, 2000; Bryant, Moulds, Guthrie, & Nixon, 2003). ASD does not lead to the automatic diagnosis of PTSD, but if symptoms are present for longer than 1 month, the *DSM* suggests that PTSD should be considered.

Generalized Anxiety Disorder

Generalized anxiety disorder (GAD) is characterized by unfounded worrying where there are no precipitants and the individual has difficulty trying to control it. The feelings of worry and apprehension are significant enough to impair the engagement of activities (APA, 2000; Ballenger et al., 2001). For a minimum of 6 months, the anxiety and worry is pronounced and excessive, and the intensity, duration, and frequency of the worrying are out of proportion to the event (real or imagined). GAD accounts for a prevalence rate of 6.8 million people with the disorder ages 18 and above with a median onset at age 31 (APA, 2000; Ballenger et al., 2001; NIMH, 2008). Symptoms of restlessness, fatigue, disturbed sleep, difficulty concentrating, irritability, muscle tension, aches, trembling, twitching, shakes, accelerated heart rate, nausea, diarrhea, shortness of breath, and dizziness are but a few of the presenting clinical features of GAD. GAD is difficult to treat because of marked fluctuations, with intervening symptoms that may be related to other disorders and alternating periods or spontaneous remission (Ballenger et al., 2001). These clinical features are not the direct physiological effects of a substance, a general medical condition, or exclusively during a mood disorder, psychotic disorder, or a pervasive

developmental disorder (APA, 2000; Hurley, 2007). Comorbidity with other disorders is present and the disorder is distinguishable from nonpathological anxiety.

Anxiety Disorder Due to a General Medical Condition and Substance-Induced Anxiety Disorder

Anxiety disorder due to a general medical condition must involve significant anxiety that is related directly to a medical condition. In substance-induced anxiety disorder, the condition results from the direct physiological effect of ingestion or exposure to a substance or toxin. Laboratory analysis must provide evidence of the presence of these conditions in order to make a diagnosis, and the disturbance cannot be explained by another mental disorder (APA, 2000). For the anxiety disorder due to general medical condition, the *DSM-IV-TR* specifies medical conditions associated but not limited to endocrine conditions, cardiovascular conditions, respiratory conditions, metabolic conditions, and neurological conditions. In substance-induced anxiety disorders, the symptoms cannot occur during the course of delirium and the anxiety presented is clearly in excess of the conditions presented (APA, 2000). Specifiers are included in each of the conditions in the *DSM*, and both require the recording of the conditions and substance with code on Axis I (and Axis III for anxiety disorder due to a general medical condition).

Anxiety Disorder Not Otherwise Specified

The last condition in this section cited in the *DSM-IV-TR* is anxiety disorder not otherwise specified (NOS). This condition is assessed when the criteria for all other anxiety disorders cannot be met, including the adjustment disorders (APA, 2000). (See Quick Reference 10.3 for summary of the Anxiety Disorders.)

QUICK REFERENCE 10.3

ANXIETY DISORDERS AND RELATED CONDITIONS

Panic disorder (with or without agoraphobia): The presence of worry or recurrent and unexpected panic, involving intense anxiety, that can be combined with fear and avoidance of places (agoraphobia) and not due to direct physiological effects of substance abuse or a general medical condition.

Agoraphobia with history of panic disorder: Fear and pervasive avoidance of places and situations where escape is difficult or help is unavailable.

Social phobia: Persistent excessive fear, anxious anticipation, and avoidance of social or performance situations where concerns about negative judgments from others are perceived.

Specific phobia (was simple phobia): Persistent fear and an immediate anxious response to a specific object or stimulus. Subtypes of this category include: animal type, natural environment type, blood-injection-injury type, situational type, and other type.

Obsessive-compulsive disorder: Persistent and reoccurring obsessions (thoughts) and compulsions (behaviors) that are severe enough to be time consuming, and to affect emotional, social, and occupational functioning.

Posttraumatic stress disorder: Exposure to a traumatic stressor directly involving personal experience, witnessing of, and learning about events and situations involving actual or threatened death, serious injury, a threat to one's physical integrity, and/or learning about the unexpected or violent death, serious harm, or threat of death or injury experienced by a family member or other close associate.

Acute stress disorder: Acute reactions to the exposure of an extreme traumatic stressor, onset within 2 days to maximum 1 month, with the development of recurrent anxiety and other avoidance symptoms secondary to the hyperarousal experienced.

Generalized anxiety disorder: Inability to control worrying, with pronounced and excessive anxiety and worry, about a number of events and activities without precipitants.

Anxiety disorder due to a general medical condition: Anxiety disorder resulting directly from a general medical condition.

Substance-induced anxiety disorder: Anxiety disorder results due to the physiological effects of the ingestion or exposure to a substance and only in association with intoxication or withdrawal states.

Anxiety disorder NOS: Similar to other NOS categories; prominent anxiety and phobic responses where symptoms do not meet the criteria for a specific anxiety disorder or adjustment disorder.

Source: Summarized criteria from the *Diagnostic and Statistical Manual of Mental Disorders, Fourth Edition, Text Revision.* Copyright 2000 by the American Psychiatric Association.

THEORIES AND ETIOLOGY OF ANXIETY DISORDERS

Theories related to the understanding of anxiety disorders provide the underlying mechanisms from which treatment, interventions, and prevention methods are based and informed. These theoretical approaches can help to explain the complex interactions and impacts that can occur among interpersonal, intrapersonal, and environmental relationships. Theories related to the understanding of anxiety disorders are often based in theories founded in the biological sciences, neuropsychology, cognitive psychology, and social psychology.

Theories from the biological sciences and the application of neuropsychology provide an understanding of the role of organ function and dysfunction related to neuropsychological response to stress. The anatomy of the brain when examined in relation to the anxiety disorders demonstrates brain-organ dysfunction of the amygdala and the frontal striatal lobe. In anxiety disorders, there is an exaggerated reactivity of the amygdala in response to facial expression. This supports the conveying of criticism or negative feedback and these behaviors are evident in brain imaging studies, when there is impaired responses in the medial prefrontal cortex (the area of the brain critical to mentalizing and forming impressions about others) (Mathew, Coplan, & Gorman, 2001; Sripada et al., 2009). The role of the direct pathways of movement, such as the striatal functions (e.g., striato-pallido-nigral and subthalamic) and basal ganglia, predicts impoverished or excessive movement. Movement difficulties can be found when this area is involved in cases of dementia, Parkinson's disease, Huntington's disease but also in OCD, where abnormalities in memory, visuospatial processing, and organizational strategies affecting timing and motor speed are present (Saint-Cyr, 2003; Simpson et al., 2006; van den Heuvel et al., 2005).

Abnormalities in the orbitofrontal-striatal function reflect the inhibited behaviors (repetitive and ritualistic) found in anxiety disorders, such as OCD (van den Heuvel et al., 2005). In conjunction with the striatal function of the frontal lobe, the basal ganglia circuits control the excitability of (and provide input to) the frontal lobes directly influencing vigilance (Saint-Cyr, 2003). Impairment to the basal ganglia is associated with disturbed implicit learning, fear recovery, hyperarousal, and hypervigilence (Huff, Hernandez, Blanding, & LaBar, 2009; van den Heuvel et al., 2005). These impairments in turn arouse the activation of the hypothalamic-pituitary-adrenal axis, which impair serotogenic functioning and dopaminergic neurotransmission, blunt prolactin release, hypersecrete cortisol, and activate the reticular activating system resulting in attentional instability, decreased performance, social withdrawal, and increased emotional reactivity in types of anxiety disorders (Mathew et al., 2001; van den Heuvel et al., 2005). Clinical correlations in *anxiety disorders* include blushing, increased substance abuse, behavioral inhibition, social incompetence, and disruption of affiliation (Mathew et al., 2001). Impairment to any of these organ and pathway systems disturbs the systematic process resulting in the clinical expression and presentation of anxiety disorders.

Plasticity, neural networks, and neurotransmitters attest to the delayed extinction and renewal of fear in normal processes but particularly in the anxiety disorders. Plasticity allows the brain to generate new neural pathways and compensates for ones damaged or injured (as seen in head trauma). When these pathways fail to regenerate, functions related to them are impaired. Altered gene expressions also affect synaptic plasticity in the brain, related to cognitive decline, changes in processing speed, and impaired executive functions. These are evident in the inability of the individual to engage in strategic planning, decision making, judgment, perception, set shifting, generativity, self-regulation, monitoring, and action (Bieberich & Morgan, 2004; Colvert et al., 2008; Goldstein et al., 2001; Hartshorne, Nicholas, Grialou, & Russ, 2007; Joseph, McGrath, & Tager-Flusberg, 2005; Santos, Rondan, Rosset, Fonseca, & Deruelle, 2008). The cognitive disruption to synaptic and cellular processes provides a new look at how memory stores fear episodes and this stored memory in turn disrupts synaptic processes. These dysfunctional stored memories result in impairment to the basal ganglia associated with implicit learning and fear recovery. In anxiety disorders, exposure to fear causes plastic changes in the frontolimbic circuits, which suppress emotional responses no longer appropriate to fear (Huff, et al., 2009).

With the assistance of cognitive and social psychology the understanding of the recognition of fear and its subsequent extinction can be addressed. Huff et al. (2009) point out in their analysis of fear extinction that learning and training of fear can be restructured. The long-term psychological effects of trauma and stress found in anxiety disorders can be ameliorated and spontaneous recovery can occur. In this type of recovery, the immediate extinction of fear arousal is weakened and with each contextual reexperience of the fear episode is controlled. The implication is that *when* the extinction, restructuring, and training take place it results in the greatest impact on the severity and duration of the trauma and stress experienced. "In anxiety, depression, and drug addiction, individuals are particularly prone to relapse when they return to setting that resemble those previously associated with stressful or drug-taking experiences" (p. 841). In terms of plasticity, this restructuring allows the physiological effects of regenerativity of the brain to create new neural pathways and new memories, which then control for the behavioral effect,

responses, and regulation of fear-inducing memories.

The implication of generativity, learning, and retraining is an important aspect of cognitive and social psychology that helps to provide a better understanding of anxiety disorders. As noted earlier, impaired responses in the medial prefrontal cortex result in impairment to metacognitions, which is critical to mentalizing and forming impressions about others (Mathew et al., 2001; Sripada et al., 2009). Metacognitions include mental processes of attribution and imputation of emotional and situational states that provide the basis for trust and safety assessments. In anxiety disorders, the shared feature among all the disorders is the presence and response to fear and the subsequent response and impairments emanating from these responses. Since basic emotions are "hardwired" and recognized among all human beings and animals, emotions are displayed that allow for adaptation to the social environment. These include emotions such as happiness, sadness, anger, fear, joy, rage, terror, love, despair, and disgust. The ability to identify and recognize these emotions provides human beings the ability to identify a threat and act correspondingly (fight or flight). Psychological theories related to the attribution of mental states lend to the understanding of cognition, mental states, and interactions. The ability to impute mental states to others provides the basis for communication and development of emotional schema providing a blueprint of memories. When influenced by these pre-programmed types of memories and a stimuli occurs, certain actions arise. In anxiety disorders, these actions would be the avoidance of harm when recognizing danger, anger, rage, terror, and disgust, and prevention, such as seeking safety.

Eliciting and misattributing meaning assignment to situations and other environmental cues is a disorder of cognition and results in maladaptation in anxiety disorders and individuals' relation to mental states. Deficits in memory and executive function impair information processing; consequently, judgment and decision making are impaired, resulting in the attribution of negative messages specific to situations or social circumstances. In the individual suffering from a type of anxiety disorder, some disruption in organic brain function has reduced his or her background capacities to process and understand information. Furthermore, the disruption affects the individual's ability to attribute meaning, motivation, and intention to cues. When this occurs, the individual may inappropriately react to perceived threats, resulting in anxiety and maladaptation, especially if the person suffers from a brain lesion or head injury. This may cause the onset of panic and social withdrawal. The emotions are constant, but their interpretation is impaired secondary to the organic brain-related processing problems that leaves the individual responding with impaired metacognitions.

There are also situations in which anxiety is experienced by an individual who has an adequate set of background capacities present and who in most cases has the ability to impute mental states attributing meaning, motivation, and intention. Situational factors such as acts of betrayal, malevolence, and deceit (e.g., war, torture), can also affect the way an individual perceives information and violate the blueprint of thought patterns and how adaptable reactions will be. "Exposure to cruelty, perversion, or betrayal may lead to a greater sense of threat or fear as this presents not just the risk of physical injury but also the breakdown of social norms as well as the sense of safety associated with being a member of rule-guided community" (Charuvastra & Cloitre, 2008, p. 305). Impairment in the cognitive process from the interaction alters the individual's schema and brain function, resulting in anxiety. The onset of panic and social withdrawal and the emotions are constant, but their interpretation is impaired secondary to the interaction that impaired the metacognitions. In working with these clients, the issue becomes one of how to restructure the metacognition and processing of novel information to reduce the anxiety.

In relation to understanding these biological, neuropsychological, cognitive, and evolutionary processes, these theories connect the factors such as onset, consequences, and impact to a greater understanding of the anxiety disorders. Attention, recall, recognition, problem solving, strategizing, visualizing, set-shift, and generativity are basic human emotions found in all living entities. These processes provide the foundation to understand what motivates and how to motivate others. The actions individuals use to respond is guided by these processes, whether in response to fear, terror, disgust, anger, or love. In anxiety disorders, recognition of these theories can assist to provide the key to best practices, treatment, and interventions for the individual suffering from anxiety disorders by addressing restructuring of cognitive processes, changes in behavioral response, and increases in the regulation of emotions. And they enable practitioners to understand human interaction, at its best and worst, and how disorders of anxiety can be prevented.

OBSESSIVE-COMPULSIVE DISORDER

Equally common in both genders in adulthood (APA, 2000), obsessive-compulsive disorder has an average age of onset between childhood and adolescence with a median age at 19 (APA, 2000; NIMH, 2008). It is an anxiety disorder featuring "recurrent obsessions or compulsions that are severe enough to be time consuming or cause marked distress or significant impairment" (APA, 2000, p. 456). Included in the *DSM-IV-TR* criteria for OCD is the recognition by the individual of the excessiveness and unreasonableness of the obsessions and compulsions, not accounted for by a medical condition or the physiological effects of a substance. The obsession and compulsion must take longer than 1 hour a day to complete. In obsessional thinking the individual acknowledges that thoughts are a product of his or her own mind and are not imposed from another source, such as thought insertion. This impairment must be severe enough to interfere with an individual's ability to perform daily activities, to impair occupational and academic functioning, and to disrupt relationships (see Quick Reference 10.4).

The *DSM-IV-TR* defines obsessions as the "ideas, thoughts, impulses or images that are experienced as intrusive and inappropriate and that cause marked anxiety or distress" (APA, 2000, p. 457). Repeated fears of contamination or of being harmed or harming others, disturbing visions of a sexual or aggressive content, doubting, need to have things in a particular order, and unacceptable impulses are present (APA, 2000; Cooper, 1999). Because the thoughts and worries are not simply about real-life problems, the individual makes attempts to ignore, suppress, or neutralize them with some other thought or action. The cognitive bias found in OCD attributes the maintenance of obsessive thoughts and

compulsive actions to the distress experienced from the actions themselves (e.g., their moral aspect); consequently, the thinking of these thoughts increases the likelihood of an event occurring (with subsequent behaviors to neutralize thoughts related to the catastrophic consequences) (Abramowitz, Whiteside, Lynam, & Kalsy, 2003).

Fears resulting in behaviors employed in the absence of objective danger or contamination, applied in a nonjudicious manner, result in the common features of anxiety disorders such as OCD (Deacon & Maack, 2008). The particular aim of OCD is to prevent or reduce distress of a dreaded event or situation in response to these thoughts (Pietrefesa & Coles, 2009). These avoidance behaviors are defined as compulsions in OCD and as repetitive behaviors or mental acts preventing or reducing anxiety or distress rather than for pleasure or gratification (e.g., hand washing, ordering, checking, praying, counting, or repeating words silently) (APA, 2000; Deacon & Maack, 2008; Pietrefesa & Coles, 2009). Common compulsions include cleaning (or avoidance of contaminated objects), checking, counting, repeating, requesting or demanding assurances, hoarding, and putting things in order (APA, 2000; Cooper, 1999). Compulsive acts are excessive, such as repeated

---

QUICK REFERENCE 10.4

OBSESSIONS AND COMPULSIONS

Obsessions: Persistent, recurring, and distressing intrusive thoughts, images, and impulses inappropriate, anxiety provoking, and contrary to the individual's free will.

Compulsions: Persistent repetitive behaviors (e.g., checking and rechecking) or mental acts (e.g., counting) in response to an obsession or to applied rigid rules, and not performed for pleasure or gratification.

Source: Summarized from the *Diagnostic and Statistical Manual of Mental Disorders, Fourth Edition, Text Revision.* Copyright 2000 by the American Psychiatric Association.

visits to physicians to seek assurance; excessive use of alcohol or of sedative, hypnotic, or anxiolytic medications; avoiding public restrooms; or avoiding shaking hands with strangers. (See Quick Reference 10.4, which defines obsessions and compulsions.)

The selective neuropsychological deficits in executive function, nonverbal memory, motor speed, and visuospatial and visuoconstructional skills (Simpson et al., 2006; van den Heuvel et al., 2005) can explain the misattribution, impaired judgment, emotional response, and inhibited behaviors. Noted is the misattribution of safety behaviors that erroneously attributed to the feared catastrophe (Abramowitz et al., 2003; Deacon & Maack, 2008). The individual engages in excess preventive measures where the presence of the fear does not exist. This unintentionally causes a negative feedback loop whereby the thought of the safety behavior and subsequent action increases and substitutes the thoughts and behaviors misattributed to danger. It has been postulated that the obsessions and compulsions found in individuals with OCD may also be in response to two underlying dimensions of harm avoidance and incompleteness, characterized by pathological doubt, perfection, and a high degree for control (Pietrefesa & Coles, 2009). In neuropsychological studies of individuals with OCD, vander Heuvel et al. (2005) noted that such individuals spent more time generating alternative solutions or checking next responses when a mistake is made (i.e., the increased performance-monitoring characteristic of the critical self-evaluation of performance, leading to self-correction and repetitive behavior).

Associated disorders in adults include other anxiety disorders (e.g., phobias, panic disorders, generalized anxiety disorder), major depression, eating disorders, substance use disorders, learning disorders, disruptive behavior disorders, and personality disorders (obsessive-compulsive personality disorder, avoidant personality disorder, and dependent personality disorder) (APA, 2000). While it is acknowledged that recurrent or intrusive thoughts may be shared in the criteria for all of these disorders, the differentiation is made in that these cognitive concerns cannot be related primarily to the symptoms captured within another disorder and care to differentiate the presence of these disorders should be compared closely to the criteria and risk factors related to the disorder.

Risk Factors Associated With Obsessive-Compulsive Disorder

It is estimated that 2.2 million people in the United States ages 18 and above have been diagnosed with obsessive-compulsive disorder (NIMH, 2008). Risk factors associated with developing and triggering OCD include genetic/environmental factors, neurobiological factors, infections, and stressful life events. These should be taken into consideration when assessing for OCD during the diagnostic evaluation.

Genetic/Environmental Factors Parents or family members with OCD place individuals with a high risk of developing the disorder (APA, 2000; Mayo Clinic, 2008). Heredity in the development of OCD has been found in concordance for obsessive-compulsive symptoms, subclinical OCD, in first-degree relatives and in twins studies (APA, 2000; Nestadt et al., 2000; Rosario-Campos et al., 2005). Genetic factors should be considered when assessing for the presence of OCD.

Neurobiological Factors The role of brain dysfunction in striatal functions (e.g., striato-pallido-nigral and subthalamic), altered gene expressions, and basal ganglia determines motor function, abnormalities in memory, visuospatial processing, executive functions affecting timing and motor speed in obsessive-compulsive disorder (Saint-Cyr, 2003; Simpson et al., 2006; van den Heuvel et al., 2005). Abnormalities found in the orbitofrontal-striatal function have been related to OCD (van den Heuvel et al., 2005). Hypothalamic-pituitary-adrenal axis impairment increases emotional reactivity, including blushing, increased substance abuse, behavioral inhibition, social incompetence, and disruption of affiliation found in obsessive-compulsive disorders and other types of anxiety disorders (Mathew et al., 2001; van den Heuvel et al., 2005). The disruption to synaptic and cellular processes in anxiety disorders, with impairment to the basal ganglia associated with implicit learning and memory storing of fear episodes, accentuates the role of organ function in the disorder. Brain dysfunction is a risk factor for the development of OCD. The evaluation should consider assessing for cognitive impairments (e.g., changes in mental status), head injury, or head trauma to evaluate the presence of organic deficits contributing to the disorder.

Stressful Life Events   Stressful life events have been associated with the intensification of ritualistic behaviors, increasing the risk of OCD. These events include important life transitions and mourning, where intrusive thoughts trigger these rituals to alleviate the emotional distress characteristic of obsessive-compulsive disorder (APA, 2000; Mayo Clinic, 2008). Events can include pregnancy (as a major life transition) or an unexpected death, particularly in cases where death has been complicated. Focus on general stress in nonclinical populations has found increased intrusive thoughts in response to stressful and aversive stimuli, highlighting the impact of the environment in inducing obsessive impulses and the link to stress and OCD (stressful life events and traumatic stress events) (Cromer, Schmidt, & Murphy, 2007). The presence of stressful life events should always be assessed in clients suffering from OCD.

Infections   Hemolytic streptococcal infection (e.g., scarlet fever and "strep throat") is a risk factor in the development of OCD (APA, 2000; Mayo Clinic, 2008). Streptococcal infections related to Pediatric Autoimmune Neuropsychiatric Disorders (PANDAS) can trigger symptoms and neurological abnormalities. Risk of OCD is increased when this is accompanied with the abrupt onset of symptoms, and the individual carries the particular gene set also found in relatives with PANDAS (APA, 2000; Mell, Davis, & Owens, 2005). As in genetic and environmental factors, the presence of these infections should be assessed in the diagnostic evaluation to differentiate diagnosis.

OCD: Completion of the Diagnostic Assessment

The assessment of OCD should take into consideration all criteria specified under the *DSM-IV-TR* and subsequent risk factors. The assessment should include all of the demographic information available, physical examinations, current and past history (medical and mental), and specific background features that contribute to understanding presenting symptoms specified in the *DSM-IV-TR* and in this book. There are no laboratory examinations to establish OCD, but the presence of dermatologic problems offers clues to the severity of symptoms present (e.g., excessive hand washing) (APA, 2000). Hereditary factors and infections in childhood, such as hemolytic streptococcal infections and PANDAS, can establish the presence of the disorder.

Various scales can be utilized to assess for obsessive-compulsive behavior during the assessment process. These include self-reported measures, which can establish the duration, intensity, and frequency of presenting symptomology.

They also assess the presence of metacognitions, attributions, harm reduction, tolerance level, and behavioral responses associated with OCD. They can establish the basis for differential diagnosis and set a baseline for treatment planning and interventions. This section describes screening instruments to assess mental status and comorbidity present in these disorders (e.g., depression and anxiety).

The Obsessional Beliefs Questionnaire (OBQ; Obsessive-Compulsive Cognitions Working Group [OCCWG]) is an 87-item, 7-point, Likert-based questionnaire that assesses beliefs considered characteristics of obsessive thinking (Moretz & McKay, 2008). Individual subscales represent the domains of cognitions related to OCD which include control thoughts (14 items), importance of thoughts (14 items), responsibility (16 items), intolerance of uncertainty (13 items), and perfectionism (16 items). Higher scores are indicative of the presence of OCD.

The Contamination Cognitions Scale (CCS) assesses the overestimation of threat from potentially contaminated objects, listing 13 common objects associated with germs (e.g., door handles, toilet seats), and asks clients to rate the likelihood and severity of contamination if they were to touch each object and refrain from washing their hands (Deacon & Maack, 2008).

The Obsessive-Compulsive Inventory (OCI) is a 42-item self-report measure of the frequency of OCD symptoms and distress experienced from them in the past month (Moretz & McKay, 2008; Pietrefesa & Coles, 2009). A total score of 168 is possible, and a score of 42 or more is indicative of the presence of OCD. Seven subscales comprise the scale, utilizing a 5-point Likert scale that measures constructs of OCD (i.e., washing, ordering, doubting, obsessing, hoarding, and mental neutralizing) (Moretz & McKay, 2008).

The Obsessive-Compulsive Trait Core Dimensions Questionnaire (OC-TCDQ) is a 20-item self-report measure comprised of two subscales, which assesses compulsive behaviors in OCD—harm avoidance and incompleteness (Pietrafesa & Coles, 2009). Each subscale is comprised of 10 items rated on a 5-point Likert scale. The scale demonstrates good internal consistency for each subscale.

The Yale-Brown Obsessive-Compulsive Scale is a 10-item, 5-point Likert scale measuring the severity and frequency of obsessions and compulsions experienced during a day. It is comprised of two subscales, obsessions and compulsions, with a score range from zero (no symptoms) to 40 (extreme symptoms) demarcating the level of severity associated with symptoms, focusing on areas of time spent, interference, distress, resistance from the obsessions and compulsions, and level of control over them (Goodman et al., 1989).

The Vancouver Obsessional Compulsive Inventory (VOCI) is a 55-item scale comprised of six subscales measuring cognitive and behavioral constructs of OCD: contamination, checking, obsessions, hoarding, just right, and indecisiveness (Moretz & McKay, 2008).

To establish mental state and areas related to cognitive functioning, the Folstein Mini Mental State Examination (MMSE) contains questions assessing orientation to time, place, attention, and memory. This measure is dependent on age and educational background and is sensitive to individuals who may not be familiar with the information presented on these tests, such as names of presidents, geographic locations, important dates and events, and also takes into account the different conceptualization of place and location with respect to an individual's background (Adler, 2007; APA, 2000; Amin et al., 2003; Insel & Badger, 2002). It addresses task completion as related to attention and memory through engaging actions of writing, copying, and observation.

Because of the shared phenomenology of anxiety disorders with other *DSM* disorders, scales that assess both clinical features of anxiety and depression have also been utilized to assess for the severity of anxiety present. Scales such as the Cognitive-Somatic Anxiety Questionnaire (CSAQ) created by Schwartz, Davidson, and Goleman (1978) may be helpful in starting this process. The CSAQ is a 14-item instrument that focuses thoughts and somatic modes of trait anxiety and is used to assess the presence of general anxiety in situations. The CSAQ has a score ranging between 7 and 35, with the higher the score, the higher the degree of cognitive and somatic complaints. The Beck Depression Inventory (BDI) is a 21-item, self-report, multiple-choice questionnaire that measures the presence of depression with items particular to anxiety (Center for Psychological Studies, 2008). It describes a specific behavioral manifestation of depression evaluated through four self-evaluative statements with ordinal measurement to assess for severity of symptoms. The Hudson's (1990) Generalized Contentment Scale (GCS) is a 25-item scale measuring the severity of nonpsychotic depression. It produces a score range of zero to 100, with higher scores indicating greater magnitude of depression. The GCS has three cutoff points: 30, 50, and 70 (all ±5). Scores below 30 indicate the absence of a clinically significant depression; scores above 50 indicate some suicidal ideation; and scores above 70 nearly always indicate severe stress and suicidal tendencies.

These scales are useful in determining the onset, frequency, and severity of OCD. The scales can also specify the type of thoughts and behaviors that cause greatest distress and emotional reactions and responses to the obsessions and compulsions found in OCD. They can be utilized to establish the diagnosis but also the level of function in Axis V of the multiaxial assessment.

K (see Case Example 10.1) is referred by his primary care physician for a mental health assessment. He reports intrusive and obsessive thoughts regarding contamination (i.e., germs, disease, bacteria, viruses) and voices concerns about harm to himself and his family. He reports engaging in compulsive behaviors such as cleaning, checking, and ordering to avoid thinking about his problems. The intrusive thoughts have been present for over 6 months with a worsening of symptoms in the last month. He currently reports morbid ideation, insomnia, agoraphobia, intrusive thoughts, excessive behaviors, stress, worry, and difficulty completing and maintain daily functions. He identifies being stressed related to his loss of employment, marital discord, and relationship concerns with his daughters. He has poor personal hygiene and states he has no medical concerns at the time of this interview. He denies any suicidal and/or homicidal ideation and having any auditory, visual, gustatory, olfactory, or tactile hallucinations. His motor function appears within normal limits. Judgment and decision making are limited.

Multiaxial Assessment of K   The presenting clinical features of K's symptoms are obsessions and compulsion. These include K's report that he experiences intrusive thoughts related to contamination—that is, he reports thinking of ways of reducing the germs, bacteria, and viruses that he "sees" all around. These thoughts are further exacerbated by his concern related to reports of germs "in the news" and how these cause death. He reports an increase intrusion of thoughts related to being harmed and/or his family being harmed. He reports the onset of these in the last month, which are related to the increased stress and pressure he is currently experiencing secondary to his loss of employment. He reports that, secondary to these intrusions, he engages in excessive safety and preventive behaviors to reduce the emotions he experiences such as worry, fear, terror, and disgust. He states that in general he has a high need for control, perfectionism, and orderliness and the onset of pressure increased his symptom severity. Due to his current symptoms, he reports experiencing marital strain as his constant requests for reassurance are frustrating and angering his wife. This concern

──────── CASE EXAMPLE 10.1 - THE CASE OF K ────────

K is a 45-year-old Caucasian male, of average height and weight, appearing of stated age, who is referred by his family physician for a mental health assessment. Client reports experiencing morbid ideation, intense stress and worry, thought intrusions, inability to sleep, difficulty leaving his house, and hypervigilance. He described his problems as "worrying about everything and not being able to relax." He reports that these symptoms have been present for over 6 months with worsening in symptoms in the last month. There is weight loss of slightly over 10 pounds in the last month and difficulties with his personal and family life secondary to employment concerns and difficulties with completing his daily tasks. He is accompanied to the mental health assessment by his wife and daughters.

K states he has difficulties with intrusive thoughts and behaviors, which he reports are "necessary." When asked to define what the nature of these thoughts are, K states he is experiencing disturbing images of disease and how the presence of these could harm him and his family. These images cause him to experience intense disgust and alarm as he can "see" the presence of these all around. When asked what occurs when he experiences these thoughts, he replies that he has to clean the bathrooms, bedrooms, and kitchen that family members had used. He also described how this morning when he pulled out of the driveway he noticed a piece of litter on the curb. He pulled back into the driveway, picked up the litter, and went into the house to throw it away. He then reports having to clean his pathway in the kitchen and is preoccupied with germs, viruses, and bacteria all around him. He is worried that the illness will come and cause death. He reports that when these thoughts are present, he must clean to relieve them. When asked what occurs when he does not clean, he reports that he is unable to stop cleaning. K reports that in the last month he has been increasingly concerned about the possibility of death and harm and worrying about the possibility of someone breaking and entering his house. He states he is constantly checking and rechecking everything after his family to make sure the house is secure. He often locks and relocks the door just to verify that it had been done correctly. He reports thoughts of horrific images of what could transpire if the checking and cleaning routines are not kept, which cause him to feel terror. He is afraid of having his residence robbed although he is living in a middle-income family neighborhood where he has not suffered any criminally related concerns to the present time. When asked to describe what occurs in response to these thoughts, he reports repeated check and rechecking that the door is locked and germ free. When he cannot complete his ritual of checking the door he feels petrified with fear. He reports knowing that his current concerns are causing him harm and reports frustration, anger, and a sense of worthlessness regarding his inability to control his thoughts and emotions. When asked how these thoughts and behaviors have affected other areas of his life, he reports that he often forgets to shower or bathe due to constant worry. Similar concerns existed in his last employment setting and these ritualistic behaviors have caused strain in his relationships and personal life.

K reports that he was employed as a manager for over 5 years. As a manager, he is under a lot of pressure to make sure things are done correctly and reports a strong sense of control and need for perfection which he states is demanded in his job. He feels he did not have difficulties with past employers, and says they were pleased with his prior performance, and losing this job has added to his stress. When describing his job he states that internal problems forced him to increasingly check and recheck his reports and figures, and he demanded more of his employees. He found it increasingly difficult to leave his office. His high need for order has become increasingly more rigid. He reports that his thoughts about disease escalated during this time period and the pressure of them conflicted with his ability to carry out tasks. He reports that he was released from his employment duties a month ago.

He denies any medical concerns at this present time and denies taking medication. He denies any allergies to medications. He reports that he was a "social drinker" and denies any past history of illicit drug use. He denies a history of treatment for substance abuse and denies any past treatment for mental health–related concerns at the time of this interview.

K reports strain in his relationship due to his intrusive thoughts and behaviors. He reports that his wife has become increasingly angry with him, yelling at him when he requests reassurance regarding his thoughts. He reports also feeling concerned about the impact this will have on the quality of their relationship. His intense desires for cleanliness while neglecting his own personal hygiene has not improved matters related to intimacy with his wife. He states that he loves his wife but is unable to stop his presenting problems. He is also concerned his relationship with his daughters has also been affected. He denies feeling suicidal and states he has no plan and would not harm himself because of the loss this would cause for his family. (See Quick Reference 10.5, for a summary of the primary and presenting problems).

K is given the Obsessive-Compulsive Inventory Scale during the interview to measure the frequency and distress experienced from symptoms within the last month. K scored a 122 out of 168, which indicates the presence of OCD, with a mean score of distress higher than 2.5 in the subscales of washing, checking, doubting, ordering, and obsessions. His overall mean score of distress is 2.9, suggestive of moderate to severe distress related to his symptoms. He is also given the Folstein Mini Mental State Examination to assess for his mental state. He is oriented, demonstrates no impairment with recall, attention and calculation are intact, and demonstrates no impairments in language, reading, writing, or copying. He is given a score of 30, indicative of normal state (see Quick References 10.6 and 10.7).

QUICK REFERENCE 10.5

IDENTIFY PRIMARY AND PRESENTING PROBLEMS FOR K

Primary problem:	Obsessive thoughts and compulsive behaviors.
Presenting problems:	Current unemployment and strained personal and family relations. Difficulty completing activities of daily living.

---

further causes him stress, which exacerbates his presenting problem.

He is cognizant of the excessive nature of his thoughts and behaviors. When he attempts to cease these repetitive behaviors he experiences strong negative emotions, which prompt him to reengage in compulsions. He is cognizant of the effect of stress exacerbating his symptoms.

Delusions and/or hallucinations are not present, and his mental state is within normal limits, so a diagnosis of schizophrenia or a psychotic disorder is not applicable for his condition. He does not present with substance use problems or a medical condition, so anxiety disorders related to these can also be ruled out. With the high score of distress symptoms on his Obsessive-Compulsive

---

QUICK REFERENCE 10.6

RISK ASSESSMENT FOR K

Document and assess suicide risk:	No ideation or intent noted.
Assess violence risk toward family:	None noted.

QUICK REFERENCE 10.7

MENTAL STATUS DESCRIPTION

Presentation	Mental Functioning	Higher-Order Abilities	Thought Form/ Content
Appearance: Unkempt	Simple Calculations: Accurate	Judgment: Impaired Insight Intact Intelligence: Average	Thought Process: Logical
Mood: Anxious			Delusions: None
Attitude: Guarded	Serial 7s: Accurate		Hallucinations: None
Affect: Appropriate	Immediate Memory: Intact		
Speech: Normal			
Motor Activity: Restless	Remote Memory: Intact		
Orientation: Fully oriented	General Knowledge: Mostly accurate		
	Proverb Interpretation: Accurate		
	Similarities/Differences Accurate		

Inventory scale, there appears to be a strong presence of OCD, and given his presenting problem and symptom duration, K is given the diagnosis of obsessive-compulsive disorder on Axis I.

K's reporting of morbid ideation is in response to his symptoms and current stressors. He reports a weight loss of slightly over 10 pounds in the last month, secondary to his loss of employment and onset of new intrusive symptoms. He reports difficulty sleeping secondary to his fear, terror, worry, and stress and reports that his symptoms are affecting all facets of his life (e.g., employment, relationship, personal satisfaction). K's current morbid thoughts are related to feeling frustrated, angry, and emotionally weak at his inability to control his intrusive thoughts. He does not ruminate about "being worthless" or engage in persistent brooding, as found in major depression. Due to his present actions, he reports evading illness and reducing potential threats for himself and his family, indicative of mood congruency with obsessions

rather than of major depression. Due to his presenting features, the diagnosis of major depression is not applicable at the time of this interview.

On Axis II, there is no diagnosis with code V71.09. Intelligence testing should be addressed when his presenting symptoms are stabilized or it appears that these are related to issues of an organic nature, including assessment of defense mechanism and personality disorders.

K denies any medical concerns at the time of the interview. He denies any allergies to any medications, and this should be written in all caps to alert other providers in his integrated care. Axis III is coded as none reported.

Various social stressors are currently affecting K and these stressors will also be applicable indirectly to establishing his Axis V. He is currently unemployed, having lost his job in the last month. Financial concerns are placing more stress on his current condition. He reports marital strain and relationship problems with his daughter related to his compulsive behaviors. His psychosocial stressors should be coded according to level of severity on Axis IV:

1. Loss of employment
2. Financial concerns
3. Marital concerns
4. Family dynamics and interpersonal relationship concerns

His current Generalized Assessment of Functioning (GAF) addresses the severity of his obsessive symptoms and how they affect his daily functioning. K does not present with suicidal ideation but does express morbid ideation. He does have obsessive rituals, which are the nature of his presenting problem. These rituals affect his daily and occupational functioning. He has been able to maintain employment for the past 5 years until the stress at his employment setting worsened his present symptoms, resulting in his employment loss last month. His mental state is within normal limits, and his impairments are not infused with delusions or hallucinations. He does have serious impairments to his personal and occupational functioning. Because of these presenting concerns, he is given a GAF current score of 50 on Axis V (see Quick Reference 10.8).

Treatment Planning, Implementation, and Evaluation

Creating a treatment plan in this area starts with identifying problematic behaviors and how to best address them (see Sample Treatment Plan 10.1). To start treatment planning, cognitive and behavioral concerns are identified. Issues in OCD are determined by the severity and intensity of the obsessions and compulsions and what the client believes about them. In OCD, clients are cognizant that their reactions to these obsessions and compulsions are beyond reason and in excess but cannot stop them. Individuals with OCD frequently present to outpatient settings rather than inpatient settings, unless the obsessions are related to themes of hurting others and cause severe distress. Assessment for the presence of these obsessions and subsequent care should be implemented. In OCD, the ability to complete tasks is present although there are inhibitions noted. Under certain conditions, the hindered visuospatial capacities and inhibitions hamper clients' ability to effectively problem-solve when under intense stress or perceived negative criticisms. It is appropriate to assess under what conditions the symptoms worsen in severity and intensity, as this information can be useful in treatment planning and implementation.

QUICK REFERENCE 10.8
MULTIAXIAL DIAGNOSTIC SYSTEM

Axis I: [300.3] Obsessive-compulsive disorder.

Axis II: [V71.09] No diagnosis.

Axis III: None reported.

Axis IV: 1. Loss of employment.
             2. Financial concerns.
             3. Marital concerns.
             4. Family dynamics concerns.

Axis V: GAF 50. (current).

SAMPLE TREATMENT PLAN 10.1

K

Long-Term Goals:

1. Develop cognitive beliefs and behavioral patterns to control, alleviate, and reduce the frequency, intensity, and duration of anxiety symptoms.
2. Increase capacity to self-regulate.
3. Increase abilities to complete activities of daily living.

Short-Term Objectives	Plan or Interventions
1. Take medications as prescribed by physician.	Assess needs for anti-anxiety medications and arrange for prescription if needed.
2. Identify anxiety-causing and/or anxiety-producing cognitive mechanisms.	Provide education to client about OCD, including but not limited to psychological and physiological symptoms.
	Encourage client to identify anxiety-producing cognitions, feelings, and emotions and distress level associated with them.
	Reality test cognitions, assisting to differentiate between functional and dysfunctional thoughts.
3. Identify behaviors in response to cognitions.	Engage client in thoughts-stopping exercises paired with anxiety-producing cognitions.
	Encourage client to identify and verbalize feeling and emotions in response and when not in response to anxiety-producing cognitions.
	Provide education on systematic desensitization, its mechanism, and applications.
4. Implement self-relaxation techniques.	Assist client to sustain negative emotions, feelings, and physical symptoms in response to not engaging in compulsive actions.
	Educate client about self-relaxation techniques to alleviate fear, worry, terror, and/or stress.
	Assist client in practicing self-relaxation techniques in session to implement as needed.
5. Engage support systems.	Provide education to family regarding OCD.
	Provide family sessions for family to voice concerns, frustrations, and thoughts regarding treatment.
	Provide family sessions to address communication patterns that facilitate healthy dynamics.
	Provide family sessions to address marital discord.

The nature of the obsessions and compulsions is usually attributed to a negative feedback loop whereby clients see and experience some relief from performing the behaviors. Also, clients might believe that performing these behaviors protects the individual from symptoms worsening. Cognitive restructuring can be used to modify the obsessions connected to the compulsion. In restructuring these thoughts, behaviors related to them will have to be extinguished. Doing this requires clients to learn new ways of processing information and regulating emotions related to thoughts and behaviors experienced. Changing a ritualized behavior is never easy; effort and patience are required for clients to implement a more constructive pattern of behavior. Treatment should address the application of extinction of behaviors and thoughts performed in response to the stressors.

Desensitizing the client from the emotions and thoughts experienced is attributed to positive and longer-lasting responses for addressing problematic behaviors. In obsessive-compulsive disorder, this desensitizing may require repeated sessions where clients are requested to hold an item that they are told is infected with germs and to sustain impulse and emotions prior to utilizing a sanitizer. Clients can learn coping skills that can be applied and generalized to other areas, such as doorknobs, until the obsession and compulsion are stabilized. The treatment plan must include addressing the obsessions and compulsions, as these are the symptoms causing the greatest amount of distress. Treatment plans should include a long-term objective that focuses on the development of beliefs and patterns that increase functioning and reduce distress. Short-term objectives can focus on the application of education, cognitive restructuring, training, and systematic desensitization.

Deep breathing and relaxation can soothe emotions associated with thoughts and actions. With the intensity of emotions and difficulty sleeping, individuals with OCD experience difficulty managing the impact of the emotions and are subject to muscle tension. Learning to tune into the physiological reactions of OCD can assist in increasing recognition and self-regulation. Ways to regulate physiological reactions include breathing exercises, massages, tension and release exercises, and general physical exercise. These should be included in the treatment planning and utilized to improve other areas disturbed in clients' lives. Included in the long-term objective of achieving self-regulation, and in relation to short-term objectives, the addition of breathing exercises and massage sessions between couples could improve daily functioning affected by the OCD.

Accurate assessment of the pressure and stress is critical to successful outcome, as this component of added stress for the client is also a source of frustration for family members. Often these stressors include ignorance regarding OCD, family dynamic dysfunction, communication difficulties, and associated social problems that result from these stressors. Family education is important when working with individuals suffering from OCD. Areas of focus include improving communication; providing a forum to vent frustrations, concerns, and problem-solving; engaging support groups; and improving the quality of relationships among family members. Objectives regarding education and maximizing healthy communication patterns should be included in the treatment plan. The quality of intimate relationships can be addressed through marital counseling. The long-term goal is to improve clients' ability to engage in activities of daily living (as outlined in Sample Treatment Plan 10.1).

As with all disorders included in this book, the record-keeping focus in OCD is "problem oriented" and directly related to documenting the problem area and providing measureable results in treatment planning. Specific information related to observable behaviors is necessary in the documentation of OCD, and the greater the specificity of the presenting problem, the greater the success in treatment implementation. Making a connection between the thoughts and resulting behavior is critical in the problem-oriented record documentation. The thoughts, as observed through behaviors, can be addressed in the treatment plan. Documentation of concrete examples of symptoms, such as motor tension (restlessness, tiredness, shakiness, or muscle tension), autonomic hyperactivity (palpitations, shortness of breath, dry mouth, trouble swallowing, nausea, or diarrhea), or symptoms of hypervigilance should be included. Once this behavior is identified and clearly outlined, a measurable treatment plan can be established.

Intervention strategies for OCD and all of the anxiety disorders are addressed later in this chapter, as they share common underlying principles and treatment venues. The application of the multiaxial system should assess criteria defined for obsessive-compulsive disorder; establish a baseline with respect to frequency, duration, and intensity of symptoms. The next section discusses posttraumatic stress disorder with its application to the multiaxial system.

POSTTRAUMATIC STRESS DISORDER

In posttraumatic stress disorder, the person has been exposed to a traumatic stressor involving direct personal experience, witnessing of, and the learning about events and situations involving actual or threatened death, serious injury, a threat to one's physical integrity (APA, 2000; Charuvastra & Cloitre, 2008). PTSD accounts for a prevalence of 7.7 million people in the United States age 18 and above and can be found in any age group, with a median onset at age 23 (NIMH, 2008). Prevalence is highest among survivors of rape, military combat and captivity, and ethnically or politically motivated internment and genocide (APA, 2000). Included in the *DSM-IV-TR* are the defined traumatic events associated with PTSD. Traumatic injuries caused by human design (e.g., manmade disasters, crimes, torture, rape) are most likely to increase the incidence of the development of PTSD in relation to the intensity and physical proximity to the stressor (APA, 2000; Charuvastra & Cloitre, 2008).

Characteristic features of the disorder include a persistent reexperiencing, avoidance, and hyperarousal of symptoms in response to stimuli associated with the traumatic event. The reexperiencing of the event, as recollections or distressing dreams in which the event is recollected, is specified in the *DSM-IV-TR*; in rare circumstances,

dissociation occurs in which the person behaves as if the event is reexperienced (e.g., "flashbacks). These attempts include avoiding thoughts, feelings, conversations, activities, situations, people, and reminders of the traumatic event. These circumstances are associated with intense physiological responses and psychological distress, in which the person then attempts to avoid any associated stimuli related to the trauma (APA, 2000; Spoormaker & Montgomery, 2008). Associated are the intense emotions of fear, helplessness, horror, distress, anxiety, irritability, and anger further specified as an acute episode (if it lasts less than 3 months), chronic (if it lasts 3 months or longer), or with delayed onset (if at least 6 months passed between traumatic event and onset of symptoms) (APA, 2000). Associated symptoms of psychological distress include but not limited to: impaired memory; impaired executive functions; impaired affect regulation; self-destructive and impulsive behavior; feelings of ineffectiveness, shame, despair, hopelessness; insomnia; nightmares; a loss of previously held beliefs; social withdrawal, and impaired relationships with others.

Risk Factors Associated With Posttraumatic Stress Disorder

Genetic/Environment Factors The *DSM-IV-TR* notes that a genetic component is attributed to the development of PTSD. A history of depression and/or PTSD in a first-degree relative increases the risk (APA, 2000; Keane, Marshall, & Taft, 2006; Mayo Clinic, 2009). Low cortisol levels are found among groups of trauma survivors and in familial transmission, indicative that the hypothalamic-pituitary-adrenal axis has become resistant to the effects of cortisol. This leaves the system consistent with the increased reactivity and hyperarousal to explicit and implicit trauma reminders in trauma survivors found in PTSD (Keane et al., 2006; Yehuda et al., 2000). The presence of these symptoms increases the risk for the development of PTSD and should be assessed in the evaluation.

Geographic Location   Geographic location is a factor that needs to be considered. "Individuals who have recently emigrated from areas of considerable social unrest and civil conflict may have elevated rates of Posttraumatic Stress Disorder" (APA, 2000, p. 465). PTSD is observed at higher rates in non-Western and developing countries (e.g., not limited to Afghanistan, Algeria, Cambodia, Ethiopia, Gaza, Latin American countries, and Rwanda) (Keane et al., 2006). Regional and world location in the risk for PTSD needs to be considered in the assessment.

Age and Gender   When looking specifically at age, there is no association of age with PTSD. The disorder can begin at any age, but a median onset is 23 years of age (APA, 2000; NIMH, 2008). In the development of PTSD, age becomes an associated risk in the presence of gender. There is an association, however, between the development of PTSD and gender according to type of trauma experienced. Men have a higher rate of PTSD secondary to life span issues and age of entry into combat; women have a higher rate of trauma related to sexual assault (Keane et al., 2006). When controlling for gender and type of trauma, there is little difference in the overall prevalence rate between men and women and the development of PTSD.

Life Stressors   Stressors that increase the risk of PTSD include dealing with extra stress after the event (i.e., loss of a loved one, pain and injury, or loss of a job or home) (NIMH, 2009c). Little or complete loss of emotional support after the event increases the risk of developing PTSD. Marital status is not significantly associated with PTSD but can confer a protective factor when exposed to a traumatic event (Keane et al., 2006). In considering this factor, unhealthy

relationships and domestic violence are risk factors in the development of PTSD.

Trauma   The type, intensity, and duration of a traumatic event increases associated risk of developing PTSD (Mayo Clinic, 2009). Types of traumatic events include combat exposure, terroristic attacks, seeing people hurt, killed, or tortured or other life-threatening events such as kidnapping, muggings and robberies, natural disasters, plane crashes, car accidents, rape, childhood neglect and abuse, or life-threatening medical diagnoses, (APA, 2000; Mayo Clinic, 2009; NIMH, 2009c). The type of trauma should always be clearly identified and assessed as a risk factor in the development of PTSD.

PTSD: Completion of the Diagnostic Assessment

The diagnostic assessment takes into consideration all risk factors and criteria specified under the *DSM-IV-TR*. It should include all of the demographic information available, physical examinations, current and past history (medical and mental), geographic location, immigration status, type of trauma experienced, and specific background features. The type of trauma experienced can be related directly to symptom severity as this will help to clarify the cognitive, behavioral, and physiological components suffered secondary to the response. General medical conditions associated or directly related to the trauma should be assessed with subsequent medical treatment provided (e.g., head injury and trauma due to a motor accident) (APA, 2000). Included in the assessment should be medical and laboratory analyses that assess the presence of autonomic functioning (e.g., increased heart rate, sweat gland activity, electromyography, and blood analysis to determine cortisol levels) (APA, 2000; Keane et al., 2006; Yehuda et al., 2000).

More rapid identification of the disorder can result in the most successful long-term results. Assessment methods can be utilized to determine the presence of PTSD. These brief measurements provide good assessments and diagnosis. They assist in providing a more comprehensive analysis of the severity in the conditions, differential diagnosis, and establishing criteria for PTSD (e.g., duration of deterioration, onset of condition). They will also assist in the determination of the GAF score when applied to the *DSM-IV-TR* multiaxial system. These scales utilize the diagnostic constructs of the *DSM-IV-TR* and the underlying principles of the components of PTSD and the anxiety disorders listed in this chapter. These scales have a high correlation to other screening scales that share phenomenology with the disorder, such as depression, anxiety, social dysfunction, avoidance, hyperarousal, cortisol levels, and alcohol and substance use (Keane et al., 2006; Sundin & Horowitz, 2002; Yehuda et al., 2000).

The Penn Inventory for Posttraumatic Stress Disorder (PI-PTSD) is a 26-item, 3-point Likert, self-report measurement that assesses *DSM-IV* symptoms of PTSD for multiple traumatic experiences (U.S. Department of Veteran Affairs, 2009a). Included are items not directly related to *DSM-IV* symptoms but components of the anxiety disorders, such as self-knowledge (Matthews & Wells, 2000). A score range of zero to 78 reflects the severity of PTSD present (higher scores reflective of severity). Because it is not specific to a type of trauma, the PI-PTSD can assess the presence of multiple traumatic experiences and their effects.

The Los Angeles Symptom Checklist (LASC) is a 43-item, 5-point Likert, self-report measure associated with 17 DSM symptoms embedded in the scale and items measuring general distress (U.S. Department of Veteran Affairs, 2009b). Each item is rated, and a score of 2 or higher is a symptom counted toward the

diagnosis. The sum of all 43 items provides a global index of distress and adjustment problems (higher scores reflective of greater distress and adjustment problems) (U.S. Department of Veteran Affairs, 2009b). In establishing a diagnosis, this scale can assist in identifying the presence and criteria of PTSD.

The Screen for Posttraumatic Stress Symptoms (SPTSS) is a 17-item, 11-point Likert, self-report measure used to measure and assess *DSM-IV* symptoms of PTSD (U.S. Department of Veteran Affairs, 2009c). Item scores can determine symptoms and criteria for the diagnosis of PTSD, and the scale is particularly useful for those with multiple traumatic events and an unknown trauma history (U.S. Department of Veteran Affairs, 2009c). Similar to the LASC, this scale is useful in establishing the presence and criteria for the disorder.

The Impact of Events Scale measures intrusion and avoidance indirectly related to traumatic events (i.e., thoughts and images, distressing dreams, waves of feelings, repetitive and inhibited behaviors) (Sundin & Horowitz, 2000). This scale can be used with other measurements and provides an assessment of the presence of symptoms associated with traumatic impact.

These scales can be utilized with other measurements included in the obsessive-compulsive disorders section of this chapter to assess for comorbidity (e.g., Beck Depression Inventory). The Folstein Mini Mental State Examination (MMSE) should be applied to address mental state and cognitive functioning. These types of rapid assessment instruments can be utilized to evaluate the level of distress and its effect on daily functioning and the information derived can be used to support the global assessment rating on Axis V.

Mrs. Radek: Multiaxial Diagnostic Assessment
In determining Mrs. Radek's presenting problem and application to the multiaxial system (see Case

CASE EXAMPLE 10.2 - THE CASE OF MRS. RADEK

Mrs. Radek is 42-year-old Nicaraguan female, of average height, overweight, and appears her stated age. She was recently referred for a mental health assessment from her primary physician at a community-based clinic. Referral records indicate she is experiencing difficulties sleeping and having crying spells. She has a history for hypertension, hypercholesterolemia, and hypothyroidism for which she receives medical treatment. She is a non-English speaker and a non-U.S. citizen. Client reports back pain and is currently suffering from nightmares, difficulty sleeping, bouts of anger, irritability, crying spells, worrying, and feeling detached. She reports these concerns have been present for over a year and she sought attention as she was finally able to acquire medical services with language accessibility and protection of her legal status.

Mrs. Radek immigrated to the United States due to political and economic concerns. Prior to coming to the United States, she resided in a small poverty-stricken village with her family in Nicaragua. While living in her village she stated that she was never harmed but lived in fear as she was surrounded in conflict that ended in numerous deaths. She stopped attending school (equivalent to secondary education, eighth grade) due to being unable to attend because of the potential danger and unrest. She migrated to the United States as other villagers had also done to escape her living conditions and gain access to better opportunity.

While en route to the United States she was raped but never reported it for fear of deportation back from where she fled. Fearing the social repercussions she would suffer if she returned to her country after the rape, she endured the event and sought the assistance of the church she attended when she arrived in the United States. She reports that she lived with other Nicaraguans until she was able to acquire a place of residence, coliving with a man whom she reports was emotionally, verbally, and physically abusive toward her. She reports that she stayed in this relationship because of limited living and economic options and after leaving this relationship she married her current husband, who is a U.S. citizen. She reports that her husband is also emotionally and verbally abusive but denies physical abuse. She reports that he has alcohol use problems and medical concerns. She reports that he becomes more abusive when under the influence but denies that he engages in physical violence toward her.

Mrs. Radek states she has experienced difficulty sleeping for "a long time." She reports that she frequently has disturbing nightmares regarding her experiences in Nicaragua. She also reports distressing nightmares regarding the rape she suffered and currently she feels detached and reports difficulties in being able to express emotions. She reports that she frequently cries, which comes in waves of sadness, and states that she does not understand why this occurs. She reports that she feels restless, irritable and angry, her heart races and she is easily startled. When she is startled she starts trembling, shaking, feels dizzy and has numbness in her extremities. She reports experiencing difficulties concentrating especially when trying to remember the circumstances surrounding the rape. She reports that she has avoided talking about her rape to family members, including her husband because she has feelings of shame and guilt. She reports that she avoids engaging in behaviors that remind her of her rape, including responding when intimately involved with her husband.

Mrs. Radek has hypertension and hypercholesterolemia and is currently prescribed Lipitor (atorvastatin) to help lower her cholesterol. She reports not taking medication for her hypertension at the time of this interview. She reports that she has been diagnosed with hypothyroidism and is currently prescribed Synthroid (levothyroxine) for this condition. She reports that she receives samples for her cholesterol medication and reports difficulty in purchasing any medications she must pay for herself. She has been warned by her physician regarding her heart problems and weight and has scheduled an appointment to see a clinic nutritionist to help modify her eating patterns. She denies receiving previous mental health treatment and substance use concerns at the time of this interview. Currently she is employed as a house assistant and cleaning woman and receives cash payments for her services. She expresses fondness for this job and the support she receives from the interaction with the people she works for. Her husband of the last five years receives disability for his

(continued)

CASE EXAMPLE 10.2
(*CONTINUED*)

medical concerns and is an insulin-dependent diabetic. She reports citizenship concerns and despite being married, her husband refuses to assist her with obtaining citizenship. They rent a basement apartment and acknowledges that her relationship has unhealthy dynamics believing that it adds to her current concerns. She reports that she remains in contact with family members in Nicaragua through telephone calls utilizing phone cards and sends money to them when possible. Her reading and writing skills are limited, although she would like to learn English to be better able to talk with others and increase her opportunities.

Upon assessment it is noted that her motor function appears to be within normal limits although her judgment and decision making is limited. She is oriented to person, place, time, and situation (oriented x 4). She was not assessed for language skills (reading and writing). She denies suicidal and/or homicidal ideation at the time of the interview. She denies auditory, visual, tactile, and/or gustatory hallucinations at the time of interview.

Example 10.2), all risk factors and presenting features are considered. Her personal and social life is filled with numerous stressors such as illegal immigration, political and civil unrest in her country of origin, and sexual assault in relation to fleeing from her country of origin. She has had limited or no support during the occurrence of these stressors to present. Her communication ability and language skills are limited. Her current stressful circumstances are compounded by what she has experienced in the past.

She reports reexperiencing disturbing dreams related to the events she has suffered with physiological responses associated with thoughts and situations that she avoids in order not to be reminded of these events (e.g., feeling startled, restless, racing heart, trembling, shaking, dizziness, and numbness). She reports a persistent avoidance of stimuli associated with trauma (i.e., she avoids talking about her rape and events she has suffered, reports feeling detached and unable to express emotions). These symptoms have been present for over a year, with client unable to seek assistance due to her language limitations and legal status. She continues to go to work because she needs the income. On differential diagnosis, she does not meet criteria for major depression, as her symptoms are a response to traumatic events. She does not report ruminations to other nonrelated factors and features

centered on the thoughts, behaviors, and physiological responses in relation to them.

Depressive symptoms should be differentiated from secondary effects of her medical condition, which would rule out major depression as a primary condition if these were the presenting features. The presenting emotions and thoughts are related to the attributions she has related to the events she has endured, which are a component of anxiety disorders. Due to the presenting clinical features that meet the criteria, she is given the diagnosis of posttraumatic stress disorder (309.81), chronic, on Axis I.

Mrs. Radek has limited education but is not cognitively impaired, as she was oriented in recall, memory, and other executive functions. She does note impairments in concentration in relation to her presenting problem. Issues related to intelligence testing will be assessed when symptoms stabilize. Issues related to personality disorders can be assessed only after symptoms have been stabilized, including associated defense mechanism. Axis II is coded no diagnosis, code V71.09.

There are medical concerns currently affecting Mrs. Radek. These include hypertension, hypercholesterolemia, hypothyroidism, and weight-related issues. She has been prescribed medications for these concerns. She reports that she has no allergies to medications. (In a medical record, this should always be written in all capital letters to facilitate treatment communication among providers involved in her integrated care.) All presenting medical conditions should be coded on Axis III.

She has a multitude of psychosocial stressors currently affecting her and requiring coding in Axis IV. Immigration status concerns restrict her ability to acquire services, including medical services, mental health services, domestic violence services, housing services, and medical and financial assistance. She is unable to acquire these as she reports her husband is unwilling to assist her with citizenship despite duration of marriage. She has language concerns as she is a non–English speaker. She has basic educational proficiency in reading and writing, including in her native language. She has limited occupational means and works as a house assistant and cleaning woman acquiring undocumented means for her subsistence. She is currently involved in an unhealthy relationship, where substance use problems are present, including emotional and verbal abuse. She denies physical abuse at the time of this interview. She reports a past history of domestic violence with emotional, verbal, and physical abuse at the time of this interview. Her current psychosocial stressors should be coded according to level of severity on Axis IV:

1. Nonlegal U.S. immigration status
2. Financial concerns
3. Current and past relationship concerns
4. Limited supportive systems
5. English as a second language (ESL) concerns

Mrs. Radek's Axis V coding should reflect the impact of her psychosocial stressors and current symptoms presented. She is socially isolated except for the contact she has with the people she works for and telephone calls to her family. She has no friends to offer support, and her current relationship does not offer this either.

She attends to her occupational duties required to maintain subsistence, despite reporting difficulties with concentration, startle responses, and other physiological responses. Her symptoms are serious secondary to the disturbing and intrusive nature of her nightmares, her inability to sleep, feeling detached, inability to express emotions, and avoiding reminders associated with attributed factors. She is not illogical nor does she neglect her responsibilities. She also does not demonstrate flat affect or circumstantial speech. The symptoms she presents are ongoing to a series of accumulated events and responses that have been compounded by her psychosocial stressors. These pose the greatest severity in conjunction to her symptoms and to her overall global functioning. She is given a GAF score of 45 coded on Axis V (see Quick Reference 10.9).

Treatment Planning, Implementation, and Evaluation

Creating a treatment plan in this area starts with identifying problematic behaviors and how to best address them (see Sample Treatment Plan 10.2). To start treatment planning for Mrs. Radek it is important to recognize that the complex problems she is experiencing will require intervention that will increase awareness of her physiological, emotional, and behavioral responses and allow her the opportunity to increase her control of them. Attendance at a support group should be discussed and considered with Mrs. Radek, in conjunction with her individual sessions, as this will increase her level of social support and facilitate introduction to future classroom learning (e.g., ESL classes she desires to attend). Because her PTSD symptoms cause her distress, treatment should focus on the constructs of the root of the disorder. This requires that she become aware and acknowledge how these past experiences influence how she feels today, and how these past experiences

---

QUICK REFERENCE 10.9

MULTIAXIAL DIAGNOSTIC ASSESSMENT FOR MRS. RADEK

Axis I: [309.81] Posttraumatic stress disorder, chronic.

Axis II: [V71.09] No diagnosis.

Axis III: 1. Hypertension.
             2. Hypercholesterolemia.
             3. Hypothyroidism.
             4. No known drug allergies.

Axis IV: 1. No legal U.S. immigration status.
             2. Financial concerns.
             3. Current and past relationship concerns.
             4. Limited supportive systems.
             5. English as Second Language (ESL) concerns.

Axis V: 45 current GAF.

---

influence her current responses. Acknowledging how the beliefs she holds currently have been affected by her previously held beliefs will allow for the development of a healthier set of cognitive interpretations. The long-term objective for Mrs. Radek is to develop cognitive beliefs that control, alleviate, and reduce the intensity and duration of her current symptoms. It is important that her treatment objectives include cognitive restructuring so that she can begin to process novel information in a more adaptive manner, increase the capacity of her cognitions and behavioral responses, and decrease her emotional reactivity.

Since she feels detached physically and socially, treatment should also focus on increasing her awareness of the relationship between her physiologic responses and her emotional responses. While systematic desensitization is an effective method to increase emotional control, there are some concerns, given Mrs. Radek's current situation. Whether this treatment is provided through imagery or through direct exposure (which is compromised, as she is unable

to return to her country of origin or to the location where the rape occurred), she has limited support systems to sustain flooding. Pushing her too fast or too intensely can decrease her overall functioning capacity, and pushing too fast could be harmful given her current circumstances. If stability of her psychosocial factors is achieved, flooding and more aggressive forms of treatment can be explored with her in the future. Other behavioral techniques that can be implemented include deep breathing and relaxation techniques, which she can utilize as needed. She reports that she has back pain and experiences paresthesias. To increase awareness of physiologic responses to stress, objectives can focus on self-massages, stretching, deep breathing, and exercises. The long-term objective is to increase her awareness and recognition of her symptoms and achieve control and regulate emotions associated with them.

Lastly, successful treatment should also address psychosocial stressors that limit or hinder her ability to complete her tasks and activities of daily living. Her situation is compromised by her

SAMPLE TREATMENT PLAN 10.2

MRS. RADEK

Short-Term Objectives	Plan or Interventions
1. Identify level of distress associated with present symptoms.	Assist client in translating and completing a self-report measure to establish baseline of symptoms (e.g., PI-PTSD or IES).
	Encourage client to identify and specify number of episodes contributing to symptomology.
	Assist client to rate the level of distress and intensity associated with factors contributing to presenting problem.
2. Identify problematic cognitives related to stress-causing feelings, events, and situations.	Provide education to client pertinent to PTSD including but not limited to psychological and physical symptoms.
	Encourage client to identify and verbalize emotions and feelings in response to cognitions.
	Encourage client to identify content of attributions in response to cognitions.
	Encourage client to connect physical symptoms associated with cognitions.
3. Identify behavioral mechanisms related to emotional causes and responses.	Encourage client to situation-specific behaviors in response to her cognitions.
	Assist client to identify and connect physical symptoms associated with behaviors and cognitions.
	Encourage client to recognize the functionality of the behaviors utilized in response to her cognitions.
	Educate client in self-relaxation to alleviate emotional and physical stressors.
	Assist client in practicing self-relaxation techniques for self-implementation as needed.
4. Sustain client's positive self-image.	Educate and encourage client to differentiate between her conditions versus personal traits.
	Encourage client to develop unconditional self-acceptance.
	Encourage client to make a positive statement about self per session.
5. Coordinate services to increase social functioning.	Schedule an appointment with immigration services agency for legal consultation to address acquisition of legal status.
	Coordinate services with corresponding documentation for immigration services and consultation.
	Coordinate services with immigrant-based social services agencies to address housing (shelter), food, clothing, and other necessities of daily living.
	Acquire and provide information for client to attend free evening ESL classes.

legal status so a referral to help her access agencies that address immigration concerns is important. Since she has been married to a U.S. citizen for over 5 years, avenues to help her obtain her citizenship can be covered and issues pertinent to her marital relationship can be addressed, always taking into account how these factors affect her current legal status.

INTERVENTION STRATEGIES

The intervention strategies discussed are applicable to all of the anxiety disorders listed in this chapter. Some require more intense application, but all are geared to target thoughts, behaviors, and emotions in response to misattributions, erroneous information processing, and environmental factors. These interventions address the neuro-psychological processes of cognition and how the combination of these thoughts are predisposed to individuals suffering from anxiety. The strategies are also guided by theories discussed in this chapter. Some interventions have already been introduced: scales utilized in obsessive-compulsive disorder and posttraumatic stress disorder, mental status screening instruments, and depression (with comorbid anxiety symptom) scales. These scales include: the Obsessional Beliefs Questionnaire (OBQ) (Obsessive-Compulsive Cognitions Working Group), the Contamination Cognitions Scale (CCS), the Obsessive-Compulsive Inventory (OCI), the Obsessive-Compulsive Trait Core Dimensions Questionnaire (OCTCDQ), the Vancouver Obsession Compulsive Inventory (VOCI), the Penn Inventory for Posttraumatic Stress Disorder (PI-PTSD), the Los Angeles Symptom Checklist (LASC), the Screen for Post-traumatic Stress Symptoms (SPTSS), the Impact of Events Scale (IES), the Folstein Mini Mental State Examination (MMSE), the Cognitive Somatic Anxiety Questionnaire (CSAQ), the Beck Depression Inventory (BDI), and the Generalized Contentment Scale (GCS). These can be utilized in conjunction with the psychosocial and models of interventions discussed in this section.

Psychosocial Intervention

Psychosocial interventions address metacognitions, emotion regulation, physiological responses, and the corresponding behaviors associated with anxiety. These interventions can involve multiple treatment modalities (e.g., individual, group, family, and through technology) all designed to increase cognitive, behavioral, and psychosocial functioning. The psychosocial interventions listed have been cited as most effective in the treatment of anxiety disorder. Often individuals with anxiety disorders do not seek treatment because they prefer psychological therapies or because the application of medication only or medication and therapies is not appealing (Layard, Clark, Knapp, & Mayraz, 2007). The psychosocial interventions listed in this chapter have demonstrated a high degree of effectiveness and efficiency at treating anxiety disorders and are considered best practices (with or without medications) at targeting the clinical components of anxiety disorders.

Cognitive-Behavioral Therapy

Cognitive-behavior therapy (CBT) has demonstrated efficacious results in the treatment of anxiety disorders and other disorders included in the *DSM-IV-TR*. CBT is associated with demonstrable results and cost effectiveness. The emphasis is on expanding the client's sense of self-efficacy, independence, participation, self-monitoring, and control in treatment. It can be utilized in various treatment modalities (e.g., individual, groups, couples, families, Internet). All psychosocial interventions need to take into account the restrictions placed by managed care organizations and insurance plans in their billing and reimbursements. CBT interventions complement other treatment modalities in an integrated approach and are equally as effective on their own to address anxiety disorders. The techniques utilized in CBT are ideal for working with anxiety problems because they allow mental health practitioners to be relatively confrontational yet respectful of the client. "Specifically, difficulties in safety, trust, power and control, self-esteem, and intimacy are targeted [cognitive component of CBT]" (Keane et al., 2006, p. 180). This relationship is essential for promoting client independence and positive self-regard.

Particularly for anxiety disorders, focusing on thoughts and their impact on emotional regulation and reactions is suited in cases where information processing is impaired (Fruzzetti, Crook,

Erikson, Lee, & Worrall, 2008). The application of the cognitive model helps to identify thoughts and the precipitation of physiological and cognitive reaction; if not identified it creates a self-perpetuating cycle which intensifies anxiety (McEvoy & Perini, 2009; Siev & Chambless, 2007). A useful component of CBT is that it addresses the misperception of threat and danger assessments (real or imagined) and the activating of fear, terror, rage, and worry common in anxiety disorders. The CBT model utilizes components to address anxiety (i.e., self-monitoring, cognitive restructuring [including evaluating and reconsidering interpretive and predictive cognitions], relaxation training, and rehearsal and coping skills) (Siev & Chambless, 2007). It is a present-based therapy that reinforces the client's focus on the now and increases reality testing in order to sustain functioning while addressing and increasing coping capabilities and restructuring thoughts and behaviors.

One cognitive-behavior–based intervention is Albert Ellis's rational emotive behavior therapy (REBT) (Ellis & Grieger, 1977; Ellis, 2008). It is particularly helpful for clients' "catastrophizing," personalizing, or imagining the worst-case events where they are responsible for identifying the catastrophic outcome. REBT focuses on clients' irrational and unrealistic thoughts. Internal rules are identified and replaced with more functional and adaptive alternatives (Ellis & Grieger, 1977). The A-B-C-D-E format provides the structure for the analysis of cognitions.

A is the activating event (real or imagined).
B is the belief that person has about A (rational or irrational belief, functional or dysfunctional).
C is the consequence (emotional, behavioral, or both).
D is the disputation of the distorted beliefs (provide evidence for belief).

E is the new effect or philosophy that evolves out of the rational belief replacing the faulty belief (Ellis, 2008; Ellis & Grieger, 1977).

Clients are taught that an irrational or faulty belief they have about A causes C. They learn that everyone, including themselves, are fallible and imperfect human beings. REBT teaches clients to develop unconditional self-acceptance and unconditional acceptance of others. REBT employs active-directive techniques, such as role playing, assertiveness training, and conditioning, and counterconditioning procedures (Ellis, 1971).

Computer-Based Treatments

Self-help interventions are cost-effective interventions that target individuals who are reluctant to enter or unsure of entering treatment or who seek affiliation (e.g., books, self-help groups). CBT interventions are increasingly applied to novel therapeutic situations utilizing Internet-based services where automatic decision making is generated (Andersson, 2009). These interventions assess individuals' decision making and provide educational protocols and support to increase awareness and motivation. Utilizing Internet-accessible self-help materials and computer-based live group exposure sessions, an identified therapist provides support, encouragement, and occasionally direct therapeutic activities via email (Andersson, 2009). In particular, computer-based therapies are used to target individuals with panic disorder, social anxiety disorder, and post-traumatic stress disorder who do not actively seek or who have reservations about treatment. Included in these interventions are mood disorders, substance use disorders, and other health-related problems (Andersson, 2009; Walker et al., 2007).

Behavior Therapies

Contemporary behavior therapies provide the active implementation of behaviors to extinguish emotions, thoughts, and behaviors that affect the individuals. They are often rehearsed in sessions, applied through imagery, modeling, and computer models to create a response in a safe setting with the actual application of the individual exposing him- or herself to the perceived threat or source of distress. Exposure therapies (e.g., systematic desensitization, also known as in vivo exposure therapy and/or eye movement desensitization and reprocessing [EMDR]) are particularly useful for individuals suffering from phobias, separation anxiety, PTSD, and OCD; these interventions can be therapist guided or self-guided. The exposure therapies that use flooding involve gradual or prolonged exposure to the focus stimuli that creates the fear or anxiety reaction (Zoellner, Abramowitz, Moore, & Slagle, 2008). Behavior therapies are particularly effective where executive functions are disturbed and the individual has difficulty imagining events or situations that can trigger fear. "*In vivo exposure* generally involves returning to the site of the traumatic event to reduce avoidance and promote mastery over the associated trauma cues" (Keane et al., 2006). *Relaxation training* is also a behavior-based therapy, where learning to control muscle tension through taught relaxation techniques reduces anxiety and physiological responses.

Family Therapy

Family therapy allows family members to verbalize thoughts, emotions, and concerns related to any mental disorder. Family members can experience difficulties secondary to rituals, fears, inability to perform functions, neglect, and violence. Codependency is a dynamic that occurs and leaves family members feeling hopeless in making life manageable. Families need education and support where they can learn skills to cope and receive help in understanding their loved one's behavior. Family therapy can offer support, education, and a forum to vent feelings and problem-solve. It is important that the family as a whole receive assistance in strengthening its own support systems.

MODELS TO TREAT ANXIETY DISORDERS

Models to treat anxiety disorders utilize a component of multiple approaches to target different components of the disorder. In general, more than one psychotherapeutic approach is used in combination with other interventions.

Self-Regulatory Executive Function Model

The Self-Regulatory Executive Function Model (S-REF) model is particularly useful in addressing metacognitive beliefs associated with rumination, major depression, panic disorder, social phobia, hypochondriasis, obsessive-compulsive symptoms, and worry. According to this model, attentional control and inflexibility, such as an inability to shift, are contributing factors in emotional disorders (McEvoy & Perini, 2009). It addresses beliefs that increase the likelihood of selecting coping strategies that promote self-focused attention (threat monitoring, thought suppression, worry, and rumination) and maintain emotional disorders (McEvoy & Perini, 2009). "The model differentiates three levels of processing: automatic, low-level processing of external and internal stimuli; controlled processing directed toward the control of action and thought; and a permanent store of self beliefs" (Matthews & Wells, 2000, p. 83). The model's treatment aim is to increase attention shifting externally, increase flexibility and control, and employ the application of cognitive-behavioral therapy and attention training. Self-knowledge driving the maladaptive responses is examined, as are metacognitive beliefs influencing thoughts that maintain dysfunction, and processing schemas are modified to provide alternative processing to problematic stimuli (Matthews & Wells, 2000). Intervention focuses on three phases of attention training, including selective attention, attention switching, and divided attention. These require that individuals focus on one particular sound to the exclusion of others for 30 seconds. Once complete attention is shifted to another sound, it is then shifted to another approximately every 5 seconds—thus dividing attention simultaneously—and focused on as many sounds as possible for approximately 15 seconds (McEvoy & Perini, 2009; Matthews & Wells, 2000). The model's CBT and attention training serves as a supplemental component and has demonstrated improvements in increased attention, self-control, and disengaging from threats in panic disorders and social phobia.

Pharmacology

Pharmacological advances are available to address aspects of brain-related dysfunction associated with the anxiety disorders. This mode of intervention is effective but not without controversy. Excessive availability and inadequate regulation has increased the consumption of psychotherapeutic drugs through prescriptions, illegal street vendors, and the Internet. Increased use of benzodiazepines and other anxiolytics has contributed to an estimated 15% to 44% of chronic benzodiazepine users becoming addicted and experiencing discontinuance problems. Upon cessation these individuals experience severe withdrawal symptoms, including emergent anxiety and depressive symptoms (Hood, et al., 2009). Benzodiazepines—for example, clonazepam (Klonopin), temazepam (Restoril), and alprazolam (Xanax)—have little effect on PTSD symptoms (Spoormaker &

Montgomery, 2007). Benzodiazepine and prescription antianxiety medications excluding non-benzodiazepine antianxiety agents (e.g., hypnotics, sedatives, and anxiolytics) can be misused and abused by individuals with anxiety disorders, which creates further problems of withdrawal and dependence (World Health Organization, 2009e).

In certain types of anxiety disorders, pharmacotherapy may be less effective when using traditional selective serotonin reuptake inhibitors (SSRIs) (Pietrefesa & Coles, 2009). SSRIs approved by the Food and Drug Administration that can be used to treat anxiety include: sertraline (Zoloft), fluoxetine (Prozac), and paroxetine (Paxil), which may exhibit modest effectiveness in treatment of PTSD (Keane et al., 2006; Spoormaker & Montgomery, 2007). Tricyclic antidepressants are used less often due to side effects and potential toxicity, specifically imipramine (Tofranil) and amitriptyline (Elavil). Efficacy of the monoamine oxidase inhibitors (MAOIs), such as phenelzine (Nardil) and brofaromine (Consonar), is not supported for certain types of anxiety disorders and used as a last resort based on the problematic side effects and dietary restrictions (Keane et al., 2006)). Other psychotherapeutic medications include antipsychotic agents, such as nefaxodone (Serzone), trazadone (Desyrel), and mirtazapine (Remeron), to treat insomnia and in rare circumstances hallucinations. Other sleep agents, such as cyproheptadine (Periactin), slightly worsened nightmares and symptom severity in anxiety disorders such as PTSD (Spoormaker & Montgomery, 2007).

Antiadrenergic agents are changing the future direction of pharmacological treatment in the anxiety disorders, as these agents target specific neurobiological components relative to the clinical presentation. The association between noradrenergic hyperactivity and pharmacological agents targeting specific adrenergic receptors (associated with hyperarousal and hypervigilance) might be more applicable and efficient and provide better clinical and treatment outcomes than traditional psycho-therapeutic drugs, such as prazosin (Minipress) (Keane et al., 2006; Strawn & Geracioti, 2007). Pharmacological interventions that target neurobiological and organic mechanisms related to the clinical presentation of anxiety disorders may also prove safer, relevant, and more appropriate than the types of pharmacological treatments currently available.

INTEGRATED APPROACH

The current approach to health care service delivery is the integrated approach, and the emphasis is on evidence-based practices. Market-based principles and application to service delivery have shifted health care to a specialization of services that emphasizes quality assurance and cost effectiveness. This is the model of health care practice that dominates all aspects and types of treatment availability emphasizing evidence and best practices, with a feedback loop between billing and reimbursement. Utilizing an integrated approach allows for expediency in treatment, through rapid identification, safety control measures among providers, and intervention techniques that reduce harm. The resultant approach is one that stresses demonstrated effectiveness while encouraging client participation. The mechanisms for the allocation of services specify not just specialization but integration as a quality control measure. All treatment is under scrutiny for reimbursement despite the implementation of the Wellstone-Domenici Mental Health and Addiction Parity Act of 2008, that emphasizes the integration of effectiveness, efficiency, need, and demonstrable results for continuation of services (More, 2008).

Due to their multifactorial aspects, anxiety disorders will require the integrated

specialization of professionals. This is already evident in the pharmacological intervention services, counseling, and screening for medication side effects and hazardous effects. The integrated approach facilitates the integration of family and a supportive system of care used to achieve more successful outcomes, reducing harm and increasing sustainability.

Internet-based anxiety disorder interventions are beneficial in targeting individuals who are reluctant to engage in treatment and/or do not desire the restrictions placed to acquire treatment. These methods offer some potential advances to identify unmet needs and integrate services through a novel application of interventions that applies best practices to address diagnostic components related to a disorder. Measures that help to identify the presence of anxiety disorders should be integrated into care to facilitate treatment acquisition, demonstrate evidence, and facilitate communication among interdisciplinary providers.

SUMMARY AND FUTURE DIRECTIONS

Anxiety disorders are a taxonomical classification of disorders found in the *DSM-IV-TR* sharing common features and criteria specifying meta-cognitions and physiological responses in common. The disorders presented in this chapter share a basis in altered physiological organ function, neurological disturbances, cognitive alterations, and behavioral disruptions. A breakdown in attention and information processing that results in physiological responses and inappropriate threat meaning assignments remain central to the clinical phenomenology of anxiety disorders. The disorders listed in this category include panic attack, panic disorder without agoraphobia, agoraphobia without history of panic disorder, phobia (specific or social), obsessive-compulsive disorder, posttraumatic stress disorder, acute stress disorder, generalized anxiety disorder, anxiety disorders due to a general medical condition, substance-induced anxiety disorder, and anxiety disorder not otherwise specified. Despite their common features, their clinical presentations vary in specificity of cognitive and behavioral responses, with intensity and excessive and inappropriate responses found in all.

The theories presented relate to the understanding of anxiety disorders and also guide their treatment, intervention, and prevention. These theories have their basis in the biological sciences, neuropsychology, cognitive psychology, evolutionary psychology, and social psychology. They provide a comprehensive analysis and understanding of the multifactorial basis of how these disorders evolve and mechanisms for their effective treatment. Brain function alterations or damage (e.g., striatal and frontal lobes), plasticity, altered genes, and hypothalamus-pituitary-adrenal axis abnormalities offer an understanding of organic dysfunction and physiological alterations in response to stressful environmental agents. These changes are also applied to address adaptation, emotions, and issues of motivation, intention, and imputation of mental states in interactions and lend to the understanding of the interaction among individuals, relationships, and environmental factors in the development of anxiety disorder. Treatments and intervention practices to address the constructs of anxiety disorders focus on cognitive restructuring, training of executive functions in new ways to process information, learned physiological responses, desensitization, and extinction of behaviors. These methods focus on the neuropsychological deficits in cognition and emphasize reducing emotional reactions that accompany these disorders, such as fear, terror, anxiety, and worry. Treatment needs to take into account associated risk factors and diagnostic measurements. A special focus on obsessive-compulsive disorder and posttraumatic stress disorder was included, with case presentations for each featured disorder, applications to the multiaxial diagnostic system, and sample treatment plans. Future directions should include research in information processing and attributions related to emotional and behavioral reactivity, accuracy in constructs of diagnostic assessments, technological models and applications, and preventive measures to reduce the onset and impact of stress responses and their progress.

Delirium, Dementia, and Amnestic and Other Cognitive Disorders

CARMEN P. CHANG-ARRATIA

Cognitive disorders compromise the vast majority of the disorders included under the *Diagnostic and Statistical Manual of Mental Disorders, Fourth Edition, Text Revision* (*DSM-IV-TR*; American Psychiatric Association [APA], 2000) taxonomical classification of the Delirium, Dementia, and Amnestic and Other Cognitive Disorders. These disorders include impairments in cognition, perceptions, language, communication, executive functions (e.g., problem solving, decision making, judgment), and behaviors. These disorders are found across all health-related conditions including postoperative, trauma, HIV, and substance abuse. The risk of developing these disorders increases with age and health-related consequences, and are a key sign that the presence of these increase the rates of morbidity and mortality. In particular, the focus of diagnostic impressions has been on the aging population due to the increase in life expectancies and the rapid growth of this population. It is estimated that by 2050, the world's population age 60 and above will triple to over 2 billion from 400 million in 2000 (World Health Organization [WHO], 2009e). The implications of this shift in epidemiologic impact and economic trends will not only impact epidemiological analyses but will shift the mechanisms of systems of care, impacting economical variables that have implications to the provisions of health care and the social system. The impact

will result in intended and unintended consequences to these systems and in substantial impairment to quality of life and associated costs, many preventable prior to their onset.

Medical advances have played a significant role in shifting the focus of models of care from terminal disease to a chronic illness model.

> As noted, care for acute episodes of illness is giving way to chronic conditions which may require clients to be seen by a number of different providers in a context where the supply of care is becoming increasingly fragmented. At the same time, older patients tend to have lower health literacy than younger cohorts. This can mean that older patients—particularly those with severe medical conditions—fail to receive coherent and patient-centered care with adequate follow up, thereby increasing the risk of unplanned hospital stays and higher overall costs. (WHO, 2009e, p. 20)

These authors express concern for the supply of care related both to the number of specialists available and to the specialized care and services needed to meet the demand.

Cognitive disorders are chronic and debilitating conditions that can present in such a way that the current system may fall short in properly diagnosing and assessing these conditions. System modifications and alterations that specifically address these conditions within our current systems of health care are needed to address the imminent basis and prognostic nature of these disorders. For those diagnosed with a cognitive disorder, cognitive impairment may be a long-standing symptom of the condition or an acute secondary reaction to an acute illness resulting in functional decline, hospital admission and stay; it may present as a risk factor for more intense and restricted quality of care affecting independent living (Thompson & Allen, 2008). Of these disorders, delirium and dementia are the most prevalent and severe. Delirium has a prevalence rate of 14% and 24% of hospital admissions; its incidence upon discharge accounts for 6% to 56% of cases (Thompson & Allen, 2008; Yang et al., 2008). The presence of delirium increases the prevalence of dementia diagnosed concurrently, as there is a certain amount of overlap. Various subtypes exist, but the most common subtype is Alzheimer's disease, a type of dementia affecting 10% of the population ages 65 and above and 50% of those 80 and above. It is the principal or additional diagnosis for 1.2% of discharged hospital patients and is associated with increases in medical services, longer hospital stays, institutionalization, and disruptive behaviors to at-home caregivers (Moyle, Olorenshaw, Wallis, & Borbasi, 2008; Nazarko, 2008). Worldwide, in 2000, 4.5 million people were diagnosed with dementia Alzheimer's type; it is estimated that this figure will rise to 13.2 million by 2050 (Chapman & Toseland, 2007).

This chapter introduces the diagnostic classification and definitions of cognitive disorders, as they are related to diagnosis, treatment planning, and interventions utilizing the *DSM-IV-TR*. An overview of the criteria of each will be presented with clinical features and a shared phenomenological analysis. Theories and etiological basis of these disorders will analyze the basis of these disorders and how they relate to the understanding of the disorders, prognosis, treatment, interventions, and preventions of the cognitive disorders. The focus of the chapter is on the cognitive disorders of delirium and dementia, each of which is explained in detail, addressing symptoms and risk factors. Current assessment instruments and neuropsychological tests are explained related to the application of the multiaxial system and the *DSM-IV-TR*. Case presentations of each of the disorders are presented. Each case highlights the application of the multiaxial assessment for each disorder and provides a sample treatment plan. Last, future directions are discussed.

INTRODUCTION TO DIAGNOSTIC CLASSIFICATION AND DEFINITIONS FOR COGNITIVE DISORDERS

The *DSM-IV-TR* specifies the disorders of delirium, dementia, amnestic disorders, and cognitive disorders not otherwise specified under the taxonomical classification of cognitive disorders, secondary to the deficits in cognition and consciousness exhibited as primary among the disorders listed and classified regardless of etiology (e.g., general medical condition), substance induced (e.g., drug abuse or exposure to a toxin), or a combination. Previously referred to as the organic mental disorders, this classification was dropped because it incorrectly implied that non-organic disorders had no biological basis (APA, 2000). The biological basis is related to effects in cognition in relation to brain trauma, deterioration and disease, and/or a response to direct physiological effects of physical multiple etiologies that cause these disorders.

Shared characteristics are found among all the disorders in the cognitive disorders, including a change in cognition, disturbance in consciousness, memory impairment, disturbance in executive functioning, impaired recognition and recall ability (agnosia), deterioration in language function (aphasia), impaired motor function (apraxia). These characteristics are not accounted for by the presence of another Axis I condition (e.g., major depressive disorder). The phenomenological basis of these disorders, with shared and overlapping specifications, further attenuates the concurrent inclusive set criteria. The *DSM-IV-TR* specifies each subtype found in these disorders, specifying definitions and criteria for each, and subgrouping them into three sections: cognitive disorder due to a general medical condition, cognitive disorder due to a substance-induced condition, and cognitive disorder due to multiple etiologies or not otherwise specified (NOS). Only cognitive disorder NOS has its own criteria and section without subtypes due to the inability of the symptoms to meet specified criteria. There are no unique diagnostic criteria specifications defined for delirium and dementia, only for the subtypes within the *DSM-IV-TR*.

Of the criteria shared among the cognitive disorders, disturbed consciousness is a key feature separating delirium and amnestic disorders from dementia. The disturbance of consciousness is followed by changes in cognition, developing over a short period of time but lasting weeks or months. Consciousness in these disorders is the ability to be aware of self, in actions and situations taking place, with the awareness of the interaction of self and environmental agents. In these disorders, disturbance in consciousness is the precipitating factor inducing changes. Changes in cognition include confusion, attention problems, inability to focus, disorientation, and an inability to sustain clarity and awareness of the environment (APA, 2000). The individual is quite aware of the self but is disoriented to surroundings and situations taking place,

without the accompanying multiple cognitive features of aphasia, apraxia, or agnosia found in dementia.

Memory deficit, recent and remote, is another indicator and a characteristic of these disorders, usually a prominent early symptom and criteria for dementia. When there is remote memory impairment, the client may not be able to place events in his or her past; recent memory is generally linked to current events, such as what just happened or awareness of what behaviors just occurred. "Memory impairment is required to make the diagnosis of a dementia and is a prominent early symptom" (APA, 2000, p. 148). While memory is impaired in delirium, in dementia, the progression of this deficit is slower and more insidious. In amnestic disorders, memory disturbance does not occur exclusively to the disorders but a lack of insight into memory deficits accentuates the denial of the presence of severe memory impairments despite evidence presented; in global amnesia, bewilderment will appear despite memory deficits and impairments disappearing with time (APA, 2000). In dementia, impairment in learning new material, inability to recall previously learned material, and forgetfulness that progresses so that the person cannot recall his or her occupation, place of residence, recent conversations, and reason and placement of belongings is pronounced (Insel & Badger, 2002; Moyle, Olorenshaw, Wallis, & Borbasi, 2008). Exhibited in memory deficit is agnosia, a criterion only for dementia, in which recognition and identification of objects, family members, and sounds decline due to brain dysfunction in the parietal, occipital, and temporal lobes responsible for storing memories despite intact sensory functions (APA, 2000; Auchus, 2008; Pasinetti & Hiller-Sturmhofel, 2008; Yankner et al., 2008). While memory deficits are a key feature of cognitive disorders, the severity in progression and course differentiates these among delirium, dementia, amnestic disorders, and cognitive disorders NOS.

Executive function encompasses an individual's ability to control, monitor, and regulate thought and action, including the coordination of cognitive abilities such as attention and memory. Various definitions of executive functions, as these have been applied theoretically to research, encompass a set combination of mental operations that help guide and understand cognitive and behavioral thought in reference to models, future goals, and actions (Colvert et al., 2008; Joseph et al., 2005). It is the ability to control and execute these cognitive functions that leads individuals to engage in strategic planning, decision making, judgment, perception, set-shifting, generativity, self-regulation, monitoring, and action (Bieberich & Morgan, 2004; Colvert et al., 2008; Goldstein et al., 2001; Hartshorne, Nicholas, Grialou, & Russ, 2007; Joseph et al., 2005; Santos, Rondan, Rosset, Fonseca, & Deruelle, 2008). Inability to execute these functions results in reduced performance, poor motivation, and impaired communication skills, lending to social isolation (Hartshorne et al., 2007). "Impairment of the supervisory system results in over reliance on routine control through a contention scheduling system, leading to higher rates of over learned responses to environmental contingencies" (p. 334). Executive functions are key abilities, but in those with the impaired ability to think abstractly, plan, organize, sequence information, and carry these thoughts coherently, developing and carrying out novel tasks is paramount (APA, 2000). While the processing of new information with all sensory inputs can be challenging to anyone, those with impaired executive functions are at a disadvantage. Executive functions play a key role in learning, remembering, and performing tasks (e.g., driving, organizing objects, finding familiar places, or even hypothesizing a problem). This is particularly the case for those with delirium and

dementia where the ability to connect this information to previously learned information or imagined is arduous and in decline (Insel & Badger, 2002; Moyle et al., 2008; Smith, 2005; Pansinetti & Hiller-Sturmhofel, 2008; Yankner et al., 2008).

Disturbances in perception are seen in misperceptions related to recognition, interpretation, and sensory modalities such as auditory, tactile, gustatory, and olfactory. Perceptual and spatial-frequency information lend further to executive function impairment. In face recognition, as a function of social communication, affective interpretation, and fear and danger appraisal, difficulties in shifts related to perceptual tasks and recognition impairing emotional processing are evident. These are associated with inability to recognize family members and related to emotional processing. Difficulty processing information on signs while driving, inability to recall how to make turns while driving, and increased passivity with suspicion of others are present in disturbances of perception (Adler, 2007; Insel & Badger, 2002). Misinterpretation of perceptions is also seen; individuals being coherent to time and place and then pull their intravenous tubes and catheters later in the same day. Disturbances in perception and difficulty processing are associated features found in dementia, where there is difficulty with spatial orientation and spatial tasks with features overlapping in symptomology with delirium.

Inability to articulate (dysarthria), to name objects (dysnomia), to write (dysgraphia), and the overall deterioration of language (aphasia) are present features of delirium and dementia but not for the amnestic disorders in the *DSM-IV-TR*. In patients with delirium, language may be incomprehensible, speech rambled, irrelevant, pressured, and incoherent. In those with dementia, finding the words to express the self is near impossible and the individual may replace statements with inappropriate words to compensate (APA, 2000; Insel & Badger, 2002). Comprehension of spoken and written language is impaired, quite severely in dementia. Vocalizations that are repetitive (echolalia or palilia) and show changes in tone and urgency are noted, and in commonly referred to end-stage dementia (subtype Alzheimer's), there is a complete loss of all communicative and verbal abilities secondary to significant and severe brain damage (APA, 2000; Lacey, 2006; Moyle et al., 2008; Yankner et al., 2008). For example, in echolalia, the repetitive tones "echo" or "pali" of the "lia" (speech) and considered vocalizations that are loud changes in speech with altered sounds and tones; language impairment is not noted in the amnestic disorders or in cognitive disorders NOS, only in the disorders of delirium and dementia.

The last featured impairment in the cognitive disorders in the *DSM -IV-TR* is a type of motor function termed *apraxia*. The *DSM-IV-TR* defines *apraxia* as the "impaired ability to execute motor activities despite intact motor abilities, sensory function, and comprehension of the required task" (APA, 2000, p. 149). Shifts from hyper- to hypomotor functions, such as sudden movements, trying to get out bed when unsafe, groping, or sluggishness and stupor are present particularly in delirium and dementia but not in the amnestic disorders. Inability to comb one's hair, cook, brush teeth, or wave good-bye, and difficulties with gait and coordination are symptoms of impaired motor function present in the cognitive disorders. In end-stage dementia, these may result in a complete loss of bladder and bowel control, loss of eating capabilities, swallowing problems, and difficulty sitting up and or holding up one's head (Lacey, 2006).

Of the criteria presented for these disorders, the *DSM-IV-TR* specifies criteria specific to the subtypes of delirium, dementia, and amnestic disorder. As previously noted, there

are no set criteria for the diagnosis of delirium or dementia. Diagnoses with criteria outlined for delirium with diagnostic codes include delirium due to a general medical condition ([293.0], substance-intoxication delirium (with codes specific to substances listed, e.g., alcohol [291.0]), substance-withdrawal delirium (with codes specifically listed for this condition, e.g., sedative, hypnotic, or anxiolytic [292.81]), delirium due to multiple etiologies (with multiple codes specific to delirium and etiologies, e.g., delirium due to viral encephalitis [293.0] and alcohol withdrawal delirium [291.0]), and delirium not otherwise specified (780.09). When coding for delirium due to a general medical condition, the medical condition should also be coded on Axis III with codes found in Appendix G of the *DSM-IV-TR* (e.g., [572.2] Hepatic Encephalopathy).

The diagnostic criteria outlined for the dementia subtypes with corresponding codes listed include dementia of the Alzheimer's type (294.1x) (with subtype code [294.10] for *without behavioral disturbance* and code [294.11] for *with behavioral disturbance*), and vascular dementia [290.4x] (with specifier of delirium coded [290.41], delusions coded [290.42], depressed mood coded [290.43], and uncomplicated coded [290.40]). All dementias due to a general medical condition are coded 294.1x with subtypes coded 294.10 for specifiers *without behavioral disturbance* and 294.11 *with behavioral disturbance*. These include dementia due to HIV disease, dementia due to head trauma, dementia due to Parkinson's disease, dementia due to Huntington's disease, dementia due to pick's disease, dementia due to Creutzfeldt-Jakob disease, and dementia due to other general medical conditions. When coding these, the medical condition should also be coded on Axis III with codes found in Appendix G of the *DSM-IV-TR* (e.g., [042] HIV infection or [332.0] Parkinson's disease). Substance-induced persisting dementia is coded specifically

QUICK REFERENCE 11.1

COGNITIVE DISORDERS

- Changes in Cognition
  Confusion, inability to focus, disorientation, inability to sustain clarity.
- Disturbance in Consciousness
  Changes in ability to be aware of self, changes in awareness of actions and situations, changes in the ability of awareness of the self in interactions with environmental agents.
- Memory Deficit
  Impaired attention; impaired recognition, recall, and retention of past and new information (agnosia); and forgetfulness with progression.
- Executive Function Impairment
  Inability to plan, organize, monitor, and strategize; impaired set-shifting; impaired judgment and decision-making; and impaired perception.
- Aphasia
  Inability to articulate (dysarthria); inability to write (dysgraphia) and to name objects (dysnomia); incoherent and pressured speech; repeated verbalizations (ecolalia); repeated sounds or words (palilalia); and loss of all ability to speak.
- Motor Function Impairment
  Inability to execute actions despite intact sensory and physical function (apraxia), sudden shift from hypo to hyper function, impaired gait and coordination, stupor, sluggishness, inability to perform activities of daily living, and loss of control of bodily functions.
- Associated Features
  Organic biological basis (brain damage and neurodegeneration).

to the substance (e.g., alcohol-induced persisting dementia [291.2]). Dementia due to multiple etiologies is coded based on specific dementias and etiologies (e.g., dementia of the Alzheimer's type [294.10], with late onset, without behavioral disturbance and vascular dementia, uncomplicated [290.40]). Dementia not otherwise specified is coded [294.8].

Two codes exist for the amnestic disorders: amnestic disorder due to a general medical condition (294.0) and amnestic disorder not otherwise specified (294.8). For the amnestic disorder due to a general medical condition, the general medical condition is also coded on Axis III using codes found in Appendix G of the *DSM-IV-TR*. Substance-induced persisting amnestic disorders are coded alongside the specific substance (e.g., alcohol-induced persisting amnestic disorder

[291.1]). Last, cognitive disorders not otherwise specified are coded 294.9 and have no specifier or subtype (see Quick Reference 11.1).

THEORIES AND ETIOLOGY OF COGNITIVE DISORDERS

Theories related to the understanding of cognitive disorders and neurodegenerative conditions lend to the understanding of the clinical course, applications to assessment, practice, interventions, and prevention methods. These theories have their basis in theories from the biological sciences, neuropsychology, and cognitive psychology related to neurodegeneration. Neurodegeneration of the brain is a predisposing factor, provides the interconnection between *delirium* and *dementia*, and reflects underlying brain vulnerability along a continuum of points in cognitive decline (Fick et al., 2009). Systems of biology and the neurodegeneration of the brain are inherent in the composition of the disorders that subsequently present the clinical features found and grouped in the *DSM*.

Biological theories of neurodegeneration of the brain and their central role in pathogenesis and morbidity result from transitions in normal brain functions to aging brain functions, toxin protein aggregates, and genetics. These theories posit that age-related memory disturbances and cognitive declines (mild to severe atrophy) are related to the altered functional activation of the prefrontal cortex, amygdala, and hippocampus resulting from loss of gray and white matter in the temporal lobes (Pasinetti & Hiller-Sturmhofel, 2008; Yankner et al., 2008). These disturbances and declines are found in delirium and dementia, not in normal brain function. Research of neurodevelopmental disorders, such as autism functional magnetic resonance imaging (fMRI), demonstrates that the amydala in the fusiform face area is less active in children with autism—an organic deficit resulting in impaired fear and danger assessments in face recognitions and facial expression in social interactions. This feature is also found in dementia but not in the other cognitive disorders. Agnosia, the exhibited memory deficits in the cognitive disorders, is a criterion only for dementia. Recognition, perception, and the identification of objects, family members, and sounds decline despite intact sensory functions due to brain dysfunction in the parietal, occipital, and temporal lobes (brain areas responsible for storing memories) (APA, 2000; Auchus, 2008; Pasinetti & Hiller-Sturmhofel, 2008; Yankner et al., 2008). With altered function and physical changes to the brain, affected memory and related cognitive functions are evident. The progressive neurodegeneration

of the brain and gradual destruction of the brain cells decline in all mental functions and alter personality and behavior (Pasinetti & Hiller-Sturmhofel, 2008). In affecting memory functions with subsequent deficits, executive functions are impaired, and task completion related to new and previously learned material cannot be performed as these require attention and memory.

Altered gene expressions also affect synaptic plasticity in the brain, related to cognitive decline, changes in processing speed, impaired executive functions, and agnosia. Reduced gene expressions impair the intraneuronal calcium buffering capacity, affecting the homeostasis and synaptic plasticity of the brain; calcium provides a filtering system for toxicity of the neural processes, resulting in neuronal loss, damage, and subsequent neurodegeneration (Yankner et al., 2008). In dementia, the presence of Lewy bodies (i.e., deposits of protein found in nerve cells) increases toxicity, disrupt normal brain function, and can be dangerous and fatal (Nazarko, 2008). Plasticity allows the brain to generate new neural pathways and compensates for ones damaged or injured (as seen in head trauma). When these fail to regenerate, functions related to these are impaired with the inability of the individual to engage in strategic planning, decision making, judgment, perception, set-shifting, generativity, self-regulation, monitoring, and action (Bieberich & Morgan, 2004; Colvert et al., 2008; Goldstein et al., 2001; Hartshorne, Nicholas, Grialou, & Russ, 2007; Joseph et al., 2005; Santos et al., 2008).

Changes in gene expressions due to mutations and characteristic in accelerated aging phenotypes include neurodegenerative disorders, mental retardation, and delayed psychomotor development contributing to the degenerative syndromes of ataxia (Pasinetti & Hiller-Sturmhofel, 2008; Yankner et al., 2008).

These are motor function disorders resulting in tics, gait and coordination impairment, and other motor disorders found in Parkinson's. For example, myoclonus dystonia, a movement disorder in which tremors is a feature closely associated with alcohol abuse, is an inherited genetic disorder resulting from gene mutations and repressed gene expressions, making this movement disorder associated with muscular dystrophies (Hess & Saunders-Pullman, 2006). Gene expression mutations in neurodegenerative disorders and degenerative syndromes are responsible for motor function disorders found in conditions such as dementia, where the inability to comb one's hair, cook, brush teeth, and wave good-bye, and gait and coordination difficulties are present. In more severe cases, the presence of these result in loss of all communicative abilities, complete loss of bladder and bowel functions, loss of eating capabilities, and complete loss of independent self-care. The biological basis of cognitive disorders explains their organic nature and their effects on cognitions, communication, and behaviors exhibited. It also provides the basis for treatment, focusing on the underlying etiology of organic mental disorders, and interventions and practices applicable to improving rehabilitation responses and preventive measures.

Another theory and model applicable to explain neurodegeneration and pathology in the cognitive disorders is the cognitive reserve theory. Structural components noted in the neurodegenerative diseases, the brain's role as an effective mechanism of capacity and regeneration, and the subsequent application to treatment, interventions, and prevention of cognitive disorders particularly in dementia are proposed in a model of reserves. This theory applies the biological basis of neural pathways and plasticity of brain functions in terms of reserves and includes variables that address

individual and environmental agents affecting neurodegeneration from an evolutionary psychology point of view. "The cognitive reserve (CR) model suggests that the brain actively attempts to cope with brain damage by using preexisting cognitive processing approaches or by enlisting compensatory approaches. Individuals with more CR would be more successful at coping with the same amount of brain damage" (Stern, 2006, p. 112). Stern (2006) states that neural compensation is the process whereby individuals with brain pathology compensate for brain damage by using cognitive strategies not used by individuals with intact brains, reaching a threshold where pathology is expressed and emerges in its clinical presentation. These cognitive strategies measured as "reserves" include anatomical features, such as brain volume, head circumference, and synaptic count, which malleable over time, influenced by, and contributing independently to life experiences. In addition, these include social variables, such as socioeconomic status, occupational status, and educational attainment and other attributes, such as level of intelligence (IQ). Accounting for individual differences, the brain reserve capacity (BRC) is said to produce different effects when held constant on different people despite the same amount of brain damage; therefore, social variables serving as proxies for life experiences are good predictors of individuals who can sustain brain damage prior to the expression and emergence of the clinical presentation of neurodegeneration and functional deficits (Stern, 2006; Valenzuela & Sachdev, 2009). The model considers these reserves as passive because they emerge and their expression evolves only when a critical threshold has been achieved.

Cognitive reserve theory has been analyzed from various perspectives, addressing the complexity of mental activities, the definition of reserves, and how these are attributed to the organization and cultivation of resources (e.g. the brain's role as a mechanism of efficiency and capacity). According to Valenzuela and Sachdev (2009), these perspectives have included the neurocentric perspective (such that brain reserves hold an advantage based on neuronal numbers), cognitive perspective (e.g., the deliberate development of cognitive strategies for solving complex problems as a measure of reserves), computational perspective (e.g., reserves revolve around computational redundancy and flexibility serving as compensatory and resistant adaptations to a functional brain network), and behavioral perspective (e.g., reserves are measured from observable complex mental activities through duration and frequency of social variables and leisure activities). Cognitive reserve theory does posit the interplay between individual differences in understanding neurodegeneration and pathology, the evolutionary compensatory mechanisms of organ function to explain changes in brain physiology, and how variability in individual human development and cognitive strategies compensate, adapt, and modify physiology.

Theoretical models provide guidance to and understanding of the underlying mechanisms of cognitive disorders. In the cognitive disorders, the basis is rooted in their organic composition, which accounts for their subgrouping within the *DSM* as well as their primary identification and differential diagnosis. By understanding their etiology, approaches targeting areas related to accuracy of diagnosing, practice and rehabilitative approaches, and preventive measures can be applied. Supportive information and tests include (a) positron emission tomography and functional magnetic resonance imaging for differential diagnosing and to measure the index of brain pathology and regeneration; (b) identifying biomarkers to monitor metabolic imbalances, protein abnormalities, gene function changes, and infections related to neurodegeneration

and brain damage; and c) cognitive retraining to improve mental states, increase reserves, and expand neural regenerative capacity through restructuring, training, and novelty task completion. Neurodegenerative disorders and how these modify and alter mental functions and behavioral responses are markedly demonstrated in delirium and dementia.

DSM-IV-TR: DEFINITION OF DELIRIUM

The *DSM-IV-TR* does not specify unique set criteria for delirium, which makes diagnosing a challenge. Often superimposed with other conditions, delirium can go misdiagnosed, if undetected, increasing the worsening of a present condition. The onset is associated with poor outcomes, functional decline, increased healthcare use, nursing home placement, and death (Fick, Kolanowski, Beattie, & McCrow, 2009; Robinson, Rich, Weitzel, Vollmer, & Eden, 2008). According to Fick, Agnostini, and Inouye (2002), the difficulty in diagnosing delirium, especially when superimposed with dementia, is that the *DSM* criteria stipulate that deficits should not occur just during the course of the episode of delirium (which establishing and identifying a baseline premorbid mental status assessment can be difficult). Delirium is often superimposed on dementia, making it more difficult to differentiate between both presenting disorders and the precipitating agent. It has been suggested that an interconnection exists between delirium and dementia, reflecting underlying brain vulnerability in early-stage dementia represented along a continuum of points in cognitive decline (Fick et al., 2009; Moyle et al., 2008). Delirium is frequently underdetected in hospital admissions, due to a lack of proper assessment, limited knowledge, and a lack of awareness of hypoactive delirium ("quiet" delirium) (Thompson & Allen, 2008). Of the 29%

QUICK REFERENCE 11.2

DELIRIUM

- Disturbance of Consciousness
  Impaired focus and attention, reduced clarity of awareness, easily distracted, awareness of self present, perceptual disturbances.
- Memory Impairment
  Disoriented to time and place, impaired recognition and recall.
- Language Disturbance
  Dysarthria, dysnomia, dysgraphia, rambling speech, irrelevant and illogical speech, unpredictable switching of topics.
- Disturbance Develops in a Short Amount of Time
  Symptoms develop over a short time (hours to days), fluctuation of symptoms during the day.
- Associated Features
  Disturbance to circadian rhythms, perceptual disturbances, disturbed psychomotor behavior, emotional disturbances (when accompanied by hallucinations), and nonspecific neurological abnormalities (tremor, myoclonus, muscle tone changes).

---

of people diagnosed as having dementia, delirium was misdiagnosed in all of these (Nazarko, 2008). Thompson and Allen (2008) posit that misdiagnosed and undetected delirium is an important marker for the risk of dementia (without prior cognitive or functional impairment) and a marker for mortality among older medical inpatients.

A common problem among those aged 65 and over, delirium's clinical course depends on the underlying causes and how quickly these are resolved. Its onset is associated with medical conditions and medications, and recovery is achieved through treatment of underlying causes. Symptoms can persist for hours, weeks, or longer, and may indicate the severity of underlying illnesses, a predictor of potential future cognitive decline, and poor prognosis (APA, 2000; Insel & Badger, 2002; Robinson et al., 2008). Diagnostic features and symptoms include disturbance in consciousness not accounted for by other preexisting or evolving dementia, impairment in recent memory, speech or language disturbance, and perceptual disturbances (APA, 2000; Fick et al., 2009). These features are considered in relation to

normal cognitive functions and symptoms presented in delirium. Cognitive functions assessed within normal limits include attention, concentration, intelligence, learning, judgment, memory, orientation, perception, problem solving, and psychomotor ability (Hjermstad, Log, & Kaasa, 2004). When these functions are impaired, these are related to a "triad disorder," which includes impairments in executive function, communication, and behaviors attributed to the spectrum of conditions found within organic brain disorders. These are included in the *DSM* criteria for delirium and associated presenting features. Because cognitive functions are an independent predictor for survival, the assessment of altered cognitive states and cognitive failure is a critical component of the assessment, treatment, and intervention (see Quick Reference 11.2).

Risk Factors

Risk factors associated with the onset of delirium include age, medical conditions, medication regimens, substance use, dietary changes, activities of daily living, gender, and iatrogenic events (APA, 2000; Amin, Kuhle, & Fitzpatrick, 2003; Insel & Badger, 2002; Robinson et al., 2008). It is important to be aware of these factors as they impact the diagnostic assessment and identification of the presence of delirium when present in individuals. Further explanation of these factors is included and their relation to assessment is described later in this chapter.

Age   Age is the indicator that places an individual at highest risk for the onset of delirium. According to the *DSM-IV-TR*, children are more susceptible when compared to adults secondary to febrile illnesses and reactions to medications. These susceptibilities are related to the developing brain and physiological differences in children to adults. Additionally, individuals aged 65 and over (advanced age > 80 years) are at high risk secondary to medical factors associated with chronic illnesses and subsequent complications of aging (Tabet et al., 2006).

Medical Conditions   Predictive conditions of medical risk include elevated Blood Urea Nitrogen [BUN]/creatinine ratio with a serum creatinine > 18 mg/mL. BUN and creatinine tests measure toxicity, serum, platelet counts as well as liver and kidney functions. If the levels are elevated, infection or organ failure is present. Low albumin level, electrolyte imbalance, bone metastasis, heart failure, low cardiac output, ischemic heart disease, atherosclerosis, HIV/AIDS, infections, gastrointestinal/genitourinary disorders, and cerebral atrophy are but a few of the associated medical conditions predisposing onset risk (Amin et al., 2003; Insel & Badger, 2002; Robinson et al., 2008; Tabet et al., 2006). The presence of urinary tract infections, surgery, and severe pain from herpes zoster infections is seen more frequently in persons with delirium, particularly in those with delirium superimposed on dementia (Fick et al., 2002). Their presence is

an indicator that the individual could be experiencing delirium in response to underlying medical conditions.

Pharmacotherapy   Medication regimens play a key role in the onset of delirium, especially among children and elderly persons. Amin et al. (2003) describe that polypharmacy is a major cause of delirium, resulting from more than five medications or nutritional supplements being prescribed to the person. Polypharmacy is often related to misdiagnosing secondary to an underreporting of symptoms. Fragmentations in the health care system have resulted in care being provided by multiple providers with a lack of access and sharing of preexisting medical records. This has resulted in prescription errors and the overprescribing of medications. Adding more than three drugs to a person's medication regimen can induce delirium—a common error in prescribing practices among physicians (Amin et al., 2003; Insel & Badger, 2002). Anticholinergic and central nervous system–active medications (psychotherapeutic medications) (e.g., antipsychotic agents, antihistamines, antianxiety agents, antidepressant drugs, cardiovascular agents, Parkinson's disease medications) and side effects increase the incidence of delirium and cognitive decline, even when recommended dosages are taken (Fick et al., 2009). The most common medications causing delirium are the benzodiazepines and sedative-hypnotic psychotherapeutic drugs.

Nutrition   Malnutrition, dehydration, and vitamin deficiencies increase the risk for the onset of delirium. Dehydration is a contested indicator of delirium. "Dehydration . . . is commonly used to reflect several related physiological states based on an imbalance between intake and loss of fluid and the accompanying sodium states" (Warren et al., 1994, p. 1266). The sodium states give way to electrolyte imbalances affecting cardiac functions and other organs. Of long-term care elderly persons hospitalized with dehydration and related onset of delirium, 50% died within a year of their admission. Dehydration was a key feature in the demise and concurrent findings with delirium. Issues become whether dehydration is an indicator of delirium or of an underlying cause that then is manifested in the onset of delirium. What may pose problems, when combining the underlying cause and onset of delirium, are problems secondary to the inability of the individual to flush fluids from the system. This inability to flush fluids can lead to toxicity in the body leading to the onset of delirium. The onset then becomes a secondary effect to the underlying cause rather than dehydration as a result of delirium (Culp et al., 2004). Vitamin deficiencies, such as thiamine deficiency, have been linked to the onset of delirium in alcohol withdrawal, with reversible consequences when quickly assessed but leading to long-term damage when untreated (e.g., Wernicke's encephalopathy progressing to Korsakoff's psychosis) (Parker et al., 2008; Pasinetti & Hiller-Sturmhofel, 2008). Weight loss with a resulting body mass index of less than 18.5 kg/m2, exceeding 5% in one month or 10% in six months, is indicative of a risk factor of poor ___ ___atus lending to an assessment for ___ ___ses related to the onset (e.g., alcohol ___abuse, cognitive dysfunction, func-___ons, chronic medical conditions, ___rces, and social isolation) (Amin ___Malnutrition secondary to vitamin ___dical conditions, and environmen-___cting human systems is a risk to the ___ ___rium.

Activities of Daily Living The association between activity and developing delirium demonstrate that risk is reduced when higher adherence to physical activity is present. Due to the pathophysiological similarities and cholinergic deficiency and cerebral metabolism, performing physical activities (or mobility intervention) and cognitive-stimulating activities three times daily reduces the risk of delirium (Stern, 2006; Yang et al., 2008). Engaging in educational and physical activities deters functional decline. Brain volume, head circumference, synaptic count, and dendritic branching are proxy measures of reserves that are malleable over time and influenced through life experiences; including socioeconomic status, occupational attainment, educational attainment, and IQ (Stern, 2006). Higher educational attainment can buffer the effects of neurological disease or injury, and activity (physical and leisure) mediates the relationship between education and onset of delirium (whereby physical activity improves cognitive functioning by increasing gray and white matter volume in the prefrontal and temporal cortices) (Yang et al., 2008). These can deter the onset of delirium and agnosia found in dementia. Assessing the baseline level of activity is important if presenting functional and cognitive decline contribute to the onset of delirium.

COMPLETION OF THE DIAGNOSTIC ASSESSMENT

As in the other *DSM* disorders in this book, the assessment of delirium and the cognitive disorders listed in this chapter considers related factors to provide the most comprehensive and accurate analysis of the presenting problem. These factors should include all of the demographic information available, laboratory findings, physical examinations, current and past history (medical and mental), and specific background features that may interfere with testing. These disorders require the assessment of cognition and consciousness as a determinant for meeting the criteria for these conditions, as they affect memory, perception, executive functions, and alteration in behavior. More importantly, the assessment serves as a key indicator to identify serious underlying medical conditions.

The clinical assessment of delirium serves as a surrogate for the identification and diagnosis, as medical measures need to be applied to determine and differentiate findings (e.g., laboratory work and imaging studies). These findings will then be integrated into the overall treatment planning and interventions. Essential and important to clinical applications in an integrated approach is the establishing of changes in mental status, onset, duration, and the severity of the change upon presentation. The more accurate and quicker the mental status examination, the less risk suffered and incurred to the individual presenting with severe underlying and reversible medical conditions, if treatment is then applied in a timely fashion. Neuropsychological tests document impairments of specific areas of cognitive abilities and test and measure visuo-spatial abilities, attention, choice, and reaction time (Adler, 2007). There are a variety of these tests, and can be utilized in various settings. A few are listed in this section and are also applicable to the other cognitive disorders in this chapter. The diagnostic category of Delirium does not have a unique set of criteria so a mental status examination is the key determinant for the identification of the disorder and differentiation from other related disorders.

The most commonly used assessment to measure cognitive decline is the Folstein Mini Mental State Examination (MMSE). It contains questions assessing orientation to time, place, attention, and memory and is dependent on age and educational background (i.e., certain individuals may not be familiar with the information presented on these tests, e.g. names of presidents, geographic locations, important dates and events, the different conceptualizations of place and location with respect to individual backgrounds) (Adler, 2007; APA, 2000; Amin

et al., 2003; Inger & Badger, 2002). The MMSE addresses task completion as related to attention and memory through engaging actions of writing, copying, and observation. Scores of 24 or less are associated with an increased incidence of delirium. In older inpatient adults, lower scores are associated with poor recovery function and increased nursing home admissions (Tabet et al., 2006). The measurement is positively correlated with other screening and mental status assessment tools, lending to corroborative analysis and increased accuracy of findings.

Other common measures used to assess mental status are the Confusion Assessment Method (CAM), the NEECHAM Confusion Scale, and the Executive Clock-Drawing Task (CLOX). The CAM is an algorithm screening method that addresses the presence and diagnosis of delirium according to features determined from baseline (i.e., acute onset and fluctuating course, inattention, and either disorganized thinking or altered level of consciousness) (Inouye, Bogardus, Williams, Leo-Summers, & Agostini, 2003; Yang et al., 2008). For the diagnosis of delirium by the CAM, an acute onset and fluctuating course in mental status results in the abnormal behavior and existing inattention, with features of disorganized thinking or change in level of consciousness (Inouye, et al., 2003). The NEECHAM Confusion Scale is a nine-item observational instrument that covers 13 of the possible 17 *DSM- IV* criteria for delirium. It is used to detect and assess the severity of delirium and acute confusion present through cognitive processing, behavior, and physiological control (Culp et al., 2004; Miller, Campbell, Moore, & Schofield, 2004). It can be administered in eight to ten minutes, has a score range of zero to 30 (with a score of 24 or less indicating delirium), and assesses components of cognitive status (attention and alertness, verbal and motor response, memory and orientation), observed behavior (general behavior and posture, sensory motor performance, verbal responses), and functions (vital signs, oxygen saturation, urinary continence) (Culp et al., 2004; Gemert van & Schuurmans, 2007). The Executive Clock-Drawing Task (CLOX) is a useful measure to assess deficits in executive functions, impairments in visual and spatial frequency and perception, and the presence of agnosia and apraxia (Amin et al., 2003). This measure asks that a clock be drawn with the hands and face set at 1:45 such that a child can read it. The scoring is based on the 15-point established criteria, with a score of below 10 demonstrating impaired executive function (Insel & Badger, 2002). This measure, like the CAM and NEECHAM Confusion Scale, correlates well with the MMSE and provides identification of delirium.

Completing a functional impairment assessment should be administered in accordance with the assessment of mental state disturbances. The Functional Activities Questionnaire (FAQ) is an informant-based measure that obtains ratings on the ability of the individual to perform ten higher-order functional activities, such as writing checks, paying bills, assembling tax records, and conducting other business-related affairs as well as preparing a meal (Amin et al., 2003; Insel & Badger, 2002). Because of the decline in function as it relates to activities of daily living, measures to assess nutritional intake should also be administered. Malnutrition in a key risk factor in delirium, represented by vitamin deficiencies, electrolyte imbalances, and social stressors directly associated with this disorder. The Nutrition Checklist for Older Adults (DETERMINE mnemonic) is a screening instrument to assess malnutrition and related social issues in older adults (American College of Physicians, 2006; Amin et al., 2003). The measure addresses key problem areas related to nutrition utilizing the mnemonic device of *DETERMINE*: *d*isease, *e*ating poorly, *t*ooth loss/mouth pain, *e*conomic hardship, *r*educed social contact, *m*ultiple medications,

*i*nvoluntary weight loss/gain, *n*eeds assistance in self-care, and *e*lder years (> age 80), with a possible score range of 0 to 20, and has a threshold of six and above determining high nutritional risk (American College of Physicians, 2006). These measures assist in providing a more comprehensive analysis of the deterioration in the conditions, identification of corresponding disorders, and criteria for other conditions (e.g., duration of deterioration, onset of condition). They will also assist in the determination of the Generalized Assessment of Functioning (GAF) score when applied to the *DSM-IV-TR* multiaxial system. In determining the decreased function of activities of daily living, changes in routines and the impact of existing economic hardship also contributing to the presenting nature and changes in symptomology must be measured. These factors also serve as determinants of the impact of and to environmental agents coded on Axis IV according to level of severity.

These assessments are included in the determination of the mental status background information and associated risk factors in relation to the presence of delirium and/or other cognitive disorders. Because of the presenting nature of delirium, the accuracy of the application and administration of a mental status examination is the most important marker to be addressed. Risk factors will help to rule out other conditions with similar clinical presentations and narrow the symptoms of features and criteria pertinent to the diagnostic categorization. In delirium, these risk factors will be applied to Axis I and Axis III respectively with the application of codes from Appendix G for Axis III found in the *DSM-IV-TR*. These codes are a diagnostic feature for general medical conditions and medication-induced disorders and a recording measure for the cognitive disorders in the *DSM-IV-TR*. An exception is substance-related delirium coded to each substance with corresponding codes assigned in the *DSM-IV-TR*. (See Case Example 11.1, The Case of Mr. Zellner.)

——— CASE EXAMPLE 11.1 - THE CASE OF MR. ZELLNER ———

Mr. Zellner is a 58-year-old, Caucasian male of European descent. He is of average weight and of tall height, appearing his stated age. He was admitted through the emergency room for a 24-hour observation in the psychiatric unit at a hospital due to rapid changes in mental status, disorientation, confusion, and agitation. He was brought to the hospital via ambulance secondary to requests from family members who noted changes and called for assistance. At the time of this interview, Mr. Zellner received preliminary laboratory work and vitals were checked in the emergency room prior to admission to the psychiatric unit. Upon assessment, he is scheduled for a full blood work and medical routine examination with further testing in the morning, pending a psychological examination and stabilization of his agitated condition in the psychiatric unit. Family is present at time of admission and this interview. Preliminary information of Mr. Zellner's condition is acquired from family and with Mr. Zellner present. Mental status examination is administered individually to Mr. Zellner at the time of this interview.

Mr. Zellner is divorced and lives alone in his home and works part time. Family members report he enjoys part-time employment, after his early retirement from military service. He took early retirement this past year. Retirement from the military has been a major change in Mr. Zellner's life but he has been adjusting well. He enjoys going to his part-time work and engaging in personal interests, which include his dogs, housework, and working on his cars. Family members state that he is frequently looked after by them as he enjoys spending time with them and eating dinner together twice a week. According to the family, Mr. Zellner gets "annoyed" frequently when they look after him but report that overall he "lets [us]" visit him. At the time of this interview, Mr. Zellner frequently looks over to family members when speaking, looks at this interviewer, smiles, and often loses focus during the interview. Mr. Zellner needs repeated reassurance that his dogs are adequately being cared for in his absence.

Mental health history reveals no previous mental health treatment, from family members' reports. Family members deny Mr. Zellner having received inpatient or outpatient treatment to their knowledge. Family members report that Mr. Zellner has had problems with alcohol abuse in the past but these concerns have been resolved for over 15 years. Family members report that his alcohol use led to difficulties with his marriage and subsequent divorce, and to their knowledge, Mr. Zellner did not receive inpatient treatment for his chemical dependency and abuse concerns. Family members report that when he drank he was "awful" and state that his temperament has improved since he has stopped drinking. Family members report that Mr. Zellner is temperamental and prone to anger easily when things "are not his way." When asked to describe how they have noted a change from his usual demeanor, family members report that over the last week Mr. Zellner's is acting "nothing like himself," exhibits inability to remember, and decreased normal functioning and agitation. When Mr. Zellner is asked if he likes to have things his way, Mr. Zellner looks and smiles at interviewer and reports, "Yes, I like working on my cars."

Medical history reveals from family report that Mr. Zellner has a history of asthma for which he takes albuterol (an inhalant medication). Past medical information includes surgery for ulcerative colitis without complication. Family members are not sure if he follows up medically for any other concerns. Family members report that Mr. Zellner does not follow any dietary regimen related to what was prescribed to alleviate his conditions. Mr. Zellner is a smoker and smokes two packs of cigarettes per week and ingests three to four cups of coffee daily. Mr. Zellner is allergic to penicillin per family report. (In a medical record, when this is written, allergies should always be capitalized so other team members will take note.) Per family report, his only current medication is albuterol.

Mr. Zellner's condition declined during the week, and family members found him at his home confused and agitated. Secondary to contacting him via telephone to converse, the family reports that Mr. Zellner was unaware of who they were and could not follow the conversation or the questions asked. Family members became concerned and went to his house, where they found Mr. Zellner confused about his surroundings, agitated, and could not be calmed. When asked if Mr. Zellner was verbalizing any hallucinations or delusions when they found him at his residence, the family reported that Mr. Zellner could not follow a conversation. His speech was altered and at times slurred. His balance was unsteady yet he frequently wanted to leave and would become angry with family who deterred him and attempted to calm him down. Family members contacted the ambulance service because of concerns that Mr. Zellner had suffered a stroke as he was slurring his speech and his inability to remain steady. Family members were unsure if Mr. Zellner attended his part-time job during the week. They noted that he had worked on his cars sometime during the past week, although his tools were in the same position as last seen. Family members noted that Mr. Zellner was now unable to feed and case for his dogs.

Mental Status Examination

The purpose of the interview was explained to Mr. Zellner. Mr. Zellner demonstrated difficulty understanding the purpose of assessment but he was aware that his family members were not present. He is unable to recall who they are by name. Mr. Zellner was administered the Folstein Mini Mental State Examination. In assessing orientation, Mr. Zellner is unable to recall events related to date, time, and month but is aware that he is in a hospital. In immediate recall, his attention is impaired, and he demonstrated difficulties with this task requiring repetition of commands. Mr. Zellner could not perform serial sevens or spell the word WORLD backward accurately. He is able to produce a few letters, but this required repetition of the instructions and word. His attention, calculation, and recall are impaired. When asked to follow the three-stage command, Mr. Zeller is able to follow the command partially but focus diminishes and he is unable to remain attentive to task at time of assessment. Mr. Zellner is unable to retain focus during the reading and writing portion of the assessment, completing only a few words during the writing portion without being able to construct a full sentence. During the copying exercise, Mr. Zellner was asked to draw the copied picture of the two superimposed pentagons but was unable to sustain concentration to do so, completing only a partial pentagon and unable to keep to the lines. Mr. Zellner's score on the Folstein MMSE is 13 at time of this interview, with mental status impaired.

Due to the degree of impairment and his pending laboratory analysis, an immediate consultation with the attending physician and psychiatrist was requested. Despite his agitation on the psychiatric unit, his past medical condition of ulcerative colitis with concerns regarding continued aggravation, an inability to acquire an immediate assessment of his medical condition, and the severity of his altered mental state, his condition appears indicative of an underlying medical concern rather than a psychiatric condition. Mr. Zellner was evaluated by medical professionals where he was found to have elevated blood pressure, fever, and elevated blood count levels. He was transferred to the intensive care unit for further analysis and care.

Application of Multiaxial Assessment

Mr. Zeller's case demonstrates the underlying multiple etiologies of delirium, as these present in hospital settings, and the severity these pose to medical stabilization when the presence of these are unknown. Most cases of delirium are seen in the emergency room, where information is limited. The onset of Mr. Zeller's case is difficult to assess, given the often-rapid changes in condition. Most important in addressing these rapid changes are the accuracy of the mental status assessment, the term of onset, and the severity of impairment, with greater severity demonstrating a more serious underlying condition. While Mr. Zeller was transferred to the psychiatric unit because of his agitation and changes in mental status, it was the mental status examination that revealed an acute clinical presentation for which medical treatment was then administered. Background information provided by the family assisted in establishing a prior level of functioning to the baseline of symptomology that the client presented with at admission.

In applying the multiaxial assessment, Mr. Zellner presents with altered consciousness, inability to sustain attention, and demonstrating disorganized thinking. He does not have hallucinations or delusions, is aware of self, but is disoriented to situations and environments. These changes in cognitions fluctuate as he is able to sustain a degree of recognition of his family members when they were absent during mental status assessment. He is unable to recognize their names at time of interview and per family members' reports. During the interview, Mr. Zellner is unable to sustain focus when asked direct questions regarding information presented

to evaluate his attention and focus. He demonstrates that his focus and attention do not follow subject matter discussed during the interview. During the MMSE, his memory is impaired as he is unable to recall, follow three-stage commands, or maintain attention during the reading exercise. He demonstrates signs of dysgraphia, as he is unable to write a full sentence or complete the copying exercise. The onset of his symptomology developed within a short period of time, a week, per family members' report. He is agitated; this is the presenting problem for admission and transfer for stabilization to the psychiatric unit, despite associated clinical features of psychomotor behaviors in delirium. Mr. Zellner has a past history of substance abuse, which has been resolved for over 15 years. Substance-induced intoxication or withdrawal is ruled out. Due to his disturbance in consciousness, impairments with memory, and recent symptomology, supported by subsequent laboratory findings and medical analysis with elevated blood pressure, fever, and abnormal blood work, Mr. Zeller meets the diagnostic criteria for Delirium due to a General Medical Condition (293.0).

The *DSM-IV-TR* specifies that when delirium is related to a general medical condition, that the medical condition be specified utilizing codes located in Appendix G. Mr. Zellner has a past history of ulcerative colitis for which he underwent surgery. Per family reports, at time of the interview, Mr. Zellner continues to suffer symptomology related to this condition and does not follow dietary instructions. Family members are unaware if he currently receives further medical treatment for this condition. Family members report that he is asthmatic and treats this condition with albuterol despite his smoking but are unaware of side effects or contraindications related to this medication at the time of this interview. Given the subsequent positive findings for elevated blood pressure, fever, and abnormal blood work, it is not possible to tentatively diagnose Mr. Zellner with Delirium Not Otherwise Specified (780.9). There is evidence that this condition may be related to an underlying medical condition. The final analysis will have to be acquired from medical to ascertain the medical condition. At the time of the interview, given history and laboratory findings, he is given the diagnosis on Axis I of Delirium due to Ulcerative Colitis (293.0) with Axis III code (556.9) for Ulcerative Colitis.

At the time of this interview, Axis II is diagnosis coded no (V71.09) for Mr. Zellner—given that his current mental status and intellectual functioning relevance of a personality disorder cannot be assessed. Furthermore, related to the etiology of his presenting problem and disorder: Assessing for a personality disorder is not an issue pertinent to delirium.

Axis III has medical concerns that require noting and these concerns need to be coded as specified in the *DSM-IV-TR* with subsequent Appendix G codes. Mr. Zellner has asthma for which he utilizes albuterol. He has a past history of surgery for ulcerative colitis with current presenting concerns related to this ongoing condition. Mr. Zellner is a cigarette smoker and smokes two packs per week. He drinks three to four cups of coffee per day despite his ulcerative colitis. He does not follow his prescribed dietary recommendations for his condition. He has a past history of alcohol abuse of which has been in remission for over 15 years. Per family members' report, he does not have a current or past history of mental health–related concerns. He is allergic to penicillin.

Mr. Zellner has few issues pertinent to his social environment on Axis IV. These issues are important in establishing prior levels of functioning and indirectly used to determine Axis V. He is retired but enjoys working part-time. He has

transitioned from his retirement with minimal difficulties, per family members' report. He is not experiencing financial difficulties and has secure housing, owning his own home. He enjoys leisure activities of working on his cars, doing housework, and relating to the care of his dogs (a concern to him during the interview despite his altered consciousness). He is divorced and acquires supportive social support from his family, spending leisure time with them, through telephone calls, visits, and eating meals together weekly. These activities ceased during the week of his admission when his condition deteriorated and his symptoms worsened. It was his family members who noted the change and acquired emergency services to transport him to the hospital for his presenting condition. Family members were present at time of admission and provided supplemental information during this interview. His current Axis IV is presented in severity:

1. Medical concerns (past and current)
2. Secure employment
3. Secure housing
4. Supportive social system

Mr. Zellner's Axis V is a current GAF score of 34. From his MMSE score of 13, he has severe impairment to his mental state, thought processes, and subsequent level of functioning. He is not suicidal, delusional, or experiencing hallucinations, but he is illogical and speech irrelevant, with an inability to focus and shift his thought process during interview and assessment. His condition deteriorated within a short length of time, demonstrating that it impaired his ability to perform his usual household activities (e.g., take care of his dogs). At the time of the interview, family members are unable to verify if his employment was affected due to his change in mental status. His agitation

---

QUICK REFERENCE 11.3

MULTIAXIAL DIAGNOSTIC ASSESSMENT FOR MR. ZELLNER

Axis I: [293.0] Delirium due to ulcerative colitis.

Axis II: V71.09 No diagnosis.

Axis III: 1. Ulcerative colitis [556.9].
               2. Asthma.
               3. ALLERGIES TO PENICILLIN.
               4. History of alcohol abuse (remission over 15 years).

Axis IV: 1. Medical concerns (past and current).
               2. Secure employment.
               3. Secure housing.
               4. Supportive social system.

Axis V: 34.

---

demonstrates altered level of function related to behaviors, with Mr. Zellner angry due to his disorientation and family attempting to calm him prior to his arrival to the hospital. He does not present with obsessions or rituals, and his behaviors are not grossly inappropriate but concurrent to symptoms of delirium related to an underlying medical condition rather than a mental disorder (e.g., depression). Given these presenting symptoms and features, at the time of the interview and assessment, Mr. Zellner is given a GAF score of 34 (see Quick Reference 11.3).

DELIRIUM: TREATMENT PLANNING, IMPLEMENTATION, AND EVALUATION

Because presenting cases of delirium predominately occur in hospital settings, accounting for many emergency room admissions, treatment will be related to the medical stabilization to the client and associated care. The cessation of these symptoms will be in response to the stabilization of a general medical condition, the removal or cessation of ingestion substance or exposure to a toxin, and the remedy of an infection. Treatment planning will be brief and supportive, and the level of care and will assure the transition of supportive services (see Sample Treatment Plan 11.1). Often delirium is highly correlated with mortality, and in these situations, focus of care and treatment will shift from maintenance and regeneration to palliative and bereavement. In cases where delirium superimposes dementia, delirium serves as an indicator substantiating the presence of dementia, usually Alzheimer's subtype; consequently, delirium also signals the progression of end-stage dementia and death. The next section highlights the clinical course and diagnosis of dementia. In the case of delirium, integrated treatment is provided through interdisciplinary teams found in a variety of settings where the onset of delirium can occur. Subsequent treatment should focus on the cessation and stabilization of underlying and overimposed etiologies, where coordination of care will be based on the prognosis and setting from where it will be administered. Depending on the severity and prognosis, long-term care may be required.

SAMPLE TREATMENT PLAN 11.1

MR. ZELLNER

Objectives	Plan or Interventions
1. Achieve medical stabilization for underlying medical condition.	Acquire medical consultation and treatment for client's medical concerns.
	Coordinate medical services between hospital medical staff and client's primary care physician.
	Encourage client to follow medical protocols for stabilization.
	Provide supportive and palliative counseling, if necessary.
2. Support family system during medical stabilization.	Encourage family member participation through education and communication of medical procedures.
	Assist family members in obtaining and providing information related to client's presenting problem.
	Provide supportive and palliative counseling, if necessary.
3. Plan and organize discharge.	Address physician-based recommendations for postcare.
	Acquire referral appointment for services and organize plans for transfer to relevant facilities such as residential, homecare, etc.
	Provide supplemental supportive resources to access post-care.

DSM-IV-TR: DEFINITION OF DEMENTIA

Dementia is varied in its subtypes and found in the most common form of *Alzheimer's* disease. It is the principal or additional diagnosis for 1.2% of discharged hospital patients, with associated increases in medical services, longer hospital stays, institutionalization, and disruptive behaviors to at-home caregivers (Moyle et al., 2008; Nazarko, 2008). And much like the symptoms of delirium, dementia does not have specific *DSM* criteria but rather associated symptoms and features that are applied to its subtypes. These subtypes include dementia of the Alzheimer's type, vascular dementia, dementia due to HIV disease, dementia due to head trauma, dementia due to Parkinson's disease, dementia due to Huntington's disease, dementia due to Pick's disease, dementia due to Creutzfeldt-Jakob disease, and dementia due to other general medical conditions. These symptoms and features include all those of

the cognitive disorders, making dementia a prominent and challenging disorder to identify due to similarity of clinical features and shared phenomenology with other disorders.

Impairments in memory, disturbances in executive functions, impaired perception (visual and spatial) despite intact sensory functions, cognitive disturbances, language deterioration, and impaired motor activities are symptoms present in dementia (APA, 2000; Smith, 2005). Unlike delirium, disturbance in consciousness results in the loss of awareness of self and to other indicators of consciousness. A chronic evolvement of impairments insidiously develops over time (spanning from 12 to 20 years), differentiating dementia from the onset of other cognitive disorders. Characteristics of personality and behavior changes, changes in comprehension, and diminished learning capacity are indicative of progressive brain malfunction and neurodegeneration (Moyle et al., 2008; Yankner et al., 2008). The progressive neurodegeneration and brain damage that occurs causes global mental and behavioral changes associated with symptoms of dementia, such as deterioration in cognition and psychomotor functions.

The criterion for all dementia subtypes includes the identification of agnosia (i.e., the presence of a memory deficit despite intact sensory functions) (APA, 2000; Auchus, 2008; Nazarko, 2008; Pasinetti & Hiller-Sturmhofel, 2008). "Memory impairment is required to make the diagnosis of dementia and is a prominent early symptom" (APA, 2000, p. 148). Included is the inability to recognize, retain, and recall objects as deficits in memory begins to emerge. This hinders the ability to learn new material and retain previously learned material, progressing to where the person is unable to recall his or her own name, occupation, conversations, placement of personal belongings, and residence (Insel & Badger, 2002; Moyle et al., 2008). Impairments to memory also cause intellectual impairments that interfere with all aspects of function and comprehension of internal states and causes loss of introspection (i.e., the person loses the ability to feel and identify sensations and experiences) (Smith, 2005). In advanced stages of severe dementia (subtype Alzheimer's), the progressive decline in mental functions results in the inability to carry out daily activities, such as dressing, eating, driving, and addressing personal hygiene (Adler, 2007; Pasinetti & Hiller-Sturmhofel, 2008). Difficulty processing information on traffic signs while driving, inability to recall how to make turns while driving, and increased passivity with suspicion of others are present in disturbances of perception (Adler, 2007; Insel & Badger, 2002). Misinterpretation of perceptions to time and place with difficulty with abstraction, spatial orientation, and spatial tasks are features that overlap with symptoms of delirium. The presence of hallucinations is a signal of more severe dementia related to further neurodegeneration and brain damage.

Motor functional impairments (i.e., apraxia) are present and a criterion in all the dementia subtypes. These impairments include the loss of motor skills affected by impaired executive functions including learning, remembering, and performing tasks. The loss of motor functions includes the inability to make eye contact, speak, and carry out tasks of daily living (e.g., dressing, bathing, combing hair). It also includes difficulties with tasks such as shopping and cooking (Nazarko, 2008). As dementia progresses, inability to produce gestures such as waving and loss of gait and coordination functions progress; at end-stage dementia, sitting up and holding one's head up is impossible. There is a loss of bladder and bowel functions and an inability to eat and swallow (Chapman & Toseland, 2007). These are all attributed to the continued brain damage and neurodegeneration.

The overall deterioration of language (aphasia) is a clinical feature present in all the dementia subtypes where comprehension of spoken and written language is impaired (see Quick Reference 11.4). These impairments include the loss of verbal ability, speech function, and communication present in delirium with the inability to articulate (dysarthria), name objects (dysnomia), and write (dysgraphia) (APA, 2000). Repetitive vocalizations (echolalia or palilia) show changes in tone and urgency is noted. In the end-stages of dementia, particularly subtype Alzheimer's, there is a complete loss of all communicative and verbal abilities in clinical presentation secondary to progressive neurodegeneration (APA, 2000; Lacey, 2006; Moyle et al., 2008; Yankner et al., 2008).

Risk Factors

The risk factors that affect and are related to the onset and progression of dementia are almost equivalent to those for delirium. This is attributed to the organic nature of the disorders

---

QUICK REFERENCE 11.4

DEMENTIA

- Memory Deficit
  Agnosia, chronic and insidious evolvement of impairment in attention, recall, recognition, progressive forgetfulness, loss of awareness of self.
- Impaired Executive Functions
  Impaired ability to organize, plan, strategize, set-shift, impaired judgment and decision making, impaired visuo-spatial orientation, changes in perception.
- Language Deterioration
  Aphasia, vague and empty speech, echolalia, palilalia, decreased communication.
- Motor Function Impairment
  Apraxia, impaired ability to carry out activities of daily living, impaired gait and loss of coordination, incontinence, inability to eat and/or swallow.
- Associated Features
  Emotional disturbances (when accompanied by hallucinations). Onset is slow and progressive with chronic duration of disorder postdiagnosing up to 20 years.

---

but also the superimposed characteristics of delirium to dementia. Understanding and knowing the risk factors associated with this disorder will provide a more accurate identification of symptoms during the assessment with subsequent appropriate administration of care.

Age Age is related to the onset and prevalence of dementia. High-risk individuals are those aged 65 and older, often referred to as the "baby boomer generations" (APA, 2000; Moyle et al., 2008; Nazarko, 2008; Pasinetti and Hiller-Sturmhofel, 2008). "The percent of the population over 65 years of age and an estimated 50% of individuals over the age of 85 are thought to have some form of dementia" (Insel & Badger, 2002, p. 365). The *DSM-IV-TR* also specifies the uncommon presence of dementia in children and adolescents secondary to general medical conditions with deterioration in school as an early sign. The disorder is predominantly found among elderly persons within the current high-risk age group.

Genetic/Environment There is some evidence that there is a genetic predisposition to dementia, subtype Alzheimer's, as related to environmental factors. These have been found in the identification of the apolipoprotein E-e4 gene, which increases the risk of developing the subtype Alzheimer's (Pasinetti & Hiller-Sturmhofel, 2008). Pasinetti and Hiller-Sturmhofel (2008) note that the involvement of inherited genes in the development of dementia, subtype Alzheimer's, is also found in individuals who developed the condition in their early 30s and 40s. Understanding the genetic component of these disorders lends to their biological basis, differential diagnosing, yet indicates preventive measures that can be taken to deter the expression and development of this condition.

Nutrition Malnutrition, dehydration, and vitamin deficiencies increase the risk and cause of the onset of dementia. Systematic conditions known to cause dementia, in that vitamin deficiencies such as vitamin B12 deficiency, are noted in the *DSM-IV-TR*. Examination and analysis of these conditions is important for the establishing of diagnostic features and differential diagnosis. And much like delirium, weight loss with a resulting body mass index of less than 18.5 kg/m^2, exceeding 5% in 1 month or 10% in 6 months, is indicative of a risk factor of poor nutrition lending to an assessment related to the onset (e.g., alcohol and substance abuse, cognitive dysfunction, functional limitations, chronic medical conditions, financial resources, and social isolation) (Amin et al., 2003; Moyle et al., 2008). Malnutrition, vitamin deficiency, medical conditions, and environmental stressors affecting human systems are factors in dementia. Noteworthy is the measure of change and impact to activities of daily living and quality of life and how these relate to self-determination and dignity. Assessment of nutrition is a factor in end-stage dementia, where force feeding and feeding tubes may be required. When this is needed to ensure the provision of care and food refusal, in patient rights, this step in treatment is a heavily debated issue in bioethics.

Activities of Daily Living   The association between activity and developing dementia can be reduced by performing physical activities and engaging in higher education pursuits. Performing physical activities (or mobility intervention) and cognitive stimulating activities three times daily may help to reduce the risk of developing both delirium and dementia (Stern, 2006; Yang, et al., 2008). Higher educational attainment can buffer the effects of neurological disease or injury, and physical activity improves cognitive functioning by increasing gray and white matter volume in the prefrontal and temporal cortices (Yang et al., 2008). Educational and physical activities can help to modify and deter functional decline. Assessing the baseline level of activity is important if functional and cognitive decline are

present and will be applied to the diagnostic assessment with subsequent implementation of type of treatment.

COMPLETION OF THE DIAGNOSTIC ASSESSMENT

Similarly to delirium, the clinical assessment for dementia will serve as a surrogate for the identification and diagnosis. Medical examinations will need to be performed to determine findings (e.g., laboratory work and imaging studies). Neuropsychological tests and screenings will need to document impairment of specific areas of cognitive abilities and test and measure visuo-spatial abilities, attention, choice, and reaction time (Adler, 2007). These are listed and explained in the delirium section and are applicable to assess the unique features and criteria of dementia. Specific to assessing dementia is the Folstein Mini Mental State Examination (MMSE), the Confusion Assessment Method (CAM), and the Executive Clock-Drawing Task (CLOX). The MMSE is the most commonly used mental status assessment and correlates well with other such measures listed. Functional impairment must also be assessed; the Functional Activities Questionnaire (FAQ) can be used to do so. Issues pertinent to nutrition and important in the diagnosing and care of dementia can be assessed utilizing the Nutrition Checklist for Older Adults (DETERMINE mnemonic) screening instrument.

Because chronic conditions often cause physical pain and worsen comorbid conditions, there is associated discomfort and symptoms attributed to the disorder indicative of pain (e. g., dysfunctional and aggressive behaviors as a protective response and depression) (Smith, 2005; Zwakhalen, Hamers, Abu-Saad, & Berger, 2006). Dementia is a chronic illness, with progressive worsening of symptoms until termination. Affecting major systems, pain and discomfort can account for related behavioral symptoms in advanced-stage dementia. Pain assessment and management can improve the quality of functioning and care, especially to persons institutionalized and uncommunicative, unable to understand or answer simple yes/no questions (Zwakhalen et al., 2006). A variety of screening tools frequently used in long-term care facilities but adaptable to other settings focus on the observation of behavior to determine pain and discomfort. The Discomfort Scale in Dementia of the Alzheimer's Type (DS-DAT) is an assessment tool that addresses discomfort based on the observation of nine behavioral indicators and their frequency, intensity, and duration (Smith, 2005). The behavioral indicators include areas of breathing, vocalization, facial expressions (content, sad, frightened, frown), body language (relaxed and tense), and fidgeting. While this scale does not measure pain but rather discomfort, it is useful in addressing quality of life in progressive stages of dementia. It has a high correlation with other pain assessment measurements and can be used in conjunction with them.

Of the various pain assessment scales available, the Checklist of Nonverbal Pain Indicators (CNPI) is a behavioral observation–based measurement for cognitively impaired older adults with dementia (Feldt, 2000). It is indicative of pain along six areas during movement or rest (Smith, 2005; Nygaard & Jarland, 2005). It has acceptable test–retest reliability and is used regularly in nursing homes. CNPI scores range from one to six, with one to two indicative of mild pain, three to four indicative of moderate pain, and five to six indicative of severe pain (Nygaard & Jarland, 2005; Warden, Huley, & Volicer, 2003; Zwakhalen, et al., 2006). The Pain Assessment in Advanced Dementia Scale (PAINAD), modified from the DS-DAT, assesses pain along five behavioral observation–based dimensions such as breathing, vocalization, facial expression, body language, and consolability (Smith, 2005; Warden et al., 2003). With a score range of zero to ten (ten indicative of severe pain), it is used in nonverbal advanced dementia and requires training to understand and use (Zwakhalen et al., 2006). The Pain Assessment for the Dementing Elderly (PADE) also measures pain in advanced dementia. Despite its wide use, it has been criticized for unclear scoring and a lack of determination of pain sensitivity (Zwakhalen et al., 2006). Last, the Visual Analogue Scale (VAS) can be particularly instrumental in assessment of pain, in conjunction with these assessments and mental status assessments, providing a semantic assessment of pain through visual simulation. The scale measures a characteristic or attitude along a continuum of values utilizing a visual representation anchored in word descriptors at each end of the continuum, capturing the idea and perception of pain with a mark along the continuum representing the perception of current state of pain (Gould, Kelly, Goldstone, & Gammon, 2001).

These assessments can be included with the mental status assessments, functional living assessments, and nutrition assessments for accurate diagnosis and to determine overall quality of life. They share a high degree of correlation to the other measures. Risk factors will rule out conditions with similar clinical presentations, narrowing the symptoms to features and criteria pertinent to the diagnostic categorization. A more comprehensive analysis of the deterioration in the conditions, identification of corresponding disorders, and criteria for other conditions (e.g., duration of deterioration, onset of when it began) will assist in the determination of the multiaxial system. (See Case Example 11.2, The Case of Mrs. Oliver.)

——— CASE EXAMPLE 11.2 - THE CASE OF MRS. OLIVER ———

Mrs. Oliver is a 59-year-old female of European Caucasian decent. She is of average height and weight, appearing her stated age. She was referred for mental health services at a community mental health clinic by her home health services for changes in mental status and a general decline in functioning. Mrs. Oliver presents to a community-based clinic with the home health worker for this assessment. Provided with the referral is medical documentation noting changes in Mrs. Oliver's condition. It states that she has achieved stabilization in last 6 months post cerebrovascular accident (CVA); she demonstrates worsening of symptoms in the past month, when the referral was scheduled. It is noted that Mrs. Oliver's present symptoms on referral information include agitation, increased lability, changes in appetite, forgetfulness, and changes in activities of daily living.

Medical factors related to Mrs. Oliver's condition are of primary concern. Her medical history is positive for heart disease with Mrs. Oliver having suffered a CVA with aphasia and ataxia in the past year. She receives home health services secondary to continued rehabilitation and is seen two to three times per week for assistance. Mrs. Oliver suffered paralysis to left side of her face and extremities (both arms and legs) for which she receives occupational rehabilitation services at the hospital. Mrs. Oliver has a history of arthritis with some swelling and deformation to hands and joints evident. She is prescribed Celebrex for her arthritis. She utilizes assisted mobility for support for both of her conditions. She is not allergic to medications. She has a history of hypertension for which she has been prescribed nitrites. She has a positive history for acid reflux disease. She is on dietary restriction secondary to her medical concerns. She was prescribed Lexapro for poststroke depression; it was discontinued due to her complaints of abdominal distention and nausea. Medication was not resumed. Per referral information, she has no past history of mental illness and/or treatment. Her current medications include nitrites and Celebrex.

At the time of the interview, Mrs. Oliver is cooperative and demonstrates slight difficulties with speech, particularly with enunciation due to physical impairment related to the CVA. During interview she is not accompanied by her home health assistant. When asked why she was referred for services, Mrs. Oliver reports problems with her home health assistant, citing ineptitude and robbery. When asked about her history and specific concerns she is experiencing, Mrs. Oliver reports she has medical problems, lives alone, and she has to monitor the assistant because she "steals." Mrs. Oliver reports she has had to "hide" her belongings, including food, which she reports are taken by the home assistant. When asked how long these concerns have been present, she is unable to state a time frame. She continues to cite her displeasure and distrust of her home assistant. Mrs. Oliver does reside alone in an apartment building per her report and referral documentation. Her immediate family does not live in the area. She is provided assistance and company from a home health assistant; she has been a recipient of services for over six months. No concerns have been noted prior to her referral for presenting symptomology.

Mrs. Oliver is asked about her medical concerns of which she reports having suffered a "stroke." When asked when this occurred, she reports "over 5 years ago." Referral information cites that Mrs. Oliver suffered a cerebrovascular accident in the last year. When asked why she receives home health services, she reports these are for assistance with "cleaning and cooking." When asked if she receives any rehabilitation services for her aphasia or ataxia, she reports she attends medical checks at her hospital where she sees "Dr. M." Referral information notes that Dr. M. is her primary care physician, but she does not see him for rehabilitation at the hospital. When asked if she has been experiencing any difficulties with remembering her appointments, she denies this at the time of the interview. When asked when she was born, she reports the incorrect year. When asked if she has contact with her family members, she reports telephone conversations with them. When asked where they reside, she reports that they do not reside in the state and has difficulty initially remembering the state but reports this correctly per referral information provided. When asked if she has been experiencing difficulties sleeping, she denies this at the time of the interview. When asked if she has been feeling frustrated or agitated, she reports that she has felt angry as her attendant continues to "take" her belongings and again suspects the attendant of robbery and purposefully obstructing access to these. When asked about her appetite, she denies problems. Referral information reports changes in appetite with decreased intake. She denies suicidal, morbid, and/or homicidal ideations at time of this interview. She denies auditory, visual, gustatory, olfactory, and/or tactile hallucinations at time of this interview.

Mrs. Oliver lives alone in her apartment. She has limited social interaction and receives most of her social contact from her home health assistant. She reports telephone contact with family members who reside in another state. She is not married but reports a "boyfriend" with whom she reports contact. Per home health assistant and Mrs. Oliver's report at time of the interview, she lives alone but receives calls from a gentleman but is not sure as to the nature of the relationship. Mrs. Oliver has extensive medical concerns for which she receives disability and public assistance. Prior to her medical issues, she worked part time as an administrative assistant at an office. She is high school educated and holds a high school diploma. She has access to ambulette transportation services to facilitate transportation to and from her appointments when necessary.

Mrs. Oliver is given an MMSE and the CLOX to assess for changes in mental status. Due to limitations secondary to her physical impairments to her extremities, time is extended for the assessment. She was asked to draw a clock with a dial at 1:45. She demonstrated difficulties with following the instruction. Modifications were made, and the CLOX was overlapped with the copying on the MMSE to address changes in visuospatial orientation and recognition, retention, and recall. Due to her limitations, the sheet was folded in four and the clock was drawn in the first quadrant of the sheet. She was asked to copy the clock, to her best ability, in the fourth quadrant as drawn by this interviewer. Mrs. Oliver drew a partial circle, as she was unable to note on the sheet, drawing outside of the page between quadrant four and three. The hands of the clock were copied incorrectly as she was unable to execute the first task of copying the clock. When she was asked to spell the word WORLD, she was able to spell a few of the letters but demonstrated difficulties with task. She was shown three objects on the desk and asked to name these; she was able to do so. She was assessed as to orientation to which she demonstrated impairments to time and date but is oriented to place, acknowledging she is at a clinic. She is unable to perform serial sevens appropriately. When asked to identify and name the three objects presented, she is unable to do so. She demonstrates impairment with reading exercise and writing limitations secondary to noted physical limitations. Physical limitations and educational background were considered in the assessment. Mrs. Oliver's current MMSE score is 17, which demonstrates moderate impairment.

Medical evidence documenting Mrs. Oliver's heart-related problems, including her cerebrovascular accident, hypertension, aphasia, and ataxia support a multifactorial medical and neurodegenerative basis for symptoms. Her mental status assessment demonstrates moderate impairment, which further supports alterations in cognitive processes attributed to physical factors.

Application of Multiaxial System

Mrs. Oliver is experiencing difficulties related to her present condition of aphasia and subsequent motor function impairments related to complications of her ataxia and arthritis. Despite the presence of these symptoms, Mrs. Oliver had achieved some stabilization within the past 6 months with an increase in symptomology within the past month. Modifications were made to the assessment to address and compensate for her physical limitations. She demonstrates difficulties with task execution and perception. Her attention and orientation related to memory are impaired, and motor function is limited. Changes are noted in her perception and alteration in behavior, secondary to her reports of increased suspicion of her home attendant within the last month not previously noted in the last 6 months. She demonstrates signs of compensation for her increased forgetfulness and problems with remote memory functions, as she is unable to state her date of birth. She notes awareness of self as she reports her actions (e.g., "hides"), but perception and cognition is altered citing increased suspicion. She reports "anger" secondary to these concerns, which is attributed to the lability noted in her referral. She has psychosocial stressors that increase her risk of dementia combined with her medical condition. "Individuals with *dementia* may be especially vulnerable to physical stressors (e.g., illness or minor surgery) and psychosocial stressors (e.g., going to the hospital, bereavement), which may exacerbate their intellectual deficits and other associated problems" (APA, 2000, p. 150). Her medical condition, physical circumstances, psychosocial changes incurred secondary to changes to her physical health, financial changes, mobility restrictions, attendance of medical appointments, and educational background place her at higher risk, and symptoms are indicative of dementia despite her age bracket. The severity of her past and current medical concerns are indicative of the diagnosis of early-stage vascular dementia (290.4x) on Axis I.

Differential diagnosis is noted as to specifier of the type of vascular dementia present. Mrs. Oliver was treated for depressive symptoms after the onset of her vascular concerns; treatment was ceased secondary to abdominal discomfort and nausea attributed to her medication. Treatment was not resumed after symptom cessation, and complications were not noted thereafter from her referral services. Mrs. Oliver currently reports altered cognitive processes and behaviors related to her memory impairment, executive functioning, changes in perception with increased anger and suspicion related to these changes. Her impaired motor function is related to a presenting neurodegenerative condition. The changes in appetite (i.e., decreased appetite) are simultaneous to the changes she presents with that also were noted by her home health assistant and referral information. These changes are also present within the time frame of onset despite prior stabilization; this is indicative of progressive neurodegenerative decompensation rather than a mental disorder. Mrs. Oliver is given the diagnosis of vascular dementia with delirium (290.41) on Axis I with subsequent medical condition coded based on Appendix G on Axis III. To retard the progression of her condition, she requires stabilization and treatment for hypertension with a full medical evaluation to rule out further concerns. No behavior disturbance specifier is noted on Axis I, as it is a component and noted feature of her degenerative condition and not a precipitating agent.

Axis II is coded V71.09 no diagnosis for Mrs. Oliver. Her current changes in personality and behavior are related to her medical condition and neurodegeneration. As dementia is a progressive and a degenerative condition, personality changes will be noted. These will not be indicative of a personality disorder but to changes related to her illness. Intellectual functioning and testing is limited due to the progressive course of her condition but is accessed at baseline per her educational background. Per background history, no concerns with intellectual functioning are noted prior to the onset of her medical concerns.

Mrs. Oliver has extensive medical concerns that are related to the primary diagnosis on Axis I. She suffered a cerebrovascular accident with subsequent complications of aphasia and ataxia. She has hypertension for which she takes medication. She is placed on dietary restriction. She suffers from acid reflux disease. She suffers from arthritis, with evidence of swelling of her joints, and is prescribed Celebrex. She has no allergies to any medications. (This should be listed in all caps to reduce medical errors and for other providers to note when integrating care.) When coding her medical concerns, the primary concerns noted on Axis III should be that related to her vascular dementia is the CVA (e.g., stroke). This is coded 436 on Axis III from Appendix G. Listed first on Axis III, she also has ataxia, which is a complication related to her CVA and a contributing condition to her neurodegeneration.

Various psychosocial stressors are applicable and affect her presenting problem on Axis IV. Of these, primary are her medical concerns. She has suffered extensive environmental and social changes secondary to her medical problems. She is receiving rehabilitation for these concerns. Her activities of daily living have been disturbed secondary to her presenting problems, and she requires assistance. Her mobility is limited due to her physical concerns, and she requires assistance and coordination of ambulette services to transport her to her medical appointments. Her financial situation has altered with her currently receiving disability and public assistance. She has multiple hospital visits, and her current social life revolves around her medical visits, with the majority of her socialization taking place with her home health assistant. Her only contact with her family members is through telephone conversations as they do not reside in the same state. Her psychosocial stressors should be listed in order of severity:

1. Medical concerns
2. Limited mobility
3. Financial concerns
4. Limited social support
5. Social isolation
6. Secure housing

Her Axis V diagnosis should note the impact of her psychosocial stressors with her current presenting symptoms. Her physical impairments cause a significant impact to her occupational and social life. She has changes in perception, executive function impairment, and memory deficits. She does not present with suicidal, morbid, or homicidal ideation at time of the interview. Changes in her personality occurred within the last month and are attributed to her medical condition. She demonstrates impairments in her judgment and thinking. She has major impairment in judgment and thinking secondary to her medical concerns and neurodegenerative condition. Her MMSE score was a 17, which is indicative of moderate impairment to her mental status. She is not incoherent or acting grossly inappropriate, and for this reason is not diagnosed with behavioral disturbances on Axis I. She has no suicidal preoccupations. Her family relations are intact, and geographic distance is the only concern noted. Relationship concerns may have been affected secondary to her medical concerns, but these are not presented by Mrs. Oliver as an issue affecting her overall social functioning. She does require assistance with activities of daily living, secondary to her mobility concerns after her CVA; she receives rehabilitation 2 to 3 days during the week. She has maintained herself the remainder of the week until further changes were noted. Due to her medical concerns and associated psychosocial stressors and impact, Mrs. Oliver is given a GAF score of 32 (see Quick Reference 11.5).

QUICK REFERENCE 11.5

MULTIAXIAL ASSESSMENT FOR MRS. OLIVER

Axis I: [290.41] Vascular dementia with delirium.

Axis II: [V71.09] No diagnosis.

Axis III: 1. Cerebrovascular accident [436].
               2. Cerebellar ataxia [334.3].
               3. Hypertension.
               4. Arthritis.
               5. Acid reflux disease.
               6. No allergies to medications.

Axis IV: 1. Medical concerns.
               2. Limited mobility.
               3. Financial concerns.
               4. Limited social support.
               5. Social isolation.
               6. Secure housing.

Axis V: 32.

DEMENTIA: TREATMENT PLANNING, IMPLEMENTATION, AND EVALUATION

Treatment planning for dementia will be set according to the stage of progression of the condition. Considering this factor, care must be taken to recognize distinctions between dementia subtypes and how these impact treatment planning and implementation according to symptomology and levels of severity (see Sample Treatment Plan 11.2). An example can be seen in the differences in levels of confusion found in early stages of dementia, Alzheimer's subtype, to those in vascular dementia (Nazarko, 2008). While distinctions are present among the subtypes, what remains constant is that dementia is a chronic condition. Much can be done to prevent the rapidity of its onset, once identified. In cases where delirium superimposes dementia, this can signal early-stage dementia and an opportunity for intervention to increase brain capacity. "Those interventions that have the strongest links to improving cognitive reserves in individuals with brain pathology, particularly dementia, include physical activity, social interaction, challenging mental activities, and avoidance of anticholinergic drugs and inappropriate medications" (Fick, Kolanowski, Beattie, & McCrow, 2009, p. 33). Reactions to pharmacological treatments which increase the risks for those that suffer from dementia and delirium and should be avoided include the use of anticholinergic drugs such as antihistamines, bronchodilator medications, antipsychotic agents, anti-anxiety agents, antidepressant drugs, cardiovascular agents, and antiparkinsonian medications (Fick et al, 2002; Reeves and Brister, 2008; Young and Inouye, 2007). (See Table 11.1.) In early-stage dementia, the primary goal of treatment planning is improving brain functions. It is achieved by improving the client's executive functions (including enhancing visuospatial functioning) and increasing memory functions through implementation of activities that increase recognition, recall, and retention capabilities.

SAMPLE TREATMENT PLAN 11.2

MRS. OLIVER

Short-Term Objectives	Plan or Interventions
1. Stabilize client's medical condition.	Schedule an appointment with primary care physician to address medical factors contributing to progression of disorder.
2. Acquire neurological testing.	Schedule an appointment for a psychiatric consult to acquire orders for neurological testing.
	Coordinate services among primary care providers, rehabilitative services, and mental health services.
	Encourage client to be compliant with her medical treatments and regimen.
3(a). Implement cognitive retraining exercises.	Engage client in sustaining completion and performance of a simple task (e.g., puzzle, board game, card game).
	Engage client in completion of a creative activity that requires readaptation and coordination of visuo-spatial skills (e.g., number-colored paintings).
	Teach and engage client to play card game "Memory" in session to improve concentration and attention.
	Engage client and home assistant in session to play game to be implemented at home.
	Encourage client to identify a hobby or activity that she enjoys and can participate in once per week.
	Facilitate meetings between home health assistant and client to address concerns.
3(b). Improve recognition, recall, and retention time.	Identify thoughts related to changes in perception that increase labile mood.
	Provide education to client regarding neurodegenerative illness and the impact on judgment and decision making.
3(c). Restructure cognitive processes.	Assist client in identifying thoughts to be utilized to increase well-being.
	Write thoughts for client to utilize so she can be be reminded.
4. Decrease client's social isolation.	Engage client in participating in a recreation activity at an assisted living community center once per week.
	Coordinate a trip for client to visit family members once per month.
	Encourage client to increase telephone contacts per week to family and relationship.
5. Increase left/right coordination to increase plasticity.	Engage client in exercises that utilize left/right coordination (e.g., holding and lifting handball with opposite predominant extremity during session).
	Engage client in exercises that utilize left/right coordination with sustained attention (e.g., focus attention to an activity opposite of requested performed activity).
6. Maintain activities of daily living.	Maintain coordination of transportation services.
	Maintain coordination of home health services.
	Monitor client's ability to maintain activities of daily living, with implementation of assisted living services if necessary.

Table 11.1.   Commonly Used Anticholinergic Drugs among Older People

Type of Drug	Example
Antihistamine	Hydroxyzine, diphenhydramine
Antispasmodic	Alverine, hyoscyamine
Benzodiazepine	Lorazepam
Analgesic	Codeine
Antiarrhythmic	Digoxin
Diuretic	Furosemide
Antiparkinsonian	Orphenadrine, benzatropine
Bladder stabilizer	Oxybutynin
Brochodilator	Theophylline

Source: Adapted from J. Young and S. Inouye (2007), "Delirium in Older People," *British Medical Journal, 334,* 842–846.

Challenging mental activities and cognitive stimulation can provide a protective treatment and intervention factor. Educational pursuits, reality orientation techniques, mental imaging, recall and delayed recall, executive exercises, and meaningful activities focusing on current interests, hobbies, and preferences improve memory in older adults with mild cognitive impairments (e.g., reading of newspapers, pursuits of hobbies, taking a class, playing board games, playing a musical instrument, and writing for pleasure) (Chapman & Toseland, 2007; Fick et al., 2009). These activities can assist to improve brain functioning with increased responsivity in areas engaged in cognitive tasks (Stern, 2006; Valenzuela & Sachdev, 2009). Short-term objectives and long-term goals that incorporate these interventions and protective features can alter the progression of the disorder and should be implemented in treatment planning.

Exercise, which takes into account the client's physical abilities and limitations, also provides a protective factor to the onset and/or speed of the progression of dementia. Engaging the client in regular physical activity two to three times per week for a minimum of 15 minutes stimulates trophic factors and neural growth mechanisms, resulting in the provision of cognitive reserves (Fick et al., 2009; Yang et al., 2008). In early-stage dementia, exercise can serve as a mediating variable between the impact of social variables, cognitive dysfunction, and the motor function impairment resulting from neurodegeneration. Physical exercise can also offset and alleviate disorders that share phenomenology with the cognitive disorders and conditions associated with the intended and unintended consequences of aging (e.g., pain, physical discomfort, and incidences of depression and/or anxiety associated with losses). Objectives and long-term goals addressing the benefits of exercise geared to increasing concentration, self-regulation, and coordination of motor functions should be implemented in the treatment plan.

Social activities promoting well-being and networking opportunities can positively impact the progressive course of dementia by enhancing reserves. These activities involve going to the movies, restaurants, clubs, and sporting events; gardening, cooking; doing volunteer activities; and decreased television watching (which increases cognitive decline) (Fick et al., 2009). Social activities provide increased support and can reduce social isolation. Support also can buffer psychosocial stressors and associated negative emotions as changes associated with the awareness of the progression of dementia become evident to the person (particularly in the dementia subtypes of a general medical condition, e.g., Vascular, Parkinson's, HIV). Increasing social activities as an objective to decrease the long-term impact of the progression of dementia should be addressed in the treatment plan.

In moderate stages, where hospitalization and institutionalization occurs secondary to the progression of the disease, treatment planning should focus on the adaptation and orientation of the client to the new setting. Addressing the external environmental stressors, modifications to the environmental setting that provide structure and reduce stimuli will increase activity and reduce disorientation. This will include assisting clients with the provision of memory cues, such as clocks, calendars, and photos (Moyle et al., 2008). In the treatment planning, this may also include walking with the client to increase awareness, visual orientation, and memorization of environmental settings (e.g., recognition, recall, and attention) to decrease disorientation and improve adaptation. Implementation of activities that enhance cognitive reserves should be considered and applied in the treatment planning based on level of capacity (e.g., considering the deterioration and atrophy caused secondary to brain damage). As communication becomes impaired, monitoring of pain, discomfort, and nutrition secondary to physical deterioration of motor functions should be routinely assessed and included as an objective and long-term goal of treatment planning.

In cases where the progression of dementia is advanced, treatment focus will need to include the degree of medical care, withdrawal of interventions, initiation of hospice, and preparation for the terminal phases of the disorder (Hurley & Volicer, 2002). In end-stage dementia, medical interventions that utilize artificial nutrition and feeding tubes, artificial hydration,

cardiopulmonary resuscitation for heart failure, and antibiotics for infections are recurrent secondary to the occurrence of severe and significant brain damage (Chapman & Toseland, 2007). This practice continues to raise ethical issues regarding patient rights, and what is deemed end-of-life decisions for older adults with dementia, and what constitutes "life sustaining." Palliative care is the dominant paradigm in end-stage dementia, but this is not without contest.

"Life sustaining" measures are of particular concern in treatment planning as these involve interaction, facilitation, and mobilization of major systems of care responding to the patient. Treatment focuses on the balance between patient rights, medical care, and family desires and centers on what is deemed "life sustaining." There is the medical oath to preserve and sustain life, utilizing medical interventions, to improve quality of life during the transition to death (e.g., tube feeding to prevent unnecessary starvation due to inability to eat or drink). From the medical perspective, the presence or absence of vitals and brain waves is a component of determining whether life-sustaining measures should be used.

Consciousness determines the awareness of the individual and actions he or she would command in the presence of it. It is difficult to assess the presence of consciousness in end-stage dementia secondary to the physical and mental deterioration. In the absence of determining the client's level of awareness, types of treatments to deliver and how, when, and what is deemed in the best interest and quality of life for the client can be problematic for family members and assisting staff. Advance Directives facilitate communication of a client's wishes prior to when in the absence of consciousness to administer these. But in the absence of Advance Directives, which implicitly state client's wishes for care and resuscitative measures, arguments against and for "sustained" life measures can infiltrate quality of care and treatment. These arguments include favoring sustained life measures in an effort to preserve at any point "life," addressing quality as the measure provided at any point of the illness's course until reaching its natural end. Those who are against sustained life measures cite that such measures do not improve quality of life; rather, these decrease it at end stages of dementia due to their invasive nature (e.g., feeding tubes are associated with higher rates of aspiration pneumonia and infections, and artificial dehydration increases swelling and worsens other symptoms associated with dehydration) (Chapman & Toseland, 2007). While these arguments continue to center on the greater aspects of bioethical debates, treatment planning can center on facilitating support and communication between family members and staff, addressing bereavement and grief issues, and providing support and respite to clients through pain monitoring and stimulation through conversation and other sensory stimuli, until further measures are administered and/or death proceeds.

INTERVENTION STRATEGIES

Interventions strategies for delirium and dementia include the mental status assessments, functional assessment measures, and quality of life measures that can be utilized to assess and identify the presence of delirium and dementia. Mental status assessment interventions include the Folstein Mini Mental State Examination (MMSE), the NEECHAM Confusion Scale, the Executive Clock Drawing Task (CLOX), and the Confusion Assessment Method (CAM). Intervention strategies that assess changes in levels of functioning include the Functional Activities Questionnaire (FAQ) and the Nutrition Check List for Older Adults. Intervention

strategies that assess quality of care associated with these disorders include the Checklist for Nonverbal Pain Indicators (CNPI), Pain Assessment in Advanced Dementia Scale (PAINAD), Discomfort Scale in Dementia of the Alzheimer's Type (DS-DAT), the Pain Assessment for the Dementing Elderly (PADE), and the Visual Analogue Scale (VAS).

Intervention strategies that target cognitive processes, restructuring, and retraining are best to complement the organic nature of these disorders. As specified in the *DSM-IV-TR,* evidence from the mental status examinations and medical findings determine the type of cognitive disorder and the level of psychosocial intervention to apply, according to the stage of progression. Centering on the biological basis of the organic nature of these disorders affecting cognitive, emotional, and psychomotor processes observed in presenting clinical features, psychosocial interventions and models which focus on the rehabilitation and reduction of discomfort are discussed in this section. Interventions and models are used interchangeably for both delirium and dementia in more advanced stages and superimposed conditions. Note that intervention for delirium will be more brief and in relation to cessation and stabilization of the underlying condition for its exacerbation (e.g., general medical condition).

Psychosocial Interventions

Psychosocial interventions address cognitive changes that affect thought processes, mood, and personality changes associated with cognitive disorders. The application of these interventions depends on type and stage of progression of the disorder. They can be used in different treatment modalities (e.g. individual, group, and family) to increase cognitive, behavioral, and psychosocial functioning. The psychosocial interventions listed have been cited as most effective in the treatment of cognitive disorders. Briefly included in this section are psychosocial interventions that have attracted some attention and following in the clinical field due to their effectiveness to deal with the organic nature of the disorder.

Cognitive-Behavioral Therapy Cognitive-Behavioral Therapy (CBT) has been useful in associated disorders that share a phenomenological basis with the cognitive disorders. The use of CBT helps to moderate the psychosocial stressors affecting the client and caregivers. Of the many associated losses occurring in older life, including marital and family conflict and major physical illnesses (e.g., cardiac diseases), the cognitive disorders share phenomenology with other disorders of cognition. This makes differential diagnosis difficult unless a mental status examination with other medical findings is performed. Generally among older adults, and also in older adults with dementia, anxiety and depression occur. In cases of dementia, depression has been incorrectly diagnosed when the correct diagnosis should have been dementia (Myers and Harper, 2004). This misdiagnosis can hinder the application of intervention methods which assist to buffer the progression of dementia. Due to the perceptual and cognitive changes in dementia, CBT has been most effective in providing relaxation training, meditation, graduated exposure therapy, and supportive group therapy to clients. CBT also addresses cognitive training and restructuring associated with memory and perceptual disturbances. Treatment focuses on orientation to reality and function and increases executive functions by engaging client in problem solving and task completion. Application of behavior modification in response to changes in cognitive processes is also the domain of CBT. This intervention can be useful to enhancing and increasing motor functions.

Reality Orientation Therapy Reality Orientation (RO) is one of the most extensively evaluated psychological approaches and is applied in a variety of settings with significant results in areas of cognitive abilities, memory, and information/orientation (Myers & Harper, 2007). It is a cognition-oriented technique for clients with memory loss and time-place disorientation and an efficacious treatment for dementia. RO utilizes continuous and repetitive orientation to the environment to reorient the client with dementia (Zanetti et al., 2002). It can be used as a 24-hour-based therapy involving patients in reality testing, such as in finding the way around the hospital setting or home to increase orientation, involving patients in continuous communication throughout the day, or in "classrooms" where orientation-related activities in group settings occur (Douglas, James, & Ballard, 2004; Spector, Davies, Woods, & Orrell, 2000; Zanetti et al., 2002). It uses signposts, notices, and other memory aids to increase orientation and encourage increases in memory through cues (Douglas et al., 2004). Mixed results have occurred with the duration of the effectiveness of the therapy after cessation, but when applied on a continuous basis, this therapeutic technique has improved areas of functioning in memory improvement and time-space orientation in clients with dementia.

Behavior Therapy Behavior therapy is noted as particularly useful in more advanced stages of dementia and acute cases of delirium. It utilizes the ABC model (*a*ntecedent, *b*ehavior, and *c*onsequences) to create structure, increase orientation, and decrease unwanted and risk behaviors. The therapy utilizes a chart-based system to track behaviors, from structuring the intake of pain medication, initiation and completion of activities of daily living, and increasing adherence to modifications that target problem areas (e.g., sleep-wake cycles, socialization, and mobility). Behavior therapy can be particularly useful in advanced stages of dementia as it allows clients to focus on the completion of a specific task related to ability and capability. As the illness progresses, or in acute stages of disorientation, narrowing and sustaining focus is key to decreasing risks and further decompensation (Spiegler & Guevremont, 1998).

Bereavement Therapy Bereavement therapy is useful in any clinical application related to loss. It can prove beneficial in addressing the multiple related losses experienced due to the course and progression of the disorder. Depending on the subtype of dementia, awareness of the losses suffered secondary to a decrease in cognition and the progressive loss of motor functioning capabilities can be emotionally overwhelming. Losses regarding changes in environment and adaptation to long-term care settings require addressing losses associated with independence, loss of familiar settings, and loss of privacy. The progressive loss associated with ongoing changes in cognition and behaviors can be taxing to family members who do not understand the nature of the illness. Bereavement therapy can be particularly helpful to family members during end-stage progression of dementia and mortality-associated delirium. In delirium, the loss of a loved one can be quite sudden. In cases where delirium superimposes another serious medical condition, the losses associated with them can overwhelm client and family members alike. And in facing the death of a loved one in end-stage dementia, bereavement therapy can offer support, understanding, and facilitate the transition for parties involved.

Family Therapy Family therapy has been a much-discussed topic in the literature of care in dementia and delirium. In particular, integrating family member participation in the care of the client has been of more intense focus to increase awareness, improve patient satisfaction, and enhance caregiving and quality of life. The Creating Avenues for Relatives model (CARE), discussed later in the chapter, addresses the importance and need in engaging families in treatment (Moyle et al., 2008). Family therapy, as discussed elsewhere in this book, acknowledges that the client is part of a larger system. Chronic illnesses, such as dementia, can be particularly overwhelming for families in terms of costs, time, and emotions. Meeting the demands of everyday life, including taking care of the loved one, can strain immediate relationships and negatively affect the quality of caregiving for all involved. Family therapy can allow members to voice their concerns, address and create strategies for effective problem solving, and provide a respite where emotions related to loss and frustrations can be voiced and explained. Family therapy can also provide a venue to increase communication among key members involved in the care of the ill family member, facilitate communication with staff, and, in the end stages of the illness, provide stage where family members can engage in decision making regarding treatment, quality of life, and life-sustaining measures.

Reminiscence Therapy, Validation Therapy, and Similar Therapies There has been some attraction of and to these therapies in the clinical field addressing the "lived experience" of individuals. Reminiscence, validation, and similar therapies address the "lived experiences" of individuals. They have often been cited as useful in treatment with the geriatric population. Rooted in humanistic and Rogerian principles (and sharing this foundation with the other psychosocial interventions included in this section), the particular application, focus, and goals of these therapies related to the needs of delirium and dementia is of key concern and question. Focus in these therapies is the "validation" of emotions and experiences of the client, through a vocalization of the client's narrative as it relates to his or her past memories, allowing the doing and undoing of past experiences and resolving emotions and concerns related to these affecting the individual. The center core is that, in the process of this reminiscent experience, the individual reaches resolution and validates his or her experience and existence. Validation is a centerpiece of all the psychosocial interventions presented in this section.

At present, no literature documents the effectiveness of these therapies in addressing the underlying components: cognitive improvement, concerns, and deficits applicable to the conditions of delirium and dementia (Douglas et al., 2004; Livingston et al., 1996/2005; Myers & Harper, 2004). A cited positive feature is that a person with dementia may enjoy and gain pleasure from listening to an old record (Douglas et al., 2004), and this is a noteworthy respite and a relaxing measure which does little to alter the progressive decline of the disorder. Perhaps this is attributed on the basis that these therapies do not address the causation of these illnesses and subsequent diagnostic features. In individuals with declined cognitive abilities, impaired memory and perceptual disturbances, and loss of or disturbed awareness of self, validation where a disturbance is present is not validation. It is questionable as to what will be achieved through the application of these types of interventions. Reminiscence and validation therapies do little to increase orientation or visual and spatial awareness when memory is impaired. When the ability to plan, organize, and strategize cannot be executed, creating narrative of a memory will be far from an achievable task. In terms of rehabilitation, when memory is impaired it is difficult to address reality or process information. How reminiscence and validation therapies address language deficiencies in the

cognitive disorders—a key component of any narrative (in either verbal, written, and/or speech applied format)—is not well-defined with this type of disorder. In terms of rehabilitation and the understanding of its effectiveness to the care of dementia and delirium, these interventions are better served with individuals who are not suffering from these cognitive disorders, focusing attention on the caregivers of individuals suffering from dementia and delirium.

Models of Care

Models of care apply multifactorial treatment methods in an integrated interdisciplinary approach to deliver comprehensive care. Rooted in various disciplines, they apply problem-solving strategies to the multifactorial basis of these disorders (i.e., cognitive decline, behavioral problems) and use an interdisciplinary method to deliver care. The models discussed in this section address the care of delirium and dementia from a variety of target foci, including reducing internal and external stressors, decreasing associated risk factors, increasing and integrating active family participation into caregiving and decision-making functions, and improving patient care through paradigmatic changes and approaches.

Progressively Lowered Stress Threshold The Progressively Lowered Stress Threshold (PLST) model applies principles that modify the environment to compensate for cognitive losses. It posits the maintenance of a structured routine, regular rest periods to address fatigue and loss of reserve capacities, and controls for factors that increase stress (Moyle et al., 2008). The basis of the model is to target and reduce stress-inducing factors, resulting in a decrease in symptomology and increased functioning. The six factors addressed and included in the model are (1) fatigue; (2) changes in routine, environment, or caregiver; (3) demands that exceed functional capacity; (4) multiple and competing stimuli; (5) affective responses to perceptions of loss; and (6) physical stressors such as pain (Gerdner, Buckwalter, & Reed, 2002; Moyle et al., 2008). Targeting the environment to reduce internal stresses experienced and exacerbated secondary to altered cognitive functioning compensates for the deficits created through neurodegeneration and facilitates adaptation to new settings. Environmental targets include decreasing disorientation by utilizing colors to highlight sensory input and increase orientation, and providing furnishings that address functional limitations (Nazarko, 2008). PLST addresses the impact levels of stress on persons with dementia and delirium and impact levels of patient behavior. It addresses the stages of progression of these disorders into subgroups based on intellectual losses, affective or personality losses, conative or planning losses, and progressively lowered stress threshold (Gerdner et al., 2002). Studies on the model are limited with respect to their outcome, but in residential settings, the model has demonstrated improvements in activity level, nutrition, and a reduction in disruptive behavior.

Hospital Elder Life Program   The Hospital Elder Life Program (HELP) was developed to reduce incidences of delirium and increase functioning in dementia. The model includes a set of protocols targeting six associated risk factors: (1) cognitive impairment, (2) sleep deprivation, (3) immobility, (4) visual impairment, (5) hearing impairment, and (6) dehydration (Robinson et al., 2008). Noted by Robinson et al (2008), the components included in the model to address these factors include:

1.   A daily visitor program to increase socialization and improve orientation and communication.

2.   Therapeutic activities program to increase cognitive stimulation and socialization.

3.   Mobilization to promote daily exercise and walking.

4.   A nonpharmacological sleep protocol to promote relaxation and sufficient sleep.

5.   A hearing and vision protocol with adaptive equipment.

6.   An oral fluid volume repletion and feeding assistance.

The aims of the model provides an interdisciplinary approach, with expert staff and highly trained and supervised volunteer staff, to (1) assess and deliver standardized protocols for the management of the six associated risk factors for delirium and (2) reduce the use of restraints, improve satisfaction with care, and increase the understanding of care of older people with confusional states (Moyle et al., 2008). Information technology supports the model and documents interventions, tracks patient progress, and reports clinical and financial performance as part of meeting integrated means of balancing practices and cost-effective measures (Bradley, et al., 2004). The model has produced favorable outcomes in reducing episodes of delirium and is used predominately in hospital settings.

Creating Avenues for Relatives   Family involvement in patient care has been determined to be an important factor in the improvement of patient outcomes. The Creating Avenues for Relatives (CARE) model addresses family involvement and increases communication between family and caregivers. The CARE model educates family members on the characteristics and behaviors found in dementia and helps them to develop strategies to take an active role in the care of their ill family member (Moyle et al., 2008). Moyle at al. (2008) noted that the model includes educational interventions and staff/family collaborations to improve care.

These interventions included audio and print information to educate family members and clients about emotional and behavioral changes and creating mutual agreements between nurses and family caregiving activities to facilitate integration of care. In the studies of effective models of care for those with dementia and delirium, Moyle et al. (2008) concluded that the impact of the model resulted in reduced incidents of acute confusion, an increase in family caregivers' understanding of dementia, and increased family caregivers' beliefs and efficacy about caring for their ill family member.

Advanced Illness Care Teams The Advanced Illness Care Team (AICT) is a model of care that applies a holistic approach utilizing medical interventions, implantation of meaningful activities, and psychological and behavioral interventions that aim to improve comfort, care, and well-being (Adler, 2007). The model applies an interdisciplinary approach to care to reduce problem behaviors, decrease the use of antipsychotic medications and reduce the excessive prescribing of psychotropic drugs, and limit the use of mechanical restraints (Adler, 2007).

Pharmacology There has been a shift in the care of delirium and dementia with respect to pharmacological treatments to a nonpharmacological approach, or rather one that utilizes less pharmacology to address components of the disorder. Side effects from the medications can decrease cognitive performance and functional capacity, increasing impairments despite recommended levels of administration, and increasing associated risk (e.g., falls, fractures) (Fick et al., 2009; Reeves & Brister, 2008). In the subtypes of dementia (e.g., Alzheimer's, vascular, and Parkinson's), delusions and hallucinations can and do occur due to neurodegeneration and progressive brain damage. "Dopaminergic agents (e.g. levodopa [Dopar]) used to treat Parkinson's

disease may cause development of psychotic symptoms" (Reeves & Brister, 2008, p. 49). Pharmacological treatments have also been a risk and precipitant of delirium. Risks associated with polypharmacological treatments include withdrawal syndromes of benzodiazepines and sedative-hypnotics and side effects of narcotic analgesics, drugs with anticholinergic effects (e.g., tricyclic antidepressants), antipsychotics, and cardiovascular drugs, resulting in discontinuation in their application to stabilization and prevention of symptomology (Fick et al., 2002; Reeves & Brister, 2008; Young & Inouye, 2007). Reactions to these medications are also present in clinical features of dementia, especially delirium superimposed dementia. Withdrawal syndromes resulting from the use of medications, such as the benzodiazepines, can result in psychotic symptoms and exacerbate the onset of delirium (Insel & Badger, 2002; Parker et al., 2008).

There are concerns regarding which types of medications are implemented if psychotic features are present. Medication cost and the U.S. Food and Drug Administration warning regarding their safety in their use and increased mortality among the elderly are key issues in their administration (Breggin, 2006; Ushijima, Yokoyama, Sugiyama, & Amano, 2008). According to some advocates for medications, reduction in acute agitation associated with perceptual disturbances, decreased wandering, increased stabilization of sleep-wake cycles, and lability of mood can be achieved with the use of perospirone and risperone (Risperdal) at low dosages (Reeves & Brister, 2007; Ushijima et al., 2008). Current emphasis is to avoid pharmacological treatments utilizing atypical antipsychotic drugs (risperidone and olanzapine) due to their associated risk of stroke (Young & Inouye, 2007). Other medications that advocates for medication cite as effective in treating symptomology include Abilify (aripiprazole), Geodon (ziprasidone), and Clozaril (clozapine). Data are not available regarding the use of Abilify in older people; prolonged use of Geodon has shown problematic results with older adults with cardiovascular disease; and Clozaril is ineffective for older patients because of toxicity (Reeves & Brister, 2007).

Advocates of nonpharmacological interventions report that use of these medications cause further physical brain deterioration and may increase the risk of injury secondary to sedation in disoriented clients, and increase the onset of other medical conditions and morbidity. Adherence to nonpharmacological treatments focuses on understanding the impact of psychosocial stressors, changes in caregiving, and cognitive and behavioral rehabilitation that provide results equivalent to the use of pharmacological treatments. The premise is that, in vulnerable populations, pharmacological treatments may not remedy the underlying basis and origin of disorders related to neurodegeneration. Their efficacy may prove temporary as an effective treatment modality in the care of those with dementia and delirium. The presence of these medications often causes further impairments and deterioration, leading to syndromes (e.g., withdrawal) not otherwise present that have further social consequences.

INTEGRATED APPROACH

Facing all health care models and treatment practices is the integrated approach. In the present-day arena of evidence-based practices, insurance and managed care restrictions, models of care that provide treatment modalities and interventions on market-based principles, with the maximum results and cost-efficiency measures at their core, affect all clients, providers, and organizations. These health care models and treatment practices require the utilization of practices that increase accuracy in diagnosing, specialization, and increased quality care through demonstrable outcomes; an interdisciplinary approach; and best practices that are required within the treatment setting. The shift of care from a multidisciplinary approach to an interdisciplinary form of care is notable. Integrated care begins with the *DSM-IV-TR*'s assertion that an interdisciplinary approach requires clinical and medical evidence of the diagnosis of these disorders (e.g., mental status assessments, magnetic resonance imaging scans, and laboratory analysis). The organic nature of the cognitive disorders is multifactorial, addressed in the subgrouping in the *DSM-IV-TR* based on their biological basis and treatment. Interdisciplinary care addressing the medical, neuropsychological, psychosocial, and functional component, from a variety of disciplines that provide client-centered care, is the paradigm operating. This approach is related to all the disorders addressed in this chapter and this book.

Paradigm changes are also emerging in the treatment of cognitive disorders and these changes posit that increased accuracy, assessment, and distribution of resources be applied to improve quality of care and increase sustainability of the client's condition while maintaining cost effectiveness. Employing assessment measures and screening tools that increase detection of early-stage dementia and the onset of delirium supports not only accuracy in evidence but cost effectiveness in treatment. Proper assessment can also lead to the managing of resources specific to the level of care and stage of progression required to engage and integrate rehabilitation and respite. Among these shifts, a greater input and involvement of family caregiving is important to the integrated approach in the treatment of cognitive disorders—achieved through education regarding dementia and delirium and integrating mutually agreed-on caregiving functions between medical staff and family members, delaying the need for early placement in long-term care and institutionalization. Client satisfaction, improved treatment participation, and increased deterrence of the progression of neurodegeneration are achieved through family involvement. Familiar settings, familiar people, in the presence of a constant care provider, decreases symptoms associated with these conditions (e.g., disorientation, mood lability, and agitation). (In institutional settings where high turnover is present, these situations increase the stress threshold.) Considering the cost-effective measure of this integrated approach, concerns will need balancing: These concerns require offsetting the costs associated with increased hospital utilization, institutionalization, and risks related to injuries to the costs incurred to caregivers in terms of allocating and mobilizing finances and resources. The aim is to reduce the inevitable circumstance of institutionalization secondary to progression of the illness. With the input of all participating parties focusing on the care of the client, a mutually agreed-on integrated goal that requires further assessment and distribution of resources is achievable.

Best practices are those that can effectively address and target the presenting pathology and individuals suffering. They bring about the most stabilization, reduce the rapidity of progression, decrease strain to caregivers, and delay the need for institutionalization. Specialization is the feature of today's current health care system that utilizes market-based principles in the allocation and distribution of services. For the treatment of delirium and dementia, provider and service specialization is required. This is applicable to all areas of client care in the current health care system. A few of these changes can be seen in the increased involvement of pharmacists in billable specialized consultation practices. Intervention services that include procedural

terminology will have an impact on the integration of care and the paradigm shift in treatment orientations, practices, and systems of care. Psychosocial interventions that complement the organic features, address rehabilitation of the clinical presentation, and utilize clinical features that expand and mobilize brain reserves and increase brain plasticity are the best practices to be integrated into care. Many of these interventions are already stipulated by insurance companies and managed care organizations and suffer the restrictions on the reimbursements and billable time allotments. Despite the changes achieved through the Wellstone-Domenici Mental Health and Addiction Parity Act of 2008, equity in the provision of services, whether medical or mental, requires extending the application of treatment through demonstrable need, effective results, and positive outcomes. Summing the overall spectrum of the application of the interventions in an integrated approach has its paradox: While the integrated approach is not a cost-effective measure, due to all the components needed to detect and differentiate in diagnosing (e.g., the cost of magnetic resonance imaging) and the costs associated with specialized services, it is overall much more cost effective than the expenses resulting from misdiagnosing, inappropriate or lack of services, and death. And due to the nature of the cognitive disorders, successful treatment can be achieved only through an interdisciplinary approach.

SUMMARY AND FUTURE DIRECTIONS

Cognitive disorders are a taxonomical classification of disorders that exhibit primarily deficits in cognition and consciousness despite their multifactorial origin (e.g., general medical condition, substance-induced [e.g., drug abuse or exposure to a toxin], or a combination). These disorders include delirium, dementia, amnestic disorders, and other cognitive disorders. Clinical presentation of these symptoms differ among subtypes and clinical presentation and include changes in cognition, disturbances in consciousness, memory deficits, impaired executive functions, deterioration of language, and impaired motor functions. They are related to the neurodegeneration and brain damage associated with loss in gray and white matter in the temporal lobes secondary to altered activation in the prefrontal cortex, amygdala, and hippocampus.

This chapter discussed theories and etiology of cognitive disorders related to systems of biology and cognitive reserve theory and how they can help to understand and explain the underlying mechanisms of cognitive disorders, best practices, treatment, and interventions to address them. Risk factors associated with these disorders include age, medical conditions, genetic and environmental risks, pharmacotherapy, nutrition, and activities of daily living; also discussed is how these factors can affect assessment and interventions. This chapter focused on the clinical presentation and diagnosis of delirium and dementia due to their higher prevalence, their chronic nature, and the rapid rise in an aging population, which will impact their incidence rates. Prognosis, clinical course, and issues in bioethics are addressed as they affect all systems of care. Case studies, application of the multiaxial system, and sample treatment plans are provided. Mental status assessments, functional assessments, nutritional assessments, and pain and discomfort assessments are discussed with subsequent interventions and best practices and models in relation to etiology. The integrated approach, as it affects care and the provisions of services for delirium and dementia, is addressed. Future research is needed that addresses improvement in the accuracy and utilization of assessment tools that detect these disorders early, best practices and models that address and complement the etiological basis of these disorders, and preventive measures that can offset the onset and delay their progression.

12

Selected Sexual Disorders

Gary Dick and Sophia F. Dziegielewski

INTRODUCTION

In the human life cycle, each individual develops into a sexual being with certain needs, desires, and expectations. The similarities as well as the differences that occur in development can be pronounced. This complex interchange of human sexual behavior is influenced by a complex interaction among physiological, behavioral, psychosocial, political, and cultural factors (Lipsith, McCann & Goldmeier, 2003). This fact makes understanding and becoming adaptable through awareness of one's sexuality a central component of productive, normal human growth and development (Dziegielewski, Jacinto, Dick, & Resnick-Cortes, 2007). Yet this development is never easy as sexual development and expression is considered a unique and private affair. Often individuals have trouble discussing sexual issues with their own intimate partners; one can only imagine the difficulty that occurs when sharing this information with professional strangers.

As individuals progress through the life cycle and seek to join sexually with a mate, problems can occur, and these problems will need to be acknowledged and discussed. Sexual health can be further complicated by previous sexual experiences that include sexual abuse, sexual behaviors, and parental attitudes toward sex as well as other environmental factors that can greatly impact individuals. If ignored, these varied factors can lead to the development of sexual disorders, where an individual is unable to participate in a sexual relationship as he or she wishes (Meston & Rellini, 2008). Since sexual development is often misunderstood, neglected, or abused within the society, individuals who suffer from sexual problems may not know how to address them. They may also simply not be comfortable telling others as so much of what could be "sexual talk" has been viewed as taboo.

The focus of this chapter is on the assessment of sexual disorders, stressing the fact that these disorders are often overlooked in the diagnostic assessment and in treatment of individuals and couples. Reasons for this can include reluctance on the part of the clinician and/or the couple or individual to talk about the problems due to embarrassment and/or shame. In order to be diagnosed as a disorder, an individual must report distress. Approaching this problem often is viewed as difficult and distressing (Meston & Rellini, 2008).

This chapter highlights the importance of assessing the onset, context, and etiology of sexual dysfunction. The nature of its onset includes determining whether the onset is of the lifelong type, meaning the problem has been present since the onset of sexual functioning, or it is acquired, meaning it developed after a period of normal sexual functioning. The assessment needs to determine the situation in which the sexual dysfunction occurs. Does it occur only with certain partners, or in specific situations, or is it associated to specific types of stimulation?

This information helps to determine if the etiological factors are psychological or a combination of psychological factors and medical or substance abuse factors (Dziegielewski, Turnage, Dick & Resnick-Cotes, 2007). When professionals agree about a consistent definition, the identification of shared meaning and the subsequent risk factors can improve treatment possibilities (Lewis et al., 2004).

The purpose of this chapter is to explore the most common sexual disorders and the criteria for completing the diagnostic assessment. It is beyond the purpose of this chapter to address all aspects of the sexual disorders; therefore, selected disorders covered in this chapter include those outlined in the fourth edition of the *Diagnostic and Statistical Manual of Mental Disorders* (*DSM-IV*) and the *DSM-IV-TR* (American Psychiatric Association [APA], 1994, 2000). The disorders termed the *sexual dysfunctions* include sexual desire disorders, sexual arousal disorders, orgasmic disorders, sexual pain disorders and sexual dysfunction disorders due to a general medical condition, substance-induced sexual dysfunction, and sexual dysfunction not otherwise specified. The extent, importance, and early predictors of problem behaviors and symptoms are explored. The various aspects of the disorder are presented along with a case application that highlights the multiaxial diagnosis as well as exploring some of the currently available evidenced-based treatments.

OVERVIEW OF THE SEXUAL DYSFUNCTIONS: ORGASMIC AND SEXUAL DESIRE–RELATED DISORDERS

According to social learning theory, individuals acquire much of their sexual behavior in large part according to socially acceptable (i.e., reinforced) or unacceptable (i.e., punished) codes of expression (i.e., contingencies). For example,

rarely is intimate sexual expression ever modeled, given this high degree of secrecy and privacy. Furthermore, the traditional modes of education are not often utilized. Schools are leery about providing this type of education and view much of it as the responsibility of the parent. Yet parents feel unprepared and uncomfortable approaching this subject (Burgess, Dziegielewski, & Green, 2005). Not only is there no parental modeling or social influence, but as result of this privatization of sexuality, children can receive inaccurate, inappropriate, or exploitive information. Accurate and honest information at this level is essential because from this starting point all expectations will be modeled.

When there is a general attempt to avoid sharing sexual information or neglect durng this phase of human development, gaps in learning are created. There exists few appropriate channels for obtaining information considered unknown, embarrassing, or forbidden. This lack of attention to the development of human sexuality can have serious, long-term effects that cause adults to struggle with unrealistic expectations or to lack the proper coping skills to deal with sexual behaviors throughout their lives (Horton, 1995). Acceptance of sexual needs, desires, and expectations can be highly variable, complicating the definition of what is normal sexual behavior and what is related to a sexual problem (Nicolson & Burr, 2003).

Sexual response is an outcome of how an individual feels toward the self as well as how he or she sexually responds toward others. The expression of human sexuality is influenced by previous sexual experiences, internal needs and desires, conflict between socialization and desire, and the relationship with the partner. It consists of cognitive, affective, and physiological components (Rowland, Tai, & Slob, 2003). When assessing an individual for any of the sexual response disorders, special attention should always be given to factors related to the human sexual response.

> ### QUICK REFERENCE 12.1
>
> #### SEXUAL DISORDERS AS CATEGORIZED IN THE *DSM-IV-TR*
>
> Orgasmic disorders
>
> Sexual desire disorders
>
> Sexual arousal disorders
>
> Sexual pain disorders
>
> Sexual dysfunction Disorders due to a general medical condition or substance-induced sexual dysfunction
>
> Sexual dysfunction not otherwise specified

These multidimensional factors can influence physiological, cognitive, affective, social, religious, situational, and environmental factors (Rowland et al., 2003). Situational and environmental factors, such as societal mores as they relate to sexual roles and expectations, family attitudes, sex education or lack of it, and religious beliefs can all affect the ability to achieve orgasm (Dziegielewski, Jacinto, et al., 2007).

Having a sexual disorder can affect quality of life and self-esteem and lead to depression and anxiety. Individuals' lack of access to information regarding the origins and treatment of sexual problems and the professional practitioner's reluctance to discuss human sexuality can further contribute to secrecy that surrounds problems with sexual functioning and sexual suffering (Dziegielewski, Turnage, Dick, & Resnick-Cotes, 2007).

When an individual believes that he or she has encountered difficulties that cause significant disturbance in the sexual relationship, are often these problems often termed *sexual dysfunctions*. In an attempt to understand problems that can develop within the human sexual response cycle, the *DSM-IV-TR* lists the essential feature of sexual dysfunction as having a "disturbance in the processes that characterize the sexual response cycle or by pain associated with sexual intercourse" (APA, 2000, p. 535). According to

the *DSM-IV-TR*, to be diagnosed with a sexual dysfunction, these symptoms must be present: (1) the problem must be persistent and recurrent; (2) it must not occur exclusively in relation to another major clinical diagnosis (such as major depression or an adjustment disorder), and it must not be caused by substance abuse or be related to a general medical condition; and (3) it must cause marked distress or interpersonal difficulty (APA, 2000). (See Quick Reference 12.1 for a listing of categories of the sexual disorders as outlined in the *DSM-IV-TR*.)

ORGASMIC DISORDERS

The *DSM-IV-TR* (APA, 2000) lists the following orgasmic disorders: female orgasmic disorder, male orgasmic disorder, and premature ejaculation. The major feature of orgasmic disorder for both men and women is the persistent or recurrent problems with the sexual response cycle, such as an orgasm that occurs too quickly with minimal stimulation in males, a delay in orgasm, or the complete absence of an orgasm following the normal sexual excitement phase.

In order to comprehend the absence of an orgasmic response, it is imperative that the existence and definition of orgasmic response be recognized. Stated simply, *orgasm* is the peak of climax or sexual excitement in sexual activity (McCary, 1973). Physiologically normal men and women are capable of achieving an orgasm. The orgasmic response generally consists of facial grimacing, generalized myotonia, carpopedal spasm, gluteal and abdominal muscle contraction, and rhythmic contractions of the orgasmic platform, which results in vaginal contractions in females and penile swelling and ejaculation in males (Anderson, 1983). Often both men and women who experience orgasmic disorders have a strong sexual drive. For example, in women, the capacity to appreciate sexual foreplay, lubricate, and enjoy phallic penetration often shows no impairment (Kaplan, 1974). One of the primary problems for researchers in understanding the orgasmic response is that it can differ among individuals with regard to intensity, length, duration, and overall pleasure. Further, the response can differ in the same individual from one act of coition to another (McCary, 1973). For example, the inability to achieve an orgasm in a female who has experienced intense and satisfying orgasms may produce a subjective state of worry and concern whereas another female who has never experienced an orgasm may be so accepting that this is the state of her sexual functioning that she may not react with the same psychological intensity.

DSM-IV-TR (APA, 2000) divides the sexual response cycle into these phases: *desire phase* (desires and fantasies about sex), *excitement phase* (subjective interpretations and actual physiologic changes take place), *orgasm phase* (generalized muscular tension and contractions in the sex organs), and *resolution phase* (general sense of relaxation and release of the previously created muscular tension). The female and male orgasmic disorders are sexual dysfunction disorders in which orgasm is delayed or absent following a normal excitement phase or the opposite reaction, which results in premature ejaculation in men (Maxmen, Ward, & Kilgus, 2009).

In diagnosing orgasmic disorder, as with all sexual dysfunctions, it is important to determine if the orgasmic disorder is lifelong or acquired, generalized or situational, and to determine the etiology of the disorder, specifically if it is psychological or a combination of factors. Additionally, it is important to determine if the dysfunction causes the subjective distress and interpersonal difficulty. Often orgasmic disorders have multiple etiologies, and a number of causal factors are believed to contribute to the diagnosis of orgasmic disorders in women and men (Dziegielewski, Jacinto, et al., 2007). For example, an individual may suffer from the side effects of medications, such as antidepressants and other types of medications used for a number of chronic conditions. Some other causes include situational factors, such as relationship conflict, traumatic experience (e.g., rape), sexual and physical abuse, menopause, surgery, hysterectomy, removal of ovaries, and incontinence surgery (FSDInfo, 2004). In both men and women, it is important to include a detailed psychological, relational, social, and medical history (McCabe, 2009).

According to *DSM-IV-TR* (APA, 2000), orgasmic disorders refer to "the persistent or recurrent delay in, or absence of, orgasm following a normal sexual excitement phase" (p. 547). This problem may be generalized, occurring throughout all an individual's sexual experiences, or situational, occurring with a specific partner or circumstance. The disorder is also distinguished by whether it is a lifelong or acquired condition and by whether it is primary or secondary. Generally, the term *primary orgasmic disorder* applies to individuals who have never been able to achieve orgasm through any means. The term *secondary orgasmic disorder* applies to individuals who have been orgasmic in the past but for whatever reason are currently anorgasmic. Secondary orgasmic dysfunction may vary in degree. It can consist of anorgasmia with a specific partner; a prior

> ## QUICK REFERENCE 12.2
>
> ### 302.73 FEMALE ORGASMIC DISORDER
>
> Female orgasmic disorder occurs when there is a lack of an orgasm or a significant delay in an orgasm following sexual activity. Since women can require varying degrees of stimulation to trigger orgasm, the assessment should be based on the woman's capacity for orgasm relative to her age, sexual experience, and the adequacy of the stimulation she receives from herself or her partner. Most female orgasmic disorders are lifelong and not acquired.
>
> Measurement instruments include:
>
> Golombok-Rust Inventory of Sexual Satisfaction (GRISS) (Kuileter, Vroege, & van Lankveld, 1993)
>
> Female Sexual Function Index (FSFI) (Rosen et al., 2000)

history of orgasm with current decreased frequency; the experience of anorgasmia only in particular contexts; or recent orgasmic dysfunction with previous orgasmic capability, on all occasions of sexual activity, including masturbation (McCabe & Delaney, 1992).

Anorgasmia, which involves difficulty achieving orgasm, is generally considered psychogenic in nature. Medical and life circumstances, such as fatigue, acute illness, medication, decreased perineal musculature, or neurological and vascular conditions, can complicate or enhance the occurrence of this difficulty. Psychological factors should also be considered essential in understanding the disorder (Fish, Busby, & Killian, 1994; Stuntz, Falk, Hiken, & Carson, 1996).

It has been estimated that, in the United States, nearly 43% of women younger than age 60 experience some type of sexual dysfunction (Laumann, Paik, & Rosen, 1999). Among all the sexual difficulties described by women, orgasmic disorder is reported to be one of the most common (Wincze & Carey, 1991), although it is difficult to calculate the exact prevalence rates (Kaplan, 1974; Kinzl, Traweger, & Biebl, 1995; Simons & Carey 2001). Morokoff and LoPiccolo (1986) suggest that 5% to 10% of American women have dealt with a lifelong inability to achieve orgasm. Palace (1995) estimates that 30% of women meet the *DSM-IV-TR* criteria for orgasmic disorder and 20% of women meet the criteria for sexual desire disorders (about 23.5 and 15 million women, respectively). In a study of women with sexual arousal and orgasmic disorders, Bechara et al. (2003) reported that the women experienced diminished clitoral vascular responses when compared with women without sexual dysfunction. (See Quick Reference 12.2 for female orgasmic disorder.)

Male orgasmic disorder is considered rare when compared to the occurrence of female orgasmic disorder. However, in a review of numerous studies in this area, Spector and Carey (1990) reported occurrence rates among men who present for treatment as similar to those for females, involving approximately 4% to 10% of males. Male prevalence rates in the general population, however, remain much lower. In a review of the literature, Simons and Carey (2001) reported prevalence rates for males who suffer from male orgasmic disorder as approximately 0% to 3% and from premature ejaculation approximately 4% to 5% of the population. This condition remains the least common of the orgasmic disorders in males (see Quick Reference 12.3).

QUICK REFERENCE 12.3

302.74 MALE ORGASMIC DISORDER

Male orgasmic disorder is the persistent and recurring inability to achieve an orgasm following normal sexual activity, whether through sexual intercourse or masturbation. Most men who complain of male orgasmic disorder are not as much concerned about the delay in orgasm as they are in the lack of an orgasm. Age, medical conditions, and use of substances are considered when diagnosing male orgasmic disorder. This disorder is often accompanied by other sexual disorders, such as hypoactive sexual desire disorder. The majority of men have a history of achieving an orgasm.

　　Measurement instruments:

Erectile Quality Scale (EQS) (Wincze et al., 2004)

Premature Ejaculation Profile (Patrick et al., 2009)

ASSESSMENT AND TREATMENT OF THE FEMALE AND MALE ORGASMIC DISORDER

Heiman (2002) observes that successful treatment for the orgasmic disorders may require a combination of psychological and physiological interventions. To address only physiologic treatment overlooks the reality that an individual's understanding of human sexuality is impacted by subjective meanings that may further interfere with sexual functioning. Psychological interventions impact sexual physiology. Heiman further recommends that future research regarding female sexual dysfunction assess the efficacy of psychological and physiological treatments separately and in combination.

In completing the diagnostic assessment for the orgasmic disorder, one factor that requires assessment is whether there is a history of sexual abuse or molestation in childhood (Kinzl et al., 1995; Saunders, Villeponteaux, Lipovsky, & Kilpatrick, 1992; Stuntz et al., 1996). These negative past psychological experiences can have a direct effect on one's experience of intimate sexual expression in adulthood (Heiman, 2002). In one report, women who recounted inadequate sex education reported orgasm disorders significantly more often than did either victims of a single incident of sexual abuse or nonvictims. The researchers concluded that "female orgasm requires the ability to be intimate, to confide in a partner, and to become dependent on another person without being afraid of the consequences" (Kinzl et al., 1995, pp. 790–791). Kinzl's work supports the recognition that healthy early family relationships are critical to adult sexual well-being. Birnbaum (2003) reported that women with female orgasmic disorder may perceive heterosexual intercourse as aversive. With regard to heterosexual intercourse, women with orgasmic disorder stated that they experienced feelings of (a) immorality or sinfulness; (b) guilt, shame, and anger; (c) derealization; (d) detachment from their partner; and (e) detachment during coitus. Attempting to address these issues by prescribing medication without including psychological intervention will lead to additional frustration for clients. Anderson (1983) and McCary (1973) outlined the major treatments for the orgasmic disorders as a combination of: (a) sexual education and skills training, (b) Kegel exercises for women, (c) sensate focus and directed masturbation, (d) systematic desensitization, and (e) general behavioral or cognitive-behavioral approaches. In the current literature, most treatments involve a combination approach.

One treatment used to assist women is Kegel exercises. Arnold Kegel believed that orgasmic difficulty in women is related to poor tone or damage of the vaginal musculature. The exercises were originally designed to address urinary stress incontinence. Women are generally taught to control and squeeze the pubococcygeal muscle (Caird, 1988) that surrounds the vagina, urethra, and anus. To start this exercise process, women may begin to urinate and to stop the urine several times while in midstream. To measure muscle strength and its relation to muscle tone, Chambless et al. (1982) and other researchers utilized a perineometer. This instrument was used to measure the response while either fantasizing or imagining sexual fantasies. Kegel exercises have been used by numerous clinicians and researchers to treat anorgasmic women with mixed results (Chambless, Sultan, & Stern, 1984).

McCabe and Delaney (1992) describe a number of therapeutic interventions that combine physiological principles with psychoeducational ones. For example, they found that sex education serves well as a component of sensate focus and directed masturbation. Utilizing the pioneering work of Masters and Johnson (1970) sensitivity teaching helps the individual to learn to recognize erotic sensations associated with orgasm. This can help to inhibit the tendency to feel the need to hold back, in order to allow the orgasmic response to occur. The individual is taught how to stimulate him- or herself intensely. Masturbation is used because: (a) it is the sexual practice most likely to result in orgasm, (b) individuals can learn to attend to their own physical sensations and sexual feelings most readily through this means, and (c) it is less anxiety producing in that partner evaluation is removed (Anderson, 1983). Males and females are taught to recognize their own erotic sensations through the use of graduated masturbation exercises. If this stimulation brings a concurrent shutting off of response, the individual must simultaneously learn self-distraction.

Generally, the first step in guided masturbation involves learning to accept and identify various parts of one's own sexual anatomy. Visual exploration is highlighted. Fantasy or sexual thinking that stimulates sexual arousal is encouraged. For women, the obvious erogenous zones, such as the clitoris, are identified (LoPiccolo & Stock, 1986). For men, direct massaging of the penis seems most beneficial. The next step generally involves direct instruction in the techniques of masturbation. Since this needs to be a very individualized process, men and women are encouraged to go slowly and to focus on the techniques that bring them the most pleasure.

Sexual fantasy and sexual imagery are highly encouraged. Clients may choose to create their own fantasies or to read sexually oriented magazines or books that can stimulate erotic thought. For some men and women who are still unable to achieve orgasm and need further assistance, electrical and vibratory stimulation can be introduced. LoPiccolo and Stock (1986) believe that, for women, it is important to begin the use of vibrators and electrical devices only at this late stage in treatment. If introduced earlier, it is believed that orgasm may become more vibrator dependent.

In both males and females, reaching orgasm alone at first, without the partner, is encouraged. Once this has been accomplished, sensate focus exercises that involve the other partner are added. These exercises focus on the development of mutual caressing, touching, and communication. Once this is accomplished, the convergence of a reciprocal learning process is encouraged. Males are encouraged to follow the instruction of the anorgasmic female partner, helping her to achieve orgasm through direct manipulation of the genital area (LoPiccolo & Stock, 1986). Females are instructed to do the same for anorgasmic males, helping the male to reach orgasm during masturbation while pulling him closer to the vaginal area. It is recommended that combined coital and manual stimulation later be used to achieve orgasm in males (Dekker, 1993). In anorgasmic females, penile-vaginal intercourse should also include direct stimulation of the clitoris. Positions that facilitate this direct stimulation of the clitoris include those with the woman kneeling above her male partner and rear-entry intercourse, where the male can reach around her body and access the clitoris for manual stimulation.

Sensate focus exercises (Masters & Johnson, 1970) and directed masturbation combine sexual skills learning approach designed to alter behavior with educational strategies that modify communications patterns. In this form of directed masturbation, partners engage in nondemand pleasure through a series of graduated tasks ranging from sensual body massage to coitus (McCabe & Delaney, 1992). Couples are treated together, generally by a male-female cotherapy team. Couples are guided through touching techniques and focus on open sharing and communication of feelings and sensations. There is movement from sensual touching to increased genital contact and eventual coitus (Anderson, 1983; Masters & Johnson, 1970). Although sensate focus and directed masturbation are used frequently in treatment, empirical testing of the techniques is still lacking (Anderson, 1983; McCabe & Delaney, 1992).

Masters and Johnson (1970) implemented a method for couples based on the assumption that all problems were assumed to reside in the relationship. The couples worked conjointly to improve sexual functioning and address sexual and marital issues, while the overall attainment of orgasm was discouraged. Whitehead, Mathews and Ramage (1987) indicate that both forms of treatment showed evidence of being effective in increasing sexual response. However, couples therapy is considered the probable model of choice when addressing women who express increased anxiety, poor attitudes regarding

masturbation, and problems with primary arousal and orgasm (Whitehead et al., 1987).

To further highlight this type of practice strategy, Morokoff and LoPiccolo (1986) compared minimal therapist contact sessions with a 15-session treatment program. Fourteen couples participated in minimal therapist contact (4 sessions) whereas 29 couples underwent full therapist contact (15 sessions). In the minimal therapist contact group, a movie titled *Becoming Orgasmic Together* was used. This movie was shown with supportive interaction and planning on the part of the therapist. In the therapist contact group, specific techniques were also highlighted, including a guided intervention focus on education, information, and systematic progression. A program originally developed by LoPiccolo and Lobitz (as cited in Morokoff & LoPiccolo, 1986) was used, and techniques similar to those described earlier in regard to direct masturbation were introduced.

Overall, both treatment programs were found to be effective in producing orgasm. Unexpectedly, the minimal treatment program produced superior results regarding the attainment of orgasm through masturbation and during coitus (with additional genital stimulation) than the full therapist contact group. The authors hypothesize that women in the minimal treatment group may have taken more responsibility for success, a factor that may have increased their motivation. The findings indicate that reduced therapist contact did not decrease effectiveness in the treatment of orgasmic dysfunction. Also, LoPiccolo and Lobitz support the use of education, information, feedback, and systematic progress through a program of directed masturbation in treating individuals who experience anorgasmia.

In the treatment of orgasmic dysfunction, a combination approach of sexual education, directed masturbation, and sensate focus exercises is common. Whitehead, Mathews, and Ramage

(1987) compared the effectiveness of conjoint therapy based on the work of Masters and Johnson with female-focused intervention designed by Heiman and LoPiccolo. In this work, Whitehead et al. differentiated between the two treatment models. The Heiman and LoPiccolo model (as cited in Whitehead et al., 1987) was primarily a female-focused program that allowed women to learn more about their own needs through a type of directed masturbation that encouraged self-exploration and self-stimulation. This learning was shared with the partner. In this form of treatment, the problem was identified as existing within the woman, and she was taught how to overcome deficits in sexual response. In this female-focused approach, the achievement of orgasm was a major goal.

One technique that has been used repeatedly throughout the years to treat orgasmic dysfunction is a variation of Wolpe's systematic desensitization (Anderson, 1983). The underlying premise in systematic desensitization is that sexual anxiety plays a central role in the dysfunction. It is assumed that the creation of sexual arousal, instead of the usual muscle relaxation, can prevent and help avoid the development of sexual anxiety (Dekker, 1993). In this type of in vivo desensitization, the client is trained to relax the muscles through a sequence of exercises. Anxiety-provoking stimuli are listed in hierarchical order, and the deeply relaxed client slowly confronts each of the anxiety-arousing stimuli until the stimuli fail to generate anxiety (Anderson, 1983). Empirical data relating to systematic desensitization have been mixed, with some studies showing increased orgasmic response and others demonstrating decreased sexual anxiety with increased sexual satisfaction but limited changes in orgasmic response (Anderson, 1983).

In assuming that there is a causal relationship between sexual anxiety and sexual dysfunction, systematic desensitization attempts to decrease levels of anxiety so that increased sexual responsiveness will result. Nevertheless, current research has been contradictory; Husted found an increase in orgasmic frequency with reduction in sexual anxiety, while both Dekker and Norton and Jehu found that systematic desensitization did decrease sexual anxiety yet did not affect orgasmic response (cited in McCabe & Delaney, 1992).

Last, to further address the treatment of anxiety in anorgasmic individuals, cognitive and cognitive-behavioral techniques have been employed. Palace and Gorzalka (1990) found that preexposure to anxiety-provoking stimuli enhanced both the rate and magnitude of genital arousal in both functional and dysfunctional women. However, both groups reported less subjective arousal after preexposure to anxiety-provoking stimuli. This study lends evidence to the observation that anxiety may enhance sexual physiological arousal without the concomitant cognitive recognition of arousal.

In research, several studies have been initiated that highlight the treatment of anorgasmic females from a behavioral or a cognitive-behavioral perspective. One of the most popular approaches is Barbach's (1980), which uses behavioral strategies in a group format. This approach has been tested by several researchers and has been found to be a useful technique for treating inorgasmic females (Bogat, Hamernik, & Brooks, 1987). It employs a supportive and educational group format in which individualized homework sessions are completed. Standardized measures are used and individuals are pretested and posttested throughout the studies. Results support that most of the women tested using this approach not only experience orgasm but seem to accept their own body parts and their own personal health.

Another study is that of G. L. Wilson and L. J. Wilson (1991), who selected 80 female subjects to evaluate two cognitive-behavioral sex therapy formats that were designed to alleviate inhibited female orgasm. Both group and individual sections were employed. Standardized measures were used to gather initial baseline data, and the resulting data were statistically analyzed. In general, the subjects chose individual therapy over group therapy. Women stated that they did not feel comfortable discussing such an intimate problem with a group of strangers.

Premature Ejaculation

Premature (rapid, early) ejaculation is thought to be the most prevalent male sexual complaint (Waldinger, 2005) and is often recognized as the most common sexual disorder among males (Ralph & Wylie, 2005). In a recent survey of 12,815 males ages 50 to 80 years, 46% reported an ejaculatory disturbance and of that number 59% reported being highly concerned about it (Rosen, Altwein, & Boyle, 2003). Hawton, Catalan, and Fagg (1992) found various forms of "erectile dysfunction as the most frequent problem in men presenting to sexual dysfunction clinics" (p. 161). Fertility is a major concern in males, and when combined with a concern about the ejaculatory process, this becomes a significant concern for all males regardless of age (Ralph & Wylie, 2005). In this society, males are generally praised for their ability to perform and are chastised when they experience difficulty. It is estimated that 75% of men will experience premature ejaculation at some point in their lives (Symonds, Roblin, Hart, & Althop, 2003). In a study conducted by Masters and Johnson (1970), 46% of the males who presented to the sexual dysfunction clinic for treatment had the presenting complaint of premature ejaculation. Premature ejaculation has an impact on a man's life, specifically on self-esteem and relationships; and the inability to maintain control over the ejaculation may lead to anxiety, shame, and embarrassment (Symonds et al., 2003).

Masters and Johnson (1970) defined a man as experiencing premature ejaculation if he could not control his ejaculation for a sufficient length of time to satisfy his partner in at least 50% of their coital connections. Using this perspective, the diagnosis of premature ejaculation was not related to the man himself but dependent on the female partner's sexual performance when, in fact, some women may require more time for an orgasm (Waldinger, 2005). This definition, however, has been criticized as it inadvertently might feed into the misperception that the longer the sexual encounter lasts, the better perception of satisfaction.

The basic criteria for diagnosing premature ejaculation include: (a) persistent or recurrent ejaculation with minimal sexual stimulation before, during, or shortly after penetration (this ejaculation must also occur before the male desires it); (b) the disturbance must cause marked distress or interpersonal difficulty; and (c) the episodes of premature ejaculation must not be related to the direct effects of any substance (*DSM-IV-TR*, 2000, p. 554). (See Quick Reference 12.4.)

In terms of possible changes for the *DSM-5*, Waldinger and Schweitzer (2006) argue that based on the current low positive predictor value of the *DSM-IV-TR* definition, especially for the clinical, epidemiological, and drug trials, a revision of this category in *DSM-5* is needed. These authors stress the importance of distinguishing between lifelong and acquired premature ejaculation. They suggest a third category, which would be termed "Natural Variable PE" (p. 702). In this category, the complaints are only transient and belong to the usual variations that can occur in performance. Furthermore, some professionals fear coding this diagnosis on Axis I may detract from the medical aspects of the condition. Not coding it on Axis III (related to a general medical condition) will focus on the mental

QUICK REFERENCE 12.4

302.75 PREMATURE EJACULATION

The basic criteria for diagnosing premature ejaculation is the persistent or recurrent ejaculation with minimal sexual stimulation before, during, or shortly after penetration. (This ejaculation must also occur before the male desires it.) Premature ejaculation must cause marked distress or interpersonal difficulty, and the episodes of premature ejaculation must not be related to the direct effects of any substance. It is important to determine the context in which premature ejaculation occurs. Is the problem lifelong or acquired, generalized or situational, or caused from only psychological factors rather than a combination of factors?

Measurement Instruments:

Premature Ejaculation Profile (Patrick et al., 2009).

health aspects only. As the term *mental disorder* continues to undergo significant changes, blurring the line between a mental health disorder and a general medical condition, this placement may require increased scrutiny.

Assessment and Treatment of Premature Ejaculation

The best assessment starts with identifying the burden of the condition from the client's perspective (Sotomayor, 2005). Once the level of stigma and embarrassment is noted, clearly defining the time period surrounding premature orgasm is essential. The majority of men complain of premature ejaculation if they orgasm within 1 minute of exposure to the sexual environment (Waldinger, 2005). Therefore, periods could vary from lasting seconds after penetration to up to 10 minutes. The range of what could be considered normal unproblematic latency is quite broad, further complicating the definition (O'Donohue, Letourneau, & Geer, 1993). Therefore, in assessing the client, understanding the shared meanings of what both partners want as well as identification of the factors that can affect the duration of the excitement phase in particular is essential to identify the factors that can lead to the occurrence of too-quick or unplanned orgasms.

Another factor to consider is whether the premature ejaculation occurred prior to contact, upon penetration or immediately following penetration, or during female coitus. The practitioner experienced in treating the sexual disorders should determine if the ejaculation was against volition and before the male wishes it (Waldinger, 2005). Factors that need to be considered include the age of the male, the novelty of the sexual partner or the situation surrounding the encounter, and the frequency of sexual behavior. It is important to note, however, that focusing on just one of the three criteria, such as the time from entry to orgasm, can result in an inaccurate diagnosis, making subsequent treatment problematic and incomplete (Dziegielewski, Jacinto, et al., 2007).

What can be considered effective psychosocial treatments for this disorder vary with a combination approach usually being considered the most effective. Types of treatment include relaxation training, enhancement arousal, pubococyygeal muscle training, and cognitive and behavioral pacing strategies. Using these strategies in combination with the couple rather than alone is considered optimal (Ralph & Wylie, 2005). For a more detailed explanation and overview of treatment in this area, the reader is referred to Metz and Pryor (2000). Furthermore, as a result of increased understanding related to the condition of premature ejaculation and based on improved information related to the efficacy of using pharmacologic treatments, such as the serotonin reuptake inhibitors (SSRIs), there is more interest treating this disorder with medication (Waldinger, Schweitzer, & Olivier, 2005; Waldinger, Zwinderman, Schweitzer, & Olivier, 2004).

Generally, the most common method used to treat premature ejaculation is sensate focus exercises incorporating the use of the squeeze technique discussed by Masters and Johnson (1970). This treatment starts with sensate focus exercises, where the couple is expected to touch each other with no expectation of reaching orgasm. This nondemanding touching should last for several days, and no direct genital penetration is encouraged. Once the female partner has assisted the male in reaching an erection and he reports feeling as if he will ejaculate, the squeeze technique is introduced.

At this stage in the ejaculatory response, the male feels that he cannot control the orgasmic experience, and he can feel the seminal fluid begin to flow. At that moment, the female partner is instructed to stop massaging the penis and to squeeze the glans, below the head of the penis. This means taking her thumb and placing it on the rear side of the shaft (toward the partner's body), opposite the frenulum (directly below the head of the penis); two fingers should be used to apply pressure on the top of the glans. This pressure should be applied for 3 or 4 seconds, or until the male reports that he feels uncomfortable enough to lose the urge to ejaculate. These training sessions should continue for 15 to 20 minutes, alternating between sexual stimulation and squeezing, without ejaculation.

Once control over manually stimulated erections has been achieved (approximately 2 or 3 days later), vaginal penetration is attempted. Generally, the woman assumes the top position so she can control the withdrawal of the penis from the vagina. The female is instructed to insert the penis into her vagina and to move as little as possible. This is to give the male time to think about other things and help distract him from the urge to ejaculate. If the male feels the urge to ejaculate, the female is instructed to withdraw the penis and implement the squeeze technique as described earlier. Eventually, thrusting and movement is added to stimulate or maintain the erection. A time span of 15 to 20 minutes is considered desirable for ejaculatory control. Masters and Johnson (1970) caution, however, that in using this technique, several considerations should be weighed. First, the female partner, not the male, should be the one to add the pressure to the penis; and, second, this technique should not be used as a sexual game. If it is overused, the male may become so skilled and insensitive during this process that he becomes able to avoid stimulation even when there is no desire to do so.

LoPiccolo and Stock (1986) believe there is little evidence for the efficacy of the squeeze technique when used as a solitary method. Further, Kinder and Curtiss (1988) question the use of this technique alone and urge that before the efficacy of this treatment modality can be measured, more research is needed to compare individuals receiving this technique with a similar control group.

In general, three behavioral treatments are associated with erectile dysfunction: (1) communication technique training (to deal with social and relationship issues), (2) sexual technique training (teaching education and the practice of sexual techniques), and (3) a combination treatment that utilizes both. Kilman et al. (1987) studied 20 couples who were tested to determine the effectiveness of several different treatments on secondary erectile dysfunction. Three treatment groups (consisting of eight 2-hour sessions) were all designed to enhance the male's sexual functioning and included: a communication education group that stressed positive communication techniques, a sexual training group that was designed to enhance positive sexual techniques, and a combination treatment group that stressed both communication and sexual training. The fourth group, referred to as the attention placebo control group, implemented controls to limit the degree of treatment received, thus constituting a less powerful treatment procedure than that given the other groups. Highly structured lectures were provided without any planned applicability or practice time being allotted for individual problem solving. The couples in the no-treatment control group were pretested and waited 5 weeks for treatment to begin. After the posttest, they were provided with the combination treatment.

Several pretest measurement inventories and questionnaires were used, including the Sexual Interaction Inventory (SII), designed by LoPiccolo and Steger (1974); the Marital Adjustment Test (MAT), developed by Locke and Wallace (1959); the Sex Anxiety Inventory (SAI), developed by Janda and O'Grady (1980); and the Sexual Behavior and Attitudes Questionnaire, developed by Sotile and Kilmann (1978). The results were statistically analyzed; in summary, the study supported the view that each of the treatments for secondary erectile dysfunction has statistically significant effectiveness when compared to no treatment at all. This study served to further support the recommendation by Eastman (1993) that the importance of education, communication, and support should not be underestimated, even when a condition is organically generated.

Goldman and Carroll (1990) also highlight the importance of including education when treating secondary erectile dysfunction in older couples. In this study, 20 couples were randomly assigned to two groups; 10 completed an education workshop and 10 were used as controls. The workshop provided a structured educational format that focused on the physiological and psychological changes that occur in the sexual response cycle during aging. Sexual behavior was measured along three dimensions utilizing three standardized scales: (1) frequency of sexual behavior, (2) sexual satisfaction, and (3) knowledge and attitudes toward sex. Pretest and posttest scores were reviewed and analyzed.

Study results suggest that couples who attended the workshop had a significant increase in knowledge levels after completion. A slight increase in sexual behavior was noted for the experimental group, with a slight decline in this behavior for the control group. Overall, the educational workshop was considered a success, with a reported increase in knowledge and positive changes as well as more realistic attitudes once the etiology of sexual satisfaction and erectile functioning was explained.

Although the literature has stressed the importance of education in the treatment of erectile difficulty, the addition of play therapy has also been considered. Shaw (1990) focused on this option in treating men who had inhibited ejaculation. The central premise of the inclusion of play therapy is the belief that sexuality should be fun and pleasurable, not performance oriented. However, the reality for many men is that the desire to perform becomes extremely anxiety provoking (Barlow, 1986). In play therapy, performance anxiety is addressed and males are taught to reduce the focus on performance. The focus of the intervention is on helping clients recognize and increase the spontaneous aspects of their personalities. In Shaw's study (1990), participants were expected to create and act on fantasies, to participate in sensate focus exercises, and to take part in sexual expression board games. Fifteen males (followed over a 3-year period) were able to successfully ejaculate with their own touch, although they were unable to do so with their partners. Of the 12 men who completed the program, all reported relief within 3 to 22 months of intervention.

SEXUAL DESIRE AND AROUSAL DISORDERS

In the *DSM-IV* and *DSM-IV-TR* (APA, 1994; 2000), the sexual desire disorders are divided into two diagnostic types: hypoactive sexual desire disorder and sexual aversion disorder. The sexual arousal disorders are also divided into two types: female sexual arousal disorder and male erectile disorder. These disorders are covered together as the sexual desire and arousal disorders are often interrelated. A lack of desire consists of the deficiency or the lack of sexual fantasies and the lack of desire for sexual activity. This low interest in sex is often related to problems with sexual arousal and orgasmic problems (Dziegie-lewski, Turnange, et al., 2007).

Hypoactive Sexual Desire Disorder

In the sexual desire disorders, hypoactive sexual desire disorder occurs at the initial (desire) phase of the sexual response cycle. It is identified when "a deficiency or absence of sexual fantasies and desire for sexual activity" exists (APA, 1994, p. 496). Leif (1977) termed this condition *inhibited sexual desire,* referring to minimal or no interest in sexual activity. Hypoactive sexual desire can be situational (occurring within a specific context) or global (occurring across situations and partners) (Fish, Busby, & Killian, 1994). In addition, hypoactive sexual desire can be primary (lifelong) or secondary (occurring after a normal period of sexual functioning) (Salonia, et al., 2004).

The criteria for diagnosing hypoactive sexual desire disorder includes the persistent and recurring deficiency or the absence of sexual fantasies and desire for sexual activity (Criterion A). Additionally, the problem has to cause significant distress for the individual or interpersonal difficulty with one's sexual partner leading to distress or interpersonal difficulty (Criterion B). Hypoactive sexual desire disorder cannot be accounted for by another Axis I disorder, other than another sexual dysfunction, and not be due to substance abuse, medication, or a medical condition (Criterion C) (see Quick Reference 12.5).

Sexual Aversion Disorder

Sexual aversion disorder is defined as "the aversion to and active avoidance of genital sexual contact with a sexual partner" (Criterion A) (APA, 1994, p. 499). For the most part, the term *sexual disorder* as it relates to a sexual aversion disorder requires a complete avoidance of genital sexual contact with a sexual partner. The disturbance must cause marked disturbance or interpersonal difficulty (Criterion B). The disorder is not better accounted for by another Axis I disorder (except another dysfunction) (Criterion C).

Sexual antipathy, which may manifest as anxiety or panic, must be intense enough to cause marked distress or interpersonal dissatisfaction and difficulty and is not directly related to another clinical diagnosis. This revulsion can be limited to a particular aspect of sexual conduct, such as vaginal secretions or genital stimulation; or it can be more diverse and include an aversion to such sexual behaviors as kissing and hugging. An outcome of this disorder is often repeated avoidance of sexual relations via coitus. Female arousal disorder presents in 62% of women seeking therapy, whereas the rates for vaginismus and dyspareunia are 12% to 17% and

---

QUICK REFERENCE 12.5

302.71 MALE HYPOACTIVE SEXUAL DESIRE DISORDER

The hypoactive sexual desire disorder is characterized by the deficiency or absence of sexual fantasy or desire for sexual activity that creates significant personal distress or interpersonal difficulty. This problem usually surfaces within an interpersonal relationship when two people have different levels of desire for sexual activity. It is important to determine if the lack of sexual desire has been a lifelong issue or acquired. For most people, the disorder develops after a period of pleasurable sexual activity.

Measurement instruments:

Sexual Interaction System Scale (SISS) (Woody, D'Souza, & Crain, 1994)

Sexual Desire Conflict Scale for Women (SDCSW) (Kaplan & Harder, 1991)

Golombok-Rust Inventory of Sexual Satisfaction (GRISS) (Kuileter, Vroege, & van Lankveld, 1993)

Female Sexual Function Index (FSFI) (Rosen et al., 2000)

Sexual Inhibition (SIS) and Sexual Excitation (SES) Scales I (Janssen, Vorst, Finn & Bancroft, 2002)

3% to 5%, respectively (Spector & Carey, 1990). Dyspareunia (which can occur in males and females) and vaginismus (which occurs only in females) are sexual pain disorders that are explained briefly in Quick References 12.6 and 12.7. Alexander (1993) found the incidence of decreased libido to be 11% to 48%, with help-seeking behavior occurring more often in women. Further, Alexander stated that 70% of those who seek assistance for sexual disorders present with decreased libido (i.e., sex drive).

Kinzl, Traweger, and Biebl (1995) estimated that nearly 20% of the total U.S. population may experience hypoactive sexual desire disorders. Regardless of specific percentages, several studies indicate that inhibited sexual desire disorders are on the rise, climbing to approximately 40% of those seeking sex therapy and 31% of couples seeking treatment (Fish, Busby, & Killian, 1994). The Sex Therapy Clinic of the University of New York at Stony Brook found reported sexual desire disorders to be 32% between 1974 and 1976, 46% in 1978, and then to 55% in 1981 and 1982 (Trudel, 1991). Although hypoactive

sexual disorders appear to be more commonly reported in women, there is a rising incidence of sexual desire disorder among men (Trudel, 1991).

Female Sexual Arousal Disorder

In the area of the sexual arousal disorders, there also appears to be an increasing rate of prevalence. Spector and Carey (1990) estimated the prevalence of inhibited female orgasm to be 5% to 10% of the general population. They also indicated that inhibited female orgasm is the most commonly presented female dysfunction, reported by 18% to 76% of females seeking sex therapy treatment.

The main feature of Female Sexual Arousal Disorder is the persistent or recurrent inability to maintain an adequate lubrication/swelling response (Criterion A). This lack of response prohibits the female from progressing through the female sexual response cycle to the stages of plateau, orgasm, and resolution. The arousal response includes the expansion and swelling of

QUICK REFERENCE 12.6

FEMALE DYSPAREUNIA AND VAGINISMUS

Dyspareunia (coded 302.76) (pronounced dis-par-oon-ya) is one of the sexual pain disorders where an individual (female or male, more common in females) reports pain that accompanies sexual intercourse. The pain is often severe and can be felt in the genital area deep inside the pelvis. This pain is very uncomfortable and the sharp painful feelings in the genital area disturb if not prohibit any enjoyment related to the sexual encounter.

In female dyspareunia, painful intercourse is often associated with a lack of lubrication, which results in a dry, burning sensation during intercourse. The causes of dyspareunia can be classified as either organic, such as physical or medical factors (e.g., illness, injury, or drug effects), or psychosocial, including psychological, interpersonal, environmental, and cultural factors. Any condition that results in poor vaginal lubrication can cause discomfort during intercourse. The most common causes are drugs that have a drying effect, such as antihistamines, certain tranquilizers, and marijuana, and disorders such as diabetes, vaginal infections, and estrogen deficiencies.

Vaginismus (coded 306.51) (pronounced vag-in-is-mus) is one of the sexual pain disorders similar to dyspareunia in that the pain is in the genital area, but the spasms occur specifically within the muscles of the vagina. In this condition, the spasms and the resulting pain are so severe that penetration is impossible. Since medical conditions and hormonal changes that can lead to vaginal dryness can also cause painful intercourse, a complete medical workup is always recommended.

Measurement instruments:

Female Sexual Function Index (FSFI): (Rosen et al., 2000)

Sexual Interaction System Scale (SISS) (Woody, D'Souza, & Crain, 1994)

Sexual Desire Conflict Scale for Women (SDCSW) (Kaplan & Harder, 1991)

Golombok-Rust Inventory of Sexual Satisfaction (GRISS) (Kuileter, Vroege, & van Lankveld, 1993)

QUICK REFERENCE 12.7

302.76 MALE DYSPAREUNIA

Male dyspareunia is sexual pain that occurs either during or after sexual intercourse. Some of the causes of male dyspareunia are an inflammation or infection in the penis, foreskin, testes, prostate, or urethra. Other causes may include sexually transmitted diseases, thrush, or a trauma. An important aspect of diagnosing male dyspareunia is to determine if the pain is external or internal. External dyspareunia is usually associated with an allergic reaction to a spermicidal, lubricants, or soap detergents. Internal dyspareunia is more likely associated with inflammation or infection.

Measurement instrument:

Golombok-Rust Inventory of Sexual Satisfaction (GRISS) (Kuileter, Vroege, & van Lankveld, 1993)

QUICK REFERENCE 12.8

302.72 FEMALE SEXUAL AROUSAL DISORDER

Female sexual arousal disorder is persistent or recurrent inability to maintain adequate lubrication-swelling response of sexual excitement to the extent that the female is unable to attain sexual activity or endure sexual activity to completion. Sexual arousal disorder is often accompanied by female orgasmic disorder. Conservative sexual beliefs have been found to be closely related to hypoactive sexual desire and to arousal difficulties in women; body image beliefs and automatic thoughts focusing on self-body appearance seem to be strongly associated with orgasmic disorder (Nobre, Pinto-Gouveia, & Nobre, 2008).

Measurement Instruments:

Golombok-Rust Inventory of Sexual Satisfaction (GRISS) (Kuileter, Vroege, & van Lankveld, 1993)

Female Sexual Function Index (FSFI) (Rosen et al., 2000)

---

external genitalia, vasocongestion in the pelvis, and increased blood flow in the vaginal walls, resulting in fluid passing through them. This is the main source of lubrication, making the vagina wet. In addition, this disturbance causes marked distress or interpersonal difficulty for the client (Criterion B). Female Sexual Arousal Disorder cannot be accounted for by another Axis I disorder, other than another sexual dysfunction, and cannot be due to a substance such as drug abuse or a response to a medication or a medical condition (Criterion C) (See Quick Reference 12.8).

Male Erectile Disorder

One of the leading causes of orgasmic disorders is erectile dysfunction, defined as the inability to achieve or maintain a penile erection sufficient for satisfactory sexual performance (Fazio & Brock, 2004). In the general population, the prevalence of male erectile disorder (ED) is estimated at 4% to 9% of all men, although it is the most common presenting complaint for males. Generally, 36% to 40% of males seeking sex therapy report having this disorder. Fifty percent of these males describe secondary erectile disorder (being able to maintain an erection at some point), whereas only 8% describe primary erectile disorder (never being able to maintain an erection) (Spector & Carey, 1990). Estimates of the prevalence rate of premature ejaculation were 36% to 38% and inhibited male orgasm 4% to 10%, which makes inhibited male orgasm the least common of the male dysfunctions (Spector & Carey, 1990). In a study of young male drug abusers, 20% reported erectile dysfunction (LePera, Giannotti, Taggi, & Macchia, 2003). The prevalence of premature ejaculation for the men in the study was 36%.

According to the *DSM-IV-TR*, Criterion A requires a persistent or recurrent inability to attain or to maintain an adequate erection during sexual activity. This disturbance must be significant enough to cause marked distress (Criterion B); and it cannot be accounted for by other Axis I mental or medical disorders or have a direct relationship to a substance (drug or medication) (APA, 2000). (See Quick References 12.9 and 12.10 for the *DSM-IV-TR* description of the disorder and a listing of possible measurement instruments to assist with an assessment.)

QUICK REFERENCE 12.9

302.72 MALE ERECTILE DISORDER

Erectile dysfunction is the inability to maintain an erection for satisfactory sexual performance. ED can occur at any age but increases with age and can be brought on by a number of physical conditions, such as diabetes, heart disease, high blood pressure, and alcoholism. Erectile dysfunction can occur periodically in all men, yet the inability to maintain an erection sufficient for sexual intercourse at least 25% of the time would be considered erectile dysfunction.

Sample measurement instruments:

Quality of Sexual Life Questionnaire (QVS) (Costa et al., 2003)

Brief Male Sexual Inventory (BMSI) (O'Leary et al., 2003)

Erectile Quality Scale (EQS) (Wincze et al., 2004)

Erectile dysfunction tends to increase with age and is common in men over 50. A number of factors are associated with ED, including demographic, medical, behavioral, and psychological variables (Moore, Strauss, Herman, & Donatucci, 2003). A host of medical conditions are associated with ED, including heart disease, diabetes, obesity, arthritis, and hypertension.

Sexual dysfunction is strongly related to the aging process. In a study of 37,742 men ranging in age from 53 to 90 years, fewer than 2% of men reported erectile problems occurring before age 40 and only 4% reported that it occurred between 40 and 49 years of age (Bacon et al., 2003). After age 50, the prevalence of erectile dysfunction was found to increase with age. Twenty-six percent of the men reported their first problem with erectile dysfunction between 50 and 59 years, and 40% in men between 60 and 69 years (Bacon et al., 2003). In a similar study of 560 aging men and ED, researchers found differences between groups of men in early adulthood, middle adulthood, and late adulthood on several dimensions of erectile functioning (Moore, Straus, Herman, & Donatucci, 2003). Younger men report greater overall rating on their sex life, greater frequency of intercourse, and better

---

QUICK REFERENCE 12.10

607.84 MALE ERECTILE DISORDER DUE TO A GENERAL MEDICAL CONDITION

Sexual dysfunction due to a general medical condition indicates that the sexual dysfunction is due exclusively to a general medical condition and is not accounted for by a mental disorder or substance abuse. The role of the clinician is to first establish the presence of a general medical condition and then to determine the onset, exacerbation, and remission of the medical condition and the onset of the sexual dysfunction.

Measurement instruments:

Brief Male Sexual Inventory (BMSI) (O'Leary et al., 2003)

Erectile Quality Scale (EQS) (Wincze et al., 2004).

overall erectile performance than older men do. However, when orgasmic disorders do occur in younger men, these men tend to experience more severe psychosocial difficulties than older men do. Younger men report greater negative partner reactions to orgasmic disorders. This factor alone may increase the risk for relationship issues and depression. ED has been reported in 10% of healthy young males and in more than 30% of males with chronic disease (Moore et al., 2003).

The dynamic model conceptualizes ED as having multiple etiological factors based on medical conditions that affect the psychosocial context in which ED is experienced. This bidirectional model between ED and psychosocial factors is such that psychosocial factors exacerbate ED and ED may increase psychosocial factors (Moore et al., 2003). Whether the etiology of ED is psychological in nature, results from acute or chronic physiological precipitants, or is a combination of relationship factors that coexist with organic causes and psychological factors, they are not mutually exclusive, and it is important for the social worker to be able to communicate openly with the men in order to assess the severity of ED (Goldstein, 2004).

ASSESSMENT AND TREATMENT OF THE SEXUAL DESIRE AND AROUSAL DISORDERS

Sexual desire and arousal disorders occur in both men and women. The sexual response of both men and women varies over time and across the life cycle. Multiple factors need to be considered in diagnosing the lack of, or diminished, sexual desire and arousal problems, including the relationship with the sexual partner, prior sexual abuse and past negative sexual experiences, poor sexual body image (small breast size for women and small penis size for men), internalized negative emotions about sexuality, life stress, fatigue, mental health issues such as anxiety and depression, as well as medical conditions. In addition, since so many individuals may not have quality sex education on what is normal and what is not, for both men and women, the practitioner needs to inquire about the effect of the aging process on sexual desire and arousal.

With all sexual dysfunctions, it is important to remember that to be considered a sexual disorder, this lack of desire must be viewed as a problem that is persistent and recurrent. It cannot be related exclusively to another major clinical diagnosis (such as major depression or an adjustment disorder), or caused by substance abuse or be related to a general medical condition; and it must cause marked distress or interpersonal difficulty (APA, 2000). Once the definition and diagnostic criteria of what constitutes a sexual disorder has been derived, special attention to the application and relevance of this definition for each individual must be explored. Special consideration always needs to be given to what constitutes a sexual desire or arousal problem. Therefore, the problem of assessing *normal* and *abnormal* sexual behavior continues to be complicated. According to Knopf and Seiler (1990), the average couple generally has sexual intercourse two to three times a week; however, this number is highly dependent on the individual couple's preferences and needs. Simply stated, the number of times couples have or do not have sexual intercourse is not considered a problem— unless it is deemed so by the participating couple (Dziegielewski, Jacinto, et al., 2007). The frequency of sexual behavior in a relationship is only one factor to be explored in the determination of a sexual arousal or desire disorder. Since it is clear that an individual's perceptions about sexual desire and arousal can be swayed by a multitude of factors, other factors to be considered are: personal beliefs, societal attitudes and mores, cultural pressure, parental influence, spiritual and religious teaching, socioeconomic status, and education level (Stuntz et al., 1996).

COMPLETING THE DIAGNOSTIC ASSESSMENT

Proper assessment requires the careful accumulation of data that are likely to affect sexual response. Age; marital status; religious beliefs; whether the couple reside together; socioeconomic status; level of education of both partners; motivation for treatment of both partners; nature of the marital relationship; functional ability of the male partner; levels of anxiety; type of anorgasmia (primary versus secondary); gynecological, physiological, and medical condition; the presence of psychosis or depression; and drug and alcohol use may all impact an individual's ability to reach orgasm (Dziegielewski, Turnage, et al., 2007). In completing the diagnostic assessment with a sexual disorder, it is important to note: (a) whether the condition is lifelong or acquired (with or without previously normal functioning); (b) whether it is generalized or situational (with a particular partner); (c) if it is conjunct (with or without a partner) or solitary (as in masturbation); and (d) if it is due to psychological, medical, substance or combined factors. In clinical assessment, it is suggested that practitioners obtain information on such qualities as the frequency, intensity, duration, setting, and degree of sexual impairment; the level of subjective distress; and the effects on other areas of functioning (e.g., social or occupational) for each client treated in practice.

Many medical problems can inhibit orgasmic responses, and failure to address them is one of the most common reasons for failure of sexual therapy. Medical conditions that can impede assessment and treatment include neurological disorders, such as multiple sclerosis; spinal cord and peripheral nerve damage; endocrine and metabolic disorders; diabetes; and thyroid deficiency. Simon et al., (2005) emphasize that in females with hypoactive sexual disorder in particular, it has been reported that there is a chronic absence of desire in 50% of postoophorectomy (ovarian removal) surgery patients. Furthermore, in women, hormonal influences and imbalances related to normal life experiences such as pregnancy and menopause should always be assessed (Barna, Patel, & Patel, 2008).

Drugs (e.g., sedatives and narcotics) and alcohol are also likely to inhibit an orgasmic response. Antidepressant medications and hypertensive medications can potentially suppress the orgasmic response (Knopf & Seiler, 1990). With the problem of premature ejaculation, a link to withdrawal from opioids should also be ruled out (Stuntz et al., 1996). Alcohol may retard orgasmic response in low doses and can inhibit response entirely in higher doses (McCabe & Delaney, 1992). When alcohol abuse is linked to anorgasmia, it is important to assess which came first, the alcohol abuse or the anorgasmia (McCabe & Delaney, 1992). There is a high incidence of alcohol abuse among women who have been sexually abused as children, and these women are also more likely to display sexual disorders (Golden, 1988; Kinzl et al., 1995; Saunders et al., 1992).

When working with couples, the importance of a first sexual encounter cannot be overstated, since it marks the initial step in deconditioning inhibition. For individuals who are unable to achieve orgasm under situational circumstances, a complete evaluation of anxiety-producing factors during the situations in question may be indicated. Also, when looking at certain sexual disorders, such as male erectile disorder, acquired cases may remit spontaneously 15% to 30% of the time (APA, 2000). This may happen simply by changing circumstances and setting up an environment that allows freedom and flexibility in the sexual routine and encounters.

The level of knowledge and education regarding sexuality and sexual behavior should be assessed prior to the implementation of a treatment program. This may include the couple's comprehension regarding male and female anatomy; male and female sexual response; the possible causes of male and female dysfunction; sexual myths and misconceptions; and discussion of masturbation, oral and anal sex, and the variety of intercourse positions (McCabe & Delaney, 1992). Although research results are conflicting, it is assumed that communication skills, marital harmony, sexual anxiety, and performance anxiety may all be important factors in sexual response (McCabe & Delaney, 1992).

Therapeutic consideration of the emotional and cognitive contributing factors to the disruption of the physiological stages of sexual arousal should be made during the assessment phase. In addition, the therapist must differentiate between sexual anxiety, low sexual desire, and the ability of the individual to achieve satisfactory arousal; the functional ability and flexibility of the partner must also be taken into consideration when evaluating an individual's ability to respond sexually (Hawton et al., 1991; Trudel, 1991). The experiences, beliefs, and cognitions an individual holds can and do impact sexual performance and ability. Within the treatment context, the concepts of desire and arousal are clearly different. *Desire* refers to a mental and emotional state, whereas *arousal* represents a physiological state, manifest in behavior. Distinguishing between the concepts of desire and arousal, much as making the differentiation between the treatments of the sexual arousal and desire disorders, is crucial in the provision of treatment for anorgasmic individuals or for males with premature ejaculation.

In addition to self-report measures and partner evaluation measures, several authors have employed assessment scales when studying sexual response and orgasmic response. The Locke-Wallace Marital Adjustment Scale, Sexual Interaction Inventory, Sexual Interaction System Scale (SISS), Sexual History Form, Women's Sexuality Questionnaire, Sexual Arousability Inventory, Derogatis Sexual Functioning Inventory, Global Sexual Satisfaction Index, Sexual Behavior and Attitudes Questionnaire, Sex Anxiety Inventory, and a variety of other scales have been developed to assess sexual functioning (Chambless et al., 1984; Janda & O'Grady, 1980; Locke & Wallace, 1959; LoPiccolo & Steger, 1974; Morokoff & LoPiccolo, 1986; Palace, 1995; Palace & Gorzalka, 1990; Sotile & Kilmann, 1978; Woody, D'Souza, & Crain, 1994). The assessment tools strive to obtain a profile of the sexual functioning of the individuals and the couple, the nature of the marital relationship (levels of marital satisfaction and happiness), levels of sexual anxiety and performance anxieties, and ratings of sexual responsiveness (orgasmic response in relation to masturbation and coitus). Generally, several assessment measures have been used in conjunction with one another.

The Sexual Interaction Inventory encompasses scales relating to frequency dissatisfaction, pleasure mean, perceptual accuracy, self-acceptance, and mate acceptance (Morokoff & LoPiccolo, 1986). The Sexual History Form rates frequency of sexual intercourse, duration of foreplay, duration of intercourse, frequency of orgasm in masturbation, partner stimulation, intercourse, and stimulation during intercourse as well as sexual relationship satisfaction and the perceived sexual relationship satisfaction of the partner (Morokoff & LoPiccolo, 1986). The SISS provides a viable measure designed to explore sexual interaction, sexual satisfaction, and overall marital adjustment (Woody, D'Souza, & Crain, 1994).

There has been an increase in research into the diagnosis and treatment of the sexual disorders in the last decade that has resulted in several new instruments designed to diagnose and monitor treatment outcomes (Meston & Derogatis, 2002). These instruments measure several aspects of human sexual dysfunction, including sexual drive, quality of erection, ejaculation, sexual satisfaction, sexual inhibition, sexual excitation, psychological and interpersonal relationships issues resulting from erectile dysfunction, quality of life and erectile dysfunction, and orgasm; all offer valid measures on multiple dimensions of sexual dysfunction. In addition to the use of instruments, a skilled, thorough clinical interview is critical to any social work assessment.Since many sexual desire disorders present concurrently with arousal and orgasm disorders (Nicolson & Burr, 2003), taking a proper history is essential to the implementation of the best treatment plan. In fact, Segraves and Segraves (1991) reported that of the 475 women they studied with a diagnosis of hypoactive sexual desire disorder, 41% had at least one other sexual disorder and 18% had sexual disorders in all three phases of the sexual response cycle (desire, arousal, and orgasm). Taking an adequate history ensures that the therapist has endeavored to ascertain all the factors that may have caused, may be related to, and may be maintaining the sexual dysfunction.

As the actual etiology of a sexual disorder may be physiological, psychological, environmental, or situational, a physical exam is critical (Borello-France, et al., 2004; Salonia et al., 2004; Zippe et al., 2004). A physical examination should always be the first line of assessment, since many diseases and physical abnormalities produce or exacerbate sexual dysfunction (age, physical health, depression, stress, and hormone insufficiency; medical illnesses, e.g., diabetes, renal failure, endocrine disorders, and neurological disorders; and psychiatric illnesses). A multitude of studies have linked sexual arousability to hormonal determinants (Rosen & Leiblum, 1987). Alexander (1993) indicates that estrogen-

androgen replacement in postmenopausal women appears to increase sexual desire, arousal, and drive. Research also has suggested that 50% to 60% of men diagnosed with psychogenic impotence may actually suffer from an organic condition (Conte, 1986). Alexander (1993) presented a comprehensive listing of the organic causes of decreased sexual desire. In this review, she delineates both reversible and irreversible organic origins for the pituitary, endocrine, neurological, renal, psychiatric, and pharmacologic determinants.

Some studies have suggested that dysfunctional individuals may experience less of a physiological response during sexual arousal or are simply less attentive to their own physiological cues than are sexually functional individuals (Barlow, 1986; Borello-France et al., 2004; Hofman et al., 2004; Palace & Gorzalka, 1992). These individuals may, in turn, also have difficulty labeling physiological genital cues relating to their own sexual arousal. However, the results from studies conducted in this area have been conflicting, and it is suggested that more research is required to establish this as a predictor for understanding sexual responses.

During the assessment process, it is important to note the use of substances that can affect sexual behavior, including prescription and nonprescription medications, drugs (certain drugs may interfere with vaginal lubrication), and alcohol (alcohol may result in difficulty gaining an erection) (Johnson, Phelps, & Cottler, 2004). It is important that persons with medical problems recognize the effects of some prescription medications on sexual response.

In assessment, the psychological aspects that can affect sexual response should be noted. For example, a type of psychological turning off can actively suppress sexual desire (Read, 1995; Salonia et al., 2004). In such cases the individual may actively learn to focus on angry, fearful, or distracting associations that result in the physiological inhibition of desire (Kaplan,

1979). Anxiety, power and control struggles, individual body image, problems with self-esteem, and a history of abuse may also serve to inhibit the sexual response. Postcolostomy and postmastectomy patients have the added complication of the likelihood of body image issues (Jensen, Klee, Thranov, & Groenvold, 2004). The fear of intimacy, inability to form commitment, dependency issues, guilt, and conflicts pertaining to sexual preference and identification can also influence the sexual response cycle (Hofman et al., 2004; Zippe et al., 2004).

In assessing sexual difficulties, it is always important to take into account the partner as well as environmental and situational issues. Partner-relationship areas that need to be considered include ways of addressing and relating to intimacy, attraction to the partner, communication problems and means of problem solving, sources of marital conflict and discord, family issues and pressure, and the presence of small children, living arrangements, and the sense of security in the relationship. It is frequently useful to gain information regarding both partners' sensitivity to stimulation and responsive body areas (Anderson, 1983). Women displaying inhibited sexual desire are more likely to report greater martial dissatisfaction and refuse sexual invitations from their spouses more often than noninhibited women (Stuart, Hammond, & Pett, 1987). Stuart et al. (1987) reported that the inhibited women in their study expressed the view that they experience lower levels of affection and emotional closeness in their marriages. Clearly, the quality and nature of the marital relationship bears relation to most sexual disorders, particularly those of sexual desire.

Parental attitudes and teachings, as well as religious indoctrination, influence lifelong sexuality. Stuart et al. (1987) compared women's perception of parental attitudes toward sex and parental displays of affection, and found significant differences between women exhibiting inhibited sexual desire and noninhibited women. The inhibited women rated parental attitudes and teachings as well as religious indoctrination much more negatively than the noninhibited women. Closely tied to the parental displays of affection and their attitudes toward sex and the women's attitudes toward parental displays of affection was the failure of parents to appropriately teach sexual education and knowledge (Stuart et al., 1987). Although beyond the scope of this chapter, two books that may be helpful in teaching adolescent sexual education are *Adolescent Sexual Health Education: An Activity Source Book* (Card & Benner, 2008a) and *Model Programs for Sexual Health* (Card & Benner, 2008b).

Another environmental and situational factor that needs to be considered in the social work assessment of sexual function is life stress (Johnson et al., 2004). Excessive life stressors frequently result in decreased sexual interest and arousal. It is important to note that environmental and situational factors, although somewhat difficult to isolate and identify clearly, can be extremely amenable to change; therefore, their contribution to intervention success should not be underestimated.

The partners' preferred frequencies of sexual interaction—defined as the frequency of the wish to have sex—should be determined. This is a critical assessment factor, since no criteria for normal sexual desire exist. In fact, when couples are comparable in their levels of desire, disorders may not be identified. Sexual differences are recognized as disorders when one partner's desire differs significantly from the other's. As Stuart et al. (1987) stated, "If both partners have a similar level of desire, there is no issue. [However, differences in the couple's] level of [sexual] desire may create a problem" (p. 93).

A critical component for thorough assessment is the client's *desire* for sexual activity along with the *frequency* of sexual activity, since desire and frequency can differ enormously. It is quite conceivable that a person might desire more sexual activity than current circumstances permit (as parents of young children understand all too clearly). In this instance, a low frequency of sexual activity might not reflect a sexual desire disorder. According to Rosen and Leiblum (1987), an individual might experience a strong sexual appetite, manifested through sexual urges, thoughts, and feelings, but fail to initiate or engage in sexual activity because he or she does not have the opportunity to do so. Perhaps a more useful measurement is *sexual fantasy*: "A conscious mental representation which translates itself in more or less imaginary form with hedonic value and is susceptible to produce sexual activity" (Trudel, 1991, p. 265). Trudel (1991) also recommended the cognitive evaluation of irrational beliefs, thoughts, and ideas impacting the cognitive-behavioral dimension of sexuality (also see Thyer & Papsdorf, 1981).

The practitioner's assessment of the sexual disorders should always include demographic information; identification of the primary and secondary nature of the problem; global versus situational description of the sexual problem; information about the specificity, intensity, and duration of the presenting problem; the antecedent circumstances at the onset of the problem as well as concurrent factors; a complete sexual history, including desired as well as actual frequency of sexual activity; and the motivation for seeking treatment. Assessing environmental and situational factors related to the sexual response as well as referral for a physical examination by a well-trained physician are also indicated.

In summary, the assessment of the sexual disorders requires that the mental health practitioner consider the primary versus secondary nature of the problem and take into account psychosocial factors, including prior history of sexual abuse as a child; the nature of the relationship with the partner; the partner's ability to

adequately perform sexually; any physiological or medical factors; and the documentation of use of substances or medications.

SELECTED ASSESSMENT SCALES AND METHODS FOR TREATING THE SEXUAL DISORDERS

In addition to a thorough clinical interview, other self-report assessment techniques include rapid assessment instruments, questionnaires, and behavioral records. There are numerous available questionnaires, including Thorne's 200-Item Sex Inventory Scale, the Sexual Orientation Method, the Self-Evaluation of Sexual Behavior and Gratification Questionnaire, the Sexual Interest Questionnaire, the Sexual Interaction Inventory, and the Derogatis Sexual Functioning Inventory (Conte, 1986). Additionally, the practitioner can develop a self-designed rating scale that allows the client to report on any aspect of sexual arousal that is of concern to him or her. Such scales are often useful, especially if the time of day can be recorded and a space to record circumstances leading up to the sexual activity or the lack thereof is provided. These self-designed rating scales are extremely useful in the assessment of sexual functioning, especially in looking at the contextual factors and the client's own perceptions of the severity of the problem. Indeed, the systematic client-reported tracking of sexual activities is essential for ascertaining whether problems exist and whether clients are benefiting from treatment.

Assessing sexual functioning of women who have been sexually abused is an important concern for practitioners working with adult survivors of childhood sexual abuse. Kinzl, Traweger, and Biebl (1995) designed a 7-item scale to measure sexual dysfunction for their study of sexual dysfunction in women who had been sexually abused as children. Items on their scale include persistent or recurrent deficiency or absence of sexual fantasy and desire for sexual activity in adulthood; aversion to and avoidance of genital sexual contact with a partner; delay in, or absence of, orgasm following normal sexual excitation; genital pain before, during, or after sexual intercourse; and a lack of a subjective sense of sexual excitation (Kinzl et al., 1995).

Understanding the relationship dynamics of couples experiencing sexual difficulties is an important component of a comprehensive assessment. It is useful to inquire about the level of commitment to the relationship; contentment; tension; communication (both general and sexual needs); enjoyment of sexual activity; frequency of sexual activity; frequency of sexual thoughts; and each partner's own desired frequency of sexual activity, along with the projected partner's desired frequency (Hawton et al., 1991).

The next questionnaires have been tested for their psychometric properties and measure multiple dimensions of sexual dysfunction.

Sexual Interaction System Scale

The Sexual Interaction System Scale (SISS) (Woody, D'Souza, & Crain, 1994) was developed to measure a couple's sexual functioning. This instrument explores the nature of the sexual relationship and interactions, sexual satisfaction, and marital adjustment. Their study found strong correlations among marital adjustment, sexual interaction, and sexual satisfaction.

Sexual Desire Conflict Scale for Women

The Sexual Desire Conflict Scale for Women (SDCSW) (Kaplan and Harder, 1991) is a 33-item scale for women that measures the subjective discomfort and conflict a woman feels in relation to her sexual arousal and desire. The scale examines the woman's subjective evaluation of her emotional being, as opposed to behavioral factors, such as orgasm. Kaplan and Harder's study (1991) found that women who have been sexually abused display the highest scores. The development of a similar scale for men to delineate male sexual desire conflicts was recommended; the authors suggested it could produce the recognition of important gender differences. These instruments are important not only for the assessment of sexual functioning; they are also important to the development of appropriate interventions.

Psychological and Interpersonal Relationships Scales

The 23-item Psychological and Interpersonal Relationships Scales (PAIRS) (Swindle, Cameron, Lockhart, & Rosen, 2004) was developed to measure psychological and interpersonal outcomes associated with erectile dysfunction and its treatment. Three domains are conceptualized within the PAIRS: sexual self-confidence, spontaneity, and time concerns. The PAIRS has demonstrative adequate psychometric properties and captures the psychological, behavioral and relationship factors necessary in assessing the concerns of men with ED.

Quality of Sexual Life Questionnaire (QVS)

The Quality of Sexual Life Questionnaire (QVS) (Costa et al., 2003) is a 27-item questionnaire designed to assess the quality of life in men with erectile dysfunction has three subscales: sexual life, skills, and psychosocial well-being. The QVS detects men with ED as well as the severity of ED. One of the strengths of this instrument is that men are asked about their perceived achievement, satisfaction, and importance of each item. For example, on the item asking about the subject's concerns about the quality of ejaculation, the questions are: (1) You think things are going: very badly, fairly badly, neither well nor badly, fairly well, or very well. You are: very dissatisfied, somewhat dissatisfied, indifferent, somewhat satisfied, and very satisfied. In your life you consider this to be: unimportant, somewhat unimportant, important, and very important.

Brief Male Sexual Inventory

The Brief Male Sexual Inventory (BMSI) (O'Leary et al., 2003) is an 11-item questionnaire measuring erectile function, ejaculatory function, sex drive, erections or ejaculations, and overall satisfaction. Regarding sexual function within the last 30 days, a sample of questions include: Over the past 30 days, when you had erections how often were they firm enough to have sexual intercourse? (Not at all, a few times, fairly often, usually, always.) In the past 30 days, to what extent have you considered a lack of sex drive to be a problem? (Big problem, medium problem, small problem, very small problem, no problem.) In the validation of the BMSI, there was an age-related decrease in erectile function and sexual functioning in all domains of sexual functioning assessed. Men in their 40s reported erections firm enough for intercourse 97% of the time, whereas men in their 80s reported erections firm enough for intercourse 51% of the time.

Erectile Quality Scale

The Erectile Quality Scale (EQS) (Wincze et al., 2004) is a 15-item self-administered questionnaire that measures the most important aspects of erectile quality. Definitions of erectile quality were developed from qualitative interviews in a sample of 93 men with and without ED. Erectile quality was defined in their own words along with their opinions about certain aspects of erectile quality that was important to

them. The constructs measured on the EQS, which were the same for both heterosexual and homosexual men, were: rigidity/hardness, duration, control/confidence, ease of obtaining/speed of onset, sensitivity/sensation, fast recovery, and appearance of penis. This instrument is useful for assessing outcome following treatment for ED.

Female Sexual Function Index

The Female Sexual Function Index (FSFI) (Rosen et al., 2000) is a 19-item self-report measure of female sexual functioning that provides scores on five domains of sexual functioning: desire, arousal, lubrication, orgasm, satisfaction, and pain (Meston & Degogatis, 2002).

Golombok-Rust Inventory of Sexual Satisfaction

The Golombok-Rust Inventory of Sexual Satisfaction (GRISS) (Kuileter, Vroege, & van Lankveld, 1993) is a 56-item self-report (28 items for males and 28 for females) developed to measure both the quality of a heterosexual relationship as well as each partner's sexual functioning within their relationship (Meston & Derogatis, 2002). The GRISS measures 12 domains of sexual functioning: five for females, five for males, and two common gender domains. The domains measuring female sexuality include anorgasmia, vaginismus, avoidance, nonsensuality, and dissatisfaction.

Sexual Inhibition and Sexual Excitation Scales I

The Sexual Inhibition (SIS) and Sexual Excitation (SES) Scales I (Janssen, Vorst, Finn, & Bancroft, 2002) is a 45-item instrument designed to measure male sexual inhibition and excitation.

The SES factor has 20 items and four subscales. The four subscales measure social interaction with a sexually attractive person, excitation as a result of visual stimuli, ease of arousal when thinking or fantasizing about sex, and excitation that is a result of nonspecific stimuli. The SIS factor has 25 items and six subscales: losing one's arousal and erection easily, inhibition due to concern about sexual interactions with a partner, performance concerns, worries and external sources of distraction, fear about the risk of being caught while performing sexual acts, negative consequences of sex, and physical pain, norms, and values.

CASE EXAMPLE 12.1 – CASE OF ROBERT

Robert and his wife came to couples counseling for marital problems. The wife had sought the therapist out and made the initial appointment. Her chief complaint at the initial contact was arguing, financial stressors, and verbal and emotional abuse. When the couple arrived for their first session, Robert appeared overweight, disheveled, angry, and depressed. The therapist asked the husband how long he had been depressed, at which time he replied, "All my life." He was not on medication at the time because he stated he could not afford it. He also reported that he was not aware of any mental health or medical conditions. He had a routine physical three months ago for his employment and no medical problems were noted.

At this point, the therapist asked Robert and his wife how things were sexually. He replied, "Not good. I am glad you asked." Four factors emerged within the first few minutes of the interview indicating that Robert was at risk for erectile dysfunction: depression, overweight, marital disatisfaction and numerous life stressors. His wife reported that Robert was depressed and that his mood seemed to improve once they had sex. She was very concerned because often they would try to have intercourse and Robert could not maintain his erection long enough. The wife reported that she felt responsible for Robert's self-esteem and for lifting his depression and was concerned his lack of sexual performance might be her fault. The therapist acknowledged the difficult dynamic this situation had put the couple in, specifically addressing how Robert's depression was being used to control his wife and her desperate need to please him. The wife explained that if she did not have sex with him, then she had to live with a depressed and cranky husband. Robert reported he felt better about himself once he achieved an orgasm, and became very frustrated when he could not make this happen.

Another presenting problem was that Robert was upset with his wife because she did not always follow through on what she promised. When the therapist asked them to explain this further, the wife reported that during the passion of their lovemaking in the past, she would verbalize her fantasies. According to the couple, she would often moan out, "Do me on the dining room table!" Robert was often upset with his wife because she hesitated to fully follow through on her fantasies and they had never done it on the dining room table. Now he felt frustrated and related his current performance to her unrealistic fantasy. Clearly, the expectations and the difficulty performing sent mixed messages, although at times inadvertently, had apparently been a source of tension for quite some time.

In assessing for sexual arousal disorder, the therapist inquired about erectile disorder. Robert revealed that he had difficulty maintaining an erection and was on Viagra to enhance his performance. The erectile dysfunction was acquired and was not present earlier in the marriage. There was significant stress within the relationship that contributed to both interpersonal conflict and the arousal disorder. The wife was having problems on the job, was unable to structure the home to meet the needs of their 3-year-old daughter, and

(continued)

they were engaging in verbal and psychological abuse with each other. The couple had financial problems, and there were overt control issues between the couple. The ED was generalized because it was not limited to intercourse with his wife. At times, he was able to achieve an erection when he masturbated.

Robert reports that he makes demands on his wife for approval and that if they continued it would make him feel better about himself. Robert reported many job stressors. He is a supervisor and states that he really does not like to interact with people and that the nature of the job is always producing stress for him. Robert reports he is fearful of his manager and hates criticism. The therapist was aware that engaging Robert, listening to his concerns, and being nonjudgmental was critical since he reported feelings of inadequacy and fears of rejection. The therapist praised the wife for caring so much for Robert as to bring him to therapy to talk more openly about their relationship (see Quick Reference 12.11 Multiaxial Diagnostic Assessment, Quick Reference 12.12 for treatment strategy and Sample Treatment Plan 12.1).

QUICK REFERENCE 12.11

MULTIAXIAL DIAGNOSTIC ASSESSMENT ROBERT

Axis I: 607.84 Male erectile dysfunction.

           V61.10 Partner relational problem.

Axis II: No diagnosis.

Axis III: No medical conditions noted.

Axis IV: 1. Problems with primary support group: Robert and his wife have long-standing marital difficulties.

           2. Occupational problems: Both Robert and his wife are experiencing job-related stress.

           3. Economic problems: Robert and his wife do not make enough money to cover basic medical expenses.

QUICK REFERENCE 12.12

TREATMENT PLAN STRATEGY

1. Couples counseling to deal with the relationship issues stemming from the male erectile dysfunction.
   a. Address marital discord.
   b. Help parents develop a structure within the home for their 3-year-old child.
2. Medical examination to assess testosterone levels.
3. Psychiatric evaluation to assess possible need for medications for depression.

SAMPLE TREATMENT PLAN 12.1

MALE ERECTILE DISORDER, ACQUIRED TYPE, GENERALIZED TYPE, DUE TO PSYCHOLOGICAL FACTORS

Definition: A disorder whose essential feature is a persistent inability to achieve or maintain an adequate erection throughout sexual activity, following a period of normal sexual functioning, is not limited to a specific type of stimulation, situation, or partner, and not due to a medical condition.

Signs and Symptoms to Note in the Record:

- Recurrent lack of physiological response to sexual intimacy.
- The inability to maintain an erection and/or during the initial stages of sexual activity.
- Loss of rigidity during the act of sexual intercourse.
- Ability to attain an erection and when/where/what activity results in attaining one.
- Avoidance of intimacy.
- Lowered self-confidence.
- Lowered self-esteem.

Goals:

1. Achieve an erection in response to sexual activity.
2. Maintain erection throughout sexual intercourse.
3. Engage in pleasure derived responsiveness to desires during intimate relations with his partner.
4. Increase self-confidence.

Objectives	Interventions
1. Client will visit primary care physician.	Routine physical examination to rule out physical causes of erectile dysfunction.
	Use self-report measure to assess degree of erectile dysfunction.
	Encourage client to discuss results of self-report measurements with primary care physician and psychiatrist to coordinate treatment.
	Assessment and appointment with psychiatrist for medication evaluation related to depressive symptoms that may have been over-looked with a general physical exam
2. Client will share feelings regarding ED.	Reduce client's feelings of embarrassment via general statements and/or nonthreatening questions.
	Encourage client to share/discuss feelings of shame, depression, and inadequacy.
	Assist client in connecting these emotions to behaviors that perpetuate relationship problems and social isolation.
	Conjugate therapeutic session to address open line of communication regarding sex, conflict resolution, and feelings with partner.
3. Client will identify perceptions of partner's needs and difficulty in satisfying these needs.	Assist client in identifying how these perceptions contribute to increased feelings of inadequacy and ED.
	Encourage client to share how feelings of inadequacy have resulted in avoidance of intimacy.
	Encourage client to share difficulties experienced in relationship due to sexual dysfunction.

(continued)

TREATMENT PLAN 12.1 *(Continued)*

Objectives	Interventions
4. Client will engage partner in professional advice and problem-solving process.	Encourage client and partner to share with one another feelings, thoughts, and emotions affecting the relationship due to ED.
	Encourage client and partner to share needs, difficulties, and desires with one another.
	Encourage client to share difficulties that are being experienced.
5. Client will journal sexual fantasies resulting in penile erection.	Focus client on the integration of sexual fantasies and successful attainment of an erection.
	Encourage client to integrate sexual fantasies into current sexual intimate relationship.
6. Client and partner will experiment with new and varying types of stimuli during sexual relations.	Encourage client and partner to explore varying positions, types of foreplay, and venues increasing and sustaining the arousal response.
7. Client will verbalize desire for and enjoyment of sexual activity to partner.	Aid client in expressing to partner his enjoyment of intimate relations to reinforce positive sexual relations.
	Address reactions and feelings associated with this verbal acknowledgment in individual therapy.

OVERVIEW OF TREATMENT METHODS FOR THE SEXUAL DISORDERS

In the treatment of the sexual disorders, attention to sex education as part of any skill training intervention needs to include information designed to build general knowledge of human sexuality. A basic knowledge of the anatomy and physiology of self and partner is essential. Most times what knowledge the client does have was received sporadically and was not learned in a nonthreatening environment. A good basis of sex education knowledge is needed to assist in further developing skills in the ability to express individual needs and desires, intimacy, affectional touching, reciprocity of sexual needs, and general sexual functioning (O'Donohue et al., 1993).

In facilitating sexual education, more has to be provided than simply teaching body awareness. Issues regarding treatment of the sexual dysfunctions must take into account physiological problems that impact sexual functioning and perceptions influencing desire that may have emotional causes, such as stress, hidden anger, resentment, intimacy issues, and family of origin issues. Most of the treatment modalities address a multiplicity of issues pertaining to the sexual disorders, and their methods of addressing the problem of sexual dysfunction can vary. Some treatments concentrate on recognizing and understanding the physiological influences alone (Chambless et al., 1984); others view sexual dysfunction as a problem of faulty early sexual development that must be identified and modified (Ravart & Cote, 1992); still other treatments emphasize addressing cognitive-behavioral influences (Palace, 1995); and many treatments use a combination approach that applies physiological, developmental, and emotional components together as they relate to sexual arousal.

In general, regardless of the sexual disorder, the strongest evidence appears related to the effectiveness of a cognitive-behavioral approach. However, more research is needed to establish whether the group or the individual format is more successful. The limited number of professionals available to lead the sessions and the cost-effectiveness of groups increases the likelihood of the use of group modalities. Despite the emphasis on groups, it is important to note that some individuals might not be receptive to or ready for participation in a group format. The results of these studies and the current concerns within the professional climate emphasizing group work augment the need to consider such issues prior to the initiation of treatment.

SUMMARY AND FUTURE DIRECTIONS

Mental health practitioners who work with individuals suffering from the sexual disorders must: develop a comprehensive assessment (including an extensive sexual history); utilize rapid assessment instruments to determine sexual status; be comfortable incorporating sex therapy to supplement individual and couples therapy; and develop a treatment plan with follow-up, all while maintaining a stepwise open communication style that is necessary for the treatment of sexual disorders. The inclusion of pharmacotherapy, along with integrating various forms of sex therapy including cognitive, educational, and behavioral techniques, remains a crucial element in the complete treatment of individuals suffering from any type of sexual difficulty and should not be forgotten or underestimated. In addition to the need for more behavioral science research in the area of sexual dysfunctions, there is the need for research replication. Many different cognitive and behavioral treatments have been conducted on either an individual or a group basis; however, the question of whether the results from these studies will remain consistent across individuals over time needs further exploration.

Each year new measurement scales and other areas to improve treatment success are developed. Staying abreast of these changes is essential to providing evidence-based practice strategy. Clients often are not comfortable discussing problems related to sexual health and performance, and creating an environment where acceptance and comfort for disclosure and discussion may be the most important aspect of ensuring treatment success. Many current social work and behavioral science researchers concur with the need for the inclusion of a psychosocial component with specific measures to address the marital, social, and personal difficulties an individual may express (Birnbaum, 2003; Goldman & Carroll, 1990; Heiman, 2002; Kaplan, 1990; Shaw, 1990). The inclusion of cognitive, educational, and behavioral techniques remains a crucial element in the complete treatment of individuals experiencing any type of sexual difficulty, not just the orgasmic disorders.

Evidence-based treatment options remain central to the successful treatment of the sexual disorders. More research is needed to determine exactly what types of cognitive-behavioral treatments work best and if the results remain consistent over time. Today, the lack of evidence-based treatments remains a major issue in practice, particularly in the area of the treatment of sexual dysfunctions. Contrary to Szasz's (1980) assertion that "the so called sexual dysfunctions (which are psychogenic in nature) are not medical diseases or problems requiring sex therapy" (p. 13), social workers and other behavioral scientists have shown this belief to be outdated and dangerous. Although the importance of including the psychosocial and psychosexual aspects in understanding sexual dysfunctions is well documented, it is frequently overlooked. The authors of this chapter support this contention and uphold the view that treatment success requires the consideration of relationship problems through a cognitive-behavioral model. If relationship problems are determined to be critical, a complete social evaluation should be conducted prior to the initiation of physical or biological treatments. A behavioral and cognitive approach to sex therapy is crucial in the treatment of sexual dysfunctions; thus, the roles of the social worker and the behavioral scientist become pivotal as well.

CHAPTER

13 Personality Disorders

SOPHIA F. DZIEGIELEWSKI AND GEORGE JACINTO

OVERVIEW

This chapter provides information on adults who suffer from the mental disorders known as the personality disorders. It is estimated that 10% of the population suffer from this group of disorders, yet the actual criteria and treatment options remain controversial (Community Care, 2006). These illnesses relate directly to an individual's personality, which defines the basic core of his or her self-identity, and how the world is interpreted, influencing all interactions that will result. When inflexible and pervasive, these enduring patterns of behavior can cause troubled and disturbed relations that touch every aspect of a person's life. Personality functioning affects the development of individual talents and responses as well as close relationships with others. The link between developing these disorders and how exhibiting these problematic behaviors affects the family system is not well known. As individuals develop, there does appear to be a correlation within early separation and loss, parental neglect, and other types of family dysfunction, although most professionals agree this factor alone could not account for the development of personality disorders (Sherry, Lyddon, & Henson, 2007). There also appears to be a strong correlation between substance use and personality disorders, so much so that some practitioners feel that when a personality disorder is assessed, so should the possibility of a substance-related disorder (McMain & Ellery, 2008).

This chapter highlights the guidelines for using the *Diagnostic and Statistical Manual of Mental Disorders* (*DSM-IV-TR*) (American Psychiatric Association [APA], 2000), to better understand and assess these conditions. The *DSM-IV-TR* describes 10 disorders in this area: paranoid, schizoid, schizotypal, antisocial, borderline, histrionic, narcissistic, avoidant, dependent, and obsessive-compulsive. There is also no one NOS category. This chapter presents the distinctions between each of these disorders, highlighting the similarities and differences within each cluster, the latest practice methods, and newest research and findings to further the understanding of these often-devastating illnesses.

PERSONALITY DISORDERS AS DEFINED WITHIN THE *DSM*

The personality of each individual mediates environmental, cognitive, emotional, spiritual, physical, and interpersonal events. When disturbed, it can negatively impact the individual's way of understanding the self and virtually all interactions in the world in which he or she lives. There is evidence from the literature that the notion of personality disorders dates back to the ancient Egyptians; some allusion to the disorders is contained in the Ebers Papyrus (Okasha & Okasha, 2000). The ancient Greeks described their god Achilles as antisocial (Walling, 2002); accounts of Alcibiades, a Greek general, described him as having had the traits of anti-social personality disorder with narcissistic features (Evans, 2006). In addition, it is not certain whether the condition runs in families; however, individuals suffering from a personality disorder may also experience a genetic predisposition to developing a similar disorder to that diagnosed previously for a first-degree relative. Research on family members and how best to treat individuals within the family system is gaining in interest (Hoffman, Buteau, & Fruzzetti, 2007).

To exemplify the recent changes in the criteria in the *DSM*, a brief historical overview of the personality disorders in the *DSM* will be presented. Over the past 50 years, the number and types of personality disorders listed in the *DSM* has changed with each new edition. In the *DSM-I* (APA, 1952), there were 17 categories of personality "disturbance." In addition, there were "transient situational personality disorders" listed, and four disorders of this category were labeled as "adjustment reactions." (Refer to Quick Reference 13.1 for the complete listing.)

The *DSM-II* (1965) is similar to the listing of the disorders in *DSM-I* (1952) with several modifications including the deletion of inadequate personality pattern disturbance, emotionally unstable personality pattern disturb-ance, dyssocial reaction under the sociopathic personality disturbance, and removes the special symptoms reactions from the listing. The term *personality disorder* appears to have replaced the headings personality pattern disturbances, personality trait disturbance, and sociopathic personality disturbance. The *DSM-II* (1965) continued to retain the sexual deviations listing and added a description of specific conditions in this section.

The *DSM-III* (1980) and *DSM-III-R* (1987) removed the Sexual Deviations and Substance Related Disorders (alcoholism and drug dependence) sections from the listings under personality disorders. In the *DSM-III-R* (1987), the three clusters of disorders were introduced.

Cluster A included those disorders with odd or eccentric behaviors. Cluster B included disorders that had dramatic, emotional, or erratic behaviors. Cluster C included those disorders characterized by anxiousness and fear.

In the *DSM-IV-TR* (2000), the personality disorders are grouped into the three clusters similar to what was previously described in the *DSM-III-R* (1987). The *DSM III-R* Cluster C disorder labeled passive aggressive personality disorder was removed from the listing of personality disorders and does not appear in the *DSM-IV-TR* (2000). Since the symptoms can still be problematic, however, it has been added to the potential list of defense mechanisms outlined in the book (see Quick Reference 13.1). This chapter provides an overview of personality disorders described in the *Diagnostic and Statistical Manual of Mental Disorders*. Each personality disorder description includes a brief introduction, the *DSM-IV-TR* (2000) criteria for each disorder, and a brief example of a client who experiences the disorder. The chapter concludes with a detailed description and suggested treatment plan of a person diagnosed with borderline personality disorder.

WHAT IS A PERSONALITY DISORDER?

The development of the current general diagnostic criteria for a personality disorder in the *DSM-IV* and the *DSM-IV-TR* more clearly prescribes the boundaries for disorders in this classification than in the earlier versions of the *DSM*. This definition assists practitioners by providing a clear listing of criteria in order to make an accurate diagnosis of a specific personality disorder (see Quick Reference 13.2).

When assessing for the symptoms relevant to the diagnosis, the practitioner needs to start first by reviewing for the presence of minimal levels

QUICK REFERENCE 13.1

PERSONALITY DISORDERS AS LISTED IN EACH EDITION OF THE DSM

DSM-I (1952)	DSM-II (1965)	DSM-III (1980) DSM-III-R (1987)	DSM-IV (1995) DSM-IV-TR (2000)

Personality Pattern Disturbance (PPD)
■ Inadequate PPD
■ Schizoid PPD
■ Cyclothymic PPD
■ Paranoid PPD
 	
Personality Trait Disturbance (PTD)
■ Emotionally unstable PTD
■ Passive-aggressive PTD
■ Compulsive PTD
■ PTD, Other
 	
Sociopathic Personality Disturbance
■ Antisocial reaction
■ Dyssocial reaction
■ Sexual deviation *Specify term*
■ Addiction
    Alcoholism
    Drug addiction
 	
Special Symptoms/ Reactions
■ Learning disturbance
■ Speech disturbance
■ Enuresis
■ Somnambulism
■ Other
	Personality Disorders (PD)
	■ Paranoid PD
	■ Cyclothymic PD
	■ Schizoid PD
	■ Explosive PD
	■ Obsessive compulsive PD
	■ Hysterical PD
	■ Asthenic PD
	■ Antisocial PD
	■ Passive-aggressive PD Inadequate PD
	■ Other PD NOS
	■ Unspecified PD
	
	Sexual Deviations
	■ Homosexuality
	■ Fetishism
	■ Pedophilia
	■ Transvestitism
	■ Exhibitionism
	■ Voyeurism
	■ Sadism
	■ Masochism
	■ Other sexual deviation
	■ Unspecified sexual deviation
	
	Alcoholism Drug Dependence
		Cluster A
		■ 301.00 Paranoid
		■ 301.20 Schizoid
		■ 301.22 Schizotypal
		Cluster B
		■ 301.70 Antisocial
		■ 301.83 Borderline
		■ 301.50 Histrionic
		■ 301.81 Narcissistic
		Cluster C
		■ 301.82 Avoidant
		■ 301.60 Dependent
		■ 301.40 Obsessive compulsive
		■ 301.84 Passive aggressive
		■ 301.90 Personality disorder NOS
		
		Note:
		301.89 Atypical, mixed or other personality disorder was listed in the *DSM-III* and changed in the *DSM III-R* to 301.90 Personality Disorder NOS
			Cluster A
			(odd-eccentric)
			301.0 Paranoid PD
			301.20 Schizoid PD
			301.22 Schizotypal PD
			
			Cluster B
			(dramatic-emotional)
			301.7 Antisocial
			301.83 Borderline
			301.50 Histrionic
			301.81 Narcissistic
			
			Cluster C
			(anxious-fearful)
			301.82 Avoidant
			301.6 Dependent
			301.4 Obsessive-compulsive
			301.9 Personality disorder NOS
			
			Note:
			301.84 Passive Aggressive Personality Disorder (listed in the *DSM-III-R*) was removed from the Personality Disorders in the *DSM-IV* and placed in the section titled Criteria Sets and Axes Provided for Further Study.

QUICK REFERENCE 13.2

GENERAL DIAGNOSTIC CRITERIA FOR A PERSONALITY DISORDER

A.   The individual suffers from an enduring pattern of inner experience and behavior that deviates markedly from the expectations of the individual's culture. This problematic pattern of behavior is manifested in two (or more) of the following areas:
   (1)   cognition
   (2)   affectivity
   (3)   interpersonal functioning
   (4)   impulse control

B.   When problematic behaviors occur, the duration involves an enduring pattern of response that is inflexible. This pervasive pattern of behavior spans across a broad range of personal and social situations.

C.   This enduring pattern of behavior is severe enough to lead to clinically significant distress or impairment in social, occupational, or other areas of functioning.

D.   The behaviors an individual experiences constitute a stable pattern exhibited over a long duration, and its onset can be traced back at least to adolescence or early adulthood.

E.   Assessment is made to ensure that this enduring pattern of behavior is not better accounted for as a manifestation or consequence of another mental disorder.

F.   There should be no connection between the behaviors exhibited and the direct psychological effects of a substance such as drug abuse or medication abuse or a general medical condition (e.g., head trauma).

Source: This information is summarized from the *Diagnostic and Statistical Manual of Mental Disorders, Fourth Edition, Text Revision.* Copyright 2000 by the American Psychiatric Association.

---

of the criteria relevant for a personality disorder. Once the symptoms are identified, the predominance of certain symptoms that form clusters of behavior are noted. To facilitate this process, a brief discussion of the personality disorders organized under Clusters A, B, and C is presented along with the diagnostic criteria outlined by the *DSM-IV-TR* (2000) for the disorder. In addition, for each personality disorder a brief case example is provided that clearly identifies how the behavior meets the criteria. Since the behaviors exhibited are often less severe, although enduring, a brief case scenario is offered that clearly outlines the occurrence of the problematic behaviors. After the criteria for the personality disorder are described, each case scenario highlights how these behaviors relate to the diagnostic assessment.

Cluster A Personality Disorders

The Cluster A personality disorders include paranoid personality disorder, schizoid personality disorder, and schizotypal personality disorder. Each of these personality disorders shares the common theme of odd or eccentric behavior. When diagnosed in this cluster, individuals have trouble relating to others. Others might comment openly or privately that the person with a Cluster A personality disorder acts strangely and others often are uncomfortable to be around them.

Paranoid personality disorder (PPD) is characterized by a general distrust and suspiciousness of others whose motives and intentions are perceived as malicious. These perceptions begin in early adulthood and are present in a number of

QUICK REFERENCE 13.3

301.0 PARANOID PERSONALITY DISORDER

A. Individuals often exhibit a pervasive distrust and suspiciousness of others. The motives of others are repeatedly questioned and are interpreted as malevolent. The onset is often in the beginning by early adulthood and present in a variety of contexts, as indicated by four (or more) of the following:

(1) The individual cannot escape the feelings and suspects, without sufficient basis, that others are exploiting, harming, or deceiving him or her.

(2) Each interaction is characterized by the person experiencing preoccupation with unjustified doubts about the loyalty or trustworthiness of friends or associates.

(3) Interactions with others are strained as the individual is reluctant to confide in others because of a consistent yet unwarranted fear that the information will be used maliciously against him or her.

(4) When included in conversations and interactions the individual reads hidden demeaning or threatening meanings into benign remarks or events.

(5) Connecting to others is very difficult and at the conclusion of the interaction the individual persistently bears grudges and is unforgiving. Interactions are difficult as they are laced with insults, seek to injure, or slight the other person.

(6) Most interactions are perceived as attacks on his or her character or reputation that are not apparent to others and is quick to react angrily or to counterattack.

(7) Intimate relationships are strained as often the individual has recurrent suspicions, without justification, regarding fidelity of spouse or sexual partner.

B. Another mental disorder is not causing the symptoms and the condition does not occur exclusively during the course of schizophrenia, a mood disorder with psychotic features, or another psychotic disorder and is not due to the direct physiological effects of a general medical condition.

Note: If criteria are met prior to the onset of schizophrenia, add "premorbid," e.g., "paranoid personality disorder (premorbid)."

Source: Information is summarized form the *Diagnostic and Statistical Manual of Mental Disorders, Fourth Edition, Text Revision.* Copyright 2000 by the American Psychiatric Association.

situations. Those with PPD assume the ill intent of others and believe that others might exploit, harm, or deceive them. At times, they may believe that they have been seriously injured by others when there is no evidence that an injury has taken place (APA, 2000). These individuals and the suspicious nature of the interactions that result can be so frustrating for others that oftentimes they are avoided. PPD is most often diagnosed in males. Refer to Quick Reference 13.3 for a description of the *DSM-IV-TR* diagnostic criteria for PPD. (See Case Example 13.1.)

Schizoid personality disorder (SPD) is characterized by detachment from social contact and a limited range of emotional expression in settings that require interpersonal exchange. Individuals with SPD do not seek or want to develop intimate relationships and do not seek romantic sexual relationships with others. They do not desire to be part of a social group and prefer to be

---
CASE EXAMPLE 13.1 - CASE OF LEON

Leon has gotten up late this morning and suspects someone meaning him harm interfered with his alarm clock so that he would be late for work (Criterion A1). He thinks it is Morgan at work, whom he believes wants to make him look bad before his boss so that he will be fired (A6). When he arrives an hour late at work, he is greeted by the receptionist, Mary, who says, "Good morning, Leon" (A4). While she was trying to be friendly, John thinks she is trying to get him in trouble with the boss by making a scene so that the boss will know he is late. Morgan, who believes she is a good friend of Leon, greets him. He ignores Morgan and goes to his workstation. He is thinking of how disloyal Morgan has been (A2). Leon notices his boss, Jacob, and Morgan were whispering about something. He believes they are discussing his tardiness this morning and plotting to "write him up" (A1 and A2). He cannot contain himself any longer and confronts his boss about his conversation with Morgan. The boss tells him they were planning a surprise for a coworker who was celebrating her 50th birthday. Leon still does not believe his boss. This incident adds to his bearing a grudge against Morgan, whom he cannot forgive for meddling with his alarm clock (A5).

    Leon meets five of the diagnostic criteria (A1, 2, 3, 5, and 6) for a diagnosis PPD. It is common for persons with PPD to blame others for their own failures. Cultural considerations when diagnosing this disorder may have to do with immigrant groups who do not understand the dominant culture and may experience language barriers, or may not understand rules and regulations of the new country. Several ethnic groups may also display behaviors that might be incorrectly misinterpreted as paranoia (APA, 2000). Persons with PPD can be very difficult to treat in psychotherapy due to their chronic suspiciousness and perception of attacks on their character (Dobbert, 2007).

---

alone. They have a preference to work with mechanical or abstract tasks and find little pleasure in hobbies or the activities of life. When others socialize, these individuals prefer to be alone. They do not connect well with others and avoid social contact whenever possible. (Refer to Quick Reference 13.4 for a description of the *DSM-IV-TR* diagnostic criteria for SPD and Case Example 13.2.)

Schizotypal personality disorder (STPD) is characterized by significant discomfort with social interaction and close personal relationships and a lack of interest in developing enduring friendships. Additionally the person with schizotypal personality disorder experiences cognitive misrepresentations and eccentric behavior. These experiences begin in early adulthood and are

---
QUICK REFERENCE 13.4

301.20 Schizoid Personality Disorder

A.   The individual experiences a lack of desire to connect with a pervasive pattern of detachment from social relationships. When attachments are made the individual exhibits a restricted range of expression of emotions in a variety of interpersonal settings. These behaviors begin by early adulthood and present in a variety of contexts. As indicated by four (or more) of the following:

    (1)   The individual shows little desire for developing or maintaining close relationships. When these relationships exist there is little enjoyment with a lack of desire to be part of a family.

    (2)   Activities of a solitary nature are often desired and chosen.

    (3)   There is little desire or interest in having sexual experiences with another person.

    (4)   Mostly prefers solitary activities and when forced receives little pleasure in few, if any, activities.

(5) Prefers to be alone and lacks close friends or confidants other than first-degree relatives.

(6) Often appears indifferent to the praise or criticism of others.

(7) When interacting with others, emotional coldness, detachment, or flattened affectivity are displayed.

B. Another mental health disorder is not causing either the symptoms or the disorder and it does not occur exclusively during the course of Schizophrenia, a mood disorder with psychotic features, another psychotic disorder, or a pervasive developmental disorder and is not due to the direct physiological effects of a general medical condition.

Note: If criteria are not met prior to the onset of schizophrenia, add "premorbid," e.g., "schizoid personality disorder (premorbid)."

Source: Information is summarized from the *Diagnostic and Statistical Manual of Mental Disorders, Fourth Edition, Text Revision.* Copyright 2000 by the American Psychiatric Association.

─── CASE EXAMPLE 13.2 – CASE OF SAL ───

Sal has just gotten off work as a night watchman at a warehouse where he is the only employee during the graveyard shift. Sal meets his brother for breakfast and tells him that he chose this job because it allows him to spend a good amount of time alone (Criterion A2). He has never dated and has lived alone in a one-bedroom apartment for 28 years. He is not interested in a sexual relationship even though his brother has attempted to set him up with dates over the years (A3). He goes from home to work and, on rare occasion, to his brother's home for dinner. He does not desire any acquaintances or friends since he just does not like being around other people (A1). He simply prefers to be alone. He has told his brother on several occasions that he does not like people. Since he entered school, he has never sought to have friends, and he contacts his brother only when he needs something and cannot figure out how to meet his need on his own (A5). Three weeks ago he was honored for 15 years' service to his company. His boss showered him with praise for keeping the company free of break-ins and stated he was one of the finest employees any employer would want to have as part of the team. After the ceremony Sal told his boss that he did not know what the ruckus was about and that he did not desire or deserve the recognition (A6). Sal made it clear to his boss he was just doing his job and nothing more and would prefer not to be subjected to another ceremony of this type again in the future.

Sal meets five of the diagnostic criteria (A1, 2, 3, 5, and 6) for a diagnosis of SPD. Persons with SPD do not see themselves as having a problem and are happy with being left alone. Some individuals who come from a variety of cultural backgrounds may display defensive behaviors and avoid social contact and may be misinterpreted as schizoid. For example, a person moving from a rural environment to New York City may react with shock at the different stressfully charged milieu of the city. An individual may appear to be cold, hostile, and distant preferring to stay to him- or herself (APA, 2000). When the patterned behavior is related to the disorder, it would not occur to them that they might benefit from psychotherapy. If a person with SPD were to see a therapist, it would be because of a referral from a health professional or relative. Psychotherapy is generally contraindicated for people with SPD due to their intense resistance to change their way of life.

present in a number of situations. This personality disorder, although not equivalent to schizophrenia, is sometimes referred to as the most similar to schizophrenia. One reason for this may rest with the experience of ideas of reference versus delusions. Those diagnosed with STPD often experience ideas of reference, which result from an attachment of meaning to casual events specific to the individual. The person focuses on the paranormal or entertains superstitions that are not within the norms of his or her cultural milieu. This is similar to schizophrenia, where individuals have a more pronounced form of delusional thinking called delusions of reference. In the personality disorder, the ideas of reference are not as pronounced and usually are related to a specific idea or item as opposed to a general theme that pervades every aspect of the person's life. When assessing for this disorder, the cultural context, including beliefs and practices need to be considered. Many religious rituals, beliefs, and practices may appear to meet criteria for STPD. For instance, the practices of shamanism, speaking and singing in tongues, magical beliefs, voodoo ritual, seeing and talking with dead relatives, and the evil eye related to mental health and physical illness are some experiences that are common in many cultures. With regard to etiology of the disorder when compared with the general population, there appears to be a familial predisposition for development of STPD when first-degree biological relatives are diagnosed with schizophrenia. The child may observe the behaviors of a relative with schizophrenia and copy the behaviors of the relative (APA, 2000; Dobbert, 2007). (Refer to Quick Reference 13.5 for a description of the *DSM-IV-TR* diagnostic criteria for STPD and Case Example 13.3.)

QUICK REFERENCE 13.5

301.22 SCHIZOTYPAL PERSONALITY DISORDER

A. This personality disorder is characterized primarily by a pervasive pattern of social and interpersonal deficits with a reduced capacity for developing and maintaining close relationships. In addition to the difficulty of relating to others, there are cognitive or perceptual distortions and eccentricities of behavior. These behaviors begin by early adulthood and present in a variety of contexts, as indicated by five (or more) of the following:

   (1) The individual experiences ideas of reference. This is different from delusions of reference which is often more pronounced and seen in schizophrenia and the other psychotic disorders.

   (2) There are patterns of behavior that reflect odd beliefs or magical thinking and these perceptions influence behavior and are inconsistent with subcultural norms (e.g., superstitious, belief in clairvoyance, telepathy, or "sixth sense" in children and adolescents, bizarre fantasies or preoccupations).

   (3) Unusual perceptual experiences occur including body- and perception-related illusions.

   (4) Episodes of odd thinking and speech that present as vague ideas, circumstantial speech, metaphorical ideas, and overelaborate or stereotyped thoughts.

   (5) Exhibiting suspicious and paranoid ideations.

   (6) The responses to stimuli that are exhibited are inappropriate or constricted affect is displayed.

   (7) Behaviors or appearance exhibited is odd, eccentric, or peculiar.

> (8) The individual has a lack of close friends or confidants, other than first-degree relatives.
>
> (9) Excessive social anxiety that does not diminish regardless of whether the situation becomes familiar and the individual tends to be associated with paranoid fears rather than negative judgments about his- or herself.
>
> B. Another mental health disorder does not account for the symptoms. The symptoms do not occur exclusively during the course of schizophrenia, a mood disorder with psychotic features, another psychotic disorder, or a pervasive developmental disorder.
>
> _____
>
> Note: If criteria are met prior to the onset of schizophrenia, add "premorbid," e.g., "schizotypal personality disorder (premorbid)."
>
> *Source:* Information is summarized from the *Diagnostic and Statistical Manual of Mental Disorders, Fourth Edition, Text Revision.* Copyright 2000 by the American Psychiatric Association.

──────── CASE EXAMPLE 13.3 – CASE OF MARGE ────────

Marge has lived alone during her adult life. She wears clothes that would have been popular in the 1920s, and her makeup causes her to stand out when she is in public (Criterion A7). She is currently suspicious of her neighbor, whom she thinks is watching her (A5). The neighbor has left his apartment the same time Marge has for the past two weeks, and she thinks he is plotting to take advantage of her (A1). Marge has no friends and says she fears people, even those she has known casually for a long time (A8). She thinks acquaintances may one day "snap" and take advantage of her (A9). To protect herself she has three large dogs in her back yard. She says they are there for protection and to keep people away from her. Marge has been known to hold odd beliefs as reported by her acquaintances (A2). She believes she is clairvoyant and makes predictions about the future that are not accurate, according to her coworkers. She recently went to a priest to discuss her "psychic gifts" but was vague and circumstantial when the priest pressed her to a clear explanation of how her psychic abilities work (A4). She was unsatisfied with her consult with the parish priest. She states openly that she does not date and does not want to have any children as she is not sure she could love a child.

Marge meets six of the diagnostic criteria (A1, 2, 4, 5, 7, and 9) for a diagnosis of STPD. Marge is uncomfortable with interpersonal relationships, entertains perceptual distortions, and appears eccentric to those around her. Treatment options for Marge may vary depending on what she is willing to tolerate. Psychotherapy, especially of resistive, is not always considered the treatment of choice and can be contraindicated for individuals who are diagnosed with STPD (Dobbert, 2007).

Cluster B Personality Disorders

The Cluster B personality disorders include antisocial, borderline, histrionic, and narcissistic personality disorders. The majority of people who suffer from a personality disorder fall in the Cluster B group (Caligar, 2006). Each of these personality disorders shares the common theme of dramatic and emotional behavior. Often individuals have intense relationships that quickly become strained with family and friends. This frustrates those in the support system, and it is not uncommon for family and friends to say that they simply cannot take the intensity and drama that typically surround relationships with a person with this type of personality disorder. Caregivers in particular may find these behavioral traits extremely frustrating (Scheirs & Bok, 2007).

Antisocial personality disorder (APD) is characterized by a history of disregarding others and violating others' rights, beginning in childhood or early adolescence and continuing into adulthood (APA, 2000). Key elements of APD include deceit and manipulation of others and failure to adhere to social norms. In order to be given a diagnosis of APD, a person has to have a history of conduct disorder symptoms prior to age 15 (APA, 2000). Somatic marker and social cognition models explain APD. Both models include the cortical (prefrontal cortex) and limbic (amygdalae) structures of the brain as integral to the underlying process involve in the development of APD (Sinclair & Gansler, 2006). Environmental factors may also contribute to the development of APD. Growing up in a home where parents demonstrate antisocial behavior, including domestic violence,

separation, divorce, and living in foster care, can deprive children of an emotional bond that may contribute to APD (Black, 2006). Confusing discipline regimes, child abuse, and inadequate supervision have been associated with development of APD (Black, 2006). There is a potential for association with others who are aggressive like themselves, and they may become gang members (Black, 2006). There may also be intense relationship problems and domestic violence related to and complicated by substance abuse, extreme jealousy, and violent responses (Costa & Babock, 2008). The key to understanding the individual who suffers from APD (the old term is *psychopath*) is watching for evidence of his or her behavioral deviations from the norm (Federman, Holmes, & Jacob, 2009). The diagnosis of APD is more common in males than in females. (Refer to Quick Reference 13.6 for a description of the *DSM-IV-TR* diagnostic criteria for APD and Case Example 13.4.)

QUICK REFERENCE 13.6

301.7 ANTISOCIAL PERSONALITY DISORDER

A. The individual suffers from a pervasive pattern of disregard for and violation of the rights of others. This pattern of behavior generally becomes noticeable around age 15 years. This personality disorder is indicated by three (or more) of the following:

(1) There is a consistent failure to conform to social norms. There is also a disrespect for lawful behaviors as evidenced by repeatedly performing illegal acts that are serious enough to end in arrest.

(2) There is a pattern of deceitfulness, as indicated by repeated lying, the use of aliases, or feeling limited guilt or concern for conning others for personal profit or pleasure.

(3) Behaviors are very impulsive and there is a failure to plan ahead.

(4) Actions show evidence of irritability and aggressiveness, as indicated by repeated physical fights or assaults.

(5) There is a reckless disregard for safety of self or others.

(6) Social behaviors often show consistent irresponsibility. A lack of concern is noted indicated by repeated failure to sustain consistent work behavior or honor financial obligations.

(7) There is a lack of remorse for mistreating or disrespecting others. When confronted, the individual is often indifferent to or rationalizes their own actions dismissing acceptance of responsibility for having hurt, mistreated, or stolen from another.

B. The individual is at least 18–21 years of age.

C. There is evidence of conduct disorder, with onset before age 15 years.

> D. The symptoms are not related directly to another mental disorder. The symptoms are not exclusively exhibited during the course of schizophrenia or a manic episode.
>
> _____
>
> *Source:* Summarized from the *Diagnostic and Statistical Manual of Mental Disorders, Fourth Edition, Text Revision.* Copyright 2000 by the American Psychiatric Association.

CASE EXAMPLE 13.4 - CASE OF DAVID

David has had lifelong problems conforming to societal rules (Criterion A1). As an adolescent he would regularly steal from parents and stores (A1). When confronted about stealing, he would lie and blame someone else (A2). He cut the family dog with a knife when he was 14 years of age; shortly thereafter he was diagnosed with conduct disorder. Conduct disorder is usually a precursor to the diagnosis of antisocial personality disorder. David has little control over his impulses; for instance, when he wants something, if he does not have the money, he would just steal it (A3). When caught he said he just focused on what he wanted and not the consequences of his stealing and breaking the law. Due to his low impulse control he had a history of starting fights in school until he was finally expelled (A4). When he stole a car, he raced the vehicle over 100 mph, placing himself and others in danger (A5). When confronted with his law violations, he never showed remorse for the harm he brought to others (A7). He would simply dismiss his wrongdoings as someone else's fault.

David meets six of the diagnostic criteria (A1, 2, 3, 4, 5, and 7) for antisocial personality disorder. Persons diagnosed with APD do not learn from experience. This coincides with the social cognition and somatic marker models that try to explain the development of APD. APD appears to be related to urban settings and low socioeconomic status. Practitioners should be careful not to diagnose APD if a person lives in a hostile environment and antisocial behavior is seen as a protective survival tactic. Often persons with APD are arrested for the same crime many times. Due to their lack of insight, individuals with APD may respond best to specific goal-directed treatments with clear goals and objectives that are linked directly to behavioral consequences.

Borderline personality disorder (BPD) is characterized as "an instability of interpersonal relationships, self-image, and affects, and marked by impulsivity that begins by early adulthood and is present in a variety of contexts" (APA, 2000, p. 706). BPD is diagnosed more frequently in females (75%) than in males. BPD begins in early adulthood and manifests with symptoms of unstability in interpersonal relationships, problems with self-image, unstable affect, and notable impulsivity (APA, 2000, p. 711). BPD is present in the many person-in-environment circumstances in which a person participates. Circumstances in which BPD symptoms are exacerbated include emotional instability, "existential" dilemmas, uncertainty, anxiety-provoking choices, conflicts about sexual orientation, and competing social pressures to decided on careers" (APA, 2000, p. 708). Difficulties are often noted in setting and establishing boundaries. Crisis situations may be generated to avoid boundaries and these types of behavior can be very frustrating to family and friends. (Refer to Quick Reference 13.7 for a description of the *DSM-IV-TR* diagnostic criteria for BPD and Case Example 13.5.)

Histrionic personality disorder (HPD) is characterized by "excessive expression of conditions and attention-seeking behavior. This

QUICK REFERENCE 13.7

308.83 BORDERLINE PERSONALITY DISORDER

In this personality disorder there is a pervasive pattern of instability. This instability is often reflected in difficulty forming and maintaining interpersonal relationships. Self-image is often poor and there is often a marked impulsivity beginning by early adulthood. This instability is presented in a variety of contexts and is indicated by five (or more) of the following:

(1)   The individual displays frantic efforts to avoid real or imagined abandonment.

(2)   There is a pattern of unstable and intense interpersonal relationships. These close personal relationships are characterized by instability with the individual alternating between extremes of idealization and devaluation.

(3)   The individual reports experiencing identity disturbance where feelings of markedly and persistently unstable self-image or sense of self become commonplace.

(4)   There is impulsivity in at least two areas that are potentially self-damaging (e.g., spending, sex, substance abuse, reckless driving, binge eating).

(5)   The individual reports incidents of recurrent suicidal feelings and subsequent behaviors consist of suicidal gestures, or threats, or self-mutilating behavior.

(6)   The individual appears unstable as mood and affect show episodes of instability due to a marked reactivity of mood (e.g., intense episodic dysphoria, irritability, or anxiety usually lasting a few hours and only rarely more than a few days).

(7)   Feelings of emptiness cannot be shaken.

(8)   With minimal if any provocation the individual responds with inappropriate, intense anger and difficulty controlling anger. These frequent displays of anger may concern those around the individual as there is often evidence of frequent displays of temper, constant angry outbursts, and the possibility of recurrent physical fights.

(9)   Symptoms include transient, stress-related paranoid ideations or severe dissociative symptoms.

Source: Summarized from the *Diagnostic and Statistical Manual of Mental Disorders, Fourth Edition, Text Revision.* Copyright 2000 by the American Psychiatric Association.

CASE EXAMPLE 13.5 - CASE OF SARAH

Sarah was chronically unemployed due to her difficulty controlling her anger (Criterion 8) and her development of intense and unstable relationships at work (2). She has been seeing a psychotherapist for 10 years. In therapy, she is working on her feelings of emptiness (7), abandonment issues (1), and unstable pattern of relationships, both romantic and nonromantic (2). While in therapy, she has attempted suicide four times (5) and states her partner is to blame for her insecurity. She deliberately planned to be available and not respond to requests by her therapist. She refused to answer the phone when her therapist tried to contact her to check on her well-being. She had cut her wrist (self-mutilating behavior), and when she saw the psychotherapist at her next appointment she said she felt such intense emotional pain she wanted to feel it physically on her body as well (5). She had numerous surface cuts to her arm from previous attempts at suicide. To hide these marks, she would often wear a long-sleeve shirt. When she would meet with her therapist, however, she would often fold up her sleeves to expose the scarring on her arms. She often demonstrates her unstable relationship patterns with her therapist. At times, she reports that she idealizes the therapist and, on other days, devalues her contributions (2). She has been addicted to prescription medication for several years. She doctor shops so she will always have a sufficient supply of medications, and she smokes marijuana (A4).

Sarah meets six of the diagnostic criteria (A1, 2, 4, 5, 7, and 8) for BPD. BPD is five times more common among first-degree relatives diagnosed with the disorder than in the general population. The research about the genetic association of families and BPD is mixed in its results. Dobbert (2007) reports that significant research reveals there appears to be an inverse relationship between the neurochemical serotonin and impulsivity. Additional research suggests that it is possible being exposed to abuse as a child could suppresses the level of serotonin, and life situations such as this can play an important role in the developing of BPD (Dobbert, 2007). BPD symptoms are reported to decline with advancing age, appropriate medication, and psychotherapy. Although BPD is chronic in nature, most people with BPD successfully emerge from psychotherapy and experience a remission of symptoms (Dobbert, 2007).

pattern begins by early adulthood and is present in a variety of contexts" (APA, 2000, p. 711). Often persons diagnosed with HPD have a dramatic flare in their self-presentation to others. They are happy being the center of attention and become uneasy and feel unappreciated when they are not the focus of attention in their environment. While they commandeer the position of life of the party, they are often inappropriately attired in sexually provocative dress and behave in a seductive manner. While they may present in a dramatic manner, they are often vague about details and extremely impressionistic. Persons with HPD are exceedingly trusting of authority figures and can be highly suggestible. (Refer to Quick Reference 13.8 for a description of the *DSM-IV-TR* diagnostic criteria for HPD and Case Example 13.6.)

QUICK REFERENCE 13.8

301.50 HISTRIONIC PERSONALITY DISORDER

Individuals with this disorder have impaired social relationships and exhibit a pervasive pattern of excessive emotionality and attention seeking behavior. This pattern of behavior is noted as beginning by early adulthood and is present in a variety of contexts, as indicated by five (or more) of the following:

(1) The individual seeks to be the center of attention and is often uncomfortable in situations in which he or she is not the center of attention.

(2) Setting appropriate social boundaries are disturbed and when interacting with others actions are often characterized by inappropriate sexually seductive or provocative behavior.

(3) When in social situations the individual displays rapidly shifting and shallow expression or emotions.

(4) Great emphasis is placed on physical appearance and often the way the person looks is used to draw attention to self.

(5) Speech is often bold and the style of speech is excessively impressionistic, although if examined closely often lacks in detail.

(6) Details and portrayal of events show self-dramatization, theatricality, and communications often consist of an exaggerated expression of emotion.

(*continued*)

QUICK REFERENCE 13.8 *(Continued)*

(7)   When socializing with others the individual is often suggestible and easily influenced by others or circumstances.

(8)   The individual has trouble establishing and understanding commitment boundaries and often considers relationships to be more intimate than they actually are.

Source: Summarized from the *Diagnostic and Statistical Manual of Mental Disorders, Fourth Edition, Text Revision.* Copyright 2000 by the American Psychiatric Association.

CASE EXAMPLE 13.6 - CASE OF CELESTE

Celeste presents herself to her vocational rehabilitation counseling having been referred by her psychiatrist. She is 42 years old, weighing 350 pounds, and about 5 foot 10 inches tall. She is dressed in a provocative outfit: short shorts and a blouse that accentuated her large breasts (Criterion 4). She privately states she seeks a job in an environment where she can be the focus of attention (1). She reports that her life is very chaotic and there is a great deal of drama in her relationships and within her life situation (6). While there is a lot of volume and excitement in her conversation, it is lacking in content. Her flamboyant hyperverbal style lacks details and is quite impressionistic (5). She talks quickly, and her emotions rapidly fluctuate back and forth and appear to be shallow and incongruent (3). As the counselor conducts the assessment, Celeste seems overly familiar blinking her eyes and touching the counselor on the shoulder in response to a question he asks her (2). When told this behavior is not appropriate, she shrugs her shoulders and smiles. When it happens again and confronted directly with this inappropriate behavior, she denies she has violated boundaries between herself and her counselor. She states that she now believes there is a special connection and that her relationship with her counselor is growing closer. She does not respond easily when boundaries are set and continues to be more intimate than is appropriate, given the professional relationship (8).

     Celeste meets seven of the diagnostic criteria (1, 2, 3, 4, 5, 6, and 8) for a diagnosis of HPD. When evaluating a person for the diagnosis of HPD, it is important to note whether the disorder is causing clinically significant impairment. Some studies suggest that HPD is of similar prevalence for males and females. The *DSM-IV-TR* (APA, p. 712) states that a man "may dress and behave in a manner often identified as 'macho' and may seek to be the center of attention bragging about athletic skills, whereas a woman, for example, may choose very feminine clothes and talk about how much she is impressed with her dance instructor."

Narcissistic personality disorder (NPD) is characterized by a grandiose sense of self-importance, need to be affirmed, and lack of empathy that emerges in early adulthood and is present in a number of situations (APA, 2000, p. 714). Individuals with NPD are boastful and pretentious and exaggerate their accomplishments to impress others. They are focused on fantasies of "unlimited success, power, brilliance, beauty, or ideal love" (APA, 2000, p. 714). A common feature of a person with NPD is emotional coldness and absence of reciprocal interests with others. (Refer to Quick Reference 13.9 for a description of the *DSM-IV-TR* diagnostic criteria for NPD and see Case Example 13.7.)

QUICK REFERENCE 13.9

301.81 NARCISSISTIC PERSONALITY DISORDER

Individuals with this disorder exhibit a pervasive pattern of grandiosity that is evident in fantasy or behavior. The individual has an intense need for admiration, and wants to be the center of attention and lacks empathy for others. The condition becomes obvious in early adulthood and remains present in a variety of contexts. It is indicated by five (or more) of the following:

(1) The individual has a grandiose sense of self-importance. He or she exaggerates achievements and talents. The sense of self-importance is strong and expects to be recognized as superior without the commensurate achievements.

(2) Often there is a preoccupation with fantasies of unlimited success, power, brilliance, beauty, or finding and experiencing the ideal love.

(3) The individual believes that he or she is special and unique and can only be understood by, or should associate with, other special or high-status people (or institutions).

(4) Interactions with others can be intense as communication often centers around acknowledging excessive self-admiration.

(5) There is often a sense of entitlement and unreasonable expectations within social contexts. For example, the individual expects favorable treatment or automatic compliance with his or her expectations.

(6) The sense of self-importance is often linked to self-idealization and this assumption can lead to social interactions that are interpersonally exploitative. This feeling of self-importance may lead the person to take advantage of others to achieve his or her own ends.

(7) The individual clearly lacks empathy for others and is unwilling to recognize or identify with the feelings and needs of others.

(8) Social engagements and interactions are often troublesome as the individual believes others are envious of him or her.

(9) Social interactions are often limited as the individual shows arrogant, haughty behaviors or attitudes toward others.

Source: Criteria summarized from the *Diagnostic and Statistical Manual of Mental Disorders, Fourth Edition, Text Revision.* Copyright 2000 by the American Psychiatric Association.

CASE EXAMPLE 13.7 – CASE OF GARY

Gary reports to family and friends that he has joined Mensa because he believes he is of high status and prefers to be around geniuses (Criterion 1). He does not tell anyone how he actually became a member of Mensa. His friend is sworn to keep confidence and not reveal that in order to get into Mensa he had his friend take the qualifying test to join the organization. In all settings he talks about his brilliance and ability to innovate. He also discusses his fantasies with family members about becoming wealthy and powerful (2). He travels in a crowd that pays him attention for his faux successes and alleged brilliance (3). The thing he enjoys most is the attention and admiration of others who believe his story (4). He has a strong sense of entitlement and believes he deserves fame, fortune, and the compliance of others to follow his wishes (5). When he does not get his way, he becomes belligerent and demands to get his way (9). At work he uses people to advance in the ranks (6). He has caused two of his supervisors over the past four years to be

(continued)

CASE EXAMPLE 13.7
(*Continued*)

fired and he assumed their positions. He coldly talks about them and shares his disgust of them as human beings. On a recent occasion at the market he met one of his former supervisors. He had actually supported the termination of employment of the supervisor. The previous supervisor told Gary that he had been unemployed for three years since he was terminated from the job where Gary still works. The man said he was in a desperate financial situation and asked if Gary could be of any help getting him back in the agency from which he was terminated. Gary shook his head no and demonstrated no empathy for his situation (7). He coldly dismissed the former supervisor and passed him by stating openly to him that this was not his problem.

Gary meets eight of the diagnostic criteria (1, 2, 3, 4, 5, 6, 7, and 9) for a diagnosis of NPD. It is important to note that adolescents display narcissistic traits; however, that does not mean that they will become adults diagnosed with NPD. People with NPD may have particular difficulty adjusting to the aging process since age limits both physical and occupational functioning (APA, 2000, p. 716). There is no consensus about the etiology of NPD. The prevalence of NPD is higher in persons who have first-degree biological relatives diagnosed with NPD (Dobbert, 2007). Therapy can be successful with those diagnosed with NPD who are seriously committed to changing their behavior. Dobbert (2007) asserts that "a consistently applied system of rewards and punishments is more effective" (p. 103).

Cluster C, Personality Disorders

The Cluster C personality disorders include avoidant, dependent, obsessive–compulsive personality disorders, and personality disorder not otherwise specified. Each of these personality disorders shares the common theme of anxious and fearful behavior.

Avoidant personality disorder (AVPD) is characterized by "social inhibition, feelings of inadequacy, and hypersensitivity to negative evaluation that begins by early adulthood and is present in a variety of contexts" (APA, 2000, p. 718). Individuals with AVPD avoid contact with others out of fear they may be criticized, rejected, or meet with disapproval. They avoid people as much as possible because if they engage in interaction, the fear of being embarrassed or rejected is too great to confront (CRS-Behavioral Health Advisor, 2009). They will not attempt to make new acquaintances unless they can be sure they will meet with approval and be liked without criticism. They are observed to be shy, inhibited, and stay in the background, seemingly invisible, since they fear being degraded or rejected. Adults with AVPD report less involvement in extracurricular activities and when compared to other mental disorders, such as major depressive disorder, are often considered less popular (Rettew, 2006). Since they have a limited support network due to isolation, they have few resources to work through a crisis. (Refer to Quick Reference 13.10 for the *DSM-IV-TR* diagnostic criteria for AVPD and see Case Example 13.8.)

Dependent personality disorder (DPD) is characterized by "a pervasive excessive need to be taken care of that leads to submissive and clinging behavior and fears of separation" (APA, 2000, p. 721). This set of behaviors starts in early adulthood and is experienced in a number of settings. The person with DPD experiences great difficulty making basic decisions, such as what to wear or what to eat, and needs strong direction and reassurance of others. Individuals with DPD require parents or spouses to make all of the decisions for them. They have great difficulty getting angry with those upon whom they depend on out of fear they may estrange them.

QUICK REFERENCE 13.10

301.82 AVOIDANT PERSONALITY DISORDER

Individuals with this disorder often exhibit a pervasive pattern of social inhibition. There are feelings of inadequacy, and hypersensitivity to being around others and getting negative evaluation. The disorder often begins by early adulthood and is evidenced in a variety of contexts, as indicated by four (or more) of the following:

(1)	The individual avoids social contact and occupational activities that involve significant interpersonal contact. This avoidance is based in fears of criticism, disapproval, or rejection.

(2)	There is an unwillingness to get involved with people unless the individual is certain of being liked.

(3)	Restraint is displayed within intimate relationships because of an intense fear of being shamed or ridiculed.

(4)	The individual is preoccupied with being criticized or rejected in social situations.

(5)	Feelings of inadequacy govern behaviors and inhibit developing new interpersonal relationships.

(6)	There is a strong self-impression that contact needs to be avoided as the individual views the self as socially inept, personally unappealing, or inferior to others.

(7)	Engagement in new activities is avoided and reluctance to approach situations where the personal risk may prove to be too embarrassing.

Source: Criteria summarized from the *Diagnostic and Statistical Manual of Mental Disorders, Fourth Edition, Text Revision.* Copyright 2000 by the American Psychiatric Association.

CASE EXAMPLE 13.8 - CASE OF LINDA

Linda is a 30-year-old British American female who has worked in a New York garment factory for 12 years. She likes her work setting and upon arriving at work she immediately goes to her workstation without having to engage in conversation (Criterion 1). She stays to herself at break time, even when invited by others to join conversation (5). Several of her coworkers are part of groups that socialize after work hours. She has been invited to join a card club, sewing circle, and service club that helps elderly persons. She says she did not join any of those groups because she was not sure the members would like her if they really got to know her (2). She also was concerned that with more than three people in a group, she greatly feared several members of the group would make fun of her (4). A coworker tried to set her up for a date with Sam, a popular employee who was handsome and kind. Linda said she could not meet Sam for a date because she was afraid she would say something that might cause him to ridicule her (3). She recently started seeing a psychotherapist because she would like to feel more confident and would like to make some "real" friends. She reports to the therapist that she sees herself as unappealing, feels interior to others (6), and fears she will be embarrassed if she tries to begin new activities, such as joining the service club that serves elderly persons (7). She is hopeful that she can make some positive changes with the help of her therapist.

Linda meets seven of the diagnostic criteria (1, 2, 3, 4, 5, 6, and 7) for a diagnosis of AVPD. People with AVPD may be disposed to the disorder if they have grown up in a home with overly anxious parents who may have been diagnosed with social phobia or AVPD. However, genetic predisposition and the impact of environmental factors have not been clearly associated with the development of AVPD (Tillfors, Furmak, Ekselius, & Fredrikson, 2001). Cultural practices may consider avoidant behaviors appropriate; conversely, avoidant behavior could be the result of acculturation following immigration to the United States. For instance, language barriers may contribute to isolation and fear of criticism when a person attempts to communicate, which may add difficulty to social situations.

QUICK REFERENCE 13.11

301.6 DEPENDENT PERSONALITY DISORDER

Individuals suffering from this disorder exhibit a pervasive and excessive need to be taken care of. This desperate need to belong leads to submissive and clinging behavior and fears of separation. The course of the disorder generally begins by early adulthood and is present in a variety of contexts as indicated by five (or more) of the following:

(1)   The individual has difficulty making everyday decisions. When faced with a decision, an excessive amount of advice and reassurance from others is needed.

(2)   There is a lack of self-sufficiency and the individual needs others to assume responsibility for most major areas of his or her life.

(3)   When disagreements occur in social relationships the individual has difficulty expressing concerns with others because of fear of loss of support or approval. Note: This does not include what could be considered realistic fears of retribution.

(4)   There is difficulty initiating projects or doing things independently because of a lack of self-confidence in his or her own judgment or abilities. This lack of confidence in the self causes the concern of a lack of motivation or energy.

(5)   The individual goes to excessive lengths to obtain nurturance and support from others. This activity is so pronounced that he or she might volunteer to do things that are unpleasant or that the individual does not really want to do.

(6)   There are intense feelings of discomfort that are uncomfortable, leaving the individual helpless when alone. When alone there are exaggerated fears of being unable to care for himself or herself.

(7)   The individual urgently seeks to be in a relationship or will seek another relationship as a source of care and support when a close relationship ends.

(8)   There is an unrealistic preoccupation with fears related to being left to take care of himself or herself.

Source: Criteria summarized from the *Diagnostic and Statistical Manual of Mental Disorders, Fourth Edition, Text Revision.* Copyright 2000 by the American Psychiatric Association.

When a close relationship ends, they frantically seek another relationship to replace the previous one. (Refer to Quick Reference 13.11 for the *DSM-IV-TR* diagnostic criteria for DPD and Case Example 13.9.)

Obsessive-compulsive personality disorder (OCPD) is characterized as "a preoccupation with orderliness, perfectionism, and mental and interpersonal control, at the expense of flexibility, openness, and efficiency. The pattern begins by

---

CASE EXAMPLE 13.9 - CASE OF MARK

Mark is a 33-year-old unemployed male who has always lived at home. His parents are in their late 60s and have supported him since birth. Over the years he has depended on his mother to manage his social and financial affairs (Criterion 2). The parents are of modest means and have tried to get Mark to work toward independence with no success. His mother has gotten tired of Mark's dependency and no longer wants to make small, everyday decisions without having to shower Mark with reassurance (1). Mark's uncle owns a survey company and he has been supportive of Mark over the years. In order to receive support and nurturance of his uncle, Mark has agreed to work on a project where he will have to go into murky swamp water up to his knees to place survey markers. Mark says he does not like going in the water since there are poisonous snakes there, but he wants to make his uncle happy (5). Mark has recently been referred to a therapist by his mother. He shares with the therapist that his greatest fear is being left alone when his parents die (8) and that he fears he will be left to care for himself one day and he will not be able to do so. He does not know who he will turn to for help when his parents die.

Mark meets six of the diagnostic criteria (1, 2, 4, 5, 6, and 8) for a diagnosis of DPD. Individuals with first-degree relatives who have a diagnosis of AVPD are at significant higher risk of developing DPD (Dobbert, 2007). It has been hypothesized that a father who is dependent on the mother models dependent traits learned by a child who is observing the parents' relationship (Dobbert, 2007). Psychotherapy with persons diagnosed with DPD is extraordinarily challenging because the client can easily transfer dependence onto the therapist.

early adulthood and is present in variety of contexts" (APA, 2000, p. 725). Individuals with OCPD are focused on control of their environment. They are preoccupied with orderliness, perfectionism, and control of mental and interpersonal aspects of their lives. Their sense of control leads to excessive attention to rules, important details, the making of lists, exact following of procedures such that the individual forgets the major reason for completing the activity. Individuals with OCPD often leave important tasks to the last minute due to poor time management. Their perfectionist approach to life and unrealistic performance expectations cause them significant stress leading to

---

QUICK REFERENCE 13.12

301.4 OBSESSIVE-COMPULSIVE PERSONALITY DISORDER

Individuals with this personality disorder exhibit a pervasive pattern of preoccupation with orderliness and perfectionism. There is a strong desire to achieve mental and interpersonal control. This desire for control is so strong it overrides any desires for flexibility, openness, and efficiency. This disorder often begins by early adulthood and is present in a variety of situations, as indicated by four (or more) of the following:

(1) The individual is often preoccupied with details and desires to have clear rules and guidelines. Oftentimes, lists are created and the need for order in all activities is pervasive. This desire to have control is significant enough to interfere with functioning and can affect individual performance in organizations. The desire for structure interferes with schedules to the extent that the major point of the activity is lost.

(2) The behaviors exhibited show perfectionism and this desire to be perfect interferes with task completion. Oftentimes, intense and impossible criteria are applied to accomplish a task and related to this self-implied structure the individual is unable to complete a project because his or her own overly strict standards are not met.

(3) Often there is excessive devotion to work and productivity and these behaviors occur to the exclusion of leisure activities and friendships. This activity however cannot be accounted for by obvious economic necessity.

(continued)

QUICK REFERENCE 13.12 (*Continued*)

(4) Activities are controlled and all actions consist of over-conscientious, scrupulous, and inflexible ideas related to morality, ethics, or values. These behaviors cannot be related or accounted for by cultural or religious identification.

(5) Objects hold importance and oftentimes the individual cannot discard worn-out or worthless objects even when they have no sentimental value.

(6) The need for control is strong and the individual has trouble delegating tasks or to work with others unless they submit to exactly his or her way of doing things.

(7) Hoarding behaviors can occur where the individual adopts a miserly spending style toward both self and others. In this disorder, money is often viewed as something to be hoarded for future catastrophes and not spent even when need dictates.

(8) Behaviors show patterns of rigidity and stubbornness.

Source: Criteria summarized from the *Diagnostic and Statistical Manual of Mental Disorders, Fourth Edition, Text Revision.* Copyright 2000 by the American Psychiatric Association.

CASE EXAMPLE 13.10 - CASE OF RAY

Ray is a middle-aged Italian American who lives in Chicago. He has lived in his condominium for the past 28 years. He has difficulty getting around his home since he has never thrown anything away that he has brought home, except for food stuffs (Criterion 5). He has difficulty from time to time at work due to his rigidity and stubbornness (8). His boss recently asked Ray to change the plans for a piece of furniture he was building. Ray refused to change the design saying that it had to be constructed that way. He was written up for being stubborn and insubordinate. Despite Ray's rigidity, his boss likes the results of his perfectionism (2) and his workaholic traits, which are evident in his high levels productivity (3). Ray works at least 12 hours a day since he is so fixed on details, the organization of his work site, and tight schedules he sets himself to meet his self-imposed deadlines (1). He rarely complains about working overtime but does find fault in the way others do the same or similar jobs as they do not always do it the way he thinks is best. Ray always volunteers to work on holidays since he says his work is his life (3).

    Ray meets five of the diagnostic criteria (1, 2, 3, 5, and 8) for a diagnosis of OCPD. OCPD is diagnosed twice as often among males than females. It is important for a practitioner to assess the client's cultural and religious background so as not to include behaviors reflecting customs, practices, habits, or interpersonal manners that are culturally sanctioned by the client's group. While successful psychotherapeutic interventions are complicated by rigidity and stubbornness (Dobbert, 2007), a combination of cognitive-behavioral therapy and selective serotonin reuptake inhibitors (e.g., fluoxetine [Prozac]) may be effective in treating OCPD (Moore & Jefferson, 2004).

dysfunctional behavior. (Refer to Quick Reference 13.12 for the *DSM-IV-TR* diagnostic criteria for OCPD and see Case Example 13.10.)

    Personality disorder not otherwise specified (PDNOS) is a category "for disorders of personality functioning . . . that do not meet criteria for any specific Personality Disorder" (APA, 2000, p. 729). This category is not a Cluster C disorder but includes traits of all of the personality disorders. Persons who are given this diagnosis would display features of more than one specific disorder without meeting the full diagnostic criteria for the disorder. PDNOS is diagnosed when there is clearly significant distress or impairment in one or more significant areas of functioning. The *DSM-IV-TR* (2000) offers examples of depressive personality disorder and passive-aggressive personality disorder in a section focusing on criteria sets and axes provided for further study.

Summary of the Personality Disorders

When assessing individuals for a diagnosis of personality disorder, it is important to collect as much information as possible about them. Understanding the dynamics in the family of origin, the environment in which the person grew up and currently resides, religious and cultural practices, current physical and mental health, recent events that may cause stress or past life experiences that continue to affect the individual in the conduct of daily affairs, interpersonal style, and currency of the person's social support system are all critical pieces to the assessment process. A more detailed case example follows and this example includes the assessment, diagnosis, and intervention planning for a client who suffers from borderline personality disorder. This case example provides an overview of the multiple factors involved in the diagnostic assessment of a client diagnosed with this type of personality disorder.

BORDERLINE PERSONALITY DISORDER

Borderline personality disorder is a mental illness with a chronic, fluctuating course. It affects an estimated 10 million Americans or approximately 2% to 3% of the population (Gershon, 2007; Goodman, Jeong, & Triebwasser, 2009). It accounts for 20% of psychiatric inpatients and 10% of psychiatric outpatient admissions, and the diagnosis is five times more common among

close relatives of a borderline patient than in the general population (Grim, 2000). It is also estimated that 75% of the clients who are diagnosed with this disorder are women (Gershon, 2007). This disorder is severe, as approximately 5% of borderline individuals will eventually kill themselves (D. Hales & R. E. Hales, 1996). Of all the personality disorders, BPD can be considered one of the most devastating and the diagnosis has begun to serve as a catchall phrase where the behaviors the individual is experiencing can start with simple threats and extend as far as verbal and physical aggressiveness as well as suicidal threats and acts (Sieleni, 2007).

BPD, similar to the other personality disorders, is generally indicative of a lifelong pattern of behavior. Therefore, when an individual is diagnosed with a personality disorder such as this one, numerous things must be considered and intervention options can vary. This section discusses one of the most common and severe forms of personality disorders known. In order to reduce the magnitude of disturbances BPD can have on the individual, the family, and society, it is critical that practitioners complete a thorough diagnostic assessment, treatment plan, and practice strategy that can efficiently identify, and effectively treat individuals who suffer from BPD.

Overview of Borderline Personality Disorder

Borderline personality disorder was first diagnosed in 1938, describing individuals who straddled the border between neurosis and psychosis (Maxmen, Ward, & Kilgus, 2009). Generally, personality disorders develop in childhood or adolescence and become apparent by young adulthood (Grim, 2000). In BPD, individuals suffer with numerous problem behaviors that impair current occupational and social functioning. The exact cause of this disorder, however, remains unknown. One study suggests that a significant number of abused and/or neglected children demonstrate the criteria for BPD during adulthood (Widom et al., 2009). BPD can be particularly frustrating in treatment as it constitutes a chronic mental illness that historically has not responded well to therapeutic or medicinal interventions.

DSM-IV-TR Multiaxial System

According to the *DSM-IV-TR*, individuals with BPD have a pervasive pattern of instability of interpersonal relationships, self-image, and affects and marked impulsivity beginning by early adulthood (APA, 2000). These individuals make frantic efforts to avoid real or imagined abandonment, sometimes resulting in a suicide attempt or self-mutilation. Additional characteristics of BPD include frequent mood changes, recurrent suicidal or self-mutilating behavior or both, chronic feelings of emptiness, and difficulty controlling inappropriate anger (Dobbert, 2007).

For individuals who suffer from BPD, the criteria outlined are prominent with at least five of these behavioral patterns being exhibited (*DSM-IV-TR*, 2000).

1. Individuals often make frantic efforts to avoid real or imagined abandonment. When this happens regularly, it can become difficult for family and friends to maintain long-term relationships as often everyday relationship fluctuations or upsets are thought of as catastrophic.

2. Relationship patterns often become unstable because of the intense responses and constant demands the individual places on his or her relationships. These intense relationships are often characterized by unstable and intense moods that alternate between the client

expressing idealization for the individual and devaluation. When utilizing the defense mechanism of idealization, the individual deals with emotional conflict or internal or external stressors by attributing exaggerated positive qualities to others. In devaluation, the individual deals with emotional conflict or internal or external stressors by attributing exaggerated negative qualities to self or others. Constant use of these types of defense mechanisms can easily strain the most caring of relationships.

3. These individuals often experience identity disturbances in which they are markedly unable to understand the relationship of the self to others. Patterns of behavior remain persistently unstable, and self-image or the sense of self is often impaired. In order to get control over these ambivalent feelings, the individual is often seen as compulsive in at least two areas, and the impulsivity is often unpredictable and self-damaging. At times these individuals have recurrent suicidal attempts and gestures, or threats, as well as self-mutilating behavior. Fears of abandonment are often articulated and cases of domestic violence can be exacerbated (Costa & Babock, 2008).

4. Moods are often unstable, and individuals often complain of chronic feelings of emptiness that are reflected in inappropriate episodes of intense anger or difficulty controlling their actions based on the fear of abandonment. At times, the fears and desperation to control the situation may become so severe that these individuals report transient, stress-related paranoid ideation or severe dissociative symptoms. When this occurs, the individual believes people are plotting to destroy his or her

relationships (e.g., paranoid ideation) or that he or she is mentally separated from the relationship when reality testing remains intact (e.g., dissociative symptoms). (See Quick Reference 13.7 listed earlier in this chapter for the criteria related to borderline personality disorder.)

The core symptom evidenced by the individual who suffers from BPD is emotion dysregulation, which constitutes a combination of an emotional response system that is oversensitive and overreactive to normal life-course events. In these cases the individual is unable to modulate the resulting strong emotions and actions associated with the feelings experienced. In addition, the developmental circumstance that produces emotional dysregulation is an invalidating environment in which individuals fail to label and modulate arousal, tolerate distress, and trust emotional responses as valid interpretations of what is happening around them (Linehan, 1993). Up to 75% of individuals with BPD experienced some sort of sexual abuse in childhood. Yet it is unclear whether the exact relationship is between being a victim of abuse and development of the disorder. Parent-child relationships are important to examine in the diagnostic assessment (Widom et al., 2009). Overall, those who suffer from BPD often have a chronic, fluctuating course that significantly impairs social and occupational functioning (Maxmen et al., 2009).

The chronic nature of progression of BPD mandates that alternative forms of treatment be explored. This population has a high rate of use of psychiatric services and emergency room visits. For these individuals, mental health utilization costs are great, treatment dropout rates are high, and estimated rates of completed suicide average aproximately 5% (Paris, 2002). In addition, for individuals with BPD, medication noncompliance is common, and the rate of substance

abuse is great (Koerner & Linehan, 2000; Stefansson & Hesse, 2008). Individuals with BPD may also use defense mechanisms to deal with their intense feelings. Common defense mechanisms used to control anxiety in BPD may include: acting out, passive aggression, projection, projective identification, and splitting (Zanarini, Weingeroff, & Frankenburg, 2009). See earlier chapter for a description of these defense mechanisms.

Measurement Instruments and Diagnostic Assessment

To facilitate the diagnostic assessment when working with individuals suffering from BPD, several clinical scales can be utilized. The overall assumption for using these scales in the self-harm risk assessment is the assumption that many negative thoughts coupled with few positive thoughts indicate a risk of suicide (Fischer, 1999). Furthermore, these measurement scales help to identify symptoms, evaluate client progress, and help to determine the direction of the therapeutic intervention. To facilitate the immediate risk assessment, scales used with individuals with BPD should address parasuicidal behavior, depression, and anxiety. In addition, scales that focus on sexual abuse can help the clinician to determine a possible history and the impact of the event on the client's current level of functioning.

One such scale, Reasons for Living Inventory (RFL), is designed to assist with measuring suicide potential by looking at the adaptive characteristics of suicide (Linehan, Goldstein, Nielsen, & Chiles, 1983). The RFL is based on cognitive-behavioral theory, which asserts that cognitive patterns influence suicidal behavior. The scale looks at the topic of suicide from the absent adaptive coping skills in the client. See Fischer and Corcoran (2007a, 2007b) for a more complete list of scales that could be of benefit in this area.

Numerous scales are available that measure one's level of depression. Differentiating chronic depression from a personality disorder is clinically important, especially from dysthymic disorder, with its long and consistent history (Farabaugh, Fava, & Alpert, 2007). These depression scales may assist with this differentiation. The Self-Rating Scale can provide the practitioner with an easy-to-complete short scale (Zung, 1965). The items on the measurement scale were selected to look at depressive symptoms and include cognitive, affective, psychomotor, somatic, and social-interpersonal items. As many individuals with BPD suffer from anxiety, appropriate scales that address this symptom are imperative. Zung also developed the Self-Rating Anxiety Scale (SAS), which assesses anxiety as a clinical disorder and quantifies the symptoms of anxiety.

The majority of individuals diagnosed with BPD may have been victims of child abuse (Widom et al., 2009). To measure a client's beliefs associated with sexual abuse, the Beliefs Associated with Childhood Sexual Abuse (BACSA) was developed (Jehu, Klassen, & Gazan, 1986). This scale helps to depict changes in clients who are receiving cognitive therapy and identifies distorted beliefs. (See Case Example 13.11.)

CASE EXAMPLE 13.11 - CASE OF C

C is a 27-year-old Caucasian woman who currently lives with her husband and three children in their own home. The client recently applied for and was approved for Social Security Disability and receives $488.00 a month. She has a medical problem related to her hip and mobility is severely limited. Her husband is employed as a long-distance truck driver who is generally away for brief periods while contracting cross-country loads. C reports a history of emotional problems in the form of anxiety and depression. She reports that she has excessive worry about a number of events in her life. She worries about her children, her mother, her husband, and herself. She often finds these symptoms hard to control and reports restlessness or feeling on edge, irritability, difficulty concentrating, but most of all fears that she will do something wrong and "everyone" close to her will leave her. She gets so concerned about this that when her husband comes off the road they often fight. He carries a cell phone but most times he does not answer it when she calls. She reports that she finds this extremely frustrating, as what if something was wrong with the children, so she calls him repeatedly. He tells her he does not answer the cell phone for safety reasons, but she is not sure she believes this. When describing her husband, she states that she loves him as he is a wonderful father. Or other times she states he cannot be trusted and expects so much from her and their relationship. She seems very conflicted about their relationship; sometimes she blames him for many of their problems and alternately she blames herself. She also talks similarly about the relationship she has with her own mother and states her mother "may not be the best but she is all I have."

She stated that she first had these problems with feelings of anxiety and abandonment when she was a child, with a recurrence of more pronounced symptoms approximately 3 years ago. C first received mental health services at age 12. She also received outpatient psychiatric treatment when 19 or 20 years old. She participated in a 2-month partial hospitalization program 3 months ago. She is currently receiving outpatient treatment, occasionally attends a weekly anxiety support group, and sees a psychiatrist every 2 months and a case manager monthly. The psychiatrist currently prescribes C the medication Paxil, and she takes it daily.

C was born in a rural town and is one of twin sisters. They were born two and a half months premature and had to stay in an incubator for 4 to 6 months following delivery. C's sister died soon after birth. C believes many of her problems in infancy are related to the fact that her mother took drugs and smoked during her pregnancy, but she states that she has learned to forgive her. The client has eight older biological siblings. Her mother left her family when the client was 2 years old. C subsequently lived with grandparents, her father, mother, and in several foster group homes. She stated that she keeps in regular contact with her mother, who has also suffered from several emotional breakdowns. She does not keep in contact with other family members although she states she has tried. She states the relationships always start out good but for some reason they do not return her calls and efforts to communicate. C also reported extensive physical, emotional, and sexual abuse during her childhood. She has addressed the abuse in individual therapy, but she continues to experience nightmares, flashbacks, and problems with sexual relations.

C attended mainstream classes in school and never had to repeat any grades. She graduated high school in 1992 as an average student. She began a medical secretarial program one year following her graduation but quit after only 6 weeks. C's employment history is sporadic. She was a waitress in the past and reports she lost the job due to her panic attacks.

C was married in May 1999. After years of marriage, she gave birth to a healthy boy several months ago. She has another son, age 2, and a daughter, age 4, with the same man. She currently lives with her husband and their three children. C takes care of her personal hygiene except when very depressed. She does some household chores, such as cooking and cleaning, only when absolutely necessary. She enjoys taking care of her children, watching TV, and listening to music. She does not have any hobbies. C forces herself to walk once or twice a week for exercise. She has no friends locally despite her attempts to make some. She stated that "people must think I am boring or screwed up." C does not belong to any clubs and does not attend church. She has a valid driver's license but drives only when she has to. She is not able to shop by herself due to panic attacks.

C reported first drinking alcohol when she was 16 years old. She admitted drinking heavily on weekends for a while after high school with friends, but she denied having a problem with alcohol abuse and denies current use. She first tried illegal drugs in the form of marijuana a few times when she was 16 years old but denies current use. C reported taking powder cocaine once when she was 22 years old. She has never been in any formal substance abuse or 12-step program. C denies any current alcohol or drug use. She smokes one pack of cigarettes daily.

C reported two incidents of trouble with the law for domestic violence when she was in her early 20s, although the charges were dropped the following day. C reported her husband has become verbally and physically abusive in the past. He refuses to participate in marital therapy. He has told her and this social worker that the "drama" surrounding his wife and her problems is just too much at times. Although he loves her and his children, he needs a break and actually looks forward to taking extended trips in his truck just to get away.

Completion of the Diagnostic Assessment for C The diagnostic assessment began with the collection of psychosocial information. C was born as one of twin sisters (the other twin died in infancy), and she has eight older biological siblings. Her mother left her family when the client was 2 years old. C subsequently had an unstable living situation growing up, having lived in several places with different people (grandparents, father, mother, foster group homes). She stated that her mother has suffered several emotional breakdowns. C also reported extensive physical, emotional, and sexual abuse during childhood. In terms of her emotional development, problems related to emotional instability can be related to experiences in her household while growing up. Unfortunately, these circumstances can complicate the diagnosis as, for many survivors of abuse, the development of chronic anxiety and depression may persist into adult life.

C clearly has difficulty forming stable relationships. Ordinary interpersonal conflicts may provoke intense anxiety, depression, or rage. She has many arguments with her husband, for which she rotates between blaming herself and blaming him. According to Herman (1992), survivors of abuse have relationships that are driven by the hunger for protection and care and are haunted by the fear of abandonment. Due to her inability to protect herself from her father during her childhood, C has difficulty in protecting herself in her current relationships. A desperate longing for nurturance and care makes it difficult to establish safe and appropriate boundaries with others. Further, she has no close friends and does not trust easily, always fearing abandonment. Effective interpersonal relationships depend on both a stable sense of self and appropriate emotional expression, which C seems to struggle with and with problems in this area.

C's presenting problems include difficulty with relationships and a strained marital relationship. She reports domestic violence concerns with her current husband and says he threatens to harm her physically when he is angry. She denies that he has hit her but fears he might. C reports that the domestic violence is generally emotional abuse, but she fears that when the fighting escalates, it might turn into mutual physical abuse. She does appear to be very concerned about her children, although all look healthy and appear to be well fed and cared for. She has a history of sexual and physical abuse and anxiety. She does not believe her partner would hurt the children.

Overall, C has a poor self-image, which is not uncommon for individuals who have suffered abuse. (See Table 13.1 for mental status description.) Like other adult survivors who have escaped from the abusive situation, C has a poor self-mage and views herself with contempt, shame, and guilt. Although C states that she has escaped the abuse from her father and brothers, her present relationship with her

husband has the potential to also become abusive. She states, "I escaped an abusive home life, only to fall into another abusive relationship where I once again have to struggle for survival and control."

Once the primary and presenting problems have been identified, the first task of the mental health practitioner, especially with the history and potential engagement in impulsive activities that could lead to self-harm or suicide attempts, is to complete a risk assessment for C. Key questions need to identify the potential for suicide risk, risk of violence to others, and the risk of her impulsive behavior and how it might lead to incidents of abuse toward her children. These questions are asked in a straightforward and direct manner. Once identified, this information needs to be clearly recorded. C states she is not suicidal and would not harm herself because of her children but shows evidence of lacerations to her wrist from a previous attempt years ago. This happened when her husband told her he was leaving her. She also reports that she would not harm her children in any way. Although she appears impulsive to action, she has no history of ever hurting them when angry or irritated. C also states that there is no current physical abuse in her marriage but the relationship and the fighting get so intense she feels there could be. She states that when they fight, her husband verbally abuses her by calling her names and telling her she is crazy.

The second step for the mental health practitioner is to identify client strengths and behaviors that contribute to impairment in daily functioning. In addition, the clinician should observe the client's appearance, mood, attitude, affect, speech, motor activity, and orientation. Mental functioning needs to be assessed in terms of the client's ability to complete simple calculations, serial 7s, immediate memory, remote memory, general knowledge, proverb interpretation, and recognition of similarities and

Table 13.1. Mental Status Description

Presentation	Mental Functioning	Higher-Order Abilities	Thought Form/Content
Appearance: Appropriate	Simple Calculations: Mostly accurate	Judgment: Impulsive	Thought process: Logical and organized
Mood: Anxious	Serial 7s: Accurate	Insight: Impaired	Delusions: None
Attitude: Guarded	Immediate Memory: Intact	Intelligence: Average	Hallucinations: None
Affect: Appropriate	Remote Memory: Intact		
Speech: Normal	General Knowledge: Accurate		
Motor Activity: Restless	Proverb Interpretation: Mostly accurate		
Orientation: Fully oriented	Similarities/Differences: Mostly accurate		

differences. In addition, questions concerning higher-order abilities, thought form, and content need to be processed.

The primary problem for C is her difficulty in establishing and maintaining healthy relationships. Her current relationships are all intense, unstable, and chaotic. She and her husband battle when he comes off the road, and she fears he will leave her if this pattern continues. Her mother provides some support; however, she reports that she and her mother "like each other one day and the next day they become sworn enemies" (see Table 13.1 for mental status description for C).

Application of the Multiaxial System

C is given two Axis I provisional diagnoses. The first is generalized anxiety disorder (GAD), as her behaviors are characterized by anxiety, worry, restlessness, or feeling on edge as well as difficulty concentrating and irritability (see Quick Reference 13.13). However, it is unclear if the anxiety-related symptoms she is experiencing are related to the anxiety disorder or better explained along with her relationship difficulties that are characteristic of the diagnosis BPD. Since she has a documented history of anxiety-related problems that cause impairment in social and occupational functioning, previous treatment, and medications, it appears prudent to list this as a possibility for further exploration. Furthermore, at this time it is difficult to tell whether the symptoms of GAD are severe enough to warrant such a diagnosis. A risk assessment related to the mood disturbance is required (see Quick Reference 13.14).

In addition, a second provisional diagnosis and the potential for posttraumatic stress disorder (PTSD) will be explored further. This diagnosis is characterized by an extremely traumatic event

---

QUICK REFERENCE 13.13

IDENTIFY PRIMARY AND PRESENTING PROBLEM

Primary problem: Borderline personality disorder.

Presenting problems: Difficulty with relationships, poor self-image.

QUICK REFERENCE 13.14

RISK ASSESSMENT

Document and assess suicide risk:	No evidence at present time.
Document and assess violence risk:	Slight with no previous history.
Document and assess child abuse risk to her children:	Slight with no previous history.

---

accompanied by symptoms of increased arousal and by avoidance of stimuli associated with the trauma, which is directly related to her history of child physical and sexual abuse. C reports that she often has an intense fear of having sexual relations with her husband and fears that he will leave her, blaming her for the problems that they are having. She says that she experiences intense distress when she hears about child abuse or thinks about what happened to her. She begins to relive the incidents in her mind. Based on this reliving of the experience, she detaches from her husband in an attempt to escape the possibility of it happening again. Although it is possible that this client meets the criteria for PTSD, it remains unclear whether the symptoms she is experiencing relate directly to the diagnosis of PTSD or to her primary diagnosis of BPD.

It appears that C's emotional development may have been stunted due to the emotional instability of her household while growing up, it is possible her feelings of chronic anxiety and depression may be related primarily to her difficulty in forming stable relationships. For C, ordinary interpersonal conflicts may provoke intense anxiety, depression, or rage. Regardless, these two diagnoses are listed as provisional and warrant further exploration and attention in the terms of treatment planning and intervention.

C's principal or primary diagnosis of BPD is placed on Axis II. Characteristics of BPD include a pattern of unstable, intense relationships, unstable self-image or sense of self, impulsivity, frequent mood changes, chronic feelings of emptiness, and difficulty controlling anger or inappropriate anger. For C, this disorder is clearly related to a history of early abandonment and physical and sexual abuse. This makes it difficult for her to maintain a firm sense of who she is or how she contributes positively or negatively in a relationship. Individuals with personality disorders live within a system of internal defense mechanisms on which they rely to avoid or overcome feelings. Although these defense mechanisms can cause a great deal of difficulty, clients like C utilize them as the only way to deal with problems.

Defense mechanisms that can be coded on this axis include idealization and devaluation. C deals with emotional conflict and internal and external stressors through idealization, where she attributes exaggerated positive qualities to family members and all relationships. She also practices devaluation in which she deals with emotional conflict or internal or external stressors by attributing exaggerated negative qualities to her own actions. For example, C has difficulty in establishing and maintaining healthy relationships. Effective interpersonal relationships depend on a stable sense of self (Linehan, 1993). Without these capabilities, it is understandable that the client develops chaotic relationships.

On Axis III, no diagnosis is noted, although there is evidence of lacerations of the right wrist noted from an attempted suicide years ago.

On Axis IV, stressors include relationship conflicts due to aggressive behaviors between her and her spouse (potential for domestic

QUICK REFERENCE 13.15		
APPLICATION OF THE MULTIAXIAL SYSTEM		
Axis I:	Generalized anxiety disorder	300.02 (provisional)
	Posttraumatic stress disorder	309.81 (provisional)
Axis II:	Borderline personality disorder	301.83 (principal diagnosis)
	Defense mechanisms: 　Idealization 　Devaluation	
Axis III:	Deferred	
Axis IV:	Limited social support, primary relationship problems	
Axis V:	50 (current level of functioning)	

violence) and social environmental pressures due to low income and a poor living environment. She has many arguments with her husband, for which she blames herself. She justifies his violent behavior by willingly faulting herself. Gregory (2008) asserts that "from our earliest recollections, we come to expect only abandonment and abuse" (p. 4). Related to her inability to protect herself from her father during her childhood, C has difficulty in protecting herself in her current relationships. She is so desperate for love and attention that it is difficult for her to establish safe and appropriate boundaries with others.

On Axis V, the Global Assessment of Functioning (GAF) rating for current = 50 is noted since C has limited access to social support (i.e., as she has few family members or friends). Current stress severity rating is moderate (see Quick Reference 13.15 for listing of the multiaxial system for C.).

Treatment Planning Considerations

Treatment of BPD is difficult, and the best approaches to practice remain a subject of debate. Further, few treatments have been accepted as designed primarily for the client suffering from BPD (Bateman, Ryle, Fonagy, & Kerr, 2007). One approach gaining in popularity is called mentalization-based therapy (MBT). In this model, the concepts relative to cognitive psychology (contingency theory) are highlighted and combined with the developments in attachment theory. This model was first developed in the context of prolonged inpatient therapy. It disregards the psychoanalytic tenets of the unconscious and focuses more on the linkages with neurophysiology (Bateman, et al., 2007). Another popular treatment method is cognitive analytic therapy (CAT), which seeks to reintroduce key psychoanalytic object relations theoretical concepts (e.g., separation and individuation) into the treatment setting along with recognizing the cognitive aspects within the treatment environment.

Although the treatments designed specifically for this population are limited, research in this area is increasing. Recently a study evaluated three treatment approaches for BPD: a transference-focused approach, a dialectical behavioral approach, and a supportive approach. When compared, the structure dynamic approach labeled transference-focused psychotherapy resulted in clients experiencing change

---

QUICK REFERENCE 13.16

IDENTIFICATION OF PROBLEMATIC BEHAVIORS

- Identify problems related to impulse control (e.g., unsafe sex, substance use, or driving recklessly).
- Identify behavioral outcomes or the problems that result when impulses are not controlled.
- Assess for history and use of substances.
- Identify episodes when explosive temper outbursts or threats based in aggression are most likely to occur.
- Identify concrete examples of low self-esteem and unstable self-image.
- Identify feelings of abandonment and attempts to diminish this feeling.
- Identify the potential for lethality or the possibility of danger to self or others.

---

in six domains; dialectical behavior therapy and supportive treatment were linked to fewer changes among clients (Clarkin, Levy, Lenzenweger, & Kernberg, 2007). Clarkin and colleagues (2007) and the research they present suggest that individualized treatments may be the most beneficial. Additional research is needed to explore the specific mechanisms of change in the application of these treatment approaches. In the "Intervention Strategy" section of this chapter, dialectical behavior therapy is discussed in greater detail.

Regardless of the method used, it appears that the most important techniques still revolve around developing a stable, trusting relationship with a mental health practitioner who does not respond punitively to provocative acts, who actively participates in therapy and provides assurance of the therapist's interest and concern, and who emphasizes the negative effects of self-destructive behavior (D. Hales & R. E. Hales, 1996). BPD is a lifelong disorder in which a pervasive pattern of disregard for and violation of the rights of others occurs that is generally noted as beginning in adolescence. The first step for the mental health practitioner is to clearly define the behaviors that the client is experiencing. Once defined, a plan for how best to address these behaviors is developed.

The goals in therapy are to decrease or eliminate these behaviors and improve the client's adaptation to change (see Quick Reference 13.16). Many clinicians refuse to see these patients or will limit the number of individuals with BPD in their practice to only one or two, as such clients are often seen as provocateurs and expert manipulators (Perry, 1997). Therefore, individuals with this disorder have reputations for being difficult, noncompliant with treatment, and manipulative. Despite these barriers to treatment, research indicates positive directions for the future and a good prognosis for these individuals (APA, 2000).

The numerous problems identified make it difficult to conclude that any one form of treatment will consistently demonstrate the greatest success (Perry, Tarrier, Morriss, McCarthy, & Limb, 1999). However, combination treatment that includes the possibility of medications and therapy seem to offer promise. Dobbert (2007) asserts that manipulation of serotonin levels and therefore the use of an antidepressant medication along with therapy could assist with reducing aggressive behavior. See Quick Reference 13.17 for an overview of therapeutic goals.

Intervention Strategy

It appears that the most effective interventions for individuals with BPD include intensive outpatient individual and group psychotherapy (see

---

QUICK REFERENCE 13.17

THERAPEUTIC GOALS

- Assess for suicide risk and stabilize.
- Develop and demonstrate coping skills to deal with mood swings.
- Develop the ability to control impulses.
- Develop and demonstrate anger management skills.
- Learn and practice interpersonal relationship skills.
- Reduce self-damaging behaviors.

Sample Treatment Plan 13.1). In addition, antidepressants, mood stabilizers, and atypical antipsychotics are often prescribed for individuals with BPD (National Institute of Mental Health [NIMH], 2009a). Therefore, the ideal treatment modality for individuals with BPD is most likely a combination approach that consists of extended individual and group therapy with psychiatric services available to those with more severe symptoms. In addition, best practice with clients diagnosed with BPD addresses suicidal and self-mutilating behavior, depression, anxiety, and issues revolving around childhood sexual abuse. Involving family members if

---

SAMPLE TREATMENT PLAN 13.1

BORDERLINE PERSONALITY DISORDER

Definition: A pervasive pattern of instability of interpersonal relationships, self-image, and affects, and marked impulsivity beginning by early adulthood and present in a variety of contexts.

Signs and Symptoms:
- Frantic efforts to avoid real or imagined abandonment.
- Pattern of unstable and intense relationships characterized by alternating between extremes of idealization and devaluation.
- Identity disturbance—unstable self-image.
- Impulsivity in at least two areas of functioning: spending, sex, substance abuse, reckless driving.
- Recurrent suicidal behavior, gestures or threats, or self-mutilating behavior.
- Affective instability due to a marked reactivity of mood.
- Chronic feelings of emptiness.
- Inappropriate anger, difficulty controlling anger.
- Stress-related paranoid ideation or severe dissociative symptoms.

Goals:
1. Client will stop self-injurious behaviors.
2. Client will maintain prescribed medication regimen.
3. Client will learn to regulate her emotions.
4. Client will learn to express emotions appropriately.
5. Client's family will increase knowledge about BPD.

Objectives	Tasks/Interventions
1. Client will cease self-injurious behaviors (cutting self, suicide attempts) as measured by client's self-report.	Practitioner will establish a no-harm, no-risk agreement with client as part of a safety plan designed to prohibit her from cutting self or attempting suicide.
	Practitioner will establish a no-harm, no-risk agreement with client as part of a safety plan designed to prohibit her from cutting self or attempting suicide.
2. Client will continue taking prescribed medications as recorded by client in daily journal.	Client to take medications as prescribed.
	Client to record in daily journal each time she takes her medication.
3. Client to have a better ability to regulate her emotions, as measured by an average score of 5 at baseline to an average of 2 at the end of treatment on client's daily report of emotional intensity.	Practitioner to use technique called dialectical behavior therapy 2 times per week with client.
4. Client to express emotions appropriately as measured by an average score of 2 at baseline to an average score of 15 at the end of treatment on clinician-developed behavior count of appropriate behaviors used during sessions.	Practitioner to facilitate client awareness of appropriate behaviors to express emotion.
	Client to evaluate the intensity of her emotions on clinician/client-developed scale 3 times per day during treatment.
	Practitioner to evaluate client progress on clinician-developed behavior count of appropriate behaviors at the end of each session.
5. Client's family will increase knowledge of borderline personality disorder, as evidenced by scores of pretest and posttest measures relative to information about the disease.	Client's family will participate in 6-week educational program about BPD.
	Client's family will network with others who have family members with BPD.

available is imperative. Doing this helps to build a support system for the client and will help to maximize the quality of interpersonal relationships. As individuals with BPD have intense, chaotic, and emotional relationships, teaching them skills to help regulate their emotions is imperative (Linehan, 1993).

Strategies for Individual Therapy and Intervention
Yen, Johnson, Costello, and Simpson (2009) reported that a 5-day dialectical behavior therapy (DBT) partial hospital program demonstrated that improvement continued over a 3-month period. Although this program had a decreased length of inpatient hospitalization days, the combined hospital and community-based model helped these individuals improve their overall level of functioning. Chronic

maladaptive relational and behavioral patterns were addressed through intense inpatient group and individual counseling.

In addition, Bateman and Fonagy (1999) evaluated the effectiveness of partial hospitalization in the treatment of BPD by comparing the effectiveness of a psychoanalytically oriented partial hospitalization program with standard psychiatric care for individuals diagnosed with BPD. Group psychoanalytic psychotherapy within a structured, flexible, consistent, limit-setting, and reliable partial hospitalization program was evaluated. In this study, individuals with BPD in a partial hospitalization program improved dramatically compared to those in standard psychiatric care. The number of suicide attempts, inpatient days of hospitalization, level of anxiety and depression, and self-mutilation acts all decreased following their participation in the partial hospitalization program. Since BPD is a chronic mental illness that requires intensive psychiatric care, long-term follow-up treatment is imperative. Those who received intensive group and individual treatment did better when community supports were included. The type of therapy most effective with individuals with BPD involves a combination of individual psychotherapy and skills training. The goal of skills training is the acquisition of adaptive skills. The goal of individual therapy is getting clients to use the skills in place of maladaptive behaviors (Linehan, 1993).

A popular type of intervention for the individual with BPD is DBT. This type of therapy is a broad-based cognitive-behavioral treatment that has diversified over time (A. R. Fruzzetti & A. E. Fruzzetti, 2009). It was developed originally for individuals with BPD. Through controlled clinical trials, it remains effective with this disorder (Feigenbaum, 2007). "The primary dialectic in psychotherapy is that of acceptance and change" (A. R. Fruzzetti & A. E. Fruzzetti, 2009, p. 230). The dialectical perspective contains three main characteristics, each of which is important in understanding BPD and the development of change behaviors.

1. Dialectics directs the client's attention to the immediate and larger contexts of behavior as well as to the interrelatedness of individual behavior patterns. Change is considered an ongoing process, and recognizing the need for change is central to the treatment process. Change is expected to occur in the client, in the therapy, and within the therapist (A. R. Fruzzetti & A. E. Fruzzetti, 2009).

2. Reality is a fundamental process of change, and recognizing the synthesis of internal opposing forces will evolve contradicting and replacing problematic thinking with a new set of opposing forces (Linehan, 1993). The identification of problematic thoughts include extreme thinking, behavior, and emotions that make progress difficult.

3. It is assumed that the individual and the environment are undergoing continuous transition. This belief aims to assist the client to become more comfortable with change.

Since the core disorder in BPD is emotion dysregulation, this type of therapy creates a type of emotional regulation by teaching the client to label and modulate arousal, to tolerate distress, and to trust his or her own emotional responses as valid interpretations and apply this awareness to events (Linehan, 1993). DBT tries to reframe dysfunctional behaviors as part of the client's learned problem-solving skills and engages both the practitioner and the client in active problem solving. At the same time, emphasis is placed on understanding the client's current emotional, cognitive, and behavioral responses. In this method, the mental health practitioner is expected to address all of the client's problematic behaviors in a systematic manner. Doing this includes conducting a collaborative behavioral analysis, formulation of hypotheses about possible variables influencing the problem, generation of possible changes, and trying out/evaluating solutions. This intervention emphasizes the necessity of teaching clients to accept themselves and their life situation as they are in the moment.

Furthermore, the criteria for BPD reflect a pattern of behavioral, emotional, and cognitive instability and dysregulation. Based on this premise, Linehan (1993) outlines four specific skills training modules aimed at treating these difficulties. In the first module, teaching core mindfulness involves learning emotional regulation skills. In the second module, the client learns interpersonal effectiveness skills to deal with chaotic and difficult relationships. The third module teaches the client emotion regulation skills. The fourth skills training module teaches the client distress tolerance skills, helping him or her to learn to consciously experience and observe surrounding events.

Dialectical behavior therapy can form the foundation of a sound practice model to follow when establishing a treatment plan for individuals with BPD. Even if the mental health practitioner is unable to engage the client in long-term therapeutic ventures utilizing the treatment methods, DBT may help by improving the client's overall level of functioning. In summary, it appears that no intervention is perfect for all disorders. According to Fruzzetti and Fruzzetti (2009), when dealing with the personality disorders, especially BPD, a dialectical approach may be most useful when:

- Change-oriented or acceptance-oriented therapy is not successful on its own.
- The treatment reaches a plateau short of its targets for improvement.
- Clients and therapists get stuck in power struggles.
- For multiproblem clients in general (p. 231).

Psychopharmacological Interventions The use of psychotropic medication may be helpful as part of the treatment plan for an individual with BPD. The wide range of symptoms apparent in individuals with this illness mandates that every avenue of treatment be explored, including mixing therapy and medication. Although the use of medication has been shown to be effective, "even with potentially effective pharmacotherapy, some form of concomitant psychosocial intervention is generally required" (Dobbert, 2007; NIMH, 2009a).

For individuals with BPD, the treatment dropout rates are high, medication noncompliance is common, and the rate of substance abuse is great

(Koerner & Linehan, 2000). Practitioners must stress the need for clients to comply with all aspects of treatment and to help monitor the client's progress, especially the potential of substance abuse. Linking the client to Alcoholics Anonymous groups or substance abuse treatment centers or both will help them develop a support system that revolves around abstinence.

In terms of specific medications for use with this disorder, attention has been given to using certain mood stabilizers and the atypical antipsychotics (Lehmann, 2003). Psychotic symptoms in these individuals include paranoia, delusions, referential thinking, and dissociations. For this reason, medication such as clozapine (Clozaril), an antipsychotic given to people with severe schizophrenia who have failed to respond to standard treatments, has been utilized in an attempt to reduce the episodes of severe self-mutilation and aggression in psychotic patients with BPD (Chengappa, Elbeling, Kang, Levine, & Parepally, 1999). Psychotic symptoms generally increase when the individual is under a great deal of stress. The symptoms related to dissociation include depersonalization, analgesia, derealization, and altered sensory perceptions, and these individuals often experience flashbacks. Research supports that flashbacks in people with PTSD were reduced (Bohus et al., 1999) using a naltrexone (ReVia). Furthermore, the study concluded that since increased activity of the opioid system contributes to dissociative symptoms, including flashbacks, that these symptoms may respond to treatments with other opiate antagonists. The one area not influenced by naltrexone was the level of tension experienced by the subjects.

Although medication management of BPD is controversial, it warrants further investigation due to the chronicity of the illness. Further research is needed in the treatment of BPD. Central to the presentations of this chronic personality disorder are unpredictability of behaviors and variations in symptomology. As many psychotherapeutic interventions are researched, medication treatment as a supplement for individuals suffering from borderline personality disorder needs further evaluation to be sure that usage extends beyond just treating the symptoms.

SUMMARY AND FUTURE DIRECTIONS

Of all the mental disorders, the personality disorders can have the most distinct impact on day-to-day functioning, often making daily functioning difficult but severe enough to stop it completely. BPD, in particular, is a chronic mental illness that historically has not responded to therapeutic or medicinal interventions. According to the DSM, the essential feature of BPD is a "pervasive pattern of instability of interpersonal relationships, self-image, affects, and marked impulsivity" (APA, 2000). Individuals diagnosed with any of the personality disorders often have reputations for being difficult, noncompliant with treatment, and manipulative. Despite these barriers to treatment, research indicates positive directions for the future and a good prognosis for these individuals.

In terms of the diagnostic assessment, once the type of personality disorder is identified, a comprehensive risk assessment is needed that can support the chronic nature of this category of disorders. Oftentimes individuals with a personality disorder end up in treatment but it is not specifically related to the personality disorder symptoms alone. Individual approaches such as dialectical behavior therapy and other psychosocial individual and group therapy approaches can assist with improvement in a client's overall general and interpersonal adjustment (A. R. Fruzzetti & A. E. Fruzzetti, 2009). Although some clients suffering from a personality disorder may be resistant to treatment at first, these treatments can be beneficial in improving levels of functioning, enhancing their social relationships, and preventing self-damaging suicidal and self-mutilating behavior.

Additional research needs to be completed in several areas to assess adequate treatment interventions. When looking specifically at BPD, more studies are needed that determine which components of DBT contribute to the positive outcomes needed. In addition, longitudinal follow-up studies are needed to determine suicide rates and maintenance of long-term treatment gains. When working specifically with BPD, the development of a treatment regimen needs to involve follow-up care and community support. Many individuals with this disorder are frequent consumers of inpatient psychiatric facilities. As a result, their chronic maladaptive relational and behavior patterns may initially need to be addressed in an inpatient setting. Outpatient follow-up treatment will help the client to reestablish his or her social network and work on behaviors that precipitated the admission. The key to best assisting individuals who suffer from the personality disorders, especially BPD, is helping to prevent a relapse.

As for the future and the *DSM-5*, Millon & Grossman (2007) criticize the *DSM-IV-TR* for not officially endorsing an underlying set of principles that integrate these topic areas and differentiate the categories. As the discussion and debate continues, what will happen in the future with these Axis II diagnoses remains to be seen.

Quick References: Criteria and Treatment Plans

SELECTED DISORDERS USUALLY FIRST DIAGNOSED IN INFANCY, CHILDHOOD, AND ADOLESCENCE

Mental Retardation: Quick Reference
Sample Treatment Plan for Mild Mental Retardation
Pervasive Disorders: Quick Reference
Sample Treatment Plan for Autistic Disorder

Additional Treatment Plans for Selected Disorders that Occur in Childhood and Adolescence

Attention-Deficit/Hyperactivity Disorder, Predominantly Inattentive Type
Attention-Deficit/Hyperactivity Disorder, Predominantly Hyperactive Impulsive Type
Separation Anxiety Disorder
Expressive Language Disorder

Additional Information for Somatoform Disorders, Facitious Disorders, and Sleep Disorders

Somatoform and Factitious Disorders Quick Reference
Sample Treatment Plan for Body Dysmorphic Disorder
Sleep Disorders: Quick Reference
Sample Treatment Plan for Insomnia

Additional Treatment Plans for Selected Anxiety Disorders, Bipolar Disorders, and the Psychotic Disorders

Generalized Anxiety Disorder
Posttraumatic Stress Disorder
Major Depressive Disorder
Bipolar Disorder
Schizophrenia-Paranoid Type
Bulimia Nervosa

Special thanks for earlier versions of these treatment plans and suggestions by Laurel Torres, J. Erin Webb, and Carmen Chang-Arriata.

QUICK REFERENCE

MENTAL RETARDATION

Abbreviated Guidelines

- If this condition is present, the practitioner should always list it with supporting information from an intelligence test to verify the Intelligence Quotient (IQ) score.
- Individuals must have significantly subaverage intelligence and deficits in adaptive functioning.
- Definition is compatible with American Association on Mental Retardation (AAMR) definition except for subtyping.
- Onset prior to age 18; if later, consider the diagnosis as possible dementia.
- Must have IQ of 70 or below on an individual intelligence test (IQ).
- This disorder is slightly more common in males.

Borderline Intellectual Functioning: IQ of 71–84, can code on Axis II.

Mild: IQ approximately (50–55) 55–70, considered *educable,* able to perform at sixth-grade level, can use minimal assistance, may need some supervision and guidance, often lives in community or in minimally supervised settings.

Moderate: IQ approximately (35–40) 35–55 (50–55), considered trainable, able to perform at second-grade level, with moderate supervision can attend to own personal care, can perform unskilled or semiskilled work, often lives in the supervised setting in the community.

Severe: IQ approximately (20–25) 20–35, (35–40) generally institutionalized, has little or no communicative speech, possible group home with extensive support and follow-up to complete activities of daily living.

Profound: IQ below 20 or 25, generally total care required.

Note: All IQ score categories can have a margin of error equivalent to a 5-point overlap.

Source: Summarized criteria from the *Diagnostic and Statistical Manual of Mental Disorders, Fourth Edition, Text Revision.* Copyright 2000 by the American Psychiatric Association.

TREATMENT PLAN

MILD MENTAL RETARDATION

Definition: The main feature of mental retardation is significantly subaverage intellectual functioning which is evidenced by an IQ score of below 70 and verified by an IQ test. Mild mental retardation occurs when the individual has an IQ between 50/55 and 70. This disorder becomes apparent in childhood, and is characterized by an inability to maintain focus/concentration, an inability to complete tasks, and poor organization skills.

Signs and Symptoms to Note in the Record:

- Subaverage intelligence; specifically, an IQ of between 50/55 and 70.
- Limitations in communication, self-care, social and interpersonal skills, self-direction, and academic skills.
- List difficulties in coping with everyday demands.
- List difficulties in functioning independently.
- Inability to follow through on assignments/tasks from beginning to end.

- Inattention to detail/often makes careless mistakes.
- Loses interest in activities/frequent shifting of focus from one project to another without completion.
- Messy working space/area.
- Dislike of activities that require sustained attention.

Goals:

1. Behavior will correspond to appropriate level of functioning within social contexts, such as school, home, and community settings.
2. Accept intellectual limitations, but also be able to express strengths.
3. Reduce the number of socially inappropriate behaviors.
4. Parents should develop a simple routine at home and positively reinforce compliance with the rules.
5. Client will take medication as prescribed by psychiatrist.
6. Client will increase attention/concentration span.
7. Client will adhere to firm limits as established by parents and teachers.
8. Client will increase self-esteem.

Objectives	Interventions
1. Client will maintain attention to activities for increasing intervals of time.	Assist parents and child in developing a routine, schedule child's chores and assignments to be completed each day, and the time frame in which each is to be completed.
	Make recreational activities contingent upon completion of daily assignment while systematically increasing the length of time required to complete such tasks.
2. Client will improve self-confidence and self-worth.	Client will list, recognize, focus on strengths, and work on building interpersonal relationships.
3. Client will be placed in an appropriate school setting and an appropriate residential setting.	Consult with teachers, parents, and mental health professionals to determine appropriate classroom setting depending on the client's intellectual capabilities and skill level.
	Determine appropriate residential setting, depending on the client's abilities and the level of care required.
4. Practitioner will introduce and help the client utilize self-monitoring techniques to help client stay on task.	Introduce the client to a nondisruptive, self-repeating tape of tones that regularly reminds the child to ask self, "Am I working on my assigned task?"
5. Teachers will develop an educational plan that focuses on the child's ability and compensates for the child's weaknesses.	Implement a reward/token system for compliant behavior and positive academic performance.
6. Parents will increase use of positive reinforcement at home.	Develop and implement a list of daily chores that the child is developmentally able to achieve and positively reinforce achievements.
7. Parents and teachers will recognize and verbally express when the child is behaving in a socially inappropriate way.	Design a reward system to reinforce the child's socially appropriate behaviors.
8. Parents will ensure that medication is taken in appropriate dosage and at specified time.	Child will adhere to a daily routine of taking medications as established by parents.
9. Parents and teachers will establish and implement rules and consequences for the child.	Assist the parents in determining clear rules for the child and developing a system of natural consequences for inappropriate behaviors.
10. Parents and teachers will positively reinforce appropriate behaviors of the child.	Utilize verbal praise to reward compliance with rules.
	Utilize a reward system to reinforce on-task behaviors and completion of tasks at home and in the classroom.

QUICK REFERENCE

PERVASIVE MENTAL DISORDERS (PDD)

Abbreviated Guidelines

- PDDs comprise a category of disorders beginning in early childhood and characterized by severe and pervasive impairment in several areas of development affecting an individual's personal, family, and occupational skills acquisition, interests, and activities.
- Characterization of PDD includes but is not limited to impaired reciprocal social interactions and stereotyped behaviors, with qualitative impairments, which deviate from expected communication and actions related to developmental stage.
- The skills exhibited are extremely limited and deficient relative to the actual developmental level.
- These disorders occur in the first few years of life and are often associated with some form of mental retardation. For this reason, the presence of mental retardation should always be assessed.
- The nature of these disorders is its lifelong component, with early and supportive assessment and intervention improvement noted.

Types of Pervasive Mental Disorders

- **Autistic disorder:** Impaired social reciprocal relationships, with impairment and/or delay in verbal and nonverbal communication, and restricted, repetitive, and nonspontaneous play, behaviors, and activities. Manifest by age 3, these result in the loss in the development of peer-appropriate relationships, delay in verbal and nonverbal communication, uneven intellectual cognitive development and impaired ability to perceive social and emotional cues facilitating communicative social, symbolic, and imaginative interactions, with ritualistic, stereotyped, and inflexible patterns of behavior and reactions.
- **Asperger's disorder:** Autistic-like symptoms, without language impairment, delays, or acquisition, with severely impaired reciprocal social interaction and restricted patterns of behavior, interests, and activities. There are no cognitive delays in cognitive development or age-appropriate self-help and adaptive skills, and no mental retardation is noted in this disorder, unlike in autistic disorder.
- **Rett's disorder:** Associated with severe and profound mental retardation, onset of disorder is prior to age 4 with a period of normal functioning after birth and subsequent deceleration of normal growth and development of head circumference between ages 5 and 48 months. A genetic disorder affecting and reported only in females, the development of the loss of psychomotor function resulting in gait and coordination loss, stereotyped hand movements, impaired expressive and receptive language and life-long diminishing interest in social interaction and responding within the social environment.
- **Childhood disintegrative disorder:** Associated with severe mental retardation, medical conditions such as *Schilder's disease* and *metachromatic leukodystrophy*, and more often found in males. Characteristic symptoms of the disorder include the loss of previously acquired developmentally appropriate skills at age 2 and before age 10, with significant impairments in at least two of the areas of development (e.g., language, social skills and behaviors, bowel or bladder control, motor skills, and/or play).
- **Pervasive developmental disorder NOS:** Impairments in the development of reciprocal social interactions, verbal and nonverbal communication, and with the presence of impaired behaviors resulting in stereotyped behaviors, not meeting the criteria specific for *PDD*, *schizophrenia*, *schizotypal personality disorder*, or *avoidant personality disorder*.

Source: These criteria are briefly summarized utilizing the *Diagnostic and Statistical Manual of Mental Disorders, Fourth Edition, Text Revision.* Copyright 2000 by the American Psychiatric Association.

TREATMENT PLAN

AUTISTIC DISORDER

Definition: The main features of autistic disorder are abnormal or impaired development in social interaction and communication as well as a strict regimen of repetitive behaviors.

Signs and Symptoms to Note in the Record:

- Lack of interest in other people.
- Failure to develop appropriate interpersonal relationships.
- Delays in communication skills and language development.
- Repetition of rituals or self-stimulating behaviors, such as rocking.
- Self-injurious behaviors, such as head banging or biting.
- Overreaction to changes in routine or environment.
- Impairment in both intellectual and cognitive functioning.

Goals:

1. Develop basic language and communication skills.
2. Parents should accept their child's capabilities and limitations.
3. Decrease and eventually eliminate all self-injurious behaviors.

Objectives	Interventions
1. Client will work with speech and language therapists.	Refer the client to a speech and language therapist to increase the child's development of speech and language skills.
2. Client will increase interactions with others, which will help to improve communication skills.	Parents should utilize positive reinforcement or modeling techniques to encourage interaction with others and increase communication skills.
3. Client will decrease any self-injurious behaviors	Teach the parents behavioral management skills and techniques to identify triggers for self-injurious behaviors and how to prevent them.
	Refer the parents and the child to a therapist who is knowledgeable about aversive therapy and can assist the practitioner/case manager to develop a plan designed to identify and decrease self-injurious behaviors.
4. Parents will develop an understanding of their child's illness and discuss coping/supportive and behavioral strategies to address it.	Educate parents about autism, explaining possible problems to anticipate as well as realistic expectations for performance.
	Refer to a support group for families to assist with learning how others address the child's individual needs.
	Encourage parents to identify when respite is needed and provide referrals as indicated.

Additional Treatment Plans for Disorders Usually First Diagnosed in Infancy, Childhood and Adolescence

TREATMENT PLAN

ATTENTION-DEFICIT/HYPERACTIVITY DISORDER, PREDOMINANTLY INATTENTIVE TYPE

Definition: A disorder that becomes apparent in childhood, must be present before the age of 7, and is characterized by an inability to maintain focus/concentration, an inability to complete tasks, and poor organization skills.

Signs and Symptoms to Note in the Record:

- Inability to follow through on assignments/tasks from beginning to end.
- Inattention to detail/often makes careless mistakes.
- Loses interest in activities/frequent shifting of focus from one project to another without completion.
- Messy working space/area.
- Dislike of activities that require sustained attention.

Goals:

1. Client will take medication as prescribed by psychiatrist.
2. Client will increase attention/concentration span.
3. Client will adhere to firm limits as established by parents and teachers.
4. Client will increase self-esteem.

Objectives	Interventions
1. Client will maintain attention to activities for increasing intervals of time.	Assist child in developing a routine, schedule child's chores and assignments to be completed each day, and the time frame in which each is to be completed.
	Make recreational activities contingent upon completion of daily assignment while systematically increasing the length of time required to complete such tasks.
2. Client will improve self-confidence and self-worth.	Client will list, recognize, focus on strengths, and utilize these in interpersonal relationships.
3. Practitioner will introduce and help the client utilize self-monitoring techniques to help client stay on task.	Introduce the client to a nondisruptive, self-repeating tape of tones that regularly reminds the child to ask self, "Am I working on my assigned task?"
4. Parents and teachers will establish and implement rules and consequences for the child.	Assist the parents in determining clear rules for the child and developing a system of natural consequences for inappropriate behaviors.
5. Parents and teachers will positively reinforce appropriate behaviors of the child.	Utilize verbal praise to reward compliance with rules.
	Utilize a reward system to reinforce on-task behaviors and completion of tasks at home and in the classroom.
6. Parents will ensure that medication is being taken in appropriate dosage and at specified time.	Child will adhere to a daily routine of taking medications as established by the prescriber with oversight by parents.

TREATMENT PLAN

ATTENTION-DEFICIT/HYPERACTIVITY DISORDER, PREDOMINANTLY HYPERACTIVE-IMPULSIVE TYPE

Definition: A disorder that becomes apparent in childhood, must be present before the age of 7, and is characterized by excessive motor activity as well as poor impulse control of emotional and physical behaviors.

Signs and Symptoms to Note in the Record:

- Inability to remain seated for an extended period of time.
- Excessive fidgeting.
- Excessive talking/noise.
- Blurting out of answers/inability to think before speaking/inability to raise hand and wait to be called on.
- Frequent interruption of conversations, activities, and so on.
- Frequent accidents.

Goals:

1. Client will take medication as prescribed by psychiatrist.
2. Client will improve impulse control.
3. Caregivers will set firm and consistent limits and reinforce positive behaviors of the child.
4. Client will improve self-esteem.

Objectives	Interventions
1. Client will increase awareness of disruptive/impulsive behavior at home and in the classroom.	Child will discuss recent disruptive behaviors and explore alternatives on how the situation could be handled better next time.
	Parents and teachers will develop a system responsible for immediately alerting the child to impulsive or off-task behaviors (i.e., attention training system) at home or in school.
2. Client will improve self-confidence, self-regard, and self-worth.	Client will be able to identify and increase the frequency of positive self-statements.
	Client will identify things that he or she does well.
3. Client will increase medication compliance and report side effects to prescriber and treatment team.	Client will adhere to a daily routine of taking prescribed medications as established by parents.
Parents will ensure that medication is taken in appropriate dosage and at specified times.	Client will be able to identify side effects related to the medications and express any concerns to prescriber and parents.
4. Parents and teachers will establish and implement rules and limitations for child.	Assist parents and teachers in determining clear rules and boundaries for the client and responsibilities of the client.
5. Parents and teachers will decide on and implement consequences for inappropriate behaviors of the client.	Develop natural and meaningful consequences for noncompliance with rules.
6. Parents and teachers will positively reinforce appropriate behaviors of the client.	Utilize verbal praise to reward compliance with rules and appropriate behaviors.

TREATMENT PLAN

Separation Anxiety Disorder

Definition: The main feature of separation anxiety disorder is an excessive anxiety and worry over being separated from the home or attachments related to parents or caregivers.

Signs and Symptoms to Note in the Record:

- High level of distress when separated from parents or other caregivers.
- Excessive worry about losing parents or something happening to them while they are away from the child.
- Fear of being alone without parents nearby.
- Frequent nightmares about separation from parents.
- Lack of participation in social activities due to excessive fear of being separated from parents.

Goals:

1. Decrease the anxiety and fear when a separation is anticipated or occurs.
2. Resolve the underlying issues that may be contributing to the fear.
3. The child should participate in activities with peers and spend time playing independently, away from parents.
4. Parents should establish clear boundaries and set firm limits on their child's acting out behaviors which occur when separation is near.

Objectives	Interventions
1. Client will describe fears and how those fears are irrational.	Encourage the child to explore the reasons why separation from parents is feared.
	Encourage the child to express how fears are irrational.
2. Client will increase the amount of time spent away from parents.	Encourage the child to spend progressively longer periods of time playing independently or with peers.
	Parents should positively reinforce autonomous behaviors.
3. Both the client and parents will examine why anxiety occurs and the factors that may contribute to its occurrence.	Encourage the child to examine and verbally express how fear may be related to past separations, trauma, or abuse.
	Encourage the parents to examine how they may be contributing to or reinforcing their child's anxiety and fears.
4. Parents will set limits on their child's crying, clinging, pleading, and temper tantrums when separation occurs.	Teach the parent to set consistent limits on their child's temper tantrums, crying, and clinging.
	Educate the parents about the need for space and privacy.

TREATMENT PLAN

EXPRESSIVE LANGUAGE DISORDER

Definition: A disorder characterized by developed expressive language substantially below the intellectual/developmental level expected of the individual. This is demonstrated by scores on the expressive language portion of standardized tests with these scores substantially below scoring on the nonverbal intellectual and language reception portions.

Signs and Symptoms to Note in the Record:

- Expressive language scoring on standardized tests is below normal range, while nonlinguistic and comprehensive scoring is often within or above the normal range.
- Limited speech, often the result of limited vocabulary, poor sentence structure, and improperly conjugated verbs.
- Children often begin speaking late and progress through language development stages behind their peers and at a slower rate.
- Difficulty introducing new vocabulary into the range of verbal expression.

Goals:

1. Parents and child will utilize the expertise of a language pathologist in determining language capabilities and assisting the child in reaching full expressive capacity.
2. Parents and child will develop an awareness/acceptance of expressive language limitations.
3. Child will utilize tools to help cope with frustrations and ridicule often associated with language deficits.
4. Child will improve self-esteem.

Objectives	Interventions
1. Client and parents will comply with all recommendations of language pathologist.	Consistent communication between parents, teachers, and therapist to reinforce learning techniques and language development.
2. Child and family will accept limitations of language deficit.	Individual therapy to eliminate denial and encourage acceptance of language deficit in order to facilitate proper educational placement and an optimal learning environment.
	Family therapy to eliminate the denial and encourage acceptance of child's language difficulties in order to facilitate proper educational placement and maximum language development.
3. Child will implement effective coping mechanisms to deal with peer ridicule due to language difficulties.	Individual therapy to introduce, practice, and encourage client use of effective coping mechanisms including: positive self-talk, deep breathing strategies, relaxation techniques.
4. Parents and teachers will reinforce client strengths.	Focus on client strengths (math, manual dexterity, creativity, etc.) and further the development of these to their full potential in order to compensate for language deficits.

QUICK REFERENCE

SELECTED SOMATOFORM DISORDERS

Somatoform disorders (unconscious awareness and response by the client): The client is unaware that he or she has a mental disorder. These disorders consist of the development of physical symptoms and somatic complaints that suggest the occurrence of a medical condition. Upon further examination, however, no known physiological cause is found. To ensure that an actual physical problem is not the cause of the symptomology, prior to diagnosis a physical exam should be completed.

Somatization disorder (300.81): Recurrent and multiple somatic complaints (over a period of years), onset before age 30 that occur over a period of several years. The symptoms are not intentionally produced or feigned, and the client is unaware that the condition or concerns may not be real. Four of these criteria must be met: pain symptoms, two gastrointestinal symptoms, one sexual symptom, and one pseudoneurologial symptom. The condition occurs with all of the four criteria not being explained by any medical condition or direct effects of a substance (drug abuse or medication); or when there is a medical condition, the physical complaints or resulting social or occupational impairment are in excess of what is associated with the medical condition.

Conversion disorder (300.11): The essential feature is the presence of one or more symptoms or deficits affecting voluntary motor or sensory function that suggest a neurological or other general medical condition. Psychological factors are judged associated with the symptom or deficit because the initiation or exacerbation of the symptom or deficit is preceded by conflicts or other stressors. Similar to the other somatoform disorders, the symptom or deficit is not intentionally produced. The symptoms are not explained by a general medical condition, direct effects of a substance, or a culturally sanctioned behavior or experience. The symptom or deficit causes clinically significant distress or impairment in social, occupational, or other important areas of functioning or warrants medical evaluation. The symptom or deficit is not limited to pain or sexual dysfunction and is not explained by any other mental disorder.

Pain disorder (307.xx) was called somatoform pain disorder: Preoccupation with pain with no known underlying cause. Pain is in one or more anatomical sites and the focus of the clinical presentation. The presumption of the pain can cause clinically significant distress or impairment in social, occupational, or other important areas of function. Psychological factors are judged to have an important role in the onset, severity, exacerbation, or maintenance of the pain. The symptom or deficit is not intentionally produced. The pain cannot be explained by a mood, anxiety, or psychotic disorder and does not meet criteria for dyspareunia.

Hypochondriasis (300.7): Preoccupation with fears of having, or ideas one has, a serious disease based on misinterpretation of bodily symptoms. The duration of the disturbance lasts at least 6 months. Preoccupation persists despite medical evaluations and reassurance. The preoccupation is not of delusional intensity for the person may acknowledge that he or she is exaggerating the extent of the fear and is not restricted to concern about appearance. The preoccupation causes significant distress or impairment in social, occupational, or other important areas of functioning. Preoccupation is not accounted for by generalized anxiety disorder, obsessive-compulsive disorder, panic disorder, a major depressive episode, separation anxiety, or another somatoform disorder.

Body dysmorphic disorder (300.7): Preoccupation with an imagined flaw in appearance. If a slight anomaly is present, the person's concern is excessive. The preoccupation causes clinically significant distress or impairment in social, occupational, or other important areas of functioning. This preoccupation is not better accounted for by another mental disorder.

Source: These criteria are briefly summarized utilizing the *Diagnostic and Statistical Manual of Mental Disorders, Fourth Edition, Text Revision.* Copyright 2000 by the American Psychiatric Association.

QUICK REFERENCE

FACTITIOUS DISORDER AND SELECTED TYPES

Factitious disorders (conscious): The essential feature is the intentional production of physical or psychological signs or symptoms. The motivation is to assume the sick role. External incentives—for example, economic gain and avoiding legal responsibility—are absent.

Factitious disorder with predominantly physical signs and symptoms (300.19): If physical signs and symptoms predominate in the clinical presentation (as in Munchausen syndrome), the person is creating these physical symptoms for attention.

Factitious disorder NOS (300.19): This category includes disorders with factitious symptoms that do not meet the criteria for factitious disorder (aka Munchausen by proxy), intentionally creating physical or psychological signs or symptoms in another person under their care for attention, therefore the client indirectly assumes the sick role by using the sickness of the other person to gain self-attention.

Source: These criteria are briefly summarized utilizing the *Diagnostic and Statistical Manual of Mental Disorders, Fourth Edition, Text Revision.* Copyright 2000 by the American Psychiatric Association.

TREATMENT PLAN

BODY DYSMORPHIC DISORDER

Definition: The essential feature of body dysmorphic disorder is a preoccupation with a defect in appearance. The defect is either imagined or, if a slight physical anomaly is present, the individual's concern is markedly excessive.

Signs and Symptoms to Note in the Record:

- Complaints commonly involve imagined or slight flaws of the face or head, such as hair thinning, acne, wrinkles, scars, vascular markings, paleness or redness of the complexion, swelling, facial asymmetry or disproportion, or excessive facial hair.
- Preoccupation with shape, size, or some other aspect of a body part seen as defective; may simultaneously focus on several body parts.
- Spending hours a day thinking or checking "defect" to the point where these thoughts and actions may dominate the individual's life.
- Feelings of self-consciousness may lead to avoidance of work, school, or public situations.

Goals:

1. Identify ways to cope with anxiety and depression.
2. Reduce preoccupation with the imagined physical defect.
3. Reduce thinking of unnecessary plastic surgery.
4. Client will gradually face feared social situations.

Objectives	Interventions
1. Client will be assessed for medication needs to address possible anxiety or depression.	Schedule client for a complete psychiatric evaluation and follow any recommendations made by the psychiatrist.
2. Client will explore origin of problem and the reasons why it exists.	Client will participate in cognitive-behavioral therapy.
	Therapist will help individual understand how thoughts and perceptions are distorted in regard to appearance and help client focus on more realistic perceptions.
3. Client will reduce obsessive behavior regarding body flaw.	Client will reduce time spent looking in mirror on elaborate grooming, repeated requests for reassurance of others, and repeated touching of defect.
	Therapist should dissuade client from plastic surgery.
4. Client will confront feared social situations.	Client will participate in a support group to discuss with others similar issues and concerns.

QUICK REFERENCE

SELECTED SLEEP DISORDERS

Dyssomnias: Primary disorders of initiating or maintaining sleep or of excessive sleepiness and are characterized by a disturbance in the amount, quality, or timing of sleep.

Primary insomnia (307.42): Primary complaint is difficulty initiating or maintaining sleep or of nonrestorative sleep that lasts for at least 1 month. The sleep disturbance or daytime fatigue causes clinically significant distress or impairment in social, occupational, or other important areas of functioning. The sleep disturbance does not occur exclusively during the course of narcolepsy, breathing-related sleep disorder, circadian rhythm sleep disorder, or a parasomnia. The disturbance does not occur exclusively during the course of another mental disorder. The sleep disturbance is not due to direct physiological effects of a substance (e.g., a drug of abuse, a medication) or a general medical condition.

Primary hypersomnia (307.44): Excessive sleepiness for at least 1 month (or less if recurrent) shown by prolonged sleep episodes or by daytime sleep episodes occurring almost daily. The age for onset is between ages 15 and 30 with a gradual progression over weeks to months. For most, the duration of the major sleep episode lasts from 8 to 10 hours with difficulty awakening in the morning. The excessive sleepiness causes significant distress or impairment in social, occupational, or other important areas of functioning. The excessive sleepiness is not better accounted for by insomnia and does not occur exclusively during the course of another sleep disorder and cannot be accounted for by an inadequate amount of sleep. The disturbance is not caused by physiological effects of a substance or general medical condition. Specify if recurrent: When there are periods of excessive sleepiness and these periods of sleepiness are repeated for at least 3 days, and these periods occur several times a year for at least a 2-year time period.

Narcolepsy (347): Irresistible attacks of refreshing sleep that occur daily over at least 3 months. The presence of one or both of the following: cataplexy and or recurrent intrusions of elements of rapid eye movement (REM) sleep into the transition between sleep and wakefulness, as manifested by either hypnopompic or hypnagogic hallucinations or sleep paralysis at the beginning or end of sleep episodes. The disturbance is not due to the direct physiological effects of a substance or another medical condition.

Breathing-related sleep disorder (780.59): Sleep disruption, leading to excessive sleepiness or insomnia, that is judged to be due to a sleep-related breathing condition. The disturbance is not better accounted for by another mental disorder and is not due to the direct physiological effects of a substance or another general medical condition (other than a breathing-related disorder).

Circadian rhythm sleep disorder (was sleep wake schedule disorder) (307.45): A persistent or recurrent pattern of sleep disruption leading to excessive sleepiness or insomnia due to a mismatch between the sleep-wake schedule required by a person's environment and his or her circadian sleep-wake pattern. The sleep disturbance causes clinically significant distress or impairment in social, occupational, or other important areas of functioning. Does not occur exclusively during the course of another sleep disorder or other mental disorder. The disturbance is not due to the direct physiological effects of a substance or another medical condition.

Source: These criteria are briefly summarized utilizing the *Diagnostic and Statistical Manual of Mental Disorders, Fourth Edition, Text Revision.* Copyright 2000 by the American Psychiatric Association.

TREATMENT PLAN

INSOMNIA

Definition: Insomnia can be either a symptom or, if severe enough, can be diagnosed as a sleep-related mental disorder. Insomnia is difficulty initiating or maintaining sleep, or it can be difficulty in both initiating and maintaining sleep. Since sleep schedules vary, an intervention plan needs to fit the individual's own needs and practices. Insomnia can occur as a symptom in many of the mental health disorders, making it an important intervention concern, whether it is the primary symptom or not.

Insomnia is generally classified based on the duration of the problem. In assessing the individual, special attention needs to be given to establishing the time frame:

- Symptoms lasting less than 1 week are classified as *transient insomnia.*
- Symptoms between 1 to 3 weeks are classified as *short-term insomnia.*
- Assessing for transient and short-term insomnia includes identifying causes such as: jet lag, changes in shift work or activities of daily living (ADLs), excessive or unpleasant noise, uncomfortable in room. Look carefully at life circumstances and life events as probable causes.
- Symptoms lasting longer than 3 weeks are classified as *chronic insomnia*

Most causes of chronic or long-term insomnia are usually linked to an underlying psychiatric or physiologic (medical) condition.

Signs and Symptoms to Note in the Record:

- Difficulty initiating or maintaining sleep or nonrestorative sleep for a period of at least 1 month (to place the diagnosis for primary insomnia).
- Note any psychological problems that may lead to insomnia, such as anxiety stressors.
- Note any mental health conditions, such as schizophrenia, mania or hypomania (bipolar disorders), and depression, as these may affect sleep patterns.
- Note any medical conditions that may cause sleep disturbances, such as chronic pain syndromes, chronic fatigue syndrome, congestive heart failure, nighttime angina (chest pain) from heart disease, acid reflux disease, chronic obstructive pulmonary disease (COPD), nocturnal asthma (asthma with night time breathing symptoms), obstructive sleep apnea, degenerative diseases (such as Parkinson's disease and Alzheimer's disease), brain tumors, strokes, or trauma to the brain.
- Note any medications or substances (legal and illegal) being taken as these could interfere with sleep, and identify and any strategy the client is using to deal with adjusting the disturbed sleep patterns (e.g., drinking herbs before bedtime, exercising before bed, etc.).

Goals:

1. Identify sleep habits and ways to increase sleep scheduling and comfort.
2. Reduce preoccupation with stressors that disturb sleep-wake schedule.
3. Reduce thinking of unnecessary events or factors.

Long-Term Goals:

1. Improve sleep-wake schedule.
2. Develop routine for initiating restful sleep.
3. Increase capacity to self-regulate thoughts and self-relaxation.
4. Increase ability to complete activities of daily living.

Objectives	Interventions
1. Client will get a physical exam to identify any medical or psychological illnesses that could contribute to sleep problems and disturbances.	Physician will conduct a thorough medical history and medical conditions that might cause insomnia-like symptoms.
2. Client will identify factors that trigger disturbed sleep patterns.	Complete a sleep diary for approximately 2 weeks, identifying events and situations that seem to contribute to sleep-wake schedule difficulties.
	Offer optional devices that can be used to assist with sleep-wake patterns in addition to the diary. Explain actigraphy (a technique to assess sleep-wake patterns over time). An actigraph is a small, wrist-worn device (about the size of a wristwatch) that measures movement. It contains a microprocessor and onboard memory and can provide objective data on daytime activity.
3. Client will identify high-risk factors when becoming overtired.	Identify high-risk factors and situations with client and problem-solve what to do if these situations occur. Situations include:
	■ Difficulty with memory.
	■ Impaired motor coordination (being uncoordinated).
	■ Irritability and impaired social interaction.
	■ Motor vehicle accidents because of fatigue or sleep-deprived driving.
4. Client will establish a sleep hygiene routine as part of the behavioral therapy routine.	Introduce important sleep hygiene components and help client develop a plan to improve sleep quality and quantity.
Steps include:	Steps include:
■ relaxation training,	■ Sleep as much as needed until the client feels rested, do not oversleep.
■ stimulus control,	■ Increase exercise and develop a routine to exercise regularly at least 20 minutes daily. This should be completed 4 to 5 hours before bedtime.
■ and sleep restrictions.	■ Avoid forcing sleep.
	■ Develop and maintain a regular sleep and awakening schedule.
	■ Avoid caffeinated beverages in the afternoon, such as tea, coffee, soft drinks, etc.
	■ Avoid nightcaps (alcoholic drinks prior to going to bed).
	■ Do not smoke, especially in the evening.
	■ Do not go to bed hungry.
	■ Adjust the environment in the room (lights, temperature, noise, etc.)
	■ Do not go to bed with your worries; try to resolve them before going to bed.

(*continued*)

TREATMENT PLAN (*Continued*)

Objectives	Interventions
5. Client will identify anxiety-causing and/or anxiety-producing cognitive mechanisms	Client will be supported as he or she identifies and verbalizes feelings and emotions in response and when not in response to anxiety producing cognitions that may affect sleep.
	Provide education on systematic desensitization, its mechanism, and applications.
	Educate client about self-relaxation techniques to alleviate fear, worry, terror, and/or stress.
	Assist client in practicing self-relaxation techniques in session to implement as needed.
6. Practitioner will engage support systems.	Educate client and family regarding signs of insomnia and importance of keeping sleep hygiene routines.
7. Practitioner will complete a mental status exam and assess for mental health–related problems and possible drug, substance, or alcohol abuse.	Assess for psychiatric disorders and drug and alcohol use. Seek input from a trained professional in psychiatry or substance abuse if needed.

TREATMENT PLAN

GENERALIZED ANXIETY DISORDER

Definition: Generalized anxiety disorder is characterized by excessive anxiety and worry about a number of events or activities that lasts for at least 6 months,

Signs and Symptoms to Note in the Record:

- Restlessness or feeling keyed up or on edge.
- Easily fatigued.
- Difficulty concentrating.
- Irritability.
- Muscle tension.
- Sleep disturbance, such as restless sleeping or difficulty falling asleep.
- Difficulty controlling the worry.

Goals:

1. Reduce overall intensity and frequency of the anxiety.
2. Increase ability to function on a daily basis.
3. Resolve the core issue that is causing the anxiety.
4. Develop coping skills to better handle anxieties encountered in the future.

Objectives	Interventions
1. Client will complete a psychiatric evaluation and take medications as prescribed.	Arrange for a psychiatric evaluation for psychotropic medications and monitor client for side effects of the medication.
2. Client will identify causes of anxious feelings.	Assign the client homework assignments to identify cognitive distortions that are causing anxiety.
	Psychotherapy to address client's cognitive distortions.
3. Client will identify how worries are irrational.	Psychotherapy to assist client in developing an awareness of the irrational nature of fears.

4. Client will utilize thought-stopping techniques to prevent anxiety.	Teach client thought-stopping techniques to prevent anxiety-producing thoughts.
5. Client will decrease level of anxiety by increasing positive self-talk.	Cognitive therapy to assist the client in developing more realistic thoughts that will increase self-confidence in coping with anxiety.
6. Client will identify alternative, more positive views of reality that oppose the anxiety-producing view.	Reframe the client's fears and anxieties by suggesting another way of looking at them and helping the client to broaden his or her perspective.
7. Client will develop a relaxation and regular exercise program to decrease anxiety level.	Teach client the technique of guided imagery. Encourage regular exercise as a means of reducing anxiety.

TREATMENT PLAN

POSTTRAUMATIC STRESS DISORDER (PTSD)

Definition: The development of fear, helplessness, or horror in response to an event, including actual life-threatening events or threatened death for self and others, the witnessing of an event involving the death or threat of harm to another, or learning of the death or threat of injury to a family member or friend.

Signs and Symptoms to Note in the Record:

- Persistent reexperiencing of the traumatic event—flashbacks.
- Continuous avoidance of persons, places, and things, emotions, and feelings associated with the traumatic event.
- Physiological response when exposed to stimuli associated with traumatic event.
- Difficulty sleeping and possible nightmares.
- Difficulty concentrating.
- Angry outbursts.

Goals:

1. Client will return to level of functioning prior to traumatic event.
2. Client will learn and utilize coping skills to assist in maintaining close relationships.
3. Client will be able to cognitively reexperience the traumatic event without a physiological response.
4. Client will exhibit acceptance of the traumatic event.

Objectives	Interventions
1. Client will identify ways in which PTSD has impaired occupational or social functioning.	Explore in individual therapy the limiting effects PTSD has had on intimate relationships, work, and recreational activities.
2. Client will describe traumatic event in detail.	Therapist will assist client in safely recalling details of the traumatic event utilizing eye movement desensitization and reprocessing.
3. Client will utilize relaxation and anger management techniques to help cope with PTSD.	Client will learn and implement imagery and deep muscle relaxation, positive self-talk, and/or deep breathing techniques in coping with physiological effects of PTSD.
4. Client will increase ability to talk about traumatic event while decreasing physiological or emotional response.	Client will engage in repeated retelling of the story of the traumatic event in order to gradually increase ability to verbalize the traumatic event in individual therapy session.
5. Client will confront physical stimuli associated with event while remaining calm.	Use of systematic desensitization to reduce emotional and physiological reactions to mentally picturing the traumatic event and physical aspects of it.
6. Client will interact with others experiencing PTSD and develop supportive network.	Refer client to a PTSD support group.

TREATMENT PLAN

MAJOR DEPRESSIVE DISORDER, RECURRENT

Definition: Major depressive disorder is characterized by one or more major depressive episodes. These episodes last for a period of at least 2 weeks and are characterized by depressed mood and/or a loss of interest or pleasure in most activities.

Signs and Symptoms to Note in the Record:

- Depressed mood for most of the day nearly every day.
- Markedly diminished interest or pleasure in all or most activities.
- Changes in appetite: eating too little or too much.
- Insomnia or hypersomnia.
- Psychomotor agitation.
- Fatigue or loss of energy.
- Feelings of worthlessness or excessive guilt.
- Difficulty with concentrating.
- Suicidal thoughts.

Goals:

1. Lessen depressed mood and return to an effective level of functioning.
2. Develop the ability to recognize and cope with feelings of depression.
3. Develop healthier cognitive patterns and more positive beliefs about self and the future.
4. Reduce suicidal thoughts.

Objectives	Interventions
1. Client will identify the source of depressed mood.	Ask client to make a list of what is causing the depression and process this list in psychotherapy.
2. Client will identify any dysfunctional self-talk that is perpetuating the depression and replace those negative thoughts with more positive and realistic self-talk.	Ask client to keep a daily record of dysfunctional thoughts. Challenge each of the client's negative thoughts through cognitive therapy.
3. Client will verbalize more positive, hopeful statements about the future.	Ask client to write at least one positive statement daily about self and the future and discuss them in psychotherapy
4. Client will engage in regular exercise and/or meditation.	Assist the client in developing an exercise routine, and teach the client meditation and/or relaxation techniques.
5. Client will reduce suicidal ideation.	Assess and monitor client for suicide ideation, and arrange for hospitalization when client is judged to be a threat to self.
6. Client will take medication as prescribed by psychiatrist	Monitor client's medications for compliance and report effectiveness and side effects to the client's psychiatrist.

TREATMENT PLAN

BIPOLAR I DISORDER, MOST RECENT EPISODE MANIC

Definition: Bipolar I disorder, most recent episode manic, is characterized by the presence of a manic episode. There has previously been at least one major depressive episode, manic episode or mixed episode, but the client is currently in a manic episode. A manic episode consists of a period of elevated, expansive, and irritable mood that lasts at least 1 week.

Signs and Symptoms to Note in the Record:

- Inflated self-esteem or grandiosity.
- Decreased need for sleep.
- Pressured speech.
- Flight of ideas or racing thoughts.
- Distractibility.
- Psychomotor agitation.
- Excessive involvement in pleasurable activities that may have harmful consequences, such as sexual promiscuity or impulse buying.

Goals:

1. Reduce uncontrollable energy, return to a normal activity level, and increase good judgment.
2. Reduce agitation, impulsive behaviors, and pressured speech, and increase sensitivity to consequences of behaviors.
3. Cope with underlying feelings of low self-esteem and fears of rejection or abandonment.
4. Increase controlled behavior, achieve a more stable mood, and develop more deliberate speech and thought processes.

Objectives	Interventions
1. Client will cooperate with a psychiatric evaluation and take medications as prescribed.	Arrange for a psychiatric evaluation for psychotropic medications and monitor client's reaction to the medication.
2. Client will reduce impulsive behaviors.	Psychotherapy to address consequences of behaviors.
3. Client will decrease grandiosity and express self more realistically.	Confront the client's grandiosity through psychotherapy and reinforce more realistic self-statements.
4. Client will be able to sit calmly for 30 minutes without agitation or distractibility.	Reinforce client's increased control over hyperactivity and help client set attainable goals and limits on agitation and distractibility.
5. Client will speak more slowly and maintain focus on one subject at a time.	Provide structure for client's thought processes and actions by directing the course of conversation and developing plans for client's behaviors.
6. Client will acknowledge the low self-esteem and fear of rejection that underlies grandiosity.	Psychotherapy to explore the psychosocial stressors that are precipitating client's manic behaviors, such as rejection by peers or past traumas.

TREATMENT PLAN

SCHIZOPHRENIA (PARANOID TYPE)

Definition: Schizophrenia of the paranoid type is characterized by delusions and auditory hallucinations. The delusions are primarily persecutory and grandiose, and the hallucinations are usually related to the theme present in the delusions.

Signs and Symptoms to Note in the Record:

- Delusions and auditory hallucinations, which are typically persecutory and/or grandiose.
- The individual typically has a patronizing and superior manner toward others, and interactions with others are either extremely formal or intense.
- Suicidal ideation as a result of the persecutory delusions.
- Anger that may result in violence toward others.
- Extreme distrust of others without sufficient basis.
- A pattern of suspiciousness toward others without reason.
- Expectation of being harmed by others.

Goals:

1. Maintain proper medication treatment for delusions and hallucinations.
2. Demonstrate more trust of others by verbalizing positive beliefs and attitudes about them.
3. Interact with others without defensiveness and/or anger.
4. Reduce suspiciousness about others by interacting with others in a more trusting, open, and relaxed manner.

Objectives	Interventions
1. Client will take medication as prescribed.	Monitor client's medications for compliance and report effectiveness and side effects to client's psychiatrist.
2. Client will identify those individuals the client distrusts and *why*.	Assist client in exploring the nature of the paranoia.
3. Client will examine the belief that others are untrustworthy.	Review client's social interactions and explore distorted beliefs directed at others.
	Encourage client to assess the distorted perceptions by verifying those conclusions with others.
4. Client will decrease accusations against others based on the belief that they will cause harm.	Provide alternative explanations for others' behaviors besides planning to bring harm to client.
	Use role playing to increase client's empathy for others.
5. Client will increase interaction with others without expression of mistrust, fear, or suspicion.	Refer client to a support group for people suffering from schizophrenia.

TREATMENT PLAN

BULIMIA NERVOSA (PURGING TYPE)

Definition: The main features of bulimia nervosa are binge eating and purging behaviors that are used as a means of preventing weight gain.

Signs and Symptoms to Note in the Record:

- Consumption of large quantities of food at one time.
- Self-induced vomiting, abuse of laxatives, or excessive exercise to prevent weight gain.
- Preoccupation with body image and body size.
- Fear of becoming overweight.
- Electrolyte imbalance and dental problems resulting from the eating disorder.

Goals:

1. Stop the pattern of binge eating and purging behavior.
2. Restore a more healthy eating pattern with appropriate nutrition to maintain a healthy weight.
3. Develop understanding of cognitive and emotional struggles that have resulted in the eating disorder, and develop alternative coping strategies.
4. Change the perception of self so that it does not focus on body weight or size as the primary means of self-acceptance.

Objectives	Interventions
1. Client will cooperate with a complete physical exam and dental exam.	Refer client to physician for a physical exam and to dentist for a dental exam.
2. Client will keep a food journal of food consumption and any methods used to control gaining weight.	Discuss with client the dysfunctional eating patterns that may have resulted in physical problems.
	Monitor client's bingeing and purging behaviors, develop a nutritional eating plan, and positively reinforce healthy eating patterns.
3. Client will identify the relationship among low self-esteem, a drive for perfectionism, a fear of failure, and the eating disorder.	Assist client in exploring how a drive for perfectionism and a need for control led to the eating disorder.
	Encourage client to identify positive qualities, and positively reinforce all of client's accomplishments.
4. Client will develop alternative coping strategies for dealing with the underlying emotional issues.	Assist client to develop assertive behaviors that will allow healthful expression of emotions. Refer client to an eating disorder support group.
5. Client will state a basis for identity that is not based on body weight or size but on personal character, values, or personality traits.	Assist client to identify a basis for self-worth that is not based on body size by assessing his or her talents, positive traits, and importance to significant others in life, such as family and friends.

References

Abramowitz, A. J. (2009, November 1). *Dulcan's Textbook of Child and Adolescent Psychiatry*. (M. K. Dulcan, Ed.). Retrieved November 1, 2009, from PsychiatryOnline .com: http://www.psychiatryonline.com

Abramowitz, J. S., Whiteside, S., Lynam, D., & Kalsy, S. (2003). Is thought-action fusion specific to obsessive-compulsive disorder?: A mediating role of negative affect. *Behaviour Research and Therapy*, 1069–1079.

Adams, G., Turner, H., & Bucks, R. (2005). The experience of body dissatisfaction in men. *Body Image*, *2*, 271–283.

Adler, G. (2007). Intervention approaches to driving with dementia. *Health and Social Work*, *32*(1), 75–79.

Adler, L. A., Spencer, T., Brown, T. E., Holdnack, J., Saylor, K., Schuh, K., et al. (2009). Once-daily atomoxetine for adult attention-deficit/hyperactivity disorder: A 6-month, double-blind trial. *Journal of Clinical Psychopharmacology*, *29*(1), 44–50.

Ahn, W., & Kim, N. S. (2008). Causal theories of mental disorder concepts. *Psychological Science Agenda*, *22*(6), 3–8.

Alegria, M., Shrout, P. E., Woo, M., Guarnaccia, P., Sribney, W., Vila, D., et al. (2007). Understanding differences in past year psychiatric disorders for Latinos living in the US. *Social Science and Medicine*, *65*, 214–230.

Alexander, B. (1993). Disorders of sexual desire: Diagnosis and treatment of decreased libido. *American Family Physician*, *47*, 832–838; discussion *49*, 758.

Allen, K., Byrne, S., Forbes, D., & Oddy, W. (2009). Risk factor for full and partial-syndrome early adolescent eating disorders: A population-based pregnancy cohort study. *Journal of the American Academy of Child & Adolescent Psychiatry*, *48*(8), 800–809.

Alperin, R. M. (1994). Managed care versus psychoanalytic psychotherapy: Conflicting ideologies. *Clinical Social Work Journal*, *22*(2), 137–148.

Altschule, M. D., Bigelow, L. B., Bliss, E. L., Cancro, R., Cohen, G., Kety, S., et al. (1976). The genetics of schizophrenia. In S. Wolf (Ed.), *The biology of the schizophrenic process*. (pp. 58–80). New York: Plenum Press.

American College of Physicians. (2006). NutritiChecklist for Older Adults: DETERMINE Mnemonic. Retrieved October 21, 2009, from American College of Physicians: http://www.acponline.org/acp_press/essentials/cdim_ch36_wed03.pdf

American Psychiatric Association. (1952). *Diagnostic and statistical manual of mental disorders*. Washington, DC: Author.

American Psychiatric Association. (1980). *Diagnostic and statistical manual of mental disorders* (3rd ed.). Washington, DC: Author.

American Psychiatric Association. (1987). *Diagnostic and statistical manual of mental disorders* (3rd ed., rev.). Washington, DC: Author.

American Psychiatric Association. (1994). *Diagnostic and statistical manual of mental disorders* (4th ed.). Washington, DC: Author.

American Psychiatric Association. (1995). *Diagnostic and statistical manual of mental disorders* (4th ed., rev). Washington, DC: Author.

American Psychiatric Association. (2000). *Diagnostic and statistical manual of mental disorders* (4th ed., text rev.). Washington, DC: American Psychiatric Press.

American Psychiatric Association. (2004). Practice guidelines for the treatment of patients with schizophrenia (2nd ed.). *American Journal of Psychiatry*, *161*, 1–56.

Amin, S., Kuhle, C., & Fitzpatrick, L. (2003). Comprehensive evaluation of the older woman. *Mayo Clinic Proceedings*, *78*(9), 1157–1185.

Anastopoulos, A. D. (1999). Attention-deficit/hyperactivity disorder. In S. D. Netherton, D. Holmes, & E. C. Walker (Eds.), *Child adolescent psychological disorders: A comprehensive textbook* (pp. 98–117). New York: Oxford University Press.

Andersen, B. L. (1983). Primary orgasmic dysfunction: Diagnostic considerations and review of treatment. *Psychological Bulletin, 93*(1), 105–136.

Anderson, D. F., Berlant, J. L., Mauch, D., & Maloney, W. R. (1997). Managed behavioral health care services. In P. R. Kongstvedt (Ed.), *Essentials of managed care* (pp. 248–273). Gaithersburg, MD: Aspen.

Andersson, G. (2009). Using the Internet to provide cognitive behavior therapy. *Behaviour Research and Therapy, 47*, 175–180.

Antonovsky, A., & Sourani, T. (1988). Family sense of coherence and family adaption. *Journal of Marriage and Family, 50*, 79–92.

APA Online. (2001a). Practice coding. Retrieved from http://www.apa.org/practice/medcoding.html

APA Online. (2001b). Practice coding. Retrieved from http://www.apa.org/practice/medbilling.html

Armenteros, J. L. (1997). Risperidone in adolescents with schizophrenia: An open pilot study. *Journal of the American Academy of Child and Adolescent Psychiatry, 36*, 694–697.

Aronson, E. (2008). *The social animal* (10th ed.). New York: Worth Publishers.

Arredondo, P. (1998, July). Integrating multicultural counseling competencies and universal helping conditions in culture-specific contexts (Reconceptualizing multicultural counseling). *Counseling Psychologist, 26*(4), 592–602.

Attia, E., Haiman, C., Walsh, B., Flater, S. R. (1998). Does fluoxetine augment the inpatient treatment of anorexia nervosa? *American Journal of Psychiatry, 155*, 548–551.

Attia, E., & Roberto, C. A. (2009). Should amenorrhea be a diagnostic criterion for anorexia nervosa? *International Journal of Eating Disorders, 42*(7), 581–589.

Auchus, A. (2008, September). *Agnosia.* Retrieved October 14, 2009, from The Merck Manuals Online Medical Library: http://www.merck.com/mmpe/sec16/ch210/ch210b.html

August, G. J., Realmuto, G. M., Hektner, J. M., & Bloomquist, M. L. (2001). An integrated components preventive intervention for aggressive elementary school children: The Early Risers program. *Journal of Consulting and Clinical Psychology, 69*, 614–626.

Austrian, S. G. (2005). *Mental disorders, medications, and clinical social work* (3rd ed.). New York: Columbia University Press.

Axelson, D., Birmaher, B., Strober, M., Gill, M. K., Valeri, S., Chiappetta, L., et al. (2006). Phenomenology of children and adolescents with bipolar spectrum disorders. *Archives of General Psychiatry, 63*, 1139–1148.

Ayuso-Gutierrez, J. L., & del Rio Vega, J. M. (1997). Factors influencing relapse in the long term course of schizophrenia. *Schizophrenia Research, 28*, 199–206.

Bacon, C. G., Mittleman, M. A., Kawachi, I., Glovannucci, E., Glasser, D. B., & Rimm, E. R. (2003). Sexual function in men older than 50 years of age: Results from the health professionals follow-up study. *Annual of Internal Medicine, 139*, 161–168.

Badger, L. W., & Rand, E. H. (1998). Mood disorder. In J. B. W. Williams & K. Ell (Eds.), *Mental health research: Implications for practice* (pp. 49–117). Washington, DC: National Association of Social Workers Press.

Baggerly, J. (2009). Play therapy research: History and current empirical support. In A. A. Drewes (Ed.), *Blending play therapy with cognitive behavioral therapy: Evidence-Based and other effective treatments and techniques* (pp. 97–115). Hoboken, NJ: Wiley.

Baldessarini, R. J., Perry, R., & Pike, J. (2007). Factors associated with treatment non-adherence among U.S. bipolar disorder patients. *Human Psychopharmacology Clinical Experience, 23*, 95–105.

Baldwin, R. L., Chelonis, J. J., Flake, R. A., Edwards, M. C., Field, C. R., Meaux, J. B., et al.(2004). Effect of methylphenidate on time perception in children with attention-deficit/hyperactivity disorder. *Experimental and Clinical Psychopharmacology, 12*(1), 57–64.

Ballenger, J. C., Davidson, J. R., Lecrubier, Y., Nutt, D. J., Borkovec, T. D., Rickels, K., et al. (2001). Consensus statement generalized anxiety disorder from the international consensus group on depression and anxiety. *Journal of Clinical Psychiatry, 62*(Suppl. 11), 53–58.

Barbach, L. (1980). *Women discover orgasm: A therapist's guide to a new treatment approach.* New York: Macmillan.

Barbarich, N. C., McConaha, C., Halmi, K. A., Gendall, K., Sunday, S. R, Gaskill, J., et al. (2004). Use of nutritional supplements to increase the efficacy of fluoxetine in the treatment of anorexia nervosa. *International Journal of Eating Disorders, 35*(1), 10–15.

Barker, R. L. (2003). *The social work dictionary* (5th ed.). Washington, DC: NASW Press.

Barkley, R. A. (2006). *Attention-deficit hyperactivity disorder: A handbook for diagnosis and treatment* (3rd ed.). New York: Guilford Press.

Barlow, D. H. (1986). Causes of sexual dysfunction: The role of anxiety and cognitive interference. *Journal of Consulting and Clinical Psychology, 54,* 140–148.

Barna, M. M., Patel, R., & Patel, M. (2008). Female sexual dysfunction: From causality to cure. *U.S. Pharmacist, 33*(11). Retrieved March 5, 2010, http://www .uspharmacist.com/content/d/feature/c/11464.

Baron, M., Gruen, R., Rainer, J. D., Kane, J., Asnis, L., & Lord, A. A. (1985). A family study of schizophrenia and normal control probands: Implication for the spectrum concept of schizophrenia. *American Journal of Psychiatry, 142*(4), 447–455.

Baroni, A., Lungsford, J. R., Luckenbaugh, D. A., Towbin, K. E., & Leibenluft, E. (2009). Practitioner review: The assessment of bipolar disorder in children and adolescents. *Journal of Child Psychology and Psychiatry, 50*(3), 203–215.

Barrera, M. Jr., Biglan, A., Taylor, T. K., Gunn, B. K., Smolkowski, K., Black, C., et al. (2002). Early elementary school intervention to reduce conduct problems: A randomized trial for Hispanic and non-Hispanic children. *Prevention Research, 3*(2), 83–94.

Basco, M. R., Ladd, G., Myers, D. S., & Tyler, D. (2007). Combining medication treatment and cognitive-behavior therapy for bipolar disorder. *Journal of Cognitive Psychotherapy: An International Quarterly, 21*(1), 7–15.

Bateman, A., & Fonagy, P. (1999). Effectiveness of partial hospitalization in the treatment of borderline personality disorder: A randomized controlled trial. *American Journal of Psychiatry, 156*(10), 1563–1569.

Bateman, A. W., Ryle, A., Fonagy, P., & Kerr, I. B. (2007). Psychotherapy for borderline personality disorder: Mentalization-based therapy and cognitive analytic therapy compared. *International Review of Psychiatry, 19*(1), 51–62.

Beauchaine, T. P., & Hinshaw, S. P. (Eds.). (2008). *Child and adolescent psychopathology.* Hoboken, NJ: Wiley.

Beauchaine, T. P., Hinshaw, S. P., & Gatzke-Kopp, L. (2008). Genetic and environmental influences on behavior. In T. P. Beauchaine & S. P. Hinshaw (Eds.), *Child and adolescent psychopathology* (pp. 58–90). Hoboken, NJ: Wiley.

Bechara, A., et al. (2003). Duplex Doppler ultrasound assessment of clitorial hemodynamics after topical administration of Alprostadil in women with arousal and orgasmic disorders. *Journal of Sex & Marital Therapy, 29*(Suppl. 1), 1–10.

Beck, A. T., Freeman, A., & Associates. (1990). *Cognitive therapy of personality disorders.* New York: Guilford Press.

Becker, A. E., Eddy, K. T., & Perloe, A. (2009). Clarifying criteria for cognitive signs and symptoms for eating disorders in *DSM-V. International Journal of Eating Disorders, 42*(7), 611–619.

Berghuis, D. J., & Jongsma, A. E. (2008a). *The severe and persistent mental illness: Treatment planner* (2nd ed.). Hoboken, NJ: Wiley.

Berghuis, D. J., & Jongsma, A. E. (2008b). *The severe and persistent mental illness: Progress notes planner* (2nd ed.). Hoboken, NJ: Wiley.

Bergstrom, R., Neighbors, C., & Malheim, J. (2009). Media comparisons and threats to body image: Seeking evidence of self-affirmation. *Journal of Social and Clinical Psychology, 28*(2), 264–280.

Bernstein, B. E., & Hartsell, T. L. (2004). *The portable lawyer for mental health professionals* (2nd ed.). Hoboken, NJ: Wiley.

Bettmann, J. E. (2006). Using attachment theory to understand the treatment of adult depression. *Clinical Social Work Journal, 34*(4), 531–542.

Bieberich, A., & Morgan, S. (2004). Self-regulation and affective expression during play in children with autism or Down syndrome: A short-term longitudinal study. *Journal of Autism and Developmental Disorders, 34*(4), 439–448.

Biederman, J. (2003). New-generation long-acting stimulants for the treatment of attention-deficit hyperactivity disorder. *Medscape, Psychiatry, and Mental Health.* Retrieved June 15, 2009, from http://www .medscape.com/viewarticle/464377.

Biederman, J., Mick, E., Faraone, S. V., Braaten, E., Doyle, A., Spencer, T., et al. (2002). Influence of gender on attention deficit hyperactivity disorder in children referred to a psychiatric clinic. *American Journal of Psychiatry, 159,* 36–42.

Birnbaum, G. E. (2003). The meaning of heterosexual intercourse among women with female orgasmic disorder. *Archives of Sexual Behavior, 32*(1), 61–71.

Bishara, D., & Taylor, D. (2009). Asenapine monotherapy in the acute treatment of both schizophrenia and bipolar I disorder. *Neuropsychiatric Disease and Treatment, 5,* 483–490.

Black, D. (2006). What causes antisocial personality disorder? Retrieved November 24, 2009, from http://www.psychcentral.com/lib/2006/what-causes-antisocial-personality-disorder/.

Bloom, B. L. (1992). *Planned short-term psychotherapy: A clinical handbook*. Boston: Allyn & Bacon.

Bloom, M., Fischer, J., & Orme, J. G. (2009). *Evaluating practice: Guidelines for the accountable professional* (6th ed.). Boston: Allyn & Bacon.

Bogat, A. G., Hamernik, K., & Brooks, L. A. (1987). The influence of self-efficacy: Expectations on the treatment of preorgasmic women. *Journal of Sex & Marital Therapy, 13*, 128–136.

Boggs, C. D., Morey, L. C., Skodol, A. E., Shea, M. T., Sanislow, C. A., Grilo, C. M., et al. (2005). Differential impairment as an indicator of sex bias in DSM-IV criteria for four personality disorders. *Psychological Assessment, 17*, 492–496.

Bohus, M., Landwehrmeyer, M., Stiglmayr, C., Limberger, M., Bohme, R., & Schmahl, C. (1999). Naltrexone in the treatment of dissociative symptoms in patients with borderline personality disorder: An open-label trial. *Journal of Clinical Psychiatry, 60*, 598–603.

Bola, J. R. (2006). Psychosocial acute treatment in early-episode schizophrenia disorders. *Research on Social Work Practice, 16*(3), 263–275.

Bola, J. R., & Mosher, L. R. (2002). Predicting drug-free treatment response in acute psychosis from the Soteria Project. *Schizophrenia Bulletin, 38*, 559–575.

Bola, J. R., & Mosher, L. R. (2003). Treatment of acute psychosis without narcoleptics. Two-year outcomes from the Soteria Project. *Journal of Nervous and Mental Disease, 191*, 219–229.

Bonn, D. (1999). New treatments for alcohol dependency better than old (News). *Lancet, 353*(9148), 213.

Borello-France, D., et al. (2004). Bladder and sexual function among women with multiple sclerosis. *Multiple Sclerosis, 10*(4), 455–461.

Boroughs, M., & Thompson, J. K. (2002). Exercise status and sexual orientation as moderators of body image disturbance and eating disorders in males. *International Journal of Eating Disorders, 31*, 301–311.

Boyd-Franklin, N. (1989). *Black families in therapy*. New York: Guilford Press.

Bradley, E., Webster, T. R., Baker, D., Shlesinger, M., Inouye, S. K., Barth, M., et al. (2004). Translating research into practice: Speeding the adoption of innovative health care programs. *Commonwealth Fund*, no. 724, 1–12.

Braithwaite, K., Duff, J., & Westworth, I. (1999). *Conduct disorder in children and adolescents*. Behavioural Neurotherapy Clinic. Available from http://www.adhd.com.au/conduct.html

Brandell, J. R. (2004). *Psychodynamic social work*. New York: Columbia University Press.

Brasher, K. L. (2009). Solution-focused brief therapy: Overview and implications for school counselors. *Alabama Counseling Association Journal, 34*(2), 20–30.

Braun, S. A., & Cox, J. A. (2005). Managed mental health care: Intentional misdiagnosis of mental disorders. *Journal of Counseling and Development, 83*, 425–433.

Breggin, P. (2006). Intoxication anosognosia: The spellbinding effect of psychiatric drugs. *Ethical Human Psychology and Psychiatry, 8*, 201–215.

Brekke, J. S., & Barrio, C. (1997). Cross-ethnic symptom differences in schizophrenia: The influence of culture and minority status. *Schizophrenia Bulletin, 23*(2), 305–316.

Brendel, D. H. (2001). Multifactorial causation of mental disorders: A proposal to improve the *DSM. Harvard Review of Psychiatry, 9*(1), 42–45.

Breslau, J., Aguilar-Gaxiola, S., Borges, G., Castilla-Puentes, R. C., Kendler, K. S., Medina-Mora, M., et al. (2007). Mental disorders among English-speaking Mexican immigrants to the US compared to a national sample of Mexicans. *Psychiatry Research, 151*(1–2), 115–122.

Briggs-Gowan, M. J., Carter, A. S., Bosson-Heenan, J., Guyer, A. E., & Horwitz, S. M. (2006). Are infant-toddler social-emotional and behavioral problems transient? *Journal of the American Academy of Child and Adolescent Psychiatry, 45*(7), 849–858.

Bromfield, R. (2007). *Doing child & adolescent psychotherapy: Adapting psychodynamic treatment to contemporary practice* (2nd ed.). Hoboken, NJ: Wiley.

Brophy, J. J. (1991). Psychiatric disorders. In S. A. Schroeder, M. A. Krupp, L. M. Tierney, & S. J. McPhee (Eds.), *Current medical diagnosis and treatment* (pp. 731–786). Norwalk, CT: Appleton & Lange.

Brower, A. M., & Nurius, P. S. (1993). *Social cognitions and individual change: Current theory and counseling guidelines*. Newbury Park, CA: Sage.

Brown, K. W., McGoldrick, T., & Buchanan, R. (1997). Body dysmorphic disorder: Seven cases treated with eye movement desensitization and reprocessing. *Behavioural and Cognitive Psychotherapy, 25*, 203–207.

Browning, C. H., & Browning, B. J. (1996). *How to partner with managed care: A "do it yourself kit" for building working relationships and getting steady referrals*. New York: Wiley.

Bruner, J. (1991). *Acts of meaning*. Cambridge, MA: Harvard University Press.

Brunk, M. (1999). *Effective treatment of conduct disorder.* Juvenile Forensic Evaluation Resource Center. Available from http://www.ness.sys.virginia.edu

Bryant, R. A., Moulds, M., Guthrie, R., & Nixon, R. D. (2003). Treating acute stress disorder following mild traumatic brain injury. *American Journal of Psychiatry, 160,* 585–587.

Brzustowicz, L., Hodgkinson, K., Chow, E., Honer, W., & Bassett, A. (2000, April 28). Location of major susceptibility locus for familial schizophrenia on chromosome 1g21-q22. *Science, 288,* 682–687.

Budman, S., & Gurman, A. (1988). *Theory and practice of brief therapy.* New York: Guilford Press.

Burck, C., & Speed, B. (1995). Introduction. In C. Burck & B. Speed (Eds.), *Gender power and relationships* (pp. 1–6). New York: Routledge.

Bureau of Labor Statistics, U. S. Department of Labor. (Last updated April 14, 2007).*Occupational Outlook Handbook, Social Workers, 2008–2009 ed.* Retrieved September 19, 2009, from: http://www.bls.gov/oco/ocos060.htm

Burgess, V., Dziegielewski, S. F., & Green, C. E. (2005). Improving comfort about sex communication between parents and their adolescents: Practice-based research within a teen sexuality group. *Brief Treatment and Crisis Intervention, 5*(4), 379–390.

Burke, C. K., Burke, J. D., Reiger, D. A., & Rae, D. (1990). Age at onset of selected mental disorders in five community populations. *Archives of General Psychiatry, 47,* 511–518.

Burner, S. T., Waldo, D. R., & McKusick, D. R. (1992). National health expenditures projections through 2030. *Health Care Financing Review, 14*(1), 1–29.

Burns, T., & Lloyd, H. (2004). Is a team approach based on staff meetings cost-effective in the delivery of mental health care? *Current Opinion in Psychiatry, 17*(4), 311–314.

Byely, L., Archibald, A. B., Graber, J., & Brookes-Dunn, J. (2000). A prospective study of familial and social influences on girls' body image and dieting. *International Journal of Eating Disorders, 28,* 155–164.

Caird, W. (1988). The modification of urinary urgency during sexual arousal. *Journal of Sex Research, 24,* 183–187.

Caligar, E. (2006). Personality disorders: Psychodynamic treatments. *Psychiatric Times, 23*(8), *12,* 17–18.

Calton, T., & Spandler, H. (2009). Minimal-medication approaches to treating schizophrenia. *Advances in Psychiatric Treatment, 15,* 209–217.

Campbell, J. A., Essex, E. L., & Held, G. (1994). Issues in chemical dependency treatment and aftercare for people with learning differences. *Health & Social Work, 19*(1), 63–70.

Canino, G., & Alegria, M. (2008). Psychiatric diagnosis—Is it universal or relative to culture? *Journal of Child Psychology and Psychiatry, 49*(3), 237–250.

Canino, I., & Spurlock, J. (1994). *Culturally diverse children and adolescents: Assessment, diagnosis, and treatment.* New York: Guilford Press.

Capriotti, T. (2006). Update on depression and antidepressant medications. *MEDSURG Nursing, 15*(4), 241–246.

Card, J. J., & Benner, T. (Eds.). (2008a). *Adolescent sexual health education: An activity source book.* New York: Springer.

Card, J. J., & Benner, T. (Eds.). (2008b). *Models programs for adolescent sexual health: Evidence-based HIV, STI, and pregnancy prevention interventions.* New York: Springer.

Carlson, G. A. (1998). Mania and ADHD: Comorbidity or confusion. *Journal of Affective Disorders, 51,* 177–187.

Carlton, T. O. (1984). *Clinical social work in health care settings: A guide to professional practice with exemplars.* New York: Springer.

Carlton, T. O. (1989). Classification and diagnosis in social work in health care. *Health and Social Work, 14*(2), 83–85.

Carpenter, J., Schneider, J., Brandon, T., & Wooff, D. (2003). Working in multidisciplinary community mental health teams: The impact on social workers and health professionals of integrated mental health care. *British Journal of Social Work, 33*(8), 1081–1193.

Carpenter, W. T., Conley, R. R., & Buchanan, R. W. (1998). Schizophrenia. In S. J. Enna & J. T. Coyle (Eds.), *Pharmacological management of neurological and psychiatric disorders.* (pp. 27–52). New York: McGraw-Hill.

Carroll, J. (2009). Concerns about aspects of harm reduction and the overselling of evidence-based practices in the treatment of alcohol/other drug problems. *Alcoholism Treatment Quarterly, 27*(3), 329–337.

Casas, J. M. (1984). Policy, training, and research in counseling psychology: The racial/ethnic minority perspective. In S. D. Brown & R. W. Lent (Eds.), *Handbook of counseling psychology* (pp. 785–831). New York: Wiley.

Case, L. P., & Lingerfelt, N. B. (1974). Name-calling: The labeling process in the social work interview. *Social Service Review, 48,* 75–86.

Cash, T. F. (1996). Treatment of body image disturbances. In J. K. Thompson (Ed.), *Body image, eating disorders and obesity* (pp. 83–107). Washington, DC: American Psychological Association.

Cassano, G. B., Pini, S., Saettoni, M., & Dell'Osso, L. (1999). Multiple anxiety disorder comorbidity with patients with mood spectrum disorders with psychotic features. *American Journal of Psychiatry, 156,* 474–476.

Center for Psychological Studies. (2008). *Beck Depression Inventory Scale.* Retrieved October 24, 2009, from Nova Southeastern University: http://www.cps.nova.edu/~cpphelp/BDI.html

Chambless, D. L., et al. (1982). The pubococcygens and female orgasm: A correlational study with normal subjects. *Archives of Sexual Behavior, 11*(6), 479–490.

Chambless, D. L., Sultan, F. E., & Stern, T. E. (1984). Effect of pubococcygeal exercise on coital orgasm in women. *Journal of Consulting and Clinical Psychology, 52,* 114–118.

Chambliss, C. H. (2000). *Psychotherapy and managed care: Reconciling research and reality.* Boston: Allyn & Bacon.

Chang-Muy, F., & Congress, E. P. (Eds.). (2009). *Social work with immigrants and refugees: Legal issues, clinical skills, and advocacy.* New York: Springer.

Chapman, D., & Toseland, R. (2007). Effectiveness of advanced illness care teams for nursing home residents with dementia. *Social Work, 52*(4), 321–329.

Charuvastra, A., & Cloitre, M. (2008). Social bonds and posttraumatic stress disorder. *Annual Review of Psychology, 59,* 301–328.

Cheisa, M., & Fonagy, P. (1999). Cassel personality disorder study methodology and treatment effects. *British Journal of Psychiatry, 176,* 485–491.

Chen, S. (1997). *Measurement and analysis in psychosocial research.* Brookfield, VT: Ashgate.

Chengappa, K., Elbeling, T., Kang, J., Levine, J., & Parepally, H. (1999). Clozapine reduces severe self-mutilation and aggression in psychotic patients with borderline personality disorder. *Journal of Clinical Psychiatry, 60,* 477–484.

Cheung, A. H., Emslie, G. J., & Mayes, T. L. (2006). The use of antidepressant to treat depression in children and adolescents. *Canadian Medial Association Journal, 174*(2), 193–200.

Chopra, D. (1994). *Alternative medicine: The definitive guide.* Fife, WA: Future Medicine.

Cicchetti, D. (2008). A multiple-levels-of-analysis perspective on research in development and psychopathology. In T. P. Beauchaine & S. P. Hinshaw (Eds.), *Child and adolescent psychopathology* (pp. 27–57). Hoboken, NJ: Wiley.

Ciminero, A. R., Calhoun, K. S., & Adams, H. E. (1986). *Handbook of behavioral assessment* (2nd ed.). New York: Wiley.

Ciompi, L., & Hoffman, H. (2004). Soteria Berne. An innovative milieu therapeutic approach to acute schizophrenia based on the concept of affect-logic. *World Psychiatry, 3,* 140–146.

Clark, A. F. (2006). Schizophrenia and schizophrenia-like disorders. In C. Gillberg, R. Harrington, & C. Steinhausen (Eds.). *A Clinicians Handbook of Child and Adolescent Psychiatry* (pp. 79–110). New York: Cambridge University Press.

Cohen, A., Patel, V., Thara, R., & Gureje, O. (2008). Questioning an axiom: Better prognosis for schizophrenia in the developing world? *Schizophrenia Bulletin, 34*(2), 229–244.

Colby, I., & Dziegielewski, S. F. (2010). *Introduction to social work: The people's profession* (3rd ed.). Chicago: Lyceum Books.

Collins, E. (1991). Body figure perceptions and preferences among preadolescent children. *International Journal of Eating Disorders, 10,* 199–208.

Colom, F., et al. (2005). Stabilizing the stabilizer: Group psychoeducation enhances the stability of serum lithium levels. *Bipolar Disorders, 7*(5), 32–36.

Colvert, E., et al. (2008). Do theory of mind and executive function deficits underlie the adverse outcomes association with profound deprivations?: Findings from the English and Romanian adoptees study. *Journal of Abnormal Child Psychology, 36*(7), 1057–1068.

Community Care. (2006). Do personality disorders exist? *Community Care, 26*(1), 28–29.

Concian, F. M. (1991). Feminist science: Methodologies that challenge inequality. *Gender and Society, 6*(4), 623–642.

Cone, J. D. (1998). Psychometric considerations: Concepts, contents and methods. In A. S. Bellack & M. Hersen (Eds.), *Behavioral assessment: A practical handbook* (4th ed., pp. 22–46). Boston: Allyn & Bacon.

Congress, E. (1997). *Multicultural perspectives in working with families.* New York: Springer.

Congress, E. (2008). Assessment of adults. In K. M. Sowers & C. N. Dulmus (Series Eds.) & W. Rowe & L. A. Rapp-Paglicci (Vol. Eds.), *Comprehensive handbook of social work and social welfare: Vol. 3. Social work practice* (pp. 310–325). Hoboken, NJ: Wiley.

Conte, H. R. (1986). Multivariate assessment of sexual dysfunction. *Journal of Consulting and Clinical Psychology*, *54*, 149–157.

Cooper, M. (1999). Treatment of persons and families with obsessive compulsive disorder: A review article. *Crisis Intervention*, *5*, 25–36.

Cooper, R. (2004). What is wrong with the *DSM*? *History of Psychiatry*, *15*(1), 5–25.

Cooper, W. O., Arbogast, P. G., Ding, H., Hickson, G. B., Fuchs, D. C., & Ray, W. A. (2006). Trends in prescribing of antipsychotic medications for US children. *Ambulatory Pediatrics*, *6*(2), 79–83.

Corey, G. (2001a). *Theory and practice of psychotherapy* (6th ed.). Belmont, CA: Brooks/Cole.

Corey, G. (2001b). *Case approach to counseling and psychotherapy* (5th ed.). Belmont, CA: Brooks/Cole.

Corya, S. A., Williamson, D., Sanger, T. M., Briggs, S. D., Case, M., & Tollefson, G. (2006). A randomized, double-blind comparison of olanzapine/fluoxetine combination, olanzapine, fluoxetine, and venlafaxine in treatment-resistant depression. *Depression and Anxiety*, *23*(6), 364–372.

Cosgrove, L., Krinsky, S., Vijayaraqhavan, M., & Schneider, L. (2006). Financial ties between *DSM-IV* panel members and the pharmaceutical industry. *Psychotherapy and Psychosomatics*, *75*(3), 154–160.

Costa, P., et al. (2003). Quality of Sexual Life Questionnaire (QVS): A reliable, sensitive and reproducible instrument to assess quality of life in subjects with erectile dysfunction. *International Journal of Impotence Research*, *15*, 173–184.

Courtney, E. A., Gamboz, J., & Johnson J. G., (2008). Problematic eating behaviors in adolescents with low self-esteem and elevated depressive symptoms. *Journal of Eating Behaviors*, *9*(4), 408–414.

Cowles, L. A. F. (2003). *Social work in the health field: A care perspective* (2nd ed.). New York: Haworth Press.

Craig, L., Attwood, A., Benton, C., Penton-Voak, I., & Munafo, M. (2009). Effects of acute alcohol consumption and alcohol expectancy on processing of perceptual cues of emotional expression. *Journal of Psychopharmacology*, *23*(3), 258–265.

Cromer, K. R., Schmidt, N. B., & Murphy, D. L. (2007). An investigation of traumatic life events and obsessive-compulsive disorder. *Behavior Research and Therapy*, *45*, 1683–1649.

Crow, S. J., Mitchell, J. E., Roerig, J. D., & Steffen, K. (2009). What potential role is there for medication treatment in anorexia nervosa? *International Journal of Eating Disorders*. *42*(1), 1–8.

CRS-Behavioral Health Advisor. (2009, January 1). Avoidant personality disorder. *Health Source: Consumer Edition*, 1.

Culp, K., Wakefield, B., Dyck, M., Cacchione, P., DeCrane, S., & Decker, S. (2004). Bioelectrical impedance analysis and other hydration parameters as risk factors for delirium in rural nursing home residents. *Journal of Gerontology: Medical Sciences*, *59A*(8), 813–817.

Cunha A., Relvas, P., & Soares, I. (2009). Anorexia nervosa and family relationships: Perceived family functioning, coping strategies, beliefs, and attachment to parents and peers. *International Journal of Clinical and Health Psychology*, *9*(2), 229–240.

Curtis, O. (1999). *Chemical dependency: A family affair*. Pacific Grove, CA: Brooks/Cole.

Dare, C., & Eisler, I. (1997). Family therapy for anorexia nervosa. In D. Garner & P. E. Garfinkel (Eds.), *Handbook of treatment for eating disorders* (2nd ed., pp. 333–349). Chichester, England: Wiley.

Dassori, A. M., Miller, A. L., Velligan, D., Saldana, D., Diamond, P., & Mahurin, R. (1998). Ethnicity and negative symptoms in patients with schizophrenia. *Cultural Diversity and Mental Health*, *4*(1), 65–69.

Davidson, L., Tondora, J., Lawless, M. S., O'Connell, M. J., & Rowe, M. (2009). *A practical guide to recovery-oriented practice: Tools for transforming mental health care*. New York: Oxford University Press.

Davis, D., Sbrocco, T., Odoms-Young, A., & Smith, D. (2010). Attractiveness in African American and Caucasian women: Is beauty in the eyes of the observer? *Journal of Eating Behaviors*. *11*(1), 25–32.

Davis, J. M., & Casper, R. (1977). Antipsychotic drugs: Clinical pharmacology and therapeutic use. *Drugs*, *12*, 260–282.

Davis, S. R., & Meier, S. T. (2001). *The elements of managed care: A guide for helping professionals*. Belmont, CA: Brooks/Cole.

Dawson, D. A. (2000, September). The link between family history and early onset alcoholism: Earlier initiation of drinking or more rapid development of dependence? *Journal of Studies on Alcohol*, *61*(5), 637.

Deacon, B., & Maack, D. J. (2008). The effects of safety behaviors on the fear of contamination: An experimental investigation. *Behaviour Research and Therapy*, *46*, 537–547.

Debonnel, G., Saint-Andre, E., Hebert, C., de Montigny, C., Lavoie, N., & Blier, P. (2006). Differential physiological effects of a low dose and high doses of venlafaxine in major depression. *International Journal of Neuropyschopharmacology*, *10*, 51–61.

Dekker, J. (1993). Inhibited male orgasm. In W. O'Donohue & J. H. Geer (Eds.), *Handbook of sexual dysfunction: Assessment and treatment* (pp. 279–302). Boston: Allyn & Bacon.

Delligatti, N., Akin-Little, K. A., & Little, S. G. (2003). Conduct disorder in girls: Diagnostic and intervention issues. *Psychology in the Schools*, *40*, 183–192.

DeRubeis, R. J., et al. (2005). Cognitive therapy vs. medications in the treatment of moderate to severe depression. *Archives of General Psychiatry*, *62*, 409–416.

de Shazer, S., & Dolan, Y. (2007). *More than miracles: The state of the art of solution-focused brief therapy*. New York: Haworth Press.

Desmond, J., & Copeland, L. R. (2000). *Communicating with today's patient*. San Francisco: Jossey-Bass.

DiClemente, C. C., Bellino, L. E., & Neavins, T. M. (1999). Motivation for change and alcohol treatment. *Alcohol Research and Health*, *23*(2), 86–92.

Dittmar, H. (2009). How do "Body Perfect" ideals in the media have a negative impact on body image and behaviors? Factors and processes related to self and identity. *Journal of Social and Clinical Psychology*, *28*(1), 1–8.

Dobbert, D. L. (2007). *Understanding personality disorders: An introduction*. Westport, CT: Praeger.

Douglas, J., James, I., & Ballard, C. (2004). Non-pharmacological interventions in dementia. *Advances in Psychiatric Treatment*, *10*(3), 171–179.

Drugs.com. (2009a). New drug approvals. Retrieved November 22, 2009, from http://www.drugs.com/newdrugs.html

Drugs.com. (2009b). FDA Approves Fanapt. Retrieved November 30, 2009, from http://www.drugs.com/newdrugs/fda-approves-fanapt-schizophrenia-1345.html

Dulcan, M. K. (2006). *Helping parents, youth, and teachers understand medications for behavioral and emotional problems* (3rd ed.). Washington, DC: American Psychiatric Publishing.

Dumont, M. P. (1987). A diagnostic parable: First edition, unrevised. *Journal of Reviews and Commentary in Mental Health*, *2*, 9–12.

Duncan, T. E., Duncan, S. C., & Hops, H. (1998, July). Latent variable modeling of longitudinal and multilevel alcohol use data. *Journal of Studies on Alcohol*, *59*(4), 399–409.

Dupper, D. (1992). Separate schools for Black males. *Social Work in Education*, *14*(12), 75–76.

Dutta, R., Greene, T., Addington, J., McKenzie, K., Phillips, M., & Murray, R. M. (2007). Biological, life course, and cross-cultural studies all point toward the value of dimensional and developmental ratings in the classification of psychosis. *Schizophrenia Bulletin*, *33*(4), 868–876.

Dziegielewski, S. F. (1996). Managed care principles: The need for social work in the health care environment. *Crisis Intervention and Time-Limited Treatment*, *3*(2), 97–110.

Dziegielewski, S. F. (1997a). Time limited brief therapy: The state of practice. *Crisis Intervention and Time Limited Treatment*, *3*(3), 217–228.

Dziegielewski, S. F. (1997b). Should clinical social workers seek psychotropic medication prescription privileges? Yes. In B. A. Thyer (Ed.), *Controversial issues in social work practice* (pp. 152–165). Boston: Allyn & Bacon.

Dziegielewski, S. F. (1998). *The changing face of health care social work: Professional practice in the era of managed care*. New York: Springer.

Dziegielewski, S. F. (2004). *The changing face of health care social work: Professional Practice in managed behavioral health care* (2nd ed.). New York: Springer.

Dziegielewski, S. F. (2005). *Understanding substance addictions: Assessment and intervention*. Chicago: Lyceum Books.

Dziegielewski, S. F. (2006). *Psychopharmacology for the non-medically trained*. New York: Norton.

Dziegielewski, S. F. (2007, December 31). *Issues in schizophrenia: The social worker's role in optimizing adherence* (special report), 1–12. Retrieved December 30, 2007, from CEZone.com

Dziegielewski, S. F. (2008). Brief and intermittent approaches to practice: The state of practice. *Journal of Brief Treatment and Crisis Intervention*, *8*(2), 147–163.

Dziegielewski, S. F. (2010). *Psychopharmacology and social work practice: A person in environment approach* (2nd ed.). New York: Springer.

Dziegielewski, S. F., & Holliman, D. (2001). Managed care and social work: Practice implications in an era of change. *Journal of Sociology and Social Welfare*, *28*(2), 125–138.

Dziegielewski, S. F., Jacinto, G., Dick, G., & Resnick-Cortes, C. (2007). Orgasmic disorders. In B. Thyer & J. Wodarski (Eds.), *Social work in mental health: An evidence-based approach* (pp. 427–456). Hoboken, NJ: Wiley.

Dziegielewski, S. F., Johnson, A., & Webb, E. (2002). DSM-IV and social work professionals: A continuing education evaluation. *Social Work in Mental Health,* *1*(1), 27–41.

Dziegielewski, S. F., & Leon, A. M. (2001a). *Psycho-pharmacology and social work practice.* New York: Springer.

Dziegielewski, S. F., & Leon, A. M. (2001b). Time-limited case recording: Effective documentation in a changing environment. *Journal of Brief Therapy, 1*(1).

Dziegielewski, S. F., Leon, A. M., & Green, C. E. (1998). African American children: A culturally sensitive model for group practice. *Early Child Development and Care, 147,* 83–97.

Dziegielewski, S. F., & Powers, G. T. (2000). Designs and procedures for evaluating crisis intervention. In A. R. Roberts (Ed.), *Crisis intervention handbook: Assessment, treatment and research* (2nd ed.). (pp. 742–773). New York: Oxford University Press.

Dziegielewski, S. F., Resnick, C. A., & Krause, N. (1995). Shelter-based crisis intervention with battered women. In A. Roberts (Ed.), *Helping battered women: New perspectives and remedies* (pp. 159–172). New York: Oxford University Press.

Dziegielewski, S. F., Turnage, B. F., Dick, G., & Resnick-Cortes, C. (2007). Sexual desire and arousal disorders. In B. Thyer & J. Wodarski (Eds.), *Social work in mental health: An evidence-based approach* (pp. 403–426). Hoboken, NJ: Wiley.

Dziegielewski, S. F., & Wolfe, P. (2000). EMDR as a time-limited intervention for body image disturbance and self-esteem: A single subject case study design. *Journal of Psychotherapy in Independent Practice, 1*(3), 1–16.

Easing the emotional cost of schizophrenia. (1997). In News in Mental Health Nursing. *Journal of Psychosocial Nursing, 35*(2), 6.

Eastman, P. (1993, May/June). Washington report: Treating erectile dysfunction. *Geriatric Consultant,* 10–13.

Ecker, B., & Hulley, L. (1996). *Depth-oriented brief therapy: How to be brief when you were trained to be deep—and vice versa.* San Francisco: Jossey-Bass.

Egan, G. (1998). *The skilled helper: A problem management approach to helping* (6th ed.). Pacific Grove, CA: Brooks/Cole.

Egger, H. L., & Angold, A. (2006). Common emotional and behavioral disorders in preschoolchildren: Presentation, nosology, and epidemiology. *Journal of Child Psychiatry, 43,* 313–337.

Einarson, A. (2009). Risks/safety of psychotropic medication use during pregnancy. *Canadian Journal of Clinical Pharmacology, 16*(1), e58–e65.

Ellis, A. (1971). *Growth through reason.* Palo Alto, CA: Science and Behavior Books.

Ellis, A. (2008). Cognitive restructuring of the disputing of irrational beliefs. In W. T. O'Donohue & J. E. Fisher (Eds.). *Cognitive behavior therapy: Applying empirically supported techniques in your practice* (pp. 91–95). Hoboken, NJ: Wiley.

Ellis, A., & Grieger, R. (Eds.). (1977). *Handbook of rational-emotive therapy.* New York: Springer.

Epstein, L. (1994). Brief task-centered practice. In R. Edwards (Ed.), *Encyclopedia of social work* (19th ed., pp. 313–323). Washington, DC: NASW Press.

Ethics meet managed care. (1997, January). *NASW NEWS, 42*(1), 7.

Evans, K. (2006). Alcibiades: Ancient Greek aristocratic idea or antisocial personality disorder? Proceedings of the Fourth International Conference on New Directions in the Humanities, Tunis, Tunisia. July 3-6, 2006.

Evans, S., Levin, F., Brooks, D., & Garawi, F. (2007). A pilot double-blind treatment trial of memantine for alcohol dependence. *Alcoholism: Clinical and Experimental Research, 31*(5), 775–782.

Eysenck, H. J., Wakefield, J. A. Jr., & Friedman, A. F. (1983). Diagnosis and clinical assessment: The *DSM-III. Annual Review of Psychology, 34,* 167–193.

Fairburn, C. G., Cooper, Z., & Shafran, R. (2003). Cognitive behavior therapy for eating disorders: A trans-diagnostic theory and treatment. *Behavior Research and Therapy, 41,* 509–529.

Fanger, M. T. (1994). Brief therapies. In R. Edwards (Ed.), *Encyclopedia of social work* (19th ed., pp. 323–334). Washington, DC: NASW Press.

Farabaugh, A., Fava, M., & Alpert, J. (2007). Differentiating chronic depression from personality disorders. *Psychiatric Times, 24*(6), 64–68.

Faraone, S. V., et al. (2005). Molecular genetics of attention-deficit hyperactivity disorder. *Biological Psychiatry, 57,* 1313–1323.

Farrelly, N., Dibben, C., & Hunt, N. (2006). Current management of bipolar affective disorder: Is it reflective of the BAP guidelines? *Journal of Psycho-pharmacology, 20*(1), 128–131.

Fassino, S., Daga, A., Boggio, S., Garzaro, L., & Pierò, A. (2004). Use of reboxetine in bulimia nervosa: A pilot study. *Journal of Psychopharmacology, 18*(3), 423–428.

Faust, J., & Stewart, L. M. (2008). Impact of child abuse timing and family environment on psychosis. *Journal of Psychological Trauma, 6*(2–3), 65–85.

Fazel, S., Gulati, G., Linsell, L., Geddes, J. R., & Grann, M. (2009). Schizophrenia and violence: Systematic review and meta-analysis. *PLoS Medicine, 6*(8), e1000120. doi: 10.1371/journal.pmed.1000120. Retrieved from http://www.power2u.org/downloads/schizophreniaandviolencejournal.pmed.1000120.pdf

Fazio, L., & Brock, G. (2004). Erectile dysfunction: Management update. *Canadian Medical Association, 17*(9), 1429–1436.

Federman, C., Holmes, D., & Jacob, J. D. (2009). Deconstructing the psychopath: A critical discursive analysis. *Cultural Critique, 72,* 36–65.

Feigenbaum, J. (2007). Dialectical behaviour therapy: An increasing evidence base. *Journal of Mental Health, 16,* 51–68.

Feisthamel, K. P., & Schwartz, R. C. (2009). Differences in mental health counselors' diagnoses based on client race: An investigation of adjustment, childhood, and substance-related disorders. *Journal of Mental health Counseling.* Retrieved December 8, 2009, from http://www.thefreelibrary.com/Differences in mental health counselors' diagnoses based on client . . . a0193182088.

Feldman, M. B., & Meyer, I. H. (2007). Eating disorders in diverse lesbian, gay, and bisexual populations. *International Journal of Eating Disorders, 40*(3), 218–226.

Feldt, K. S. (2000). Checklist of Nonverbal Pain Indicators (CNPI). *Pain Management Nursing, 1*(1), 13–21.

Ferriman, A. (2000). The stigma of schizophrenia. *British Medical Journal, 320*(8), 522.

Fick, D., Agostini, J., & Inouye, S. (2002). Delirium superimposed on dementia: A systematic review. *Journal of the American Geriatrics Society, 50,* 1723–1732.

Fick, D., Kolanowski, A., Beattie, E., & McCrow, J. (2009). Delirium in early-stage Alzheimer's disease: Enhancing cognitive reserve as a possible preventative measure. *Journal of Gerontological Nursing, 35*(3), 30–38.

Field, A. E., Austin, S. B., Frazier, A. L., Gillman, M. W., Camargo, C. A. Jr., & Colditz, G. A. (2002). Smoking, getting drunk, and engaging in bulimic behaviors: In which order are the behaviors adopted? *Journal of the American Academy of Child & Adolescent Psychiatry, 41*(7), 846–853.

Fimerson, S. S. (1996). Individual therapy. In V. B. Carson & E. N. Nolan (Eds.), *Mental health nursing: The nurse patient journey* (pp. 367–384). Philadelphia: Saunders.

Findling, R. L. (2000). A double-blind pilot study of risperidone in the treatment of conduct disorder. *Journal of the American Academy of Child and Adolescent Psychiatry, 39*(4), 509–516.

First, M. B., Frances, A., & Pincus, H. A. (1995). *DSM-IV handbook of differential diagnosis.* Washington, DC: American Psychiatric Press.

First, M. B., & Westen, D. (2007). Classification for clinical practice: How to make *ICD* and *DSM* better able to serve clinicians. *International Review of Psychiatry, 19*(5), 473–481.

Fish, L. S., Busby, D., & Killian, K. (1994). Structural couples therapy in the treatment of inhibited sexual drive. *American Journal of Family Therapy, 22,* 113–125.

Fischer, J. (Ed.). (1999). *Measures for clinical practice a sourcebook* (3rd ed., Vol. 2). New York: Free Press.

Fischer, J. (2009). *Toward evidence-based practice: Variations on a theme.* Chicago: Lyceum Books, Inc.

Fischer, J., & Corcoran, K. (2007a). *Measures for clinical practice: A source book. Volume 1: Couples, families, and children* (4th ed.). New York: Oxford University Press.

Fischer, J., & Corcoran, K. (2007b). *Measures for clinical practice: A source book. Volume 2: Adults* (4th ed.). New York: Oxford University Press.

Fischer, J. S. (2000). Taking the shock out of electroshock. *U.S. News & World Report, 128*(3), 46.

Flaum, M. (1995). Schizophrenia. In C. L. Shriqui & H. A. Nasrallah (Eds.), *Contemporary issues in the treatment of schizophrenia* (pp. 83–108). Washington, DC: American Psychiatric Press.

Floersch, J., et al. (2009). Adolescent experience of psychotropic treatment. *Transcultural Psychiatry, 46*(1), 157–179.

Fountoulakis, K. N. (2008). The contemporary face of bipolar illness: Complex diagnostic and therapeutic challenges. *International Journal of Neuropsychiatric Medicine: CNS Spectrums, 13*(8), 763–774, 777–779.

Foxcroft, D., Kypri, K., & Simonite, V. (2009). Bayes' Theorem to estimate population prevalence from alcohol use disorders identification test (AUDIT) scores. *Addiction, 104*(7), 1132–1137.

Frager, S. (2000). *Managing managed care.* New York: Wiley.

Frances, A., Pincus, H. A., Davis, W. W., Kline, M., First, M. B., & Widiger, T. A. (1991). The *DSM* field trials: Moving towards an empirically derived classification. *European Psychiatry, 6,* 307–314.

Frances, A., Pincus, H. A., Widiger, T. A., Davis, W. W., & First, M. B. (1990). DSM-IV: Work in progress. *American Journal of Psychiatry, 147,* 1439–1448.

Frances, A., & Ross, R. (1996). *DSM-IV case studies: A clinical guide to differential diagnosis.* Washington, DC: American Psychiatric Press.

Frese, F. J. III, Knight, E. L., & Saks, E. (2009). Recovery from schizophrenia: With views of psychiatrists, psychologists, and others diagnosed with this disorder. *Schizophrenia Bulletin, 35*(2), 370–380.

Friedman, S. (1997). *Time-effective psychotherapy: Maximizing outcomes in an era of minimizing resources.* Needham Heights, MA: Allyn & Bacon.

Froehlich, T. E., Lanphear, B. P., Epstein, J. N., Barbaresi, W. J., Katusic, S. K., & Kahn, R. S. (2007). Prevalence, recognition, and treatment of attention-deficit/hyperactivity disorder in a national sample of U.S. children. *Archive of Pediatric and Adolescent Medicine, 161*(9), 857–864.

Fruzzetti, A. E., Crook, W., Erikson, K. M., Lee, J. E., & Worrall, J. M. (2008). Emotion regulation. In W. T. O'Donohue & J. E. Fisher (Eds.). *Cognitive behavior therapy: Appling empirically supported techniques in your practice* (pp. 174–186). Hoboken, NJ: Wiley.

Fruzzetti, A. R., & Fruzzetti, A. E. (2009). Dialectics in cognitive and behavior therapy. In W. T. O'Donohue & J. E. Fisher (Eds.). General principles and empirically supported techniques of cognitive behavior therapy (pp. 230–239). Hoboken, NJ: Wiley.

FSDInfo. (2004). Information on female sexual dysfunction. Retrieved August 29, 2004, from http://www.fsdinfo.org/orgasmic_disorders.html

Fuller, R. K., & Hiller-Sturmhofel, S. (1999). Alcoholism treatment in the United States: An overview. *Alcohol Research and Health, 23*(2), 69–77.

Furnham, A., Badmin, N., & Sneade, I. (2002). Body image dissatisfaction: Gender differences in eating attitudes, self-esteem, and reasons for exercise. *Journal of Psychology, 136*(6), 581–596.

Gamino, L. A., & Ritter, R. H. Jr. (2009). *Ethical practice in grief counseling.* New York: Springer.

Gardner, W., Pajer, K. A., Kelleher, K. J., Scholle, S. H., & Wasserman, R. C. (2002). Child sex differences in primary care clinicians' mental health care of children and adolescents. *Archives of Pediatric and Adolescent Medicine, 156,* 454–459 [Electronic version]. Retrieved April 26, 2009, from http://www.archpediatrics.com

Garner, D. M. (1991). *Eating Disorders Inventory: Manual.* Odessa, FL: Psychological Assessment Resources.

Garner, D. M., & Garfinkel, P. E. (1997). *Handbook of treatment for eating disorders.* New York: Guilford Press.

Garner, D. M., Olmsted, M. P., & Polivy, J. (1983). Development and validation of a multidimensional eating disorder inventory for anorexia and bulimia. *International Journal of Eating Disorders, 2,* 15–34.

Gau, S. S. F., Shen, H., Chou, M., Tang, C., Chiu, Y., & Gau, C. (2006). Determinants of adherence to methylphenidate and the impact of poor adherence on maternal and family measures. *Journal of Child and Adolescent Psychopharmacology, 16*(3), 286–297.

Gavin, M. (2007, December). Kids health—pica. Retrieved November 7, 2009, from http//www.kidshealth.org

Gaw, A. C. (1993). *Culture ethnicity, and mental health illness.* Washington, DC: American Psychiatric Press.

Gelhorn, H., et al. (2006). Common and specific genetic influences on aggressive and nonaggressive conduct disorder. *Journal of the American Academy of Child & Adolescent Psychiatry, 45*(5), 570–577.

Gemert van, L. A., & Schuurmans, M. J. (2007). The Neecham Confusion Scale and the Delirium Observation Screening Scale: Capacity to discriminate and ease of use in clinical practice. *BioMed Central Nursing, 6*(3). doi: 10.1186/1472-6955-6-3

Gerdner, L., Buckwalter, K., & Reed, R. (2002). Impact of a psychoeducational intervention on caregiver response to behavioral problems. *Nursing Research, 51*(6), 363–374.

Gershon, J. (2007, May). The hidden diagnosis. *USA Today, 135,* 72–74.

Ghizzani, A., & Montomoli, M. (2000). Anorexia nervosa and sexuality in women: A review. *Journal of Sex Education and Therapy, 25,* 80–88.

Gilbert, D. J., Abel, E., Stewart, N. F., & Zilberman, M. (2007). More than drugs: Voices of HIV-seropositive individuals with a history of substance use reveal a range of adherence factors. In L. S. Ka'opua, & N. L. Linsk (Eds.), *HIV treatment adherence: Challenges for social services* (pp. 161–179). Binghamton, NY: Haworth Press.

Gilbert, L. A. (1991). Feminist contributions to counseling psychology. *Psychology of Women Quarterly, 15,* 537–547.

Gilliland, B., & James, R. (1997). *Crisis intervention strategies.* Pacific Grove, CA: Brooks/Cole.

Gingerich, W. J. (2002). Computer applications for social work practice. In A. R. Roberts & G. J. Greene (Eds.), *Social workers desk reference* (pp. 23–28). New York: Oxford University Press.

Gitlin, M. J. (1996). *The psychotherapist guide to psychopharmacology* (2nd ed.). New York: Free Press.

Glick, I. (2005). *New schizophrenia treatments.* Presentation at the Schizophrenia and Bioplar Education day. Stanford University, Palo Alto, CA.

Goldberg, J. F. (2007). What psychotherapists should know about pharmacotherapies for bipolar disorder. *Journal of Clinical Psychology: In Session, 63*(5), 475–490.

Goldberg, J. F., & Garno, J. L. (2009). Age at onset of bipolar disorder and risk for comorbid borderline personality disorder. *Bipolar Disorders, 11,* 205–208.

Golden, J. (1988). A second look at a case of inhibited sexual desire. *Journal of Sex Research, 25,* 304–306.

Goldman, A., & Carroll, J. (1990). Educational intervention as an adjunct to treatment of erectile dysfunction in older couples. *Journal of Sex & Marital Therapy, 16,* 127–141.

Goldman, S. M. (1998). Preface. In G. P. Koocher, J. C. Norcross, & S. Sam (Eds.), *Psychologists' desk reference* (1–2). New York: Oxford University Press.

Goldstein, E. G., & Noonan, M. (2001). The framework: Theoretical underpinnings and characteristics. In B. Dane, C. Tosone, & A. Woolson (Eds.), *Doing more with less: Using long-term skills in short-term treatment* (pp. 2–55). Northvale, NJ: Jason Aronson.

Goldstein, G., Beers, S., Siegel, D., & Minshew, J. (2001). A comparison of WAIS-R profiles in adults with high-functioning autism or differing subtypes of learning disabilities. *Applied Neuropsychology, 8*(3), 148–154.

Goldstein, I. (2004). Epidemiology of erectile dysfunction. *Sexuality & Disability, 22*(2), 113.

Gonzalez, H. M., et al. (2008). Antidepressant use among Blacks and Whites in the United States. *Psychiatric Service, 59*(9), 1131–1138.

Goodman, M., Jeong, J. Y., & Triebwasser, J. (2009). Borderline personality disorder and bipolar disorder distinguishing features of clinical diagnosis and treatment. *Psychiatric Times, 26*(7), 55–59.

Goodman, S. H., & Tully, E. (2006). Depression and women who are mothers: An integrative model of risk for the development of psychopathology in their sons and daughters. In C. L. M. Keys & S. H. Goodman (Eds.), *Women and depression: A handbook for the social, behavioral, and biomedical sciences* (pp. 241–280). New York: Cambridge University Press.

Goodman, W. K., et al. (1989). Yale-Brown Obsessive Compulsive Scale. 1. Development, Use, and reliability. *Archives of General Psychiatry, 46*(11), 1006–1011.

Gottesman, I. I. (1991). *Schizophrenia genesis: The origins of madness.* New York: Freeman.

Gould, D., Kelly, D., Goldstone, L., & Gammon, J. (2001). Examining the validity of pressure ulcer risk assessment scales: Developing and using illustrated patient simulations to collect data. *Journal of Clinical Nursing, 10*(5), 697–706.

Green, A. I. (2007). Substance abuse and schizophrenia: Pharmacological approaches. *Journal of Dual Diagnosis, 3*(2), 63–72.

Green, D. L., & Roberts, A. R. (2008). *Helping victims of violent crime: Assessment, treatment, and evidence-based practice.* New York: Springer.

Greenberg, G., Ganshorn, K., & Danilkewich, A. (2001). Solution-focused therapy: Counseling model for busy family physicians. *Canadian Family Physician, 47*(11), 2289–2295.

Gregory, D. (2008). *Broken bones, broken lives: Adult recovery from childhood abuse.* Bloomington, IN: AuthorHouse.

Greydanus, D. E., Nazeer, A., & Patel, D. R. (2009). Psychopharmacology of ADHD in pediatrics: Current advances and issues. *Neuropsychiatric Disease and Treatment, 5,* 171–181.

Grigorenko, E. L. (2009). *Multicultural psychoeducational assessment.* New York: Springer.

Grills-Taquechel, A., & Ollendick, T. H. (2008). Diagnostic interviewing. In M. Hersen & A. M. Gross (Eds.), *Handbook of clinical psychology: Vol. 2. Children and adolescents.* (pp. 458–479). Hoboken, NJ: Wiley.

Grim, P. (2000, July). Cut to the quick. *Discover, 21,* 38.

Griswold, K. S., & Pessar, L. F. (2000). Management of bipolar disorder. *Family Physician, 62,* 1343–1353, 1357–1358.

Grohol, J. M. (2006). Schizophrenia treatment. Retrieved March 22, 2010, from http://www.psychcentral .com/disorders/sx31t.htm

Gross, R., Rabinowitz, J., Feldman, D., & Boerma, W. (1996). Primary health care physicians' treatment of psychosocial problems: Implications for social work. *Health and Social Work, 21,* 89–94.

Guilmatre, A., et al. (2009). Recurrent rearrangements in synaptic and neurodevelopmental genes and shared biological pathways in schizophrenia, autism, and mental retardation. *Archives of General Psychiatry, 66*(9), 947–956.

Gur, R. E., & Pearlson, G. D. (1993). Neuroimaging for schizophrenia research. *Schizophrenia Bulletin, 19*(2), 337–353.

Haas, M., et al. (2009). Risperidone for the treatment of acute mania in children and adolescents with bipolar disorder: A randomized, double-blind, placebo-controlled study. *Bipolar Disorders, 11,* 687–700.

Hajeka, T., et al. (2008). Rapid cycling bipolar disorders in primary and tertiary care treated patients. *Bipolar Disorders, 10,* 495–502.

Hales, D., & Hales, R. E. (1996). *Caring for the mind: The comprehensive guide to mental health.* New York: Bantam Books.

Hamamci, Z. (2006). Integrating psychodrama and cognitive behavioral therapy to treat moderate depression. *Arts in Psychotherapy*, *33*, 199–207.

Hamilton, S., & Armando, J. (2008). Oppositional defiant disorder. *American Family Physician*, *78*(7), 861–866.

Hamrin, V., & Pachler, M. (2007). Pediatric bipolar disorder: Evidence-based psychopharmacological treatments. *Journal of Child and Adolescent Psychiatric Nursing*, *20*(1), 40–58.

Hansen, N. B., Lambert, M. J., & Forman, E. M. (2002). The psychotherapy dose-response effect and its implication for treatment delivery services. *Clinical Psychology: Science and Practice*, *9*(3), 329–343.

Hansen, R. A., Gartlehner, G., Lohr, K. N., Gaynes, B. N., & Carey, T. S. (2005). Efficacy and safety of second-generation antidepressants in the treatment of major depressive disorder. *Annals of Internal Medicine*, *143*(6), 415–426.

Harel, E. V., & Levkovitz, Y. (2008). Effectiveness and safety of adjunctive antidepressants in the treatment of bipolar depression: A review. *Israel Journal of Psychiatry and Related Sciences*, *45*(2), 121–128.

Harper-Dorton, K. V., & Herbert, M. (1999). *Working with children and their families* (Rev. ed.). Chicago: Lyceum.

Harrison, D., Thyer, B., & Wodarski, J. (1996). *Cultural diversity and social work practice*. Springfield, IL: Charles C Thomas.

Harrow, M., Goldberg, J. F., Grossman, L. S., & Meltzer, H. Y. (1990). Outcome in manic disorders: A naturalistic follow-up study. *Archives of General Psychiatry* (47), 665–671.

Hartley-Brewer, E. (2008, April). What your tween sees in the mirror: Looks matter enormously to your tween. Here's how to promote a positive body image. *Scholastic Parent & Child*, 78–79.

Hartmann, D. E. (1995). *Neuropsycological toxicology* (2nd ed.). New York: Plenum Press.

Hartsell, T. L., & Bernstein, B. E. (2008). *The portable ethicist for mental health professionals: A complete guide to responsible practice*. Hoboken, NJ: Wiley.

Hartshorne, T., Nicholas, J., Grialou, T., & Russ, J. (2007). Executive function in charge syndrome. *Child Neuropsychology*, *13*, 333–344.

Hartung, C. M., & Widiger, T. A. (1998). Gender differences in the diagnosis of mental disorders: Conclusions and controversies of the *DSM-IV*. *Psychological Bulletin*, *123*, 260–278.

Hawton, K., Catalan, J., & Fagg, J. (1991). Low sexual desire: Sex therapy results and prognostic factors. *Behaviour Research and Therapy*, *29*, 217–224.

Hawton, K., Catalan, J., & Fagg, J. (1992). Sex therapy for erectile dysfunction: Characteristics of couples, treatment outcome, and prognostic factors. *Archives of Sexual Behavior*, *21*, 161–175.

Heiman, J. R. (2002). Psychologic treatments for female sexual dysfunction: Are the effective and do we need them? *Archives of Sexual Behavior*, *31*(5), 445–450.

Heiman, J. R., & Meston, C. M. (1997). Empirically validated treatment for sexual dysfunction. *Annual Review of Sex Research*, *8*, 148–195.

Helms, J. E. (Ed.). (1990). *Black and White racial identity: Theory, research, and practice*. Westport, CT: Praeger.

Helzer, J. E., Kraemer, H. C., Krueger, R. F., Wittchen, H. U., Sirovatka, P. J., & Regier, D.A. (Eds.). (2008). *Dimensional approaches in diagnostic calssification: Refining the research agenda for DSM-V*. Washington, DC: American Psychiatric Association.

Henderson, R., Landry, M., Phillips, C., & Shuman, D. (1994). *Intensive outpatient treatment for alcohol and other drug abuse: Treatment improvement protocol (TIP)* (Series No. 8, Publication No. SMA 94B2077). Rockville, MD: U.S. Department of Health and Human Services.

Hepworth, D. H., Rooney, R. H., & Larsen, J. (2002). *Direct social work practice: Theory and skills*. Pacific Grove, CA: Brooks/Cole.

Hepworth, D. H., Rooney R. H., Rooney, G., Gottfried, K., & Larsen, J. A. (2010). *Direct social work practice: Theory and skills* (8th ed.). Belmont, CA: Brooks/Cole.

Herbert, J. D., Forman, E. M., & England, E. L. (2008). Psychological acceptance. In W. T. O'Donohue & J. E. Fisher (Eds.), *Cognitive behavior therapy: Applying empirically supported techniques in your practice* (2nd ed., pp. 4–16). Hoboken, NJ: Wiley.

Herman, J. L. (1992). *Trauma and recovery: The aftermath of violence from domestic abuse to political terror*. New York: Basic Books.

Hess, C., & Saunders-Pullman, R. (2006). Movement disorders and alcohol misuse. *Addiction Biology*, *11*(2), 117–125.

Herzog, D., & Eddy, K. (2009). Eating disorders: What are the risks? *Journal of American Academy of Child & Adolescent Psychiatry*, *48*(8), 782–3.

Higgins, E. (1994). A review of unrecognized mental illness in primary care: Prevalence, natural history, and efforts to change the course. *Archives of Family Medicine*, *3*, 899–907.

Hinshaw, S. P. (1994). *Attention deficit and hyperactivity in children*. Thousand Oaks, CA: Sage.

Hinshaw, S. P. (2008). Developmental psychopathology as a scientific discipline: Relevance to behavioral and emotional disorders of childhood and adolescence. In T. P. Beauchaine & S. P. Hinshaw (Eds.), *Child and adolescent psychopathology* (pp. 3–26). Hoboken, NJ: Wiley.

Hinshaw, S. P., & Stier, A. (2008). Stigma in relation to mental disorders. *Annual Review of Clinical Psychology*, *4*, 269–293.

Hirschfeld, R. M., et al. (1997). The National Depressive and Manic-Depressive Association consensus statement on the undertreatment of depression. *Journal of the American Medical Association*, *277*, 333–340.

Hirschfeld, R. M., et al. (2000). Development and validation of a screening instrument for bipolar spectrum disorder: The mood disorder questionnaire. *American Journal of Psychiatry*, *157*(11), 1873–1875.

Hjermstad, M., Loge, J., & Kaasa, S. (2004). Methods for assessments of cognitive failure and delirium in palliative care patients: Implications for practice and research. *Palliative Medicine*, *18*(6), 494–506.

Hodson, D. S., & Skeen, P. (1994). Sexuality and aging: The hammerlock of myths. *Journal of Applied Gerontology*, *13*, 219–234.

Hoek, H.W. (2006). Incidence, prevalence and mortality of anorexia nervosa and other eating disorders. *Current Opinion in Psychiatry*, *19*(4), 389–394.

Hoffer, A. (2008). Child psychiatry: Does modern psychiatry treat or abuse? *Journal of Orthomolecular Medicine*, *23*(3), 139–152.

Hoffman, P. D., Buteau, E., & Fruzzetti, A. E. (2007). Borderline personality disorder: Neo-Personality inventory ratings of patients and their family members. *International Journal of Social Psychiatry*, *53*(3), 204–215.

Hoffman, R. E. (2000, March 25). Transcranial magnetic stimulation and auditory hallucinations in schizophrenia. *Lancet*, *355*, 1073–1076.

Hofman, M., et al. (2004). Cancer patients' expectations of experiencing treatment-related side effects. *Cancer*, *100*(4), 851–857.

Holcomb-McCoy, C. C., & Myers, J. E. (1999). Multicultural competence and counselor training: A national survey. *Journal of Counseling and Development*, *77*, 294–302.

Hollis, C. (1995). Child and adolescent (juvenile onset) schizophrenia. A. case controls study of premorbid developmental impairments. *British Journal of Psychiatry*, *166*, 489–495.

Hong, C. J., Lee, Y. L., Sim, C. B., & Hwu, H. G. (1997). Dopamine D4 receptor variants in Chinese sporadic and familial schizophrenics. *American Journal of Medical Genetics (Neuropsychiatric Genetics)*, *74*, 412–415.

Hood, S., O'Neil, G., & Hulse, G. (2009). The role of flumazeil in the treatment of benzodiazepine dependence: Physiological and psychological profiles. *Journal of Psychopharmacology*, 401–409.

Horn, P. (2008). Psychiatric ethics consultation in light of the *DSM-V*. *HEC Forum*, *20*(4), 315–324.

Horton, A. L. (1995). Sex related hot-line calls: Types, interventions and guidelines. In A. Roberts (Ed.), *Crisis intervention and time limited cognitive treatment* (pp. 290–312). Thousand Oaks, CA: Sage.

Houmanfar, R., Maglieri, K. A., Roman, H. R., & Ward, T. A. (2008). Behavioral contracting. In W. T. O'Donohue & J. E. Fisher (Eds.), *Cognitive behavior therapy: Applying Empirically Supported Techniques in your practice* (2nd ed., pp. 53–59). Hoboken, NJ: Wiley.

Hsia, C. C., & Barlow, D. H. (2001). On the nature of culturally bound syndromes in the nosology of mental disorders. *Transcultural Psychology*, *38*(4), 474–476.

Hudson, W. W. (1990). *The WALMYR Assessment Scale Scoring manual*. Tempe, AZ: WALMYR Publishing.

Huff, N. C., Hernandez, J. A., Blanding, N. Q., & LaBar, K. S. (2009). Delayed extinction attenuates conditioned fear renewal and spontaneous recovery in humans. *Behavioral Neuroscience*, *123*(4), 834–843.

Huggins, J. E., Grant, T., O'Malley, K., & Streissguth, A. P. (2008). Suicide attempts among adults with fetal alcohol spectrum disorders: Clinical considerations. *Mental Health Aspects of Developmental Disabilities*, *11*(2), 33–41.

Huguelet, P., Mohr, S., & Borras, L. (2009, January). Recovery, spirituality and religiousness in schizophrenia. *Clinical Schizophrenia & Related Psychoses*, 307–316.

Humeniuk, R., et al. (2008). Validation of the alcohol, smoking and substance involvement screening test (ASSIST). *Addiction*, *103*(6), 1039–1047.

Hurley, A. (2007). A case of panic disorder treated with cognitive behavioral therapy techniques. *Mental Health Aspects of Developmental Disabilities*, *10*(1), 25.

Hurley, A., & Volicer, L. (2002). Alzheimer disease: "It's okay, mama, if you want to go, it's okay." *Journal of the American Medical Association*, *288*(18), 2324–2331.

Hutchings, J., et al. (2007). Parenting intervention in sure start services for children at risk of developing conduct disorder: Pragmatic randomized controlled trial. *British Medical Journal*, *334*, 678–682.

IMS. (2009). IMS Health reports U.S. prescription sales grew 1.3% in 2008 to $291 billion. Retrieved

December 9, 2009, from http://www.imshealth.com/ portal/site/imshealth/menuitem.a46c6d4df3db4b3d8 8f611019418c22a/?vgnextoid=078ce5b87da10210Vgn VCM100000ed152ca2RC RD &vgnextfmt=default

Inouye, S. K., Bogardus, S. T., Williams, C. S., Leo-Summers, L., & Agostini, J. V. (2003). The role of adherence on the effectiveness of non-pharmacologic interventions: Evidence from the delirium trial. *Archives of Internal Medicine, 163*(8), 958–964.

Insel, K., & Badger, T. (2002). Deciphering the 4 D's: Cognitive decline, delirium, depression, and dementia—a review. *Journal of Advanced Nursing, 38*(4), 360–368.

Iveson, C. (2002). Solution-focused brief therapy. *Advances in Psychiatric Treatment, 8*, 149–157.

Ivezaj, V., Saules, K. K., Hoodin, F., Alschuler, K., Angelella, N. E., Collings, A., et al. (2010). The relationship between binge eating and weight status on depression, anxiety, and body image among a diverse college sample: A focus on Bi/Multiracial women. *Journal of Eating Behaviors. 11*(1), 18–24.

Jacobs, M. H. (1995). What is schizophrenia. In S. Vinogradov & I. D. Yalom (Eds.), *Treating schizophrenia* (pp. 1–25). San Francisco: Jossey-Bass.

Jacobs, N. N. (2008). Bibliotherapy utilizing cognitive behavior therapy. In W. T. O'Donohue & J. E. Fisher (Eds.), *Cognitive behavior therapy: Applying Empirically Supported Techniques in your practice* (2nd ed., pp. 60–67). Hoboken, NJ: Wiley.

Janda, L. H., & O'Grady, K. E. (1980). Development of a sex anxiety inventory. *Journal of Consulting and Clinical Psychology, 48*, 169–175.

Janikowski, T. P., Donnelly, J. P., & Lawrence, J. (2007). The functional limitations of clients with co-existing disabilities. *Journal of Rehabilitation, 73*, 15–22.

Janowsky, D. S., Hong, L., Morter, S., & Howe, L. (1999). Underlying personality differences between alcohol/ substance-use disorder patients with and without an affective disorder. *Alcohol and Alcoholism, 34*(3), 370–377.

Janssen, E., Vorst, H., Finn, P., & Bancroft, J. (2002). The Sexual Inhibition (SIS) and Sexual Excitation (SES) Scales: I. Measuring sexual inhibition and excitation proneness in men. *Journal of Sex Research, 39*(2), 114–126.

Jehu, D., Klassen, C., & Gazan, M. (1986). Cognitive restructuring of distorted beliefs associated with childhood sexual abuse. *Journal of Social Work and Human Sexuality, 4*(1), 49–69.

Jensen, C. E. (2004). Medication for children with attention-deficit hyperactivity disorder. *Clinical Social Work Journal, 32*(2), 197–214.

Jensen, P. T., Klee, M. C., Thranov, I., & Groenvold, M. (2004). Validation of a questionnaire for self-assessment of sexual function and vagnial changes after gynaecological cancer. *Psycho-Oncology, 13*(8), 577–592.

Johnson, B. A., & Ait-Daoud, N. (1999). Medications to treat alcoholism. *Alcohol Research and Health, 23*(2), 99–106.

Johnson, F., & Wardle, J. (2005). Dietary restraint, body dissatisfaction, and psychological distress: A prospective analysis. *Journal of Abnormal Psychology, 114*(1), 119–125.

Johnson, J. G., Cohen, P., Kasen, S., & Brook, J. S. (2002). Childhood adversities associated with risk for eating disorders or weight problems during early adolescence or early adulthood. *American Journal of Psychiatry, 159*(3), 394–400.

Johnson, L., & Tucker, C. (2008). Cultural issues. In M. Hersen & A. M. Gross (Eds.), *Handbook of clinical psychology: Vol. 2. Children and adolescents* (pp. 789–832). Hoboken, NJ: Wiley.

Johnson, R. (1998). Clinical assessment of ethnic minority children using the *DSM-IV*. In G. P. Johnstone (1999, February). Adverse psychological effects of ECT. *Journal of Mental Health, 8*(1), 69–86.

Johnson, S. D., Phelps, D. L., & Cottler, L. B. (2004, February). The association of sexual dysfunction and substance use among a community epidemiological sample. *Archives of Sexual Behavior, 33*(1), 55–63.

Johnston, J., Roseby, V., & Kuehnle, K. (2009). *In the name of the child: A developmental approach to understanding and helping children of conflicted and violent divorce* (2nd ed.). New York: Springer.

Jones, E. (1995). The construction of gender in family therapy. In C. Burck & B. Speed (Eds.), *Gender power and relationships* (pp. 7–23). New York: Routledge.

Jones, K. (1969). *Drugs and alcohol.* New York: Harper & Row.

Jones, S. (2003). Psychotherapy of bipolar disorder: A review. *Journal of Affective Disorders, 80*, 101–114.

Jones, S. H., Sellwood, W., & McGovern, J. (2005). Psychological therapies for bipolar disorder: The role of model driven approaches to therapy integration. *Bipolar Disorders, 7*, 22–32.

Jongsma, A. E., Jr., & Peterson, L. M. (1995). *The complete psychotherapy treatment planner.* New York: John Wiley & Sons.

Jongsma, A. E., Jr., Peterson, L. M., & Bruce, T. J. (2006). *The complete adult psychotherapy treatment planner* (4th ed.). Hoboken, NJ: Wiley.

Jordan, C., & Franklin C. (Eds.). (2003). *Clinical assessment for social workers: Quantitative and qualitative methods* (2nd ed.). Chicago: Lyceum Books.

Joseph, R. M., McGrath, L. M., & Tager-Flusberg, H. (2005). Executive dysfunction and its relation to language ability in verbal school-age children with autism. *Developmental Neuropsychology, 27*(3), 361–378.

Jureidini, J. (2009). How do we safely treat depression in children, adolescents and young adults? *Drug Safety, 32*(4), 275–282.

Kane, M. N., Houston-Vega, M. K., & Nuehring, E. M. (2002). Documentation in managed care: Challenges for social work education. *Journal of Teaching in Social Work, 22*(1/2), 199–212.

Kaplan, A., & Dziegielewski, S. F. (1999). Graduate social work students' attitudes toward spirituality and religion: Issues for education and practice. *Social Work and Christianity: An International Journal, 26*(1), 25–39.

Kaplan, H. S. (1974). *The new sex therapy.* New York: Random House.

Kaplan, H. S. (1979). *Disorders of sexual desire.* New York: Simon & Schuster.

Kaplan, H. S. (1990). The combined use of sex therapy and intra-penile injections in the treatment of impotence. *Journal of Sex & Marital Therapy, 16*, 195–207.

Kaplan, L., & Harder, D. W. (1991). The sexual desire conflict scale for women: Construction, internal consistency, and two initial validity tests. *Psychological Reports, 68*, 1275–1282.

Kaplan, M. (1983a). A woman's view of *DSM-III. American Psychologist, 38*, 786–792.

Kaplan, M. (1983b). The issue of sex bias in *DSM-III:* Comments on articles by Spitzer, Williams, and Kass. *American Psychologist, 38*, 802–803.

Karls, J. M., & O'Keefe, M. E. (2008). *The PIE Manual.* Washington, DC: NASW Press.

Karls, J. M., & O'Keefe, M. E. (2009). Person in environment system. In A. R. Roberts (Ed.), *Social workers' desk reference* (2nd ed., pp. 371–376). New York: Oxford University Press.

Karls, J. M., & Wandrei, K. M. (Eds.). (1996a). *Person-in-environment system: The PIE classification system for social functioning problems.* Washington, DC: NASW Press.

Karls, J. M., & Wandrei, K. M. (1996b). *PIE manual: Person-in-environment system: The PIE classification system for social functioning problems.* Washington, DC: NASW Press.

Karper, L. P., & Krystal, J. H. (1996). Augmenting antipsychotic efficacy. In A. Breier (Ed.), *The new pharmacotherapy of schizophrenia* (pp. 105–132). Washington, DC: American Psychiatric Press.

Karpowicz, E., Skärsäter, I., & Nevonen, L. (2009). Self-esteem in patients treated for anorexia nervosa. *International Journal of Mental Health Nursing, 18*(5), 318–325.

Kass, F., Spitzer, R. L., & Williams, J. B. W. (1983). An empirical study of the issue of sex bias in the diagnostic criteria of *DSM-III* Axis II personality disorders. *American Psychologist, 38*, 799–801.

Katsounari, I. (2009). Self-esteem, depression and eating disordered attitudes: A cross-cultural comparison between Cypriot and British young women. *European Eating Disorder Review, 16*(6), 455–461.

Kaye, W. H., Nagata, T., Welzin, T. E., Hsu, L. K., Sokol, M.S., McConoha, C., et al. (2001). Double-blind placebo-controlled administration of fluoxetine in restricting- and restricting-purging-type anorexia nervosa. *Biological Psychiatry, 49*, 644–652.

Kazdin, A. E. (2002). Psychosocial treatments for conduct disorder in children and adolescents. In P. E. Nathan & J. M. Gorman (Eds.), *A guide to treatments that work* (2nd ed., pp. 57–85). New York: Oxford University Press.

Keane, T. M., Marshall, A. D., & Taft, C. T. (2006). Posttraumatic stress disorders: Etiology, epidemiology, and treatment outcome. *Annual Review of Clinical Psychology, 2*, 161–197.

Kearney, C. A., Cook, L. C., Wechsler, A., Haight, C. M., & Stowman, S. (2008). Behavioral assessment. In M. Hersen & A. M. Gross (Eds.), *Handbook of clinical psychology: Vol. 2. Children and adolescents* (pp. 551–574). Hoboken, NJ: Wiley.

Keck, P. E. (2005). Bipolar depression: A new role for atypical antipsychotics? *Bipolar Disorders, 7*(4), 34–40.

Keel, P. K., Dorer, D. J., Eddy, K. T., Franko, D., Charatan, D. L., & Herzog, D. B. (2003). Predictors of mortality in eating disorders. *Archives of General Psychiatry, 60*(2), 179–183.

Keenan, K., & Wakschlag, L. (2000). More than the terrible twos: The nature and severity of disruptive behavior problems in clinic-referred preschool children. *Journal of Abnormal Child Psychology, 28*, 33–46.

Keenan, K., & Wakschlag, L. S. (2002). Can a valid diagnosis of disruptive behavior disorder be made in preschool children? *American Journal of Psychiatry, 159*(30), 351–358.

Keenan, K., Wakschlag L. S., Danis, B., Hill, C., Humphries, M., Duax, J., et al.(2007). Further evidence of the reliability and validity of *DSM-IV* ODD and CD in preschool children. *Journal of the American Academy of Child and Adolescent Psychiatry, 46,* 457–468.

Keeping Kids Healthy. (2009). Adolescent-onset schizophrenia: 1 in every 100 young people. Retrieved November 19, 2009, from http://www.keepingkidshealthy.org/topics/schizophrenia-adolescent-onset/.

Keller, M. B., Hanks, D. L., & Klein, D. N. (1996). Summary of the mood disorders field trial and issue and overview. *Psychiatric Clinics of North America, 19*(1), 1–28.

Keller, M. B., Klein, D., Hirschfeld, R. M., Kocsis, J. H., McCullough, J. P., Miller, I., et al. (1995). Results of the *DSM-IV* mood disorders field trial. *American Journal of Psychiatry, 152,* 843–849.

Keller, M. B., & Wunder, J. (1990). Bipolar disorder in childhood. In M. Hersen & C. G. Last (Eds.), *Handbook of child and adult psychopathology* (pp. 69–81). New York: Pergamon Press.

Kelly, J. J., & Rice, S. (1986). The aged. In H. L. Gochros, J. S. Gochros, & J. Fischer (Eds.), *Helping the sexually oppressed* (pp. 99–108). Englewood Cliffs, NJ: Prentice-Hall.

Keltner, N. L., & Folks, D. G. (Eds.). (2001). *Psychotropic drugs* (3rd ed.). St. Louis, MO: Mosby.

Kendler, K. S., & Diehl, S. R. (1993). The genetics of schizophrenia: A current, genetic epidemiological perspective. *Schizophrenia Bulletin, 19*(2), 261–286.

Kendler, K. S., Gruenberg, A. M., & Tsuang, M. T. (1985). Psychiatric illness in first degree relatives of schizophrenic and surgical control patients: A family study using *DSM-III* criteria. *Archives of General Psychiatry, 42*(8), 770–779.

Kendler, K. S., McGuire, M., Gruengerg, A. M., O'Hare, A., Spellman, M., & Walsh, D. (1993). The Roscommo family study. 1: Methods, diagnosis of probands and risk of schizophrenia in relatives. *Archives of General Psychiatry, 50*(7), 527–540.

Kennedy, S. H., Anderson, H. E., & Lam, R. W. (2005). Efficacy of escitalopram in the treatment of major depressive disorder compared with conventional selective serotonin reuptake inhibitors and venlafaxine XR: A meta-analysis. *Journal of Psychiatry and Neuroscience, 31*(2), 122–131.

Kent, J. D., Blader, J. C., Koplewicz, H. S., Abikoff, H., & Foley, C. A. (1995). Effects of late-afternoon methylphenidate administration on behavior and sleep in attention-deficit hyperactivity disorder. *Pediatrics, 96,* 320–325.

Keough, M. E., Timpano, K. R., & Schmidt, N. B. (2009). Ataques de nervios: Culturally bound and distinct from panic attacks? *Depression and Anxiety, 26*(1), 16–21.

Kern, R. S., Glynn, S. M., Horan, W. P., & Marder, S. R. (2009). Psychosocial treatments to promote functional recovery in schizophrenia. *Schizophrenia Bulletin, 35*(2), 347–361.

Keshavan, M., Marshall, W., Shazly, M., & Paki, M. (1988). Neuroendocrine dysfunction in schizophrenia: A familial perspective. *Psychiatry Research, 23*(5), 345–348.

Keshavan, M. S., Montrose, D. M., Pierri, J. N., Dick, E. L., Rosenberg, D., Talagala, L., et al. (1997). Magnetic resonance imaging and spectroscopy in offspring at risk for schizophrenia: Preliminary studies. *Progressions in Neuro-Psychopharmacological and Biological Psychiatry, 21,* 1285–1295.

Keski-Rahkonen, A., Hoek, H. W., Susser, E. S., Linna M. S., Sihvola, E., Raevuori, A., et al. (2007). Epidemiology and course of anorexia nervosa in the community. *American Journal of Psychiatry, 164*(8), 1259–1265.

Kessler, R. C., Chiu, W. T., Demler, O., & Walters, E. E. (2005). Prevalence, severity, and comorbidity of twelve-month DSM-IV disorders in the national comorbidity survey replication (NCS-R). *Archives of General Psychiatry, 62,* 617–627.

Kessler, R. C., Heeringa, S., Lakoma, M. D., Petukhova, M., Schoenbaum, M., Wang, P. S., et al. (2008). Individual and societal effects of mental disorders on earnings in the United States: Results from the national comorbidity survey replication. *American Journal of Psychiatry, 165*(6), 703–711.

Kielbasa, A. M., Pomerantz, A. M., Krohn, E. J., & Sullivan, B. F. (2004). How does clients' method of payment influence psychologists' diagnostic decisions? *Ethics and Behavior, 14,* 187–195.

Kilman, P. R., Milan, R. J., Boland, J. P., Nankin, H. R., Davidson, E., West, M. O., et al. (1987). Group treatment for secondary erectile dysfunction. *Journal of Sex and Marital Therapy, 13,* 168–180.

Kilpatrick, A. C., & Holland, T. P. (1999). *Working with families: An integrative model by level of need.* Boston: Allyn & Bacon.

Kim-Cohen, J., Arseneault, L., Caspi, A., Taylor, A., Polo-Tomas, M., & Moffitt, T. E. (2005). Validity of DSM-IV conduct disorder in 4.5–5 year old children: A longitudinal epidemiological study. *American Journal of Psychiatry, 162,* 1108–1117.

Kinder, B. N., & Curtiss, G. (1988). Specific components in the etiology, assessment, and treatment of male sexual dysfunctions: Controlled outcome studies. *Journal of Sex & Marital Therapy, 14,* 40–48.

King, G., & Lorenson, J. (1989, June). Alcoholism training for social workers. *Social Casework: Journal of Contemporary Social Work,* 375–385.

Kinzl, J. F., Traweger, C., & Biebl, W. (1995). Sexual dysfunctions: Relationship to childhood sexual abuse and early family experiences in a nonclinical sample. *Child Abuse and Neglect, 19,* 785–792.

Kirst-Ashman, K. K. (2008). *Human behavior, communities, organizations, and groups in the macro social environment: An empowerment approach* (2nd ed.). Belmont, CA: Wadsworth Publishing/Brooks Cole.

Kislal, F., Kanbur, N., Derman, O., & Kutluk, T., (2003). Diagnostic appearance of abdominal roentgenogram in pica. *Pediatrics International, 45,* 491–493.

Klein, D. A., & Walsh, B. T. (2003). Eating disorders. *International Review of Psychiatry, 15*(3), 205–216.

Kluck, A., (2008). Family factors in the development of disordered eating: Integrating dynamic and behavioral explanations. *Journal of Eating Behaviors, 9,* 471–483.

Knopf, J., & Seiler, M. (1990). *ISD: Inhibited sexual desire.* New York: Morrow.

Koerner, K., & Linehan, M. (2000). Research on dialectical behavior therapy for patients with borderline personality disorder. *Psychiatric Clinics of North America, 23*(1), 151–167.

Koocher, G. P., Norcross, J. C., & Sam, S. S., III (Eds.). (2010). *Psychologists' desk reference* (pp. 103–108). New York: Oxford University Press.

Kraemer, H. C. (2005). A comparison of short- and long-term family therapy for adolescent anorexia nervosa. *Journal of the American Academy of Child and Adolescent Psychiatry, 44,* 632–639.

Kraemer, H. C., Shrout, P. E., & Rubio-Stipec, M. (2007). Developing the diagnostic and statistical manual V: What will "statistical" mean in the *DSM V? Social Psychiatry and Psychiatric Epidemiology, 42,* 259–267.

Kronenberger, W. G., & Meyer, R. G. (1996). *The child clinician's handbook.* Needham Heights, MA: Allyn & Bacon.

Krupinski, J., & Tiller, J. W. G. (2001). The identification and treatment of depression by general practitioners. *Australian and New Zealand Journal of Psychiatry, 35,* 827–832.

Kuileter, M. M., Vroege, J. A., & van Lankveld, J. J. D. M. (1993). *The Golombok-Rust Inventory of Sexual Satisfaction. Nederlandse vertalilng enaapassignnen.* Leiden: Netherlands University Medical Center [Dutch translation and adaption].

Kushner, J. N., & Associates.(1995). *Purchasing managed care services for alcohol and other drug treatment: Technical Assistance Protocol (TAP)* (Series No. 16, Publication No. SMA 96-3091). Rockville, MD: U.S. Department of Health and Human Services.

Kutchins, H., & Kirk, S. A. (1986). The reliability of *DSM-III:* A critical review. *Social Work Research and Abstracts, 22,* 3–12.

Kutchins, H., & Kirk, S. A. (1988). The business of diagnosis. *Social Work, 33,* 215–220.

Kutchins, H., & Kirk, S. A. (1993). DSM-IV and the hunt for gold: A review of the treasure map. *Research on Social Work Practice, 3*(2), 219–235.

Kutchins, H., & Kirk, S. A. (1997). *Making us crazy. DSM: The psychiatric bible and the creation of mental disorders.* New York: Free Press.

Lacey, D. (2006). End-of-life decision making for nursing home residents with dementia: A survey of nursing home social services staff. *Health and Social Work, 31*(3), 189–199.

Lahey, B. B. (2008). Oppositional defiant disorder, conduct disorder, and juvenile delinquency. In T. P. Beauchaine & S. P. Hinshaw (Eds.), *Child and adolescent psychopathology* (pp. 335–369). Hoboken, NJ: Wiley.

Lambert, L. (1998). New medications aid cognition in schizophrenia. *Journal of the American Medical Association, 280*(11), 953.

Lambert, M. J., Bergin, A. E., & Garfield, S. L. (2004). Introduction and historical overview. In M. J. Lambert (Ed.), *Bergin and Garfield's handbook of psychotherapy and behavior change* (5th ed., pp. 3–15). Hoboken, NJ: Wiley.

Lankshear, A. J. (2003). Coping with conflict and confusing agendas in multidisciplinary community mental health teams. *Journal of Psychiatric and Mental Health Nursing, 10*(4), 457–464.

Latorre, M. A. (2000, April/June). A holistic view of psychotherapy: Connecting mind, body, and spirit. *Perspectives in Psychiatric Care, 36*(2), 67.

Laumann, E. O., Paik, A., & Rosen, R. C. (1999). Sexual dysfunction in the United States: Prevalence and predictors. *Journal of the American Medical Association, 281,* 537–544.

Laurens, I., Hodgins, B., Maughan, R., Rutter, M., & Taylor, E. (2009). Community screening for psychotic-like experiences and other putative antecedents of schizophrenia in children aged 9–12 years. *Schizophrenia Research, 90*(1), 130–146.

Lauver, P., & Harvey, D. R. (1997). *The practical counselor: Elements of effective helping.* Pacific Grove, CA: Brooks/Cole.

Lawrie, S. M., & Abukmeil, S. S. (1998). Brain abnormality in schizophrenia: A systematic and quantitave review of volumetric magnetic resonance imaging studies. *British Journal of Psychiatry, 172,* 110–120.

Layard, R., Clark, D., Knapp, M., & Mayraz, G. (2007). Cost-benefit analysis of psychological therapy. *National Institute Economic Review, 202,* 90–98.

Leach, M. M. (2006). *Cultural diversity and suicide: Ethnic, religious, gender, and sexual orientation perspectives.* Binghamton, NY: Haworth Press.

Leahy, R. L. (2007). Bipolar disorder: Causes, contexts, and treatments. *Journal of Clinical Psychology: In Session, 63* (5), 417–424.

LeCroy, C. W., & Okamoto, S. K. (2009). Guidelines for selecting and using assessment tools with children. In A. Roberts (Ed.), *Social workers desk reference* (2nd ed., pp. 381–389). New York: Oxford University Press.

Lee, J., & Bean, F. D. (2004). America's changing color Lines: Race/Ethnicity, immigration, and multiracial identification. *Annual Review of Sociology, 30,* 221–242.

Lee, J., Jang, M., Lee, J., Kim, S., Kim, K., Park, J., et al. (2005). Clinical predictors for delirium tremens in alcohol dependence. *Journal of Gastroenterology and Hepatology, 20*(12), 1833–1837.

Lefley, H. P., & Pederson, P. B. (1986). *Cross-cultural training for mental health professionals.* Springfield, IL: Charles C Thomas.

Le Grange, D., Binford, R., & Loeb, K. L. (2005). Manualized family-based treatment for anorexia nervosa: A case series. *Journal of the American Academy of Child and Adolescent Psychiatry, 44*(1), 41–46.

Lehmann, C. (2003). Antipsychotics appear effective for borderline personality disorder. *Psychiatric News, 38*(2), 18.

Lehmann, H. E., & Ban, T. A. (1997, March). The history of the psychopharmacology of schizophrenia. *Canadian Journal of Psychiatry, 42*(2), 152–162.

Lehne, R. A., & Scott, D. (1996). Psychopharmacology. In V. B. Carson & E. N. Arnold (Eds.), *Mental health nursing: The nurse patient journey* (pp. 523–570). Philadelphia: Saunders.

Leif, H. (1977). What's new in sex research. *Medical Aspects of Human Sexuality, 7,* 94–95.

Leit, R. A., Pope, H. G., Jr., Gray, J. J. (2001). Cultural expectations of muscularity in men: The evolution of *Playgirl* centerfolds. *International Journal of Eating Disorders, 29*(1), 90–93.

Lemanek, K. L., Brown, R. T., Armstrong, F. D., Hood, C., Pegelow, C., & Woods, G. (2002). Dysfunctional eating patterns and symptoms of pica in children and adolescents with sickle cell disease. *Clinical Pediatrics, 41*(7), 493–500.

Lemke, J. L. (2006). Clinical trials and the drugging of our children. *Journal of Orthomolecular Medicine, 21*(3), 152–156.

Leon, A. M., & Dziegielewski, S. F. (1999). The psychological impact of migration: Practice considerations in working with Hispanic women. *Journal of Social Work Practice, 13*(1), 69–82.

LePera, G., Giannotti, C. F., Taggi, F., & Macchia, T. (2003). Prevalence of sexual disorders in those young males who later become drug abusers. *Journal of Sex and Marital Therapy, 29*(2), 149–156.

Lerner, J. W., Lowenthal, B., & Lerner, S. R. (1995). *Attention deficit disorders: Assessment and teaching.* Belmont, CA: Wadsworth.

Lewinsohn, P., & Striegel-Moore, R. (2000). Epidemiology and natural course of eating disorders in young women from adolescence to young adulthood. *Journal of the American Academy of Child & Adolescent Psychiatry, 39*(10), 1284.

Lewis, R. W., Fugl-Meyer, K. S., Bosh, R., Fugl-Meyer, A. R., Laumann, E. O., Lizz, E., et al. (2004). Epidemiology/Risk factors of sexual dysfunction. *Journal of Sexual Medicine, 1*(1), 35–39.

Libassi, C., & Parish, M. S. (1990). Strengthening the "bio" in the biopsychosocial paradigm. *Journal of Social Work Education, 26,* 109–123.

Liberman, R. (1973). Behavioral approaches to family and couple therapy. In J. Fischer (Ed.), *Interpersonal helping: Emerging approaches for social work practice* (pp. 200–229). Springfield, IL: Charles C Thomas.

Lieberman, J. A., Alvir, J. M. J., Woerner, M., Degreef, G., Bilder, R. M., Ashtari, M., et al. (1992). Prospective study of psychobiology in first-episode schizophrenia at hillside hospital. *Schizophrenia Bulletin, 18*(3), 351–371.

Lilienfeld, S. O., & Landfield, K. (2008). Issues in diagnosis: Categorical vs. dimensional. In W. E. Craighead, D. J. Miklowitz, & L. W. Craighead (Eds.), *Psychopathology: History, diagnosis, and empirical foundations* (pp. 1–33). Hoboken, NJ: Wiley.

Lin, K., & Kleinman, A. M. (1988). Psychopathology and clinical course of schizophrenia: A cross-cultural perspective. *Schizophrenia Bulletin, 19*(2), 371–430.

Lindeman, M., Stark, K., & Latvala, K. (2000). Vegetarianism and eating-disordered thinking. *International Journal of Eating Disorders, 8*, 157–165.

Linehan, M. (1993). *Skills training manual for treating borderline personality disorder.* New York: Guilford Press.

Linehan, M. N., Goldstein, J. L., Nielsen, S. L., & Chiles, J. A. (1983). Reasons for staying alive when you are thinking of killing yourself: The Reasons for Living Inventory. *Journal of Counseling and Clinical Psychology, 51*, 276–286.

Lipsith, J., McCann, D., & Goldmeier, D. (2003). Male psychogenic sexual dysfunction: The role of masturbation. *Sexual and Relationship Therapy, 18*(4), 447–471.

Liu, C. F., Campbell, D. G., Chaney, E. F., Li, Y. F., McDonnell, M., & Fihn, S. D. (2006). Depression diagnosis and antidepressant treatment among depressed VA primary care patients. *Administration Policy Mental Health & Mental Health Services Research, 33*, 331–341.

Lock, J. (2009). Eating disorders in children and adolescents. *Psychiatric Times, 26*(10). Retrieved from http://www.searchmedica.com/resource.html?rurl=http%3A%2F%2Fwww.psychiatrictimes.com%2Fspecial-reports%2Fcontent%2Farticle%2F10168%2F1471354%3FpageNumber%3D2&q=Lock%2C+J.+%282009%29.+Eating+disorders+in+children+and+adolescents.+Psychiatric+Times%2C+26%2810%29.&c=ps&ss=psychTimesLink&p=Convera&fr=true&ds=0&srid=3

Lock, J., & Le Grange, D. (2005). Family-based treatment of eating disorders. *International Journal of Eating Disorders, 37*(Suppl.), 564–567.

Lock, J., Le Grange, D., Agras, W. S., & Dare, C. (2001). *Treatment manual for anorexia nervosa: A family-based approach.* New York: Guilford Press.

Locke, H. J., & Wallace, K. M. (1959). Short marital and prediction tests: Their reliability and validity. *Journal of Marriage and Family Living, 21*, 251–255.

Loeber, R., Pardini, D., Homish, D. L., Wei, E. H., Crawford, A. M., Farrington, D. P., et al. (2005). The prediction of violence and homicide in young men. *Journal of Consulting and Clinical Psychology, 73*, 1074–1088.

Long, P. W. (2000). *Schizophrenia: A handbook for families: Schizophrenia youth's greatest disaster.* Retrieved from http://www.mentalhealth.com/dis/p20-ps01.html

LoPiccolo, J., & Steger, J. C. (1974). The Sexual Interaction Inventory: A new instrument for assessment of sexual dysfunction. *Archives of Sexual Behavior, 3*, 585–595.

LoPiccolo, J., & Stock, W. E. (1986). Treatment of sexual dysfunction. *Journal of Consulting and Clinical Psychology, 54*, 158–167.

Lorr, M., & Wunderlich, R. A. (1988). A Semantic Differential Mood Scale. *Journal of Clinical Psychology, 44*, 33–38.

Loth, K. A., Neumark-Sztainer, D., & Croll, J. K. (2009). Informing family approaches to eating disorder prevention: Perspectives of those who have been there. *International Journal of Eating Disorders, 42*(2), 146–152.

Lott, B. (1991). Social psychology: Humanist roots and feminist future. *Psychology of Women Quarterly, 15*, 505–519.

Lukoff, D. (2007). Spirituality in the recovery from persistent mental disorders. *Southern Medical Journal, 100*(6), 642–646.

Lum, D. (Ed.). (2003). *Culturally competent practice: A framework for understanding diverse groups and justice issues* (2nd ed.). Pacific Grove, CA: Brooks/Cole, Thomson Learning.

Lum, D., & Lu, Y. E. (2003). Skill development. In D. Lum (Ed.), *Culturally competent practice: A framework for understanding diverse groups and justice issues* (2nd ed.). (pp. 128–164). Pacific Grove, CA: Brooks/Cole, Thomson Learning.

MacCluskie, K. C., & Ingersoll, R. E. (2001). *Becoming a 21st century agency counselor.* Belmont, CA: Brooks/Cole, Thompson Learning.

MacLaren, C., & Freeman, A. (2007). Cognitive behavior therapy model and techniques. In T. Ronen & A. Freeman (Eds.), *Cognitive behavior therapy in clinical social work practice.* (pp. 25–44). New York: Springer.

MacPhee, A. R., & Andrews, J. (2006). Risk factors for depression in early adolescence. *Adolescence, 41*(163), 435–466.

MacPhillamy, D. J., & Lewinsohn, P. M. (1982). The Pleasant Events Schedule: Studies on reliability, validity and scale intercorrelation. *Journal of Consulting and Clinical Psychology, 50*, 363–380.

Maïano, C., Morin, A., Monthuy-Blanc, J., Garbarino, J., (2009). The Body Image Avoidance Questionnaire: Assessment of its construct validity in a community sample of French adolescents. *International Journal of Behavioral Medicine, 16*(2), 125–135.

Maier, W., Hallmeyer, J., Minges, J., & Lichtermann, D. (1990). Morbid risks in relatives of affective, schizoaffective, and schizophrenic patients: Results of a family study. In A. Maneros & M. T. Tsuang (Eds.), *Affective and schizoaffective disorders: Similarities and differences.* New York: Springer-Verlag.

Malhotra, A. K., Pinsky, D. A., & Breier, A. (1996). Future antipsychotic agents: Clinical implications. In A. Breier (Ed.), *The new pharmacotherapy of schizophrenia* (pp. 41–56). Washington, DC: American Psychiatric Press.

Malone, D., Marriott, S., Newton-Howes, G., Simmonds, S., & Tyrer, P. (2009). Community mental health teams for people with severe mental illnesses and disordered personality. *Schizophrenia Bulletin, 35*(1), 13–14.

Mancoske, R., Standifer, D., & Cauley, C. (1994). The effectiveness of brief counseling services for battered women. *Research on Social Work Practice, 4*(1), 53–63.

Mandell, B. R., & Schram, B. (2006). *An introduction to human services: Policy and practice* (6th ed.). Boston: Pearson.

Masters, W. H., & Johnson, V. D. (1970). *Human sexual inadequacy.* Boston: Little, Brown.

Mathew, S. J., Coplan, J. D., & Gorman, J. M. (2001). Neurobiological mechanisms of social anxiety disorder. *American Journal of Psychiatry, 158*(10), 1558–1567.

Matthews, G., & Wells, A. (2000). Attention, automaticity, and affective disorder. *Behavior Modification, 24*(1), 69–93.

Mattoo, S., Singh, S., Bhardwaj, R., Kumar, S., Basu, D., & Kulhara, P. (2009). Prevalence and correlates of epileptic seizure in substance-abusing subjects. *Psychiatry and Clinical Neuroscience,* 580–582.

Maxmen, J. S., & Ward, N. G. (1995). Schizophrenia and related disorders. In J. S. Maxmen & N. G. Ward (Eds.), *Essential psychopathology and its treatment* (pp. 173–194). New York: Norton.

Maxmen, J. S., Ward, N. G., & Kilgus, M. (2009). *Essential psychopathology and its treatment* (3rd ed.). New York: Norton.

Mayes, R., & Horwitz, A. V. (2005). DSM III and the revolution in the classification of mental illness. *Journal of the History of the Behavioral Sciences, 41*(3), 249–267.

Mayo Clinic. (2008, December 18). *Obsessive Compulsive Disorders: Risk Factors.* Retrieved March 22, 2010, from Mayo Clinic: http://www.mayoclinic.com/health/obsessive-compulsive-disorder/DS00189/DSECTION=risk-factors

Mayo Clinic. (2009, 10 April). *Post Traumatic Stress Disorder (PTSD): Risk Factors.* Retrieved March 22, 2010, from Mayo Clinic: http://www.mayoclinic.com/health/

post-traumatic-stress-disorder/DS00246/DSECTION=risk-factors

Mays, V. M., Ponce, N. A., Washington, D. L., & Cochran, S. D. (2003). Classifications of race and ethnicity: Implications for public health. *Annual Review of Public Health, 24,* 83–110.

McAdoo, H. (1997). *Black families.* Thousand Oaks, CA: Sage.

McAllister, R., & Caltabiano, M. L. (1994). Self-esteem, body image and weight in noneating-disordered women. *Psychological Reports, 75,* 1339–1343.

McBride, C., Atkinson, L., Quilty, L. C., & Bagby, M. R. (2006). Attachment as moderator of treatment outcome in major depression: A randomized control trial of interpersonal psychotherapy versus cognitive behavior therapy. *Journal of Consulting and Clinical Psychology, 74*(6), 1041–1054.

McCabe, M. P. (2009). Anorgasmia in Women. *Journal of Family Psychotherapy, 20*(2/3), 177–197.

McCabe, M. P., & Delaney, S. M. (1992). An evaluation of therapeutic programs for the treatment of secondary inorgasmia in women. *Archives of Sexual Behavior, 21,* 69–89.

McCary, J. L. (1973). *Human sexuality.* New York: D. Van Nostrand.

McCaulay, M., Mintz, L., & Glenn, A. (1988). Body image, self-esteem, and depression-proneness: Closing the gender gap. *Sex Roles, 18*(7/8), 381–391.

McElroy, S. L., Strakowski, S. M., West, S. A., & Keck, P. E. (1997). Phenomenology of adolescent and adult mania in hospitalized patients with bipolar disorder. *American Journal of Psychiatry, 154*(1), 44–49.

McEvoy, P. M., & Perini, S. J. (2009). Cognitive behavioral group therapy for social phobia with or without attention training: A controlled trial. *Journal of Anxiety Disorders, 23,* 519–528.

McGoldrick, M., Giordano, J., & Garcia-Preto, N. (Eds.). (2005). *Ethnicity and family therapy.* New York: Guilford Press.

McMahon, R. J., Wells, K. C., & Kotler, J. S. (2006). Conduct problems. In E. J. Mash & R. A. Barkley (Eds.)., *Treatment of childhood disorders* (3rd ed., pp. 137-270.). New York: Guilford Press.

McMain, S., & Ellery, M. (2008). Screening and assessment of personality disorders in addiction treatment settings. *International Journal of Mental Health Addiction, 6,* 20–31.

McMaster, S. A. (2004). Harm reduction: A new perspective on substance abuse services. *Social Work, 49*(3), 356–363.

Meeks, S. (1999). Bipolar disorder in latter half of life: Symptom presentation, global functioning, and age of onset. *Journal of Affective Disorders, 52*(2), 161–167.

Mell, L. K., Davis, R. L., & Owens, D. (2005). Association between streptococcal infection and obsessive compulsive disorder, Tourette's syndrome, and tic disorder. *Pediatrics, 116*(1), 56–60.

Mellsop, G., Menkes, D., & El-Badri, S. (2007). Releasing psychiatry from the constraints of categorical diagnosis. *Austrian Psychiatry, 15*(1), 3–5.

Mendelson, J., & Mello, N. (1992). *Medical diagnosis and treatment of alcoholism.* New York: McGraw-Hill.

Menezes, N. M., Arenovich, T., & Zipursky, R. B. (2006). A systematic review of longitudinal outcome studies of first-episode psychosis. *Psychological Medicine, 36*(10), 1349–1362.

Mental Health America. (2009). Factsheet: Schizophrenia in children. Retrieved November 22, 2009, from http://www.mentalhealthamerica.net/go/information/get-info/schizophrenia/schizophrenia-in-children

Merck. (2000). *The physician guide to diagnosis and treatment.* Whitehouse Station, NJ: Author.

Meston, C. M., & Derogatis, L. R. (2002). Validated instruments for assessing female sexual function. *Journal of Sex and Marital Therapy, 28,* 155–164.

Meston, C. M., & Rellini, A. (2008). Sexual dysfunction. In W. E. Craighead, D. J. Miklowitz, & L. W. Craighead (Eds.), *Psychopathology: History, diagnosis, and empirical foundations* (pp. 1–33). Hoboken, NJ: Wiley.

Metcalf, L. (1998). *Solution-focused group therapy.* New York: Free Press.

Metz, M. E., & Pryor, J. L. (2000). Premature ejaculation: A psychophysiological approach for assessment and management. *Journal of Sex and Marital Therapy, 26,* 293–320.

Mezzich, J. E. (2005). Values and comprehensive diagnosis. *World Psychiatry, 4,* 91–92.

Mezzich, J. E., & Salloum, I. M. (2007). Towards innovative international classification and diagnostic systems: ICD-11 and person-centered integrative diagnosis [Editorial]. *Acta Psychiatrica Scandinavica, 116*(1), 1–5.

Miasso, A. I., Cassiani, S. H., & Pedrao, L. J. (2008). Bipolar affective disorder and medication therapy: Identifying barriers. *Revista Latino-Americana De Enfermagem, 16*(4), 739–745.

Miklowitz, D. J. (2008). Adjunctive psychotherapy for bipolar disorder: State of the evidence. *American Journal of Psychiatry, 165*(11), 1408–1419.

Miklowitz, D. J., et al. (2007). Psychosocial treatments for bipolar depression: A 1-year randomized trial from the systematic treatment enhancement program. *Archives of General Psychiatry, 64*(4), 419–426.

Milkman, H., & Sederer, L. (1990). *Treatment choices for alcoholism and drug abuse.* New York: Lexington Books.

Miller, J., Campbell, J., Moore, K., & Schofield, A. (2004). Elder care supportive interventions protocol: Reducing discomfort in confused, hospitalized older adults. *Journal of Gerontological Nursing, 30*(8), 10–18.

Miller, N. S., & Gold, M. S. (1998, July). Management of withdrawal syndromes and relapse prevention in drug and alcohol dependence. *American Family Physician, 58*(1), 139–147.

Millon, T., & Grossman, S. (2007). *A personalized psychotherapy approach.* Hoboken, NJ: Wiley.

Mitchell, A. J., Vaze, A., & Rao, S. (2009). Clinical diagnosis of depression in primary care: A meta-analysis. *Lancet, 374,* 609–619.

Mitchell, A. M., & Bulik, C. M. (2006). Eating disorders and women's health: An update. *Journal of Midwifery & Women's Health, 51*(3), 193–201.

Mitchell, R. W. (1991). *Documentation in counseling records.* Washington, DC: American College Association.

Modesto-Lowe, V., & Kranzler, H. R. (1999). Diagnosis and treatment of alcohol-dependent patients with comorbid psychiatric disorders. *Alcohol Research and Health, 23*(2), 144–150.

Moffitt, T. E., Caspi, A., Rutter, M., & Silva, P. (2001). *Sex differences in antisocial behavior.* Cambridge, UK: Cambridge University Press.

Moise, F. N., & Petrides, G. (1996). Case study: Electroconvulsive therapy in adolescents. *Journal of the American Academy of Child and Adolescent Psychiatry, 35*(3), 312–319.

Moline, M. E., Williams, G. T., & Austin, K. M. (1998). *Documenting psychotherapy: Essentials for mental health practitioners.* Thousand Oaks, CA: Sage.

Molodynski, A., & Burns, T. (2008). The organization of psychiatric services. *Medicine, 36*(8), 388–390.

Moore, D. P., & Jefferson, J. W. (1997). *Handbook of medical psychiatry.* St. Louis, MO: Mosby.

Moore, D. P., & Jefferson, J. W. (2004). Obsessive-compulsive personality disorder. In D. P. Moore & J. W. Jefferson (Eds.), *Handbook of medical psychiatry* (2nd ed., chap. 142). Philadelphia: Mosby Elsevier.

Moore, T. M., Straus, J. L., Herman, S., & Donatucci, C. F. (2003). Erectile dysfunction in early, middle, and late adulthood: Symptoms patterns and psychosocial correlates. *Journal of Sex & Marital Therapy, 29,* 381–399.

Moradi, B., Dirks, D., & Matteson, A. V. (2005). Roles of sexual objectification experiences and internalization of standards of beauty in eating disorder symptomotology: A test and extension of objectification theory. *Journal of Counseling Psychology, 52*(3), 420–428.

More, J. (2008). Wellstone-Pete Domenici mental health parity and addiction equity act of 2008: Explained in brief. Retrieved November 30, 2009, from http://www.treatmentsolutionsnetwork.com/blog/index.php/2008/12/16/wellstone-pete-domenici-mental-health-parity-and-addiction-equity-act-of-2008-explained-in-brief/.

Moreno, C., Arango, C., Parellada, M., Shaffer, D., & Bird, H. (2007). Antidepressants in child and adolescent depression: Where are the bugs? *Acta Psychiatrica Scandinavica, 115*(3), 184–195.

Moretz, M., & McKay, D. (2008). Disgust sensitivity as a predictor of obsessive-compulsive contamination symptoms and associated cognitions. *Journal of Anxiety Disorders, 22*(4), 707–715.

Morokoff, P. J., & LoPiccolo, J. (1986). A comparative evaluation of minimal therapist contact and 15 session treatment for female orgasmic dysfunction. *Journal of Consulting and Clinical Psychology, 54*, 294–300.

Morrison, J. (1995). *DSM-IV Made Easy: The Clinician's Guide to Diagnosis.* New York: Guilford Press.

Moses, T. (2009). Stigma and self-concept among adolescents receiving mental health treatment. *American Journal of Orthopsychiatry, 79*(2), 264–274.

Moyle, W., Olorenshaw, R., Wallis, M., & Borbasi, S. (2008). Best practice for the management of older people with dementia in the acute care setting: A review of the literature. *International Journal of Older People Nursing, 3*(2), 121–130.

Muller, R. J. (2008). *Doing psychiatry wrong: A critical and prescriptive look at a faltering profession.* New York: Analytic Press.

Munby, J., & Johnson, D. W. (1980). Agoraphobia: The long term follow-up of behavioural treatment. *British Journal of Psychiatry, 137*, 418–427.

Munro, A. (1999). *Delusional disorder: Paranoia and related illnesses.* New York: Cambridge University Press.

Munro, A., & Mok, H. (2006). An overview of treatment in paranoia/delusional disorder. *Canadian Journal of Psychiatry, 40*, 616–622.

Murrie, D. C., Boccaccini, M. T., McCoy, W., & Cornell, D. G. (2007). Diagnostic labels in juvenile court: How do descriptions of psychopathy and conduct disorder influence judges? *Journal of Clinical Child and Adolescent Psychology, 36*, 228–241.

Myers, D. (1992). *Psychology* (3rd ed.). New York: Worth.

Myrick, H., & Anton, R. F. (1998, Winter). Treatment of alcohol withdrawal. *Alcohol Health and Research World, 22*(1), 38–44.

National Alliance on Mental Illness. (2003). *Tardive dyskinesia.* Retrieved June 10, 2009, from http://www.nami.org/Content/ContentGroups/Helpline1/Tardive_Dyskinesia.htm.

National Institute for Clinical Excellence. (2004). *Eating disorders: Core interventions in the treatment and management of anorexia nervosa, bulimia nervosa, and related eating disorders* (Clinical Guideline No. 9). London: Author. (Available at http://www.nice.org.uk/guidance/CG9)

National Institute of Mental Health. (2000). *Bipolar disorder research at the National Institute of Mental Health* (NIH Publication NO. 00-4500). Bethesda, MD: Author.

National Institute of Mental Health. (2008). The numbers count: Mental disorders in America. Retrieved November 22, 2009, from http://www.nimh.nih.gov/health/publications/the-numbers-count-mental-disorders-in-america/index.shtml

National Institute of Mental Health. (2009a). Borderline personality disorder. Retrieved November 29, 2009, from http://www.nimh.nih.gov/health/publications/bor derline-personality-disorder-fact-sheet/index.shtml

National Institute of Mental Health. (2009b). *How is bipolar disorder treated?* Retrieved June 22, 2009, from http://www.nimh.nih.gov/health/publications/bipolar-disorder/how-is-bipolar-disorder-treated.shtml

National Institute of Mental Health. (2009c, February 24). *Post Traumatic Stress Disorder (PTSD).* Retrieved March 22, 2010, from http://www.nimh.nih.gov/health/topics/post-traumatic-stress-disorder-ptsd/index.shtml

National Institute of Mental Health. (2009d). Schizophrenia. Retrieved November 22, 2009, from http://www.nimh.nih.gov/health/publications/schizophrenia/index.shtml

National Institute of Mental Health. (2009e). What medications are used to treat depression? Retrieved December 9, 2009, from http://www.nimh.nih.gov/health/publications/mental-health-medications/what-medications-are-used-to-treat-depression.shtml

National Institute of Mental Health. (2009f). What medications are used to treat schizophrenia? Retrieved March 22, 2010, from http://www.nimh.nih.gov/health/publications/mental-health-medications/what-medications-are-used-to-treat-schizophrenia.html

Nauert, R. (Ed.). (2007). New genetic link for schizophrenia. Retrieved November 22, 2009, from http://www.psychcentral.com/news/2008/02/28/new-genetic-link-to-schizophrenia/1977.html

Nazarko, L. (2008). A manager's guide to dementia care. *British Journal of Healthcare Management*, *14*(7), 275–279.

Nemeroff, C. B. (2007). The burden of severe depression: A review of diagnostic challenges and treatment alternatives. *Journal of Psychiatric Research*, *41*, 89–206.

Nestadt, G., Samuels, J., Riddle, M., Bienvenue, J. O. 111., Liang, K., LaBuda, M., et al. (2000). A family study of obsessive compulsive disorder. *Archives of General Psychiatry*, *57*(4), 358–363.

Netherton, S. D., Holmes, D., & Walker, C. E. (1999). *Child and adolescent psychological disorders: A comprehensive textbook*. New York: Oxford University Press.

Newcombe, D., Humeniuk, R., & Ali, R. (2005). Validation of the World Health Organization alcohol, smoking and substance involvement screening test (ASSIST): Report of results from the Australian site. *Drug and Alcohol Review*, *24*(3), 217–226.

Newman, B. M., & Newman, P. R. (2009). *Development through life: A psychosocial approach* (10th ed.). Belmont, CA: Wadsworth/Cengage Learning

Nichols, M. P., & Schwartz, R. C. (2005). *The essentials of family therapy* (2nd ed.). Boston: Allyn & Bacon/Pearson Education.

Nicolson, P., & Burr, J. (2003). What is "normal" about women's (hetero)sexual desire and orgasm?: A report of an in-depth interview study. *Social Science & Medicine*, *57*(9), 1735–1745.

Nigg, J., & Nikolas, M. (2008). Attention-deficit/hyperactivity disorder. In T. P. Beauchaine & S. P. Hinshaw (Eds.), *Child and adolescent psychopathology* (pp. 301–334). Hoboken, NJ: Wiley.

Nilsson, K., & Hagglof, B. (2005). Long-term follow-up of adolescent anorexia nervosa in northern Sweden. *European Eating Disorders Review*, *13*(2), 89–100.

Nobre, P. J., & Pinto-Gouveia, J. (2008). Cognitive and emotional predictors of female sexual dysfunctions: preliminary findings. *Journal of Sex & Marital Therapy*, *34*(4), 325–342.

Nock, M. K., Kazdin, A. E., Hiripi, E., & Kessler, R. C. (2007). Lifetime prevalence, correlates, and persistence of oppositional defiant disorder: Results from the national comorbidity survey replication. *Journal of Child Psychology and Psychiatry*, *48*(7), 703–713.

Noggle, C. A., & Dean, R. S. (2009). Use and impact of antidepressants in the school setting. *Psychology in the Schools*, *46*(9), 857–868.

Nugent, W. (2004). A validity study of two forms of the self-esteem rating scale. *Research on Social Work Practice*, *14*(4), 287–294.

Nunes, E. V., & Rounsaville, B. J. (2006). Comorbidity of substance use with depression and other mental disorders: From diagnostic and statistical manual of mental disorders, fourth edition (*DSM-IV*) to *DSM-V*. *Addiction*, 101(Suppl. 1), 89–96.

Nygaard, H., & Jarland, M. (2005). Are nursing home patients with dementia diagnosis at increased risk for inadequate pain treatment? *Geriatric Psychiatry*, *20*, 730–737.

Ochner, C. N., Gray, J. A., & Brickner, K., (2009). The development and initial validation of a new measure of male body dissatisfaction. *Journal of Eating Disorders*, *10*(4), 197–201.

O'Donnell, M. P. (1994). Preface. In M. P. O'Donnell & J. S. Harris (Eds.), *Health promotion in the work place* (pp. ix–xvi). Albany, NY: Delmar.

O'Donohue, W., & Fisher, J. E. (2008). Introduction. In W. T. O'Donohue & J. E. Fisher (Eds.), *Cognitive behavior therapy: Applying empirically supported techniques in your practice* (2nd ed., pp. 1–3). Hoboken, NJ: Wiley.

O'Donohue, W., Letourneau, E., & Geer, J. H. (1993). Premature ejaculation. In W. O'Donohue & J. H. Geer (Eds.), *Handbook of sexual dysfunctions: Assessment and treatment* (pp. 303–334). Boston: Allyn & Bacon.

Okasha, A., & Okasha, T. (2000). Notes on mental disorders in pharaonic Egypt. *History of Psychiatry*, *11*, 413–424.

O'Leary, M. P., et al. (2003). Distribution of the Brief Male Sexual Inventory in community men. *International Journal of Impotence Research*, *15*, 185–191.

Olfson, M., Marcus, S., & Wan, G. (2009). Stimulant dosing for children with ADHD: A medical claims analysis. *Journal of the American Academy of Child Psychiatry*, *48*(1), 51–59.

Orovwuje, P. R. (2008). Contemporary challenges in forensic mental health: The ingenuity of the multidisciplinary team. *Mental Health Review Journal*, *13*(2), 24–34.

Oshodi, A., Bangaru, R., & Benbow, J. (2005). A paranoid migrant family: Folie a famille. *Irish Journal of Psychological Medicine*, *22*, 26–29.

Owen, J. (2008). The nature of confirmatory strategies in the initial assessment process. *Journal of Mental Health Counseling, 30*(4), 362–374.

Packard, T., Jones, L., & Nahrstedt, K. (2006). Using the image exchange to enhance interdisciplinary team building in child care. *Child and Adolescent Social Work Journal, 23*(1), 86–106.

Pagan, J., Rose, R., Viken, R., Pulkkinen, L., Kaprio, J., & Dick, D. (2006). Genetic and environmental influences on stages of alcohol use across adolescence and into young adulthood. *Behavior Genetics, 36*, 483–497.

Palace, E. M. (1995). Modification of dysfunctional patterns of sexual response through autonomic arousal and false physiological feedback. *Journal of Consulting and Clinical Psychology, 63*, 604–615.

Palace, E., & Gorzalka, B. B. (1990). The enhancing effects of anxiety on arousal in sexually dysfunctional and functional women. *Journal of Abnormal Psychology, 99*, 403–411.

Palace, E., & Gorzalka, B. B. (1992). Differential patterns of arousal in sexually functional and dysfunctional women: Physiological and subjective components of sexual response. *Archives of Sexual Behavior, 21*, 135–159.

Pande, P. (1987). Personality patterns of alcoholics [CD-ROM]. *Journal of Psychological Research, 31*(1), 1–3. Abstract retrieved from PsychLIT: AN 75–36076.

Pandya, M., Pozuelo, L., & Malone, D. (2007). Electroconvulsive therapy: What the internist needs to know. *Cleveland Clinical Journal of Medicine, 74*(9), 679–685.

Papadatou, D. (2009). *In the face of death: Professionals who care for the dying and the bereaved.* New York: Springer.

Papworth, M. (2006). Issues and outcomes associated with adult mental health self-help materials: A "second order" review or "qualitative meta-review." *Journal of Mental Health, 15*(4), 387–409.

Parad, H. J., & Parad, L. G. (1990). *Crisis intervention: The practitioner's sourcebook for brief therapy.* Milwaukee, WI: Family Service America.

Paris, J. (2002). Chronic suicidality among patients with borderline personality disorder. *Psychiatric Services, 53*, 738–742.

Parker, A., Marshall, E., & Ball, D. (2008). Diagnosis and management of alcohol use disorders. *British Medical Journal, 336*, 496–501.

Pasinetti, G., & Hiller-Sturmhofel, S. (2008). Systems biology in the study of neurological disorders: Focus on Alzheimer's disease. *Alcohol Research & Health, 31* (1), 60–65.

Patrick, D. L., Giuliano, F., Ho, K. F., Gagnon, D. D., McNulty, P., & Rothman, M. (2009). The Premature Ejaculation Profile: Validation of self-reported outcome measures for research and practice. *BJU International, 103*(3), 358–364.

Paul, A. M. (1999). *Painting insanity black.* Retrieved from Salon.com Health & Body Web site: http://www.salon.com/books/it/1999/12/01/schizo/?CP=SAL&DN=110.

Pearson, G. S. (2008). Advocating for the full-frame approach [Editorial]. *Perspectives in Psychiatric Care, 44*(1), 1–2.

Peele, S. (1996, September/October). Recovering from an all-or-nothing approach to alcohol. *Psychology Today, 29*(5), 35–42.

Peplau, L. A., Frederick, D. A., Yee, C., Maisel, N., Lever, J., & Ghavami, N., (2009). Body image satisfaction in heterosexual, gay, and lesbian adults. *Archives of Sexual Behavior, 38*(5), 713–725.

Perlman, H. H. (1957). *Social casework: A problem solving process.* Chicago: University of Chicago Press.

Perry, A., Tarrier, N., Morriss, R., McCarthy, E., & Limb, K. (1999). Randomised controlled trial of efficacy of teach patients with bipolar disorder to identify early symptoms of relapse and obtain treatment. *British Medical Journal, 218*(7177), 149–154.

Perry, B. D. (2008). Child maltreatment: A neurodevelopmental perspective on the role of trauma and neglect in psychopathology. In T. P. Beauchaine & S. P. Hinshaw (Eds.), *Child and adolescent psychopathology* (pp. 93–128). Hoboken, NJ: Wiley.

Perry, P. (1997, July/August). Personality disorders: Coping with the borderline. *Saturday Evening Post, 269*(4), 44–54.

Petitclerc, A., Boivin M., Dionne, G., Zoccolillo, M., & Tremblay, R. E. (2009). Disregard for rules: The early development and predictors of a specific dimension of disruptive behavior disorders. *Journal of Child Psychology and Psychiatry, 50*(12), 1477–1484.

Petrakis, I., & Krystal, J. (1997, Spring). Neuroscience: Implications for treatment. *Alcohol Health and Research World, 21*(2), 157–161.

Physicians' desk reference (63rd ed., 2009). Montvale, NJ: Medical Economics.

Pietrefesa, A. S., & Coles, M. E. (2009). Moving beyond an exclusive focus on harm avoidance in obsessive-compulsive disorder: Behavioral validation for the separability of harm avoidance and incompleteness. *Behavior Therapy, 40*(3), 251–259.

Pliner, P., Chaiken, S., & Flett, G. (1990, June). Gender differences in concern with body weight and physical appearance over the life span. *Personality and Social Psychology Bulletin, 16*(2), 263–273.

Pollak, J., Levy, S., & Breitholtz, T. (1999, Summer). Screening for medical and neurodevelopmental disorders for the professional counselor. *Journal of Counseling Development, 77,* 350–357.

Pollatos, O., et al. (2008). Reduced perception of bodily signals in anorexia nervosa. *Science Direct: Eating Behaviors, 9*(4), 381–388.

Pomerantz, A. D., & Segrist, D. J. (2006). The influence of payment method on psychologists' diagnostic decisions regarding minimally impaired clients. *Ethics and Behavior, 16*(3), 253–263.

Pomeroy, C. (1996). Anorexia nervosa, bulimia nervosa, and binge eating disorder: Assessment of physical status. In J. K. Thompson (Ed.), *Body image, eating disorders and obesity* (pp. 83–107). Washington, DC: American Psychological Association.

Pope, H. G., Phillips, K. A., & Olivardia, R. (2000). *The Adonis complex: The secret crisis of male body obsession.* New York: Free Press.

Potenza, M. (2006). Should addictive disorders include non-substance-related conditions? *Addiction, 100*(Suppl. 1) 142–151.

Pottick, K. J., Kirk, S. A., Hsieh, D. K., & Tian, X. (2007). Judging mental disorder in youths: Effects of client, clinician, and contextual differences. *Journal of Consulting and Clinical Psychology, 75*(1), 1–8.

Powers, G. T., Meenaghan, T., & Toomey, B. (1985). *Practice-focused research.* Englewood Cliffs, NJ: Prentice-Hall.

Poznyak, V., Saraceno, B., & Obot, I. (2005, November). Breaking the vicious circle of determinants and consequences of harmful alcohol use. *Bulletin of the World Health Organization, 83*(11), 803–804.

Pozzi, G., Martinotti, G., Reina, D., Dario, T., Frustaci, A., Janiri, L., et al. (2008). The assessment of post-detoxification anhedonia: Influence of clinical and psychosocial variables. *Substance Use & Misuse, 43*(5), 722–732.

Prince, M., Patel, V., Saxena, S., Maj, J., Phillips, M. R., & Rahman, A. (2007). No health without mental health [Global Mental Health Series Article 1]. *Lancet, 370,* 859–877.

Prout, H. T. (2007). Counseling and psychotherapy with children and adolescents: Historical developmental, integrative, and effectiveness perspectives. In H. T. Prout & D. T. Brown (Eds.), *Counseling and psychotherapy with children and adolescents: Theory and practice for school and clinical settings* (4th ed., pp. 1–31). Hoboken, NJ: Wiley.

Pumariega, A. J., Rogers, K., & Rothe, E. (2005, October). Culturally competent systems of care for children's mental health: Advances and challenges. *Community Mental Health Journal, 41*(5), 539–555.

Qiu, A., et al. (2009). Neuroanatomical asymmetry patterns in individuals with schizophrenia and their non-psychotic siblings. *NeuroImage, 47*(4), 1221–1229.

Queralt, M. (1996). *The social environment and human behavior: A diversity perspective.* Boston: Allyn & Bacon.

Qureshi, A., Collazos, F., Ramos, M., & Casas, M. (2008). Cultural competency training in psychiatry. *European Psychiatry, 23*(Suppl. 1), 49–58.

Rabinowitz, A. (2009). Enhancing medication-assisted treatment: Success beyond harm reduction. *Journal of Social Work Practice in the Addictions, 9,* 240–243.

Ralph, D. J., & Wylie, K. R. (2005). Ejaculatory disorders and sexual fuction. *BJU International, 95,* 1181–1186.

Rankin, E. A. (1996). Patient and family education. In V. B. Carson & E. N. Arnold (Eds.), *Mental health nursing: The nurse patient journey* (pp. 503–516). Philadelphia: Saunders.

Rashidian, A., Eccles, M. P., & Russell, I. (2008). Falling on stony ground? A qualitative study of implementation of clinical guidelines' prescribing recommendations in primary care. *Health Policy, 85,* 148–161.

Rauch, J. (1993). Introduction. In J. Rauch (Ed.), *Assessment: A sourcebook for social work practice.* (pages unknown). Milwaukee, WI: Families International.

Ravart, M., & Cote, H. (1992). Sexoanalysis: A new insight-oriented treatment approach for sexual disorders. *Journal of Sex and Marital Therapy, 18,* 128–140.

Raz, S., & Raz, N. (1990). Structural brain abnormalities in the major psychosis: A quantitative review of the evidence from computerized imaging. *Psychological Bulletin, 108*(1), 93–108.

Read, J. (1995). Female sexual dysfunction. *International Review of Psychiatry, 7,* 175–182.

Reamer, F. G. (2001). Ethics and values in clinical and community social work practice. In H. Briggs & K. Corcoran (Eds.), *Social work practice: Treating common client problems* (pp. 85–106). Chicago: Lyceum.

Reamer, F. G. (2005). Documentation in social work: Evolving ethical and risk-management standards. *Social Work, 50*(4), 325–334.

Reamer, F. G. (2009). Ethical issues in social work. In A. Roberts (Ed.), *Social workers desk reference* (2nd ed., pp. 115–120). New York: Oxford University Press.

Reeves, R., & Brister, J. (2008). Psychosis in late life: Emerging issues. *Journal of Psychosocial Nursing, 46* (11), 45–52.

Reid, W. H., Keller, S., Leatherman, M., & Mason, M. (1998). ECT in Texas. *Journal of Clinical Psychiatry, 59*, 5–13.

Resnick, C., & Dziegielewski, S. F. (1996). The relationship between therapeutic termination and job satisfaction among medical social workers. *Social Work in Health Care, 23*(3), 17–35.

Resnick, W. M., & Carson, V. B. (1996). The journey colored by mood disorders. In V. B. Carson & E. N. Arnold (Eds.), *Mental health nursing: The nurse patient journey* (pp. 759–792). Philadelphia: Saunders.

Rettew, D. C. (2006). Avoidant personality disorder: Boundaries of a diagnosis. *Psychiatric Times, 23*(8).

Riccio, C. A., Hynd, G. W., Cohen, M. J., & Gonzalez, J. J. (1993). Neurological basis of attention deficit hyperactivity disorder. *Exceptional Children, 60*, 118–124.

Ridley-Siegert, D. (2000). Anorexia nervosa: Treatment with olanzapine. *British Journal of Psychiatry, 177*, 87.

Roberts, A., & Dziegielewski, S. F. (1995). Foundation skills and applications of crisis intervention and cognitive therapy. In A. Roberts (Ed.), *Crisis intervention and time-limited cognitive treatment* (pp. 3–27). Thousand Oaks, CA: Sage.

Roberts, A. R. (2005). Bridging the past and present to the future of crisis intervention and crisis management. In A. R. Roberts (Ed.), *Crisis intervention handbook: Assessment, treatment, and research* (3rd ed., pp. 3–34). New York: Oxford University Press.

Robertson, S., Davis, S., Sneed, Z., Koch, D., & Boston, Q. (2009). Competency issues for Alcohol/other drug abuse counselors. *Alcoholism Treatment Quarterly, 27*(3), 265–279.

Robinson, S., Rich, C., Weitzel, T., Vollmer, C., & Eden, B. (2008). Delirium prevention for cognitive, sensory, and mobility impairments. *Research and Theory for Nursing Practice, 22*(2), 103–113.

Roemmelt, A. F. (1998). *Haunted children: Rethinking medication of common psychological disorders.* Albany: State University of New York Press.

Romano, E., Zoccolillo, M., & Paquette, D. (2006). Histories of child maltreatment and psychiatric disorder in pregnant adolescents. *Journal of the American Academy of Child and Adolescent Psychiatry, 45*(3), 329–336.

Room, R. (2006). Taking account of cultural and societal influences on substance use diagnoses and criteria. *Addiction, 101*(Suppl. 1), 31–39.

Rosario-Campos, L., et al. (2005). A family study of early onset obsessive compulsive disorder. *American Journal of Medical Genetics (Neuropsychiatric Genetics Part B), 136B*(1), 92–97.

Rosen, A., & Callaly, T. (2005). Interdisciplinary teamwork and leadership: Issues for psychiatrists. *Australasian Psychiatry, 13*(3), 234–240.

Rosen, J. (1995). Assessment and treatment of body image disturbance. In K. Brownell & C. Fairburn (Eds.), *Eating disorders and obesity: A comprehensive handbook* (pp. 369–373). New York: Guilford Press.

Rosen, R., Brown, C., Heiman, J., Leiblum, S., Meston, C. M., Shabsigh, R., et al. (2000). The Female Sexual Function Index (FSFI): A multidimensional self-report instrument for the assessment of female sexual function. *Journal of Sex and Marital Therapy, 26*, 191–208.

Rosen, R., et al. (2003). Lower urinary tract symptoms and male sexual dysfunction: The multinational survey of the aging male (MSAM-7). *European Urology, 44*(6), 637–649.

Rosen, R. C., & Leiblum, S. R. (1987). Current approaches to the evaluation of sexual desire disorders. *Journal of Sex Research, 23*, 141–162.

Rounsaville, B. J., O'Malley, S., Foley, S., & Weissman, M. M. (1988). Role of manual-guided training in the conduct and efficacy of interpersonal psychotherapy for depression. *Journal of Consulting and Clinical Psychology, 56*(5), 681–688.

Rowland, D. L., Tai, W. L., & Slob, A. K. (2003). An exploration of emotional response to erotic stimulation in men with premature ejaculation: Effects of treatment with clomipramine. *Journal of Sexual Behavior, 32*(2), 145–153.

Rude, S. S., & Bates, D. (2005). The use of cognitive and experiential techniques to treat depression. *Clinical Case Studies, 4*(4), 363–379.

Rudman, W. J. (2000). *Coding and documentation of domestic violence.* Retrieved October 12, 2009, from http://www.endabuse.org/userfiles/file/HealthCare/codingpaper.pdf

Rudolph, C. S. (2000). Educational challenges facing health care social workers in the twenty-first century. *Professional Development, 3*(1), 31–41.

Ruffolo, M. C. (1998). Mental health services for children and adolescents In J. B. W. Williams & K. Ell (Eds.), *Advances in mental health research: Implications for practice* (pp. 333–419). Washington, DC: NASW Press.

Russell-Chapin, L., & Ivey, A. (2004). *Your supervised practicum and internship: Field resources for turning theory into action.* Belmont, CA: Thomson Learning.

Sadler, J. Z. (Ed.). (2002). *Descriptions & prescriptions: Values, mental disorders and the DSMs.* Baltimore: Johns Hopkins University Press.

Sadler, J. Z., Fulford, B., & Phil, M. B. (2004). Should patients and their families contribute to the *DSM-V* process? *Psychiatric Services, 55,* 133–138.

Sadock, B. J., & Sadock, V. A. (2008). *Kaplan and Sadock's comprehensive textbook of psychiatry.* Baltimore: Lippincott, Williams, & Wilkins.

Saint-Cyr, J. A. (2003). Frontal-striatal circuit functions: Context, sequence, and consequence. *Journal of the International Neuropsychological Society, 9*(1), 103–127.

Sajatovic, M., Valenstein, M., Blow, F., Ganoczy, D., & Ignacio, R. (2007). Treatment adherence with lithium and anticonvulsant medications among patients with bipolar disorder. *Psychiatric Services, 58*(6), 855–863.

Saklad, S. R. (2000). APA studies focus on side effects, efficacy of antipsychotics. *Psychopharmacology Update, 11*(1), 1.

Salesby, D. (1994). Culture, theory and narrative: The intersections of meanings in practice. *Social Work, 39*(4), 351–359.

Salonia, A., Munarriz, R. M., Naspro, R., Nappi, R. E., Briganti, A., Chionna, R., et al. (2004). Women's sexual dysfunction: A pathophysiological review. *BJU International, 93*(8), 1156–1164.

Santos, A., Rondan, C., Rosset, D., Fonseca, D., & Deruelle, C. (2008). Mr. Grimace or Ms. Smile: Does categorization affect perceptual processing in autism? *Psychological Science, 19*(1), 70–76.

Satterly, B. A. (2007). The alternative lenses of assessment: Educating social workers about psychopathology. *Teaching in Social Work, 27*(3/4), 241–257.

Saunders, B. E., Villeponteaux, L. A., Lipovsky, J. A., & Kilpatrick, D. G. (1992). Child sexual assault as a risk factor for mental disorders among women: A community survey. *Journal of Interpersonal Violence, 7,* 189–204.

Schapman-Williams A. M., & Lock, J. (2007). Using cognitive-behavioral therapy to treat adolescent-onset bulimia nervosa: A case study. *Clinical Case Studies, 6*(6), 508–524.

Schatzberg, A. F., Cole, J. O., & Debattista, C. (2007). *Manual of clinical psychopharmacology* (6th ed.). Washington, DC: American Psychiatric Press.

Scheirs, J. G. M., & Bok, S. (2007). Psychological distress in caretakers or relatives of patients with Borderline Personality Disorder. *International Journal of Social Psychiatry, 53*(3), 195–203.

Schlundt, D. G. (1989). Computerized behavioral assessment of eating behavior in bulimia: The self-monitoring analysis system. In J. W. Jornson (Ed.), *Advances in eating disorders 2: Bulimia* (pp. 1–23). New York: JAI Press.

Schmajuk, N. A. (2001). Hippocampal dysfunction in schizophrenia. *Hippocampus, 11*(5), 599–613.

Schoenwald, S. K., Kelleher, K., & Weisz, J. R. (2008). Building bridges to evidence-based practice: The MacArthur foundation child system and treatment enhancement projects (Child STEPs). *Administration and Policy in Mental Health and Mental Health service research, 35,* 66–72.

Schulte, M., Ramo, D., & Brown, S. (2009). Gender differences in factors influencing alcohol use and drinking progression among adolescents. *Clinical Psychology Reviews, 29*(6), 535–547.

Schulz, S. C. (2000). New antipsychotic medications: More than old wine and new bottles. *Bulletin of the Menninger Clinic, 64*(1), 60–75.

Schur, S. B., Sikich, L., Findling, R. L., Malone, R. P., Crismon, M. L., & Derivan, A., et al. (2003). Treatment recommendations for the use of antipsychotics for aggressive youth (TRAAY). Part I: A review. *Journal of the American Academy of Child and Adolescent Psychiatry, 42,* 132–44.

Schutte, N. S., & Malouff, J. M. (1995). *Sourcebook of adult assessment strategies.* New York: Plenum Press.

Schwartz, G. E., Davidson, R. J., & Goleman, D. J. (1978). Patterning of cognitive and somatic processes in self-regulation of anxiety: Effects of meditation versus exercise. *Psychosomatic Medicine, 40*(1), 321–328.

Schwebel, D., & Gaines, J. (2007, June). Pediatric unintentional injury: Behavioral risk factors and implications for prevention. *Journal of Developmental and Behavioral Pediatrics, 38*(3), 245–254.

Segal, Z., Vincent, P., & Levitt, A. (2002). Efficacy of combined, sequential, and crossover psychotherapy and pharmacotherapy in improving outcomes in depression. *Journal of Psychiatry Neuroscience, 27*(4), 281–290.

Segraves, R. T., & Segraves, K. B. (1991). Hypoactive sexual desire disorder: Prevalence and comorbidity in 906 subjects. *Journal of Sex and Marital Therapy, 17,* 55–58.

Seligman, L., & Reichenberg, L. W. (2007). *Selecting effective treatments: A comprehensive, systematic guide to treating mental disorders* (3rd ed.). Hoboken, NJ: Wiley.

Shindul-Rothschild, J. A., & Rothschild, A. J. (1998). Psychotropics in primary care. In L. A. Eisenbauer & M. A. Murphy (Eds.), *Pharmacotherapeutics and advanced nursing practice* (pp. 37–51). New York: McGraw-Hill.

Shlonsky, A. (2009). Evidence-based practice in social work education. In A. Roberts (Ed.), *Social workers desk reference* (2nd ed., pp. 1169–1176). New York: Oxford University Press.

Siebert, C. (2006). Functional assessment: Process and product. *Home Health Care Management and Practice, 19*(1), 51–57.

Seibert, S., & Gruenfeld, L. (1992). Masculinity, femininity, and behavior in groups. *Small Group Research, 23*(1), 95–112.

Shannon, S., & Heckman, E. (2007). *Please don't label my child: Break the doctor-diagnosis-drug cycle and discover safe, effective choices for your child's emotional health.* New York: Rodale.

Shapiro, F. (2001). *Eye movement desensitization and reprocessing: Basic principles, protocols, and procedures* (2nd ed.). New York: Guilford Press.

Shapiro, F., Kaslow, W., & Maxfield, L. (Eds.). (2007). *Handbook of EMDR and family therapy processes.* Hoboken, NJ: Wiley.

Shapiro, J. P., Friedberg, R. D., & Bardenstein, K. K. (2006). *Child and adolescent therapy: Science and art.* Hoboken, NY: Wiley.

Shapiro, S. (1981). *Contemporary theories of schizophrenia.* Hightstown, NJ: McGraw-Hill.

Shaw, D. S., Gilliom, M., Ingoldsby, E. M., & Nagin, D. S. (2003). Trajectories leading to school-age conduct problems. *Developmental Psychology, 39*(2), 189–200.

Shaw, J. (1990). Play therapy with the sexual workhorse: Successful treatment with 12 cases of inhibited ejaculation. *Journal of Sex & Marital Therapy, 16,* 159–164.

Sheafor, B. W., & Horejsi, C. R. (2008). *Techniques and guidelines for social work practice* (8th ed.). Boston: Allyn & Bacon.

Sheafor, B. W., Horejsi, C. R., & Horejsi, G. A. (1997). *Techniques and guidelines for social work practice* (4th ed.). Needham Heights, MA: Allyn & Bacon.

Sheikh, J. I., Cassidy, E. L., Doraiswamy, M. P., Salomon, R. M., Hornig, M., Holland, P. J., et. al. (2004). Efficacy, safety, and tolerability of sertraline in patients with late-life depression and comorbid medical illness. *Journal of the American Geriatrics Society, 52*(1), 86–92.

Sherry, A., Lyddon, W. J., & Henson, R. K. (2007). Adult attachment and developmental personality styles: An empirical study. *Journal of Counseling and Development, 85*(3), 337–348.

Siegelman, L. (1990). *Selecting effective treatments.* San Francisco: Jossey-Bass.

Sieleni, B. (2007). Borderline personality disorder in corrections. *Corrections Today, 69*(5), 24–25.

Siev, J., & Chambless, D. L. (2007/2008). Specificity of treatment effects: Cognitive therapy and relaxation for generalized anxiety and panic disorder. *Journal of Consulting and Clinical Psychology, 75*(4), 513–522.

Simon, G. E., & Savarino, J. (2007). Suicide attempts among patients starting depression treatment with medications or psychotherapy. *American Journal of Psychiatry, 164*(7), 1029–1034.

Simon, J., et al. (2005). Testosterone patch increases sexual activity and desire in surgically menopausal women with hypoactive sexual desire. *Journal of Endocrinology and Metabolism, 90*(9), 5226–5233.

Simon, J. K. (2010). *Solution focused practice in end-of-life & grief counseling.* New York: Springer.

Simons, J. S., & Carey, M. P. (2001). Prevalence of sexual dysfunctions: Results from a decade of research. *Archives of Sexual Behavior, 30*(2), 177–219.

Simpson, E., Pistorello, J., Begin, A., Costello, E., Levinson, J., Mulberry, S., et al. (1998). Use of dialectical behavior therapy in a partial hospital program for women with borderline personality disorder. *Psychiatric Services, 49*(5), 669–673.

Simpson, H. B., Rosen, W., Huppert, J. D., Lin, S., Foa, E. B., & Liebowitz, M. R. (2006). Are there reliable neuropsychological deficits in obsessive-compulsive disorder? *Journal of Psychiatric Research, 40*(3), 247–257.

Sinclair, S. J., & Gansler, D. A. (2006). Integrating the somatic marker and social cognition theories to explain different manifestations of antisocial personality disorder. *New School Psychology Bulletin, 4*(2), 40–47.

Siris, S. G. (2000). Management of depression in schizophrenia. *Psychiatric Annals, 30*(1), 13–17.

Skidmore, R. A., Thackeray, M. G., & Farley, O. W. (1997). *Introduction to social work* (7th ed.). Boston: Allyn & Bacon.

Skinner, B. F. (1953). *Science and human behavior.* New York: Macmillan.

Skovgaard, A. M., Houmann, T., Christiansen, E., Landorph, T., Jorgensen, T., Olsen, E. M., et al. (2007). The prevalence of mental health problems in children

1(1/2) years of age—the Copenhagen child cohort 2000. *Journal of Child Psychology and Psychiatry, and Allied Disciplines, 48*(1), 62–70.

Skultety, K. M., & Zeiss, A. (2006). The treatment of depression in older adults in the primary care setting: An evidence-based review. *Health Psychology, 25,* 665–674.

Slomski, A. J. (2000, January 5). Group practice economics. *Medical Economics Archive.*

Smajkic, A., Weine, S., Djuric-Bijedic, Z., Boskailo, E., Lewis, J., & Pavkovic, I. (2001). Sertraline, paroxetine, and venlafaxine in refugee posttraumatic stress disorder with depression symptoms. *Journal of Traumatic Stress, 14*(3), 445–452.

Smith, M. (2005). Pain assessment in older adults with advanced dementia. *Perspectives in Psychiatric Care, 41*(3), 99–113.

Smith, R. C., & Hughes, C. C. (1993). Culture bound syndromes. In *Culture, ethnicity, and mental illness* (p. 75). Washington, DC: American Psychiatric Press.

Smock, S. A., Trepper, T. S., Wetchler, J. L., McCollum, E. E., Ray R., & Pierce, K. (2008). Solution-focused group therapy for level 1 substance abusers. *Journal of Marital and Family Therapy, 34*(1), 107–120.

Sohrabji, F. (2002). Neurodegeneration in women. *Alcohol Research & Health, 26*(4), 316–318.

Sommers-Flanagan, J., & Sommers-Flanagan, R. (2009). *Clinical interviewing* (4th ed.). Hoboken, NJ: Wiley.

Sommers-Flanagan, R. S., & Sommers-Flanagan, J. (2007). *Philosophical foundations.* Hoboken, N.J: Wiley.

Soni, A. (2009, July). The five most costly conditions, 1996 and 2006: Estimates for the U.S. civilian non-institutionalized population [Statistical Brief #248]. Agency for Healthcare Research and Quality, Rockville, MD. Retrieved November 24, 2009, from http://www.meps.ahrq.gov/mepsweb/data_files/publications/st248/stat248.pdf

Sorensen, M. J., Mors, O., & Thomsen, P. H. (2005, Sept.). *DSM-IV* or *ICD-10-DCR* diagnoses in child and adolescent psychiatry: Does it matter? *European Child and Adolescent Psychiatry, 14*(6), 335–340.

Sotile, W. M., & Kilmann, P. R. (1978). The effects of group systematic desensitization on orgasmic dysfunction. *Archives of Sexual Behavior, 7,* 477–491.

Sotomayor, M. (2005). The burden of premature ejaculation: The patient's perspective. *Journal of Sex Medicine* (Suppl. 2), 110–114.

Spector, A., Davies, S., Woods, B., & Orrell, M. (2000). Reality orientation for dementia: A systematic review of the evidence of effectiveness from randomized controlled trials. *Gerontologist, 40,* 206–212.

Spector, I. P., & Carey, M. P. (1990). Incidence and prevalence of sexual dysfunctions: A critical review of the literature. *Archives of Sexual Behavior, 19,* 389–408.

Spetie, L., & Arnold, L. E. (2007). Ethical issues in child psychopharmacology research and practice: Emphasis on preschoolers. *Psychopharmacology, 191*(1), 15–26.

Spiegler, M., & Guevremont, D. (1998). *Contemporary behavior therapy* (3rd ed.). Pacific Grove, CA: Brooks/Cole.

Spitzer, R. L., Williams, J. B. W., & Skodol, A. E. (1980). *DSM-III:* The major achievements and an overview. *American Journal of Psychiatry, 137,* 151–164.

Spokas, M. E., Rodebaugh, T. L., & Heimberg, R. G. (2004). Cognitive biases in social phobia. *Psychiatry, 3,* 51–55.

Spoormaker, V. I., & Montgomery, P. (2008). Disturbed sleep in post-traumatic stress disorder: Secondary symptom of core feature? *Sleep Medicine Reviews, 12,* 169–184.

Sripada, C. S., Sehkar, C., Angstadt, M., Banks, S., Nathan, P. J., Liberzon, I., et al. (2009). Functional neuro-imaging of mentalizing during the trust game in social anxiety. *NeuroReport, 20*(11), 984–989.

Sroufe, L. A., Carlson, E. A., Levy, A. K., & Egeland, B. (1999). Implications of attachment theory for developmental psychopathology. *Development and Psychopathology, 11,* 1–13.

Stefansson, R., & Hesse, M. (2008). Personality disorders in substance abusers: A comparison of patients treated in a prison unit and patients treated in inpatient treatment. *International Journal of Mental Health Addiction, 6*(3), 402–406.

Stein, B. D., Zima, B. T., Elliott, M. N., Burnam, M. A., Shahinfar, A., Fox, N. A., et al. (2001). Violence exposure among school-age children in foster care: Relationship to distress symptoms. *Journal of the American Academy of Child and Adolescent Psychiatry, 40*(5), 588–594.

Steinglass, P. (1976). Experimenting with family treatment approaches to alcoholism, 1950-1975: A review [CD-ROM]. *Family process,* 97–123. Abstract retrieved from PsychLIT: AN 3882.

Steinhausen, H. C. (2002). The outcome of anorexia nervosa in the 20th century. *American Journal of Psychiatry, 159*(8), 1284–1293.

Steps taken to watchdog managed care. (1997, January). *NASW News, 42*(1), 12.

Stern, Y. (2006). Cognitive reserve and Alzheimer disease. *Alzheimer Disease & Associated Disorders, 20*(2), 112–117.

Strawn, J. R., & Geracioti, T. D., Jr. (2007). The treatment of generalized anxiety disorder with pregabalin, an atypical anxiolytic. *Neuropsychiatric Disease and Treatment, 3*(2), 237–243.

Striegel-Moore, R. H., Dohm, G., Kraemer, H., Taylor, C., Daniels, S., Crawford, P., Schreiber, et al., (2003). Eating disorders in white and black women. *American Journal of Psychiatry, 160*, 1326–1331.

Striegel-Moore, R. H., Franko, D. L., Thompson, D., Barton, B., Schreiber, G. B., & Daniels, S. R. (2005). An empirical study of the typology of bulimia nervosa and its spectrum variants. *Psychological Medicine, 35*, 1563–1572.

Strober, M., Freeman, R., DeAntonio, M., Lampert, C., & Diamond, J. (1997). Does adjunctive fluoxetine influence the post-hospital course of restrictor-type anorexia nervosa? A 24-month prospective, longitudinal follow-up and comparison with historical controls. *Psychopharmacology Bulletin, 33*, 425–436.

Stuart, F. M., Hammond, D. C., & Pett, M. A. (1987). Inhibited sexual desire in women. *Archives of Sexual Behavior, 16*(2), 91–106.

Stuntz, S. S., Falk, A., Hiken, M., & Carson, V. B. (1996). The journey undermined by psychosexual disorders. In V. B. Carson & E. N. Arnold (Eds.), *Mental health nursing: The nurse patient journey* (pp. 879–895). Philadelphia: W. B. Saunders.

Substance Abuse and Mental Health Services Administration. (1998). *Treatment Episode Data Set (TEDS)*. Available from http://www.oas.samhsa.gov/DASIS.htm.

Substance Abuse and Mental Health Services Administration. (2009a). *The NSDUH report: Concurrent illicit drug and alcohol use.* Research Triangle Park, NC: Office of Applied Studies and Substance Abuse and Mental Health Services Administration.

Substance Abuse and Mental Health Services Administration. (2009b). *Results from the 2008 National Survey on Drug Use and Health: National findings.* Research Triangle Park, NC: Office of Applied Studies and Substance Abuse and Mental Health Services Administration.

Substance Abuse and Mental Health Services Administration. (2009c). *The NSDUH Report: Nonmedical use of Adderall among full-time college students.* Research Triangle Park, MD: Office of Applied Studies and Substance Abuse and Mental Health Services Administration.

Sue, D. W., & Sue, D. (Eds.). (2008). *Counseling the diverse: Theory and practice* (5th ed.). Hoboken, NJ: Wiley.

Sundin, E. C., & Horowitz, M. J. (2002). Impact of event scale: Psychometric oroperty. *British Journal of Psychiatry, 180*, 205–209.

Sutton, M. (2000, October). Cultural competence: It's not just political correctness: It's good medicine. *Family Practice Management* (pp. 1–6). Available online: http://www.aafp.org/fpm/20001000/58cult.html.

Swartz-Kulstad, J. L., & Martin, W. E. (1999). Impact of culture and context on psychosocial adaption: The cultural and contextual guide process. *Journal of Counseling and Development, 77*, 281–293.

Swendsen, J., Conway, K., Degenhardt, L., Dierker, L., Glantz, M., Kin, R., et al. (2009). Socio-demographic risk factors for alcohol and drug dependence: The 10-year follow-up of the National Comorbidity Survey. *Addiction, 104*(8), 1346–1355.

Swindle, R. W., Cameron, A. E., Lockhart, D. C., & Rosen, R. C. (2004). The Psychological and Interpersonal Relationship Scales: Assessing psychological and relationship outcomes associated with erectile dysfunction and its treatment. *Archives of Sexual Behavior, 33*(1), 19–30.

Szasz, T. (1980). *Sex by prescription: The startling truth about today's sex therapy.* New York: Doubleday.

Tabet, N., Stewart, R., Hudson, S., Sweeney, V., Sauer, J., Bryant, C., et al. (2006). Male gender influences response to an educational package for delirium prevention among older people: A stratified analysis. *International Journal of Geriatric Psychiatry, 21*, 493–497.

Tarasoff v. The Regents of the University of California, 551 P.2d 334 (Calif. 1976).

Taylor, S. (1996). Meta-analysis of cognitive-behavioral treatments for social phobia. *Journal of Behavioral Therapy and Experimental Psychiatry, 27*(1), 1–9.

Taylor, T. K., Schmidt, F., Pepler, D., & Hodgins, H. (1998). A comparison of eclectic treatment with Webster-Stratton's Parents and Children Series in a Children's Mental Health Center: A randomized controlled trial. *Behavior Therapy, 29*, 221–240.

Terry, L. L. (1992). Gender and family therapy: Adding a bi-level belief systems component to assessment. *Contemporary Family Therapy: An International Journal, 14*(3), 199–210.

Thomas, C. P., Conrad, P., Casler, R., & Goodman, E. (2006). Trends in the use of psychotropic medications among adolescents, 1994 to 2001. *Psychiatric Services*, *57*(1), 63–69.

Thomas, N. L. (2000). Parenting children with attachment disorders. *Handbook of attachment interventions* (pp. 261–277; DHHS Publication). *Healthy people 2000: National health promotion disease and prevention objectives*. Washington, DC: Department of Health and Human Services.

Thomas, V. (1989). Body-image satisfaction among Black women. *Journal of Social Psychology*, *129*(1), 107–112.

Thompson, K., & Allen, S. (2008). Outcomes of emergency admission of older patients: Impact of cognitive impairment. *British Journal of Hospital Medicine*, *69*(6), 320–323.

Thorens, G., Gex-Fabry, M., Zullino, D. F., & Eytan, A. (2008). Attitudes toward psychopharmacology among hospitalized patients from diverse ethno-cultural backgrounds. *BMC Psychiatry*, *8*, 55.

Thyer, B. A., & Papsdorf, J. D. (1981). Relationship between irrationality and sexual arousability. *Psychological Reports*, *48*, 834.

Thyer, B. A., & Wodarski, J. S. (1998). *Handbook of empirical social work practice: Mental disorders* (Vol. 1). New York: Wiley.

Tierney, L. M., McPhee, S. J., & Papadakis, M. A. (Eds.). (1997). *Current medical diagnosis and treatment* (36th ed.). Stamford, CT: Appleton & Lange.

Tillfors, M., Furmark, T., Ekselius, L., & Fredrikson, M. (2001). Social phobia and avoidant personality disorder as related to parental history of social anxiety: A general population study. *Behviour Research and Therapy*, *39*, 289–298.

Timko, C., Moos, R. H., Finney, J. W., Moos, B. S., & Kaplowitz, M. S. (1999, July). Long-term treatment careers and outcomes of previously untreated alcoholics (ST). *Journal of Studies on Alcohol*, *60*(4), 437–445.

Timonen, M., & Liukkonen, T. (2008). Clinical review management of depression in adults. *British Medical Journal*, *336*, 435–439.

Tompkins, M. A. (2004). *Using homework in psychotherapy: Strategies, guidelines, and forms*. New York: Guilford Press.

Ton, H., & Lim, R. F. (2006). The assessment of culturally diverse individuals. In R. F. Lim (Ed.), *Clinical manual of cultural psychiatry* (pp. 3–31). Arlington, VA: American Psychiatric Press.

Tonigan, J. S., Conners, G. J., & Miller, W. R. (1998). Special populations in Alcoholics Anonymous. *Alcohol Health and Research World*, *22*(4), 281–285.

Torpy, J. M. (2009). Bipolar disorder. *Journal of the American Medical Association*, *301*(5), 564.

Tracker, C. M. E. (2009). Violence in schizophrenia rare in the absence of substance abuse. *JAMA*, *301*, 2016.

Trautmann, J., Rau, S., Wilson, M., & Walters, C., (2008). Vegetarian students in their first year of college: Are they at risk for restrictive or disordered eating behaviors? *College Student Journal*, *42*(2), 340–347.

Tremblay, R. E., Nagin, D. S., Séguin, J. R., Zoccolillo, M., Zelazo, P. D., Boivin, M., Pérusse, D., & Japel, C. (2004). Physical aggression during early childhood: Trajectories and predictors. *Pediatrics*, *114*(1), e43–e50.

Trudel, G. (1991). Review of psychological factors in low sexual desire. *Sexual and Marital Therapy*, *6*, 261–272.

Tsou, J. Y. (2007). Hacking on the looping effects of psychiatric classifications: What is an interactive and indifferent kind? *International Studies in the Philosophy of Science*, *21*(3), 329–344.

Tsuang, D. (2004). Rates of schizophrenia among relatives of schizophrenic patients. Retrieved November 20, 2009, from http://www.schizophrenia.com/research/hereditygen.htm.

Turner, F. J. (Ed.). (1996). *Social work treatment: Interlocking theoretical approaches* (4th ed.). New York: Free Press.

UNAIDS. (2006). *AIDS epidemic update: Special report on HIV/AIDS: December 2006*. Geneva: UNAIDS.

University of Virginia Health System. (2006). *Adolescent medicine: Schizophrenia*. Retrieved November 18, 2009, from http://www.healthsystem.virginia.edu/uva health/peds_adolescent/schiz.cfm

U.S. Department of Health and Human Services. (2006). *Detoxification and substance abuse treatment: A Treatment Improvement Protocol (TIP) 45*. Rockville, MD: Substance Abuse and Mental Health Services Administration.

U.S. Department of Health and Human Services. (2008). Substance abuse treatment for persons with HIV and AIDS: Treatment Improvement Protocol Series (37). Rockville, MD: Substance Abuse and Mental health Services Administration.

U.S. Department of Health and Human Services. (2009). A provider's introduction to substance abuse treatment for lesbian, gay, bisexual and transgender individuals. Rockville, MD: Substance Abuse and Mental Health Services Administration.

U.S. Department of Veterans Affairs. (2009a). Penn Inventory for Posttraumatic Stress Disorder. Retrieved October 26, 2009, from U.S. Department of Veterans Affairs: National Center for PTSD: http://www.ptsd.va.gov / professional / pages / assessments / penn-inventory-ptsd.asp

U.S. Department of Veteran Affairs. (2009b). Los Angeles Symptom Checklist (LASC). Retrieved October 26, 2009, from U.S. Department of Veterans Affairs: National Center for PTSD: http://www.ptsd.va.gov/professional/pages/assessments/lasc.asp

U.S. Department of Veteran Affairs. (2009c). Screen for Posttraumatic Stress Symptoms (SPTSS). Retrieved October 26, 2009, from US Department of Veteran Affairs: National Center for PTSD: http://www.ptsd.va.gov/professional/pages/assessments/sptss.asp

Usery, J. B., Lobo, B., & Self, T. (2008). Pitfalls in prescribing: How to minimized drug therapy risks. *Consultant*, *48*(1).

Ushijima, M., Yokoyama, S., Sugiyama, E., & Amano, N. (2008). Contribution of perospirone and risperidone to reduce delirium in senile patients. *Psychogeriatrics*, *8*, 4–7.

Valenstein, M., McCarthy, J. F., Austin, K. L., Greden, J. F., Young, E. A., & Blow, F. C. (2006). What happened to lithium? Antidepressant augmentation in clinical settings. *American Journal of Psychiatry*, *163*(7), 1219–1225.

Valenzuela, M., & Sachdev, P. (2009). Harnessing brain and cognitive reserve for the prevention of dementia. *Indian Journal of Psychiatry*, *51*(5), 16–21.

Valtonen, H. M., Suominen, K., Haukka, J., Mantere, O., Leppamaki, S., Arvilommi, P., et al. (2008). Differences in incidence of suicide attempts during phases of bipolar I and II disorders. *Bipolar Disorders*, *10*, 588–596.

Van Balkom, A. J. L. M., & Van Dyck, R. (1998). Combination treatments for obsessive-compulsive disorder. In R. P. Swinson, M. M. Antony, S. Rachman, & M. A. Richter (Eds.), *Obsessive-compulsive disorder: Theory, research, and treatment* (pp. 349–366). New York: Guilford Press.

Van Balkom, A. J. L. M., Van Oppen, P., Wermeulen, A. W. A., Van Dyck, R., Nauta, M. C. E., & Vorst, H. C. M. (1994). Meta-analysis on the treatment of obsessive-compulsive disorder: A comparison of antidepressants, behavior, and cognitive therapy. *Clinical Psychology Review*, *14*, 359–381.

Van den Bergh, N. (Ed.). (1991). *Feminist perspectives on addictions*. New York: Springer.

Van den Heuvel, O. A., et al. (2005). Frontal-striatal dysfunction during planning in obsessive-compulsive disorder. *Archives of General Psychiatry*, *62*(3), 301–310.

Vandereycken, W. (2006). Media influences and body dissatisfaction in young women. *Eating Disorders Review*, *17*(2), 5.

Van Lier, P. A., van der Ende, J., Koot, H. M., & Verhulst, F. C. (2007). Which better predicts conduct problems? The relationship of trajectories of conduct problems with ODD and ADHD symptoms from childhood into adolescence. *Journal of Child Psychology and psychiatry, and Allied Disciplines*, *48*(6), 601–608.

Van Wormer, K. (2008). Counseling family members of addicts/alcoholics: The states of change model. *Journal of Family Social Work*, *11*(2), 202–221.

Vaughan, B. S., Roberts, H. J., & Needelman, H. (2009). Current medications for the treatment of attention-deficit/hyperactivity disorder. *Psychology in the Schools*, *46*(9), 846–856.

Versiani, M., Moreno, R., Ramakers-van Moorsel, C. J. A., & Schutte, A. J. (2006). Comparison of the effects of mirtazapine & fluoxetine in severely depressed patients. *CNS Drugs*, *19*(2), 137–146.

Vidair, H. B., & Gunlicks-Stoessel, M. L. (2009). Innovative child and adolescent treatment research for anxiety and depressive disorders. *Depression and Anxiety*, *26*(4), 307–308.

Vieta, E., Suppes, T., Eggens, I., Persson, I., Paulsson, B., & Brecher, M. (2008). Efficacy and safety of quetiapine in combination with lithium or divalproex for maintenance of patients with bipolar I disorder (International Trial 126). *Journal of Affective Disorders*, *109*, 251–263.

Villa, V., Manzoni, G. M., Pagnini, F., Castelnuovo, G., Cesa, G. L., & Molinari, E. (2009). Do coping strategies discriminate eating disordered individuals better than eating disorder features? An explorative study on female inpatients with anorexia and bulimia nervosa. *Journal of Clinical Psychological Medical Settings*, *16*(4), 297–303.

Vitousek, K. M., Watson, S., & Wilson, G. T. (1998). Enhancing motivation for change in treatment-resistant eating disorders. *Clinical Psychology Review*, *18*(4), 391–420.

Waldinger, M. (2005). Lifelong premature ejaculation: current debate on definition and treatment. *Journal of Men's Health & Gender*, *2*(3), 333–338.

Waldinger, M. D., & Schweitzer, D. H. (2006). Changing paradigms from a historical *DSM-III* and *DSM-IV* view: Toward and evidence-based definition of premature ejaculation: Part II—Proposals for *DSM-V* and *ICD-11*. *Journal of Sexual Medicine, 3*, 693–705.

Waldinger, M. D., Schweitzer, D. H., & Olivier, B. (2005). On-demand SSRI treatment of premature ejaculation: Pharmacodynamic limitations for relevant ejaculation delay and consequent solutions. *Journal of Sex Medicine, 2*, 120–130.

Waldinger, M. D., Zwinderman, A. H., Schweitzer, D. H., & Olivier, B. (2004). Relevance of methodological design for the interpretation of efficacy of drug treatment of premature ejaculation: A systematic review and meta-analysis. *International Journal of Impotence Research, 16*, 369–381.

Walitzer, K. S., & Connors, G. J. (1999, Fall). Treating problem drinking. *Alcohol Research and Health, 23*(2), 138–145.

Walker, D., Roffman, R., Picciano, J., & Stephens, R. (2007). The check-up: In-person, computerized, and telephone adaptations of motivational enhancement treatment to elicit voluntary participation by the contemplator. *Substance Abuse Treatment, Prevention, and Policy, 2*, 1–10.

Walker, E., Mitial, V., Tessner, K., & Trotman, H. (2008). Schizophrenia and the psychotic spectrum. In W. E. Craighead, D. J. Miklowitz, & L. W. Craighead (Eds.), *Psychopathology: History, diagnosis, and empirical foundations* (pp. 402–434). Hoboken, NJ: Wiley.

Walker, T. (2000). MCOs begin to recognize the reality of schizophrenia. *Managed Healthcare, 10*(6), 43–46.

Walkup, J., Bernet, W., Bukstein, O., Walter, H. (Work Group on Quality Issues), Arnold, V., & Benson, R. S. (Co-Chairs), et al. (2009). Practice parameter on the use of psychotropic medication in children and adolescents. *Journal of the American Academy of Child and Adolescent Psychiatry, 48*(9), 961–973.

Wallace, J. (1989). A. biopsychosocial model of alcoholism. *Social Casework: The Journal Of Contemporary Social Work, 70*(6), 325–331.

Walling, H. W. (2002). Antisocial personality disorder: A new heel for Achilles? *Western Journal of Medicine, 176*(3), 213–214.

Walsh, B. T., et al. (2006). Fluoxetine after weight restoration in anorexia nervosa. *JAMA, 295*(22), 2605–2612.

Walsh, J. (2000). *Clinical case management with persons having a mental illness: A relationship-based perspective*. Belmont, CA: Wadsworth/Thompson Learning.

Walsh, J. (2002). Shyness and social phobia: A social work perspective on a problem in living. *Health and Social Work, 27*(2), 137–144.

Walsh, T. (2008). Recovery from eating disorders. *Australian and New Zealand Journal of Psychiatry, 42*(2), 95–96.

Walsh, T. (2009). Eating disorders in *DSM-V*: Review of existing literature (Part 1). *International Journal of Eating Disorders, 42*(7), 579–580.

Walter, C. A., & McCoyd, J. L. M. (2009). *Grief and loss across the lifespan: A biopsychosocial perspective*. New York: Springer.

Wambach, K. G., Haynes, D. T., & White, B. W. (1999). Practice guidelines: Rapprochement or estrangement between social work practitioners and researchers. *Research on Social Work Practice, 9*(3), 322–330.

Warden, V., Hurley, A., & Volicer, L. (2003). A pain assessment tool for people with advanced Alzheimer's and other progressive dementias. *Home Healthcare Nurse: The Journal of the He Home care and Hospice Professional* , 32–37.

Ware, J. E., & Sherbourne, C. D. (1992). The MOS 36 Item Short Form Health Survey (SF-36): Conceptual framework and item selection. *Medical Care, 30*(2), 473–483.

Warren, J., Bacon, E., Harris, T., McBean, A., Foley, D., & Phillps, C. (1994). The burden of outcomes associated with dehydration among US elderly, 1991. *American Journal of Public Health, 84*(8), 1265–1269.

Watson, L. (1991). Paradigms of recovery: Theoretical implications for relapse prevention in alcoholics [CD-ROM]. *Journal of Drug Issues, 21*(4), 839–858. Abstract retrieved from PsychLIT: AN 79–17576.

Weaver, H., & Wodarski, J. S. (1996). Social work practice with Latinos. In D. F. Harrison, B. A. Thyer, & J. S. Wodarski (Eds.), *Cultural diversity and social work practice* (2nd ed.). Springfield, IL: Charles C Thomas.

WebMD. (2008). *Webster's New World Medical Dictionary* (3rd ed.). Hoboken, NJ: Wiley.

WebMD. (2009a). Could you have adult ADHD? Recognizing signs and symptoms. Retrieved November 29, 2009, from http://www.webmd.com/add-adhd/adult-adhd-symptoms-9/causes?ecd=wnl_emw_111109

WebMD. (2009b). Schizophrenia medications. Retrieved November 22, 2009, from http://www.webmd.com/schizophrenia/guide/scizophrenia-medications

Weiner, I. B. (1987). Identifying schizophrenia in adolescents. *Journal of Adolescent Health Care, 8*(4), 336–343.

Weisman, A. G. (1997). Understanding cross-cultural prognostic variability for schizophrenia. *Cultural Diversity and Mental Health, 3*(1), 23–35.

Weissman, M. M., Markowitz, J. C., & Klerman, G. L. (2007). *Clinician's quick guide to interpersonal therapy.* New York: Oxford University Press.

Wekerle, C., MacMillan, H. L., Leung, E., & Jamieson, E. (2008). Child maltreatment. In M. Hersen & A. M. Gross (Eds.), *Handbook of clinical psychology: Vol. 2. Children and adolescents.* (pp. 856–903). Hoboken, NJ: Wiley.

Weller, E. B. (1995). Bipolar disorder in children: Misdiagnosis, underdiagnosis, and future directions. *Journal of the American Academy of Child and Adolescent Psychiatry, 34,* 709–715.

Wells, R. A. (1994). *Planned short-term treatment* (2nd ed.). New York: Free Press.

Wesson, D. R. (1995). *Detoxification from alcohol and other drugs* (Publication No. SMA 95-3046). Rockville, MD: Department of Health and Human Services.

West, M., Prado, R., & Krystal, A. D. (1999). Evaluation and comparison of EEG traces: Latent structure in nonstationary time series. *Journal of the American Statistical Association, 94*(446), 375–394.

Westermeyer, J. (1990). Treatment for psychoactive substance use disorder in special populations: Issues in strategic planning [CD-ROM]. *Advances in Alcohol and Substance Abuse, 8*(3/4), 1–8. Abstract retrieved from PsychLIT: AN 24228.

Whitaker, L. P. (1992). *Schizophrenic disorders: Sense and nonsense in conceptualization, assessment and treatment.* New York: Plenum Press.

White, R. M. B., Roosa, M. W., Weaver, S. R., & Nair, R. L. (2009). Cultural and contextual influences on parenting in Mexican American families. *Journal of Marriage and Family, 71*(1), 61–79.

Whitehead, A., Mathews, A., & Ramage, M. (1987). The treatment of sexually unresponsive women: A comparative evaluation. *Behaviour Research and Therapy, 25*(3), 195–205.

Whittington, C. J., Kendall, T., Fonagy, P., Cottrell, D., Colgrove, A., & Boddington. E. (2004). Selective serotonin reuptake inhibitors in childhood depression: Systematic review of published versus unpublished data. *Lancet, 363,* 1341–1345.

Whyte, L., & Brooker, C. (2001). Working with a multidisciplinary team: In secure psychiatric environments. *Journal of Psychosocial Nursing and Mental Health Services, 39*(9), 26–34.

Wickramaratne, P. J., Greenwald, S., & Weissman, M. M. (2000). Psychiatric disorders in the relatives of probands with prepubertal-onset or adolescent-onset major depression. *Journal of the American Academy of Child and Adolescent Psychiatry, 39*(11), 1396–1404.

Widom, C. S., Czaja, S. J., & Paris, J. (2009). A prospective investigation of borderline personality disorder in abused and neglected children followed up into adulthood. *Journal of Personality Disorder, 23*(5), 433–446.

Wiger, D. E. (2005). *The clinical documentation sourcebook.* (3rd ed.). Hoboken, NJ: Wiley.

Wild, T. C., & Cunningham, J. (2001, January). Psychosocial determinants of perceived vulnerability to harm among adult drinkers [Abstract]. *Journal of Studies on Alcohol, 62*(1), 105.

Wilfley, D., & Rodin, J. (1995). Cultural influences on eating disorders. In K. Brownell & C. Fairburn (Eds.), *Eating disorders and obesity a comprehensive handbook* (pp. 78–82).

Williams, J. B. W., & Spitzer, R. L. (1983). The issue of sex bias in *DSM-III*: A critique of "A woman's view of *DSM-III*" by Marcie Kaplan. *American Psychologist, 38,* 793–798.

Williams, J. M., et al. (2008). Mindfulness-based cognitive therapy (MBCT) in bipolar disorder: Preliminary evaluation of immediate effect on between-episode functioning. *Journal of Affective Disorders, 107,* 275–279.

Willie, C., Kramer, B., & Brown, M. (1973). *Racism and mental health.* Pittsburgh, PA: University of Pittsburgh Press.

Willoughby, C. L., Hradek, E. A., & Richards, N. R. (1997). Use of electroconvulsive therapy with children: An overview and case report. *Journal of Child and Adolescent Psychiatric Nursing, 10*(3), 11–18.

Wilson, G. L., & Wilson, L. J. (1991). Treatment acceptability of alternate sex therapies: A comparative analysis. *Journal of Sex & Marital Therapy, 17,* 35–43.

Wincze, J., et al. (2004). *Erection Quality Scale: Initial Scale Development and Validation. Adult Urology, 64*(2), 351–356.

Wincze, J. P., & Carey, M. P. (1991). *Sexual dysfunction: A guide for assessment and treatment.* New York: Guilford Press.

Wise, V., McFarlane, Clark, C. R., & Battersby, M. (2009). Event-related potential and autonomic signs of maladaptive information processing during and auditory oddball task in panic disorder. *International Journal of Psychophysiology, 74*(1), 34–44.

Wittchen, H. U., & Jacobi, F. (2005). Size and burden of mental disorders in Europe—A clinical review and appraisal of 27 studies. *European Neuropsychopharmacology, 15*(4), 357–376.

Wodarski, J., & Dziegielewski, S. F. (2002). *Human growth and development: Integrating theory and empirical practice.* New York: Springer.

Wodarski, J. S., & Megget, K. E. D. (1996). Social work practice with African Americans. In D. F. Harrison, B. A. Thyer, & J. S. Wodarski (Eds.), *Cultural diversity and social work practice* (2nd ed.). Springfield, IL: Charles C Thomas.

Woo, S. M., & Keatinge, C. (Eds.). (2008). *Diagnosis and treatment of mental disorders across the lifetime.* Hoboken, NJ: Wiley.

Woodruff, T. J., Axelrad, D. A., Kyle, A. D., Nweke, O., Miller, G. G., & Hurley, B. J. (2004). Trends in environmentally related childhood illnesses. *Pediatrics, 113*(Suppl. 4), 1133–1140.

Woody, J. D., D'Souza, H. J., & Crain, D. D. (1994). Sexual functioning in clinical couples: Discriminant validity of the sexual interaction scale. *American Journal of Family Therapy, 22*, 291–303.

Woolston, J. L. (1999). Combined psychopharmacotherapy: Pitfalls of treatment. *Journal of the American Academy of Child and Adolescent Psychiatry, 38*(11), 1455.

Worden, M. (1999). *Family therapy basics* (2nd ed.). Pacific Grove, CA: Brooks/Cole.

World Health Organization. (2006a). *Interpersonal violence and alcohol.* Geneva: Author.

World Health Organization. (2006b). *Youth violence and alcohol.* Geneva: Author.

World Health Organization. (2007). *Alcohol and injury in emergency departments.* Geneva: Author.

World Health Organization. (2009a). *Alcohol.* Retrieved September 5, 2009, http://www.who.int/substance_abuse/facts/alcohol/en/index.html

World Health Organization. (2009b). Depression. Retrieved December 9, 2009 from http://www.who.int/mental_health/management/depression/definition/en/print.html

World Health Organization. (2009c). *Facts and figures.* Retrieved September 12, 2009, from http://www.who.int/substance_abuse/facts/en

World Health Organization. (2009d). *The global burden.* Retrieved September 12, 2009, from http://www.who.int/substance_abuse/facts/global_burden/en/index.html

World Health Organization. (2009e). *Organization for Economic Co-operation and Development Health Working Papers No. 42—Policies for Healthy Aging: An Overview.* Paris: Organization for Economic Co-operation and Development.

World Health Organization. (2009f). *Other psychoactive substances.* Retrieved September 12, 2009, from http://www.who.int/substance_abuse/facts/psychoactives/en/index.html

Wynne, L. C. (1987). A. preliminary proposal for strengthening the multi-axial approach of the *DSM-III*: Possible family-oriented revisions. In G. L. Tischler (Ed.), *Diagnosis and classification in psychiatry: A critical appraisal of DSM-III* (pp. 477–488). Cambridge, England: Cambridge University Press.

Yackobovitch-Gavan, M., et al. (2009). An integrative quantitative model of factors influencing the course of anorexia nervosa over time. *International Journal of Eating Disorders, 42*(4), 306–317.

Yalisove, D. (1998, July). The origins and evolution of the disease concept of treatment. *Journal of Studies on Alcohol 59*(4), 469–477.

Yang, F., Inouye, S., Fearing, M., Kiely, D., Marcantino, E., & Jones, R. (2008). Participation in activity and risk for incident delirium. *Journal of the American Geriatric Society, 56*(8), 1479–1484.

Yang, J. A., & Kombarakaran, F. A. (2006). A practitioner's response to the new health privacy regulations. *Health & Social Work, 31*(2), 129–136.

Yankner, B., Lu, T., & Loerch, P. (2008). The aging brain. *Annual Review of Pathology: Mechanisms of Disease, 3*, 41–66.

Yeager, K. R., Roberts, A. R., Grainger, W. (2008). Crisis intervention. In K. M. Sowers, & C. N. Dulmus (Series Eds.) & W. Rowe & L. A. Rapp-Paglicci (Vol. Eds.), *Comprehensive handbook of social work and social welfare: Vol. 3. Social work practice* (pp. 179–198). Hoboken, NJ: Wiley.

Yeager, K. R., Roberts, A. R., & Saveanu, R. (2009). Optimizing the use of patient safety standards, procedures, and measures. In A. Roberts (Ed.), *Social workers desk reference* (2nd ed., pp. 175–186). New York: Oxford University Press.

Yehuda, R., Bierer, L. M., Schmeidler, J., Aferiat, D. H., Breslau, I., & Dolan, S. (2000). Low cortisol and risk for PTSD in adult offspring of holocaust survivors. *American Journal of Psychiatry, 157*, 1252–1259.

Yen, S., Johnson, J., Costello, E., & Simpson, E. B. (2009, May). A 5-day dialectical behavior therapy partial hospital program for women with borderline personality disorder: Predictors of outcome form a 3-month follow-up study. *Journal of Psychiatric Practice, 15*(3), 173–182.

Young, J., & Inouye, S. (2007). Delirium in older people. *British Medical Journal, 334*, 842–846.

Zachar, P., & Kendler, K. S. (2007). Psychiatric disorders: A conceptual taxonomy. *American Journal of Psychiatry*, *164*, 557–565.

Zanarini, M. C., Weingeroff, J. L., & Frankenburg, F. R. (2009). Defense mechanisms associated with borderline personality disorder. *Journal of Personality Disorders*, *23*(2), 113–121.

Zanetti, O., et al. (2002). Predictors of cognitive improvement after reality testing in Alzheimer's disease. *Age and Aging*, *31*, 193–196.

Zeiss, A. M., & Gallagher-Thompson, D. (2003). Providing interdisciplinary geriatric team care: What does it really take? *Clinical Psychology: Science and Practice*, *10*(1), 115–119.

Zeng, M., Li, Y., Chen, C., Lu, L., Fan, J., Wang, B., et al. (2008). Guidelines for the diagnosis and treatment of alcohol liver disease. *Journal of Digestive Diseases*, *9*, 113–116.

Zielinski, D. S., & Bradshaw, C. P. (2006). Ecological influences on the sequelae of child maltreatment: A review of the literature. *Child Maltreatment*, *11*(1), 49–62.

Zimberg, S. (1996, October). Treating alcoholism: An age-specific intervention that works for older patients. *Geriatrics*, *51*(10), 40–45.

Zimmerman, M. (1988). Why are we rushing to publish DSM-IV? *Archives of General Psychiatry*, *45*, 1135–1138.

Zippe, C. D., et al. (2004). Female sexual dysfunction after radical cystectomy: A new outcome measure. *Adult Urology*, *63*(6), 1153–1157.

Zoellner, L. A., Abramowitz, J. S., Moore, S. A., & Slagle, D. M. (2008). Flooding. In W. T. O'Donohue & J. E. Fisher (Eds.). *Cognitive behavior therapy: Appling empirically supported techniques in your practice* (pp. 202–210). Hoboken, NJ: Wiley.

Zuckerman, E. L. (1995). *Clinician's thesaurus* (4th ed.). New York: Guilford Press

Zung, W. K. (1965). A self-rating depression scale. *Archives of General Psychiatry*, *12*, 63–70.

Zwakhalen, S., Hamers, J., Abu-Saad, H., & Berger, M. (2006). Pain in elderly people with severe dementia: A systematic review of behavioural pain assessment tools. *BioMed Geriatrics*, *6*(3), doi: 10.1186/1471-2318-6-3. Retrieved from http://www.biomedcentral.com/content/pdf/1471-2318-6-3.pdf

About the Author

Sophia F. Dziegielewski, PhD, LISW, is a professor in the School of Social Work, University of Cincinnati (UC), in Cincinnati, Ohio. She also serves as editor of the *Journal of Social Service Research*. Dr. Dziegielewski is a licensed independent social worker in the State of Ohio and has been licensed for clinical practice in Tennessee, Georgia, and Florida. Prior to arriving at UC she was chairperson for the University of Central Florida Human Subjects Review Board, where she presided over all human subjects research at this large (43, 000 students) metropolitan university. In addition to her duties as Dean (2004–2008) of the School of Social Work, she also served as chair the UC Institutional Review Board (IRB) Behavioral Science Review Board in 2006 and as a board member until 2008. Prior to this appointment, Dr. Dziegielewski had faculty appointments in the School of Social Work at the University of Central Florida, the University of Alabama, the Department of Family and Preventive Medicine and Psychiatry at Meharry Medical College, the University of Tennessee, and in the U.S. Army Military College at Fort Benning, Georgia.

Dr. Dziegielewski has her MSW and PhD in Social Work from Florida State University, Tallahassee. Professional honors include the College and University Award for Excellence in Graduate Teaching at the University of Central Florida (2002) and the University Faculty Leadership Award (2002). In the national magazine *Social Worker Today* (2003), a feature story about Dr. Dziegielewski referred to her as a "legend" in her field. She is the recipient of numerous other awards and supports her research and practice activity with over 120 publications, including 7 textbooks, 79 articles, numerous book chapters, and hundreds of workshops and community presentations.

Her professional social work interests primarily focus on two major areas: health and mental health issues and time-limited evidence-based practice strategy. As a licensed clinical social worker, she is firm on the importance of joining practice and research and applying the concepts of measurement to establish treatment effectiveness in time-limited intervention settings.

Author Index

Subject Index

STUDY PACKAGE
CONTINUING EDUCATION
CREDIT INFORMATION

DSM-IV-TR™ In Action, 2nd Edition

Our goal is to provide you with current, accurate and practical information from the most experienced and knowledgeable speakers and authors.

Listed below are the continuing education credit(s) currently available for this self-study package. *Please note: Your state licensing board dictates whether self study is an acceptable form of continuing education. Please refer to your state rules and regulations.*

COUNSELORS: PESI, LLC is recognized by the National Board for Certified Counselors to offer continuing education for National Certified Counselors. Provider #: 5896. We adhere to NBCC Continuing Education Guidelines. This self-study package qualifies for **7.5** contact hours.

SOCIAL WORKERS: PESI, LLC, 1030, is approved as a provider for continuing education by the Association of Social Work Boards, 400 South Ridge Parkway, Suite B, Culpeper, VA 22701. www.aswb.org. Social workers should contact their regulatory board to determine co approval. Course Level: All Levels. Social Workers will receive **7.5** cal) continuing education clock hours for completing this self-study age.

PSYCHOLOGISTS: PESI, LLC is approved by the American Psy logical Association to sponsor continuing education for psycholog PESI, LLC maintains responsibility for these materials and their c PESI is offering these self- study materials for **7.5** hours of contin education credit.

ADDICTION COUNSELORS: PESI, LLC is a Provider approved NAADAC Approved Education Provider Program. Provider #: 366. self-study package qualifies for **9.0** contact hours.

Procedures:

1. Review the material and read the book.

2. If seeking credit, complete the posttest/evaluation form:

    -Complete posttest/evaluation in entirety; including your email address to receive your certificate much faster versus by mail.

    -Upon completion, mail to the address listed on the form along with the CE fee stated on the test. Tests will not be processed without the CE fee included.

    -Completed posttests must be received 6 months from the date printed on the packing slip.

Your completed posttest/evaluation will be graded. If you receive a passing score (70% and above), you will be emailed/faxed/mailed a certificate of successful completion with earned continuing education credits. (Please write your email address on the posttest/evaluation form for fastest response) If you do not pass the posttest, you will be sent a letter indicating areas of deficiency, and another posttest to complete. The posttest must be resubmitted and receive a passing grade before credit can be awarded. We will allow you to re-take as many times as necessary to receive a certificate.

If you have any questions, please feel free to contact our customer service department at 1.800.844.8260.

PESI LLC
PO BOX 1000
Eau Claire, WI 54702-1000

DSM-IV-TR™ In Action, 2nd Edition

PO BOX 1000
Eau Claire, WI 54702
800-844-8260

Any persons interested in receiving credit may photocopy this form, complete and return with a payment of $25.00 per person CE fee. A certificate of successful completion will be sent to you. To receive your certificate sooner than two weeks, rush processing is available for a fee of $10. Please attach check or include credit card information below.

Mail to: PESI, PO Box 1000, Eau Claire, WI 54702 or fax to PESI (800) 554-9775 (both sides)

CE Fee: $25: (Rush processing fee: $10)   **Total to be charged** _____

Credit Card #: _____   **Exp Date:** _____ **V-Code*:** _____
(*MC/VISA/Discover: last 3-digit # on signature panel on back of card.) (*American Express: 4-digit # above account # on face of card.)

	LAST	FIRST	M.I.

Name (please print): _____   _____   _____

Address: _____ Daytime Phone: _____

City: _____ State: _____ Zip Code: _____

Signature: _____ Email: _____

Date Completed: _____ Actual time (# of hours) taken to complete this offering: _____hours

Program Objectives After completing this publication, I have been able to achieve these objectives:

1. Clarify the difference between diagnosis, assessment, and utilizing a combination approach referred to as the diagnostic assessment.   1. Yes No

2. Identify the steps for completing the diagnostic assessment.   2. Yes No

3. Recognize the importance of including information related to culture in completing the diagnostic assessment.   3. Yes No

4. Describe the basic steps for utilizing the multiaxial diagnostic system.   4. Yes No

5. List and provide interpretation for the GAF, GARF, and SOFAS scales listed in the DSM-IV-TR.   5. Yes No

6. Apply ethical and legal considerations for application to the diagnostic assessment.   6. Yes No

7. Explain several guiding principles for efficient documentation.   7. Yes No

8. Clarify the difference between substance abuse and substance dependence as described in the DSM-IV-TR.   8. Yes No

9. Identify the most common psychotic disorders.   9. Yes No

10. Identify the most common mood disorders and the symptoms related to proper diagnostic assessment.   10. Yes No

PESI LLC
PO BOX 1000
Eau Claire, WI 54702-1000

ZNT042555   CE Release Date: 6/16/2010

Participant Profile:
1. Job Title: _____ Employment setting: _____

1. What diagnostic changes have been made to the criteria of the diagnostic categories between the DSM-IV and the DSM-IV-TR?
A. Major changes were made to all the diagnostic criteria for the major clinical syndromes
B. Most of the changes have been made in the supporting information and not to the diagnostic criteria
C. Changes have been made to the personality disorders categories only
D. No changes were made to any parts of the books and both versions are considered identical

2. What is a culture-bound syndrome?
A. This is a diagnostic category that involves race relations
B. This is a section of the DSM that seeks to explain further reactions that can be related to someone's cultural identity and behavior, rather than a mental disorder
C. This is an area of counseling where diagnostic labels are placed
D. This is a country where mental disorders are often misunderstood

3. One major change expected in the DSM-5 is the shift from:
A. A categorical presentation of the diagnostic categories to a behavioral one
B. A behavioral presentation of the diagnostic categories to a non-behavioral one
C. There are no expected changes in the presentation of the diagnostic categories
D. A categorical presentation of the diagnostic categories to a dimensional one

4. The term "Diagnosis Deferred" is used to:
A. Help clinician's decide if something is important for billing
B. Help clients examine their own biases
C. Assist the clinician to determine whether the information is inadequate to make a formal diagnostic judgment
D. Apply this information to past incidences of the problem

5. From the choices below, where are Other Disorders that may be the Focus of Clinical Treatment coded?
A. Axis I
B. Axis II
C. Axis III
D. Axis IV

6. Which of the other disorders that may be the focus of clinical treatment is a severe response related to the death of a loved one?
A. Childhood or Adolescent Antisocial Behavior: isolated acts
B. Adult Antisocial Behavior
C. Borderline Intellectual Functioning
D. Bereavement

7. In DSM-5, what is the new name expected to replace Mental Retardation?
A. Mentally Challenged
B. Intellectual Disability
C. Mental Inability
D. Dementia

8. Women of what race are most likely to develop an eating disorder such as anorexia nervosa or bulimia nervosa?
A. African American women
B. Native American women
C. Asian women
D. Caucasian women

9. Which of the disorders is MOST LIKELY related to a fear of a social situation or being in public places where performance would be required?
A. Generalized Anxiety Disorder
B. Social Phobia
C. Specific Phobia
D. Post-Traumatic Stress Disorder

10. Of the conditions listed below, which ones constitute the Personality Disorder referred to as Cluster B and is characterized by emotional and erratic behavior?
A. Paranoid Personality Disorder, Schizoid Personality Disorder, and Schizotypal Personality Disorder
B. Antisocial Personality Disorder, Borderline Personality Disorder, Narcissistic Personality Disorder, and Histrionic Personality Disorder
C. Avoidant Personality Disorder, Dependent Personality Disorder, Obsessive and Compulsive Personality Disorder
D. Bereavement, Malingering, and Adolescent Antisocial Act

PESI LLC
PO BOX 1000
Eau Claire, WI 54702-1000